BRITISH AND METRIC WEIGHTS, MEASURES AND TEMPERATURES

Weights and Measures

  1 centimetre = 0·39 inch
  1 metre = 1·09 yards
  1 gramme = 0·035 oz.
  1 litre = 1·76 pints

Temperatures

Centigrade	Fahrenheit
100°	212°
90	194
80	176
70	158
60	140
50	122
40	104
30	86
20	68
10	50
0	32

THE NEW METHOD
ENGLISH DICTIONARY

The New Method English Dictionary

EXPLAINING THE MEANING OF OVER
24,000 ITEMS
WITHIN A VOCABULARY OF
1,490 WORDS

MICHAEL PHILIP WEST, M.A., D.Phil.
AND
JAMES GARETH ENDICOTT, M.A.

FOURTH EDITION
Completing 4,980,000

With illustrations

LONGMAN

LONGMAN GROUP LTD
London

*Associated companies, branches and representatives
throughout the world*

Fourth Edition © Michael Philip West and James Gareth Endicott 1961

All rights reserved. No part of this publication may be reproduced, stored in a retrieval system, or transmitted in any form or by any means, electronic, mechanical, photocopying, recording, or otherwise, without the prior permission of the Copyright owner.

First Published	*1935*
Fourth edition	*1961*
Seventeenth Impression	*1973*

ISBN 0 582 52561 6

PRINTED AND BOUND IN ENGLAND BY
HAZELL WATSON AND VINEY LTD
AYLESBURY, BUCKS

PREFACE

This English Dictionary is written specially for the foreigner. It explains to him, in words which he knows, the meaning of words and idioms which he does not know.

It is not a translation or adaptation of any older book, but a new and original work.

This revised edition has been brought up to date (1961) by improving the definition of some words and adding a number of new words, or words which have become more important today. Many new or improved pictures have been placed close to the words which they help to explain.

The Words Defined

The dictionary defines over 24,000 items—some 18,000 words and 6,000 idioms. Its special features are its richness in examples and the care devoted to the meanings and idioms of the commoner words, such as Get, Put, Take, etc. Most small English dictionaries economise space by compressing these commonest words (for the English-speaking person knows them); yet these words are the most troublesome to the foreigner and the most likely to be encountered. This dictionary economises space by omitting the rare and highly technical words which the foreigner is unlikely to meet either in reading or in conversation. At the same time this revised edition takes into account the fact that certain technical and scientific words (Atomic, Nuclear, for example) are now commonly used in newspapers and books and are often heard in conversation and radio broadcasts. Space is further economised by omitting those derivatives and compounds whose meaning can readily be guessed.

Foreigners are often troubled by slang expressions of very common use, yet unexplained even by the larger dictionaries. Special attention is given to ordinary slang, also to such Americanisms as are commonly read or heard outside the U.S.A.

The Defining Words

All explanations are written within a vocabulary of 1,490 words. A list of these words will be found at the end of the dictionary, placed there largely for the convenience of teachers. Anyone who knows these 1,490 words will be able to understand every explanation given in this dictionary.

Moreover, by getting practice in this vocabulary the learner can convey the meaning where he does not know the English word and so get the English word from the person he is talking to.

Cross references are reduced to a minimum. That is to say that (with certain very few exceptions) the user will not find this type of definition: "NUDGE—to touch with the elbow (*see* elbow)", meaning that he has then to turn to E to find out what an elbow is. The meaning of a word outside the 1,490 defining words is given in brackets immediately following the word: "NUDGE—to touch with the *elbow* (=middle joint of the arm)".

Pronunciation

Pronunciation is indicated by a very simple system, easily learnt, and unmistakably clear. A guide to this system is given in two places: inside the front cover and inside the back cover, so that the user who is not yet familiar with the system can consult the guide in one or other of these places in connection with a word found either on a right-hand or on a left-hand page.

THE NEW METHOD ENGLISH DICTIONARY

A

a (9) *£1 a day* = £1 for each day.

a- (9) e.g. *a-building* = in the act of being built; *a-singing* = in the act of singing.

A.B. (21 + 11) able-bodied = seaman who has learnt the necessary duties.

abacus (3-9-9) frame with balls on wires, used for teaching children to count; instrument used in calculating.

ab'ack (9-3) backwards; *Taken aback* = surprised.

ab'andon (9-3-9) give up; *He abandoned his wife* = left her without arranging for her support; n. **ab'andon,** lack of control; *He spoke with abandon* = in a wild uncontrolled way; **ab'andoned** (person), given up to bad ways.

ab'ase (9-21) make low—in office, honour, or in one's self-respect.

ab'ash (9-3) make ashamed.

ab'ate (9-21) make less; become less.

abattoir (3-9-74) place where animals are killed for food.

abbey (3-1) place where religious men (or women) live apart, giving their lives to God; church used or once used by such people; **abbot** (3-9) (man), **abbess** (3-1) (woman), head of an abbey.

abbr'eviate (9-11-121) make shorter, e.g. a speech; **an abbr'evi'ation,** shortening, e.g. adj. = adjective.

A.B.C. (21 + 11 + s11) the *alphabet* (3-9-2) (= the 26 letters used in writing English); *The A.B.C. of Science* = simplest parts of —.

abdicate (3-1-21) give up a power or right; cease to be king.

abd'omen (3-67-2) the stomach; adj. **abd'ominal** (3-5-1).

abd'uct (9-8) carry away (steal) a person, e.g. a child or young woman.

ab'ed (9-2) in bed.

aberr'ation (3-9-21shn) wandering from the right or expected course, e.g. of a star; *An aberration of the mind* = mistake caused by wandering attention.

ab'et (9-2) help in doing something, usually bad.

ab'eyance (9-219-s) *In abeyance* = not in use, not at present in force, e.g. *That law is in —*.

abh'or (9-55) to hate; n. **abh'orrence** (9-5-s).

ab'ide (9-41) stay; *I cannot abide him* = I cannot bear him, hate him; *To abide by an agreement* = do what was promised.

ab'ility (9-1-1-1) state of being able; cleverness.

ab in'itio (3 + 1-1sh167) from the beginning.

abject (3-2) without value; without self-respect; *In abject poverty* = very poor.

abj'ure (9-779) *swear* (= promise in the name of God) to give up.

abl'aze (9-21) burning.

able (21) *I am able to* = I can; *An able man* = clever man; **'able-b'odied** (+ 5-1) strong, in good health; **'able-bodied s'eaman** (+ 11-9) one who has learnt all the necessary duties.

abl'ution (9-77shn) washing.

ably (21-1) in an able way.

abnegate (3-1-21) give up, not allow oneself to have.

abn'ormal (9-55) different from the usual.

ab'oard (9-55) travelling on a ship or train; *All aboard!* = all must now get into the train (on to the ship).

ab'ode (9-67) p.t. of Abide.

ab'ode (9-67) home; place in which people (or animals) live, house, tent, etc.; *My present abode* = place in which I am living now.

ab'olish (9-5-1) destroy; put an end to; **abol'itionist** (3-9-1sh9-1) person who wants to abolish something.

ab'ominate (9-5-1-21) feel great hatred for; **ab'ominable** (9-5-1-9) very bad, hateful.

abor'igines (3-9-1j1-11z) people who have lived in a country from the beginning; **an aboriginal.**

ab'ortive (9-55-1) *attempt* = unsuccessful —.

ab'ound (9-47) be in plenty; contain plenty of, e.g. *The river abounds in fish.*

ab'out (9-47) (1) on all sides, here and there, e.g. *Trees growing about the house*; (2) in various directions, e.g. *To walk about*; (3) nearly, e.g. *About a mile; Just about enough* = quite enough; (4) concerning, e.g. *To talk about a subject*; (5) in the opposite direction, *About turn!* = (order to soldiers) turn round the other way; *to come about* = happen; *to bring about* = cause; *to set about* (a piece of work) = begin; *I am about to go* = shall go very soon.

ab'ove (9-8) (1) higher than, e.g. *The sky above my head*; (2) more than, e.g. *Above 200 persons*; *This book is above me* = too difficult for me to understand; *He's a bit above himself* = too proud and pleased with his own cleverness; *Mentioned above* = spoken of on an earlier page of the book; *Above board* = fair, honest; *Keep one's head above water* = keep safe.

abr'ade (9-21) rub away; **abr'asion** (9-21-3n) rubbing away, painful rubbed place on the skin; **abr'asive** (9-21z1) rubbing; **an abr'asive,** material used for rubbing, e.g. sand.

abr'east (9-2) side by side; *Abreast of the times* = knowing the latest things which are being done.

abr'idge (9-1j) make (a book or story) shorter.

abr'oad (9-55) out of the house, out of one's own country; *There is a rumour abroad that —* = there is a story going about, being told by one person to another.

abrogate (3-9-21) cause (a law, a power) to cease, put an end to a law.

abr'upt (9-8) sudden; steep; *An abrupt manner* = impolite —.

absçess (3-1) painful poisoned place in or on the body.

absc'ond (9-5) run away quickly and secretly, e.g. *He absconded with the money.*

absęnt (3) not here, not present; *Absent-minded* = not thinking of what one is doing; **to abs'ent** (9-2) (oneself), to stay away from, not be present; n. **absęnce** (3-s) state of being absent; **absent'ee** (3-11) one who is absent (e.g. owner of land).

absolute (3-9-77) **(1)** free, uncontrolled, *An absolute ruler;* **(2)** perfect, complete, *An absolute fool;* real, *An absolute fact.*

absol'ution (3-9-77shn) forgiveness.

abs'olve (9-z5) set free, e.g. from blame or debt.

abs'orb (9-55) drink-in liquid, e.g. *The dry earth absorbs water, To absorb learning* = take — into the mind; *Absorbed in a task* = giving one's whole mind to —; **abs'orption** (9-55-shn) drinking in of liquids by dry matter, the building up of the body by food and drink.

abst'ain (9-21) keep away from, e.g. *Abstain from strong drink;* **abst'emious** (9-11-19) not drinking or eating much; **abstinence** (3-1-9-s) keeping oneself from food or drink; careful in one's eating and drinking.

abstr'act (9-3) take out from; **an 'abstract** (3-3) *of a book* = a short açcount of the ideas of —; *An abstract idea* or **an abstr'action** (9-3-shn) idea in the mind only, e.g. goodness, beauty, not the thought of any actual thing; **'abstract 'art** (+ 44) patterns and carvings which are not like real things but are meant to show the artist's ideas and feelings; **ab-·str'acted** (9-3-1) thinking of something else.

abstr'use (9-77) hidden, hard to understand.

abs'urd (9-99) very foolish, unreasonable, causing people to laugh.

ab'undance (9-8-9-s) plenty; **ab'undant** (9-8-9) plentiful.

ab'use (9-177z) **(1)** make a wrong use of; **(2)** speak rudely (to a person); n. **ab'use** (9-177s).

ab'ut (9-8) touch at one end, e.g. *My house abuts on the church;* **an ab'utment** (9-8-9) stones on each side at the bottom of an arch which prevent the arch from spreading, or falling apart.

ab'yss (9-1) very deep hole; **ab'ysmal** (9-1z) *ignorance* = complete lack of knowledge.

A.C. (21 + s11) see Alternating current.

a/c account (money).

ac- to, e.g. *accede* = (come to) to agree; *accretion,* an adding or growing on to.

ac'acia (9-21sh19) plant found mainly in hoṭ countries: liquid from it is used to make *gum* (= yellow liquid used for sticking paper, etc.).

ac'ademy (9-3-9-1) **(1)** school for higher learning; **(2)** *society* (= group) of learned men; **acad'emic** (3-9-2-1) of an academy; *A merely academic question* = question which may be talked about but which has no real importance in practice.

acc'ede (3ks11) **(1)** agree; **(2)** yield to a person's wishes; *I accede to your request* = will do what you ask; **(3)** come into an office.

acc'elerate (3ks2-9-21) make quicker; **the acc'elerator** (3ks2-9-21-9) small handle, or thing moved by the foot, which increases the speed of a motor-car.

accent (3ks) **(1)** special weight given by the voice to one part of a word, e.g. *to acc'elerate;* -el- is the accented *syllable* (= group of sounds); **(2)** mark (') showing this; **(3)** peculiar way of speaking, e.g. *He has a foreign accent;* **to acc'ent** (9ks2) put on force; **to acc'entuate** (3ks2-1721) lay special weight on a word; make much of, e.g., an opinion.

acc'ept (9ks2) take, receive, believé, agree to; *An accepted truth* = idea upon which all agree; **acc'eptable** (3-2-9) pleasant to receive, accepted gladly.

accęss (3ks2) act of coming to a place; entrance or way in; *To give access to* = allow into, lead into.

acc'essary (9ks2-9-1) helper in any act, generally wrong-doing.

acc'essible (9ks2-1) easy to reach; (person) whom one can easily go and see.

acc'ession (9ks2shn) **(1)** *The accession of King George* = time when King George became king; **(2)** increase, e.g. *accession of wealth.*

acc'essory (9ks2s9-1) helpful thing added, *The accessories of a motor-car* = lamps, instruments used in repair, and other special things added to the car.

accidence (3ks1-9-s) set of rules about changes in the form of words, e.g. *horse—horses, do —did,* etc.

accident (3ks1-9) **(1)** event which happens by chance; **(2)** unfortunate event; **(3)** something not necessary or important.

accl'aim (9k-21) receive with shouts of joy or praise; n. **acclam'ation** (3-9-21shn).

accl'imatize (9k-41-9-41) accustom to the *climate* (= heat, cold, weather) of a place.

accl'ivity (9k-1-1-1) a slope up, e.g. the side of a hill.

accol'ade (3k9-21) act of making a person a knight by laying a sword on his shoulder.

acc'ommodate (9k5-9-21) **(1)** make a thing fit; **(2)** settle (a quarrel); **(3)** supply as a kindness, e.g. money; **(4)** give lodgings to; **acc'ommodating,** kind, helpful; **accommod'ation** (9-5-9-21shn) lodgings (also meanings 1 and 3).

acc'ompany (9k8-9-1) go with; *A song with an acc'ompaniment* (9k8-9-1-9) = — with music played with it.

acc'omplice (9k5-1s) companion in wrong-doing.

acc'omplish (9k5-1) do, finish successfully; *An* **acc'omplished** *dancer* = perfect —; *She has many* **acc'omplishments** (9k5-1-9) = skilled in many arts, e.g. music, painting, etc.

acc'ord (9k55) (1) agree; (2) agreement; *To accord praise to* = to give —; *Of one's own accord* = by one's own wish; *In* **acc'ordance** (9k55-9-s) *with* = in agreement with; **acc'ording** *to his orders* = just as he ordered; **acc'ordingly** (9k55-1-1) for that reason.

acc'ordion (9k55-19) musical instrument played by pulling the ends out and pressing them together, thus forcing air under thin metal plates which make the musical sounds.

acc'ost (9k5) greet, speak to.

ACCORDION

acc'ount (9k47) story, description; **acc'ounts**, report of money received and spent; *On this account* = for this reason; *To take into account* = consider; *Of no account* = not important; *To account for* = explain; *You are* **acc'ountable** (9-47-9) *for it* = you will be asked to explain why it was done, you may be blamed.

acc'ountant (9k47-9) one who keeps accounts of money; n. **acc'ountancy** (9k47-9-sI) art of keeping accounts.

acc'outrement(s) (9k77-9-9) all the things used by a soldier in war except his clothes and weapons; **to acc'outre** (9k77-9) supply with everything necessary for war.

accr'edit (9k-2-1) *Mr. A. was accredited to London* = was given a letter to the British Government saying that he might be trusted.

accr'etion (9k-11shn) an increase in size caused either by growth or by adding bits on; matter so added.

accr'ue (9k-77) to increase; *The money which accrues* = — which comes as *interest* (= money paid for the use of money) when money is lent.

acc'umulate (9k177-17-21) grow into a mass, become greater in amount; **an acc'umulator** (9k177-17-21-9) instrument used for storing electricity.

accurate (3k17-1) exact, correct.

acc'ursed (9k99-1), **acc'urst**, under a curse; hateful.

acc'use (9k177z) say that a person has done wrong, to blame; n. **accus'ation** (3k17z21-shn).

acc'ustom (9k8-9) make used to.

ace (21s) playing card with one spot; very good fighting airman; *Within an ace of death* = in great danger of being killed; *tennis ace* = very good player.

ac'erbity (9s99-1-1) (1) sourness; (2) sharpness and ill-temper shown in the looks, or in speech.

ac'etic (acid) (9s11-1-1) having to do with *vinegar* (= very sour liquid).

acetone (3s1-67) substance used to dissolve fats (make fats liquid).

ac'etylene (9s2-1-11) gas which burns with a bright white light.

ache (21k) continuous pain.

ach'ieve (9-11) finish successfully, gain; **an ach'ievement** (——9) thing successfully done.

'achrom'atic (3k-67-3-1) colourless.

acid (3s1) sour, sharp-tasting; ill-tempered or sharp in speech; **an acid**, powerful liquid (some acids burn holes in cloth, wood, iron, etc.); *The acid test* = finding out with the help of an acid whether a metal is gold, anything which shows whether a thing is really true or not; **ac'idulate** (9s1-17-21) make acid-tasting, *Acidulated drops* = pieces of sugar with a slightly sour taste added.

'ack-'ack guns (3 + 3 + 8) anti-aircraft guns which shoot up at aeroplanes.

ackn'owledge (9-5-1j) recognize, allow as being true; *Acknowledge receipt of a letter* = say that one has received it; n. **ackn'owledgment** (——9) (above meanings), also = gift given as a sign of *gratitude* (= gratefulness).

acme (3-1) highest point, the greatest amount; *It is the acme of perfection* = — as perfect as it can possibly be.

acne (3-1) small hard spot on the skin of the face.

acolyte (3-9-41) person who is not a priest who helps in a religious ceremony.

aconite (3-9-41) (1) poison acting on the eyes and slowing the heart and breathing; (2) plant.

acorn (21-55) fruit of the *oak* (= English tree, with hard yellow wood, which grows to a great age).

ac'oustic (9-47-1 or 9-77-1) having to do with hearing; **ac'oustics**, science of sound.

ACORN

acqu'aint (9-21) make known; *I acquainted him with the facts* = told him; *To acquaint oneself with* = learn; **an acqu'aintance** (9-21-9-s) person whom one knows, but not a close friend.

acqui'esce (3-12) agree silently.

acqu'ire (9-419) gain, get; **acqu'isitive** (9-1z1-1) eager to get and own.

acqu'it (9-1) set a prisoner free in a court of law; *The court (or judge) acquitted the prisoner* = said he had done nothing wrong and set him free; *To acquit oneself well* = behave, work, well; n. **an acqu'ittal**.

acre (21-9) 4840 square yards (of land); **acreage** (21-9-1j) number of acres in a piece of land.

acrid (3-1) sour; bad-tempered; cruel (speech); **acrimony** (3-1-9-1) bitterness of words or feeling; unkindness of speech.

acrobat (3-9-3) person who can do clever things with his body, e.g. throwing and twisting himself about, walking on a rope, etc.

acr'oss (9-5) from one side to the other; over; *To come across a thing* = find; *To get across a person* = quarrel.

acr'ostic (9-5-1) game in which one has to find certain words which, written one below another, make other words with their letters; poem in which the first letters of the lines make a word.

act (3) **(1)** thing done; *An act of God* = results of natural forces, harm done by storm, wind, etc.; *An act of grace* = thing done out of kindness, not because it must be done; **(2)** part of a play; **(3)** law.

act (3) **(1)** perform a play; perform one part (one character) in a play; pretend; *To act the part of* = serve as, do the duties of —, e.g. *Acting Headmaster* = the man who is working as headmaster, the real headmaster being absent; **(2)** do, e.g. *The time for thinking is past; we must now act; Act up to one's reputation* (= good or bad name) = do what people would expect one to do; *The machine won't act* = — will not work, will not move; *To act upon the stomach* = have an effect on —; *To act upon advice* = do as advised.

action (3-shn) **(1)** movement, work, the producing of an effect; *To take action* = begin to do something; **(2)** natural working, e.g. *The action of the heart*; way of acting, e.g. *The horse has a graceful action*, movement; *Out of action* = not able to work or be used; *The action of a medicine* = effect produced by —; *The soldiers are in action* = — fighting; *An action* = a battle; *Bring an action against* = go to law against.

active (3-1) quick and full of life, full of action.

actor (3-9) man who acts in plays; **actress** (3-1) woman who acts in plays.

actual (3-179) real, as a fact; **actually** (——1) really, in fact; *He actually ran* = he really did run, though you would not have expected it.

'actu'ality (3-17-3-1-1) realness; *actuality film* = cinema film about real things, not just a story.

actuary (3-179-1) person who *calculates* how much must be paid for an *insurance* (to *insure* one's life = pay some money each year so that, when one dies, an agreed amount may be paid to one's family).

actuate (3-1721) cause to act.

ac'uity (3-1771-1) n. of *acute*.

ac'umen (9-177-2) keenness of mind; cleverness and quick understanding.

ac'ute (9-177) sharp; *An acute angle* = angle which is less than a *right angle* (e.g. the corner of a square is a r.a.); *An acute mind* = keen mind; *An acute pain* = sharp, sudden pain; *Acute illness* = serious —.

ad. (3) *advertisement* (= printed notice of goods to be sold, or needed, of a servant needed, etc.).

ad- to, e.g. *addition* (9-1shn) = giving to = adding.

A.D. (21 + 11) see Anno Domini.

adage (3-1j) wise saying.

adamant (3-9-9) very hard stone; (of character) hard, unyielding.

'Adam's 'apple (3-9-z + 3) part of a man's throat which stands out and moves during speech and swallowing.

ad'apt (9-3) to fit; to change and fit to a new use.

add (3) join one thing to another; find the whole amount of several numbers, e.g. *2 added to 2 makes 4*; to increase, e.g. *The joy of others adds to my pleasure*; **add'endum** (9-2-9) thing to be added, e.g. to a book.

adder (3-9) small poisonous snake.

add'icted (to) (9-1-1) given over to —, e.g. to drink, e.g. *He is addicted to drink* = he drinks too much wine; **an 'addict** (3-1) person who is —.

add'ition (9-1shn) act of adding; that which is added; adj. **add'itional** (9-1shg).

addle (3) *An addled egg* = bad egg; **addle-head** (+ 2) person who cannot think clearly; *To become addled* = become mixed in thought.

addr'ess (9-2) to aim; *To address a ball* = aim and get ready to hit; send or direct, e.g. to write on a letter where it is to be sent; *To address oneself to a task* = to begin to work at; *To address a person, a meeting* = to speak to; **an addr'ess**, speech; writing on a letter showing where it is to be sent; **addr'ess**, manner, e.g. *A man of pleasing address*; skill and grace; *To pay one's addresses to a lady* = make love to; **address'ee** (9-2-11) person to whom a letter is addressed.

add'uce (9-177s) *To adduce reasons* = to bring forward —.

adenoids (3-9-51-z) soft masses growing at the back of the nose; when diseased they cause difficult breathing.

adept (3-2) one who is very skilled; adj. **ad'ept** (9-2).

adequate (3-1-9) enough; good enough.

adh'ere (3-19) stick to, belong to a party, hold to an opinion; **adh'esive** (3-11-1) sticky.

ad hoc (3 + 5) for this special purpose.

adi'eu (3-177) good-bye.

ad infin'itum (3 + 1-1-41-9) for ever, without stopping.

ad 'interim (+ 1-9-1) for the present, but not for always.

adipose (3-1-67z) fat.

adj'acent (9-21s) lying near.

adjective (3-1-1) word added to a noun telling more about it, e.g. a BIG table.

adj'oin (9-51) be next to.

adj'ourn (9-99) put off to (delay until) another day, e.g. *The meeting is adjourned* = is ended now but will be continued on another day; *Let us adjourn to the next room* = let us go into —, continue our talk in —.

adj'udge (9-8j) (1) decide; (2) to judge, give to a person as the result of a judgment.

adj'udicate (9-77-1-21) give a judgment settling a claim or quarrel.

adjunct (3-8ngkt) joined; added; a thing added, or joined on to.

adj'ure (9-779) pray, ask very solemnly.

adj'ust (9-8) set right; make a thing fit.

adjutant (3-7-9) officer who helps a Commanding Officer in the army; **adjutant-bird** (+ 99) large Indian bird.

ad l'ibitum (ad lib.) (3 + 1-1-9) as much as you like.

adm'inister (9-1-1-9) look after, settle, carry on the business of —; *To administer a country* = to rule; *To administer justice* = carry on the work of a judge; *To administer medicine to* = give medicine to; **the adm'instr'ation** (9-1-1-21shn) that part of a government which carries out the laws.

admiral (3-9) highest rank of officer in the navy (= the king's warships); **The Admir'alty** (——1) office which controls the navy.

adm'ire (9-4119) look upon with wonder and pleasure; **admirably** (3-9-9-1) *done* = very well done; n. **admir'ation** (3-9-21shn).

adm'it (9-1) allow a person to come in; take into, e.g. *Admit a boy into a school*; receive as true or just, e.g. *I admit that I did it* = I say it is true that —; *I admit the claim* = I accept — as just; *It admits of doubt* = it is doubtful; n. **adm'ission** (9-1shn) act of admitting; **adm'ittance** (9-1-s) right to enter; **adm'issible** (9-1-9) which may be admitted.

adm'ixture (9-1-tsh9) act of mixing; things mixed; one thing mixed in with others.

adm'onish (9-5-1) warn, advise, tell a person that he is doing wrong.

ad'o (9-77) trouble and excitement.

ad'obe (3-67) sun-dried bricks.

adol'escent (3-9-2) growing to manhood; boy or girl aged about 12 to 18.

Ad'onis (9-67-1) very good-looking man.

ad'opt (9-5) take another person's child as one's own; accept (an idea).

ad'ore (9-55) (1) honour greatly; (2) love very much; **ad'orable** (9-55-9) very nice; very lovable; **ador'ation** (3-9-21shn) feeling of great love and respect for, the act of showing love and respect.

ad'orn (9-55) make beautiful, to ornament, e.g. *The room was adorned with roses*.

adr'enal gl'ands (3-11 + 3-z) part of the body which produces a liquid which tightens the blood-vessels and stops the flow of blood, causing the skin to become white; **adr'enalin** (9-2-9-1) liquid so produced.

adr'ift (9-1) floating about freely; *To turn adrift* = send away from home or employment.

adr'oit (9-51) clever, skilful.

adul'ation (3-17-21shn) giving praise in which one does not believe, in order to gain favour.

adult (9-8) fully grown; grown-up person.

ad'ulterate (9-8-9-21) make impure by mixing in other cheaper things; n. **ad'ulterant**, impurity so mixed in.

ad'ultery (9-8-9-1) unfaithfulness of a husband or wife.

adumbrate (3-8-21) show the general form or character of—especially of a future event.

'ad val'orem (3 + 3-55-9) according to the value.

adv'ance (9-44-s) move forward; raise to a higher rank; increase (prices); lend (money); an **adv'ance**, a going or moving forward; *In advance of* = in front of, before; *To make advances to* = try to gain the friendship of; *An advanced idea* = very new, not generally accepted.

adv'antage (9-44-1j) gain, anything likely to produce gain or success, e.g. being stronger, wiser; *To gain an advantage over* = do better than; *Take advantage of* = deceive; *You have the advantage of me* = you seem to know me, but I do not know you; adj. **advant'ageous** (3-9-21j9) helpful.

advent (3-2) coming, the act of arriving; coming of Christ; **Advent**, time from the 4th Sunday before Christmas to Christmas Day.

advent'itious (3-2-1sh9) happening by chance.

adv'enture (9-2-tsh9) dangerous or exciting deed or event; **adv'enturer** (9-2-tsh9-9) one who lives a dangerous (and perhaps dishonest) life; **adv'enturess** (9-2-tsh9-1) woman who lives a dangerous and dishonest life; **adv'enturous** (——9) **adv'enturesome** (——9) eager for adventure.

adverb (3-99) an adverb is a word added to a verb, adjective or another adverb to tell us something about it, e.g. run *quickly*, *very* big, *very* slowly.

adverse (3-99s) turned against, not in favour of, e.g. *Adverse fate, wind*, etc.; **adversary** (3-9-9-1) enemy; **adv'ersity** (9-99-1-1), unhappiness, misfortune.

adv'ert (9-99) turn the mind to; speak about.

advertise (3-9-41z) make known, bring to people's notice, e.g. by notices in the newspapers, pictures on walls, etc.; **adv'ertisement** (9-99-1z-9), act of advertising, a printed notice.

adv'ise (9-41z) tell a person what you think he ought to do; **adv'ice** (——s) opinion so given; **adv'isable** (9-41z9) which should be done; **adv'isedly** (——z1-1), after having considered the matter.

advocate (3-9-1) one who speaks for another, e.g. in a law court; **to advocate** (3-9-21) speak in favour of an idea.

adze (3) curved instrument used for shaping wood.

aegis (11j1) a shield; *Under the aegis of* = under the protection of —.

aeon (11-9) long time—longer time than can be measured.

aerate (29-21) drive air, or gas into; *Aerated water* = water filled with gas.

aerial (29-19) (1) belonging to the air; (2) wire hung in the air to receive radio signals.

aerie, aery, eyrie, eyry (29-1) nest of a bird in a high tree or on a high rock; young of a meat-eating bird which builds such a nest.

aero- (29-9-) having to do with the air; **aeroplane** (29-9-21) flying machine which is heavier than air; **aeronaut** (29-9-55) one who goes in aeroplanes or airships; **aeron'autical** (29-9-55-1) having to do with aeroplanes; **aerodrome** (29-9-67), **airdrome** (29-67) place where aeroplanes come to earth, or from which they set out on journeys.

aesth'etic (11-2-1) having to do with beauty; **an 'aesthete** (11-11) one who pretends to love art and beauty very much.

aether (11-9) see Ether.

aeti'ology (11-15-9j1) study of the cause or beginnings of things.

af'ar (9-44) at a distance.

affable (3-9) easy to talk to, friendly; n. **affab'ility** (3-9-1-1-1).

aff'air (9-29) matter of business; event; Sl. *Her hat was a strange affair* = — thing.

aff'ect (9-2) (1) act on, have a result on; (2) move the feelings; (3) pretend; (4) like, love; **aff'ected** (——1) not natural, pretending; **affect'ation** (3-2-21shn) unnatural way of behaving, pretending to be different from one's real self, pretending to feel, e.g. *An affectation of kindness*; **aff'ection** (9-2-shn) love; *An affection of (the throat)* = illness or disease; **aff'ectionate** (9-2-sh9-1) loving.

aff'iance (9-41 9-s) promise to marry.

affid'avit (3-1-21-1) written account of an event sworn in the presence of an officer of the law to be true.

aff'iliate (9-1-12 1) (take as a son) join on to, e.g. *Our school is affiliated to the university* = the university allows the children of the school to take certain examinations.

aff'inity (9-1-1-1) nearness in blood or in natural character; being of the same family; sameness; friendliness.

aff'irm (9-99) say with certainty, say solemnly; *To answer in the* **aff'irmative** (9-99-9-1) = say " yes "; **affirm'ation** (3-9-21shn).

aff'ix (9-1) fix to; *To affix one's signature* = write one's name at the bottom of a paper.

affl'ict (9-1) give pain to; **affl'iction** (——shn) pain, sorrow.

affluent (3-79) flowing freely; rich; **an affluent,** stream which flows into another.

aff'ord (9-55) to produce; *The trees afford us shade* = give —; be able to pay for, e.g. *I can't afford to buy a car* = have not enough money to buy —; *He afforded me no chance of* — = gave me no chance.

aff'orest (9-5-1) to plant with trees.

affr'ay (9-21) a fight.

affr'ight (9-41) frighten; n. fear.

affr'ont (9-8) be very rude and impolite to; **an affr'ont**, impolite act or saying.

af'ield (9-11) in the field; far away from home.

af'ire (9-419) on fire.

afl'ame (9-21) in flames, burning.

afl'oat (9-67) floating; on a ship; *There is a story afloat that* = people are saying that —.

af'oot (9-7) on foot, walking; being planned or done; *There is mischief afoot* = some evil is being planned.

af'oresaid (9-55-2) said before.

af'oretime (9-55-41) in old times.

a forti'ori (21 + 55-155-41) with still greater reason.

afr'aid (9-21) frightened.

afr'esh (9-2) again.

'Afrik'aner (3-1-44-9) a descendant of the European, mostly Dutch people who made South Africa their home, generally used of those who speak **Afrikaans**, sometimes used of any South African.

aft (44) towards the back of a ship.

after (44-9) later in time; behind; *To look after* = take care of, be in charge of; *To ask after* = ask for news about; *After a manner* = not very well; *Each after his kind* = —according to his nature.

aftermath (44-9-3) result of some event.

afterthought (44-9-55) something thought of after an act or a speech; something thought of too late, after the chance of saying it or doing it has gone.

afterwards (44-9-9-z) later.

ag'ain (9-21 or 9-2) (1) back to the first place, as before, e.g. *To be home again, To be well again*; (2) a second time; *Now and again* = sometimes; *Again and again* = often; *And, again, But then, again* = as a further thought.

ag'ainst (9-21) opposite, as an enemy, striking from the other direction; *To run up against* = meet by accident; *Lay up money against a rainy day* = — in preparation for bad times in future.

ag'ape (9-21) with the mouth open.

agar-agar (21-44 + 21-44) jelly got from seaplants used in science and medicine.

agate (3-9) very hard stone used as a jewel.

age (21j) (1) length of time; (2) length of one's life; *To come of age* = reach the age of 21, the age of manhood according to the law; **to age**, become old; **aged** (21j1) old; **ageless** (21j-1) never becoming old; **agelong** (21j-5) lasting through all time.

agency (21j9-s1) power or means by which something is done; work of an *agent* (see below); place where an *agent* (see below) works.

ag'enda (9j2-9) list of things to be settled at a meeting.

agene (21j11) chemical used to whiten flour (it is bad for animals).

agent (21j) person who acts for another; a cause, e.g. water is the agent which wears away the rocks; *A house-agent* = one who arranges the selling and renting of houses.

aggl'omerate (9-5-9-21) gather into a mass; *Agglomerate rock* = rock made up of bits of other rocks melted together.

aggl'utinate (9-77-1-21) stick together; become a sticky or jelly-like mass.

aggr'andize (9-3-41) make greater in size, power, or rank; **aggr'andizement** (9-3-1z-9).

aggravate (3-9-21) make worse; make angry; *How aggravating!* = this makes me angry.

aggregate (3-1-21) gather into a group or mass; **the aggregate** (3-1-1) whole amount; *In the aggregate* = looked at as a whole; **aggregates** = broken stone to be mixed with *cement* (= powder which, with water, makes stone-like material).

aggr'ession (9-2shn) an attack; **aggressive** (——1) quick to attack; *To take the aggressive* = to attack; **the aggressor** (——9) first to attack, the one who starts a fight.

aggr'ieved (9-11) feeling that one has good reason for complaint.

agh'ast (9-44) struck with sudden surprise or terror.

agile (3j41) quick-moving; **ag'ility** (9j1-1-1) quickness.

agitate (3j1-21) cause to move; shake; excite; cause people to fight against the government to make a change in the laws, etc.

agl'ow (9-67) shining; heated; excited.

agn'ostic (9-5-1) one who believes that nothing can be known about God or the future life.

ag'o (9-67) in the past.

ag'og (9-65) eager, excited.

agony (3-9-1) great pain; terrible struggle; **agonizing** (3-9-41-1) causing terrible pain, or sorrow.

agr'arian (9-29-19) having to do with land.

agr'ee (9-11) have the same opinion as; be friendly with; *Your story does not agree with the facts* = is different from —; *This place agrees with me* = suits me, is good for my health; **agr'eeable** (9-19) nice, ready to agree; *I am quite agreeable* = I will do as you wish; *I was agreeably surprised* = I found it better than I expected; *Agreeable to* = according to; **agr'eement** (9-11-9) agreeing; written promise made by two or more people.

agriculture (3-1-8-tsh9) art of making things grow on the land, farming; **an agric'ulturist** (3-1-8tsh9-1) farmer.

agr'ound (9-47) (used of a ship) stuck on the ground.

ague (21-17) fever.

ah'ead (9-2) in front of, e.g. *To go ahead of the rest*; forward; *Go ahead* = continue your story (work, etc.).

ah'em (9-9) sound made with the throat as a warning; the written form of a *cough* (= sudden driving of air from the throat).

ah'oy (9-51) shout used at sea for calling a ship.

aid (21) help.

aide-de-camp (21 + 9 + 44ⁿ) officer who attends on the leader of an army or officer of high rank and carries his orders.

AIGRETTE

aigrette (21-2) bunch of feathers worn in a hat; ornament of this shape.

ail (21) to trouble; be ill; *What ails you?* = what's the matter?; **ailing**, ill; **ailment** (——9) an illness.

aileron (21-9-5) edge of the wing of an aeroplane moved to control the aeroplane.

AILERON

aim at (21) try to reach, try to hit; *point a gun at;* **an aim**, thing aimed at; purpose; **aimless** (——1) without purpose.

air (29) mixture of gases which we breathe; *There are many plans in the air* = plans not yet ready for action; *To take the air* = go out for a walk; Sl. *Hot air* = proud or useless talk; *Tread on air* = be happy and excited; *Castles in the air* = plans which can never be acted upon; **to air**, put out in the air to get dry; let air into a room; *To air one's opinions* = talk about —; *On the air* = being heard by radio.

air (29) manner; e.g. *He has a proud air*; *To put on airs* = act in a proud way; *Airs and graces* = foolish unnatural ways of behaving.

air (29) music of a song without the words.

airborne (29-55) carried in aeroplanes; flying; *airborne disease* = illness carried from person to person through the air.

'air-cond'itioning (+ k9-1-sh9-1) keeping the air in houses cool (warm) dry (less dry) by a machine.

aircraft (29-44) airships and (or) aeroplanes.

airdrome (29-67) **aerodrome** (29-9-67) place where aeroplanes come to earth and set off.

air force (+ 55s) the strength of a country in machines and men for fighting in the air.

airgun (29-8) gun worked by air.

airing (29-1) *to give clothes an airing* = dry thoroughly.

airline (29-41) number of aeroplanes carrying goods and people at regular times from one place to another.

airlock (29-5) small amount of air in a pipe which prevents the regular flow of liquid.

airmail (29-21) letters carried by aeroplanes.

airman (29-9) man who flies in an aeroplane.

airplane (29-21) flying machine which is heavier than air.

airport (29-55) place where aeroplanes come to earth, set off, are repaired, etc.

air-raid (+ 21) attack by aeroplanes or airships.

airscrew (29-77) blade driven by the engine to drive an aeroplane.

airship (29-1) gas-filled ship which floats in, and moves through, the air.

air-strip (+ 1) long hard road along which aeroplanes go up or come down.

airtight (29-41) keeping air in (or out).

aisles (41) of a church = the parts which lie on either side of the nave (= central space).

aj'ar (9-44) not quite shut, e.g. door, window.

ak'imbo (9-1-67) with the arms bent and hands on the sides—like a pot with two handles. AISLE

ak'in (9-1) of the same family; alike.

alabaster (3-9-44-9) soft white stone like rather white glass.

à la c'arte (4 + 4 + 4) (meal) ordered dish by dish, not as a whole.

al'ack (9-3) cry of grief.

al'acrity (9-3-1-1) quickness.

à la m'ode (4 + 4 + 5) according to the latest ideas or customs.

al'arm (9-44) warning of danger; feeling of fear; call to arms; **to al'arm**, give warning of danger, frighten; **an al'armist**, one who is always warning people that terrible things are going to happen.

al'arm-clock (9-44) clock which rings a bell to waken one in the morning.

al'as (9-44) cry of grief.

albatross (3-9-5) large white sea-bird.

alb'eit (55-11·1) although.

alb'ino (3-11-67) person with white skin and hair and light red eyes; person or animal lacking colouring matter in the body.

album (3-9) book of plain, unprinted pages for collecting stamps, pictures, etc.

albumen (3-17-2) white liquid in an egg; material of the same kind as this.

alchemist (3-k9-1) one who in old times studied the nature of matter, chiefly with the aim of changing other materials into gold, or of finding a liquid which would make men live for ever; **alchemy** (——1) study of such things.

alcohol (3-9-5) pure form of that liquid which gives wine its power; **alcoh'olic** (3-9-5-1) containing alcohol; *An alcoholic* = one who drinks too much wine and strong drink.

alcove (3-67) part of a room cut off from the rest, e.g. for a bed; small house in the garden for sitting in.

alder (55-9) tree which grows in wet land.

alderman (55-9-9) member of the *city-council* (= group of men who govern a city), or of a *county* council.

aldis lamp (55-1 + 3) lamp used for sending messages by long and short flashes.

ale (21) drink with a bitter taste made from grain.

al'ert (9-99) watchful.

alf'alfa (3-3-9) green plant used for feeding cattle.

alfr'esco (meal) (3-2-67) (meal) in the open air.

alga (3-9) **(-ae)** (3-ji) water-plant(s) of very simple form.

algebra (3-ji-9) way of calculating in which letters stand for numbers and quantities; adj. **algebraic** (3-ji-21·1).

alias (21-13) name other than the real name, e.g. *Jones alias Smith* = Jones who called himself Smith.

alibi (3-1-41) *To prove an alibi* = prove that one was somewhere else, not in the place where a bad deed was done.

alien (21-19) foreign; **an alien**, foreigner; **to 'alien'ate** (——21) give to another, to turn away from; **in'alienable** (1-21-19-9) which cannot be given or taken away; **alienist**, doctor who treats mad people.

al'ight (9-41) get down from a carriage, horse, etc.; (of a bird) come to earth, settle.

al'ight (9-41) on fire.

al'ike (9-41) like each other; *Share and share alike* = share equally.

aliment (3-1-9) food; *The* **alim'entary** (3-1-2-9-1) *canal* = pipe leading from the mouth to the stomach and onwards.

alimony (3-1-9-1) money which must be paid to a woman by her husband to support her after she has been separated from him by law.

al'ine, al'ign (9-41) bring into line.

al'ive (9-41) living; active; *Look alive!* = be quick; *Alive with (fish)* = full of —; *I am alive to possible danger* = I know of —.

alkali (3-9-41) opposite of an acid (an alkali mixed with an acid forms a salt); adj. **alkaline.**

alkaloids (3-9-51-z) certain very poisonous materials obtained from plants and much used in medicine, e.g. to produce sleep.

all (55) whole amount; *For good and all* = for ever; *Once for all* = this time and not again; *All in good time* = do not be in a hurry; all will be done if you wait; *After all* = after considering everything; *My all-in-all* = dearly loved one; *36 in all* = 36 counting them all; *Not at all good* = not good in any part or in any way; *All but lost* = very nearly —; *All over* = over the whole surface; *It's all over* = quite finished; *That's him all over* = that is just the kind of thing he would do; *It's all over (all up) with him* = he is ruined, or dying; *All fours* (see below); Sl. *Go all out* = use all one's strength.

Allah (3-9) God (Arabic word).

all'ay (9-2I) make less, to calm, e.g. *To allay pain, to allay the storm.*

all'ege (3-2j) say as a fact, e.g. *He alleges that he was there;* bring forward as a reason; n. **alleg'ation** (3-2-2Ishn).

all'egiance (9-IIj9-s) loyalty, duty to one's ruler (king, etc.).

allegory (3-I-9-I) story in which persons and things stand for special ideas; lesson taught in the form of a story; adj. **alleg'orical** (3-I-5-I).

all'ergic to (3-99jI) even a very small amount of (e.g. egg-white, animal hair, etc.) causes serious effects in the body of a person who is allergic to it; n. **'allergy** (3-9-I).

all'eviate (9-II-I2I) make less, or easier to bear, e.g. *To alleviate pain.*

alley (3-I) (1) small round ball of stone or glass used by children in playing the game of "Marbles"; (2) narrow path or road between buildings; *A blind alley* = road which ends in a wall or building so that one cannot pass through, but must turn back; employment which does not lead on to other, better work.

all f'ours (on) (55 + 55z) down on the hands and knees; *On all fours with* = exactly equal to or like.

all'iance (9-4Ij9-s) union between families by marriage; promise between governments to help each other.

allies (3-4Iz) pl. of ally.

alligator (3-I-2I-9) creature with four legs, a long tail, a large mouth, living in rivers; it sometimes eats men.

ALLIGATOR

all-in wrestling (55 + I + r2slI) two men fighting with hands and feet, almost all forms of attack allowed.

alliter'ation (9-I-9-2Ishn) beginning several words with the same sound, e.g. Sing a Song of Sixpence; **to all'iterate**.

allocate (3-9-2I) set apart for a special person, or special purpose.

all'ot (9-5I) give a part to each person; **an all'otment** (——9) share, part of a field divided up among many persons, so as to give each a small vegetable garden.

all'ow (9-47) (1) to permit, let a person have or do; (2) give, e.g. *He allows his son £200 a year;* **all'owance**—*Make him an allowance of £200 a year* = pay regularly; *Make allowances for his youth* = remember it and so forgive his mistakes; (3) agree that a thing is true, e.g. *I allow that I was wrong; I have allowed for 20 people* = have prepared for.

alloy (3-5I) metals mixed together; **to all'oy** (9-5I) mix metals; *Unalloyed pleasure* = —— with no pain in it at all.

allspice (55-4Is) fruit of a tree called the "Pimento" used to give a pleasant taste to food.

all'ude to (9-77) speak of indirectly; e.g. *He did not say Mr. Smith's name, but it was clear he was alluding to him.*

all'ure (9-I79) charm, draw on, win the love of.

all'usion (9-773n) *To make an allusion to* = speak of not directly but in passing.

all'uvial (9-77-I9) *Alluvial soil* = soil left by rivers.

all'y (9-4I) unite, e.g. families in marriage, countries in making war; *Closely allied to* = very like, of the same kind; **an 'ally** (3-4I) one who is allied with another.

'Alma M'ater (3-9 + 2I-9) (Latin, kind mother) school or university at which a person was taught.

almanac (55-9-3) list of days, months, etc.

alm'ighty (55-4I-I) having all power, e.g. *Almighty God.*

almond (44-9) tree; nut of the almond tree.

almoner (3-9-9) officer in charge of the giving of money and help to the poor; person who arranges help for the families of people in hospital or for people after they leave hospital.

almost (55-67) nearly.

alms (44-z) gifts to the poor; **an 'almshouse**, house used as a home for the old poor.

aloe (3-67) plant with thick leaves, growing chiefly in hot countries, from which a very bitter liquid is obtained and used as a medicine.

al'oft (9-5) high up, especially on a ship, up among the sails.

al'one (9-67) separate, not with others; *Leave me alone* = do not trouble me; *He did not speak to me, let alone help me* = did not help me, did not even speak to me.

ALOE

al'ong (9-5) (1) following the length of, from end to end, e.g. *To walk along the road;* (2) on, forward, e.g. *Let's get along* = let us start; *I knew it all along* = — all the time; *James along with Alice* = together with.

alongs'ide (of) (9-5-4I) by the side (of).

al'oof (9-77) at a distance from; *To hold aloof* = keep separate from.

alop'ecia (3-67-IIsI9) lack of hair on the head.

al'oud (9-47) with a loud voice.

Alp (3) high mountain; **The Alps,** high mountains in Switzerland.

alp'aca (3-3-9) (1) South American animal, like a sheep, with long fine wool; (2) cloth made from this wool—often mixed with silk or cotton.

alpenstock (3-9-5) stick with an iron point used in mountain-climbing.

alpha (3-9) first Greek letter; *I am Alpha and Omega* = — the beginning and the end; *Alpha* = good, first class (examination mark); *Alpha minus* = less good than Alpha; *Alpha plus* = very good.

alphabet (3-9-2) letters, A.B.C., etc.; *In alphab'etical order* = in A.B.C. order.

Alpine (3-41) having to do with mountains, e.g. The Alps in Switzerland; **alpinist** (3-1-1) mountain-climber.

alr'eady (55-2-1) before this time.

alr'ight (55-41) Sl. in good order, correct, I agree; (correct form, All right).

also (55-67) too, added to.

altar (55-9) raised place on which offerings are made to a god; table at the end of a Christian church; *To lead to the altar* = marry.

alter (55-9) to change, become changed; **an alter'ation** (——21shn) a change.

alterc'ation (55-9-21shn) a quarrel.

'alter 'ego (3-9 + 2-67) (Latin, one's other self) a very close friend.

alt'ernately (5-99-1-1) first one, then the other; **to 'alternate** (5-9-21) use first one, then the other; happen in turn.

alternating current (55-9-21-1 + 8-9) flow of electricity to and fro along a wire about 50 times per second.

alt'ernative (5-99-9-1) offering the choice of two things; *I have no alternative* = I have no choice, there is no other thing which I can do.

alth'ough (55-067) though; *Although it is raining, I shall go* = it is raining, but —.

altitude (3-1-177) height, e.g. of mountains.

alto (3-67) very deep voice of boy, or very high voice of a man.

'altog'ether (55-9-209) completely; *Well, altogether, I'm glad* = after considering all things —.

altruist (3-771) one who thinks of the good of others rather than of his own; **altruism** = thinking of — one's own.

alum (3) hard bitter salt which hardens and draws together the skin.

alum'inium (3-19-1-19) (**al'uminum**) white metal, very light.

al'umnus (9-8-9) member of a school or university.

always (55-21z) at all times, for ever.

A.M. (21 + 2) see *'Ante mer'idiem*.

am'ain (9-21) with all one's force; at full speed.

am'algam (3-9-9) *mercury* (= heavy white liquid metal) mixed with another metal; **to am'algam'ate** (9-3-9-21) mix together, to unite, e.g. *To amalgamate two businesses so as to form one business company*.

am'anu'ensis (9-3-17:2-1) one employed to help in writing.

amaranth (3-9-3) flower, spoken of by poets, which never fades.

am'ass (9-3) collect a large quantity of.

amateur (3-9-9) one who studies an art, or plays a game, for the love of it, not for money; **amat'eurish**, not perfect, done by an unpractised person.

amatory (3-9-9-1) having to do with love, causing love.

am'aze (9-21) surprise greatly.

Amazon (3-9) woman-soldier; tall, strong, man-like woman.

amb'assador (3-3-9-9) officer of the government sent to another country to act for his own government; **amb'assadress** (——1) (1) wife of an ambassador; (2) woman acting as an ambassador.

amber (3-9) clear yellow stone-like material, formed of the liquid of a tree changed in the course of thousands of years into this stone-like condition.

ambergris (3-9-1) grey fat found floating in the sea, valued for making scents. (A *whale* is a large sea creature; *ambergris* is matter thrown up from the stomach of a whale.)

ambid'extrous (3-1-2-9) able to do things equally well with either hand.

amb'iguous (3-1-179) not clear as to meaning, which may be understood in more than one way.

ambit (3-1) the space round about, e.g. a house; a circle round.

amb'ition (3-1shn) desire for success and power; the success desired, e.g. *It is my ambition to be a great singer*; adj. **amb'itious** (3-1sh9s).

amble (3) (of a horse) move the two right legs, then the two left; go at an easy pace.

ambr'osia (3-67z19) food of the gods.

ambulance (3-17-9-s) carriage for the sick or wounded; hospital moved about with an army.

ambulant (3-17-9) able to walk about although ill; not kept in bed.

ambusc'ade (3-9-21) **ambush** (3-7) hiding of men in a secret place in order to attack by surprise.

am'eliorate (9-11-19-21) make better.

'am'en (44-2 or 21-2) word said at the end of a prayer, meaning "So may it be."

am'enable (9-11-9) able to be controlled, or led.

am'end (9-2) grow better, make a thing better; change the words of a law or rule which is being considered in a meeting; **amendment** (——9) = such a change; *To make amends* = do something to pay for, or make good some harm done to another.

am'enity (9-11-1-1) pleasantness; **am'enities** pleasant conditions.

Am'erican cl'oth (9-2-1-9 + 5) cloth covered with special material which makes it look like leather.

amethyst (3-1-1) red-blue jewel.

amiable (21-19) friendly, kind.

amicable (3-1-9) friendly.

am'id (9-1) in the middle of; **am'idships** (9-1-1) in the middle of a ship; **am'idst** (9-1) in the middle of.

am'ir (9-19) ruler, king, e.g. of Afghanistan.

am'iss (9-1) wrong, wrongly; *Nothing comes amiss to him* = he is prepared for, able to deal with, anything.

amity (3-1-1) friendship.

ammeter (3\-I\-9) instrument for measuring electric flow in *amperes* (see Ampere).

amm'onia (9-67-19) strong-smelling *alkaline* (= adj. of alkali, opposite of an acid) gas, often used in making ice.

ammonite (3-9-4I) shell-fish which lived long ago; its shell turned to stone.

amm'onium (9-67-19) *ammonia* gas (see Ammonia above) *combined* (= mixed, joined) with water, or an acid; liquid used for cleaning clothes.

ammun'ition (3-17-Ishn) powder and shot for guns; *Ammunition boots* = soldier's *boots* (= high shoes covering part of the leg).

amn'esia (3-11z19) loss of memory.

amnesty (3-I-I) setting free of all prisoners, a general forgiving of wrong-doers by a ruler (e.g. king).

am'oeba (9-11-9) simplest living creature, found in water (seen through the microscope it looks like a little glass ball).

amok (9-8) see Amuck.

am'ong, am'ongst (9-8) mixed with, in the middle of, between.

amorous (3-9-9) easily moved to love.

am'orphous (9-55-9) shapeless.

am'ount (9-47) add up to; become equal to; *Your words amount to this* = this is the real meaning of all that you have said; **am'ount**, n., the whole, the result of adding; certain quantity or number.

am'our-pr'opre (4-779 + 5-9) self-respect.

ampere (3-29) measure of the amount of electricity passing along a wire.

ampersand (3-9-3) sign & (= and).

amph'ibious (3-I-19) living both on land and in water; **an amph'ibian** (——19) creature which lives —.

amphitheatre (3-I-19-9) building with rows of seats all round an open space in the middle, used for public games and shows; upper seats in a theatre.

ample (3) big enough, large; **amply** (3-I) fully; **amplify** (3-I-I) make larger or louder; **amplitude** (3-I-177) great space, enough space; **an amplifier** (3-I-419) electric instrument used to make sounds louder.

amputate (a limb) (3-17-2I) cut off (a limb).

am'uck, amok (9-8) *To run amuck* = become *mad* and try to kill people.

amulet (3-17-I) thing worn as a magic charm.

am'use (9-177z) cause a person's time to pass pleasantly; make a person laugh; **am'usement** (9-177z-9) feeling of *laughter*; pleasant way of passing time.

-ana (44-9) e.g. *Johnsoniana*, stories about and sayings of Dr. Johnson.

an'achronism (9-3k-9-Iz) thing which could not happen at the date supposed, e.g. "Julius Caesar got into his motor-car."

'anac'onda (3-9-5-9) large snake.

an'aemia (9-11-19) lack of blood; weakness or bad quality of the blood.

anaesth'esia (3-I-11z19) loss of all the senses in a deep sleep, caused by doctors before they cut open the body of a sick person; **anaesth'etic** (3-I-2-I) causing such a state; **an anaesth'etic**, any liquid or gas used for this purpose; **to an'aesthetize** (9-11-9-4Iz) cause such a state; **an an'aesthetist** (9-11-9-I) one who causes —.

anagram (3-9-3) new word made up out of the letters of another, e.g. Name—Mean.

an'alogy (9-3-9jI) agreement or likeness in certain ways, e.g. *On the analogy of Tough, "Cough" should be said as "Cuff."*

analyse (3-9-4Iz) divide up a thing into the parts of which it is made; separate out the different materials of which a mixed material is made up, e.g. *The scientist analysed the liquid and found that it was made up of A, B, and C (various materials)*; n. **an'alysis** (9-3-I-); **an 'analyst** (3-9-I) one who analyses; **anal'ytical** (3-9-I-I).

'Anan'ias (3-9-419) one who tells untruths.

anarchy (3-9kI) state of having no government at all; **an anarchist** (3-9kI) one who wishes to destroy all government.

an'athema (9-3-I-9) solemn curse, thing cursed.

an'atomy (9-3-9-I) (1) study of the parts of the body; (2) cutting up a dead body so as to learn its parts; **an an'atomist**, one who studies or teaches anatomy; **anat'omical** (3-9-5-I).

ancestor(s) (3-s2-9z) those persons from whom one is descended, e.g. great-great-grandfather, etc.; **anc'estral** (3-s2); **'ancestry** (——I) one's ancestors.

anchor (3ngk9) instrument let down to the bottom of the sea to prevent a ship from moving; **to anchor**, fix a ship in one place with an anchor; **an anchorage** (3ngk9-Ij) good place in which to anchor a ship.

anchorite (3ngk9-4I) man who lives alone for religious reasons.

ANCHOR

anch'ovy (3-67-I) small fish having a very strong taste, salted and used for food.

ancient (2I-sh9) old, belonging to a time long ago; *The ancients* = those who lived long ago.

and'ante (3-3-I) (Music) gently, without hurry.

andiron (3-419) iron instrument used for holding the logs in a fire.

anecdote (3-I-67) short story; **anecdotage** (3-I-67-Ij) that age at which old people tell long uninteresting stories (*dotage* = old age).

an'emia (9-11-19) see Anaemia.

an'emone (9-2-9-I) flower; **sea-anemone**, creature like a flower, living in the sea.

an'ent (9-2) about, on the subject of.

aneroid (barometer) (3-9-5I) instrument used to measure the *pressure* (= pressing down) of the air, e.g. so as to show what the weather will be; it does this by means of a box from which most of the air has been driven out.

ANEROID

anesth'etic (3-1-2-1) see Anaesthetic.
an'ew (9-177) again.
angel (2Inj) spirit who carries God's messages; *She is an angel* = — is a very good woman; adj. **ang'elic** (3nj2-1).
Angelus (3nj9-9) *The Angelus* = prayer said in memory of the birth of Jesus Christ at the beginning, middle and end of the day, at the sound of the Angelus bell; Angelus bell.
anger (3ngg) feeling which makes people want to quarrel, fight and do harm.
ang'ina p'ectoris (3nj41-9 + 3-9-1) disease of the heart which causes great pain.
angle (3ngg) catch fish with a hook; *To angle for* = try to lead a person on to give one some desired thing; **an angler**, man who catches fish.
angle (3ngg) meeting of two lines; corner.
Anglican (3ngg-1-9) having to do with the Church of England.
anglicize (3ngg-IS4Iz) make English in form or custom.
Anglo- (3ngg-67) English. **An Anglo-Indian** (+ 1-19) (1) Englishman who has lived long in India; (2) one of mixed English and Indian birth; **'Angloph'obia** (3ngg-67-67-19) hatred of England; **'Anglom'ania** (3ngg-67-21-19) great love of England and English ways.
'Ang'ora (3ngg55-9) (name of the city, = 'Ankara, from which Turkey is governed); cat, rabbit or goat with long hair.
angry (3ngg-1) being in a state of anger; *An angry wound* = red and painful —.
Ångström unit (2ngstr5m) one hundred-millionth of a centimetre.
anguish (3nggwI) great pain, or sorrow.
angular (3nggI7-9) having many sharp corners.
anh'ydrous (3-41-9) containing no water and so in powder (not crystal) form.
aniline (dye) (3-1-11) *dye* is a colouring matter, e.g. for colouring cloth; aniline dyes are made from coal.
'animadv'ert (3-1-3-99) to blame.
animal (3-1) living thing which is not a plant; adj. *Animal desires* = — like those of an animal; **anim'alcule** (3-1-3-I77) animal too small to be seen by the eye without a microscope.
animate (3-1-21) give life to; *Animated talk* = talk which is full of life, clever, amusing; **animated cartoon** (3-1-21-1 + 44-77) cinema film of drawings which move, e.g. Donald Duck.

animism (3-1-Iz) belief that all objects have souls.
anim'osity (3-1-5-1-1) strong hatred; **'animus** (3-1-9) hatred of a particular person, group or thing so that one is not just in dealing with it (him).
anise (3-1) plant whose seeds taste nice; **aniseed** (3-1-11) seeds of anise used in making sweets and strong drink.
ankle (3ngk) part of the leg where the foot is joined on; **anklet** (3ngk-1) jewelled band worn on the ankle.
anna (3-9) Indian *coin* (= piece of money made of metal), value about one penny.
annals (3-z) history written down year by year.
ann'eal (9-11·9) make glass, iron, etc., strong by heating it and cooling it slowly.
ann'ex (9-2) (1) add, join on; (of governments) add to one's own country; (2) seize land; **'annexe** (3-2), small building added to, or used as well as, a larger one, e.g. *The annexe of a hotel*.
ann'ihilate (9-419-21) destroy completely.
anniv'ersary (3-1-99-9-1) return each year of a certain date; date on which some great event is remembered each year.
'Anno D'omini (3-67 + 5-1-41) A.D., in the year of Our Lord, e.g. A.D. 1900 = 1900 years since Christ was born.
annotate (3-67-21) add *explanatory* (= explaining) notes to.
ann'ounce (9-47-s) make (news or facts) known; say the name of a guest when leading him into a room; n. **an ann'ouncer** (radio).
ann'oy (9-51) trouble, make angry; **ann'oyance** (9-5I9-9) feeling of anger.
annual (3-I79) happening every year; **an annual**, plant which grows up and dies in a year; book of facts, stories or pictures printed and sold every year.
ann'uity (9-I7I-1) amount of money paid every year; **ann'uitant** (9-I7I-9) one who receives an annuity.
ann'ul (9-8) bring to nothing, destroy; *That law has been annulled* = has been crossed off the book of laws.
ann'unci'ation (9-8-sI2Ishn) a telling, e.g. of important news, especially the telling to Mary that she would become the Mother of Jesus Christ.
anode (3-67) the + plate, e.g., in a radio valve (tube) to which electricity flows.
anodyne (3-67-4I) thing which makes pain less.
an'oint (9-5I) put oil on, make holy by putting oil on.
an'omalous (9-5-9-9) unusual, irregular, not according to natural law, e.g. *A wingless bird is an* **an'omaly** (——-I).
an'on (9-5) after a short time; *Ever and anon* = from time to time, sometimes.
an'on (9-5) short for Anonymous (see below).

an'onymous (9-5-1-9) nameless, without the name of the writer; **anon'ymity** (3-5-1-1-1) state of being nameless.

an'opheles (mosquito) (9-5-9-11z) kind of *mosquito* (= small flying insect) whose bite causes *Malaria* (= fever common in Africa, India and other hot countries).

ANOPHELES

an'oxia (3-5-19) lack of oxygen.

answer (44-9) speak or write in return; *To answer the bell* = go to the door when the door bell rings; *That will answer my purpose* = will be useful for my need; *Our plan has not answered* = has been unsuccessful; *I can answer for his skill* = I can promise that he is skilful; *He must answer for all the wrong which he has done* = be punished —; *He answers to your description* = is as you described; *You will be* **answerable** (——9) *for this* = will be asked to explain this, may be blamed for this; n. an answer.

ant(s) (3) small creatures which build their nests in the ground, or hill-like nests above ground.

ant'agonist (3-3-9-1) *My antagonist* = person who is struggling against me; **ant'agonize** (——41) make a person one's enemy.

ant'arctic (3-44-1) very cold part in the farthest southern part of the earth.

ante- (3-1) before; **antec'edent** (3-1s11) going before, before in time; **'ante-chamber** (+ 21-9) small room through which one enters some larger room; **'anted'ate** (3-1-21) give an earlier date than the real date; **antedil'uvian** (3-1-1-77-19) before the days of Noah, in whose time all the world was supposed to have been covered with water.

antelope (3-1-67) animal like a deer.

'ante mer'idiem (3-1 + 9-1-19) *a.m.*, in the morning, before 12 o'clock.

'anten'atal (3-1-21) before birth.

ant'ennae (3-2-11) (1) things like two long hairs fixed on the front of the head of an ant, bee, or other insect; the creature feels its way with its antennae; (2) fine wires used in electrical instruments.

ant'erior (3-19-19) earlier.

anteroom (3-1-7) small room through which one enters a larger room; waiting-room.

anthem (3-9) piece of music sung in a church; *The National Anthem* = special song of a country, e.g. " God save the Queen " is the English national anthem.

anther (3-9) that part of a flower which carries the *pollen* (= yellow dust which bees carry from flower to flower, and so start the growth of the seeds).

anth'ology (3-5-9j1) collection of poems or other written pieces.

anthracite (3-9s41) very hard coal.

anthrax (3-3) dangerous disease (a form of blood-poisoning) in cattle; it also attacks man.

anthropoid (3-9-51) like a man, e.g. *An anthropoid ape* = large monkey-like creature.

anthropo- having to do with man, e.g. **anthrop'ology** (3-9-5-9j1) study of the races of Man.

anti- (3-1) against, e.g. *anti-smoking* = not in favour of people smoking pipes or cigarettes.

'antibi'otic (3-1-415-1) substance produced by a living thing (e.g. by a fungus) which prevents the growth of other living things, e.g. penicillin prevents growth of germs.

'anti'body (3-1-5-1) material formed in the body to fight against a disease.

antic (3-1) strange trick, peculiar movement.

ant'icipate (3-1s1-21) take before the proper time; think of or enjoy a thing before it actually comes; expect; know what an enemy is going to do and make preparations to prevent it.

'anticl'imax (3-1-41-3) sudden and laughable loss of force in a speech, e.g. foolish saying following much good sense.

antidote (3-1-67) something given to prevent the effects of a poison or disease.

antimony (3-1-9-1) blue-white metal which becomes a little larger when it grows solid after melting; mixed with other metals makes them harder.

ant'ipathy (3-1-9-1) a dislike.

ant'ipodes (3-1-9-11z) that part of the world just on the opposite side from our own part.

antiqu'arian (3-1-29-19) **'antiquary** (3-1-9-1) one who studies or collects old things; **ant'ique** (3-11k) old; **'antiquated** (3-1-21-1) old, not such as is used today; **ant'iquity** (3-1-1-1) (1) old times long ago; (2) thing which is of value or interest because of its age.

'antis'eptic, an (3-1-2-1) liquid or powder which kills the seeds of disease; adj. **antiseptic**, having the power to kill seeds of disease.

ant'ithesis (3-1-1-1) exact opposite; adj. **antith'etical** (3-1-2-1).

'antit'oxin (3-1-5-1) material, usually liquid, which is able to destroy the poison (of disease) in the body; antitoxins are usually made from the blood of animals which have got well after suffering from that same disease.

antlers (3-9z) horns of a deer.

antonym (3-9-1) word meaning the opposite, e.g. " bad " is the antonym of " good."

antrum (3-9) hollow inside bone, e.g. above the teeth, also above the eyes.

anus (21-9) opening through which waste matter leaves the body.

ANTRUM

anvil (3-1) large mass of iron on which pieces of hot iron (etc.) are hammered into shape.

anxiety   18   **appliance**

anx'iety (3ngz419-1) feeling of fear and doubt about the future; *My chief anxiety is to* = I am above all eager to; **anxious** (3ngsh9) feeling anxiety, causing anxiety.

a'orta (2155-9) great pipe through which blood leaves the heart.

ap'ace (9-21s) swiftly, quickly.

ap'ache (4-44sh) (1) name of an American-Indian people; (2) dangerous thief or murderer in Paris.

ap'art (9-44) separately; *To set apart* = keep for some special purpose; *Joking apart* = not trying to be amusing, but speaking seriously.

'aparth'eid (3-4t·h2I) separation of white and coloured peoples in South Africa into different areas (places).

ap'artment (9-44-9) (1) room; (2) lodgings; (3) (in America) several rooms all on one floor, used as a home.

apath'etic (3-9-2-I) lacking feeling or interest; n. **'apathy** (3-9-I) lack of —.

ape (2I) large monkey-like creature with no tail; **to ape**, behave just like another person, to copy exactly.

ap'erient (9-19-19) liquid or powder given by a doctor to clear the waste matter downwards out of the bowels.

ap'eritive (9-2-9-I) pleasant bitter drink taken before a meal so as to increase one's hunger.

aperture (3-9-179) opening.

apex (2I-2) pointed top of anything.

aph'asia (9-21zI9) loss of power of speech.

aphis (2I-I) (pl. **aphides**) (2I-I-IIz) very small creature found living on roots or leaves of plants.

aphorism (3-9-Iz) short wise saying.

apiary (2I-19-I) place where bees are kept.

ap'iece (9-IIs) for each; *a penny apiece*.

aplomb (3-5) boldness and faith in oneself, in speaking or manner.

ap'ocryphal (9-5-I) of doubtful truth; not contained in that part of the Bible which is generally accepted.

apogee (3-6jII) greatest distance of a star (etc.) from the Earth.

ap'ologize (9-5-9j4I) say that one is sorry for something which one has done; **an ap'ology** (9-5-9jI) saying that —; adj. **apolog'etic** (3-5-9j2-I).

apoplexy (3-9-2-I) bursting of a blood-vessel in the brain, causing loss of power to move or feel.

ap'ostate (9-5-2I) one who changes from one form of belief to another; **ap'ostasy** (9-5-9-I) act of turning away from something in which one used to believe.

ap'ostle (9-5) person sent to teach men about God.

ap'ostrophe (9-5-9-I) written or printed mark, ', e.g. man's.

ap'ostrophize (9-5-9-4Iz) break off a general speech in order to speak to some particular person or group of persons.

ap'othecary (9-5-9-9-I) old name for one who sells medicines.

'apothegm, 'apophthegm (3-6-2) a short practical clever saying.

apotheo'sis (9-5-167-I) act of making a person into a god; giving of great glory to a person.

app'al (9-55) make very frightened or shock greatly.

appanage, apanage (3-9-Ij) anything taken as a natural right because of one's birth or office.

appar'atus (3-9-2I-9) instruments and machines, especially those used by doctors and scientists.

app'arel (9-3) clothes; put clothes on to.

app'arent (9-3) seeming; very clear to see or understand; **app'arently** (——I) as it seems.

appar'ition (3-9-Ishn) appearance, e.g. of the spirit of a dead man.

app'eal (9-II) (1) ask eagerly and anxiously; (2) ask a higher court of law to change the judgment given already by a lower court; *This book does not appeal to me* = does not interest —; **app'ealing**, worthy of pity, moving the heart.

app'ear (9-I9) come before, be seen by, seem; *Appear before a judge* = come before —; **app'earance** (——9-s) an appearing, a look; *He has an unpleasant appearance* = does not look nice.

app'ease (9-IIz) make peaceful, satisfy; **app'easement** (——9) trying to keep peace by giving way to an enemy.

app'ellant (9-2-9) adj. of Appeal (2) (see 3rd above); e.g. *The appellant, An appellant court* = court of appeal.

appell'ation (3-2-2Ishn) name.

app'end (9-2) join on, add; **app'endage** (9-3-Ij) thing added to or hanging from another thing.

app'endix (9-2-I) (1) long note added at the end of a book; (2) the **app'endix**, small pipe, about 1½ inches × ¼ inch wide, leading off the bowel; **app'endic'itis** (9-2-Is4I-I) disease of the appendix; **app'endices** (9-2-IsIIz) pl. of Appendix (of book).

appert'ain (3-9-2I) belong to.

appetite (3-I-4I) desire (e.g. for food); **appetizing**, causing desire (for food); **appetizer**, something which causes desire for food.

appl'aud (9-55) to praise; praise loudly by shouting or other noises; **appl'ause** (——z), praises, shouts of praise.

apple (3) fruit; *Apple of my eye* = most dearly loved person; *Apple of discord* = cause of quarrelling; *I upset his apple-cart* = ruined his plans.

'apple p'ie (3 + 4I) apples cooked in a dish with *pastry* (= mixed flour, butter, etc.) above (Am. pastry above and below); *In apple-pie order* = in perfect order.

appl'iance (9-4I9-s) instrument used for some special purpose.

applicable, applicant, etc., see below, Apply.
appl'iqué work (3-11k2 + 99) cloth or wood ornamented by pieces fixed on to it.
appl'y (9-41) (1) cause to touch, put on, e.g. *To apply paint*; (2) put into practice; (3) *To apply oneself to study* = give oneself keenly to ―; (4) *To apply for* = ask for (e.g. employment); (5) *This does not apply to you* = this does not concern you, this has nothing to do with you; **'applicable** (3-1) able to be applied; **an applicant** (3-1) one who asks for employment, etc.; n. **applic'ation** (3-1-21shn).
app'oint (9-51) fix, set down as a duty, e.g. *Prayers appointed to be read in churches*; *My appointed task* = work fixed for me to do; fix a time and place for a meeting; choose a person for an office; **app'ointment** (―9) meeting arranged, e.g. *To keep an appointment* = be present as arranged; office for which one is chosen; **app'ointments** (of a house), furniture and ornaments.
app'ortion (9-55shn) divide out into shares.
apposite (3-9zI) well chosen, just right, e.g. word or saying.
appos'ition (3-9zIshn) putting of one thing or word next to another.
appr'aise (9-21z) set a price on; **appraisal,** the setting of ―.
appr'eciate (9-11sh1z1) (1) judge the value of; feel that a thing is good and understand in what way it is good; (2) understand, e.g. *I appreciate your difficulty*; (3) to increase in price; **appr'eciable** (9-11sh19) enough to be noticed; **appr'eci'ation** (9-11sh121shn) favourable judgment showing pleasure in ―; **appr'eciative** (9-11sh19-1) able to understand and be pleased by ―.
appreh'end (3-1-2) (1) take hold of, seize; (2) understand; (3) to fear; **appreh'ension** (―shn) understanding; fear; **appreh'ensive** (―1) afraid.
appr'entice (9-2-1s) one who has promised to serve a master for a number of years in order to learn an art or trade.
appr'ise (9-41z) tell, warn.
appr'oach (9-67) move towards; come near to; *I will approach him on the matter* = will ask him about it.
approb'ation (3-9-21shn) thinking well of, thinking that a thing is good.
appr'opriate (9-67-19) proper, right for the purpose; **to appr'opriate** (9-67-121) take as one's own; **appr'opri'ation** (1) act of taking for oneself; (2) act of setting a thing apart for a special person or purpose.
appr'ove (9-77) think well of, say that a thing is good; **appr'oval,** act of thinking well of; *Goods on approval* = ― which may be sent back to the shop if not liked.
appr'oximate (9-5-1-9) **-ly** (――1) nearly, not exactly but almost; **to appr'oximate** (9-5-1-21) be near to (the truth).

app'urtenance (9-99-1-9-s) thing which belongs to another thing, e.g. *The house and its appurtenances* = the house and all the things which usually belong to a house.
apricot (21-1-5) orange-yellow fruit with a large stone in it.
'a pri'ori (21 + 41·55-41) (Latin = from the former) (reasoning) from a general rule to special example, from cause to effect.
apron (21-9) piece of cloth worn in front to protect the clothes; anything of this shape and serving to protect some other object; *Tied to his mother's apron strings* = too long depending on his mother.
aprop'os (3-6-67) (French = on the subject of) adj. well suited to the subject which is being *discussed* (= spoken about); *apropos of* = in regard to, about (some subject about which we have just been speaking).
apse (3) east end of a church which is half-round, instead of square.
apt (3) (1) well suited; (2) *Apt to give trouble* = which will probably ―; **aptitude** (3-1-177) natural cleverness in some particular work.
aqualung (3-9-8) instrument used for breathing under water.
aqu'arium (9-29-19) place specially made for keeping fishes, water-plants and water-animals.
aqu'atic (9-3-1) having to do with water; living in water.

AQUALUNG

aqueduct (3-1-8) pipe or *channel* (=path for liquid) made for bringing water.
aqueous (21-19) watery.
aquiline (3-1-41) *Aquiline nose* = hooked nose like the beak of an *eagle* (= large meat-eating bird).
arab'esque (3-9-2-k) kind of fanciful Arabian painting of flowers and leaves.
arable (3-9) fit for *ploughing* (*a plough* = instrument pulled by horses or cattle for breaking up the ground before planting seeds).
arbiter (44-1-9) man who judges; **arb'itrament** (44-1-9-9) act of judging; **to 'arbitrate** (44-1-21) judge, decide who is right or wrong; **an 'arbitrator** (44-1-21-9) man who decides ―; **'arbitrary** (44-1-9-1) acting not according to rules but according to one's own ideas.
arbor (44-9) rod on which a wheel turns.
arb'oreal (44-55-19) having to do with trees.
arbour (44-9) seat or walk in a garden shaded by trees.
arc (44) part of the *circumference* (= edge) of a circle; **arc-light** (+ 41) electric lamp which gives a very powerful white light.
arc'ade (44-21) row of arches; covered street with shops on both sides.
arch (44) curved part of a building which carries weight, e.g. above a door or window;

curved part of the bottom of the foot; **to arch**, a cat arches its back.

arch (44) chief, head, e.g. *My arch-enemy* = chief enemy; *She gave him an arch look* = an inviting look.

archae'ology (44kI5-9jI) study of ancient things, e.g. art, graves, ruins, etc.

arch'aic (44k2I·I) very old, not used any more; **archaism** (44-2I·Iz) use of an old word or form of words no longer in common use.

archangel (44k2Inj) chief *angel* (= heavenly spirit).

'archb'ishop (44-I-9) high officer in the Christian Church.

archd'uke (44-I77) prince in Austria.

archer (44-9) one who shoots with a bow and arrows; **archery** (———I) art of shooting with bows and arrows.

archip'elago (44kI-2-I-67) sea with many small islands in it; group of small islands.

architect (44kI-2) man who makes the plans for new buildings; **architecture** (44-I-2ktsh9) art of planning buildings, especially beautiful buildings.

architrave (44kI-2I) cross-beam, usually of stone, resting upon two pillars.

archives (44k4I-z) government reports and notes; place where they are kept.

archway (44-2I) way by which one passes under an arch.

arctic (44-I) very cold part in the farthest north.

ardent (44-9) hot, eager; **ardour** (44-9) eagerness.

arduous (44-I79) steep; difficult; causing much labour.

area (29-I9) length × breadth = area; low courtyard between a house and the street.

ar'ena (9-II-9) central space with seats all round it, used for games or public shows.

argon (44-5) gas.

argosy (44-9-I) large ancient ship filled with valuable goods.

argot (44-67) slang, thieves' talk.

argue (44-I7) talk to a person trying to prove or disprove something; **argument** (44-I7-9) talk of this kind; reason for a belief; **argum'entative** (44-I7-2-9-I) eager to argue, loving to argue.

aria (44-I9) music for one voice or instrument.

-arian (29-I9) one who believes in, e.g. **Unit'arian** (I77-I-29-I9) one who believes in the unity of God.

arid (3-I) dry, having no rain; uninteresting or useless (talk).

ar'ight (9-4I) in the right way.

ar'ise (9-4Iz) come up, rise up; appear or be noticed.

arist'ocracy (3-I-5-9sI) (1) government by persons of noble rank; (2) lords and people of highest rank; (3) best of any group of people; **an 'aristocrat** (3-I-9-3) person of high rank;

'aristocr'atic (3-I-9-3-I) acting or being like a lord.

ar'ithmetic (9-I-9-I) art of working with numbers, e.g. adding, dividing, etc.; **'arithm'etical** (3-I-2-I).

-arium (29-I9) place in which ... are kept, e.g. **aqu'arium** (9-29-I9) place in which water-creatures are kept (Latin, *aqua* = water).

ark (44) kind of box; **Noah's Ark** (55z + 44) = big ship in which Noah is said to have put two of all living creatures when water covered all the earth (see the Bible, Genesis 6, 7).

arm (44) (1) part of the body from the hand to the shoulder; *Arm in arm* = arm of one person being under the arm of another; *To receive with open arms* = to welcome; *To keep at arm's length* = treat a person coldly; *A child in arms* = child too young to walk; (2) that part of a garment which covers the arm; (3) anything of the shape of an arm.

arm'ada (44-44-9) large number of warships.

armament (44-9-9) act of getting ready for war; a nation's armies, warships; guns on a ship or in a fort.

'armad'illo (44-9-I-67) South American animal which has a ringed shell.

ARMADILLO

armature (44-9tsh9) part of an electric machine, e.g. that part which is caused to move when electricity is passed through it.

armistice (44-I-Is) agreement to stop fighting for a short time.

armlet (44-I) band worn round the arm.

armour (44-9) iron covering to protect against weapons or shot; **armourer** (44-9-9) one who makes and repairs armour; **armoury** (44-9-I) place where weapons are made or stored; **arm'orial** (44-55-I-9) having to do with " coats of arms " (see below).

armpit (44-I) hollow under the arm near the shoulder.

arms (44-z) instruments for fighting, weapons; *Small arms* = guns which are carried in the hand, not big guns on wheels; *Take up arms against* = get ready to fight against; *Lay down arms* = stop fighting; *Up in arms against* = complaining angrily against; **coat of arms**, figures on a shield or flag as a sign of noble birth, rank and good family; **to arm**, take weapons, give weapons to; provide with necessary instruments for a piece of work.

army (44-I) large number of soldiers ready for war; *Standing army* = paid soldiers who are always ready (not those called up only when there is a war); large number of persons employed in some special work, e.g. *An army of workmen; The Salvation* (= saving) *Army* = number of persons joined in a sort of army whose purpose is to teach men to believe in Christ and to save their souls.

ar'oma (9-67-9) sweet smell; adj. **arom'atic** (3-9-3-1).

ar'ose (9-67z) p.t. of Arise.

ar'ound (9-47) on all sides; in a circle.

ar'ouse (9-47z) awaken; excite to action.

arpeggio (4-2j167) (Music) playing a set of notes quickly one after another, not all together.

arquebus (44-1-9) ancient kind of gun. ARQUEBUS

arrack (3-9) strong drink used in the East.

arr'aign (9-21) call a prisoner into a court of law, examine a supposed wrong-doer in public.

arr'ange (9-21nj) set in order; settle or decide; change a thing so as to suit it to a new purpose, e.g. *To arrange a story as a play in the theatre*; make plans and carry them out, e.g. *I will arrange everything for the dinner*; *To come to an* **arr'angement** (——9) = make an agreement.

arrant (3) well-known; *An arrant thief* = very bold thief; *Arrant nonsense* = very foolish talk.

arras (3-9) ornamental cloth used for hanging on the wall.

arr'ay (9-21) put in order, e.g. soldiers for battle; to dress, e.g. *She arrayed herself in all her finery* = dressed herself in all her fine clothes.

arr'ears (9-19z) work left undone; money owed which has not yet been paid.

arr'est (9-2) stop; seize; *He was arrested* = was seized by an officer of the law; *An arresting speech* = one which caused people to stop and listen.

'arrière 'pensée (3-129 + 44ⁿ-2) secret unexpressed thought, behind a thought which is expressed.

arr'ive (9-41) get to a place; **arr'ival**, act of arriving; *New arrivals* = persons who have just arrived.

arrogant (3-9-9) claiming honour to which one has no right, very proud.

arrogate (3-9-21) claim power which does not belong to one.

arrow (3-67) stick pointed at one end, with feathers on the other end, shot from a bow; **the broad arrow**, mark on government stores and formerly on prisoners' clothing in England. THE BROAD ARROW

arrowroot (3-9-77) West Indian plant boiled with milk or water as a food for sick persons.

arsenal (44-9) place where governments make and store instruments and materials of war.

arsenic (44-9-1) (1) metal; (2) **white arsenic**, poisonous powder made from arsenic used sometimes as a medicine for the skin.

arson (44) unlawful act of setting fire to buildings or goods.

art (44) (1) human skill; work of man (not of natural forces); (2) knowledge and skill necessary for carrying out a certain kind of work, e.g. *The art of painting, The art of writing, The art of war*; **the Arts**, certain subjects of study, e.g. language, history, etc., opposite of the Sciences; (3) cleverness, power of deceiving or of winning people over to one's opinion. *Thou art* = you are.

artefact, artifact (44-1-3) thing made by ancient man, not by nature.

art'erioscler'osis (44-111167-2-67-1) hardening of the *arteries* (= tubes carrying blood from the heart).

artery (44-9-1) blood vessel through which blood runs from the heart; *An artery of trade* = important road for trade; **art'erial** (44-19-19) having to do with arteries, like an artery; *An arterial road* = large and important road.

art'esian (44-11z19) well made by driving a pipe so deep that the water presses itself up it from below.

artful (44) having great skill in deceiving.

arthr'itis (44-41-1) painful disease of the joints.

artichoke (44-1-67) plant with thick leaves, the lower ends of which are eaten; *Jerusalem artichoke* = white root used as a vegetable.

article (44-1) one thing; written account of one subject, e.g. in a newspaper; one part of a written agreement; one of a list of beliefs accepted by the Church; *An articled clerk* = writer in a (law-)office who is bound by a written agreement with his employer; *The indefinite article* = the words "a," "an"; *The definite article* = the word "the."

art'iculate (44-1-17-21) join together; speak clearly; **articul'ation**, act of speaking, speaking clearly; act of joining, the way in which things (e.g. bones) are joined.

artifice (44-1-1s) trick; **art'ificer** (44-1-1s9) good workman; **artif'icial** (44-1-1shl) made by art, not by nature; pretended, not real.

art'illery (44-1-9-9-1) big guns and the men in charge of them.

artis'an (44-1z3) workman, skilled workman.

artist (44-1) one who practises drawing, painting, music and the making of beautiful things; one who is specially clever in work of this kind; **art'istic** (44-1-1) having to do with the making of beautiful things; beautiful; loving beautiful things made by man; **'artistry** (44-1-1) skill and good taste of an artist.

artless (44-1) simple and natural.

Aryan (29-19) (1) having to do with the Indo-European languages (Sanscrit, Persian, Greek, Latin, Italian, English, German); (2) race speaking any of these languages; adj. belonging to such a race.

asaf'oetida (3-9-11-1-9) medicine with a very bad smell.

asb'estos (3z-2-5) soft, white, wool-like material which cannot burn.

asc'end (9-2) climb, go up; *Ascend the throne*

= become king; **asc'ent**, act of going up a hill; a slope; *In the asc'endant* (9-2-9) = increasing in power and importance; **asc'endancy** (9-2-9-si) being at the top, having the power; **asc'ension** (9-2-shn) going up; *The Ascension* = going up of Christ into heaven.

ascert'ain (3-9-21) find out; make sure.

asc'etic (9-2-1) one who gives up all pleasures and controls his desires; **asc'eticism** (9-2-isiz) belief that it is better not to enjoy the pleasures of this world.

ascr'ibe (9-41) point to a thing as the cause of something; believe that a thing belongs to —.

asdic (3z-1) instrument used to find underwater things (e.g. submarines) by sound waves.

'as'eptic (21-2-1) free from seeds of disease or decay.

ash (3) tree whose wood is used for making bows, handles of spears, etc.

ash (3) fine dust left after something has been burnt; *His ashes* = dust left after the body has decayed or been burnt.

ash'amed (9-21) having a feeling of shame.

ashen (3-9) of the colour of ashes, grey.

ash'ore (9-55) on the shore.

as'ide (9-41) on one side; *He said this aside* = he said it so that no one else could hear; *To lay aside* = give up as of no more use; *To set aside* = keep for use later on; *To set aside a judgment* = decide differently from some judgment given already.

asinine (3-1-41) like an ass (donkey), very foolish.

ask (44) ask a question; *Ask a person to dinner* = invite; *Ask after Mr. X* = ask for news about his health.

ask'ance (9-3-s) *To look askance* = look to one side, as if something were wrong or untrue.

ask'ew (9-177) not straight; out of order.

asl'ant (9-44) not straight up and down; sloping.

asl'eep (9-11) sleeping, at rest.

asp (3) small poisonous snake.

asp'aragus (9-3-9-9) vegetable whose tops are eaten for food.

aspect (3-2) (1) appearance; *Of gentle aspect* = having a gentle look; (2) direction in which a thing faces, e.g. *The house has a north aspect*; (3) way of considering or looking at a thing, e.g. *To consider a question in all its aspects*.

aspen (3-9) tall tree whose leaves shake easily, even in still air.

asp'erity (3-2-1-1) roughness, bitterness; **asp'erities** (——z) discomforts.

asp'erse (9-99) say cruel things about a person; **an asp'ersion** (——shn) untrue report about a person's character; *Cast aspersions on a person's character* = say bad things about —.

ASPEN

asphalt (3-3) hard black material used in making roads.

asph'yxia (3-1-19) **asphyxi'ation**, fainting or death caused by lack of air.

aspic (3-1) meat-jelly.

aspid'istra (3-1-1-9) plant often kept in the house as an ornament.

aspirate (3-9-1) the sound H; **to aspirate** (3-9-21) draw gas or liquid out of the body.

asp'ire (9-419) desire eagerly to seek some high aim; **aspir'ation** (3-1-21shn) hope; **an 'aspirant** (3-1) one who hopes.

aspirin (3-9-1) medicine used to drive away pain, e.g. pain in the head.

ASPIDISTRA

ass (3 or 44) a donkey; Sl. *You ass!* = fool.

assagai (3-1-41) African spear.

ass'ail (9-21) to attack.

ass'assin (9-3-1) secret and disloyal murderer, usually of some important person; **to ass'assinate**, to murder as the result of secret planning.

ass'ault (9-55) sudden attack.

ass'ay (9-21) *test* (= to examine, try, prove) whether a metal is pure.

assegai = assagai.

ass'emble (9-2) come together in a group; bring people together in a gathering; fit together a machine; **ass'embly** (——1), **ass'emblage** (——ij) group of people who have come together for some purpose; the act of bringing the parts of a thing together; **ass'embly-l'ine** (9-2-1 + 41) engines are moved along a line, parts being added as they go along.

ass'ent (9-2) agreement, agree.

ass'ert (9-99) declare solemnly and with certainty; *To assert one's rights* = claim or defend —; *To assert oneself* = try to become important.

ass'ess (9-2) find out or fix the value; **ass'essment** (——9) act of fixing a value, the value which is fixed; **an ass'essor** (——9) one who fixes values.

assets (3-2) things which belong to a man (and which may be used to pay his debts); **an asset**, a help.

ass'everate (9-2-9-21) declare solemnly.

ass'iduous (9-1-179) keeping steadily to a piece of work; n. **assid'uity** (3-1-1771-1).

ass'ign (9-41) give; *He assigned each person to a task* = gave; *Assigned a task to each person* = set each person to work on; fix, e.g. a time for a meeting; **assign'ation** (3-1-21shn) arrangement to meet a lover; also the act of assigning; **ass'ignment** (9-41-9) setting aside of a thing for a person; (in law) something given, the giving of a thing; lesson or part of a lesson-book given to a child to be studied.

ass'imilate (9-1-1-21) make one thing like something else; as food becoming part of the body.

ass'ist (9-1) to help; *Assist at a meeting* = be present at —.

Ass'izes (The) (9-4IzIz) sitting of a special court of law in country towns for the purpose of examining and judging people thought to be wrong-doers.

ass'ociate (9-67sI2I) join with a person, usually for a special purpose; join together ideas in the mind; **an ass'ociate** (9-67sI2I) person joined with others, member of a group; **associ'ation** (9-67sI2Ishn) group of persons acting together for some special purpose; joining of ideas in the mind; an idea so joined; **ass'oci'ation f'ootball** (+ 7-55) kind of football in which the ball may not be touched with the hands, except by the *goal-keeper* (= man who stands between the posts).

ass'ort (9-55) divide into separate kinds or classes; **ass'orted** (—-I) various; *Ill-assorted persons* = not such as should be put together, e.g. of different tastes or opinions.

assu'age (9swzIj) make less, e.g. pain, sorrow, etc.

ass'ume (9-177) take to oneself; *Assume the offensive* = attack; *The matter assumes a grave character* = looks serious; *To assume an air of importance* = try to look important; *Assume for the sake of argument* = let us reason as if this had been proved true; n. **ass'umption** (9-8-shn).

ass'ure (9sh779) make certain; *I assure you* = I say as a sure fact —; **to ass'ure**, *To assure (insure) one's life* = pay money each year so that an agreed amount may be paid to one's family when one dies; **ass'urance** (9sh77-9) (1) belief in one's self; (2) old word for insurance, e.g. Life Assurance; **ass'uredly** (9sh77-I-I) without doubt.

aster (3-9) plant with bright-coloured flowers.

asterisk (3-9-I) star (*) used in printing.

ast'ern (9-99) at or towards the back end of a ship.

asthma (3-9) disease which makes breathing noisy and difficult.

ASTER

ast'igmatism (9-I-9-Iz) fault in the eyes which causes one to see certain parts of a thing less clearly than the rest.

ast'ir (9-99) moving, excited.

ast'onish (9-5-I) to surprise.

ast'ound (9-47) surprise greatly.

astrakh'an (3-9-3) black fur with many curls.

astral (3) having to do with the stars.

astr'ay (9-2I) wandering out of the right way.

astr'ide (9-4I) with the legs apart, as in horse-riding.

astr'ingent (9-Inj9) tightening, e.g. *An astringent liquid for the skin* = one which makes the skin tighter and harder.

astr'ology (9-5-9jI) study of the stars in order to learn the future.

astr'onomy (9-5-9-I) scientific study of the stars; **'astron'omical f'igure** (3-6-5-I + I-9) very large figure, an unimaginable amount.

ast'ute (9-177) very clever; *An astute person* = keen business man.

as'under (9-8-9) into pieces; apart.

as'ylum (9-4I-9) place where mad or helpless people are taken care of.

'asymm'etrical (2I-I-2-I) having the two sides unequal or different.

'asympt'otic line (2I-I-5-I + 4I) line which nears but never touches another line.

atavism (3-9-Iz) appearance in a child's body or character of something found in the family many years ago.

ate (2I or 2) p.t. of Eat.

atelier (3-9-I2I) room in which a painter works or teaches.

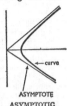

ASYMPTOTE
ASYMPTOTIC
LINE

atheist (2I-II·I) one who does not believe that there is a God.

ath'irst (9-99) wanting to drink; thirsty.

athlete (3-II) man who has a well-trained body, who is good at outdoor games; **athl'etic** (3-2-I) having to do with outdoor games.

at-h'ome (9 + 67) party to which guests are asked.

athw'art (9-55) across.

atlas (3-9) book of maps.

atmosphere (3-9-I9) air round the earth; forces which help to make one's character; *There was an electric atmosphere in the meeting* = general feeling of excitement; adj. **atmosph'eric** (3-9-2-I); **'atmosph'erics** (3-9-2-I-I) radio noises made by electricity in the air.

at'oll (3-5) coral (= rocklike material made by sea-creatures) island.

atom (3-9) part of matter so small that it cannot be divided, except into *particles* (= bits) of electricity; any very small amount; **at'omic bomb** (3-5-I + 5) Bomb = thing which explodes when dropped from an aeroplane, etc. In the atomic bomb the explosion is caused by the breaking up of atoms of a very heavy metal (uranium); **at'omic pile** (+ 4I) instrument in which the break-up of atoms is used to produce heat, or to make substances *radioactive* (= giving off particles of electricity like radium).

atomizer (3-9-4I-9) instrument which blows out liquid in very small drops.

at'one (9-67) make repayment for wrongdoing.

atr'ocious (9-67sh9) very cruel or bad.

atrophy (3-9-I) (of a part of the body) wasting away because of lack of use or lack of blood supply.

atropine (3-5-II) poisonous medicine which makes the heart beat quickly (the mouth

att'ach (9-3) join, fasten; seize goods or money according to law; **an att'achment** (——9) thing fixed on to something else; friendship.

att'aché (9-3sh2) man who goes with an *ambassador* (= officer of the government sent to another country to act for his own government).

att'ack (9-3) go and fight against; speak or write against; *To attack a task* = begin a piece of work; *An attack of illness* = sudden on-coming of —.

att'ain (9-21) arrive at, to reach; *He has many* **att'ainments** (——9) = he has learnt to do many things very well.

att'ainder (9-21-9) loss of all rights because of breaking the law.

attar (3-9) sweet-smelling oil made from flowers, e.g. from roses.

att'empt (9-2) to try.

att'end (9-2) (1) fix the mind on, listen to, e.g. *Attend to the lesson*; (2) take care of, e.g. *Attend to one's children*; (3) wait upon, e.g. *To attend on the Queen*; **an att'endant** (——9) servant or nurse; *To attend a school* = go regularly to —; **att'endance** (——9-s) act of attending, the persons present at (a meeting).

att'ention (9-2-shn) giving of the mind to a subject; *To attract attention* = cause oneself to be noticed; *He showed me many little attentions* = was kind in many small ways; *To pay attentions to a lady* = make love to —.

att'enuate (9-2-1721) make thin or less.

att'est (9-2) write one's name on a paper to show that what is said in the paper is true and correct; to prove.

attic (3-1) room just under the roof of a house.

att'ire (9-419) dress; put clothes or put ornaments on.

attitude (3-1-177) way in which one stands, sits, etc.; *To strike an attitude* = stand like an actor waiting for *applause* (= shouts of praise); way in which one feels or thinks about something.

att'orney (9-99-1) lawyer; **power of attorney**, power to act for another person.

attr'act (9-3) pull towards; cause to come near, e.g. *The earth attracts the moon*; **attr'actions** (——sh9-z) things which draw crowds together, e.g. public shows, cheap things in the shops.

attribute (3-1-17) special part of the character of something, e.g. *Politeness is the attribute of a gentleman*; **to attr'ibute** (9-1-17) say that a thing is part of the character of; say that a thing is caused by, e.g. *I attribute my success to hard work*.

attr'ition (3-1shn) rubbing away.

att'une (9-177) make the sounds of one musical instrument agree with those of another; cause people's feelings to agree.

'auberg'ine (67-29j11) purple, egg-shaped vegetable.

auburn (55-9) red-brown.

auction (55-shn) public selling of goods by asking for offers and selling for the highest offer; **'auction'eer** (——19) one who sells things in this way; **'Auction Br'idge** (+ 1j) card game.

aud'acious (55-21sh9) very daring, shameless; n. **aud'acity** (55-3s1-1).

audible (55-1) loud enough to be heard.

audience (55-19-s) hearers, people in a meeting; *The King granted an audience to Mr. X* = allowed Mr. X to come and speak to him.

audit (55-1) examination of accounts.

aud'ition (55-1shn) hearing of a singer, actor, etc., to discover whether he is good enough for employment.

'audit'orium (55-1-55-19) large hall for meetings; that part of a hall in which the hearers sit.

au f'ait (67 + 21) knowing all about, e.g. *To put a person au fait with the business* = to tell him all the latest facts about —.

auger (55-9) instrument for making holes in wood.

aught (55) anything; any part, nothing, none.

augm'ent (55-2) increase.

augur (55-9) one who in Roman times told the future; sign of the future; **to augur**, be a sign of the future, e.g. *This augurs no good*.

aug'ust (55-8) solemn, causing a feeling of fear and respect.

auk (55) sea-bird.

'Auld l'ang s'yne (55 + 3 + 41) Scottish words = old days gone by; song sung at midnight on December 31st–January 1st.

aunt (44) father's or mother's sister; wife of one's uncle; *Aunt Sally* = wooden figure at which one throws sticks, as a game; any person or thing whom (which) everyone attacks.

aura (55-9) faint smell or feeling lying around any object—like the smell round flowers.

aureole (55-167) circle of bright light round the head of a holy person as shown in a picture.

aur'iferous (55-1-9-9) (rock) producing gold.

aur'ora (9-55-9) light of early morning; **the Aur'ora Bore'alis** (+ 5-1-21-1) arch of light seen in the sky in the far north.

auspices (55-1s1) signs of good fortune; *Under the auspices of* = with the favour and help of; **ausp'icious** (55-1sh9) promising good fortune.

aust'ere (55-19) very plain and simple in appearance; hard in character or manner; **aust'erity** (55-2-1-1).

austral (55) of the morning; of the south.

auth'entic (55-2-1) proved to be real or true; **to auth'enticate** (——21) show without doubt that a thing is real; **'authent'icity** (——1s1-1).

author (55-9) first beginner of a new thing; writer of a book, story, etc.; **authoress** (——1) woman writer.

auth'ority (55-5-1-1) right and power to give

orders; such right given to another; person or group of persons having the right to govern; person or book which may safely be believed on a certain subject, e.g. *He is a great authority on children's diseases*; **auth'oritative** (55-5-1-9-1) (above meanings and especially —) said or written by a person who ought to be believed; **authorize** (55-9-4I) give to another the right and power to act.

auto- (55-) self-, own-.

'autobi'ography (55-9-415-9-1) story of a man's life written by himself.

autocrat (55-9-3) ruler who has complete and uncontrolled power.

autocycle (55-9-4I) bicycle which has a petrol motor to drive it along.

autograph (55-9-44) person's own handwriting; person's name written by himself.

autom'atic (55-9-3-1) self-moving, e.g. machine which works by itself; *An automatic movement* = — done without thinking; *Automatic pistol* = hand-gun which puts a new shot in place after each shot has been fired.

AUTOMATIC

'autom'ation (55-6-21shn) making machines which work by themselves under the control of electric instruments instead of men.

aut'omaton (55-5-9-9) machine made to act like a man; man who works like a machine without thought.

automobile (55-9-67-11) motor-car.

aut'onomy (55-5-9-1) power of self-government.

autopsy (55-5-1) examining a body to find the cause of death.

'autosugg'estion (55-6-9j2stshn) putting ideas into one's own mind, e.g. trying to make oneself well from illness by saying, "I am getting better."

autumn (55-9) season between summer and winter; **aut'umnal** (55-8).

aux'iliary (5gz1-19-1) helping; a help.

av'ail (9-21) be of use or value; *To avail oneself of* = make use of; *Available*=which can be used, e.g. *Available fats* = — which the body can use.

avalanche (3-9-44) sudden slipping of a mass of snow down a mountain; *An avalanche of letters* = many letters coming at one time.

avarice (3-9-1s) great desire for wealth.

av'ast (9-44) stop!

av'aunt (9-55) go away!

ave (21-1) cry of greeting (in ancient Rome).

Ave. (3) short for *avenue* (= broad street).

av'enge (9-2nj) pay back a hurt or wrong by hurting the person who did the wrong.

avenue (3-1-177) broad street; road with trees on both sides.

av'er (9-99) declare.

average (3-9-1j) like most others; common; middle value of a set of numbers, e.g. the average of 3, 6, 9 is $\frac{18}{3}$ = 6.

av'erse to (from) (9-99) very unwilling to.

av'ert (danger) (9-99) turn away, e.g. one's eyes; prevent some bad thing from happening.

aviary (21-19-1) place for keeping birds.

avi'ation (21-12Ishn) science of flying by machines; **'aviator** (21-121-9) man skilled in using flying-machines.

avid (3-1) hungry; eager for.

avoc'ation (3-9-21shn) (1) one's regular business; (2) second business less important than one's chief or regular business.

av'oid (9-51) keep away from; escape.

'avoirdup'ois (3-9-9-51z or 3-74-7-74) way of measuring in pounds made up of 16 ounces; *Too much avoirdupois* = (of a person) too fat.

av'ouch (9-47) declare; say that one has knowledge of a thing.

av'ow (9-47) declare openly that something is true; *an av'owal*, saying in public, e.g. that one has done wrong.

av'uncular (9-8ngk17-9) having to do with an uncle.

aw'ait (9-21) wait for; *A real welcome awaits you* = you may expect to receive —.

aw'ake (9-21) wake from sleep; excite to action; adj. not sleeping, active in mind; **aw'aken**, to awake.

aw'ard (9-55) give by judgment of a court of law; give as a result of careful thought; **aw'ard**, thing so given.

aw'are (9-29) having knowledge of; ready and watching.

aw'ash (9-5) level with the surface of the water.

aw'ay (9-21) not at home or in the usual place; apart; *To throw away* = throw out as of no further use; *Pass away* = die; *Fall away* = desert, not to support any more; *To work away* = continue working; *Right away, Straight away* = at once, now; *Far and away the best* = much the best.

awe (55) feeling of respect mixed with fear; **awesome**, causing awe.

awful (55) causing great fear; Sl. very, e.g. *awfully good, awfully bad*.

awh'ile (9-4I) for a short time.

awkward (55-9) ungraceful; not clever in doing or making things; difficult to deal with; *To be in an awkward situation* = to be in difficulties.

awl (55) instrument for making holes.

awning (55-1) covering to shade windows or doors of a house from the sun.

aw'oke (9-67) p.t. of Awake.

awr'y (9-41) bent to one side, not straight.

axe (3) heavy blade fixed to a handle used for cutting down trees, etc.

ax'illa (3-1-9) hollow under the arm where it meets the body.

axiom (3-19) truth which everyone accepts

axis as true without proof; adj. **axiom'atic** (3-19-3-1).
axis (3-1) imaginary straight line round which a thing turns, e.g. *The axis of the earth.*
axle (3) bar on which a wheel turns.

ay, aye (21 or 41) yes; *For aye* = for ever.
ayah (419) Indian nurse.
az'alea (9-21-19) bush with sweet-smelling flowers.
azure (3379) sky-blue; light blue.

B

B.A. (11 + 21) see Bachelor of Arts.

baa (44) cry of a sheep.

babble (3) speak like a baby; talk foolishly; tell a secret; make a sound as of running water.

babe (21), **baby** (21-1) very young child; inexperienced person, e.g. *A babe in the ways of the world*.

babel (21) disorder; *Tower of Babel* = high building in the city of Babel where (according to the Bible) disorder started because everybody spoke a different language.

bab'oon (9-77) kind of large monkey.

babu (44-77) former Indian title = Mr.; Indian *clerk* (= worker in an office).

baby (21-1) see Babe.

BABOON

baby-sitter (21-1 + 1-9) person who sits by the baby while the parents are out of the house.

baccarat (3-9-44) card game played for money.

bacchan'alian (3-9-21-19) having to do with songs, dances and drinking much wine.

bachelor (3-9-9) unmarried man; **Bachelor of Arts**, title given to a person who has finished a course of study at a university.

bac'illus (9sI-9) very small living thing, often causing disease; pl. **bac'illi** (9sI-41).

back (3) (1) that part which is behind, e.g. part of the body, of hand, of chair, of house, etc.; (2) towards the back; to the place in which it was first, e.g. *To go back*; *Pay back* = to pay money owed; *Go back on one's friends* = be unfaithful to; *Never look back* = never have any bad fortune; **to back**, cause to go backwards, e.g. *He backed the car into the side-street*; support, e.g. *Back me up, won't you?* = please support me in all ways; *Back a bill* = write one's name on the back promising to pay if the first person fails to pay; *Back horses* = pay money which will be lost if the horse loses in a race, and will be paid back, together with more money, if it wins; *Back down* = give up a claim; *Back out of* = say one cannot do as promised.

back-bencher (+ 2-9) member of Parliament who does not hold and has not held office and therefore sits at the back.

backbite (3-41) speak unkindly of an absent person.

back-blocks (+ 5) land far from a town or river-front in Australia.

backbone (3-67) long row of bones in the middle of the back.

back-fire (+ 419) explosion inside a car-engine which comes too soon and so does not drive the car forward.

b'ackg'ammon (3-3-9) indoor game played with wooden pieces on a special board.

background (3-47) more distant part of a view; that part of a picture against or upon which the chief figures are painted; *One's background* = one's past experience, education, etc.; *To keep in the background* = try not to be noticed.

BACKGAMMON

b'ackh'and (3-3) done with the back of the hand; *A back-handed compliment* = a saying which may be understood either as praise or blame.

backing (3-1) help, e.g. in money matters.

back-log of orders (+ 5) orders for goods which the shop has not yet been able to send.

b'acks'ide (3-41) Sl. the part of the body on which one sits.

b'acksl'ider (3-41-9) one who turns away from true faith or good behaviour.

backward (3-9) not equal to others; *A backward child* = one who is not level in his power of thought or strength with other children of the same age; slow, not eager to act; **backwards** (——z) towards the back.

backwater (3-55-9) small stream leading out of a river and fed by its water; *To live in a backwater* = in a quiet place away from the stream of new ideas and interesting people such as one meets in a city.

backwoods (3-7-z) distant uncleared forest land.

bacon (21-9) salted meat from the back and sides of a pig.

bact'eria (3-11-19) microscopic living things which cause disease and decay.

bad (3) opposite of good.

badger (3j9) small night animal that lives in a hole in the ground; **to badger**, trouble a person and make him angry, e.g. by continuing to ask questions.

BADGER

badinage (3-1-443) playful talk.

badminton (3-1-9) game played by hitting a small feathered object over a net.

baffle (3) make too difficult; turn off the right path; prevent from carrying out a plan; **baffling**, impossible to understand.

baffle-plate (+ 21) plate used to make gas or liquid flow in a different direction.

bag (3) container made of paper, cloth, leather, etc., in which things are carried; *Bag of bones* = very thin person; *Whole bag of tricks* = all the necessary things; *Let the* *cat out of the bag* = tell a secret; *Clear out bag and baggage* = go, taking all one's things; *Get a good bag* = shoot many birds or animals; Sl. *Bags* = trousers; **to bag,** kill birds, etc., collect, obtain; Sl. steal, or take, e.g. *He bagged my seat.*

b'agat'elle (3-9-2) game played on a special table with nine balls and a stick; *A mere bagatelle* = unimportant thing.

baggage (3-1j) collection of bags, etc., of a traveller.

baggy (3-1) hanging down loosely like a bag.

bagman (3-9) travelling *salesman* (= man who sells things).

bagpipe (3-41) Scottish instrument of music.

bail (21) money given by a prisoner or his friends to a court of law so that the prisoner may be set free until he is judged; if he does not come back when called the money is seized by the law; *I'll go bail that —* = I am sure.

BAGPIPE

bail, bale (21) throw water out, e.g. from a boat; **bail out,** get out, e.g. from an aeroplane when in the air.

bail (21) small piece of wood laid on top of the *stumps* (= three upright pieces of wood used in the game of *Cricket*).

bailey (21-1) court-yard in a castle; **Old Bailey,** court of law where law-breakers are judged in London.

bailey-bridge (21-1 + 1) bridge which can be quickly pushed across a river.

BAILEY-BRIDGE

bailiff (21-1) officer of the law; man who looks after a farm or lands for the owner.

bairn (29) child.

bait (21) (1) food for horses; (2) food put in a *trap* in order to catch animals, or on a fishing-*line* (= string for catching fish); something which causes desire; *Ground-bait* = food thrown into the water to bring fish to that place; **to bait,** set upon a person or animal so as to make him (it) angry.

baize (21) thick cloth made of wool.

bake (21) cook by dry heat in a closed box; *Half-baked* = imperfect, unfinished; **baker** (21-9) one who makes bread; *Baker's dozen* = 13; **bakery** (——11) place where bread is made or sold.

bakelite (21-9-41) hard brown substance made from phenol (got from coal), used for electric fittings.

balance (3-9-s) instrument for measuring weight; have the same amount on both sides; *To keep one's balance* = keep calm; *Lose one's balance* = become excited; *Trembling in the balance* = undecided, about to be decided; *To balance an account* = add up the two sides of an account and show the difference between them; *My bank balance* = money which I still have in the bank; *A debit balance* = money owed to the bank; *A balance sheet* = paper showing money spent and received, owed by and owed to a business company.

balcony (3-9-1) shelf-like place built out from the wall of a house for people to stand or sit on; upstairs seats in a theatre.

bald (55) having no hair—especially on the head; *To speak baldly* = speak plainly, even cruelly; Sl. *Go for (at) it bald-headed* = try for it with all one's strength.

balderdash (55-9-3) senseless talk.

baldric (55-1) band over the shoulder from which a sword or horn is hung.

bale (21) goods enclosed in cloth and tied with rope for sending by ship, train, or on the back of an animal.

bale (21) see Bail.

baleful (21) evil, full of desire to do harm.

balk, baulk (55) a narrow piece of ground between two fields; large beam of wood; **to balk,** prevent a person from doing what he wishes to do.

ball (55) round object used in play; any round thing; shot from a gun; *To have the ball at one's feet* = have a good chance of being successful; *Keep the ball rolling* = continue, continue talking.

ball (55) large number of people gathered for dancing; *Open the ball* = make a beginning.

ballad (3-9) short story told in the form of a poem; simple song.

ballast (3-9) heavy material put in the bottom of a ship to keep it steady; road material.

b'all-b'earing (+ 29-1) metal balls moving in a ring round a bar in a machine so that the bar may turn more easily, with less rubbing.

baller'ina (3-9-11-9) woman who dances in a *ballet* (see below).

ballet (3-21) show-dancing by very well-trained dancers to good (not jazz) music.

ball'istics (9-1-1) science of gun-fire.

ball'oon (9-77) large bag filled with gas to make it lighter than air.

ballot (3-9) elect secretly by writing names on pieces of paper, or putting a mark against printed names.

b'allyh'oo (3-1-77) Sl. noisy way of calling attention to some subject or person.

ballyrag (3-1-3) scold angrily; to play in a rough and disorderly way.

balm (44) oily liquid obtained from a tree, used as a medicine, especially to lessen pain; anything which lessens pain.

balmy (wind) (44-1) gentle, sweet-smelling.

balsam (55) sweet-smelling material that comes from a tree; kind of tree; a flower.

b'alustr'ade (3-9-21) row of upright pieces of stone or wood with a bar along the top, guarding the outer edge of stairs or steps, or of any place from which people might fall.

b'amb'oo (3-77) tall hollow tree, formed like grass, found in hot countries.

bamb'oozle (3-77) deceive, make a fool of.

ban (3) an order; a notice; **to ban**, forbid.

ban'al (3-44) very common and uninteresting.

ban'ana (9-44-9) common fruit, long and yellow, having a soft white centre.

band (3) anything used for fastening things together; flat long piece of any material used for fastening, or forming part of a garment; long narrow line of colour different from that round it; group of persons united for some special purpose; group of persons playing musical instruments; *to band together*, = join in a group.

bandage (3-1j) long piece of cloth for tying up a wound; to tie up in a bandage.

band'anna (3-3-9) brightly coloured handkerchief.

bandbox (3-5) light box for holding a hat; *As if she's just come out of a bandbox* = very clean and new-looking.

bandeau (3-67) narrow piece of cloth worn round a woman's head.

bandicoot (3-1-77) large Indian rat; kangaroo-like animal found in Australia (see Kangaroo).

bandit (3-1) armed thief; **band'itti** (3-1-1), members of a group of armed thieves.

b'andol'ier, -eer (3-9-19) broad band with pockets for holding *cartridges* (= little boxes of powder and shot put into a gun for firing).

bandy (3-1) throw about, e.g. *To bandy words* = talk and answer and talk again, quarrel; *To bandy a story about* = spread —.

BANDOLIER

bandy-legged (+ 2) having legs curved outwards at the knees.

bane (21) (1) poison; (2) ruin, cause of ruin, e.g. *Disease is the bane of life*; **baneful**, causing ruin.

bang (3) loud noise caused by a heavy blow, bursting, or exploding; shut with a loud noise; Sl. *It hit me bang in the eye* = exactly —.

bangle (3-1) ring of metal worn on the arm or leg.

banian, banyan (3-19) Indian trader; Indian name for a tight garment worn near the skin; **banian tree**, see Banyan.

banish (3-1) drive away; send away to live in a foreign country.

banister (3-1-9) upright pieces of wood or metal with a bar along the top guarding the outer edge of stairs.

banjo (3-67) musical instrument with four strings and a body (main part) like a drum.

bank (3ngk) mass of earth raised up above the level of the ground; side of a river; *Banks of seats* = rows of seats rising one behind another; **to bank up**, raise up into a bank; **to bank** (in flying) make an airplane slope when turning.

BANJO

bank (3ngk) place in which money is kept and paid out on demand; *To bank* = pay money into a bank; *"I bank on you"* = depend —; **bank holidays**, special days on which banks and all businesses are closed.

banknote (3ngk-67) piece of printed paper for which money is paid on demand at any bank.

bankrupt (3ngk-8) having failed in business; unable to pay one's debts.

banner (3-9) flag with a special sign on it.

banns (3-z) *To put up (call) the banns* = give notice of a marriage.

banquet (3ngkwI) a feast.

bansh'ee (3-11) strange spirit or fairy supposed (in Ireland) to cry out sadly when a member of the family dies.

bantam (3-9) very small kind of cock or hen; small fighter with the *fists* (= tightly closed hands); *Bantam weight* (of a *boxer* (= fighter)) = 116 pounds.

banter (3-9) be merry and laugh at a person.

B'ant'u (languages) (3-77) group of African languages.

banyan (3-9) tree whose branches go down into the ground and form many roots (see also Banian).

baobab (21-67-3) African tree.

bapt'ize (3-41) put in the water, or put water on, as a sign of receiving as a Christian; **b'aptism** (3-Iz) practice of the Christian Church concerned with putting water on a child at the time of naming it; **bapt'ismal name** (3-Iz) name given at baptism.

BAOBAB

bar (44) (1) stiff long piece of wood, metal, etc.; (2) long piece of wood or metal used to prevent people from passing, e.g. *A bar across the road*; shelf of sand at the mouth of a harbour; (3) place where the prisoner stands in a court of law; *The bar* = all the lawyers; *To join the bar* = become a lawyer; (4) place where wine and strong drink is sold; (5) long mark on cloth, etc.; (6) *Bar of music* = few notes of music marked off with downward lines; **to bar**, fix bars in, e.g. a window; to keep people out; mark (cloth, etc.) with bars; *I bar that!* = I cannot allow that; *Barring* = not counting.

barb (44) point of an arrow turned backwards to prevent it being pulled out of a wound; *Barbed words* = very cruel —; *Barbed wire* = wire with sharp points on it intended to tear the skin or clothes.

barb'arian (44-29-19) man without laws, manners or good customs; adj. **barbarous** (44-9-9), **barb'aric** (44-3-1).

barbecue (44-1-177) (1) frame on which things are dried or cooked; (2) animal cooked whole; out-of-door feast.

barbel (44) large fresh-water fish.
barber (44-9) one who cuts hair.
barbican (44-1-9) strong outer gateway or tower for defending a city or castle.

BARBICAN

bard (44) a poet or singer.
bare (29) (1) having no clothes or covering; *To pick a bone bare* = get all the meat off; *To lay bare* = uncover, show what was hidden; (2) just enough; *A bare hundred pounds* = only just £100, no more; *A bare possibility* = some hope, but very little; *Believe his bare word* = believe it because he says so, but without other proof; **to bare**, uncover, show.
barefaced (29-21st) without shame.
barefooted (29-7-1) with no shoes on; **bareheaded** (29-2-1) without a hat on.
barely (29-1) only so much and no more; *Barely enough* = only just enough.
bargain (44-1) (1) agreement about buying and selling; *Into the bargain* = also; (2) something bought at a low price; **to bargain**, talk about the price before buying; *I did not bargain for that* = did not expect; *More than one bargained for* = unpleasant surprise.
barge (44j) large boat with a flat bottom; *To barge into* = run into; **a bargee** (——11) one who has charge of a *barge* (= boat).

BARGE

baritone (3-1-67) male voice not high or low but in the middle; singer with such a voice.
barium (29-19) silver-like heavy metal.
bark (44) noise which a dog makes when excited; **to bark**, make such a noise.
bark, barque (44k) sailing-ship with three, four or five *masts* (= upright posts for sails), with square sails on all masts except the last (or *mizzen*) mast.
bark (44) skin on the outside of a tree; *To bark one's shins* = knock the skin off the surface of the front bone of one's leg.
barley (44-1) kind of grain; plant which produces this.
barman (44-9) man who serves drinks in a *bar* (= drinking place); **barmaid** (44-21) woman who serves drinks in a *bar* (see just above).
barmy (44-1) Sl. mad, foolish.
barn (44) building used for storing things on a farm.
barnacle (44-9) kind of shell-fish which fixes itself on to the bottoms of ocean-going ships and rocks.
barndoor (fowl) (44-55) (hen) of the usual kind; *He can't hit a barn door* = he shoots badly with a gun.
bar′ometer (9-5-1-9) instrument for telling how heavily the air is pressing down, and, from this, what the weather will be.
baron (3-9) title of a nobleman; **baroness** (-9-1) wife of a baron; woman who has the title in her own right; **bar′onial** (9-67-19) adj. having to do with a baron, good enough for a baron, fine; **barony** (3-9-1) rank of baron.
baronet (3-9-1) titled man below a baron and above a knight.
bar′oque (9-67k) much ornamented form of building.
bar′ouche (9-77sh) kind of horse carriage.
barque (44k) see Bark.
barrack(s) (3-9) long buildings in which soldiers live; **to barrack**, shout rudely at players in a game.

BAROQUE

barrage (3-443) (1) bar across a river; (2) line of falling shots from many guns; **barrage balloons** = gas-bags in the sky to protect a city from air attack.
barrel (3) round wooden container with curved sides; long round pipe of a gun through which the shot passes; *A barrel organ* = wind-instrument of music played by turning a handle round.

BARRAGE BALLOON

barren (3) having no fruit, children, or young; useless.
b'arric′ade (3-1-21) quickly built wall of trees, earth, etc., used in fighting; *A barricade across the street*; **to b'arric′ade**, make such walls for defending a place.
barrier (3-19) rough fence set across a path or road to prevent people from passing; anything which prevents people from passing.
barrister (3-1-9) lawyer who speaks in a law-court.
barrow, wh′eelbarrow (11-3-67) box with two handles at the back and one wheel in front used for moving soil, etc. in a garden, pushed by one man.

WHEELBARROW

barrow (3-67) small hill made over an ancient grave.
barter (44-9) to trade with things without using money.
barytone (3-1-67) see Baritone.
basal (21) at the bottom, as something upon which other things are built up.
basalt (3s55) kind of hard black rock.
base (21) bottom—upon which other things are built up; most important part of a mixture, that into which other things are mixed; line from which a runner, an army, etc., starts; *I base my belief upon this fact* = this fact is the chief reason for my belief.
base (21) opposite of noble, bad; *Base coin* =

baseball money which is not made of real gold or silver.

baseball (21-55) American game.

basement (21-9) rooms of a house below the ground.

bash (3) Sl. hit with great force.

bashful (3) (of a girl) afraid to meet people, easily frightened.

basic (21-1) having to do with the bottom, upon which other things are built up.

basil (3z) sweet-smelling plant.

bas'ilica (9z1-1-9) large hall built by the Romans; kind of church.

basilisk (3z1-1) imaginary creature whose look was supposed to cause death.

basin (21) small open dish; hollow place containing water; valley of a river.

basis (21-1) bottom; that upon which anything is built up; chief thing in a mixture, into which the other things are mixed.

BASIN

bask (44) lie in the warm sun.

basket (44-1) container made of bent sticks used for carrying things.

basket-ball (+ 55) game in which each side tries to throw the ball up into a net on a high post.

bas-relief (3 + 1-11) wall pictures in which the figures are not fully cut out nor raised very much from the surface, e.g. the head on a penny is a low bas-relief.

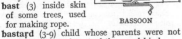
BASKET-BALL

bass (21) very low male voice; low notes in music.

bass (3) kind of fish.

Bass (3) kind of *beer* (= strong bitter drink made from grain).

b'assin'et (3-1-2) large basket for a baby to sleep in; *baby-carriage* (= carriage for a baby, pushed by hand).

basso (3-67) see Bass, 4th above.

bass'oon (9-77) *wind-instrument* (= one blown with the mouth) of music which produces a very low note.

bast (3) inside skin of some trees, used for making rope.

BASSOON

bastard (3-9) child whose parents were not married; not real; not of the usual kind.

baste (21) join cloth together loosely when starting to make clothes; pour melted fat over meat while it is cooking; Sl. hit hard.

bastin'ado (3-1-21-67) beat upon the bottom of the feet as a punishment.

bastion (3-19) tower as part of a fort.

bat (3) small flying creature like a mouse with large wings.

BAT

bat (3) stick used for hitting the ball in play; Sl. sharp blow; Sl. *To go full bat* = very fast.

batch (3) group of things of one kind; number of cakes or loaves of bread baked at one time.

bate (21) make less; *With bated breath* = holding in the breath in great fear; Sl. *To get into a bate* = become angry.

bath (44) act of washing the body; large vessel in which one washes; water used in washing the body; building in which one has a bath, or in which one swims; container for liquid, e.g. the special liquids used in science.

B'ath-ch'air (+ 29) three-wheeled chair for a sick or old person.

bathe (21δ) go into water; put in water; go for a swim in the sea; *Bathed in sunshine* = standing in full sunshine.

bathos (21-5) sudden change from very beautiful thoughts to very common or foolish thoughts.

bathysphere (3-1-19) steel ball inside which a man goes deep down in the sea.

bat'iste (3-11) thin, white cloth made of cotton.

batman (3-9) officer's servant.

baton (3-9) stick used by policemen and by leaders of music; also sign of high rank in the army.

bats (3) Sl. mad.

batsman (3-9) man who hits a ball with a *bat* (= wooden instrument).

batt'alion (9-3-19) group of about 1,000 soldiers.

batten (3) board; fix firmly with boards; *Batten down the hatches* = close firmly with boards the openings in the *deck* (= top floor) of a ship.

batten (3) become fat; *To batten on* = live in comfort at another's cost.

batter (3-9) hit hard and often; eggs, milk and flour mixed together for cooking; man who hits a ball with a *bat* (= wooden striker).

battering-ram, large heavy log with an iron end used for breaking the doors and walls of towns and castles.

battery (3-9-1) (1) (of guns) number of big guns together with the men and officers who serve them; set of guns mounted in a warship or in a fort; (2) (electric) box containing metal plates and acid used to produce or store electricity; (3) (in law) striking another person; (4) (poultry) line of small boxes: one hen is kept in each box; food is put in front; eggs roll down below.

BATTERY (POULTRY)

battle (3) fight between armies or between ships; any struggle, e.g. *The battle of life*; to battle, fight.

b'attle-arr'ay (+ 9-21) order or line all ready for battle.

battlement (3-9) wall on top of a castle with openings for shooting out.

b'attle r'oyal (+ 519) fierce battle.

batty (3-1) Sl. mad.

bauble (55) pretty thing of no value; stick carried in old days by the king's *Fool* (= man dressed in strange clothes, paid to amuse people in a king's court).

baulk (55) see Balk.

bauxite (55-41) earth from which aluminium is obtained.

bawb'ee (55-11) (Scottish) halfpenny.

bawdy (talk) (55-1) dirty talk about things not spoken of by nice people; n. **bawdry**.

bawl (55) shout very loud.

bay (21) (1) inward curve in the shore of a lake or sea; (2) part of a building; built-out part of a room; *Railway bay* = side-line in a railway station.

bay (21) tree whose leaves in old times were made into crowns for conquerors, successful poets and winners of races.

bay (21) red-brown colour; horse of this colour.

bay (21) low cry of a hunting dog; *To keep at bay* = keep at a safe distance away; *To bring to bay* = cause an animal to fight for its life.

bayonet (219-1) knife fixed on the end of a gun.

b'ay-w'indow (21 + 1-67) window which is built out from the wall.

baz'aar (9-44) (1) (in the East) part of the town where the shops are; (2) (in Europe, etc.), a shop where many kinds of useful things and play-things are sold; *sale* (= selling) of home-made things to get money for a church, school or other good cause (purpose).

be (11) *Be he alive or be he dead* = whether he is — or —.

beach (11) shore of a lake or sea; *A beach-comber* = large wave rolling up on the shore; poor homeless man in the islands of the Pacific.

beacon (11) high hill or other object which can be seen from far away; light or fire on a high place to give warning.

bead (11) ball of glass or other material with a hole through it for a string, used for ornament; *To tell one's beads* = say one's prayers; **beading** (——1) long narrow ornamental piece of wood fixed at the top of a wall.

beadle (11) officer who helped the priest of a church in old days in keeping order in church, in giving money to the poor, etc.

beagle (11) dog used for hunting *hares* (= animals like rabbits).

beak (11) horny mouth of a bird; any sharp point of this shape; Sl. school-master, judge.

beaker (11-9) wine cup, glass cup.

beam (11) (1) thick piece of wood, e.g. that holding up the roof of a house; *Broad in the beam* = of a ship, or person, broad at the widest part; *On one's beam ends* = without money and helpless; (2) stream of light; *To beam at* = smile in a very kind way.

bean (11) seed used for food; Sl. *Full of beans* = very active, full of spirit; Sl. *To give a person beans* = punish fiercely; Sl. *Old bean* = ——fellow; *Beanfeast* = any merry gathering; *French beans* = green seed-containers which are boiled and eaten as a vegetable.

bear (29) large wild animal with long hair, which presses people to death with its front legs; *He's a bear* = is rough and rude in speech and manner; *The Great Bear* = group of stars; *To bear the market* = keep selling so as to lower the price, and at last buy back at a lower price a larger amount than that sold.

bear (29) (1) carry, e.g. *Bear the marks of* = show —; *Bear a grudge against* = feel hatred for; *Bear a hand* = help; *Bear him company* = go with him; *Bear out what was said* = give proof of the truth of, be an example of; (2) suffer, e.g. *To bear pain*; *Bear the brunt* = suffer the first and fiercest attack; *Bear up against* = show courage in suffering; *I can't bear him* = hate, dislike strongly; (3) behave, e.g. *He bears himself like a man*; (4) to produce, e.g. *The tree bears much fruit*; *To bear children*; (5) go, e.g. *Bear down on* = go towards.

BEAR

beard (19) hair on the face below the mouth; *Beard the lion in his den* = go and see a person and show no fear.

bearing (29-1) (1) manner, way of behaving, e.g. *A proud bearing*; (2) meaning; *What you say has no bearing on the subject* = has nothing to do with; (3) direction; *To take bearings* = discover where a ship is; *I've lost my bearings* = do not know where I am; (4) suffering; *Past all bearing* = more than can be suffered or allowed; **ball-bearings**, balls of metal set round a bar in a machine so that the bar may turn more easily, with less rubbing; **ar-m'orial bearings** (44-55-19) figures painted on a shield as the sign of a certain person of a certain family.

beast (11) animal; cattle; *Beasts of burden* = horses, asses (donkeys), etc., which carry things; *Beasts of prey* = animals which eat other things, e.g. lions; (2) low person who behaves like an animal; Sl. any person whom one does not like; **beastly** (——1) like a beast; Sl. unpleasant; *Beastly hard* = very hard.

beat (11) (1) strike; *To follow a beaten track* = —— path travelled by many before, do what others have done before; Am. Sl. *Beat it!* = go away; *To beat up an egg* = mix thoroughly; (2) conquer, win against; *This beats everything* = is the most surprising thing I have ever heard; *This beats me* = is too difficult for me; (3) move regularly, e.g. *The heart beats*; *To beat time to music*; n. **beat**, regular movement of the heart, sound of a drum; *Policeman on his beat* = officer of the law going round those streets which he must watch; **a beater,** one who drives animals or birds out of a wood so that they may be shot by those standing outside.

be′atitude (11·3-1-177) blessedness, great happiness.

beau (67) good-looking man, lover; **b′eau id′eal** (+ 41-19) = best that can be imagined.

bea′uty (177-1) that quality which gives pleasure to the eye or ear; *A beauty* = beautiful woman, fine thing; *Beauty sleep* = sleep early in the night, before midnight; *Beauty spot* = small piece of black material stuck on to the face as an ornament; specially beautiful piece of country; **beauteous** (177-19) beautiful.

beaver (11-9) animal with valuable fur, living on land and in the water, where it builds wonderful houses; Sl. man with a beard.

bec′almed (1-44) (ship) having no wind for movement.

beck (2) sign made to call someone; small stream; *To be at a person's beck and call* = always ready to do everything they ask.

beckon (2) make a silent sign with the finger, calling a person.

bec′ome (1-8) to change from one state to another; *What will become of me?* = what will happen to me?; *What's become of him?* = where is he?; *It does not become me* = it is not right that I should; **becoming,** proper, *suitable* (= which suits well).

bed (2) thing on which one sleeps; *A bed of roses* = happy comfortable state; the course of a river or the hollow in which a sea lies; *A flower-bed* = part of garden used for growing flowers; *To bed out flowers* = to plant —; solid bottom built of brick upon which a machine will rest (stand); **bedclothes** (2-67öz) coverings for a bed; **bedding,** coverings for a bed; dry grass, etc., as a bed for an animal.

bed′eck (1-2) to ornament.

bed′ew (1-177) to wet with drops of water.

bed′izen (1-41) put on many fine, costly things, but without a sense of beauty.

bedlam (2-9) place for madmen; place of noise and disorder.

Bedouin (2-77I) wandering Arab(s) of the desert.

bedr′aggled (1-3) having the dress and hair in disorder.

bed-ridden (2 + 1) unable to get up from bed; ill, having to spend one's life in bed.

bed-rock (+ 5) rock at the bottom; *To get down to bed-rock* = get to the real facts and truth.

bedroom (2-7) room for sleeping.

bedspread (2-2) ornamental cloth spread over a bed.

bee (11) small flying creature that makes *honey* (= very sweet yellow liquid); *Have a bee in one's bonnet* = have some mad idea always in the mind.

beech (11) tree with hard wood and nuts that can be eaten.

bee-eater (11·11-9) bird.

beef (11) meat of a cow, *bull,* or *ox* (*bull, ox* = male forms of cattle); *A beefy fellow* = very strong —; *Put beef into* — = put strength into a stroke.

BEEF-EATER

b′eef-′eaters (11 + 11-9z) soldiers who wear a special dress, as in ancient times, and are seen in the Tower of London.

b′eefst′eak (11-21) thick piece of *beef* (see 2nd above).

beefy (11-1) Sl. strong.

beehive (11-41) little hut made as a home for bees.

b′ee-l′ine (+ 41) straight line, the shortest way.

been (11) p.p. of Be.

beer (119) bitter drink made from grain; Sl. *He's very small beer* = unimportant.

beet (11) (1) plant with a large, round, red root, cooked and eaten as a vegetable; (2) *Sugar-beet* = the same plant, but the root is white, used for sugar-making.

beetle (11) small creature with six legs and hard skin.

beetling (11-1) leaning out over the edge; *Beetling brows* = the *forehead* (= front part of the head above the eyes) standing out far above the eyes.

BEETLE

befall (1-55) happen.

befit (1-1) be proper for.

before (1-55) in front of; earlier than; **beforehand,** earlier.

befoul (1-47) make dirty.

befriend (1-2) help, treat in a friendly way.

beg (2) ask, ask as a kindness; *I beg leave to* = I ask if I may; *I beg your pardon* = I ask you to forgive me, or, kindly repeat what you said (also other meanings depending on the way in which it is said, e.g. *I beg your pardon!* = how dare you say that!); **to beg,** ask for food or money; (of goods) *To go begging* = not to be bought or wanted by anyone; *Beg the question* = take as true just that fact which is being questioned and to reason from it as if it were accepted.

beg′an (1-3) p.t. of Begin.

beg′et (1-2) cause to be born, to produce; p.t. **beg′at.**

beggar (2-9) one who asks for money or food; *To beggar description* = be impossible to describe; **beggarly** (——1) very poor, worthless.

beg′in (1-1) start; **beg′inning,** the start.

beg′one (1-5) Go!

beg′onia (2-67-19) plant with bright red (etc.) leaves and flowers, about 1 ft. high.

beg'otten (1-5) p.p. of Beget.
begr'ime (1-41) cover with dirt.
begr'udge (1-8j) give unwillingly; be unwilling to let someone have something.
begu'ile (1-41) deceive a person; find some means of making time pass pleasantly, e.g. on a long journey.
begum (11-8) title of a Muslim lady of high rank.
beg'un (1-8) p.p. of Begin.
beh'alf (1-44) *On his behalf* = for the purpose of helping him.
beh'ave (1-21) to act; to act with good (or bad) manners; **beh'aviour** (1-21-19) way in which one acts.
behead (1-2) cut off the head.
beh'eld (1-2) p.t. of Behold.
beh'est (1-2) a command, an order.
beh'ind (1-41) at the back of; *He has someone behind him* = supporting —; *Behind time* = late; *Behind with my work* = late in finishing; **beh'indhand** (1-41-3) late.
beh'old (1-67) see, watch.
beh'olden (1-67) feeling grateful to.
beh'oof (1-77) *On your behoof* = to help you.
beh'oove (1-77) be necessary; be right for; p.t. **beh'ove** (1-67).
beige (213) colour of dark sand.
being (11·1) creature with life; life; *The Supreme Being* = God; *To come into being* = be made, begin to live or be.
bel'abour (1-21-9) hit hard.
bel'ated (1-21-1) very late; darkness falling before the end of a journey; *Belated efforts* = attempts made too late.
bel'ay (1-21) fasten a rope round; *Belay there!* = stop! enough!; **bel'aying pin,** bar of wood or iron to which ropes are fastened.
belch (2) send wind from the stomach out through the throat; throw out with force or in large quantities, e.g. *Chimneys belch smoke, Guns belched shot.*
beldam(e) (2-9) ugly old woman.
bel'eaguer (1-11-9) attack (a city) on all sides.
belfry (2-1) part of a tower in which the bells hang.
bel'ie (1-41) show to be untrue.
bel'ief (1-11) act of regarding as true; thing regarded as true; **to bel'ieve,** regard as true; *Believe in* = have faith in.
bel'ittle (1-1) cause to seem small or unimportant.
bell (2) round, hollow, metal vessel, which makes a ringing sound when struck; *Cap and bells* = dress of a Fool; *Passing bell* = bell sounded at death; *Bells* (on a ship, e.g. "*Eight Bells*") bells sounded every half-hour; **bell-wether** (+ 2∂9) sheep with a bell round its neck which acts as leader.
b'ellad'onna (2-9-5-9) poisonous plant from which a medicine (*atropine*) is obtained; it makes the eyes bright, the mouth dry, the heart beat quickly, and the black centres of the eyes larger.

belle (2) beautiful young woman.
b'elles-l'ettres (2 + 2-9) writing, such as poetry, stories, etc.; not scientific writing.
bellicose (2-1-67) fierce, eager for war.
bell'igerent (1-1j9-9) making war; taking part in war.
bellow (2-67) make a loud deep roar.
bellows (2-67z) instrument used for blowing air into a fire to make it burn quickly.
belly (2-1) that part of the body between the breast and legs which contains the stomach, etc.; **to belly,** swell out, like a sail in the wind.
bel'ong (1-5) have to do with; be owned by; *This belongs to me* = is mine; *I belong to this school* = I am a member of —; **belongings** (——1-z) those things which are one's own.
bel'oved (1-8) much loved.
bel'ow (1-67) under; lower than; *Hit below the belt* = give an unfair blow, to attack in an unfair way.
belt (2) band put around the waist; long piece of leather used to drive a machine; *The Corn Belt* = that narrow band of country in which corn grows; *Below the belt* (see Below); **to belt,** strike with a belt. Sl. run fast.
bem'oan (1-67) be very sorry because of something.
bem'use (1-177z) make unable to think properly, e.g. *Bemused with wine* = made foolish with —.
bench (2) long seat; seat of a judge, and so = the judge; table at which a workman (e.g. shoemaker) works.
bend (2) **(1)** force out of a straight line, e.g. *To bend a bar of iron;* (on a ship) tie, e.g. a rope on to a wooden bar; to direct, e.g. *He bent his steps towards; He bent his mind to the work;* **(2)** become curved, to yield; **a bend,** thing bent; knot.
b'enedi'ction (2-1-1-shn) blessing.
b'enefa'ction (2-1-3-shn) doing good; giving money for some good purpose; **b'enefactor** (2-1-3-9) one who does good, who gives money for a good purpose.
ben'eficent (1-2-1s) doing good, kind.
benef'icial (2-1-1shl) helpful, useful.
benef'iciary (2-1-1sh9-1) one who receives money, etc., at a person's death.
benefit (2-1-1) do good, be of service to; a gift or favour; *I get no benefit from the medicine* = — does me no good; *For your benefit* = to help you; *benefit performance* = show in the theatre when all the money taken is given to one particular actor, or to help some good work.
ben'evolence (1-2-9-9-s) the desire to do good; adj. **ben'evolent.**
ben'ighted (1-41-1) in the dark; in a state of darkness of the mind, untaught.
ben'ign (1-41) **ben'ignant** (1-1-9) of a kind or gentle nature; (of a disease) not dangerous.
benison (2-1z) a blessing.
bent (2) forced out of a straight line, not straight; *He has a bent for art* = special natural

benumbed 35 **bevy**

skill or cleverness in —; *To follow one's bent* = do the work in which one has a natural skill or power.

ben'umbed (1-8) having lost all feeling, e.g. because of cold.

b'enz'ene, benzine (2-11) **'benzol** (2-5) light natural oil which burns easily.

bequ'eath (1-11ð) give or pass on a thing to others after death; **bequ'est** (1-2) that which is given to others after death.

ber'ate (1-21) to scold.

Berber (99-9) one of a people living in the hilly parts of North Africa.

ber'eave (1-11) take away; **ber'eaved**, having lost one's (wife, husband, etc.); **ber'eavement** (——9) loss of a loved person by death.

ber'eft (1-2) p.p. of Bereave.

beret (2-2) *or* **beret** (2-21 or 2-1) flat cap.

berg, iceberg (99) (41s-99) large mass of ice floating in the sea.

b'eri-b'eri (2-1) disease caused by eating food which lacks certain things necessary for health, e.g. polished *rice* (= a white grain commonly used as food in India).

berry (2-1) small fruit.

berserk (99-99) ancient *Norse* (= of Scandinavia) fighter who fought with great strength and fierceness like a mad person; pl. *berserkir* (——19); *Berserk rage* = wild, uncontrolled anger.

berth (99) place where a ship can stop and be tied up, e.g. in a harbour; *To give a person a wide berth* = keep at a safe distance from; a sleeping place in a ship or train; *To get a good berth* = get good employment.

beryl (2-1) precious stone—usually green.

bes'eech (1-11) ask eagerly and anxiously.

bes'eem (1-11) to suit; *It ill beseems you to —* = it is not proper that you should.

bes'et (with dangers) (1-2) having (dangers) on every side.

bes'ide (1-41) by, at the side of; *Beside oneself* = almost mad with trouble or excitement; *Beside the point* = having nothing to do with the subject.

bes'ides (1-41-z) also, in addition to what has been said.

bes'iege (1-11j) attack a town on all sides; *He was besieged with letters (questions, etc.)* = has received letters (etc.) in large numbers from all parts.

besm'ear (1-19) cover with (dirt).

besm'irch (1-99) make dirty.

besom (11z) brush made of sticks tied together.

bes'otted (1-5-1) foolish from drinking too much wine.

bes'ought (1-55) p.t. of Beseech.

besp'eak (1-11) order a thing to be prepared, made, or kept ready; *To bespeak your help* = ask you to be ready to help; *His appearance bespeaks illness* = shows signs of illness; *Bespoke shoes* = made specially.

best (2) most good; *It's all for the best* = it may not do us any harm in the end; *Have the best of it* = win, succeed; *Make the best of it, Make the best of a bad business (bargain)* = be cheerful in misfortune; *Make the best of one's time* = do as much as possible in the time; *Make the best of one's way, Put one's best foot forward* = go as fast as possible; *The best man* = friend who helps a man at his marriage; adv. **best**; *Best-hated man* = most hated; *We had best do something* = we ought to —, it would be wise to —; *to best*, win against, e.g. by a trick.

bestial (2-19) like an animal.

best'ir (1-99) cause to move quickly.

best'ow (1-67) put; *Bestow upon* = give.

bestr'ide (1-41) sit or stand over a thing with legs apart as in sitting on a horse; p.t. **bestr'ode** (1-67).

bet (2) pay money which will be paid back, together with more money if a certain event happens, but will be lost if it does not happen; a **bet**, making of such an agreement, the money so paid; *To bet one's bottom dollar on, To bet one's shirt on* = bet all one's money, to be very sure that it will happen.

beta (11-9) second Greek letter; of second-class quality; *Beta plus* = a little better than second class; *Beta minus* = just below second class.

betel (11) leaf which is filled with pieces of *areca-nut* (= red hard fruit), etc., and *chewed* (= kept in the mouth and bitten continually) by Indians.

b'ête n'oire (21 + 74) person or thing specially hated.

bethel (2) *A little bethel* = small church-like building (the word is often used in disrespect).

bet'ide (1-41) *Woe betide you* = may sorrow come to you.

bet'imes (1-41-z) early.

bet'oken (1-67) be a sign of.

betr'ay (1-21) sell one's country or a friend to the enemy; tell a secret; n. **betr'ayal** (1-219).

betr'othed (11-67ð) promised in marriage.

better (2-9) more good; *No better than she should be* = of doubtful character; *Better half* = wife (or husband); *Do better than one's word* = more than was promised; *One's betters* = persons older or higher in rank; *Think better of* = change one's opinion; *For better for worse* = in good or bad fortune; *We had better go* = it would be wise to go; **to better**, make better; *To better oneself* = get better employment.

betw'ixt (1-1) between.

bevel (2) sloping edge; *A bevel wheel, A bevel gear* = wheel which drives another wheel set corner-ways to it.

beverage (2-9-1j) à drink, e.g. tea, wine, etc.

bevy (2-1) group (of girls, birds, etc.).

bew'ail (1-21) to cry, be sorry because of.
bew'are (1-29) be careful of, to guard against.
bew'ilder (1-1-9) make difficult for a person to understand.
bew'itch (1-1) have a magic effect on.
bey (21) title of a governor or officer in the East.
bey'ond (1-5) on the farther side; farther away; *It's beyond me* = I do not understand it; *The back of beyond* = very distant place; *Beyond compare, Beyond praise* = very good; *Beyond hope* = more than can be hoped for; *Beyond all reason* = quite unreasonable.
bezel (2) sloping surface of a jewel; turned-up metal edge that holds a jewel in place.
bez'ique (2-11k) a card game.
bi- (4I) twice, e.g. **bi-weekly** (+ 11-1) = twice a week or once in two weeks.
bias (419) turning away from the straight line; weight on one side of a ball which causes it to roll away from the straight course; *He has a bias, He is biased* = he has an idea fixed in his mind, and will not judge fairly.
bib (1) cloth to keep a child clean when eating.
Bible (4I) holy book of the Christian Church; adj. **Biblical** (1-1).
b'ibli'ography (1-15-9-1) list of books on some special subject.
bibulous (person) (1-17-9) one who drinks 'wine freely.
biceps (41s2) large muscle on the front of the upper arm.
bicker (1-9) to quarrel about small matters.
bicycle (41s1) two-wheeled machine, which one drives along by turning a chain-wheel with the feet.
bid (1) to command; an offer to buy; *To bid to a feast* = to invite; *To bid goodbye* = to say —; p.p. **bidden**.
bide (4I) wait; remain; *To bide one's time* = wait till a good chance (of doing something) comes.
bi'ennial (4I2-19) every two years; plant which lives for two years and then dies.
bier (19) wooden carrier or table for a *coffin* (= box containing a dead body).
biff (1) Sl. a blow.
bifurcate (41-99-21) divide into two branches, e.g. a road.
big (1) large, great.
bigamy (1-9-1) act of having two wives or husbands at the same time; adj. **bigamous** (1-9-9).
bight (4I) bend in the shore; circle made in a rope.
bigot (1-9) one who believes strongly in a thing and will not listen to reason; **bigotry** (1-9-1) act of believing in a thing without reason.
bigwig (1-1) important person.
bijou (11377) French for a jewel; *A bijou residence* = nice small house.
bike (4I) Sl. bicycle.
bil'ateral (41-3-9) two-sided.
bile (4I) bitter, yellow-green liquid which changes fatty food in the body into a form in which it can be used by the body; bad temper.
bilge (1-j) dirty water in the bottom of a ship; broad bottom of a ship; Sl. foolish talk.
bil'ingual (4I-1nggw9) having two languages.
bilious (attack) (1-19) illness, with sickness and pains in the head, caused by too much *bile* (see 3rd above).
bilk (1) trick a person by running (going) away without paying what is owed.
bill (1) (**1**) plan for a law, written down for government to consider; (**2**) list of things bought and the money owed or paid for them; *To foot the bill* = pay —; (**3**) printed notice; *Bill of exchange* = written order to pay money on a certain date; *Bill of health* = list of people on a ship showing whether ill or well; *Bill of lading* = list of things loaded on a ship; *Bill of fare* = list of foods.
bill (1) horny mouth of a bird; *To bill and coo* = make love as birds do.
billet (1-1) lodging-house for a soldier; *To billet on* = send soldiers for lodging to a person's house; *A good billet* = well-paid employment.
billet (of wood) short log.
b'illet-d'oux (1-1 + 77) love letter.
billhook (1-7) curved knife used for cutting bushes or rough grass.
billiards (1-19-z) game played on a table with balls pushed with long sticks against each other or into pockets at the corners and sides.
Billingsgate (1-1-z-21) part of London; Sl. very bad language (cursing).
billion (1-19) one thousand million in France and America; one million million in England and Germany.
billow (1-67) big wave.
bill-poster (1 + 67-9) **bill-sticker** (+ 1-9) man who sticks printed notices on to walls.
billy-goat (1-1 + 67) male goat.
biltong (1-5) meat dried in the sun.
b'im'etallism (41-2-9-1z) idea that both silver and gold should have real value as money.
bin (1) large box used to contain bread, flour, coal, etc.
bind (4I) to tie; *Bind oneself to* = promise; fasten together pages and make them into a book; *To bind over* = order to appear before a judge when called; come together into a solid mass (e.g. snow, earth)—see also p.p. **bound**.
binding (4I-1) cover of a book; adj., e.g. *A promise given under force is not binding* = need not be fulfilled.
bindweed (4I-11) unwanted plant which grows along the ground and curls itself round other plants.
binge (1nj) heavy drinking.
binnacle (1-9) box with a glass top in which the compass of a ship is kept with a lamp for use at night.

BINNACLE

bin'oculars (4I-5-I7-9) glass (for both eyes) used to see distant objects.
bio- having to do with life.
bi'ography (4I5-9-I) written story of a person's life.
bi'ology (4I5-9jI) science of living things.
biped (4I-2) creature having two legs.
biplane (4I-2I) aeroplane with two wings, one above the other.

BINOCULARS

birch (99) a tree; handful of sticks tied together used for punishing; to hit with a birch.
bird (99) feathered creature which lays eggs; Sl. *A dear old bird* = — fellow; *A bird of prey* = bird which kills birds and small animals; *A bird of passage* = person who travels often from one place to another; *Birds of a feather* = persons of the same kind (usually bad); *A bird in the hand* = something which one has really got; Sl. *I'll do it like a bird* = very willingly; Sl. *To give an actor the bird* = make rude noises at—; **bird-lime** (+ 4I) sticky material spread on branches to catch birds; **bird's-eye view** (99-z + 4I + I77) = view seen from high up, general view of a subject.
birth (99) act of being born; **birthday** (99-2I) day of the year on which one was born; **birthmark** (99-44) mark on the body at birth; **birth-rate** (+ 2I) number of births in each I,000 people in a country; **birthright** (99-4I) that which belongs to one because of one's birth (e.g. as a member of a certain nation).
biscuit (I-I) (I) flat dry cake, as sold in tins. (In America "biscuit" means only unsweetened biscuits); Sl. *This takes the biscuit* = is the best (worst) thing I have heard; (2) cups, plates, etc., made of baked earth, after their first heating in the fire before the *glaze* (= glasslike surface-covering) is put on.
bis'ect (4I-2) to cut into two equal parts.
bishop (I-9) high officer in the Church; **bishopric** (——I) office of a bishop, the part of the country in which a bishop has power.
bismuth (Iz-9) grey metal, salts of which are used to calm the stomach.
bison (4I) large wild cow-like animal.
biss'extile (year) (I-2-4I) year in which there is February 29th.
bit (I) (I) piece; *To give him a bit of one's mind* = scold; *Bit by bit* = slowly, one piece after another; *Do one's bit* = one's share of the duty; (2) *Wait a bit* = a short time.
bit (I) instrument used for making holes in wood.
bit (I) metal bar put in a horse's mouth for riding or driving it; *To take the bit between one's teeth* = get out of control.
bit (I) p.t. of Bite.
bitch (I) a female dog; Sl. a nasty woman.

bite (4I) (I) to cut with the teeth; *To bite the dust* = fall on the ground, be killed; *Bite one's thumb at* = show disrespect; *Bite one's lips* = show self-control; *Bite off more than one can chew* = promise to do more than one can; (2) attack with the teeth—or as an insect does; (3) cause pain; *Biting words* = cruel —; (4) take the food on a hook as a fish does; *I offered it but he would not bite* = would not accept; p.p. **bitten.**
biz'arre (I-44) of peculiar appearance.
blab (3) tell a secret.
black (3) opposite of white; *I'm in his black books* = he is angry with me; *Black and blue* = having suffered many blows; *The Black Arts* = magic; *The black cap* = cap worn by a judge when ordering the death of a prisoner; *Black sheep* = person of bad character; *Look black* = appear angry; *The future looks black* = troubles seem probable.
blackball (3-55) show that one does not want a person elected as a member of a group.
Bl'ack D'eath (3 + 2) disease which passed over Europe about A.D. I349 and caused the death of many people.
blackguard (3-44) very bad man.
blackhead (3-2) small swelling on the skin, usually having a black top.
blacking (3-I) black material used for polishing shoes.
blackjack (3-3) cup or drinking vessel made of leather; short weapon for striking; flag of a *pirate* (= sea-thief).
bl'ackl'ead (3-2) black material like that found inside a pencil.
blackleg (3-2) man who offers to work when all his fellow workers are " *on strike* " (= refusing to work so as to get more pay, etc.).
blackmail (3-2I) demand money saying that one will tell some bad thing about the person if it is not paid.
black market (+ 44-I) unlawful sale of goods at high prices.
blacksmith (3-I) man who works with iron and makes shoes for horses.
bladder (3-9) bag, e.g. of skin or leather, used to contain liquid; *The bladder* = that part of the body which contains waste liquid before it is passed out.
blade (2I) (I) narrow leaf of a plant; (2) cutting part of a knife or sword; any narrow flat object.
blah (44) Am. Sl. foolish talk or writing, e.g. great praise intended to sell an article.
blame (2I) say that a person is the cause of a certain trouble.
blanch (44) make white; become white.
blancm'ange (9-5"3) mixture of flour, sugar, milk and other materials which sets in stiff fancy shape when cold.
bland (3) soft in speech; gentle; *Bland diet* = simple food for a sick person.
blandishments (3-I-9) arts of pleasing used to

blank   38   **blood**

make a person agree—usually to a wrong act.

blank (3ngk) with no writing on it, e.g. *A blank sheet of paper*; *To fire blank* = fire a gun with powder but no shot; *My mind was blank* = I had no ideas; *A blank look* = face showing no feeling or understanding; *To draw a blank* = be unsuccessful; *Blank verse* = unrhymed poetry.

blanket (3ngkI) thick woollen cloth, e.g. one used as a bed covering; *A wet blanket* = person who makes others feel sad or hopeless; *A blanket code* = one set of rules covering everything.

blare (29) loud noise of a horn.

blarney (44-1) soft, pleasant speech; tell a person how beautiful, clever, etc., he is.

blasé (44z21) uninterested through having enjoyed too much of anything.

blasph'eme (3-11) say evil or foolish things about God; n. **blasphemy** (3-9-1); adj. **blasphemous** (3-9-9).

blast (44) strong rush of wind or hot air; *He blew a blast on his horn* = — loud note —; to break rock with gun-powder; do great damage to, to ruin; *Blast you!* (= a cry of anger); **blasting powder,** powder like gun-powder, used for breaking rocks.

blatant (21-9) noisy, rough and having bad manners.

blather (3ðg) foolish talk.

blaze (21) bright fire; burn brightly; *To blaze a trail* = mark trees showing the way to one who follows; Sl. *Go to blazes!* = go away, do not trouble me!; *Blaze of colour* = much colour.

blazer (21-9) woollen coat, usually of bright colour, worn at games.

blazon (21) put figures on a shield; *To blazon abroad* = tell everywhere.

bleach (11) make white; become white.

bleak (11) cold and *cheerless* (= not cheerful).

bleary (eyed) (19-1) having red, painful eyes; not seeing well.

bleat (11) cry of a sheep.

bleed (11) lose blood; draw blood from; get too much money from; p.t. and p.p. **bled.**

blemish (2-1) broken place or ugly mark on a beautiful thing.

blench (2) move back in fear.

blend (2) mix together; look well together, e.g. colours; a mixture.

bless (2) ask God to show favour to; *Bless me! Bless my soul!* (= cries of surprise); *Not a penny to bless oneself with* = very poor; Sl. *To bless one's stars* = be grateful for one's good fortune; **blessed** (2-1) holy, happy, having good fortune; Sl. *The whole blessed lot* = all; *A state of single blessedness* = unmarried; **a blessing,** act of blessing, thing which brings happiness; *What a blessing it is that* — — = how fortunate —; *A blessing in disguise* = something that looked bad but was found to be very fortunate.

blew (77) p.t. of Blow.

blight (41) a disease of plants; *To cast a blight on the party* = destroy the happiness of —; *Blighted hopes* = ruined —; Sl. *Blighter* = unpleasant person.

Blighty (41-1) Sl. England; war-wound causing return to England.

blimp (1) a small airship; *Colonel Blimp*: see Colonel.

blind (41) unable to see; Sl. *Blind to the world* = having drunk too much wine.

blind (41) cloth pulled down from a roller to cover a window; *His kindness was merely a blind* = was only used to hide his real purpose.

blindfold (41-67) having the eyes covered with a cloth.

bl'ind-man's-b'uff (41 + 3-z + 8) game played by children in which one child, having the eyes covered with a cloth, tries to catch the others.

blink (1ngk) open and close the eyes quickly; (of lights) shine unsteadily; *It's no good blinking the fact* = refusing to see.

blinkers (1ngk9z) pieces of leather fixed at the sides of a horse's eyes.

bliss (1) great happiness.

blister (1-9) raised spot on the skin with clear liquid under it.

blithe (41ð) happy; **blithesome** (41ð-9) happy.

blitz, very destructive attack, e.g. from aeroplanes.

blizzard (1-9) storm with a strong, cold wind and much snow.

bloated (67-1) swollen up (= p.p. of Swell), unhealthily fat.

bloater (67-9) salted fish.

blob (5) small round mass, e.g. of wax or paint.

bloc (5) group (e.g. of countries) united by some common interest, e.g. the Sterling Bloc.

block (5) mass of wood, stone, etc.; *A chip of the old block* = child like its parents; *To go to the block* = go to have one's head cut off; an unbroken line of houses between two streets; **to block,** e.g. *To block a pipe* = prevent (water) from passing; *To block in a picture* = draw or paint roughly, showing the general arrangement; BLOCK LETTERS— as here.

block and tackle (5 + 3) an arrangement of wheels and rope for lifting heavy things.

block'ade (5-21) the shutting up of a place by warships or soldiers to prevent any persons or goods coming or going.

blocked currency (5-t + 8-9-1) money which cannot be spent outside its own country.

blockhead (5-2) fool.

bloke (67) Sl. man.

blond(e) (5) light brown, fair (hair, skin).

blood (8) (**1**) red liquid in the body; (**2**) family; *He is of good blood* = comes of good family; *Blue-blooded* = of noble family; *A blood-horse* = horse whose parents were of some special kind; *Make bad blood between* = cause a quarrel; *More than flesh and blood can stand* =

blood-bank / **board**

unbearable; *One's flesh and blood* = members of one's family; **to blood,** give a dog its first taste of blood, to give a person a new experience.

blood-bank (+ 3) store of blood used for *blood-transfusion* (= putting blood into the body of a sick or wounded person).

bloodhound (8-47) special kind of dog which can follow a smell for many hours.

blood-money (+ 8-1) money paid for giving a person over to the law.

bloodshed (8-2) killing people.

bloodshot (eyes) (8-5) white part of the eyes red with blood.

blood-vessel (+ 2) pipe through which blood flows in the body.

bloody (8-1) covered with blood; red like blood; Sl. (rude word) = very bad, much disliked.

bloom (77) flower of a plant; *The tree is blooming* = has flowers on it; *Blooming health* = perfect —; Sl. *Every blooming person* (no special meaning; the word adds force) = every person.

bloomer (77-9) Sl. foolish mistake.

bloomers (77-9z) loose trousers worn by women, tight round the waist and the knees.

blossom (5) flower of a plant.

blot (5) mark, e.g. of ink on paper; *A blot on one's character* = fault; *A blot on the landscape* = ugly thing which ruins the view; **to blot,** make ink-marks on; *To blot out* = take out words already written, destroy; *Blot one's copy-book* = spoil one's record for good character; *Blotted out with mist* = covered so that one cannot see; **bl'otting-paper** (5-1 + 21-9) special kind of paper for drying ink; **a blotter,** a book of blotting-paper.

blotch (5) ugly spot, e.g. on the skin.

blouse (47z) loose outer garment worn by women on the upper half of the body.

blow (67) send forward a stream of air; *To blow a horn* = sound — by means of the breath; *I blow my nose* = I send air through my nose to clean it; *To blow up a balloon* (= gas bag) = fill it with air; *To blow up a bridge* = fire a lot of explosive under it and destroy it; *Blow out a lamp* = put out the flame by blowing; Sl. *Blow it!* = curse it; *I'm blowed if I will* = I certainly will not.

blow (67) sudden hard stroke; *Come to blows* = begin fighting; *A terrible blow* = sudden and surprising misfortune or loss.

blower (67-9) instrument for making a fire burn quickly by blowing air through the coals.

blowfly (67-41) blue fly which lays eggs in meat.

blown (67) p.p. of Blow.

blowpipe (67-41) pipe used to drive air through burning gas so as to get a very hot flame.

blowzy (47-1) (of a woman) badly dressed, not neat, dirty-looking.

blubber (8-9) fat of a *whale* (= largest creature living in the sea); **to blubber,** weep noisily.

blucher(s) (77k9z) boots which come half way up to the knee.

bludgeon (8j9) short thick stick; strike with a stick.

blue (77) colour of the clear sky; *Look blue* = look sad; *Till all is blue* = for a long time; *Once in a blue moon* = not often, very uncommon; *True blue* = loyal; *A bolt from the blue* = great surprise; *Out of the blue* = as a surprise; *Get the blues* = feel sad; Sl. *To blue money* = spend wildly; *An Oxford (Cambridge) blue* = one who plays a game for the university.

bluebell (77-2) wild flower.

bluebook (77-7) book printed by the British government.

bluebottle (77-5) large blue fly, often seen near sweet things or meat.

bluejacket (77j3-1) sailor.

blue-print (+ 1) plan used in making a machine or building a house; any plan.

BLUEBELL

bl'ue r'ibbon (+ 1) mark of great honour.

bluestocking (77-5-1) woman who is or pretends to be very learnèd.

bluff (8) cliff; steep place; *A bluff man* = one who has a rough and noisy manner.

bluff, to — (8) deceive by pretending to be very strong and sure of oneself.

blunder (8-9) foolish mistake; **to blunder,** make a foolish mistake, move in a rough and unskilful way.

blunderbuss (8-9-8) old kind of gun with a wide end to the barrel.

BLUNDERBUSS

blunt (8) not having a sharp edge; rough and plain in speech, saying what one means without trying to be kind or polite to the hearer.

blurb (99) short piece of writing telling what a book is about and how good it is.

blurred (99) not clear in shape — as if seen through a mist.

blurt (out) (99) speak out suddenly; tell a secret.

blush (8) become red in the face, e.g. as a sign of shame, happiness, surprise; *Spare my blushes* = do not praise me in my own hearing.

bluster (8-9) (of wind) blow hard; (of a person) try to get out of a difficulty by talking noisily.

boa (679) long rope-shaped garment made of feathers worn by women about the neck.

boa-constrictor (679 + 9-1-9) large South American snake.

boar (55) wild pig; male pig.

board (55) **(1)** long flat piece of wood; *To tread the boards* = be an actor; **(2)** table of food; *Groaning board* = table with a lot of food on it; *Above board* = not secretly; *Board and lodging* = food and house-room, **(3)** group of persons sitting round a table, controlling group, e.g. *School Board* = group of persons who control the schools; (4) side of a ship; *On board* = on a ship or train; *To go by the board* = fall off a ship, to fail completely; **to board**, *To board up* = cover (a window) with boards; *To board out* = get one's food outside the house; *Board with* = get one's food with; *To board a ship* = go on to a ship (e.g. in order to attack it).

boarder (55-9) one who pays to live and have meals in another person's house, or lodging-house.

b'oarding-house (55-1 + 47) lodging-house which supplies meals.

b'oarding-school (55-1 + sk77) school in which children live.

b'oard-school, formerly a government school controlled by the School Board (see Board).

b'oard-w'ages (+ 21j1z) money paid to servants while the master of the house is away.

boast (67) speak proudly of; possess and feel proud of.

boat (67) thing moved by a sail, or a motor, or by rowing, used for travelling on water; any ship; *All in the same boat* = — same danger; *I've burnt my boats* = it is too late to turn back from this task.

boater (67-9) hard hat for wear in summer, made of *straw* (= dry yellow stems of plants).

boatswain (67) chief seaman who calls the men to work.

bob (5) (1) move quickly up and down; (2) cut short the hair of a woman; *Bob-tailed* = having a short tail.

bob (5) Obs. sl. shilling.

bobbin (5-1) small roller holding many turns of cotton, silk or wool used in a machine for making cloth, also in a *sewing machine* (= machine for joining cloth by means of thread).

bobby (5-1) Sl. policeman.

bobby-soxer (+ 5-9) Am. Sl. girl aged about 10 to 15.

bobolink (5-9-1ngk) small singing bird.

bobsled (5-2), **bob-sleigh** (5-21) small car running on iron or wooden blades, with space for three or four persons on it, guided by a moveable front part—used for sliding down a snowy slope.

BOBSLEIGH

bode (67) be a sign of what will happen, especially of evil.

bodice (5-1s) upper part of a woman's dress.

bodkin (5-1) long needle without a sharp point.

body (5-1) (1) the whole of a man or animal; (2) central part of a man or animal, without the limbs or head; (3) central part of anything, e.g. *The body of the hall* = large central part of —; *The body of a car* = that part of a motor-car in which one sits; (4) solid *material* (= made of matter) part of a man, not the spirit; (5) dead person or animal; (6) mass, e.g. *heavenly bodies* = the stars, etc.; (7) group of persons, e.g. *The Governing Body of the school*; (8) strong taste, e.g. *This wine has a full body*; (9) a person, e.g. *An honest body*.

bodyguard (5-1-44) soldiers to guard (protect) a person.

Boer (679) (1) one of the Afrikaans-speaking people of South Africa; (2) farmer in S. Africa.

boffin (5-1) Sl. scientist.

bog (5) soft, wet ground.

bogey (67g1) evil spirit; imagined fear.

boggle at (5) show unwillingness to act; make difficulties about.

bogie (67g1) four or six wheels set in a frame turning on a central pin under a railway engine or carriage.

BOGIE

bogus (67-9) not real but pretending to be real.

boh'emian (67-11-19) person (e.g. a painter or writer) who lives a free life not according to the usual customs of those around him.

boil (51) painful poisoned swelling on the body.

boil (51) make water very hot; cook in water; *Make one's blood boil* = make very angry; *Boil down* = make less by boiling, make shorter, e.g. *Boil down a book*.

boiler (51-9) iron container for holding hot water or water which is being turned into steam—e.g. as part of a steam-engine.

boisterous (51-9) wild, rough, noisy.

bold (67) full of courage, fearless; clear and easily seen.

bole (67) thick stem of a tree.

bol'ero (5-29-67) Spanish dance; **b'olero** (5-9-67) Spanish coat.

boll (5) seed-container of the cotton plant.

bollard (5-9) post on to which ships are tied.

bol'ogna (9-67-9) *sausage* (= meat cut small and packed into a long skin); Am. *Boloney!* = foolishness.

bolster (67-9) long soft *cushion* (= bag filled with wool or feathers) for putting under the head when sleeping; *To bolster up* = support.

bolt (67) (1) short arrow; *I've shot my bolt* = have made my attempt and can do no more; *Bolt upright* = straight up; *A thunderbolt* = mass of metal said to fall from the sky during a storm; *A bolt from the blue* = great surprise; (2) bar used for fastening a door; sliding bar which closes one end of a gun before the shot is fired; iron pin used in holding together pieces of metal; **to bolt**, run away; swallow food quickly.

bomb (5) hollow iron container filled with explosive material which bursts after being thrown or dropped from the air; **to bomb**, attack with bombs.

bomb'ard (5-44) to attack with guns, to fire many shots into; *Bombarded him with questions* = asked many questions of him.

bombast (5-3) big words or big talk with little meaning.
bombshell (5-2) *bomb* (see 3rd above); *He dropped a bombshell* = he said something very surprising.
b'ona f'ide (67-9 + 41-1) in good faith, real, really.
bon'anza (5-3-9) great good fortune.
bonbons (5ⁿ-5ⁿ) sweets.
bond (5) something which ties or holds firm; written promise, especially of a government, promising to pay money; *His word is as good as his bond* = his spoken promise is enough, he is very honest; money given to a court of law to make sure that a prisoner will return when called; *Goods in bond* = goods coming into a country held by government until money is paid on them.
bondage (5-1j) state of being a slave.
bondslave (5-2I) slave.
bone (67) part of the hard frame of the body; the material of which this is made; *A bone of contention* = cause of quarrelling; *I have a bone to pick with you* = something to complain about; *Make no bones about* = feel no doubt or fear in doing; *Bone-dry* = quite dry; **to bone**, take the bones out of; Sl. *to bone* = steal.
boner (67-9) Sl. schoolboy's foolish mistake.
bonfire (5-419) large fire made out of doors for pleasure or to burn dead leaves in a garden.
bonhomie (5-5-1) pleasantness of manner, cheerfulness.
b'on m'ot (5ⁿ + 67) clever saying.
b'onne b'ouche (5n+77sh) specially nice piece of food.
bonnet (5-1) hat tied on the head with strings; the covering over the engine of a motor-car; *To have a bee in one's bonnet* = have some mad idea fixed in the mind.
bonny (5-1) pretty, gay and healthy.
bonus (67-9) special payment above what is necessary.
b'on viv'ant (5ⁿ + 11-44ⁿ) one who loves good food and comfort.
boo (77) sound used to express dislike, or to drive away an animal.
booby (77-1) foolish person; *Booby prize* = something given to the last runner in a race or person who does worst in a game; *Booby trap* = foolish trick, e.g. placing a book above a door to fall on the head of a person entering.
book (7) collection of sheets of paper fastened together as a thing to be read, or to be written in; *To bring to book* = punish, make a person pay; *He is in my black books* = I am angry with him; *It suits my book* = suits my plans; *The books* = account books; **to book** *a seat* = pay for and arrange to have a seat.
bookcase (7-21) set of shelves for books.
bookie (7-1) see Bookmaker.
b'ooking-clerk (7-1 + 44) man who sells tickets (= printed cards giving the right to travel by train, enter theatre, etc.).
bookish (7-1) liking books very much.
b'ook-keeping (+ 11-1) keeping of accounts of money.
booklet (7-1) small book.
b'ookmaker (7-21-9) one who receives *bets* (= money paid which will be lost if the horse loses a race, but will be paid back with more money if the horse wins).
bookworm (7-99) paper-eating insect; person who is always reading.
boom (77) deep sound, as of a large bell or big gun.
boom (77) long pole on a ship used in loading; long pole to which a sail is fastened; chain fixed across a river to stop things, e.g. logs floating down.
boom (77) time of quick money-making in business; **to boom** (of business) be good, successful; *To boom a person* = praise and make known to all.
boomerang (77-9-3) curved stick used by Australian natives which makes a circle and comes back when thrown; used to kill birds, etc.
boon (77) a favour; a blessing, e.g. *A good book is a great boon on a long journey*.
boon comp'anion (+ 9-3-19) pleasant —.
boor (79) uninteresting person, one with bad manners.
boost (77) push upwards or forwards; increase the selling of goods; increase the value or power of.
boot(s) (77) coverings for the feet, usually made of leather, having an upper part covering part of the leg; *The boot is on the other foot* = the other person now has the blame; Sl. *To get the boot* = lose one's employment; *Have one's heart in one's boots* = be afraid; *The boots* = man in a hotel who cleans boots and shoes; *Boot of a car* = place at the back for bags and boxes.
booth (77ð) hut; shop in a hut.
bootlegger (77-2-9) one who breaks the law by making or selling wine and strong drink.
bootless (77-1) useless; *What boots it?* = of what use is it?
booty (77-1) goods stolen by thieves.
booze (77) Sl. to drink; strong drink.
bor'acic (9-3sI) acid powder used to keep food from decay, also to put on small wounds.
borax (55-3) white salt-like powder used for cleaning.
border (55-9) edge; be on the edge; *The Border* = land near the line between England and Scotland; **b'orderline c'ase** (55-9-41 + 21) question which is just on the edge, difficult to decide, e.g. borderline pass (or fail) in an examination.
bore (55) make a hole; tire a person by talking to him in an uninteresting way; **a bore,** uninteresting person.

bore (55) very large wave caused by the *tide* (= movement of the sea caused by the moon) running up a narrow river.

bore (55) (of a gun) measure across the inside of the barrel.

boredom (55-9) state of being tired and not interested.

boric (5-1) having to do with *Borax* (see 6th above).

born (55) p.p. of Bear = produce young; e.g. *He was born in 1888.*

borne (55) p.p. of Bear = carry, support, produce young; e.g. *He had borne a heavy load, She had borne many children.*

borough (8-9) town which has powers of self-government.

borrow (5-67) obtain the use of a thing on the understanding that it will be given back.

bosh (5) foolish talk.

bosom (7z9) human breast; place where one feels joy or sorrow; *Bosom friend* = close friend.

boss (5) round part which stands up from a flat surface, like the head of a very large nail.

boss (5) man in charge of workmen; head of any business; **to boss**, be head-man; to control; make oneself unpleasant by trying to control too much.

botany (5-9-1) science of plants.

botch (5) do work badly; repair roughly.

both (67) the two; as well.

bother (5ŏ9) be a trouble to; cause trouble; be anxious; *Bother!* = cry of anger.

bottle (5) container (usually of glass) for liquids; **to bottle**, put liquid or fruit into a bottle; *To bottle up one's anger* = control, hide —.

bottle-neck (+ 2) narrow space in a road which slows down cars; part of a factory where production is slow, so slowing down the whole.

bottom (5) lowest part of anything; ground under the sea, a river, etc.; Sl. the part of the body on which one sits.

b'ottom-dr'awer (+ 55) A girl puts things in her — for use when she is married.

boudoir (77-w44) lady's sitting-room.

b'ougainv'illea (77-9-1-19) climbing plant with big flowers which grows in hot countries.

bough (47) branch of a tree.

bought (55) p.t. of Buy.

bouillon (7775ⁿ) clear *soup* (= liquid food made by boiling meat and vegetables in water).

boulder (67-9) large stone.

b'oulevard (77-44) broad street, usually having trees on each side.

bounce (47-s) (of a ball) spring back or up again from the floor; (of a person) move in a rough and noisy way; try to hurry a person into some unwise action; *He has too much bounce* = is noisy and pushes himself forward; *Two bouncing boys* = strong and healthy —; Sl. *The cheque bounced* = the bank refused to pay the *cheque* (= order to pay money).

bound (47) mark the edges of; keep within a certain space; control; **bounds** (——z) edges so marked, edges beyond which one may not go; *To overstep the bounds of common sense* = behave in a foolish way.

bound (47) to jump; *By leaps and bounds* = very quickly.

bound (47) p.p. of Bind; *Bound up in his family* = very interested in; *The ship is bound for England* is going to —; *Outward bound* = going away from home; *He is bound to win* = sure to —.

boundary (47-9-1) fixed and agreed outside edge of a field, country; space within which a game is played.

bounder (47-9) Sl. person with bad manners.

bounteous (47-19) generous.

bounty (47-1) gift; act of being generous.

bouqu'et (7kz1) flowers tied together for holding in the hand.

b'ourgeois (79374), middle-class person, shopkeeper.

bourne (79) small stream.

bourse (779) place in foreign countries in which business men meet together to buy and sell, e.g. to buy and sell shares in business companies.

bout (47) short time during which there is action, e.g. *A bout of fighting, A short bout with the enemy* = little battle; *A drinking bout; A bout of illness* = short attack of —.

bovine (67-41) having to do with cattle; slow and heavy like a cow.

bow (47) bend, e.g. as a sign of respect; *I bow to your opinion* = I yield —; *Bow down to* = show great respect to, pray to.

bow (67) piece of wood held in a curve by a string, used for shooting arrows, also for rubbing strings to play music; *To have two strings to one's bow* = several plans for one purpose; *Draw the long bow* = tell an untrue story, making things bigger than they really were.

bow (67) knot such as is used for the shoes, also for a *tie* (= silk band round the neck).

bow(s) (47) front end of a ship.

bowdlerize (47-9-41) take out from a book those parts unfit for young readers.

bowel (479) long pipe continuing from the stomach and leading the waste matter out of the body.

bower (479) shaded place under the trees.

bowl (67) round deep dish.

bowl (67) large ball rolled along the ground in a game; **to bowl**, roll a ball; send a ball to the striker (in cricket); *Bowl along* = move smoothly along; *Bowled over* = knocked down, made helpless, e.g. by illness, sorrow.

b'ow-l'egged (67 + 2) having the legs curving outwards at the knee.

bowler (hat) (67-9) man's round hard hat, usually black.

bowline (67-1) rope running from the edge of a sail to the *bow* (= front part of a ship); special sort of knot which does not slip.

bowls (67-z) game in which one tries to roll a big ball as near as possible to a small ball called "the jack."

bowshot (67-5) about 300 yards.

bowsprit (67-1) pole running out from the front of a ship.

b'ow-w'indow (67 + 1-67) curved window standing out from the wall; Sl. large stomach of a fat man.

box (5) small bush; tree with very hard wood.

box (5) case or container; small room amongst the seats in a theatre; small house in the country; *A Christmas box* = present given at Christmas; *On the box* = on the driver's seat in a carriage; *Boxed up in* = shut up closely in; *Box the compass* = say all the directions of the compass, e.g. North, North-north-east, etc.

box (5) to fight with the *fists* (= tightly closed hands); *Box a person's ears* = strike him on the ears or head.

B'oxing day (5-1 + 21) December 26.

b'ox-'office (+ 5-1s) place in a theatre at which seats for a play are sold.

b'oycott (51-9) join together and refuse to buy from or sell to a person or do any business with him.

boy-sc'out(ing) (51 + 47-1) way of training boys in character and self-help through camp life, giving help to others, etc.

bra (44) see Brassière.

brace (21s) post or rope used to hold something firmly; **to brace**, hold in place firmly; *To brace oneself for a task* = gather one's strength; **a pair of braces** (——1z) bands over the shoulders which hold up the trousers.

br'ace and b'it (21s + 1) instrument used for making holes in wood.

brace (21s) *A brace of* = two.

bracelet (21s-1) band worn around the arm as an ornament.

bracing (air) (21s1) making one feel strong and well.

bracken (3) kind of wild plant whose seeds are found on the under-side of the leaves.

bracket (3-1) piece of iron or wood put in or on a wall to support something; mark in books ( ) or { }; **to bracket**, join together with a bracket.

brackish (3-1) salt-tasting.

brad (3) small, headless nail.

bradawl (3-55) instrument used for making small holes.

brag (3) express a very good opinion of one's own powers; **a braggart** (3-9) noisy fellow with a good opinion of himself; **braggad'ocio** (3-9-67tsh167) noisy bragging.

Brahmin (44-1) member of the highest, priestly, class of Hindus in India.

braid (21) narrow band of cloth used for making an edge to cloth, also for binding things together; **to braid**, twist together into one string or band; *To braid hair* = tie up or twist together in a beautiful way.

braille (21) way of writing with raised dots so that *blind* (= not able to see) people can read it with their fingers.

brain (21) grey matter inside the head with which we think; *Blow out one's brains* = shoot oneself through the head; *Cudgel* (*Rack*) *one's brains* = try hard to think; *Pick his brains* = make use of a man's knowledge.

Brains Trust (+ 8) group of four (or more) learnèd persons who talk about questions put to them on the radio.

braise (21z) cook meat very slowly in a closed pot.

brake (21) block or band pressing upon a wheel which lessens or stops movement.

brake (21) place overgrown with wild plants.

bramble (3) common wild prickly bush which bears a red fruit which later becomes black.

bran (3) skin of wheat and other grain separated from the flour.

branch (44) limb of a tree growing out from the trunk; *Branch of a river* = side stream; anything divided off from the chief part, e.g. *Branch road*; *Branch of a subject*; *Branches of a shop* = small shops controlled by one big shop; **to branch**, divide into branches; *To branch out* = start many new businesses; spend much money.

brand (3) piece of burning wood; *To snatch a brand from the burning* = save a person from great danger; mark put upon prisoners, also on cattle as a sign of ownership; *To brand a man as a thief* = show that he is —; *A brand of tea* = special kind shown by some special mark or sign on the paper or box; (in poetry) sword.

brandish (3-1) to wave (a sword) about.

brand-new (3 + 177) quite new.

brandy (3-1) strong drink made from wine.

brash (3) pushing oneself forward rudely.

brass (44) mixture of *copper* (= red metal) and *zinc* (= light easily burnt white metal); Sl. *Plenty of brass* = — of money; Sl. *Brass* = shameless daring; Sl. *A Brass hat* = high officer in the army; Sl. *Get down to brass tacks* = talk about the real facts.

brassière (3-1-29) bra (44) small tight undergarment worn by women over the breasts.

brat (3) bad-mannered child.

brav'ado (9-44-67) show of *bravery* (= braveness) and courage.

brave (21) having courage in face of danger; able to suffer without complaint; *A brave show* = fine —.

br'av'o! (44-67) shout of joy because someone has done well.

bravo (44-67) hired murderer.

brawl (55) quarrel with much noise; (of water) to flow noisily.

brawn (55) (1) strength; (2) pig-meat boiled and pressed into a pot.
bray (21) the noise made by an ass.
braze (21) join two pieces of metal with the help of melted brass.
brazen (21) made of brass; shameless.
brazier (21-19) (1) one who works with brass; (2) pot used to contain burning coals.
breach (11) act of breaking—e.g. the law; *Breach of promise* = breaking a promise to marry; *Breach of faith* = disloyal act; *Breach of the peace* = fighting; *To throw oneself into the breach* = come forward and help in time of need or danger; **to breach** (a wall), break a hole in.
bread (2) common food made of flour; food generally, e.g. *Our daily bread*; *To break bread with* = eat with; *He has eaten my bread and salt* = has been my guest; *Quarrel with one's bread and butter* = with the person who supplies one's *living* (= the money on which one lives); *Take the bread out of one's mouth* = take away one's *living* (see above); *Know on which side one's bread is buttered* = know who or what will be of most gain to oneself; **br'ead-winner** (+ 1-9) person who works to supply the family with food.
breadfruit (2-77) fruit of a tree in the South Sea Islands (the inside of it looks like and tastes like bread).
breadth (2) distance across, broadness.
break (21) (p.t. **broke**) (1) cause to separate into pieces—by force; *Break one's heart* = suffer great sorrow; *Break the back of a task* = do the hardest part; *Break the ice* = begin; *Break bread with* = eat with; (2) to ruin; (3) bring under control; *To break in a horse* = train for riding or driving in a carriage; *Break his spirit* = bring under control; (4) go beyond, not keep within, e.g. a promise or law; *Break a record in running* = run faster than anyone before; (5) cause to stop for a time, *Break one's rest* = wake up; *Break one's journey* = stop at a place on the way; *The tree broke his fall* = made him fall less heavily on the ground; *To break down* = be unable to continue (working, speaking, etc.); *Break off* = stop suddenly; *Break out* = begin suddenly; *Break up* = break into small pieces; (of a school) end for the *holidays* (= time of rest); *Break with* = stop being friendly with; **a break**, a breaking; change of direction of a ball on hitting the ground; *Make a break* = go on playing and winning points for a long time, *Break one's rest* = wake up; Sl. *A bad break* = bad mistake; Sl. *Give him a break* = give him a chance; *Break of day* = earliest daylight.
break (21) horse carriage for many people.
breakdown (21-47) accident or *failure* (n. of fail); *A nervous breakdown* = disorder of the mind caused by too much work or by *anxiety* (n. of anxious); *Breakdown of figures* = rearrangement of figures so as to show their meaning, e.g. opinions—of men/women, old/young.
breaker (21-9) large wave rolling on the shore.
breakfast (2-9) first meal of the day.
breakwater (21-55-9) wall of stone built to stop waves.
bream (11) fresh-water fish.
breast (2) front part of the body between the neck and the stomach; that part of the body which produces milk; place where the feelings are, e.g. *A troubled breast* = anxious mind; *To make a clean breast of it* = tell all one's faults; **to breast**, stand up fearlessly against.
breastwork (2-99) low wall built as a *defence* (n. of defend) in fighting.
breath (2) air drawn into the body; *To speak under one's breath* = very quietly; *With bated breath* = anxiously; *Take one's breath away* = surprise.
breathe (11ð) draw air into the body.
bred (2) p.t. of Breed; *A well-bred person* = of good family and careful training.
breech (11) back part of a thing; end of a gun into which the shot is put.
breeches (1-1z) garment covering a man's legs as far down as the knees.
breed (11) produce young; cause to be born; *To breed trouble* = cause —; **a breed**, certain kind or class of animal.
breeze (11) light wind; slight quarrel; *A breezy person* = cheerful and amusing; Sl. *Breeze along* = go quickly.
breeze-blocks (+ 5) light-weight grey blocks used in building, made from *breeze* (= small pieces of burnt coal).
brethren (2ð-1) brothers.
brevet rank (2-1 + 3ŋgk) (e.g. in the army) rank without the *extra* (= more) pay usually given to a person of that rank.
breviary (11-19-1) book of prayer.
brevity (2-1-1) shortness of speech or writing.
brew (77) boil a mixture of vegetables, etc., in liquid; make wine or strong drink; *Trouble is brewing* = is being planned.
brewery (77-9-1) place in which *beer* (= strong drink with a bitter taste) is made.
briar (419) see Brier.
bribe (41) offer money to cause another to do what is wrong; n. **bribery** (41-9-1).
bric-à-brac (1 + 9 + 3) small ornaments in a house.
brick (1) hard piece of baked earth used for building houses; *To make bricks without straw* = do work without the necessary instruments or money; Sl. *He's a brick* = very nice fellow; Sl. *Drop a brick* = make a foolish remark which hurts someone's feelings; **brickbat** (1-3) a broken piece of brick; **brickyard** (1-y44) place where bricks are made.
bride (41) woman about to be married, or newly married; adj. **bridal** (41); **bridegroom** (——77) man about to be married, or newly

married; **bridesmaid** (——z-21) girl who attends on a woman who is being married.
bridge (1j) thing built of wood, stone, iron, etc., carrying a road over a valley, river, etc.; that part of a ship where the captain stands; *The bridge of the nose* = upper *bony* (= made of bone) part of —; **to bridge**, make a bridge across.
bridge (1j) card game.
bridgehead (1j-2) strong place far forward in enemy country from which an attack will be made.
bridle (41) leather bands put on a horse's head; *To bridle one's desires* = control; *He bridled at these words* = drew himself up stiffly, showing anger; *A bridle-path* = narrow path just wide enough for a horse.
brief (11) short.
brief (11) written notes used by a lawyer speaking in a court of law; *Brief an airman* = tell him necessary facts and what he has to do.
brier (419) small bush which pricks the skin; the root of this; a pipe for smoking made from Erica root.
brig (1) ship with two *masts* (= poles carrying sails) and large square sails on both of them.
brig'ade (1-21) part of an army, about 5000 soldiers; **brigad'ier** (1-9-19) officer in command of a brigade.
brigand (1-9) thief, often one of a band of thieves living in mountains.
br'igan'tine (1-9-11) ship like a *brig* (see 3rd above) but without the lowest square sail on the second (or *main*) mast.
bright (41) having light; having clear, easily seen colours; quick at learning.
Bright's dis'ease (41 + 1z11z) disease of the *kidneys* (= parts of the body which separate waste matter from the blood).
brill (1) flat sea-fish.
brilliant (1-19) very bright; very clever; causing one to admire; **a brilliant**, precious stone cut in a pointed shape; common stone cut to make it look like a precious stone.
brilliantine (1-19-11) oily mixture for making the hair shine.
brim (1) edge, e.g. of a cup, hat, etc.; **br'im'f'ul** (——7) full to the edge; *To brim over with* = be more than full of.
brimstone (1-9) yellow material (*sulphur*) which burns with a blue flame and a strong, unpleasant smell.
brindled (1) marked with brown bands (e.g. a cow's skin).
brine (41) salt water; Sl. *The briny* = sea.
bring (1) (1) carry to the place where the speaker is; (2) to cause, e.g. *Bring to pass; Bring about a quarrel; Bring on an illness; Bring a person to do it* = cause him to —; *Bring off* = succeed in doing; *Bring to, Bring round a person who has fainted* = make him well again; *Bring up children* = take care of and train —; *Bring home a fault to* = prove that he did it, or make him understand that it was wrong.
brink (1ngk) edge, e.g. of a cliff.
briqu'ette (1k2) coal dust pressed into the form of a brick for burning.
brisk (1) quick, active.
brisket (1-1) meat from the breast of an animal.
bristle (1) stiff hair; **to bristle**, make the hair stand up; *Bristle with* = have many sharp points, difficulties.
brittle (1) hard and easily broken, like glass.
broach (67) open (a barrel of liquid); begin to talk about a subject.
broad (55) (1) wide; *It's as broad as it's long* = there is much to be said on both sides of the question; (2) open, free, generous in judgment, e.g. *Broadminded* = able to understand the opinions of others and their reasons for holding them, even if one does not agree; *Broad arrow* = mark put on government stores and formerly prisoners' clothing in England.
broadcast (55-44) scatter in all directions; send words and music through the air by electric waves.
broadcloth (55-5) thick cloth, made of wool, of very good quality.
broadside (55-41) the whole side of a ship; all the guns on one side of a warship fired at once; a sheet of paper printed on one side.
broc'ade (9-21) ornamental silk material often with gold and silver in it.
brochure (67sh779) small book.
brogue (67) kind of shoe; the way in which the Irish speak English.
broil (51) noisy quarrel.
broil (51) cook meat by holding it close to the fire.
broke (67) p.t. of Break; Sl. *Broke, Stony broke* = having no money; **broken**, p.p. of Break; *A broken man* = ruined; *A broken reed* = weak person, or one not to be trusted; *Broken down* = in a bad state, unfit for work; *Broken-hearted* = very unhappy.

BROGUE

broker (67-9) one who does business for another, especially in buying and selling foreign money or shares in businesses; **brokerage** (67-9-1j) money paid to a broker for buying and selling.
bromide (67-41) medicine used to produce a feeling of calm.
bronchi (5ngk41) two branches of the *windpipe* (= breath-pipe) in the body; **bronch'itis** (5ngk41-1) illness in the bronchi.
bronco (5ngk67) half-wild horse.
bronze (5) nine parts of *copper* (= red metal) mixed with one part of *tin* (= white metal used to cover sheets of iron made into boxes); **to bronze**, give a red-brown colour to.
bronzed (5) brown-skinned because of the sun.
brooch (67) ornamental pin worn on the clothes.

brood (77) group of young ones; **to brood,** sit on eggs as a hen does; *To brood over a subject* = think deeply about; *To brood over one's troubles* = continue to think angrily or sadly about —.

brook (7) small stream.

brook (7) suffer, allow.

broom (77) plant with yellow flowers; large brush used for making the floor clean; *A new broom sweeps clean* = a young officer is always eager to make great changes.

broth (5) liquid made by boiling meat, etc.

brother(s) (8ōgz) son(s) of the same parents; a person who is a member of the same group, e.g. *A brother doctor; Brothers in arms* = soldiers who have served together; **brotherhood** (8-9-7) group of men formed for some special purpose.

brougham (77) light closed carriage.

brought (55) p.t. of Bring.

brow (47) front of the head above the eyes; *Brow of a hill* = steep slope of —; **eyebrows** (41-47z) the half-circles of hair above the eyes.

browbeat (47-11) shout at a person and treat him unkindly.

brown (47) colour of the earth; *In a brown study* = deep in thought; Sl. *To do brown* = to trick; Sl. *Browned off* = angry and tired.

brownie (47-1) fairy, said to work in the house at night; young member of the *Girl Guides* (= girl's branch of the Boy Scouts).

browse (47z) feed on young plants; read here and there in books.

bruin (77I) a bear.

bruise (77z) coloured place on the skin caused by a blow; **to bruise,** cause a bruise; *A bruiser* = one who fights with his *fists* (= tightly closed hands) for money.

bruit (77) *To bruit abroad* = tell everyone.

brunette (7-2) woman with dark eyes and hair.

brunt (8) *To bear the brunt* = suffer the heaviest part of the attack.

brush (8) (1) instrument for cleaning or smoothing, made of sticks or stiff hair; (2) rough low bushes; (3) fox's tail; *A brush with the enemy* = small fight; Sl. *Give him a brush-off* = show rudely that one is not friendly; **to brush,** clean or make smooth with a brush; *Brush aside a difficulty* = not treat seriously; *Brush up your French* = learn it up again; *To brush past a person* = push past; **brushwood** (8-7) small sticks.

brusque (7-k) quick and rough in manner.

brussels spr'outs (8slz + 47) small tight *bunches* (= collections of things fastened tightly together) of leaves growing on the sides of a high stem, used as a vegetable. BRUSSELS SPROUTS

brute (77) animal; cruel man; **brutal,** cruel.

bubble (8) hollow ball of liquid containing air; anything easily broken, likely to disappear at any moment; Sl. **bubbly** (——1) costly gaseous wine (*Champagne*).

bubo (177-67) swelling under the arm or just where the leg joins the body; **Bub'onic Plague** (177-5-1 + 21) dangerous disease spread by rat-*fleas* (= small, jumping and biting insects) of which buboes are a sign.

b'uccan'eer (8-9-19) sea *robber* (= a thief who uses force).

buck (8) male; **a buck,** male deer; Am. Sl. dollar.

buck (8) (of a horse) jump up with all four feet off the ground; Sl. *Buck up* = be quick, be cheerful, work harder; Sl. *Very bucked* = pleased.

bucket (8-1) container with a handle for carrying water; Sl. *Kick the bucket* = die; *To bucket* = ride, or row a boat, badly.

bucket-shop (+ 5) place where shares in business are sold by persons who are not to be trusted.

buckle (8) metal fastener used for joining the ends of two bands, or for ornament; *Buckle to, Buckle down to it* = set to work hard.

buckler (8-9) shield.

buckram (8-9) stiff cloth, used for covering books, etc.

buckskin (8-1) leather made of deer-skin.

buckwheat (8-11) small black grain much used as food for hens, and in America for making cakes.

buc'olic (177-5-1) having to do with the country and countrymen.

bud (8) young tightly rolled up flower before it opens; *A budding poet* = young poet who is just beginning to show his powers.

Buddha (7-9) great religious teacher honoured by many people in China and the East.

buddy (8-1) Sl. friend.

budge (8) move a little, cause to move; *He won't budge* = won't change his plans, or opinions.

budgerigar (8j9r1g44) small bright-coloured bird.

budget (8j1) (1) collection of news or letters; (2) accounts of government money as shown at the end of the year with plans for money matters during the next year.

buff (8) faded yellow colour; yellow leather made from cow-skin; *Strip to the buff* = take off all one's clothes; **to buff,** to polish metal.

BUDGERIGAR

BUFFALO

buffalo (8-9-67) large black cow-like animal.

buffer (8-9) bar put on the front and back of a motor-car to protect the car when it knocks

buffet against or runs into anything; springs on railway engines; *A buffer state* = peaceful country between two nations which may wish to make war on each other; Sl. *Old buffer* = kind but rather foolish old man.

buffet (8-1) a blow with the hand; to hit; *To buffet about* = hit and throw from side to side.

buffet (7-21) room or table where one can get meals which one eats standing up.

buff'oon (8-77) rough and noisy fool.

bug (8) dirty, wingless insect which drinks blood; Am. any insect or small creature; Sl. *A big bug* = important person.

bugbear (8-29) imagined cause of fear.

buggy (8-1) small carriage.

bugle (177) metal horn used in the army to call soldiers.

bugle (177) glass ornament on a dress.

build (1) put together materials in order to make a thing, e.g. a house; *To build upon* = put faith in, expect a person to help; *Of the same build* = of the same general shape and size; **a building**, house, hall, etc.

BUGGY

bulb (8) round root of certain flowers; any object of this shape; electric lamp.

bulbul (7-7) Indian bird which sings sweetly.

bulge (8-j) swell outward; swelling.

bulk (8) size; *To sell in bulk* = in large amounts; *To bulk large* = seem —.

b'ulkhead(s) (8-2-z) walls which divide a ship into separate parts, so that, if one part is damaged, water may not fill the whole ship.

bulky (8-1) large and difficult to carry.

bull (7) male; male form of any large animal; Sl. useless and unnecessary work in the army; *Talk a lot of bull* = — nonsense; *To take the bull by the horns* = face difficulties without fear; *A bull in a china-shop* = rough and careless person in a place where skill and care are needed; *To bull shares* = buy many shares in businesses at a low price and, by going on buying, force up the price.

bull (7) very foolish mistake in speaking, e.g. *He has a great future behind him.*

bull (7) order from the *Pope* (= head of the Church of Rome).

b'ulldog (7-5) large powerful dog; brave man who will not yield.

b'ulld'ozer (7-67-9) big machine for moving earth.

bullet (7-1) shot as fired from a *rifle* (= kind of gun used by soldiers and hunters).

BULLDOZER

bulletin (7-1-1) short printed or written report.

bullfinch (7-1) singing bird.

bullfrog (7-5) very large kind of *frog* (= cold blooded, jumping creature with four legs which lives partly on land, partly in water, often green in colour).

bullion (7-19) quantity of gold or silver which has not been made into money.

bullneck (7-2) having a very thick neck.

bullock (7-9) young *bull* (= male form of cattle) which cannot become a father.

bull's-eye (7-z + 41) (1) centre of a *target* (= board with rings on it aimed at with a gun); (2) a kind of sweet.

bully (7-1) one who uses his strength to hurt weaker persons.

bully-beef (+ 11) meat preserved in a tin.

bulrush (7-8) tall, grass-like water plant with a brown or black woolly head.

bulwark (7-9) wall built to defend a place; side of a ship above the deck.

bum (8) Sl. back part of the body on which one sits; Am. poor man who begs for money or food.

b'umble-b'ee (8 + 11) large hairy bee which makes a loud noise when flying.

bumboat (8-67) boat which brings fresh vegetables to a ship.

bump (8) swelling caused by a blow; **to bump against**, knock against.

bumper (8-9) large drinking vessel full of wine; *A bumper crop* = very large crop.

bumper (8-9) bar fixed on the front and back of a motor-car to protect the car when it knocks against anything.

bumpkin (8-1) foolish fellow from the country.

bumptious (8-sh9) pushing oneself forward; believing too much in one's own powers.

bun (8) small round piece of sweetened bread; Sl. *This takes the bun* = this wins; this is very good, very surprising.

bunch (8) group; number of things of the same kind fastened together.

buncombe (8ngk9) see Bunkum.

bundle (8) quantity of things tied together.

bung (8) round piece of wood used to stop the hole in a barrel; **bung hole** (+ 67) hole in a barrel; *His eyes were bunged up* = closed up by swelling; Sl. throw.

bungalow (8ngg9-67) low small house with no upper floor.

bungle (8nggl) do a piece of work badly.

bunion (8-19) swelling on a joint of the foot.

bunk (8ngk) narrow bed fixed to the wall of a ship or car; **to bunk**, sleep in such a bed; Sl. run away; Sl. short for **bunkum** (8ngk9) (see below).

bunker (8ngk9) a place for storing coal in ships; low long hill on a *golf*-course (see Golf), set there to make play more difficult.

BUNSEN BURNER

bunkum, buncombe (8ngk9) foolish talk; pleasant but untrue things said to please a person.

bunny (8-1) child's word for rabbit.

b'unsen b'urner (8-9 + 99-9) lamp which mixes air and gas to make a hot blue flame.

bunting (8-1) kind of cloth used for making flags; flags and cloth-ornaments for buildings on some special day.

buoy (51) floating object fastened to the bed of the sea to show ships where there are rocks; floating ring used to save persons who fall into the water; *To buoy up one's hopes* = keep up —.

buoyant (519) very light, which cannot sink; gay, full of hope and high spirits; n. **buoyancy** (519nsɪ) power of floating; high spirits.

bur, burr (99) seed-container of certain plants covered with prickles which make it hang on to the clothes; plant which has such seeds.

burberry (99-9-1) *rain-coat* (= coat which protects one from rain) made by Burberry & Co., London.

burden (99) heavy load; load heavily; *The burden of proof lies with you* = it is your duty to prove it.

burden (99) part of a song which is repeated often.

burdock (99-5) see Bur.

bureau (17-67) large writing-table with wooden cover which slides over the top to close it; a government office; **bureaucracy** (17-5-9sɪ) government by the paid officers of government rather than by persons elected by the people; **bureaucrat** (177-9-3) member of a bureaucracy; officer who tries to centre power in himself.

burgee (99jɪɪ) pointed flag.

burgess (99jɪ) free man of a city or country, having the right to elect persons to the government.

burgh (99) town; **burgher** (99-9) one who lives in a town (especially a German or Dutch town).

burglar (99-9) thief who breaks into houses, shops, etc.

burgomaster (99-9-44-9) chief man in a town in Germany or Holland.

burgundy (99-1) kind of wine.

burial (2-19) act of putting a dead body into a grave.

burlap (99-3) very rough kind of cloth.

burl'esque (99-2-k) speech or play in which a serious thing is made to seem foolish or a foolish thing is treated solemnly so as to make people laugh.

burly (99-1) large, fat, strong.

burn (99) small stream.

burn (99) set on fire, be in flames; *Burn one's boats* = do something which makes it impossible to draw back from a piece of work already begun; *Burn the candle at both ends* = stay up late and get up early, do too much both of work and play; *Sunburnt* = made brown by sunlight.

burnish (99-1) make a metal bright by rubbing.

burnous(e) (9-77) long coat of an Arab.

burnt (99) p.t. of Burn.

burp (99) (Am.) *belch* (= let out air upwards from the stomach).

burr (99) **burdock** (99-5) see Bur.

burrow (8-67) hole in the ground made by rabbits, foxes, etc.; make a hole in the ground.

bursar (99-9) man in a university or school who has charge of the money.

burst (99) be broken open by force coming from the inside; break; *My heart will burst* = I am very sad or excited; *Ready to burst* = very excited; *To burst into tears* = suddenly begin to cry; **a burst**, sudden outbreak, e.g. *A burst of laughter*.

bury (2-1) put a dead body into the grave; cover from sight; hide away; *To bury oneself in the country* = go to a distant country-place; *To bury the hatchet* = put an end to a quarrel.

bus (8) large motor-car which carries the public on payment of small amounts; *Busman's holiday* = taking a holiday by doing one's ordinary work in another place.

busby (8z-1) tall fur hat worn by certain soldiers.

bush (7) small low tree; **the bush** = uncleared wild country in Australia or Africa.

bush, bushing (7) plate of soft metal put between two parts of a machine which rub against each other.

bushel (7) measure of grain, about $36\frac{1}{2}$ litres; *To hide one's light under a bushel* = not let people know one's cleverness.

b'ushranger (7-21njg) escaped prisoner or robber living in the Bush (Australia).

bushy (7-1) (of country) having many bushes; (of hair) growing thickly; *Bushy tail* = tail covered with thick hair.

business (1z-1) (1) one's work or employment; (2) trade and the getting of money; particular money-getting work, e.g. a shop; *Business is business* = when dealing with money we must not think of other matters, e.g. friendship; (3) duty, e.g. *It is a teacher's business to make boys learn*; *This is no business of yours* = nothing to do with you; *Mind your own business* = look to your own matters and do not ask about mine; *You have no business to —* = have no right to —; (4) matter, event; *I don't understand this business* = this matter, subject; (5) (in acting a play) things done by an actor other than speaking, e.g. movements of the hands, look on the face, etc.

businesslike (1z-1-41) doing things carefully and with common sense.

bust (8) head, shoulders and breast; person's head and shoulders cut in stone; Sl. (for burst) *Go on the bust* = go out for a merry time; *The business is bust, — is gone bust* = has failed.

bustle (8) (1) noisy movement; be busy with

much noise; (2) formerly, frame used to hold out the back part of a woman's dress.

busy (1z1) working hard; having little time for play.

busybody (1z1-5-1) one who interests himself too much in other people's concerns.

butcher (7-9) one who kills and sells animals for food; **to butcher,** murder cruelly.

butler (8-9) man-servant in charge of the dining-room and wine.

butt (8) large barrel.

butt (8) thick end of.

butt (8) give a blow with the head; hit with the heavy end of; Sl. *To butt in* to come when not wanted.

butter (8-9) yellow fat made from milk; *Look as if butter would not melt in his mouth* = seem very gentle; *He knows on which side his bread is buttered* = knows who will help him most, or bring him most gain.

buttercup (8-9-8) yellow wild flower.

butter-fingers (+ 1ngg9z); Sl. one who cannot catch a ball, or lets things fall easily.

butterfly (8-9-41) insect with large, beautifully-coloured wings.

buttermilk (8-9-1) liquid which remains after butter is made from milk.

buttery (8-9-1) room from which food and drink are served.

buttock (8-9) one side of that part of the body on which one sits.

button (8) small round fastener on clothes; any small round object used for pushing, pulling or fastening; **buttons** (——z) boy servant in a hotel or large house; **buttonhole** (+ 67) hole for a button; flower to put on the front of one's coat; *To buttonhole a person* = catch him and force him to listen.

buttress (8-1) support for a wall; **flying buttress** (41·1 +) half-arch built against a wall to support it; **to buttress,** support.

butts, the (8) place at which soldiers shoot for practice.

buxom (8-9) fat and healthy-looking.

buy (41) obtain by giving money (or other value); *To buy off* = get free from a claim by paying money; *To buy up* = buy all that can be obtained.

buzz (8) noise which an insect makes when flying; Sl. *To buzz along* = move quickly.

buzzard (8-9) meat-eating bird.

buzzer (8-9) electrical instrument which makes a *buzzing* (see 2nd above) sound.

bwana (b744-4) African word for "Sir".

by-, bye- (41) e.g. *A by-product* = second thing produced in the course of producing some other important thing; *A by-road* = small unimportant road; *A by-pass* = new road built specially for motor-cars to keep away from towns.

b'y-and-b'y afterwards.

bye (41) (1) man left over when all the other players in a game are arranged in pairs (or fours); (2) point gained in *cricket* when the ball is not hit.

b'ye-b'ye (41 + 41) good-bye; (to children) time to go to bed; bed.

bygone (41-5) something in the past.

by(e)-law (41 + 55) special law or rule made, not by the government of the whole country, but by a town or railway, etc.

byre (419) cow-house.

byway (41-21) small path leading away from the main path.

byword (41-99) common saying; person or thing to be laughed at, and thought little of.

C

C (s11) Roman figure, 100.

cab (3) (1) public carriage; (2) that part of the engine of a train in which the driver stands; **a cabby** (——1) driver of a public carriage.

cab'al (9-3) secret plan; small group of persons joined in a secret plan.

cabal'istic (signs) (3-9-1-1) magic or secret writing.

cabaret (3-9-21) *restaurant* (= eating place) where there is singing and dancing; show of dancing, etc., as given in such a place.

cabbage (3-1j) vegetable of which the leaves are boiled for food.

cabin (3-1) small house; room in a ship or aeroplane; **cabin ship** (+ 1) ship carrying people in one class only, not 1st, 2nd, 3rd.

cabinet (3-1-1) small box; piece of furniture with glass windows used to contain ornaments and objects of interest.

cabinet (3-1-1) special group of the chief men who control the government.

cable (21) thick strong rope; strong wire laid under the sea or over the land for sending electric messages; message sent by electricity; **to cable**, send such a message; **cablegram** (21-3) message sent by electricity across the ocean.

cab'oose (9-77) kitchen on deck of ship; Am. train-man's carriage at the end of a train.

cache (3sh) secret place in which stores are hidden by travellers.

c'achinn'ation (3k1-21shn) loud laughing.

cackle (3) noise made by a hen; noisy talking.

cac'ophony (3-5-9-1) unpleasant noise.

cactus (3-9) plant with thick leaves having on them many needle-like prickles.

cad (3) bad-mannered fellow.

cad'astral s'urvey (9-3 + 99-21) making of a map of land showing the ownership.

cad'averous (9-3-9-9) looking like a dead body.

caddie (3-1) boy who carries the instruments used in playing golf.

caddy (3-1) small ornamental box, e.g. for tea.

cadence (21-s) rise and fall of the voice.

cad'et (9-2) youth learning to be an officer in the army or on the king's warships.

cadge (3j) ask for money, etc.

cadi (44-1) judge among the Arabs or Turks.

caes'ura (s11z17-9) break in a line of poetry, e.g. *To be or not to be—that is the question.*

café (3-21) place which sells meals and coffee; **cafet'eria** (3-1-19-19) place for meals where those who eat serve themselves; **caffeine** (3-1-11) medicine obtained from coffee.

cage (21j) (1) box with bars for holding birds and animals; (2) box used to take workers down into a *mine* (= deep hole from which coal, etc., is obtained).

cagey (21j1) Sl. unwilling to answer questions.

cairn (29) number of stones built up, wide at the bottom and pointed at the top.

caisson (21) box on wheels containing powder and shot for guns.

caiss'on (9-77) iron box in which men work under water.

caitiff (21-1) (1) man who has no courage; (2) low and bad person.

caj'ole (9-67) get a person to do a thing by deceiving him with sweet speeches.

cake (21) sweet bread made with eggs, butter, etc.; *A cake of soap* = a piece of soap; *Caked with dirt* = thickly covered with —.

calabash (3-9-3) bottle or container made of the hard shell of a *gourd* (= large watery fruit which grows on the ground).

calamine (3-9-41) a powder, made chemically from zinc, put on the skin when it is burnt by the sun.

cal'amity (9-3-1-1) any cause that produces great evil, e.g. war, fire, etc.

calci- (-s1) having to do with chalk or lime; **calc'iferous** (3-s1-9-9) producing lime; **c'alcify** (3-s1-41) make (or be made) hard by means of lime, e.g. the bones of old persons calcify; **c'alcine** (3-s41) burn bones to become lime; **c'alcium** (3-s19) pure material obtained from lime.

calculate (3-17-21) add, divide, etc., and work with numbers; examine and tell; Am. to guess, hold an opinion that —.

calculus (3-17-9) (1) way of calculating the speed of growth, or speed of very small changes; (2) stone formed in the body.

caldron (55) see Cauldron.

Caled'onian (3-1-67-19) Scottish.

calendar (3-1-9) list of days, weeks and months printed year by year.

calf (44) (1) young of a cow or of other animals; (2) leather made from this; *Calf love* = youthful love.

calf (44) back of the leg between the knee and the foot.

calibrate (3-1-21) (1) measure the width of the hole in the barrel of a gun; (2) see whether a measuring instrument is correct.

calibre (3-1-9) width of the hole in a gun; *Of great mental calibre* = — powers of mind.

calico (3-1-67) kind of cotton cloth.

caliph (3-1) title given to descendants of Muhammad.

c'alisth'enic(s) (3-1-2-1) see Callisthenic(s).

call (55) (1) cry out in a loud voice; (2) make a short visit at a person's house; (3) cause a person to come, e.g. *Call people together to a* meeting; *Call over the coals* = scold; *Call in question* = doubt; *Call to order* = tell to behave properly; (4) to give a name to; *He called me names* = used rough language to me; *Call a spade a spade* = speak plainly; (5) waken a sleeping person; *This will call for a lot of money* = need; *To call off an attack* (etc.) = say it will not be made, cause it to stop while being made; n. **a call** (meanings as above); *A close call* = narrow escape; *There is no call to* = no need; *Many calls on one's money* = demands for; *One's calling* = one's business or employment; *Call at cards, call your hand* = say how many tricks (points) you expect to win; *Call up on the telephone* = cause a person's telephone bell to ring so as to speak to him; *Call up men* = for service in the army, *the call-up*, n.

call'igraphy (9-1-9-1) good hand-writing.

calliper(s) (3-1-9z) instrument used for measuring round objects, objects of irregular shape and the insides of holes.

CALLIPERS

c'allisth'enics (3-1-2-1) exercises which produce grace and strength of body.

callous (3-9) (1) hardened (skin); (2) without feeling for the sufferings of others.

callow (3-67) young and inexperienced.

calm (44) quiet; not rough; Sl. *It was very calm of him to* = very daring.

calomel (3-9-2) white powder taken as a medicine to clear waste matter from the body.

calorie (3-9-1) measure of heat, especially of the heat-value of food.

calumet (3-17-2) long pipe smoked by American Indians.

cal'umniate (3-8-121) tell untrue stories about a person in order to do harm to his good name; **a c'alumny** (3-9-1) untrue story.

calve (44) (of a cow) give birth to young; **calves** (——z) pl. of calf.

cal'ypso (9-1-67) West Indian singing.

calyx (21-1) circle of small leaves under a flower.

cam (3) part of a machine used for changing circular movement from circular to straight.

camar'aderie (3-9-44-9-1) friendship and good feeling.

cambric (21-1) thin white cloth.

camel (3) animal with one or two raised parts on its back.

CAMEL (ONE HUMP)

cameo (3-167) jewel with figures cut on it.

CAMEL (TWO HUMPS)

camera (3-9-9) instrument used for making pictures by means of light, e.g. *a Kodak*; *In camera* = in secret.

camisole (3-1-67) small coat of cotton or silk worn under a woman's dress.

camouflage (3-7-443) way of using paint, leaves, etc., on guns, ships or roads to prevent the enemy from seeing them; any form of *pretence* (= pretending) or hiding.

camp (3) open space with tents or huts in which soldiers or travellers live for a short time; *In the same camp* = of the same party, holding the same opinions; **to camp**, form a camp, fix a camp in a certain place, live in a camp.

camp'aign (3-21) movements and battles of an army in a war; *He is making a great campaign against drink* = making speeches, writing in the papers, etc., etc.

camphor (3-9) (1) white strong-smelling material used to keep insects out of clothes in store; (2) medicine.

campus (3-9) grounds round a school or university in America.

can (3) small metal container, usually round, for holding fruits and foods; **to can**, put into small containers, e.g. *Cannod food* = food kept good by being shut up in tins.

can'al (9-3) waterway dug by man; *The alimentary canal* = path for food in the body from the mouth to the stomach and on through the bowel.

canard (3-44) untrue report.

can'ary (9-29-1) yellow, singing bird.

cancel (3-s) draw a line through a written word; undo what has been done, put an end to, e.g. *To cancel a debt*.

cancer (3-s9) painful illness caused by uncontrolled growth of some part of the body; any growing evil.

candel'abrum (pl. **-bra**) (3-1-44-9) (9) ornamental article with many branches used for holding candles.

candid (3-1) honest, speaking the truth.

candidate (3-1-1) one who offers himself for an office; one who tries to be elected; one who sits for an examination.

candied fruit (3-1 + 77) boiled in sugar.

candle (3) round bar of wax with a string in the middle, used to give light; *Not fit to hold a candle to* = not nearly so good as; *Not worth the candle* = not worth the necessary work or cost; *Burn the candle at both ends* = sit up late and get up early; work too hard and play too hard at the same time.

candlestick (3-1) instrument used for holding a candle.

candour (3-9) honesty, plain-speaking.

candy (3-1) Am. sweets.

cane (21) (1) easily bent stick; walking-stick; (2) sugar plant; to hit with a cane.

canine (3-41) having to do with dogs; *Canine teeth* = pointed teeth third from the front in one's mouth.

canister (3-1-9) wooden or metal box, e.g. for tea.

canker (3ngk9) (1) painful place in the body of an animal where the skin is eaten away by disease; so also on a plant; (2) any evil which slowly grows and destroys.

cannibal (3-1) one who eats human meat.

cannibalize (3-1-9-41) take parts from one machine to repair another machine.

cannon (3-9) (1) large gun; (2) striking one ball against another in the game of *billiards* (see Billiards).

c'annon'ade (3-9-21) continued firing of large guns.

canny (3-1) careful; wise.

can'oe (9-77) light boat moved by a *paddle* (= stick with a broad, flat end); *To paddle one's own canoe* = work alone unhelped.

canon (3-9) (1) rule of the Church; (2) officer of the Church; (3) list of books accepted as really written by (Shakespeare, etc.); **can'onical** (9-5-1) according to the rules of the Church; *In full canonicals* = in full dress as a priest.

cañon (3nyg) see Canyon.

canopy (3-9-1) (1) curtain hung above a *throne* (= seat of a king) or bed; (2) small roof over something, e.g. over a grave inside a building.

cant (3) (1) speaking in such a way as to make people believe that one is very good; (2) the special talk of any particular group of men, e.g. thieves.

cant (3) lean over to one side; cause to slope.

can't (44) cannot.

cantaloup (3-9-77) large watery fruit which grows on the ground.

cant'ankerous (3-3ngk9-9) bad-tempered, eager to quarrel.

cant'ata (3-44-9) piece of music in the form of a play which is sung but not acted.

cant'een (3-11) (1) drink shop in a soldier's camp; (2) soldier's water bottle; (3) dining-room for workers in an office, factory, etc.; *A canteen of silver* = box of silver spoons, etc., as used at the table.

canter (3-9) (of a horse) run slowly, moving the two front and back legs together; *Win at a canter* = — easily.

canticle (3-1) song sung in church.

canto (3-67) part of a song or long poem.

cant'onment (3-77-9) place given to soldiers to live in.

canvas (3-9) strong cloth used for ship's sails, tents, etc.

canvass (3-9) (1) examine carefully; (2) go from house to house asking people to buy, or to elect a person to the government.

canyon (3nyg) deep narrow valley with steep rocky sides.

cap (3) (1) hat with no *brim* (= standing-out edge); *To set one's cap at* (of a woman) = try to get a man as an admirer; *A feather in one's cap* = something to be proud of; (2) anything fitted on to the top or end of another object, e.g. *Toe-cap* = cap on the end of a shoe; *To cap a joke* (= amusing story) = tell a better joke; *Cap and gown* = dress of a teacher —of one who has a university *degree* (= B.A., M.A., etc.).

capable (21-9) clever, able to do things well; *He is capable of such an act* = bad enough to do —; *Capable of improvement* = able to be made better.

cap'acious (9-21sh9) able to contain a large amount.

cap'acity (9-3s1-1) (1) power of doing things well; (2) amount which any container can hold; *In the capacity of* = acting as.

c'ap à p'ie (3 + 9 + 11) from head to foot = fully armed, prepared, ready.

cap'arison (9-3-1z) beautiful clothes for people or coverings for horses worn in ancient time.

cape (21) covering for the shoulders.

cape (21) point of land which goes out into the water.

caper (21-9) to jump, to dance; *To cut capers.* = to jump about.

caper (sauce) (21-9) green seeds used in making a *sauce* (= pleasant-tasting liquid) eaten with boiled *mutton* (= meat of a sheep).

cap'illary (9-1-9-1) having to do with the hair; like a hair; *Capillary attraction* = drawing-up of water through a hair-like pipe.

capital (3-1) very important; *Paris is the capital of France* = city of government of —; *A capital letter,* e.g. a big letter, A, B, etc.; *Capital punishment* = death as a punishment; *A capital speech* = very good —; n. **capital,** the above meanings, city, letter—also the whole amount of money used by a business or owned by a person (not the smaller amount coming in from year to year); *Capital goods* = machines, etc., used for manufacturing things, opposite of *Consumer goods* = things used up, e.g. food, clothes.

capitalist (3-1-9-1) one who controls large amounts of money; **capitalism** (3-1-9-1z) *private* (= not public) ownership of business— the opposite of capitalism is **socialism** (67sh19-1z) = public ownership of all business: that is, all business owned by the government.

Capitol (3-1-5) Am. name given to any important public building, e.g. that used by the government of America (U.S.A.) in Washington.

cap'itulate (9-1-17-21) yield to the enemy.

capon (21-9) *cock* (= male bird) with male parts cut so as to make it grow large and fat.

capr'ice (9-11s) sudden unreasonable idea or change of purpose.

capsicum (3-1-9) plant with a seed-container

(usually red) with a very hot taste, used for food and medicine.

caps'ize (3-41) (of a boat) turn over in the water.

capstan (3-9) upright iron roller with a rope round it, turned round by bars, used for winding in a rope.

CAPSTAN

capsule (3-177) small case, e.g. that containing seeds on a plant; case containing a measured amount of a medicine ready for swallowing.

captain (3-1) one who commands about 120 men in an army; master of a ship; leader of a group of players in a game.

caption (3-shn) a few words telling the subject of what follows in a book, newspaper, or moving-picture.

captious (3-sh9s) eager to find fault.

captive (3-1) prisoner.

captivate (3-1-21) hold as a prisoner, by beauty or charm of manner.

captor (3-9) one who seizes a prisoner; **capture** (3-tsh9) seize a prisoner; the act of seizing as prisoner.

car (44) carriage; motor-car.

car'afe (9-44) ornamental glass bottle for water.

caramel (3-9-2) sugar heated in such a way that it becomes very sticky but not hard; a sweet so made.

carat (3-9) measure of weight used for precious stones and gold; 24-carat gold is pure gold.

c'arav'an (3-9-3) company of travellers across the desert; covered cart on wheels in which one can live.

carav'anserai (3-9-3-9-41) inn in the East.

caraway (3-9-21) small seed used in cakes.

carbide (44-41) coal-like material which, mixed with water, gives off a gas that burns with a white flame.

carbine (44-41) short gun, e.g. one used by horse-soldiers.

carb'olic 'acid (4-5-1 + 3s1) brown liquid obtained from coal, used for killing germs (= seeds of disease).

carbon (44) material found in coal, wood, and the bodies of animals; **carbon paper** (+ 21-9) black paper put between two sheets of white paper to get a second copy of writing.

carbuncle (44-8ngk) (1) red precious stone; (2) hard painful spot on the skin.

carburettor (-er) (44-9-2-9) part of motor-car in which the liquid to be burnt (*petrol, gasoline*) is mixed with air.

carcass, carcase (44-9) dead body of an animal.

card (44) (1) small stiff piece of paper; (2) small stiff piece of paper with one's name on it; (3) printed paper for playing games; *Put one's cards on the table* = make one's plans known; Sl. *A queer card* = peculiar person.

card (44) prepare wool, etc., for making into thread; treat cloth in such a way as to make it soft and hairy.

cardamom (44-9-9) seed with a strong taste.

cardboard (44-55) very thick stiff paper-like material.

cardiac (44-13) having to do with the heart.

cardigan (44-1) short coat made of wool.

cardinal (44-1) (1) chief, very important; (2) red colour; (3) *Cardinal numbers*, 1, 2, 3, etc. (the *ordinals* are 1st, 2nd, 3rd, etc.); (4) high officer in the Church of Rome; (5) *The cardinal points* = north, south, east and west.

care (29) feel strongly; *I don't care* = it does not matter to me; *To care for* = love, also to take charge of and support; n. **care**, anxious feeling; watchfulness and serious thought.

car'een (9-11) lay a ship over on her side for cleaning.

car'eer (9-19) one's way through life; what one works at in life; speed; move quickly.

careful (29) taking trouble over a piece of work; exact; wise; **careless** (29-1) thoughtless; inexact; free from *anxiety* (n. of anxious).

car'ess (9-2) any act of touch expressing love.

caret (3-9) mark (∧) to show that something has been left out in writing.

caretaker (29-21-9) one who remains in charge of an empty building; one who has charge of a building and keeps it clean, warm, etc.

cargo (44-67) goods carried in a ship.

c'arib'ou (-oo) (3-1-77) kind of deer found in North America.

c'aricat'ure (3-1-9-179) picture drawn to make people laugh at the person shown in it.

caries (29-1-11z) decay in a tooth or bone.

CARIBOU

car'illon (9-1ly9) bells on which *tunes* (e.g. music of songs) can be played; a tune so played.

carmine (44-41) deep red.

carnage (44-1j) killing of many persons.

carnal (44) having to do with the body.

carn'ation (44-21shn) white or coloured sweet-smelling flower.

carnival (44-1) joyful time of feasts and games.

carn'ivorous (44-1-9-9) meat-eating.

carol (3) joyful song, e.g. one sung at Christmas.

car'ouse (9-47z) feast in which much wine is drunk; to feast.

carp (44) big fresh-water fish.

CARP

carp (44) find fault or blame without reason.

carpenter (44-1-9) one who works with wood.

carpet (44-1) thick cloth covering for the floor; *The question on the carpet* = — being considered.

carriage (3-1j) (1) act of carrying; (2) cost of carrying; (3) way of holding one's body and walking; (4) wheeled car, e.g. a horse carriage, the part of a train in which one sits.

carrion (3-19) dead or decaying meat.

carrot (3-9) red vegetable-root boiled for food; Sl. *Carrots* = red hair.

carry (3-1) support the weight of a thing; support and move from one place to another; *Carry coals to Newcastle* = supply that of which there is already enough; *He carried everything before him* = was successful in everything; *He carries himself well* = walks and stands gracefully; *To carry one's point* = lead people to agree with one's opinion; *The sound carried 3 miles* = was heard at a distance of —; *To carry on* = behave in a foolish way; *Carry on with* = go on doing; *Carry on!* = continue; *Carry out an order* = do as ordered; *Carry through a piece of business* = finish.

cart (44) thing with wheels for carrying goods pulled by a horse; *Put the cart before the horse* = do things in the wrong order; **to cart**, carry in a cart; **cartage** (44-1j) cost of carrying in a cart.

c′arte bl′anche (44 + 44ⁿsh) written order that — be done, or that — be killed; the person who receives the order may write what he wishes in the space left; *To give a person carte blanche* = to give full powers of action.

cart′el (44-2) union to keep cost of making a thing down and the price up.

cartilage (44-1·1j) strong bendable material found at the end of bones in the body.

carton (44-9) box made of *cardboard* (= strong card).

cart′oon (44-77) drawing for the purpose of making people laugh or think—generally of a present event.

cartridge (44-1j) small, round box, holding powder and shot, put into a gun for firing.

carve (44) cut a picture or figure into or out of stone, wood, etc.; cut up meat for eating; **a carver**, knife used for cutting up meat; person who carves.

cary′atid (3-1·3-1) stone support (as part of a building) cut in the shape of a woman.

casc′ade (3-21) small waterfall.

CARYATID

case (21) box; covering; **b′ook-case**, set of shelves for books.

case (21) particular set of events which demands action or thought, e.g. *A doctor's cases* = the sick persons whom he has to see; *A case in a law court* = claim made before a judge, or the trying of a wrong-doer; *To state one's case* = say the facts in one's favour; *As the case stands* = as matters are now; *That is not the case* = not the fact; *In your case* = in dealing with you; *In case it rains* = if —; *Case of a noun* = ending of a noun showing its relation to the other words.

casein (21-1·1) solid part of milk of which cheese is made.

casement (21-9) window which opens like a door.

cash (3) real money (silver, gold or paper); *Pay cash, Cash down* = pay at once on receiving the goods; **to cash**, get money for a paper promising or demanding money, e.g. *To cash a* cheque (= written order to pay money); Sl. *To cash in on it* = gain money as a result of it.

cash′ier (3-19) person in an office or shop who has charge of the money; **to cashier** (an officer of the army), send out of the army because of wrong-doing.

cashmere (3-19) soft woollen cloth.

c′ash r′egister (3 + 2j1-9) all money paid in a shop is put in the machine (as shown) and it prints the amounts on a roll of paper.

CASH REGISTER

casing (21-1) covering; frame.

cas′ino (9-11-67) hall for dancing and playing games for money; name of a game played for money.

cask (44) barrel for holding liquids.

casket (44-1) small box for precious stones; costly box for a dead body.

casserole (3-9-67) pot in which food is cooked and brought to the table.

cassock (3-9) long garment, usually black, worn in church, e.g. by a priest.

cast (44) (1) throw; *To cast it in his teeth* = blame him for it; (2) throw away as useless, e.g. *Cast-off clothing*; *A snake casts its skin*; (3) pour liquid (e.g. hot metal) into a shape in which it becomes solid; *A cast-iron case* = law-case which is certain to be won; *To cast about for* = look for; *Cast down* = sad; *the cast in a play* = actors taking the various parts; *A cast in the eye* = one eye turned to the side; *A casting-vote* (*vote* = opinion shown in a meeting) = opinion given by the head of a meeting when the people in the meeting are equally divided.

castaway (44-9-21) person who has come to land from a wrecked ship.

caste (44) custom of dividing people into separate ranks or groups, as in India; the groups so formed.

castellated (3-1-21-1) like a castle; having raised parts along the top of the wall to protect men defending it.

CASTELLATED

castigate (3-1-21) beat; punish.

casting (44-1) throwing; metal object formed by melting and pouring into a shape; **casting-vote**, see Cast.

c'ast-'iron (44 + 419) iron which has been shaped by melting; *Cast-iron rules* = hard and unchangeable.

castle (44) strong building; fort; fine house looking like an ancient castle; *Castles in the air* (— *in Spain*) = useless plans and hopes.

castor (44-9) bottle with holes in the top, e.g. for powdered sugar.

castor(s) (44-9z) small wheels put on the bottom of beds, tables, etc., to make them move easily.

c'astor-'oil (44-9 + 51) medicine produced from the *castor* plant, used to clear waste or poisonous matter downward through the bowels.

c'astor s'ugar (44-9 + sh7-9) very finely powdered sugar.

casual (331779) happening by accident; not planned; not regular; careless and rude in manner.

casualty (——-1) one who is killed or wounded in war or in an accident, etc.

casuist (3z1771) one who studies questions of right and wrong; person who reasons to prove his point rather than to prove the truth.

c'asus b'elli (21z9 + 2-4I) cause of war.

cat (3) animal which lives in the house and catches mice; other wild animals of this class; *Let the cat out of the bag* = tell a secret; *Rain cats and dogs* = — heavily; *Wait and see which way the cat jumps* = see people's opinion before acting; *To lead a cat and dog life* = be always quarrelling; Sl. woman who says unkind things about others.

cataclysm (3-9-1z) a sudden change which causes suffering, e.g. the overflow of a river, a war, etc.

catacomb (3-9-67) underground caves in which dead bodies are put.

catafalque (3-9-3-k) ornamental table on which a *coffin* (= box for a dead body) is put.

catalepsy (3-9-2-1) illness in which the whole body appears to be dead, though life still remains.

catalogue (3-9-5) list of things to be shown, or for sale, of books, etc.

cat'alysis (9-3-1-1) change in materials caused by some material which itself remains unchanged, e.g. steam passed over hot *platinum* (= heavy valuable metal) changes into two gases, *oxygen* and *hydrogen*; *platinum* is here the **c'atalyst** (3-9-1).

CATAMARAN

c'atamar'an (3-9-9-3) boat made in two parts, like two boats fixed together by a bridge.

catapult (3-9-8) instrument used for throwing stones; Y-shaped stick on which a piece of rubber is tied, used by boys for shooting (throwing) stones.

cataract (3-9-3) large waterfall; disease in which the glass-like part of the eye becomes white, causing loss of sight.

cat'arrh (9-44) illness of the nose and throat, with flowing of liquid from the nose and pain in the throat.

cat'astrophe (9-3-9-1) event which causes great suffering or ruin.

catcall (3-55) rude, noisy cry given in a theatre when an actor or the play is displeasing.

catch (3) p.t. p.p. **caught** (55) (1) run after and seize; (2) seize and hold, e.g. *To catch a ball*; (3) meet and stop, e.g. *I caught him just as he was going out*; *To catch a train* = be in time for; Sl. *You'll catch it* = be blamed; (4) receive the effect of some cause; *To catch an illness* = get an illness from another person; *To catch fire* = be made to burn; (5) discover, e.g. *To catch a person in the act* = just as he is doing wrong; *I don't catch your meaning* = understand; Sl. *To catch-on* = understand, also to take the fancy of, be liked by many people, e.g. a play; *Catch up* = come level with a person in walking; **a catch**, act of catching; fastener, e.g. *The catch of a window*; *There is a catch in it somewhere* = some trick; thing caught (p.p. of Catch); Sl. *That's no catch* = not worth anything, not worth money; **catchword** (3-99) word which sticks in the mind and is often used without proper thought of its real meaning; **catchy** (3-1) (music) such as pleases and is easily remembered.

catechize (3-1k41) to question; **catechism** (3-1-k1z) set of questions, e.g. about one's duty to God and the Church.

category (3-1-9-1) class; sort or kind of.

cater for (to) (21-9) provide food; supply what is wanted.

caterpillar (3-9-1-9) (1) creature with many legs which later changes into a flying insect; (2) kind of motor-car with wheels moving inside a band, so making the car able to go over rough ground.

catgut (3-8) strong string made of the inside parts of a sheep, etc., used in musical instruments, etc.

cath'artic (medicine) (9-44-1) medicine for driving out waste or poisonous matter from the body.

cath'edral (9-11) church in which is the chair of a *bishop* (= high officer of the church).

catheter (3-1-9) small pipe used by doctors to draw liquid out of the body.

cathode (3-67) negative (—, minus) plate from which electricity flows to the anode (+), e.g. in radio.

CAT'S EYE REFLECTORS

c'at's-eye refl'ectors (3 + 41 + 1-2-9) line

of things fixed in the middle of the road which shine in the light of the car-lamps.

catholic (3-9-1) found everywhere; very wide; having all kinds; having to do with the whole Church; having to do with the Church of Rome; *Catholic in one's tastes* = liking all sorts of people (or things).

c′at-o′-n′ine-t′ails (3 + 9 + 41 + 21-z) nine pieces of leather tied to a stick used for beating as a punishment.

cat's-paw (3 + 55) simple person used by a cleverer one to carry out a wrong act.

catsup, ketchup (2-9) hot-tasting liquid put on meat.

cattle (3) cows and other animals of the same kind.

caucus (55-9) small group within the government which meets to decide on future plans.

caudal (55) having to do with the tail.

caught (55) p.t. of Catch.

cauldron, caldron (55) large pot for boiling liquids.

cauliflower (5-1-479) vegetable with large white head, boiled for food.

CAULIFLOWER

caulk (55) press sticky, oily material into the cracks of a ship to keep out water.

cause (55z) that which produces an effect; *In the cause of science* = so as to help —; *In a good cause* = in order to do good.

causeway (55z-21) road running along the top of a bank.

caustic (55-1) having the power of slowly eating material away; burning; bitter (speech); **cauterize** (55-9-41) burn away (skin).

caution (55shn) sign or word which tells of danger; carefulness; **to caution,** warn; Sl. *He's a caution* = a peculiar, amusing person; **cautious** (55sh9) careful; afraid of danger.

c′avalc′ade (3-9-21) long line of moving people, usually riding on horses.

c′aval′ier (3-9-19) soldier on a horse; follower of King Charles I; knight; adj. gay; *In a cavalier manner* = in a proud and rough way.

cavalry (3-1) soldiers on horses.

cave (21) large hollow place in a rock or hillside; **to cave in,** fall inwards like the falling roof of a cave; to yield.

cavern (3-9) large cave.

caviare, caviar (3-144) eggs of certain fish used as food; something too good or costly for common use.

cavil at (3-1) find fault without good reasons.

cavity (3-1-1) hole.

cav′ort (9-55) Am. Sl. jump about in a noisy, uncontrolled way.

caw (55) sound made by some birds, e.g. *crows* (= very common, large black birds).

cay′enne (212) hot-tasting red powder eaten with food.

cease (s11) to stop.

cedar (s11-9) tree which has sweet-smelling wood of which pencils, etc., are made.

cede (s11) give up.

ceiling (s11-1) inside roof of a room; *Ceiling of an aeroplane* = greatest height to which it can fly; *Price ceiling* = highest price allowed.

celandine (s2-9-41) kind of flower.

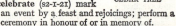

CEDAR TREE

celebrate (s2-1-21) mark an event by a feast and rejoicings; perform a ceremony in honour of or in memory of.

celebrated (s2-1-21-1) famous; **cel′ebrity** (s1-2-1-1) fame, a famous person; **celebrant** (s2-1) priest who performs the main part of the church ceremony in which Christ's last supper is remembered.

cel′erity (s1-2-1-1) speed.

celery (s2-9-1) vegetable stem generally eaten uncooked, often with cheese.

cel′estial (s1-2-19) heavenly, of the sky.

celibacy (s2-1-9-1) state of being unmarried, usually for a religious reason; **celibate** (s2-1-9) not married.

cell (s2) (1) small room, e.g. in a prison; (2) small container, e.g. those built by bees to hold *honey* (= a sweet liquid); (3) small pieces of living matter of which the body is built up; (4) box containing metal plates and acid used to produce or store electricity; *Communist cell* = group of communists working together in a non-communist country.

cellar (s2-9) room below the ground in a house.

cello (tsh2-67) (violoncello) musical instrument with four strings, giving deep notes when rubbed.

cellophane (s2-67-21) glass-like paper used for putting round food, etc.

cellular (s2-17-9) made up of *cells* (see 4th above).

celluloid (s2-17-51) material which looks like glass, but can be bent and burns very easily.

cellulose (s2-17-67s) plant matter used to make paper, *artificial* (= not real) silk, etc.

cem′ent (s1-2) any powder which, mixed with a liquid, becomes a solid mass after a time, e.g. that used in building, that used to fill holes in teeth, etc.; sticky liquid used to repair broken glass, etc.; **to cem′ent,** join firmly.

cemetery (s2-1-1) piece of land (separate from a church) where there are many graves.

cenotaph (s2-9-44) large stone put up in memory of a person or persons whose bodies lie in some other place.

censer (s2-9) container in which sweet-smelling powder is burned.

censor (s2-9) officer who examines books and pictures to prevent bad ones from being sold;

in war, one who reads all letters and newspapers so that secret plans may not become known to the enemy; **to censor,** examine books, etc., as above; **cens'orious** (s2-55-19) quick to find fault.

censure (s2-sh9) blame; to blame.

census (s2-9) counting of the people in a country.

cent (s2) 1/100th; **per cent.,** in each 100; **a cent,** one-hundredth part of a *dollar*.

centaur (s2-55) imaginary creature, half horse, half man.

c'enten'arian (s-2-1-29-19) person who is 100 years old.

cent'enary (s-2-11-9-1) hundredth year after an event; public ceremonies and feasting on this date; adj. **cent'ennial** (s-2-2-19).

centi-, $\frac{1}{100}$th part of —, e.g. *centimetre* = $\frac{1}{100}$th of a metre.

centigrade (s-2-1-21) French way of measuring heat by means of one hundred *degrees* (= steps).

centipede (s-2-1-11) insect with many (a hundred) legs.

centre (s2-9) the middle; person or thing in the middle; adj. **central** (s2); **centralize** (s2-9-41) bring to a centre; control a business (or the work of government) from the centre, leaving little freedom to officers to use their own judgment or act differently from others.

centr'ifugal (force) (s2-1-17) force which makes things fly off from the edge of a quickly turning wheel; **centr'ipetal** (2-1-1-9) (force) pulling towards the centre.

cent'urion (s2-177-19) captain of a hundred men in the Roman army.

century (s2-tsh9-1) one hundred years.

cer'amic (s1-3-1) having to do with *pottery* (= cups, pots, etc., made of burnt earth).

cereal (s11-19) food made from grain, e.g. corn and other grain used as food.

cerebrum (s2-1-9) upper brain; **cereb'ellum** (s2-1-2) small brain at the back of the head; adj. **cerebral** (s2-1).

CEREBRUM, CEREBELLUM

ceremony (s2-1-9-1) set of solemn acts as in a church or at a great public show; polite forms of behaviour; *To stand upon ceremony* = behave in a stiff and solemn way; **a cerem'onial** (s2-1-67-19) performing of a ceremony; adj. **cerem'onial, cerem'onious** (s2-1-67-19) stiff, solemn, serious; *Master of Ceremonies* = man in charge of a meeting (e.g. a dance) who sees that all goes on happily and successfully.

cer'ise (s9-11z) clear light red colour.

certain (s99) (1) sure, without doubt; (2) agreed on; *On a certain day* = on a day not named or described, but supposed to be known to the hearer; *A certain amount* = some;

certainly, without doubt; *Will you come?— Certainly* = gladly, willingly.

cert'ificate (s9-1-1-1) writing declaring a certain fact, e.g. *A birth certificate.*

certify (s99-1-41) say or write that a certain fact is true.

certitude (s99-1-177) sureness.

cer'ulean (s2-77-19) sky-coloured, blue.

cess'ation (s2-21shn) act of stopping.

cession (s2shn) agreement by law to give up something.

cesspit (s2-1) **cesspool** (s2-77) deep hole for holding the dirty water which flows out of a house.

cet'acean (s1-21sh19) of a *whale* (= the largest creature living in the sea).

chafe (21) make hot by rubbing, make painful by rubbing.

chaff (44) (1) covering separated from grain by beating; (2) worthless matter; (3) say things with a playful meaning.

chaffer (3-9) talk about the price of a thing.

chafing dish (21-1 + 1) dish with a lamp under it for cooking food at the table.

ch'agrin (sh3-11) feeling of anger and shame.

chain (21) (1) number of rings joined together to make one long piece; (2) *A chain of mountains* = one long line of —.

ch'ain-st'ores (+ 55z) number of shops in different places all owned and controlled by one business company.

chair (29) seat which can be moved, with a back; *He holds the Chair of History* = he is the chief teacher of history in a university; *To take the chair at a meeting* = be chief person controlling the speakers.

chairman (29-9) one who has charge of a meeting.

chaise (sh21z) carriage, usually for two people.

chalet (sh3-2) wooden house as in Switzerland.

chalice (3-1s) tall metal cup, used in a church.

chalk (55) white material, used by teachers for writing on a blackboard; Sl. *Better by a long chalk* = far better; *To chalk up* = write up figures, e.g. of money owed or points won in a game.

challenge (3-1nj) (1) a call to fight; to call to fight or play a game; (2) show disbelief or distrust and demand proof.

chamber (21-9) (1) room; (2) group of persons who make laws; (3) hollow space, e.g. that part of a gun in which the powder and shot are put; *A chamber, A chamber-pot* = pot kept under the bed for use during the night.

chamberlain (21-9-1) officer in charge of the king's palace.

chambermaid (21-9-21) woman who takes care of the sleeping rooms in a hotel, lodging-house.

cham'eleon (k9-11-19) cold-blooded animal with four legs, which has the power of changing its colour.

chamois (sh3-74) (1) deer found on high moun-

champ   58   **chat.**

tains; (2) (sh3mI) soft leather made from the skin of sheep, goats, etc.

champ (3) (used of a horse) bite noisily; show eagerness to start.

champ'agne (sh3-2I) high-priced yellow wine which has much gas in it.

champion (3-I9) (1) one who defends or fights for some other person or for some good cause; (2) best of all players at a certain game.

chance (44-s) (1) event which happens by accident; *probability* (n. of probable); **to chance,** happen by accident, do a thing unexpectedly and without purposing to do it, e.g. *I chanced to meet him;* (2) *Give me a chance* = make it possible for me to show that I can work well; *I'll chance it* = I will take the risk.

chancel (44-s) east end of a church.

chancellor (44-s9-9) chief man in the government; special officer who looks after the king's business; highest judge of law; head of a university.

chancery (44-s9-I) high court of law.

ch'andel'ier (sh3-9-I9) frame with branches for holding many candles or other lights.

chandler (44-9) maker or seller of candles; *A ship's chandler* = seller of all sorts of things (food, ropes, cleaning materials, etc.) to ships.

change (2Inj) take one thing instead of another; become different; make different; *Change for a pound* = .100 pence instead of —; *All change* = this train does not go any farther; **changeling** (2Inj-I) in fairy stories a baby which has been left by the fairies in place of the real baby stolen by them.

channel (3) course in which a river flows; course a ship must follow in coming to harbour to keep clear of rocks, etc.; any course made for liquid; *The channel through which I got this news* = way in which —; narrow piece of water joining two seas, e.g. *The English Channel*

chant (44) slow song; sing softly or slowly.

ch'anticleer (3-I-I9) cock (= the male form of a hen).

chanty (sh3-I) song sung by sailors to keep time in pulling a rope.

chaos (k2I5) condition of no law or order; time before the world began.

chap (3) young fellow; *Old chap* (= friendly form of address).

chap(s) (3) cheeks.

chapel (3) small church; part of a larger church in which *services* (= religious ceremonies) can be held for a few people.

chaperon (sh3-9-67) older or married person in charge of young unmarried women.

chaplain (3-I) priest of a *chapel* (2nd above); priest in the army or on one of the king's ships.

chaplet (3-I) crown of flowers; string of *beads*

CHANDELIER

(= glass balls with holes for a string, used for ornament).

chapped (3-t) (of the skin) rough and cracked by wet and cold.

chapter (3-9) one of the parts into which a book is divided; group of officers of a church.

char (44) blacken in the fire.

ch'ar-a-banc (sh3 + 9 + 3ng) long carriage or motor-car, seating many people on seats arranged across it, from side to side.

character (k3-I-9) (1) printed or written letter (A, B, C, etc.) or other mark; (2) one's nature as shown by one's acts; a person in a book or play; adj. **character'istic** (k3-I-9-I-I).

char'ade (sh9-44) game in which a word is acted part by part, then as a whole (e.g. carpet, carpet), and those watching guess the word.

charcoal (44-67) wood blackened by heating it without air, used for burning.

charge (44j) fill a gun with powder; fill with electricity; tell a person his duty; ask money as payment for; *To charge in a court of law* = say that a person has done wrong; *To charge the enemy* = run at and attack; *In charge of the children* = being trusted to take care of —.

charger (44j9) officer's horse.

chariot (3-I9) car with two wheels used in war in ancient times; **ch'ariot'eer** (3-I9-I9) driver of a —.

charity (3-I-I) kindness; giving money to the poor.

charlatan (sh44-9-9) dishonest person who pretends to have knowledge which he does not possess.

charm (44) (1) magic song; (2) magic; (3) object which has magic powers; **to charm,** work magic on; cause great pleasure to; *She has great charm,* — *is very charming* = is very pleasing in manner.

charnel-house (44 + 47) place for the dead or the bones of the dead.

chart (44) map for the use of ships; paper showing the increase or *decrease* (= becoming less) of anything.

charter (44-9) written paper from the government giving certain rights, or giving land to a person or group of persons; *To charter a ship* = to hire.

charwoman (44-7-9) servant who is employed by the hour or day to do house-cleaning.

chary (29-I) careful.

chase (2I) run after; try to catch.

chase (2I) cut lines or figures on metal or other hard material as an ornament.

chasm (k32m) deep valley with steep sides.

chassis (sh3-I) wheels and frame on which the body of a car rests.

chaste (44) pure in body; (of ornament) simple; n. **chastity** (3-I-I).

chasten (2I) punish for the purpose of making better.

chast'ise (3-4Iz) scold or beat as a punishment.

chat (3) friendly unimportant talk.

château (sh44-67) French castle or large country-house.
châtelaine (sh3-9-21) lady of the château (see above); chain hanging from the waist of a woman for carrying keys.
chattel(s) (3-z) movable things in a house; goods and chattels.
chatter (3-9) talk quickly; foolish talk; make a noise with the teeth when cold; **chatterbox** (3-9-5) person who talks a great deal.
chauffeur (sh67-99) paid driver of a motor-car.
chauvinist (sh67-1-1) one who loves something (e.g. his country) in a wild and unreasonable way, and has no respect for other countries.
cheap (11) of low price; of little value.
cheapjack (11-3) travelling seller of cheap, bad goods.
cheat (11) deceive; get money (etc.) by a trick.
check (2) prevent another person from doing what he wishes to do; see that a person has done his work correctly; *Check in* = show in a book or on a special machine that one has come into the factory or office; so also *Check out*; **a check**, paper given to prove ownership, e.g. of one's bag or hat when given for safe keeping; *Check* (*cloth*) = cloth with black and white (or coloured) squares on it.
check (2) see Cheque.
checker (2-9) see Chequered.
checkers (2-9z) Am. = *Draughts*, game played with two sets of twelve round wooden pieces on a squared board.
checkmate (3-21) arrange so that the other person must lose his king at the next move in the game of *Chess* (see —); cause a person to fail completely in his plans.
cheek (11) part of the face between the nose and ears; *Cheek by jowl* = close together; Sl. *To have the cheek to* = dare to; Sl. **cheeky** (——-1) rude and daring.
cheer (19) joy; that which makes one happy; to shout for joy; *Good cheer* = plenty of good food; *Cheer up* = do not be so sad; **cheerful**, happy.
cheese (11z) milk made into a hard mass and kept so that it gets a pleasant strong taste; **cheeseparing** (11z-29-1) very careful, especially of money.
ch'eesecl'oth (11z-5) very thin kind of cloth.
cheetah (11-9) fierce, cat-like animal found in Africa and Southern Asia.
chef (sh2) a male cook.

CHEETAH

chemical (k2-1) matter in its pure form as used by scientists; having to do with **chemistry** (see 3rd below).
chem'ise (sh9-11z) lady's undergarment.
chemist (k2-1) (1) one who studies **chemistry** (——-1); (2) one who keeps a shop for selling medicines.
chemistry (k2-1-1) that part of science which deals with the nature of various forms of matter and how these are made up, and of their action when mixed.
cheque (2k) an order to pay money.
chequered (2k9) marked in squares of different colours; *A chequered career* = life in which there have been many changes of fortune, good and bad.
cherish (2-1) to love; take care of or protect; keep in the mind, e.g. *Cherish a hatred of —*.
cher'oot (sh1-77) roll of *tobacco* (= leaves used for smoking; usually one open at both ends.
cherry (2-1) small red fruit with a stone in it; a clear light red colour.
cherub (2-9) spirit with wings, told of in the Bible; baby with wings, supposed to live in heaven.
chess (2) game; **chessmen**, the pieces used in chess.
chest (2) strong box; part of the body, the breast.
chesterfield (2-9-11) soft seat for two or three persons in a sitting-room.
chestnut (2-8) tree; nut; story, once amusing, but told too often; brown colour of a horse.
chest of drawers, as shown.
chev'al glass (sh9-3 + 44) large looking-glass showing the whole body.
cheval'ier (sh2-9-19) knight in France.
chevron (sh2-9) V-shaped piece of cloth worn as a sign of rank in the army.
chew (77) break up food with the teeth.
chi'arosc'uro (k144-9-17-67) light and shade in a picture.
chic (sh1) charming and new in dress and appearance.
chic'anery (sh1-21-9-1) dishonest reasoning; attempts to deceive.
chick (1) newly-born hen.
chicken (1-1) young *fowl* (e.g. hen); its meat; *Count one's chickens before they are hatched* = be too hopeful; *Chicken-hearted* = not brave.
chicken-pox (+ 5) disease causing red spots on the body.
chicory (1-9-1) plant with bright blue flowers eaten uncooked; the root dried and powdered is added to give a bitter taste to coffee.
chide (41) to blame for a fault.
chief (11) most important; leader; **chieftain** (——-9) head-man of a large group.
chiffon (sh1-5) very thin kind of cloth used in women's clothes.
chiffon'ier (sh1-9-19) piece of furniture used for storing small things in a sitting-room.
chilblain (1-21) painful spot on the skin caused by cold.
child (41) young son or daughter; baby; pl. **children** (1-9).
chill (1) coldness; illness caused by cold.

chilli (1-1) fruit (usually red) with a very hot taste.

chime (41) musical sound made by bells; *To chime in* = break in on the talk of others.

chim′era (**-aera**) (k41-19-9) imaginary beast which breathed smoke; impossible fancy.

chimney (1-1) that through which the smoke goes up from the fire in a building; the tall round glass part of a lamp; narrow crack in a mountain-side.

ch′impanz′ee (1-9-11) large monkey-like creature.

chin (1) that part of the face below the mouth.

china (41-9) special white earth of which plates, cups, etc., are made; cups, plates, etc., made of such material.

CHIMPANZEE

chine (41) back-bone; the back.

chink (1ngk) a crack.

chink (1ngk) sound of pieces of money striking together; Sl. money.

chintz (1-s) cotton material used for curtains and chair-covers.

chip (1) small piece; break off a small piece; *A chip of the old block* = son like the father; *To chip in* = suddenly to join in the talk of others.

chipmunk (1-8ngk) small tree-animal with a large *bushy* (= hairy) tail.

CHIPMUNK

chirp (99) **chirrup** (1-9) cry of a small bird.

chisel (1z) instrument with a sharp flat end used for cutting wood.

chisel (1z) deceive, get money by unjust means, especially by finding out some weakness in the law.

chit (1) (Indian) short letter; written promise to pay.

chit (1) *A chit of a girl* = young girl.

chivalry (shi-1) laws and customs of knights in ancient times; all the knights, e.g. *The chivalry of England*; character of a good knight —courage, politeness, *generosity* (n. of generous).

chlorine (k-55-11) heavy gas which makes things lose their colour and become white.

chloroform (k-5-9-55) liquid used to make one lose all feeling, so that doctors may cut the body without causing pain.

chlorophyll (k-5-9-1) green colouring matter of plants.

chock (5) wooden block used to prevent things from rolling; Sl. *Chock-full, Chock-a-block* = very full, packed tight.

chocolate (5-1) brown sweet; sweet hot drink.

choice (51s) act of choosing; what is chosen; *Hobson's choice* = no chance of choosing, only one thing to choose; adj. carefully chosen, good, e.g. *choice flowers* = carefully chosen, specially good flowers.

choir (kw41 9) group of singers, e.g. in a church; place where the singers sit in a church.

choke (67) (**1**) be unable to breathe, e.g. because a piece of food has gone into the *windpipe* (= breath-pipe); (**2**) hold a person's *windpipe* so as to prevent breathing; (**3**) **to choke up**, stop up a pipe; *The house is choked up with things* = filled with many things so that one cannot move about.

choler (k5-9) anger.

cholera (k5-9-9) disease found in hot countries, causing sickness and continuous passing of waste matter from the body, ending in death caused by loss of liquid.

choleric (k5-9-1) easily made angry.

choose (77z) show that which is *preferred* (= liked better) among several objects; to elect; *There is nothing to choose between them* = they are equal.

chop (5) to cut, e.g. with an axe; *To chop and change* = keep changing; *A choppy sea* = rough; **chops** (of an animal) = mouth; *To lick one's chops* = pass the tongue round the outside of the mouth, show pleasure in or desire for food; **a chop**, piece of meat cut from the back or neck with its bone; **chopsticks**, sticks used by the Chinese in eating.

choral (k55) having to do with singing in a *choir* (= group of persons who sing together, e.g. in a church).

chord (k55) straight line joining two points of a circle; string of a musical instrument; certain string-like parts of the body, e.g. *the vocal chords* = voice-producing strings in the throat.

chord (k55) group of musical sounds which are pleasing when played together.

chore (55) a small duty, e.g. in the house.

chorister (k5-1-9) member of a group of singers in a church.

chortle (55) laugh by making a peculiar noise in the throat and through the nose.

chorus (k55-9) group of singers; part of a song which is repeated; *Chorus of praise* = everyone praising something.

chosen (67zn) p.p. of Choose.

chose (67) p.t. of Choose.

chow (47) dog as shown.

chowder (47-9) fish and vegetables cooked in milk.

christen (k-1) give a name to a child.

CHOW

Christendom (k-1-9) that part of the world which believes in Christ.

Christian (name) (k-1-19) first or given name; **Christmas** (k-1-19) Dec. 25th, feast in honour of the birth of Christ.

chrome-, **chromo-**, **chromato-** (k-67-9-6) having to do with colour, e.g. **chromatics** (k-9-3-1) science of colour.

chromium (k-67-19) grey white metal.
chromosome (k-67-6-67) the body is built up of millions of cells. The chromosomes can be seen as coloured *particles* (= bits) in a cell; they carry its special character. The chromosomes in sex—mother/father—cells carry the character of the young one who will be born of their union.
chronic (illness) (k-5-1) continuing a long time.
chronicle (k-5-1) account of events set down in order of time.
chrono-, of time.
chr'onol'og'ical (k-5-9-5j1) having to do with past events in their order of time.
chron'ometer (k-9-5-1-9) clock made to keep very exact time.
chrysalis (k-1-9-1) shell-like form taken by a creeping insect before changing into a flying one.
chrys'anthemum (k-1-3-9-9) flower (brought from Japan — it flowers in the autumn).
chub (8) fresh-water fish.
chubby (8-1) fat.
chuck (8) to touch gently under the *chin* (= part of face below the mouth); Sl. *To chuck away* = throw away; Sl. *To chuck up* (*one's job*) = give up (one's employment).

CHRYSANTHEMUM

chuck (8) instrument which holds a piece of wood or metal while it is turned round and round for cutting into shape.
chuckle (8) quiet laugh.
chum (8) good friend.
chump (8) large piece of (wood); fool.
chunk (8ngk) large piece (e.g. of cake).
church (99) building in which Christians meet in order to pray to God and praise Him; all the persons who hold certain beliefs in God; *To enter the Church* = become a priest.
ch'urchw'ard'en(s) (99-55-z) persons chosen each year to help and advise the priest of a church; very long pipe used for smoking.
churlish (99-1) bad-mannered.
churn (99) machine for making *cream* (= fatty part of milk) into butter; to shake.
chute (sh77) sloping board down which articles slip, or down which water flows.
chutney (8-1) mixture of fruits and hot-tasting seeds, made in India.
cic'ada (s1-44-9) tree-insect which makes a loud noise.
cicatrix (-ce) (s1-9-1) (-1s) mark of an old wound.

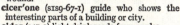
CICADA

cicer'one (s1s9-67-1) guide who shows the interesting parts of a building or city.
cider (s41-9) light drink made from apples.

cig'ar (s1-44) short thick roll of tobacco leaves closed at one end.
cigar'ette (s1-9-2) finely cut tobacco rolled in paper.
cinch (s1-sh) band holding seat on a horse; Sl. *It's a cinch* = an easy and certain success.
cinch'ona (s1ngk67-9) tree from which *quinine* (= bitter medicine used for fever) is obtained.
cincture (s1ngktsh9) band worn round the middle of the body.
cinder(s) (s1-9z) hard burnt remains of coal.
C'inder'ella d'ance (s1-9-2-9 + 44-s) gathering for dancing which ends at 12 o'clock at night.
cinema (s1-1-9) moving picture; building in which moving pictures are shown; **cinem'atograph** (s1-1-3-9-44) instrument used in taking moving pictures; instrument used for showing such pictures.
cinnamon (s1-9) brown powder made from the inner covering of a tree in India and Ceylon and used to give cakes a yellow colour and special taste; medicine.
cipher, cypher (s41-9) secret writing; figure o; person of no importance.
circa (s99-9) (Latin) about.
circle (s99) figure, every point on the edge of which is the same distance from the centre; go round; *A circle of friends* = group of friends; **c'ircuit** (s99k1) path round; set of places through which a judge (or other officer) must travel; *Electric circuit* = path of electricity along a wire from where it is produced, through a lamp (machine, etc.) and back to the producer; **circ'uitous** (s99k1771-9) going a long way round; adj. **c'ircular** (s99k17-9); *A circular* = printed letter or notice sent to many people; **to c'irculate** (s99k17-21) go round, pass from one person to another; *The circul'ation of a newspaper* = number of persons to whom it is sold.
c'ircumc'ision (s99-9-s13n) cutting round; act and ceremony of taking a boy into the Jewish religion.
circ'umference (s99-8-9-9-s) line round the outside; outside edge of a circle.
circumflex (s99-9-2) mark over a letter to show the sound, e.g. ô.
c'ircumloc'ution (s99-9-67-177shn) roundabout way of expressing some simple idea.
c'ircumn'avigate (s99-9-3-1-21) sail round the world.
circumscribe (s99-9-41) (draw a line round); keep within a certain space.
circumspect (s99-9-2) careful.
circumstance (s99-9-9-s) all the facts which are concerned with an act, e.g. place, time, events coming before; *In* (*under*) *the circumstances* = since these things are so; *Under no circumstances* = never; *In reduced circumstances* = poor; *Pomp and circumstance* = fine public ceremonies; *Circumstantial evidence* = number of facts which, taken together,

make it seem very probable that a person did a certain wrong act.

c'ircumv'ent (s99-9-2) by cleverness prevent a person from carrying out some plan.

circus (s99-9) show with animals which do clever things.

cirrus (sI-9) very high white clouds.

cissy, sissy (sI-I) a boy who behaves like a girl.

cistern (sI-9) large container built to hold water.

citadel (sI-9) strong fort in a city.

cite (s4I) call a person into a law court; repeat words from a book written by someone else as a proof of one's opinion; **a cit'ation** (s4I-2Ishn) words so repeated.

citizen (sI-I) one who lives in a city; one who has rights in a country.

citron (sI) a sour yellow fruit.

citrus fruits (sI-9 + 77) citrons, oranges, lemons, grape-fruits.

city (sI-I) London, Paris, etc., are cities; **the City,** business part of London.

civet (sI-I) fox-like animal with a peculiar smell. CIVET

civic (sI-I) having to do with a city.

civics (sI-I) study of government, especially city government.

civil (sI-I) (1) having to do with *citizens* (= people who live in a city or members of a nation); (2) not having to do with soldiers or fighting; (3) polite; **Civil Servant** (sI + 99) person employed by the government—not a member of the army or *navy* (= warships).

civ'ilian (sI-I-I9) any member of a country who is not a soldier; officer of government not in the army.

civilize (sI-I-4I) change from being wild; teach good customs, manners, laws, science and art; adj. **civilized.**

clad (3) having clothes; covered.

claim (2I) say; demand as one's right; say "That thing is mine"; **a claim,** thing claimed; piece of land marked out as belonging to one man, e.g. to a *gold-miner* (= one who gets gold out of the earth).

cl'airv'oyant (29-5I9) person (said to be) able to see distant or future events—usually by looking into a glass ball.

clam (3) large shell-fish.

clamber (3-9) climb up with difficulty.

clammy (3-I) wet, cold and sticky.

clamour (3-9) loud noise of people shouting.

clamp (3) instrument used for holding things very tightly.

clan (3) family group.

cland'estine (3-2-I) secret.

clang (3) **clank** (3ngk) sound made by striking metal against metal.

clannish (3-I) keeping closely within one's own small group and having little to do with other persons.

clap (3) make a noise by striking the hands together; *To clap — on =* to put on quickly or with force, e.g. *Clapped his hat on*; *Clap eyes on =* catch sight of.

claptrap (3-3) parts in a speech spoken to make people *clap* (see above); any simple and foolish trick to get praise; adj. meant for show but of no real value.

claret (3-9) kind of red wine; dark red colour; Sl. blood.

clarify (3-I-4I) make clear.

cl'arin'et (3-I-2) musical wind instrument.

clarion (3-I9) small horn (music); adj. clear and loud.

clarity (3-I-I) clearness.

clash (3) come together with force; quarrel.

clasp (44) join tightly together, e.g. hold one hand in the other; **a clasp,** metal instrument for joining things; **a clasp-knife** (+ 4I) a knife whose blade can be shut inside the handle.

class (44) (1) kind of; (2) group of things all of the same kind; (3) group of learners, e.g. in a school; (4) rank, e.g. *The upper classes =* lords, etc.; *The middle classes =* people who are not very rich or poor; *First class =* best.

classic (3-I) having to do with the ancient learning of Greece and Rome; work of art which will always be considered as good.

classify (3-I-4I) arrange things in classes.

clatter (3-9) noise of falling things, of feet on a stone floor, of many people talking.

clause (55z) group of words not complete in itself; one part of an agreement.

cl'austroph'obia (47-6-67-I9) fear of being shut in a small space.

claw (55) sharp, horny point on the foot of a bird or beast (e.g. cat); tear with the claws.

clay (2I) soft sticky earth used for making pots and bricks.

claymore (2I-55) Scottish sword.

clean (II) (1) not dirty; *Make a clean breast of it =* tell all one's faults; Sl. *Show a clean pair of heels =* run away; *A clean stroke =* skilful; Sl. *Come clean =* speak the truth, tell truthfully what bad thing you have done; **to clean, to cleanse** (2-z) make clean.

clear (I9) (1) easy to hear; easy to understand; easy to see through, e.g. *Clear glass*; *A clear sky* = — without clouds; (2) easy or safe to pass along, e.g. *The streets are clear*; *To keep clear of* = keep at a safe distance from; (3) complete, whole, e.g. *A clear month =* full month; **to clear,** make clear, become clear; *These goods must be cleared =* sold off; *Clear one's character* = prove that one did no wrong; *My car just cleared the other car =* just missed, did not hit —; *To clear one's costs =* gain as much as one spent; *Clear away the dishes =* take —; *Clear off (work) =* finish; or go away leaving unfinished; *Cleared me out completely =* used up all my money; *Clear up =* set things in order;

Sl. *Clear out!* = go away; **clearance** (——9-s) act of clearing, e.g. selling or throwing away things not needed; cutting down trees to clear land; distance between a moving object and some other thing, e.g. the side of a bridge; **clearing** (——1) piece of treeless land in a forest.

cleat (11) (**1**) V-shaped piece of wood; (**2**) as in the picture for fixing a rope in an 8 shape.

CLEAT

cleave (11) divide by a heavy blow, e.g. with a sword; **cleaver** (——9) heavy knife.

cleave (11) stick to; keep near.

clef (2) the sign ——— or ——— in music.

cleft (2) p.t. of Cleave.

clematis (2-9-1) plant which grows up walls, etc., and has beautiful flowers.

clemency (2-9-s1) forgiveness, mercy.

clench (2) press together firmly, e.g. the fingers or hands; settle an agreement.

clergy (99j1) priests of a Church, e.g. of the Church of England.

clerical (2-1) having to do with one who writes; having to do with *clergy* (see above); *He put on his clericals* = dress of a priest.

clerk (44) one who keeps accounts, writes letters, etc., in a business-house.

clever (2-9) quick in learning or understanding.

clew (77) (**1**) roll up a sail; (**2**) Am. for Clue.

click (1) sudden slight noise.

client (419) one who gets advice, e.g. from a doctor, lawyer, etc.; **client'èle** (119-21) group of clients.

cliff (1) steep bank.

climate (41-1) weather conditions of a country.

climax (41-3) most exciting of a number of exciting events following each other.

climb (41) go up—a mountain, tree, etc.; Sl. *To climb down* = yield.

clime (41) *climate* (see 3rd above), countries having a certain climate, e.g. *In sunny climes.*

clinch (1) drive in a nail and then knock the point sideways; fasten; decide once and for ever.

cling (1) hold firmly to.

clinic (1-1) place in which doctors examine sick people and give advice; **clinical**, at the bedside, e.g. *Clinical teaching of medicine.*

clink (1ngk) small sharp noise like that made by small pieces of metal or glass falling on a hard surface.

clinker (1ngk9) mass of hard burnt brick or coal.

clip (1) fasten together, e.g. pieces of paper with bent pieces of metal.

clip (1) cut the edge off; **a clipper** (——9) instrument for clipping; fast sailing-ship; *Newspaper clippings.* = interesting pieces cut out from a newspaper.

clique (11k) small closely-united group of persons who have the same interests, and who keep all others out of the group.

cloak (67) loose outer garment; *To cloak* = hide; *He uses long words as a cloak for his ignorance* (= not knowing things) = — as a means of hiding; **a cloakroom** (67-7) place where one leaves one's coat and hat before going into a hall; place in England where travellers' bags, etc., are taken care of, e.g. in a railway station.

clobber (5-9) Sl. clothes.

cloche (5sh) glass cover to help early plants.

clock (5) instrument for showing the time in hours and minutes; an ornament on the outside of a *sock* or *stocking* (= covering of wool or silk worn on the feet and legs); **clockwork** (5-99) machine like that of a clock used for some other purpose, e.g. to move a child's plaything; *To clock in* = show on a special clock the time when one went into the factory or office.

CLOCHE

clod (5) hard piece or mass of earth; fool; **clodhopper** (5-5-9) rough fellow from the country; unskilful person.

clog (5) cause difficulty in moving or working, e.g. *The machine is clogged with thick oil*; heavy wooden shoe.

cloister (51-9) covered pathway joined to a church; place where men or women live lives of study and prayer apart from the world.

clone (67) plant which grows from cut pieces (e.g. potato).

close (67z) to shut; to finish; *Close up!* = move or sit closer together; *Close with* = settle an agreement; *Closed shop* = factory in which all workers must belong to a *Trade Union* (see Trade —).

close (67s) (**1**) lacking space, e.g. *Close quarters* = small rooms for living in; (**2**) near, e.g. *Close to the church*; *A close friend* = near and dear friend; *A close call* = narrow escape; (**3**) tightly made, thick, near together, e.g. *To sit close*; *The room is close* = the air is not fresh; *Close-fisted* = too careful of money; *A close-up* = cinema photograph with the camera near to the face, showing it very big; **a close**, court-yard; court-yard near a *cathedral* (= large important church) in which the priests live.

closet (5z1) small room for *private* (= not public) use; place where one leaves the waste matter of the body; very small room in which things are stored, e.g. as part of a bedroom and used for storing and hanging up one's clothes; water-closet (see —).

closure (67z9) act of stopping; time in government business when speeches are stopped and the number of those saying " yes " or " no " to a question is counted.

clot (5) become thick as blood does in air; solid piece of material in liquid.

cloth (5) material made of cotton, wool, silk, etc.; *American cloth* = cloth with paint-like

matter on the surface to keep out water; *To lay the cloth* = get the table ready for a meal;
clothe (67ð) put clothes on; **clothes** (67ðz) garments; *Bed-clothes* = sheets and other coverings of a bed; **clothier** (67ðıg) one who sells clothes; **clothing** (67ðı) garments.
cloud (47) mist floating high up in the air; *In the clouds* = thinking one's own thoughts, dreaming when awake.
clout (47) rough piece of cloth; Sl. to hit; a blow.
clove (67) dried flower of a certain tree used to give a special taste to cooked fruits, etc.
clove (67) p.t. of Cleave.
cl'ove-h'itch (+ 1) knot used for tying a rope on to a post.
cloven (67) divided into two parts, e.g. the foot of a cow is a *Cloven hoof*; *He showed the cloven hoof* = showed that he was really a devil, really a bad man.
clover (67-9) plant with leaves in sets of three, having sweet-smelling flowers, used for feeding cattle.
clown (47) man who amuses people by acting in a foolish way.
cloy (51) cause dislike because of too much sweetness.
club (8) heavy stick; hit with a heavy stick; playing card marked thus:—♣
club (8) number of people joined together for a common purpose, e.g. *A football club*; meeting-house for the members of a club.
cluck (8) noise made by a hen.
clue (77) that which leads one to find the answer to a question; *The murderer left one clue—a finger-mark* = one thing helping the police to discover who did the murder.
clump (8) group (of trees); **to clump** (along), walk heavily.
clumsy (8-21) rough and unskilful in work; badly made.
clung (8) p.t. of Cling.
cluster (8-9) number of flowers or plants growing close together, any close group of things.
clutch (8) seize; *The clutch of a motor-car*— when the clutch is "let in", the car moves forward, when it is "taken out", the car stops, but the engine goes on running.
clutter (8-9) disorder; fill with a disorderly mass of things.
Co. (67) short for Company (in business); also for *County* (= part of a country, e.g. of Ireland).
co- (67) together, with each other.
coach (67) (1) large four-wheeled carriage; car or carriage in a train; (2) person who gives special training, e.g. to players for a game, to people for an examination; **to coach**, train or teach; **coachman** (———9) driver of a horse-carriage.
co'agulate (673-17-21) become thick, as blood does in air.
coal (67) black material used for burning; *Carry coals to Newcastle* = supply something of which there is already plenty; *Heap coals of fire on someone's head* = do good to a person who has done one harm.
coal'esce (679-2) grow together; unite.
coalite (67-41) coal from which some of the gas has been taken so that it makes very little smoke when burning.
coal'ition (679-1shn) joining of different or (till now) unfriendly groups.
coalscuttle (67-8) box for coal in a room.
coarse (55) not fine, rough, not polite.
coast (67) edge of a country next to the sea; *The coast is clear* = all is safe, there is no one to be seen; **to coast**, go down hill freely, e.g. on a *bicycle* (=machine with two wheels).
coat (67) outer covering; **coat of arms** (+ 9v + 44-z) figures painted on a shield as the sign of a certain person of a certain family.
coax (67) beg sweetly—like a child.
cob (5) round piece, e.g. of coal; fruit of Indian corn; strong, short-legged horse.
cob'alt (9-55) blue matter; metal.
cobble (5) make or repair shoes.
cobblestones (5-67-z) round stones used in road-making.
cobra (67-9) poisonous snake found in India.
cobweb (5-2) fine silk-like net made by a *spider* (= small animal which catches flies).

COBWEB

coc'aine (5-21) powerful medicine which takes away all feeling from the skin.
cochin'eal (5-1-11) red colouring matter obtained by drying the bodies of certain insects.
cock (5) male bird; Sl. *Cock of* —— = head of; Sl. *Old cock* = disrespectful form of address; *Cock-and-bull story* = unbelievable ——; *Cock-a-hoop* = pleased with success; *Cock-sure* = always very sure of one's opinions.
cock (5) *hammer* of a gun (= L-shaped part which is made to come down with force in order to fire the gun); raise the hammer of a gun; turn upwards and sideways, e.g. the ear of a dog.
cock'ade (5-21) ornament worn on the hat.
cockat'oo (5-9-77) brightly-coloured bird with feathers standing up on its head.
cockatrice (5-9-41s) imaginary creature, said to cause death by looking at a person.
cockboat (5-67) small boat tied to a ship.
cockchafer (5-21-9) large flying insect.
COCKATOO
c'ocked h'at (5-t + 3) hat with its edges turned up.
cockerel (5) young *cock* (= a male bird).

cockle (5) a shell-fish.
cockloft (5-5) small upper room.
cockney (5-1) (accent) special way of speaking English common among the lower classes in London; person born in London.
cockpit (5-1) (1) place used for fights between *cocks* (= male birds); (2) part of a sailing-ship; (3) scene of any great war; (4) place in which the driver of an aeroplane sits.
cockroach (5-67) large black or brown insect found in kitchens.
cockscomb (5-67) red growth on the top of the head of a male bird; see also Coxcomb.
cocktail (5-21) mixture of strong drinks and other liquids, taken before a meal; Am. mixture of foods served in a glass at the beginning of a meal.

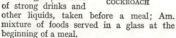
COCKROACH

cocoa (67-67) fruit of a tree, powdered and boiled with milk and sugar to make a sweet hot drink.
coconut (67-9-8) large round fruit in a hard shell, used as a food (the outer covering is used to make rope).
coc'oon (9-77) silk covering which a creeping insect makes for itself before it changes into a flying insect.
cod (5) large sea-fish, used as food.
coddle (5) treat gently, as one would a baby.
code (67) laws written down in a certain order; form of secret writing; agreed arrangement by which certain signs are given a special meaning.
codex (67-2) ancient book written by hand.
codicil (5-1s1) something added to a *Will* (= paper showing what is to be done with money, etc., after the owner's death).
codling (5-1) kind of apple used for cooking; young *cod* fish.
coelacanth (s11-6-3) ancient form of fish as shown.
COELACANTH
co'erce (6799s) force a person to do something.
co'eval (6711) of the same time in history.
coffee (5-1) small brown seeds of a bush powdered and boiled to make a rather bitter hot drink.
coffer (5-9) large strong box used for keeping things of value.
coffin (5-1) box in which a dead body is put.
cog(s) (5-z) teeth on a wheel which enable it to move another wheel.
cogent (67j9) (piece of reasoning) strong, making one agree.
cogitate (5j1-21) think.
cognac (67ny3) very strong drink made from wine.
cognate (5-21) of the same group or family; *A cognate word* = word which is the same, or almost the same, in two languages.

cogn'ition (5-1shn) act of knowing or noticing; *Not to take c'ognizance* (5-1) *of* = pretend not to notice.
coh'ere (67-19) stick together; *Coherent speech* = well joined, well reasoned —; **coh'esion** (67-11ʒn) condition or act of sticking together.
cohort (67-55) company of soldiers in the Roman army.
coiff'eur (kw4-99) person who cuts, curls, etc., women's hair; **coiffure** (kw4-179) way of doing this.
coil (51) gather (a rope, etc.) up in circles; set of circles so made; electrical instrument made of *coiled* wire.
coin (51) any piece of money made of metal; *to coin*, make money out of metal; *I'm simply coining money* = getting a lot of —; *To coin a word* = make a new word; **coinage** (——1j) money used in a country.
c'oinc'ide (671-s41) (of two spaces or drawings) fit exactly the one upon the other; (of events in time) happen at the same time; (of tastes or opinions) agree; **a co'incidence** (671-s1-s) something which happens, by accident, just at the same moment.
coir (519) brown material made up of many threads, used to make ropes (see Coconut).
coke (67) coal from which the gas has been driven by heat.
colander, cullender (8-1-9) metal pot with holes in it, used to get the water out of boiled vegetables, etc.
cold (67) illness causing pain in the throat and running of liquid from the nose.
cold (67) opposite of hot; calm and without feelings; not showing love; *In cold blood* = when quite calm; *Throw cold water on (a plan)* = say that it is useless or impossible.
colic (5-1) pain in the stomach or bowel.
col'itis (5-41-1) disease of the *colon* (= part of the bowel).
coll'aborate (9-3-9-21) to work with another, especially in writing books.
coll'apse (9-3) fall down; lose strength suddenly; fail in business.
coll'apsible (9-3-1) which can be folded into a small space, e.g. *A collapsible boat*.
collar (5-9) band worn round the neck; *to collar*, seize a person; press meat into a roll; Sl. steal.
coll'ate (5-21) examine two written papers carefully side by side.
coll'ateral (5-3-9-9) side by side; supporting or making sure.
colleague (5-11) one who works with another in an office, school, etc.
coll'ect (9-2) gather together; **a c'ollect** (5-1) short prayer.
coll'ective (9-2-1) of all, of all in the group; *Policy of collective ownership of land* = idea that land should be owned by the nation, not by single persons.
colleen (5-11) pretty Irish girl.

college (5-1j) school; part of a university; adj. **coll'egiate** (9-11j1·1).

coll'ide (9-41) run into, e.g. two trains into each other

collie (5-1) long-haired dog which drives and guards sheep.

collier (5-19) one who brings coal from the ground; a ship for carrying coal; **colliery** (——11) place from which coal is obtained.

coll'ision (9-13n) act of *colliding*.

colloc'ation (5-6-21shn) setting together in order; things set together.

coll'oquial (9-67-19) used in common speech.

coll'usion (9-773n) secret agreement for a wrong purpose.

colon (67-9) mark (:).

colon (67-5) large lower part of the bowel.

colonel (99) one who commands about 1,000 men in the army; *Colonel Blimp* (+ 1) old fat army officer who cannot change his ideas.

col'onial (9-67-19) having to do with a *colony* (2nd below).

colonn'ade (5-9-21) row of pillars usually supporting arches.

colony (5-9-1) land settled in by people from another country; people who so settle; number of foreign persons living in a city, sometimes all in one part of the town.

COLON

col'ossus (9-5-9) very large figure cut in stone; very great man; adj. **col'ossal**, very great or large.

colour (8-9) e.g. Red, Green, Blue, etc.; materials used in painting; *He has a high colour* = a red face; *Some colour of truth* = appearance of —; *Under colour of* = while pretending to; *Local colour* = description of the place where the events of a story happened; **colours** (——z) flag of a ship; special dress of a person riding a horse in a race; *Come off with flying colours* = be very successful; *Nail one's colours to the mast* = refuse to yield; *Colourable imitation* = copy good enough to deceive.

colt (67) a young male horse.

column (5-9) large round post in a building; long line of soldiers; *A column of figures* = numbers in rows one below the other.

coma (67-9) deep sleep in which all feeling is lost; **comatose** (67-9-67) in a condition of coma.

comb (67) toothed instrument used for putting the hair in order; *comb out* = search thoroughly.

combat (8-9) a fight; to fight; **combatant** (8-9) one who fights.

combin'ation (5-1-21shn) joining together; *A pair of* ——s = an upper and lower undergarment made in one piece; **to comb'ine** (9-41) join together; agree to work together; *a c'ombine* (5-41) joining together and working together of several persons or business companies; **c'ombine h'arvester** (+ 44-1-9) machine as shown which cuts corn and takes out the seeds while moving round the field.

COMBINE HARVESTER

comb'ustion (9-8stshn) act of burning; **comb'ustibles** (9-8-9-z) materials which burn easily.

come (8) (1) move in the direction of the speaker; arrive; *Your letter has just come* = has reached me; *Come to life* = become alive, become well again after fainting; *Come to terms* = make an agreement; (2) happen; *How did you come to do that?* = how did it happen that you did it?; *To come true* = happen as expected or hoped; (3) arrive from; be caused by; *He comes of a good family* = is born of, a member of —; *The money came to him from his mother* = was received when his mother died; *An idea came into my head* = was thought of by me, *Come into use* = begin to be used; *Come into play* = begin to have an effect; *He will come to no good* = not be successful; *Three years old come January* = — when January comes; *Come, come!* = be calm; **come across** = meet by accident; **come by** = obtain, e.g. *Good cooks are hard to come by*; **come down**, *Come down on a person* = punish, scold; *The custom has come down to us* = been received from our fathers, grandfathers, etc.; **come forward** = offer to help; **come in**, *Come in useful* = be found useful; *Come into money* = receive money from a dead relation; **come off** = happen; *Come off with flying colours* = be very successful; **come on**, *The fruit is coming on nicely* = growing so that the harvest will be good; **come out** = be made public; **come round**, **come to** = become well again after fainting; **come up** (of plants) = grow up out of the ground; **come up to** = be level with, be equal to.

com'edian (9-11-19) actor in light amusing parts; singer of amusing songs; **comedi'enne** (9-2-12) woman who acts such parts or sings amusing songs.

comedy (5-1-1) amusing play.

comely (8-1) pretty.

com'estibles (9-2-1-z) food.

comet (5-1) kind of heavenly body with a tail of light.

comfits (8-1) sweets.

comfort (8-9) to care for the well-being of a person; cheer a person when sad; state of being comfortable; **comfortable** (8-9-9) pleasant and causing comfort.

comic (5-1) making people laugh; *A comic* = children's paper with many coloured pictures in it.

C'ominf'orm (5-1-55) office for giving out Communist news and talks.

comity (5-1-1) politeness, friendliness.

comma (5-9) mark (,).

comm'and (9-44) order; *In command of* = in charge of, acting as chief officer of (e.g. soldiers); **to comm'and,** order, have control of; *He commands respect* = deserves and gets the respect of all.

command'eer (5-9-19) take for the use of the army, e.g. during war.

comm'andment (9-44-9) law or order.

comm'ando (5-44-67) small party of specially trained soldiers used for very dangerous attacks into the enemy country; a soldier specially trained for such work.

c'omme il f'aut (5 + 11 + 6) as it should be, correct.

comm'emorate (9-2-9-21) make people remember a certain event or person by meetings, feasts, etc., or by a building (or other object) set up in memory of it (him).

comm'ence (9-2-s) to start.

comm'end (9-2) to praise; *To commend A to B,* give A in charge of B, asking B to take great care of A.

comm'ensurate (9-2-sh9-1) of like measure or size.

comment (5-2) that which is said about a thing, usually to explain it; **to comment,** explain or speak about a subject; **commentary** (5-9-9-1) notes, or book of notes which explain another book, e.g. *A commentary on the Bible*;

commentator (5-2-21-9) radio speaker who describes games, races, etc., while looking at them.

commerce (5-99) trade, especially with other countries.

comm'iserate (9-1z9-21) express sorrow at another's troubles.

commiss'ariat (5-1-29-19) that part of an army which arranges the supply of the food.

commissary (5-1-9-1) officer having some special duty; **commiss'ar** (5-1-44) officer of the Russian government.

comm'ission (9-1shn) duty; appointment to an office; paper of appointment, e.g. of an officer in the army; payment for doing business for another; *A Royal Commission* = group of persons given the duty of enquiring into some special matter and of making a report to the government; **comm'ission'aire** (——29) servant (usually an old soldier) who stands at the door (shop, etc.); **comm'issioner** (——9) officer appointed by the government to do certain work.

comm'it (9-1) do, usually do a wrong; give in charge of; *To commit to prison* = send —; *To commit oneself to an action* = promise to do a thing, to act or speak in such a way that one will be forced to do it.

comm'ittee (9-1-1) small number of persons appointed to consider some matter and report on it.

comm'odious (9-67-19) having plenty of room.

comm'odity (9-5-1-1) article of trade; anything in daily use.

commodore (5-9-55) officer in the *navy* (= king's warships) higher than a captain.

common (5-9) general; public; found everywhere; *A common* = public land; *A common person* = one whose manners are not polite; *common sense* = good judgment; *Common or garden* = very usual and well-known.

commoner (5-9-9) one who has no title or rank as a nobleman.

commonplace (5-9-21s) such as is often seen or heard; **a commonplace,** uninteresting saying.

commons (5-9-z) **House of Commons,** group of elected persons in the British government; *On short commons* = getting little food.

commonwealth (5-9-2) group of self-governing countries united under one central government, e.g. Australia and the British Commonwealth of Nations.

comm'otion (9-67shn) great noise and much movement.

communal (5-17-9) having to do with a way of living in which all things are owned in common by all.

commune (5-177) self-governing group in a country; **to comm'une** (9-177) speak together as close friends.

comm'unicate (9-177-1-21) **(1)** pass something to another person, e.g. news, disease; **comm'unicative** (9-177-1-9-1) eager to talk, loving talking; **(2)** be joined with, e.g. *Three comm'unicating rooms* = 3 rooms opening into each other; **communic'ation cord** (9-177-1-21shn + 55) string to be pulled on a train if there is danger.

comm'union (9-177-19) sharing of thoughts and feelings; all those of the same belief in a church; *service* (= religious ceremony) held in the Christian Church in memory of Christ's last supper before His death.

comm'unique (9-177-1k21) news given out by the government.

communism (5-17-1z) form of government, e.g. in Russia, in which all power is in the hands of the workers, and all land, buildings, etc., are owned by the public.

comm'unity (9-177-1-1) group of people living in one place or having the same interests.

comm'ute (9-177) make a punishment less; Am. use a monthly *ticket* (= printed card allowing one to travel) on a railway.

comp'act (9-3) pressed closely together; **c'ompact** (5-3) box of face-powder carried in the bag by ladies.

comp'anion (9-3-19) friend; one who goes with another.

comp'anion-w'ay (+ 21) stairs on a ship.

company (8-9-1) group of people; number of invited guests; group of 100-250 men in the army commanded by a captain; group of persons united for purposes of business; *In the company of* = with; *To keep bad company* = have bad friends.

comp'are (9-29) look for and point out a likeness or difference; adj. **comp'arative** (9-3-9-1); **comp'arison** (9-3-1) act of showing the likeness or difference.

comp'artment (9-44-9) one of the small divided parts (rooms) in a carriage in a railway train; any part which has been divided and closed off.

compass (8-9) instrument with a bar of iron which always points north and south; **compasses** (8-9-1z) instrument for drawing circles; *Within the compass of* —— = inside, not beyond.

comp'assion (9-3shn) feeling of pity for the sorrows of others; **comp'assionate** (9-3sh9-1) having pity.

comp'atible (9-3-1) agreeable; having the same character.

comp'atriots (9-3-19) natives of the same country.

compeer (5-19) an equal.

comp'el (9-2) force a person to act.

comp'endium (9-2-19) short account of a book; **comp'endious** (9-2-19) containing much (knowledge) in a little space.

compensate (5-9-21) pay for; when one has done wrong or hurt someone, do something to make it right, or pay for damage.

comp'ete (9-11) work, play or run with other persons and try to be best; try to win something desired by several other persons, e.g. trade.

competent (5-1-9) able or fit for certain work; having the necessary power or right to do an act; **competency** (5-1-9-si) enough skill or knowledge for a task; enough money to live on.

compet'ition (5-1-1shn) act of *competing* (2nd above).

comp'ile (9-41) collect and arrange facts in order.

compl'acent (9-21s) satisfied with oneself.

compl'ain (9-21) express dislike, pain, etc.; make one's difficulties or troubles known; n. **a compl'aint**, act of complaining; illness.

compl'aisant (9-21z) yielding to the wishes of others and eager to please.

complement (5-1-9) that thing or amount necessary to make up a whole; all the officers and men necessary for a ship.

compl'ete (9-11) to finish; make whole; adj. whole, finished.

complex (5-2) not simple; having many parts; **a complex** (in the mind), set of ideas or desires (which one does not know that one possesses, yet which have an effect upon one's behaviour).

compl'exion (9-2kshn) colour of the face; *To put a different complexion on it* = to make a thing appear different.

compl'iance (9-419-s) agreement; yielding; **compl'iant**, ready to agree.

complicate (5-1-21) make difficult or hard to understand; n. **complic'ation**.

compl'icity (9-1s1-1) share in wrong-doing.

compliment (5-1-2) express admiration for another; **a compliment** (5-1-9) expression of ——.

compl'y (9-41) to yield; agree.

comp'onent (part) (9-67-9) a necessary part which makes up the whole.

comp'ort (oneself) (9-55) behave.

comp'ose (9-67z) put together; *To compose poetry, music* = to write; **comp'osed**, calm.

composite (5-9zI) made up of different parts.

compos'ition (5-9zIshn) act of putting together; arrangement of objects in a picture; way in which things are mixed to make something, e.g. a dish of food, earth for growing plants, a medicine, etc.; short piece of writing or music; agreement about paying debts.

comp'ositor (9-5zI-19) one who sets up *type* (=metal letters from which books are printed).

c'ompos m'entis (5-5 + 2-1) not mad.

comp'osure (9-6739) calmness.

comp'ound (9-47) mix together; *To compound a debt* = pay off a debt by one large payment less than the whole amount owed; *To compound a felony* = help in an unlawful act.

c'ompound (5-47) adj. made up of several different materials; n. a mixture; (chemical) joining of two substances so that a new substance is produced, e.g. acid + metal.

compreh'end (5-1-2) take all into consideration; understand.

compr'ess (9-2) press tightly together; **a c'ompress** (5-2) piece of wet cloth tied tightly on to a wound; **compr'ession** (9-2shn) act of pressing together; (in a motor-car) mixing and pressing of gases before firing.

compr'ise (9-41z) contain; be made up of.

compromise (5-9-41z) give up a part of one's beliefs in order to agree with another person; *To compromise oneself* = make people think that one may have done wrong.

comptr'oller (9n-67-9) public officer who examines accounts of money.

comp'ulsory (9-8-9-1) that which must be done; brought about by force.

comp'unction (9-8ngkshn) pity; sorrow for a cruel act.

comp'ute (9-177) find out the amount; add, divide, etc.

comrade (5-1) friend, fellow-worker.

con- with, together.

con (5) learn by reading over and over.

concaten'ation (9-3-1-21shn) chain of (events).

c'onc'ave (5-21) curved inwards.

conc'eal (9-s1I) hide; keep from being known.

conc'ede (9-s1I) give away; yield after disagreeing.

conc'eited (9-s11-1) having too good an opinion of oneself.

conc'eive (9-s11) think of; imagine; begin to produce young.

concentrate (5-s9-21) bring together (e.g. soldiers) to one point; increase the strength of a liquid by boiling it down; *I shall concentrate on* = give my whole mind to.

c'oncentr'ation camp (5-9-21shn + 3) prison camp for people who give trouble to the government.

conc'entric (5-s2-1) having the same centre.

concept (5-s2) idea.

conc'eption (9-s2-shn) act of *conceiving* (5th above); *A splendid conception* = a good idea.

conc'ern (9-s99) have to do with; *To be concerned about* = be anxious about; *A matter of great concern* = serious matter, my business or duty; *A going concern* = active business now really working; *A paying concern* = successful business.

concert (5-s9) meeting for hearing music; *Done in concert* = done by all in agreement with each other; **to conc'ert** *plans* (9-s99) = talk together and arrange things.

conc'ession (9-s2shn) act of yielding after a disagreement; special right given by government, e.g. the right to get oil in a certain place.

conch (5ngk) a long shell pointed at one end, sometimes blown like a horn.

conc'iliate (9-s1-121) gain the friendship of.

conc'ise (9-s41s) short, putting much meaning into a few words or small space.

conclave (5-21) secret meeting.

concl'ude (9-77) bring to an end; decide;

concl'usion (9-773n) end, result obtained after reasoning.

conc'oct (9-5) make by mixing; *Concoct a story* = make up an untrue —.

conc'omitant (9-5-1-9) that which goes with something else, e.g. *Music is the usual concomitant of feasting.*

concord (5ngk55) agreement; peace; **conc'ordat** (5-55-3) friendly agreement, e.g. between governments.

concourse (5ngk55s) meeting of many people.

concrete (5ngk-11) formed into one mass; real; stone-like material used for roads, buildings, etc.; *A concrete noun* = word which is the name of a real thing, not of a quality.

conc'ur (9-99) meet at one point; agree.

conc'ussion (9-8shn) a shaking; loss of all the senses caused by a blow on the head.

cond'emn (9-2) to blame; declare punishment for wrong-doing; declare as not fit for use.

cond'ense (9-2) press together; express the meaning in fewer words.

cond'enser (9-2-9) part of a machine which makes gas into liquid; instrument which stores electricity; curved glass which brings light together into a beam.

condesc'end (5-1-2) bring oneself down to the level of a person of less wisdom or importance, and make clear one's greatness in doing so.

cond'ign (punishment) (9-41) well deserved, and well suited to the wrong act.

condiment (5-1-9) matter added to food to make it taste nicer.

cond'ition (9-1shn) (1) state; *In good condition* = clean, strong, etc.; (2) rank; (3) *On condition that* = if; *To impose conditions* = promise to do A if B and C are done.

cond'itioned r'eflex (9-1shnd + 11-2) the flow of liquid to the mouth at the sight of food is a reflex; this reflex may be changed (conditioned) so that there is a flow at the sound of a dinner bell. So also other reflexes.

cond'ole (9-67) express pity for.

cond'one (9-67) forgive; pretend not to see.

cond'uce (9-177s) help to produce; adj. **cond'ucive** (——1).

cond'uct (9-8) lead a person (e.g. to a seat); allow to pass, e.g. *Metal conducts electricity*; control and lead persons playing music; *To conduct oneself* = behave; *To conduct a business, a war* = carry on; **a cond'uctor** (——9) man controlling players of music, the man in charge of a street-car; **c'onduct** (5-9) behaviour.

CONE

conduit (5-1) large pipe or underground way for water, etc.

cone (67) figure (drawing) or shape with a round bottom and pointed top; fruit of a certain kind of tree, e.g. *fir*-trees.

conf'abulate (9-3-17-21) talk together; **a confabul'ation**—this word is used in speaking lightly of a serious talk.

FIR-CONE

conf'ectionery (9-2-sh9-1) cakes and sweets; **conf'ectioner** (9-2-sh9-9) one who sells —.

conf'ederate (9-2-9-9) joined by agreement for a common purpose; **confeder'ation** (——21shn) group formed in this way.

conf'er (upon) (9-99) give (an honour) to; *Confer with* = talk to and get the ideas of; **c'onference** (5-9-9-s) meeting for talking about some business or for learning each other's ideas on some subject.

conf'ess (9-2) tell one's faults and wrong-doings; tell one's beliefs; **conf'essor** (——9) a priest who hears others confess.

conf'etti (9-2-1) small pieces of coloured paper which are thrown at newly-married people as they leave the church.

conf'ide (9-41) to trust; tell secrets to a trusted person.

confid'ential (5-1-2-shl) told as a secret; **c'onfidence** (5-1-s) feeling of trust; a secret told to another person; *I tell this in confidence* = I tell this to you but you must keep it secret; *A confidential manner* = — as of telling a secret.

conf'ine (9-41) keep shut in, e.g. *Confined to the house by illness*; **conf'ined**, in the act of giving birth to a child; **conf'inement** (——9) state of being shut in; act of giving birth.

conf'irm (9-99) make sure; **confirm'ation** (5-9-21shn) *service* (= religious ceremony) held in the Christian Church at which a child makes a solemn promise to live a good life; *A confirmed bachelor* (= unmarried man) = one who will never marry.

confiscate (5-1-21) seize a person's land or goods as a punishment.

conflagr'ation (5-9-21shn) great fire.

conflict (5-1) a fight; disagreement; **to confl'ict** (9-1).

confluence (5-79-s) a flowing together, e.g. of rivers into one stream.

conf'orm (9-55) to be shaped according to the form of —; to act according to law or custom; *In* **conf'ormity** (9-55-1-1) *with* = according to.

conf'ound (9-47) mix together and cause disorder; make one unable to understand; *Confound you!* = cry of anger; Sl. *A confounded long time* = a very —.

confrère (5-29) one who does the same kind of work as another.

confr'ont (9-8) bring face to face with; meet face to face.

conf'use (9-177z) mix together; throw into disorder; mistake one thing for another.

conf'ute (9-177) prove to be untrue.

congé, to take one's — (k5ⁿ321) say good-bye.

cong'eal (9nj11) become thick, as blood does in air; become hard.

cong'enial (9nj11-19) suiting one's likes and dislikes.

cong'enital (9nj2-1) inborn, e.g. disease.

conger (5ngg9) large snake-like fish caught for food.

cong'est (9nj2) collect into a mass; **cong'ested** (——1) too full, e.g. of people, of blood.

congl'omerate (9n·g-5-(-21) collect into a mass; adj. made of differe. t things or materials stuck together.

congr'atulate (9n·g-3-17· .1) express pleasure at another's good fortur.e.

congregate (5ngg-1-21) meet together; **congreg'ation**, large gathering of people, e.g. in a church for prayer.

congress (5ngg-2) a coming together of people; group of persons who make laws in America.

congruent (5ngg-79) being in agreement; able to be fitted one on the top of another.

conic, conical (5-1) having to do with a *cone* (= a figure round at the bottom and pointed at the top).

conj'ecture (9-2-tsh9) to guess, a guess.

conjugal (5-7) having to do, with marriage.

conjugate (5-7-21) give the forms of a *verb* (= a kind of word, e.g. "to be," "to do").

conj'unction (9-8ngkshn) a joining; kind of word which joins words or groups of words, e.g. "And", "But".

conjure (8-9) call up a spirit of the dead; **conjuring** (——1) *tricks* = clever tricks of a magical kind done to amuse; **conj'ure** (9-79) give a solemn order.

conk out (5ngk + 47) Sl. (of a car or machine) fail, stop.

conn'ect (9-2) join together; **conn'exion**, **conn'ection** (9-2-shn) state of being joined; way in which one thing or idea depends on another; a person who belongs to one's family by marriage, not by blood; *She is well-connected* = comes of a good family and has married into a good family; *The shop has a good connexion* = is known and used by a large number of people.

conning-tower (5-1 + 479) low armoured tower on a warship used by the officers guiding the ship.

conn'ive (9-41) help wrong-doers secretly; pretend not to see wrong-doing.

connoiss'eur (5-1-99) one who has special taste in, and knowledge of objects of art and beauty.

conn'ote (9-67) have another meaning besides the main or direct meaning, e.g. "Feminine" means of a woman, of a female — it *connotes* also gentleness and women's arts of pleasing.

conn'ubial (9-177-19) having to do with marriage.

conquer (5ngk9) take (a country) by force, e.g. by an army; win a victory over; **conquest** (5ngkw2) thing conquered.

consangu'ineous (5-3nggwi-19) of the same blood or family.

conscience (5-shg-s) inner feeling which tells one about matters of right and wrong; *Conscience money* = money paid because one feels one ought to pay it, not because one is forced.

conscious (5nsh9) awake and knowing; known to the thinking mind, e.g. *He did it consciously, not unconsciously* = he did it and knew that he was doing it; **consciousness** (——1) power of the mind to feel and know; *To lose consciousness* = to faint.

conscript (5-1) one who is forced by law to become a soldier; n. **conscr'iption** (9-1-shn).

consecrate (5-1-21) make holy; give for the use of God and the Church; n. **consecr'ation**.

cons'ecutive (9-2-17-1) following in order.

cons'ensus (of opinion) (9-2-9) a general agreement.

cons'ent (9-2) agree; allow; be willing; n. permission.

consequence (5-1-9-s) result; *Of no consequence* = unimportant; **consequent**, following as a result; **consequ'ential** (5-1-2-shl) following as a result, having important effects.

cons'ervancy (9-99-9-s1) group of persons given the duty of preserving forests or rivers; group of men who keep a town clean.

c'onserv'ation (5-9-21shn) keeping from decay or from being destroyed.

cons'ervative (9-99-9-1) wishing to keep things as they are; one who does not want to make many or large changes in the laws.

cons'ervatoire (9999-9-744) school of music or art.

cons'ervatory (9-99-9-9-1) glass house for flowers; school of music or art.

cons'erve (9-99) keep safe; keep from decay; cook fruit with sugar so that it can be kept for a long time; **cons'erves** (——z) fruit so cooked.

cons'ider (9-1-9) think about; hold a certain opinion; *To consider others* = think of the feelings and wishes of others.

cons'iderable (9-1-9) worth considering; rather important; large.

cons'iderate (9-1-9-1) kind, thinking of other people's good.

cons'ign (9-41) send; put in charge of a person; **a consignment** (——9) set of goods sent, e.g. to a trader for selling.

cons'ist (9-1) be made up of.

cons'istency (9-1-9-s1) (of matter) thickness, solidity; (of a person) quality of being *consistent* (below).

cons'istent (9-1-9) agreeing with oneself; acting according to one's ideas.

cons'ole (9-67) to help or comfort in sorrow; n. **consol'ation** (5 9 21shn).

cons'olidate (9-5-1-21) bring together and make strong; make firm.

cons'ols (9-5-z). In 1751 all the different debts of the British Government were made into one single debt at the same *interest* (= yearly payment on a debt). These united debts are called *Consols*.

cons'ommé (9-5-21) clear *soup* (= water in which meat and vegetables have been boiled).

consonant (5-9-9) (in music) pleasant when sounded together; speech sound of a letter, other than a, e, i, o, u (y, w).

consort (5-55) husband or wife of a king or queen or ruler; ship sailing under the protection of another; *To cons'ort with* (9-55) = go about in the company of.

consp'ectus (9-2-9) general view, idea, or short account of a whole subject.

consp'icuous (9-1-179) very noticeable, clearly seen.

consp'iracy (9-1-9s1) secret plan to do an unlawful act; secret plan to change the government by force; **to consp'ire** (9-419).

constable (8-9) policeman; **const'abulary** (9-3-17-9-1) all the police; adj. having to do with the police.

constant (5-9) remaining unchanged; faithful.

c'onstell'ation (5-9-21shn) group of stars.

c'onstern'ation (5-9-21shn) feeling of great surprise and fear.

constipated (5-1-21-1) having great difficulty in clearing waste matter from the body; n. **constip'ation**.

const'ituency (9-1-179-s1) group of people who elect a man to the government; the people who support a business, e.g. buying from it.

const'ituent (9-1-179) forming part of a whole; *Constituent assembly* = group of law-givers who have power to change the form of government.

constitute (5-1-177) set up; appoint a person or group and give power to act; *Her gentleness constitutes her real charm* = makes up, is.

c'onstit'ution (5-1-177shn) a setting up; *He has a good constitution* = he has good health; *The Constitution* = laws upon which the government of a country is built up; *A constitutional* = a walk.

constr'ain (9-21) use force and make a person do a certain act.

constr'ict (9-1) press together tightly.

constr'uct (9-8) build; **constr'uction** (——shn) anything built; the act or way of building; *He put a bad construction on my words* = he gave them a bad meaning; **constr'uctive** (——1) which helps to build up rather than break down or destroy.

constr'ue (9-77) explain part by part; put into another language; *His speech was construed as an attack on the government* = was understood as —.

consul (5) elected judge or officer of government in ancient Rome; government officer living in a foreign city to help the trade and people of his country; **consulate** (5-17-1) house and office of a consul.

cons'ult (9-8) seek the advice of another.

cons'ume (9-177) use up, destroy.

cons'umer goods (9-177-9 + 7) see Capital goods.

c'onsummate (5-9-21) make perfect; to finish; **cons'ummate** (9-8-1) adj. perfect, complete; *A consummate ass* = very foolish person.

cons'umption (9-8-shn) act of using up; amount used; disease of the *lungs* (= that part of the body with which we breathe); **a cons'umptive** (9-8-1) one who is suffering from consumption (*tuberculosis*).

contact (5-3) a touching; spot where something touches; joining-place of two electric wires; *To contact him* = go and talk to him.

cont'agious (disease) (9-21j9) able to be passed on by touch.

cont'ain (9-21) hold within itself; hold in; *He could scarcely contain himself* = prevent himself speaking; **a cont'ainer** (——9) vessel used to contain anything.

cont'aminate (9-3-1-21) make dirty; have a bad effect on.

cont'emn (9-2) consider bad or worthless.

contemplate (5-9-21) look at and think about; *I contémplate giving up my work here next year* = I am planning to —.

cont'empor'aneous (9-2-9-21-19) living at the same time; happening at the same time.

cont'emporary (9-2-9-9-1) one who lives at the same time as another; *A contemporary account* = story of an event told by one who lived at that time.

cont'empt (9-2) feeling caused by something low, worthless and wholly bad; the act of showing this feeling; *Contempt of court* = disobeying a judge; **cont'emptible** (———1) worthy of *contempt*.

cont'end (9-2) to struggle; struggle to make another believe in one's opinions; *I contend that* —— = I am trying to make you believe that ——; to quarrel.

cont'ent (9-2) satisfied; feeling easy in one's mind; *I am content to* —— = willing ——.

c'ontent (5-2) what is contained (in a book, speech, etc.); **the Contents,** a list of the chapters at the beginning of a book.

cont'ention (9-2-shn) opinion; quarrel or disagreement; **cont'entious** (9-2-shs) causing disagreement; eager to start a quarrel or disagreement.

cont'est (9-2) disagree with an opinion; struggle or fight against others in order to gain something; **a c'ontest** (5-2) struggle or fight.

context (5-2) place in a book or speech in which a particular word or group of words is found.

cont'iguous (9-1-179) near; touching.

continence (5-1-9-s) control of one's desires; adj. **continent** (5-1-9).

continent (5-1-9) one of the six large bodies of land in the world.

cont'ingent (9-1nj9) uncertain; which will happen if some other thing happens.

cont'inue (9-1-177) go on without stopping; go on again after a pause.

c'ontin'uity (5-1-1771-1) whole story written out ready for making into a cinema film.

cont'ort (9-55) bend out of natural shape; **a cont'ortionist** (———sh9-1) one who bends his (her) body into strange shapes to amuse people.

contour (5-79) shape, e.g. of land, mountains, etc.; line on a map showing all parts of the country which are of the same height.

contra- against; opposite.

contraband (5-9-3) goods which may not be brought into a country (or taken out) especially in time of war; unlawful trade in such goods.

contr'act (9-3) draw together and become smaller as metal does when cold; *To contract an illness* = become ill; **a c'ontract** (5-3) promise to do something, e.g. a written promise to supply goods or do work at a certain price.

c'ontrad'ict (5-9-1) declare that a thing just said is not true; say the opposite.

contr'alto (9-44-67 or 9-3-67) deep singing voice of a woman.

contr'aption (9-3-shn) Sl. any new and strange-looking machine or instrument.

contr'ariwise (9-29-1-41z) in the opposite way; looking at the question in the opposite way.

c'ontrary (5-9-1) opposite; unfavourable; **contr'ary** (9-29-1) *a contrary person* = one who always does the opposite of what is wanted.

contr'ast (9-44) put side by side so as to show the difference; appear very different when set side by side; n. **c'ontrast** (5-44) a very noticeable difference.

contrav'ene (5-9-11) go against, e.g. break a law or go against a custom.

c'ontret'emps (5ⁿ-9-44ⁿ) unexpected and unfortunate event.

contr'ibute (9-1-17) give with others for a common purpose, e.g. for some good cause; *To contribute to a newspaper* = write something for ——; **a contrib'ution** (5-1-177shn).

contrite (5-41) sorry for wrong-doing.

contr'ive (9-41) think of a clever way of doing; cause an event to happen by some clever plan, or after some difficulty; *He contrived to ruin the whole business* = the result of his work was that he ruined ——.

contr'ol (9-67) to direct, guide, rule; *A control experiment* (= trial) = doing the same work twice to be sure it is right.

controversy (5-9-99-1) disagreement; quarrelling; **controv'ersial** (5-9-99shl) difficult and causing controversy; **c'ontrov'ert** (5-9-99) show that an opinion is not correct.

c'ontum'acious (5-17-21sh9) not willing to obey; **c'ontumely** (5-17-1) state of being proud, rude and unwilling to obey orders.

cont'use (9-177z) cause damage to the body by a blow without breaking the skin.

con'undrum (9-8-9) clever saying the meaning of which must be guessed; a question to which there is an amusing answer, e.g. "When is a door not a door? When it's *ajar*" (= half-open) (a jar = a pot).

c'onval'esce (5-9-2) get better by resting after an illness.

conv'ene (9-11) call together the members for a meeting.

conv'enient (9-11-19) suiting one's time and needs, causing comfort; **conv'enience** (———s) quality of being convenient; comfort; *At your convenience* = when and how you choose; *A marriage of convenience* = —— not for love; any useful thing which causes comfort; *A convenience* = a *lavatory*; *Make a convenience of a person* = use to suit one's own purposes.

convent (5-9) building, usually with high walls round it, in which religious women live apart from the world, giving their time to prayer, study and good works.

conv'enticle (9-2-1) small building used for prayer to God, e.g. by persons who are not members of the Church of England.

conv'ention (9-2-shn) (1) large meeting usually

continuing for several days; (2) custom or rule of good behaviour; **conv'entional**, usual, according to the general rules, manners or ideas.
conv'erge (9-99j) come together at one point.
conv'ersant with (5-9-9 + 1ŏ) having a knowledge of.
c'onvers'ation (5-9-21shn) act of talking; friendly talk; **to conv'erse** (9-99) talk together in a friendly way.
c'onverse (5-99) the opposite; opposite.
conv'ert (9-99) to change from one state into another, e.g. *Convert the sitting-room into a bedroom*; change beliefs or opinions, especially one's beliefs in God; cause another to change his beliefs; use another person's money or public money as one's own; a **c'onvert** (5-9) one who has changed his beliefs; n. **conv'ersion** (9-99shn).
c'onv'ex (5-2) curved outwards like an o.
conv'ey (9-21) carry; take from one place to another; give ideas to another; give land or a house to another by a written paper according to law; **conv'eyance** (9-219-s) carriage; act of conveying.
conv'ict (9-1) prove wrong-doing in a court of law; a **c'onvict** (5-1) one who is being punished in prison for breaking the law.
conv'iction (9-1-shn) what one believes to be true or right; act of proving wrong-doing in a court of law.
conv'ince (9-1-s) satisfy by showing proof; to cause to believe.
conv'ivial (9-1-19) merry; being happy together.
c'onvoc'ation (5-9-21shn) act of calling together a meeting; a meeting; **conv'oke** (9-67) call together.
c'onvol'ute(d) (5-9-177) rolled together, rolled up; **c'onvol'utions** (——shnz)—of the brain, *wrinkles* (= small fold on the surface of material) in the grey matter of the brain.
convoy (5-51) go with in order to protect; number of soldiers going with supply-carts as a guard — also of warships going with supply ships.
conv'ulse (9-8) shake with great force, e.g. *He was convulsed with laughter*; *The country was convulsed with war*; **conv'ulsion** (9-8-shn) shaking of the limbs or whole body caused by illness.
cony, coney (67-1) wild rabbit.
coo (77) noise made by a certain kind of bird (e.g. a *dove*); *To bill and coo* = to make love.
cook (7) prepare food by boiling, baking, etc.; **a cook**, servant who prepares and cooks food; *To cook accounts* = make accounts of money look correct although they are untrue; *I'll cook his goose* = ruin his plans; **cookery** (7-9-1) art of cooking.
cookie, cooky (7-1) Am. thin, dry, sweet cake.
cool (77) not warm; calm; Sl. *I call that pretty cool*; *He's a cool customer* = daring (in a bad meaning).

coolie (77-1) old word for one who did rough work in India, China, etc.
coon (songs) (77) songs of African slaves in America.
coop (77) cage for animals, especially hens; *To coop up* = enclose in a small space.
cooper (77-9) one who makes barrels.
co-'operate (675-9-21) help one another in a common aim; **co-'operative** (675-9-9-1) working together; **co-'operative store**, special kind of shop where those who buy have a share of the money which is gained by selling.
co-'opted (member) (675-1) member of a group elected by those already in the group.
co-'ordinate (6755-1-21) cause to work together for the same purpose.
coot (77) water bird like a duck with a white spot on its head.
cop (5) Sl. catch, catch a wrong-doer; Sl. a policeman.
cope with (67 + 1ŏ) deal successfully with a difficulty.
coping (67-1) sloping stones on the top of a wall to throw off the rain.
copious (67-19) plentiful, found in plenty.
copper (5-9) red metal; piece of money of low value; large container in which clothes are boiled to clean them.
c'opper-plate (5-9 + 21) flat piece of metal on which fine writing is cut, used in printing; **c'opper-pl'ate wr'iting** (41-1) very good handwriting.
coppice (5-1s) group of bushes or small trees.
copra (5-9) dried inside of the *coconut* (= a large nut found in hot countries) used to make soil rich.
copse (5-s) group of bushes or small trees.
copy (5-1) thing made exactly like something else; make a thing just like another; write exactly what is set down on another paper; written matter ready to be printed; one printed book, e.g. *A copy of the Bible*; **copyright** (——41) protect by law something which one has written so that others may not print it without asking and being allowed; **the copyright**, right of printing a work. (Copyright covers also pictures and music.)
coqu'ette (67k2) woman who amuses herself by making men fall in love with her.
coracle (5-9) boat made of a large basket covered with leather.
coral (5) white or red stone-like material made by creatures in the ocean; red-brown colour.

CORACLE

cord (55) thick string; string-like part of the body; *Corded cloth* = having raised lines on it like strings; measure of wood cut ready for burning (128 *cubic feet*; *cubic foot* = 1 ft. × 1 ft. × 1 ft.).

cordage (55-1j) number of cords and ropes, e.g. those on a sailing ship.

cordial (55-19) (1) friendly; warm (feelings); (2) pleasant drink, e.g. made from fruit.

cordite (55-41) yellow glass-like threads or plates made from cotton and certain acids and used in place of gunpowder.

cordon (55-9) line of soldiers, policemen, etc., set round as a guard; broad band of silk worn as a mark of rank or honour.

corduroy (55-9-51) thick (cotton) material with raised lines on it.

core (55) heart or centre of a thing; in fruit, part where the seeds are.

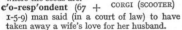

CORGI (SCOOTER)

c'o-respondent (67 + 1-5-9) man said (in a court of law) to have taken away a wife's love for her husband.

corgi (55-1) small dog; small motor-cycle, as shown.

cork (55) bark (= outside covering) of a tree, often made into round pieces used to close the hole in a bottle; **to cork**, put a cork in a bottle; *Corked wine* = wine which has got a bad taste because of a bad cork;

CORGI (DOG)

corkage (55-1j) money paid on strong drink brought by a guest into a hotel; **corkscrew** (55-77) instrument for pulling corks from bottles.

cormorant (55-9) bird used by the Chinese to catch fish.

corn (55) (English) any grain-bearing plant; grain of any such plant; Am., plant bearing a large yellow grain (called in England Maize or Indian corn);

CORKSCREW

c'ornc'ob (55-5) head of this plant; pipe (for smoking) made of it.

corn (55) hard thick skin on the foot caused by rubbing of the shoe; *Tread on a person's corns* = cause anger by speaking ill of his strongest opinions.

cornea (55-19) thin glassy covering of the eye.

corned (meat) (55) cooked salted meat, usually in a square tin.

corner (55-9) that part of a room where two sides meet; bend in a road; *To turn the corner* = get out of danger (e.g. in an illness);

CORNCOB

to corner, drive a person into a difficult place from which he cannot get out; buy up the whole supply of something so as to raise the price.

cornerstone (55-9-67) special stone put at a corner of a new building.

cornet (55-1) brass instrument of music— a kind of horn.

cornflour (55-479) flour made from *Indian corn* (see 7th above).

cornice (55-1s) ornamental line of wood or stone, put at the top of a building or at the top of a wall in a room.

corny (joke) (55-1) Am. Sl. old, often heard before.

cor'olla (9-5-9) ring of *petals* (= coloured leaves) round the seed-forming part of a flower.

cor'ollary (9-5-9-1) result which follows naturally from proving something else.

coron'ation (5-9-21shn) crowning of a king.

COROLLA

coroner (5-9-9) officer of the law who inquires into the causes of sudden death, fires, and judges the ownership of any money, gold, jewels, etc., found by accident, e.g. hidden in the ground.

coronet (5-9-1) small crown worn by a nobleman.

corporal (55-9) having to do with the body; *Corporal punishment* = punishment by beating.

corporal (55-9) rank in the army (1. common soldier, 2. lance-corporal, 3. corporal).

corporate (55-9-9) united in a group and given power by law to do business acting as one person; forming one group.

corpor'ation (55-9-21shn) number of persons allowed by law to act as one, e.g. for purposes of business; group of persons who have charge of the public business of an English town; Sl. *He has a big corporation* = stomach.

corp'oreal (55-55-19) having a material body.

corps (55) large body of soldiers; of officers of government; of dancers.

corpse (55) human dead body.

corpulent (55-17-9) fat, especially round the middle of the body.

corpuscle (55-8) very small piece of matter, e.g. red and white corpuscles of the blood.

corr'al (5-44) circular fence in which animals are kept prisoners.

corr'ect (9-2) right; according to rule or custom; **to corr'ect**, set right; mark the mistakes in written work; punish.

correlate (5-9-21) show how two things depend on each other.

corresp'ond (5-1-5) write letters to and receive letters from a person; be in agreement with, e.g. *His house corresponds to his wealth* = he has a big house because he is very rich; *Correspondent of a newspaper* = person who sends news and other writings to be printed in the paper.

corridor (5-1-55) narrow covered way joining two buildings, or two parts of one building; narrow piece of land; *A corridor train* = train with a place along which one can walk from one carriage to another.

corrig'endum (5-1j2-9) mistake pointed out for correction in a printed book.

corr'oborate (9-5-9-21) find further proof strengthening proof obtained already; make sure.

corr'ode (9-67) eat away slowly; e.g. an acid acting on metal.

corrugated (iron) (5-7-21-1) sheets of iron pressed into many small waves.

corr'upt (9-8) decayed; doing wrong for money; **to corr'upt,** *bribe* (= to give money to) a person to make him do wrong; make someone evil.

corsage (55-443) upper part of a woman's dress.

corsair (55-29) one who attacks and steals from ships at sea.

corset (55-1) stiff under-garment worn by women to give a good shape to the body.

corslet, corselet (55-1) armour for the body.

cortège (55-213) number of persons following solemnly one behind another, e.g. at a funeral.

cortex (55-2) outer shell of anything.

coruscate (5-9-21) to flash, shine.

corv'ée (55-21) forced labour.

cosh (5) instrument used for hitting a person on the head.

cosm'etics (5z-2-1) liquids, powders, etc., used by women to make the skin, hair and face beautiful.

cosmic (5z-1) having to do with the *universe* (= all the worlds and stars in the sky, everything that is).

cosmic rays (+ 21z) waves of force, like radio waves but much shorter, coming into the air around the earth from outside.

cosmop'olitan (5z-9-5-1) having the world for one's country; feeling at home in any country; *Cosmopolitan city* = a city in which peoples of many nations live.

cosmos (5z-5) order; all the stars and worlds in the sky considered as an ordered arrangement.

cosset (5-1) treat very tenderly, e.g. a sick child.

cost (5) price to be paid; *Cost price* = selling price equal to the cost of making; *Costs* = the cost of having a *case* (= question, quarrel, matter) decided in a court of law; *At all costs* = the cost does not matter; **to cost,** cause payment of money, or work; cause loss; count the cost.

coster, costermonger (5-9-8ngg9) one who sells fruit, plants, etc., on the street from a cart.

costly (5-1) sold at a high price.

costume (5-177) dress, especially of woman; special dress, e.g. that of an actor.

cost'umier (5-177-19) one who makes and sells women's dresses.

cosy (67zI) comfortable; cloth covering put over a tea-pot to keep it hot.

cot (5) small bed, e.g. for a child; small house.

-cote, house or shelter for birds or animals, e.g. **d'ovecote** (8-9) = house for *doves* (= kind of bird).

c'oterie (67-9-11) group of people who are very friendly and help each other.

cottage (5-1j) small house; *Cottage loaf* = bread made in the shape of two round masses stuck one on top of the other.

cotton (5) soft white material obtained from a plant; cloth made of this material; thread made from this material; Sl. *I don't cotton on to him* = do not like him.

couch (47) low bed; long low chair; **to couch,** lay oneself down; hold a spear ready for attack; *A demand couched in very polite form* = expressed very politely.

cough (5f) force air from the throat suddenly and with noise, usually in trying to get some matter out of the throat.

council (47-s) a meeting for making plans; group of elected persons, or persons chosen to carry on some special business.

counsel (47-s) advice; *To keep one's own counsel* = say nothing about one's plans; *A counsel of perfection* = good plan which cannot be carried out; **a counsel,** adviser on matters of law, a lawyer who speaks in the law-courts.

count (47) say the numbers in order; add up or find the whole number of a set of things; take into one's counting, e.g. *I did not count the baby*; *He does not count* = is of no importance; *To count oneself fortunate* = consider —; *May I count on you?* = trust you to help me.

count (47) title of a foreign nobleman.

countenance (47-1-9-s) appearance of the face; *Keep one's countenance* = show no feeling; *Put out of countenance* = cause to show shame; *I cannot countenance it* = not say that I am in favour of it.

counter (47-9) long table, e.g. in a shop where goods are shown or money is paid.

counter (47-9) small circular piece of bone or other material used instead of money in playing any game.

counter (47-9) make an opposite movement of any kind; strike back at.

counter- (47-9) used to make meanings that have the idea of opposite, fighting against, e.g. **c'ounter'act** (47-9-3) act against and bring to nothing.

counterfeit (47-9-1) bad money made for a dishonest purpose; any bad thing made like a good one for a dishonest purpose.

counterfoil (47-9-51) part of a written piece of paper, e.g. receipt torn off and kept for making up accounts.

c'ounterm'and (47-9-44) give a command to stop another command.

counterm'ine (47-9-41) make a *mine* (= deep hole under the ground used for putting explosives under a wall to blow it up) under the ground in order to destroy another mine being made by the enemy.

counterpane (47-9-21) outer covering on a bed.

counterpart (47-9-44) that which is exactly like something else; thing which is like another but just opposite, e.g. the right and left hand.

counterp'oised (47-9-5ɪz) condition of having the same weight on both ends; **a c'ounterpoise,** weight used for this purpose.

countershaft (47-9-44) the engine turns a wheel on the countershaft and the countershaft turns one of several wheels on the machine or car, so giving changes of speed.

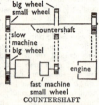
COUNTERSHAFT

countersign (47-9-4ɪ) write one's name as second name on a paper; *Give the countersign* = give the correct answer to a soldier on guard, thus showing that you are not an enemy.

countersink (47-9-ɪngk) make a hole for the head of a screw so that it may go down level with the surface.

countess (47-ɪ) title of the wife of an *earl* (in Britain), of a *count* (in other countries).

countrified (8-ɪ-4ɪ) as of the country, without the manners and customs of the city.

country (8-ɪ) piece of land; land of one nation; open land, not town; adj. of the country—not town, e.g. *A country house and a town house*; **a countryman** (——9) one who is not of the town; one who is from the same country or nation.

county (47-ɪ) one of the parts into which England is divided, e.g. Yorkshire, Devonshire, etc.

coup (77) a blow; successful piece of business; **coup d'ét'at** (+ 2ɪ-44) sudden act of government making a great change; **coup de grâce** (+ 9 + 44s) finishing stroke causing death.

coupé (77-2ɪ) closed carriage or motor-car with only one seat, usually for two persons; carriage in a train having a seat on one side only.

couple (8) two; put together in pairs.

couplet (8-ɪ) pair of lines in a poem that end with the same sound and usually contain a complete idea.

coupling (8-ɪ) joining of two things; an instrument on the end of a railway carriage which joins it on to the next carriage.

coupon (77-5) any small printed paper showing that one has a right to goods, a seat, payment, etc.

courage (8-ɪj) quality of being brave; *Dutch courage* = feeling of courage produced by strong drink; adj. **cour'ageous** (9-2ɪjə).

courier (7-ɪ9) runner who carries important messages; one who goes with travellers to help them and show them the sights.

course (55s) (ɪ) onward movement e.g. *The course of life*; *In the course of* = during; *In due course* = at the proper time; (2) the path of movement, e.g. *The course of a river*; *The course of a ship*; *A course of action* = plan of action; (3) space specially marked out for a game or for races; (4) set of things which follow one after another, e.g. *A course of lessons*; *A four-course dinner* = dinner with four different sets of dishes served one after another; *Of course* = naturally, certainly; *A matter of course* = the natural thing; **to course,** hunt, run quickly; **courser** (55-9) swift horse.

court (55) small open place with walls or buildings on all sides; meeting of law officers to question and punish wrong-doers or to decide quarrels; level place marked with lines for playing a game; king, his family and officers living in the palace; *To hold a court* = hold a gathering in the presence of the king.

court (55) attend a lady and give her favours in order to win her in marriage; seek a person's favour.

courteous (99-ɪ9) very polite; **courtesy** (99-ɪ-ɪ) politeness.

courtier (55-ɪ9) person who attends at a king's court.

courtly (55-ɪ) very polite.

c'ourt m'artial (+ 44shl) court of law in the army; **to court-m'artial,** try a soldier in such a court.

c'ourt plaster (+ 44-9) specially prepared silk used for sticking on to a small cut or wound.

c'ourtyard (55-44) space with walls or buildings on all sides.

cousin (8z) child of the brother or sister of one's parents; *Second cousin* = child of one's parent's first cousin.

cout'urier (77-ɪ79-ɪ9) maker of expensive dresses for women.

cove (67) small *bay* (= inlet in the coast); Sl. *A queer cove* = — fellow.

covenant (8-ɪ-9) solemn promise or agreement.

Coventry (5-9-ɪ) *to send to* —, refuse to speak to a person.

cover (8-9) (ɪ) put one material over the surface of another, e.g. *The snow covered the hills*; (2) protect, hide; (3) protect oneself from loss; *I am covered against fire* = I have made arrangements so that I shall be paid any losses caused by fire (see Insurance); (4) deal with; *This law covers all such matters* = all such matters come under the law; *This book covers the whole subject* = tells about; (5) pass over, e.g. *To cover the distance*; **a cover,** top, e.g. for a pot; outside boards of a book; cloth put on a bed; place set for one person at table; *Under cover of darkness* = hidden by; *Under cover of friendship* = while pretending to be a friend; *To break cover* = run out of hiding.

coverlet (8-9-ɪ) outer covering of a bed.

covert (8-9) covered, secret; wood where birds and small animals take shelter.

covet (8-ɪ) desire greatly something which belongs to another.

covey (8-ɪ) group of birds, especially those shot for food.

cow (47) female animal; animal (not a goat) from which we usually get milk.
cow (47) frighten, make a person spiritless and yielding by frightening him greatly.
coward (47-9) man of no courage; **cowardice** (——1s) act of being afraid when one ought to be brave.
cower (47-9) lower the head and shoulders as from fear or shame.
cowl (47) piece of clothing worn over the head by members of certain religious groups; metal top for a chimney; metal cover, e.g. over a machine.
cowrie, cowry (47-1) small shell used as money in parts of Asia and Africa.
cowslip (47s-1) small yellow flower found in the fields of England.
cox (5) short for *Coxswain* (k5ksn).
coxcomb (5-67) foolish fellow dressed in a foolish way.
coxswain, cockswain (k5ksn) person in command of and *steering* (= guiding) a small boat.
coy (51) (of a woman) easily frightened by a man; pretending to be afraid of men so as to draw them on.
coyote (41-67) wild wolf-like dog found in North America.
cozen (8) deceive.
crab (3) creature with a hard shell and ten legs found in water, it usually walks sideways;*To walk crab-wise* = —— sideways; **to crab**, speak ill of, to find fault with; **crabbed**, bad-tempered.

COWSLIP

CRAB

crack (3) break but not fall apart; narrow opening, e.g. made by breaking; make a noise like breaking; Sl. *He's cracked* = —— mad; *To crack jokes* = say amusing things; Sl. *To crack up a person* = praise; *To crack up* = show signs of age or decay; *A crack on the head* = hard blow; *A crack player* = very good ——
cracker (3-9) small pipe of paper containing gunpowder which makes a loud noise when fired; *A Christmas cracker* = ornamented pipe of paper containing a small gift—the two ends are pulled apart and break with a sharp noise; Am. unsweetened *biscuit* (= thin dry cake).
crackle (3) make a noise like walking on dry leaves.
cracksman (3-9) thief who breaks into houses.
cradle (21) bed for a small baby which can be swung or rolled gently from side to side to put the child to sleep; frame, e.g. for a broken limb, for a ship while building.

CRACKER

craft (44) any kind of ship.
craft (44) cleverness with the hands, e.g. in art; work, especially in art; cleverness in deceiving; **a craftsman** (——9) one who practises an art; **crafty** (——1) deceiving.
crag (3) high, steep rock.
cram (3) fill very full; press into a small space; learn a subject hastily for an examination.
cramp (3) prevent movement or growth of; hold firm; **cramped**, pressed into a small space.
cramp (3) tool for holding or pressing things together; painful uncontrolled hardening of the muscles.
cranberry (3-9-1) small red fruit.
crane (21) water bird with long legs and neck; machine used for raising heavy things; *To crane one's neck* = stretch out so as to see better.
cranium (21-19) bony container of the brain.
crank (3ngk) handle used for turning a wheel; part of a machine which changes an up and down movement into a circular movement, e.g. in a steam engine.
crank (3ngk) person with peculiar ideas, usually on one subject.
cranny (3-1) small crack.
crape (21) black cloth worn at a funeral.
crapulent (3-17-9) feeling ill after drinking too much.
crash (3) fall heavily and break with great noise; failing of a business; *A crash dive* = coming straight down in an aeroplane; *Crash helmet* = strong round hat worn by a motor-cyclist to protect his head.
crash (3) rough kind of cotton cloth, used for men's clothes in hot countries.
crass (3) complete, e.g. *Crass ignorance* (= state of not knowing).
crate (21) box made of narrow boards which do not fit closely together.
crater (21-9) hole in the top of a *volcano* (= mountain that sends out fire).
cravat (9-3) piece of cloth worn round the neck.
crave (21) ask eagerly for; have a great desire for.
craven (21) without courage.
crawl (55) move along the ground slowly, e.g. as legless creatures do; way of swimming.
crayfish (21-1), **crawfish** (55-1) fresh-water creature with a shell and ten legs.
crayon (215) coloured pencil.
craze (21) cause to become mad; *A craze* = something everybody does for a short time; **crazy** (21-1) mad.
creak (11) sharp high sound made by one thing rubbing on another.
cream (11) thick oily part of milk which

CRAYFISH

comes to the top; soft fat used as a medicine for the skin; best part of anything; (colour) yellow-white.

crease (11s) line made by folding; mark on the ground in *cricket*.

cre'ate (1121) cause to be; make; Sl. to become excited and angry; **cre'ation** (1121shn) act of creating; thing created; all things created by God; **creature** (11tsh9) any living thing.

crèche (21sh) place where children are looked after while the mothers are at work.

credence (11-s) act of believing.

cred'ential(s) (1-2-shlz) papers which prove that one may be trusted.

credible (2-1) which can be believed.

credit (2-1) trust; good name; *Money at my credit* = money which I have; *My credit is good* = people believe that I will pay back money lent to me; *To get goods on credit* = get goods promising to pay later; *The credit side of an account* = page showing money received by or owed to a business; *To give a man credit for some sense* = expect him to have —; *To give a man credit for what he has done* = praise —; **creditable** (——9) worthy of praise; **creditor** (——9) person to whom one owes money.

cred'ulity (2-177-1-1) too great willingness to believe; adj. **cr'edulous** (2-17-9).

creed (11) that which is believed; beliefs of a Church.

creek (11) Am. small stream; Eng. deep, narrow inlet on sea-coast or lake-shore.

creel (11) basket for carrying fish.

creep (11) move with the body near the ground, e.g. as a legless creature moves; to move slowly and quietly; *Make one's flesh creep* = frighten; **a creeper** (——9) plant which grows along the ground or up the wall; **creepy** (——1) causing fear.

crem'ate (1-21) burn a dead body; **cremat'orium** (2-9-55-19) place where dead bodies are burnt.

creole (1167) person born in the West Indies.

creosote (119-67) oily liquid obtained from coal, used for killing seeds of disease and protecting things from decay.

crêpe (21) thin cloth or paper with many small folds or waves in it.

crept (2) p.t. of Creep.

cresç'endo (1sh2-67) (Music) becoming louder and louder.

crescent (2) shaped like a new moon.

cress (2) hot-tasting plant.

crest (2) top edge of a wave or hill; top feathers on a bird's head.

CREST

crest (2) sign which serves as the special mark of a family, e.g. one printed on a piece of letter-paper.

cr'estfallen (2-55) feeling sad and ashamed.

cretonne (2-5) printed cotton cloth.

crev'asse (9-3) deep crack in a great mass of ice on a mountain side.

crevice (2-1s) small crack.

crew (77) p.t. of Crow.

crew (77) men working together, e.g. on a ship.

crib (1) part of a house for cattle in which one beast stands; small room; hut or small house; child's bed; **to crib;** take another boy's work out as one's own; look secretly at a book or at another boy's paper in an examination.

cribbage (1-1j) game played with cards and a board with many holes in it, a small stick being moved from one hole to another to count points won.

crick (1) painful stiffness of the neck.

cricket (1-1) game played by 22 men with a ball, a flat piece of wood (called a *bat*) and two sets of three upright sticks in the ground; one player tries to knock down the sticks with the ball while another tries to hit or stop the ball; *That's not cricket!* = not fair.

cricket (1-1) small insect which makes a loud high sound.

cried (41) p.t. of Cry.

crime (41) act of breaking the law; **criminal** (1-1) law-breaker.

crimp (1) put curves or curls into, e.g. hair.

crimp (1) person who caught men and put them by force or tricks on ships to serve as seamen.

crimson (1-z) deep red colour.

cringe (1nj) bend low or go down on the knees because of fear or shame.

crinkle (1ngk) bend into many small folds.

crinoline (1-9-11) woman's garment with large circles of wire to hold it out in a bell-like shape.

cripple (1) one whose body is not perfect, e.g. with a useless arm or leg; to hurt and make useless.

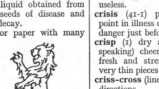

CRINOLINE

crisis (41-1) pl. **crises** (41-11z) turning-point in illness or in history; moment of great danger just before great changes.

crisp (1) dry and easily broken; (way of speaking) cheerful and short; *Crisp air* = fresh and strength-giving; *Potato-crisps* = very thin pieces of potato cooked in fat.

criss-cross (lines) (1 + 5) crossing in different directions.

crit'erion (41-19-19) pl. **criteria**, rule or example by which correct judgment can be made.

critic (1-1) one who judges works of art, or other work; one who points out faults; **to criticize** (1-1s41z).

critical (1-1) (1) e.g. *Critical moment* = very important time just before great changes for the better or for the worse; (2) having to do

with judging writings or works of art; eager to judge unfavourably, fault-finding.

crit′ique (1-11k) writing expressing an opinion of a work of art, book or play.

croak (67) noise made by a *frog* (= a green creature living near water which has long back legs and moves by jumping).

crochet (67sh21) way of making thread into garments by passing one ring or curl of thread through another.

crock (5) earthen vessel; old broken down animal or person; Sl. *To crock up* = become ill and useless.

crockery (5-9-1) earthen dishes used in eating.

crocodile (5-9-41) large water animal. *To shed crocodile tears* = pretend to be sorry (the crocodile was said to weep while eating a man).

crocus (67-9) spring flower.

croft (5) very small farm—sometimes only one small field; **crofter** (——9) owner of a croft.

crone (67) very old woman.

crony (67-1) old friend, especially one with the same interests.

crook (7) a bend; stick with a curve at one end; Am. law-breaker, dishonest person; *By hook or by crook* = by some means or other; **crooked** (7-1) not straight; Sl. not honest.

croon (77) to sing softly; **Crooner** = person who sings love-songs to dance-music.

crop (5) (1) pocket in the throat of birds in which the food is broken up; *Neck and crop* = the whole lot; (2) stick with a piece of leather on the end, carried while riding horseback.

crop (5) fruits, grain, etc., produced by the earth in one year or season; collection of things all arising at the same time, e.g. *A crop of spots on the face*, *A crop of troubles*; *To crop up* = appear unexpectedly.

crop (5) cut or bite off short, e.g. *Sheep crop the grass*.

cropper (5-9) *To come a cropper* = fall, e.g. from a horse; fail badly.

croquet (67k21) game played by striking wooden balls and making them roll through *hoops* (= ∩-shaped wire) in the ground.

croqu′ette (67k2) ball of meat baked or cooked in fat.

crore (55) (Indian) ten million.

CROQUET

cross (5) mark made by drawing one line across another; one piece of wood fastened across another; **the Cross**, wooden cross upon which Christ died; anything of this shape.

cross (to) (5) lay across; go across; *Cross one's t's* = be very exact; *Cross off*, *Cross out* = strike out a word by drawing a line through it; *To cross one plant with another* = produce a plant of a mixed kind.

cross (5) angry.

crossbow (5-67) bow (= curved piece of wood with a string joining the two ends, used for shooting arrows) fixed across a piece of wood shaped like a gun, and held as a gun is when aiming.

CROSSBOW

cr′ossbr′ed (5-2) person, animal or plant come from parents of different races or kinds.

cr′oss-ex′amine (+ 1gz3-1) continue to question in order to prove or disprove the truth of what has already been said.

cr′oss-p′urposes, at — (+ 99-9-1z) trying to work together but actually working with different aims and misunderstanding each other.

cr′oss-qu′estion (+ 2stshn) see Cross-examine (2nd above).

cross-section (+ 2-shn) picture of a thing as seen if cut across.

cr′ossword p′uzzle (5-99 + 8) square to be filled in with letters to make words reading up and down as well as across; below this square are given a few ideas to help one guess the words needed.

crotch (5) branch or stick that divides at the top, used to support cross-bars, etc.

crotchet (5-1) very short note in music; strange fancy; **crotchety** (——1) full of strange fancies; bad-tempered.

crouch (47) bend down, as a cat does before jumping.

croup (77) disease of the throat in children.

croupier (77-19) man who takes in and pays out the money at a game played for money.

crow (67) black bird which cries " Caw! Caw!" (55).

crow (67) make a noise like a *cock* (= male form of hen); express joy at one's own success.

crow-bar (+ 44) long bar of iron used for breaking stone and moving heavy things.

crowd (47) large number of people; too many people in a small place; **to crowd**, come together in large numbers, to press forward in numbers, to press into a small space.

crown (47) (1) circle of flowers, gold or other material worn on the head, usually as a sign of victory or kingship; **the crown**, state of being king, the king himself, e.g. of a hill, of a hat, of a head; **to crown**, put a crown on; h′alf a cr′own—Obs. Worth 12½ pence.

cr′ow's-feet (67z + 11) little lines in the skin at the corners of the eyes.

cr′ow's-nest (67z + 2) box-like place high on the *mast* (= a pole carrying sails) of a ship used for looking out over the sea.

crucial (77sh19) cross-like; *A crucial moment* = — when one must decide a serious matter one way or the other.

crucible (77s1) pot for melting metals.

crucifix (77s1-1) cross with the figure of Christ on it; **crucify** (77s1-41) kill by nailing on a wooden cross; n. **crucif′ixion** (77s1-1kshn).

crude (77) rough and bitter to taste; in the natural state; (of work or speech) not well finished; not polished; bad-mannered.

cruel (779) taking pleasure in giving pain to others; hard-hearted; causing pain.

cruet (771) set of small glass bottles for oil, *vinegar* (= very sour liquid), etc., used on the table at meals.

cruise (77z) journey by sea; **to cruise**, travel in a ship; **cruiser** (———9) fast warship with big guns.

crumb (8) very small piece of bread; very small piece of anything.

crumble (8) break into small pieces; decay slowly.

crumpet (8-1) flat round bread-like cake eaten hot with butter.

crumple (8) roll up and press in the hand, e.g. a sheet of paper; become bent into many folds; *To crumple up* = break or yield completely and suddenly.

crunch (8-sh) sound made by biting hard food, or by walking on small stones; bite making this sound.

crupper (8-9) leather band which goes under a horse's tail; part of a horse's back behind the *saddle* (= leather seat on horse).

crus′ade (77-21) war which the Christians fought to win back the Holy City, Jerusalem; fight against some evil or for some good cause.

cruse (77z) small pot.

crush (8) press together and break with great force; press out of shape, press carelessly into folds (e.g. a dress) as is done by careless packing; force the liquid out of, e.g. fruit; make into powder; beat an enemy completely; Sl. **a crush**, crowded gathering of guests.

crust (8) hard outer part, e.g. of bread.

crust′acean (8-21sh19) hard-shelled water creature.

crusty (8-1) having a hard *crust* (2nd above); easily made angry.

crutch (8) stick to help one walk when the legs are hurt or useless.

crux (8) difficult point to decide; most important point on which some action or idea depends.

cry (41) (1) speak in a loud voice; (2) weep; *To cry off* = say that one will not fulfil a promise; *A crying evil* = —— which should be set right at once; *In full cry* = (of dogs) going after an animal and making much noise; *Hue and cry* = hunting a person (e.g. a thief) with much shouting; show of public anger.

crypt (1) room under the main floor of a church, sometimes used for graves.

cryptic (1-1) secret, difficult to understand.

crypto- secret; **a crypto-Communist** (1-67 + 5-17-1) secret ——; **cryptogram** (1-6-3) secret writing.

crystal (1) hard stone, clear like glass; glass on a *watch* (= pocket clock); regular shape which salt and other materials take when they cease to be liquid and become solid.

crystallized fruit (1-9-41zd + 77) fruit boiled in sugar so that there are *crystals* (see above) of sugar on it.

cub (8) young of a meat-eating animal, e.g. lion; a young man, e.g. *An ill-mannered cub; Cub reporter* (of a newspaper).

cubby hole (8-1 + 67) small useful store-place or room.

cube (177) square block; $3\ cubed = 3^3 = 27$; **cube root** (+ 77) e.g. cube root of 27 is 3; **cubic** (177-1) e.g. *A cubic foot* = 1 foot long × 1 foot broad × 1 foot high; space 2 feet × 2 feet × 2 feet contains 8 cubic feet.

cubicle (177-1) small sleeping-room divided off from a larger place.

cubit (177-1) ancient measure, about 18 inches.

cuckoo (7-77) bird which makes a sound like its name and lays its eggs in the nests of other birds.

cucumber (177-9-9) creeping plant with a long green fruit.

cud (8) food which some grass-eating animals bring back from the stomach and bite again and again.

cuddle (8) lie close and warm as a baby does with its mother; make love to.

cudgel (8j) thick stick, e.g. one used as a weapon; *To take up the cudgels for* = defend; *Cudgel one's brains* = try hard to find the answer to a difficult question.

cue (177) long stick used to strike a ball with its point in *billiards* (= game, see Billiards); word or sign given to make an actor remember the following words, as in a play.

cuff (8) band on clothing just above the hand.

cuff (8) strike with the hand.

cuir′ass (kwI-3) armour protecting the breast and back; **cuirass′ier** (kwI-9-19) horse-soldier wearing armour on the breast.

cuis′ine (kwIzII) quality of cooking.

c′ul-de-s′ac (7 + 9 + 3) street open only at one end.

culinary (8-1-9-1) having to do with cooking.

cull (8) pick out; choose the good and leave the bad.

cullender, colander (8-1-9) metal pot with holes in it, used to get the water out of boiled vegetables, etc.

culminate (8-1-21) reach the highest and last point.

culpable (8-9) who (which) ought to be blamed.

culprit (8-1) wrong-doer.

cult (8) certain set of religious ceremonies and beliefs; love for a teacher or idea, e.g. *A cult of*

cultivate | 81 | **curtsy**

Browning; To make a cult of card-playing = treat it with too much seriousness, as if it were a religious duty.

cultivate (8-1-21) (1) prepare land for crops; (2) cause to grow, e.g. *To cultivate roses*; *To cultivate one's mind* = study so that one's mind may become better; *To cultivate a person's friendship* = try to become a friend of —; *A cultivated person* = one with a cultivated mind, with knowledge of music, art, etc.

culture (8-tsh9) manners and customs of a people; growing of anything which needs special care; making oneself better by study, e.g. *Voice culture; A cultured person; A person of culture* = one who has knowledge and taste in the arts.

culvert (8-9) bridge built to allow water to run under the road.

cumber (8-9) load up with useless things, and so prevent easy movement; **cumbersome**, large and difficult to move or deal with.

cummerbund (8-9-8) broad band of silk worn round the waist.

cumulative (177-17-9-1) slowly increasing by being added to.

cuneiform (177-1-55) shape of ancient writing in Asia; shaped like an arrow-head.

cunning (8-1) clever, deceiving; Am. pretty, pleasing.

cup (8) small drinking vessel; large silver or gold vessel given to the winner in games; *A bitter cup* = something very unpleasant which has to be suffered; **to cup**, draw blood through the surface of the skin by means of cups put on the skin hot and allowed to cool.

cupboard (8-9) piece of furniture with doors used for storing things; *Cupboard love* = show of love (e.g. by a child or animal) in order to get sweets or food from the store cupboard.

cupid (177-1) beautiful boy with a bow and arrows; Cupid, the son and message-bearer of Venus, the Goddess of Love.

cup'idity (177-1-1-1) strong desire, especially for wealth.

cupola (177-9-9) small round top on a building.

cupreous (177-19), **cupric** (177-1) having to do with copper.

cur (99) worthless dog.

curate (1779-1) (usually younger) priest who helps another priest.

curative (1779-9-1) helping to make sick persons well.

cur'ator (1779-21-9) one who has charge of —e.g. a building—where objects of interest are kept.

curb (99) to control; **a curb**, metal band under a horse's mouth which helps to control it; **the curb, the c'urbstone** (99-67) = kerb, line of raised stones separating the footpath (= path for walkers) from the street.

curd (99) thickened part of sour milk used to make cheese.

curdle (99) cause milk to thicken by making it sour; *To make his blood curdle* = make him afraid.

cure (179) cause a return to health; *To cure meat* = preserve with salt; *To cure a skin* = make into leather; **a cure**, way of making sick persons well; act of curing or being cured; medicine; (of a priest) *To be given a cure* = be given charge of a church.

curfew (99-177) bell rung in the evening to warn people to put out lights and fires.

curio (179-16) strange and interesting object.

curious (179-19) eager for knowledge; strange.

curl (99) make into waves and circles, e.g. hair; bend up; turn in curves, as a plant growing round a stick.

curlew (99-177) water-bird with long legs and a long curved beak.

curling (99-1) making into curls; game played by pushing round stones over ice.

curm'udgeon (99-8j) bad-tempered person—usually old man.

currant (8-9) small fruit of a bush; small dried fruit put in cakes.

currency (8-s1) money; that which is used for money.

current (8) in general use, e.g. *The current opinion* = that held by most people; now passing, e.g. *The current week; The current number of a newspaper* = to-day's —.

current (8) stream; flow of electricity along a wire.

curr'iculum (9-1-17-9) fixed course of study.

curry (8-1) brush and clean a horse; *To curry favour* = seek favour by admiring or serving a person.

curry (8-1) meat (or fish, etc.) cooked in a hot-tasting yellow liquid, much used in India.

currycomb (8-1-67) set of metal teeth fixed to a handle used for cleaning the hair and skin of horses.

curse (99) call down evil upon; say bad words in anger; **a curse**, calling down of evil; expression of anger; cause of trouble or evil; Sl. **cursed** (99-1) hateful.

cursive (99-1) writing in which the letters join on to one another.

cursory (99-9-1) quick and careless, e.g. *A cursory glance* (= look).

curt (99) short in manner; too short to be polite.

curt'ail (99-21) cut off part of a thing so as to shorten it.

curtain (99-1) covering for a window; large piece of cloth hung up to hide or cover anything; *The curtain rises* = the play begins; *A curtain lecture* = scolding given by a wife to her husband when they are alone; *A curtain raiser* = short play given before the chief play in a theatre.

curtsy (99-1) bending of the knees made by women as a sign of respect; *To drop a curtsy* = make —.

curvature (99-9tsh9) bending or curving, e.g. of the back-bone.

curve (99) line which is not straight; part of a circle; bend into a circular shape; be so bent.

curv'et (99-2) movement of a horse like a short jump over nothing; *to curv'et*, move thus.

cushion (7) soft object for sitting on or putting behind the back; any soft thing which makes a shock less.

cusp (8) point made by the meeting of two curved lines, e.g. like the horns of the moon.

custard (8-9) yellow food made with milk, egg, sugar, etc.

custody (8-9-1) safe-keeping; *To take into custody* = put in prison.

cust'odian (8-67-19) keeper, e.g. of some public building.

custom (8-9) usual or common way of doing things; thing usually done, e.g. *It is the custom for Englishmen to raise their hats to a lady*; *To take away one's custom from a shop* = not buy there any more; adj. **customary** (——9-1);

customer (8-9-9) one who buys regularly at a shop; *A queer customer* = peculiar person;

custom-house (8-9 + 47) office where money is paid on goods brought into a country; **customs duty** (8-9-z + 177-1) money paid on goods brought into a country.

cut (8) (1) divide with a knife; Sl. *That cuts no ice* = has no effect; *That cuts both ways* = has an equal effect on you and me; *Cut and dried (plan)* = all fixed and not to be changed; (2) shape by cutting; *To cut a coat* = cut out cloth for a coat; *Cut one's coat according to one's cloth* = make one's plans suit one's powers or money; *Cut out for* = well suited to; (3) make shorter; *Cut a story; Cut down a story* = make shorter; *Cut prices* = make less; *Cut across the grass* = go across and so make one's path shorter; *Cut a class* = not go to a lesson; (4) to wound, e.g. *I've cut my finger*; *To cut a person; To cut him dead* = pretend not to see; (5) give a blow to—especially hitting sideways, e.g. *To cut a ball; To cut with a stick; To cut off with a shilling* = leave no money to a son (etc.) at one's death; *He cut me out* = was more successful, e.g. in winning the favour of a lady; *That car has cut in* = has turned sharply in front of my car, so causing me to slow down; Sl. *Very cut up at* = sad; Sl. *To cut up rough* = be angry; **a cut**, result of cutting; wound; stroke; *A cut above* = better than; *The cut of a coat* = shape; *Cut along* = run along.

cute (177) clever at seeing how to gain money; Am. clever and pleasing.

cuticle (177-1) outer skin.

cutlass (8-9) short sword used by seamen.

cutlery (8-9-1) instruments for cutting.

cutlet (8-1) cooked meat from the neck of an animal.

cutter (8-9) one who cuts; person who cuts out (men's) clothes; instrument for cutting; sailing boat.

cutting (8-1) adj. cruel, causing pain; n. piece cut out, e.g. *A newspaper cutting* = interesting piece cut out from a newspaper; road cut through a hill.

cuttlefish (8-1) jelly-like creature floating in the sea (it sends out brown ink and its chalky bone is used for cleaning hands).

cwt. = *hundredweight* (8-9-21) = 112 pounds (Am. 100 pounds).

c'ybern'etics (s41-9-2-1) study of instruments used for controlling machines; see Automation.

cycle (s41) *In cycle* = in a circle; *A cycle of events* = things happening one after another as if in a circle; two-wheeled machine driven with the feet along the roads.

cyclone (s41-67) powerful wind blowing in a circle.

c'yclop'aedia (41-6-11-19) **enc'yclop'aedia** (1-s41-6-11-19) book or set of books supplying knowledge on all subjects.

cyclostyle (s41-6-41) (= wheel pen) instrument for printing by pressing ink through writing on wax paper.

cyclotron (s41-6-5) instrument which causes particles of electricity to travel faster and faster, used in breaking up atoms; see Fission.

cyder (s41-9) see Cider.

cygnet (s1-1) young *swan* (see Swan).

cylinder (s1-1-9) roller-shaped object; round hollow box in which the steam or other gas pushes forward the bar which turns the wheel in an engine.

cymbal (s1) one of two brass plates struck together to make music.

cynical (s1-1) not believing in the goodness of people; always pointing out the bad; n. **a cynic.**

cynosure (s1-9z179) object at which everyone looks.

cypher, cipher (s41-9) secret writing; the figure 0; person of no importance.

cypress (s41-1) dark green tree often planted in grave-yards, poisonous to horses.

cyst (s1) small bag-like growth in the body, usually containing liquid.

cyt'ology (s41-5-9j1) study of the *cells* (= particles of living matter) of which the body is built.

Czar (44) see Tsar.

D

dab (3) touch gently as one does when washing a wound; Sl. *A dab at* — = very clever at.
dab (3) flat sea-fish.
dabble (3) play in the water; *To dabble in (art)* = work at — but not seriously or continuously.
dabchick (3-1) small water bird.
dace (21s) small, freshwater fish.
dachshund (4ks-7) German dog with a long body and short legs.
dactylo-, having to do with the fingers.
dad (3) **daddy** (3-1) a child's word for father.
d'addy-l'ong‹l'egs (+ 5 + 2-z) small flying creature with six very long legs.
dado (21-67) band of different coloured paint or wood round the lower part of a wall of a room.
daffodil (3-9-1) yellow, spring flower.
daft (44) foolish; mad.
dagger (3-9) pointed knife used as a weapon; *Look daggers at* = show hatred.

DAFFODIL

dago (21-67) dark-skinned person, e.g. from the south of Europe.
dahlia (21-19) beautiful flower.
daily (21-1) happening every day; a newspaper.
dainty (21-1) beautiful and neat; **daintily** (——1) *dressed* = beautifully and carefully dressed; beautiful and easily broken or damaged, e.g. an ornament; *She is very dainty* = very careful in choosing; (food) hard to please; **a dainty** = specially nice piece of food.

DAHLIA

dairy (29-1) place where cows are kept for producing milk; milk-shop or milk-business.
dais (21-1) raised part of the floor.
daisy (21z1) very common small flower, yellow in the centre and white round it.
dale (21) valley.
dally (3-1) be slow or waste time; *To dally with* = play carelessly with, e.g. with love; **dalliance** (3-19-s) playing in a loving way.
dalm'atian (3-21shn) white dog with black spots.
dam (3) wall or bank built to keep back water.
dam (3) mother animal.
damage (3-1j) break, hurt or destroy; n. hurt, loss, etc.; **damages** (3-1jiz) money paid to make good a loss (e.g. to pay for repairing).
damasc'ene (3-9-11) ornament metal by cutting lines in the surface and putting other metal in the hollows so cut.
damask (3-9) beautiful silk with raised figures worked into it; fine steel made in Damascus; light rose-colour.

dame (21) an *elderly* (= rather old) lady; title of honour given to women; *A dame school* = small school kept by an old woman.
damn (3) to curse; send to everlasting punishment; *That damns it for me* = proves to me that it is bad; **damn!**, cry of anger.
damp (3) slightly wet; **firedamp** (419-3) poisonous gas found in the coal *mines* (= holes in the ground from which coal is obtained); **to damp**, make slightly wet; **to damp (down)**, make a fire burn more slowly; make an instrument sound less loudly; *To damp a person's feelings* = cause loss of joy or hope.
damper (3-9) door in a chimney or fire-place used to make the fire burn more slowly; *Cast a damper on a party* = cause it to be less merry; **a damper**, thin cake of flour and water (Australian).
damsel (3-z) girl.
damson (3-z) small dark blue stone-fruit.
dance (44-s) jump about; move to the time of music; *To give a dance* = invite guests to one's house for dancing; *Lead a person a dance* = cause much trouble to —; cause to follow one about from place to place.
dandelion (3-1-419) small, yellow, wild flower.
dandle (3) to dance (move) a small child up and down on the knee.
dandruff (3-9) small dry pieces of skin found among the hairs of the head.

DANDELION

dandy (3-1) man who gives too much time and thought to his clothes.
dangerous (21nj9-9) risky, which may cause harm; n. **danger** (21nj9).
dangle (3ngg) hang down and swing loosely.
dank (3ngk) cold and wet.
d'ans'euse (44ⁿ-99z) female dancer.
dapper (3-9) (usually of a small person), neat and well-dressed.
dappled (3) spotted.
Darby and Joan (44-1 + 67) old and loving husband and wife.
dare (29) be brave enough to do; *I dared him to do it* = I told him that he was not brave enough to —; *I dare say* = I believe it possible that —; **daredevil** (29-2) person who is not afraid of the greatest danger.
dark (44) without light; secret or unknown; evil; brown or black (eyes, hair or skin); (of colour) deep, e.g. *Dark red* = deep red.
darkling (44-1) in the dark.
darky, darkey (44-1) man with a black skin.
darling (44-1) one who is greatly loved.
darn (44) repair a hole in cloth by passing

dart 84 **dearth**

threads through and across; **darn it!**, cry of anger.

dart (44) run quickly; throw out quickly, e.g. *A snake darts out its tongue.*

dart (44) sharp-pointed weapon thrown by hand; **darts**, a game played by throwing darts at a circular board.

dash (3) make a sudden quick run; throw or be thrown with force, e.g. *The waves dashed against the cliff; To dash off a letter* = write quickly; *His hopes were dashed* = ruined; **a dash**, quick movement, e.g. *A dash for safety* = rush —; spirit, activity, e.g. *A soldier of great dash and skill*; small amount of liquid, e.g. *Whisky* (= *strong drink*) *with a dash of water*; *To cut a dash* = make oneself noticed as a fine fellow; **Dash!**, a cry of slight (not great) anger.

dashboard (3-55) board fixed in front of a carriage; instrument-board in a motor-car.

dashing (fellow) (3-1) spirited, gay, active.

dastard (3-9) low fellow without courage.

data (21-9) facts taken as true as the starting-point of a piece of reasoning.

date (21) time shown by the day, month and year; **to date**, write or show the date of, e.g. a letter; *Out of date* = not in present use, or useless; Sl. *Make a date* = make an agreement to meet at a certain time; *Up-to-date* = new, as now used.

date (21) a small brown sweet fruit with a long stone, much eaten in Egypt, etc.

datum (21) a known fact (see Data, 3rd above).

daub (55) make dirty marks on; paint badly.

daughter (55-9) female child.

daunt (55) prevent a person from acting by fear; control by fear; *Nothing daunted* = not frightened; *Dauntless* = not afraid of anything.

dauphin (55-1) eldest son of the King of France.

davenport (3-55) small writing-table.

davits (3-1) curved bars on the edge of a ship by means of which a boat is swung out and lowered.

D'avy J'ones's L'ocker (21-1 + 67-z1z + 5-9) bottom of the sea (Davy Jones is an imaginary spirit of the sea who has a large box into which he puts everything that sinks).

dawdle (55) waste time; stand about doing nothing.

dawn (55) coming of day; *It began to dawn on him* = he began to understand.

day (21) time from sunrise to sunset; *This day week* = on the same day of next week; *Days of grace* = further days allowed beyond the fixed time for paying a debt; *To win the day, The day is ours* = battle —; *Every dog has his day* = all persons have some happy times; **daybook** (21-7) account-book in which each day's business is written; **daybreak** (21-21) sun-rise; **daydream** (21-11) think pleasant but useless thoughts when awake; **daylight-saving** (21-41 + 21-1) putting the clock forward one hour in summer so as to start work earlier and get more daylight after work.

daze (21) make foolish, e.g. by a sudden shock.

dazzle (3) make a person unable to see by throwing a strong light in the eyes; cause wonder by some act of great cleverness or power.

D.C. (11-11) see Direct current.

D.D. (11 + 11) Doctor of *Divinity* (= study of man's belief in God)—title given by a university to priests and officers of the Church.

D.D.T. (d1d1d1t11) substance used for killing insects (it acts on their nerves).

de- from; of; down; to cause lack of.

deacon (11) officer of the Church below a priest.

dead (2) lifeless; having ceased to live; *A dead sleep* = very deep —; *Dead* = complete, completely, e.g. *Dead tired*; *A wind dead against us*; *A dead calm*; *Dead beat* = tired out; *The dead centre* = exact middle point; *A dead-centre* = position of the wheel of an engine in which the engine cannot turn it forwards or backwards; **dead heat** (+ 11) two runners coming in level with each other so that both win; **dead-line** (+ 41) last date for signing or paying; Am. Sl. **dead pan** (+ 3) face with no show of feeling in it; **deadlock** (2-5) disagreement which cannot be settled; *Dead of night* = darkest part of the night; *Make a dead set at* = go straight towards; *A dead shot* = sure —, never failing to hit; **deaden** (the senses), make one feel less; (a sound) make less loud; **deadly** (2-1) as if dead, e.g. *Deadly pale* = white-faced; causing death, e.g. *Deadly poison.*

DEAD-CENTRE·

piston
crank

deaf (2) unable to hear; *Turn a deaf ear to* = refuse to listen; **d'eaf-m'ute** (+ 177) unable to hear or speak.

deal (11) **(1)** give, e.g. *To deal a blow*; **(2)** give each a share, e.g. *To deal cards*; **(3)** do business with, e.g. *To deal with Mr. A.*; *To deal at a shop* = buy —; *To deal in corn* = buy and sell —; arrange, do what is necessary, e.g. *To deal with a matter* = settle —; *Deal with a question* = decide, answer; **a deal**, act of business, buying or selling; *To make a deal* = arrange to sell or buy a certain thing.

deal (11) a certain amount, e.g. *A great deal, A good deal* = rather a lot.

deal (11) soft white wood.

dealt (2) p.t. of Deal.

dean (11) officer in the Church in charge of several priests; the head of a part of a university, teaching a certain subject or group of subjects.

dear (19) **(1)** loved; **(2)** costly or precious; *Oh dear!, Dear me!, Dear, dear!* = cries of grief, wonder, surprise, etc.

dearth (99) lack of.

death (2) act of dying; state of having no life; *Death-duties* = share of a dead man's wealth taken by the government; *The death of all his hopes* = end —; *Death rattle* = sound heard in a person's throat at the moment of death.

deb (2) Sl. = débutante.

déb'âcle (21-44) sudden ruin, e.g. when an army runs away in disorder.

deb'ar (1-44) shut out from:

deb'ark (1-44) go on shore from a ship.

deb'ase (1-21) make of less value.

deb'ate (1-21) consider and talk about a question; **a deb'ate**, public meeting in which a· question is talked over by two parties, each party taking one side.

deb'auch (1-55) lead away from goodness or honesty; feasting and drinking too much.

deb'enture (1-2-tsh9) written promise of a government or of a business company to pay a debt (a debenture holder is paid a fixed amount yearly for the use of his money, and the amount does not increase if the company gains more money).

deb'ilitate (1-1-1-21) weaken.

debit (2-1) write down as a debt, as money owed, in an account-book; *The debit side of an account* = page showing payments and debts owed to others.

d'ebonair (2-9-29) light-hearted, having nice manners.

deb'ouch (1-47) flow out of; (of men) to come out from a small space, e.g. soldiers ... from a wood.

débris (2-11) broken, useless pieces.

debt (2) anything owed, e.g. *A debt of money, A debt of thanks*, etc.; *A bad debt* = one which will never be paid.

d'eb'unk (11-8) show an over-praised person as he really is.

début (21-77) person's first performance or appearance.

d'ébut'ante (21-77-44ⁿ) young woman in her first year of being invited as a guest to parties other than children's parties.

dec-, deca-, having to do with ten, e.g.

decade (2-9) ten years.

decadent (2-9) decaying; becoming worse.

decalogue (2-9-5) the Ten Commandments in the Bible.

dec'amp (1-3) run away secretly, e.g. with money.

dec'ant (1-3) pour liquid carefully from one vessel into another; **dec'anter** (——9) ornamental glass wine-bottle.

dec'apitate (1-3-1-21) cut off the head.

dec'arbonize (11-44-9-41) take away the *carbon* (= coal-like material) from—especially from inside the engine of a motor-car.

DECANTER

dec'ay (1-21) go bad; fall into ruin; become worse or less, e.g. *Man's powers decay in old age*.

dec'ease (1s11s) die; death.

dec'eive (1s11) cause a person to believe what is untrue; to trick; n. **dec'eit** (1s11).

d'ec'elerate (11s2-9-21) cause to go more slowly.

decent (11s) fitting, right; good enough; not causing shame or shock to others; n. **decency** (11s-s1).

dec'eption (1s2-shn) act of deceiving.

dec'ide (1s41) judge and settle a question; **dec'ided** (——1) fixed, settled; **dec'idedly** (——1-1) clearly and undoubtedly.

dec'iduous (trees) (1s1-179) trees whose leaves fall off in winter.

decimal (2s1) having to do with the number "10"; **a decimal**, e.g. 1·3 (·3 is a decimal and means $\frac{3}{10}$ths).

decimate (2s1-21) kill large numbers.

dec'ipher (1s41-9) discover the meaning of difficult or secret writing.

dec'ision (1s13n) act of deciding (see 5th above).

deck (2) floor of a ship; complete set of playing-cards.

deck (2) dress in fine clothes; to ornament, e.g. with flowers.

decl'aim (1-21) speak with strong feeling; n. **declam'ation** (2-9-21shn).

decl'are (1-29) say solemnly; make known to all; *Have you anything to declare?* (question asked at time of entering a country) = have you any goods on which you ought to pay?; *Well, I declare!* cry of surprise; n. **declar'ation** (2-9-21shn).

decl'ension (1-2-shn) giving the different forms of a noun or adjective.

decl'ine (1-41) (1) to slope downwards; (2) fail in health; (3) refuse; (4) give the different forms of a noun or adjective; **a decl'ine**, slow loss of strength or goodness.

decl'ivity (1-1-1-1) a slope, e.g. of a mountain-side.

d'ecl'utch (11-8) loosen the *clutch* (see Clutch) of a motor-car so that the engine goes on running but the car stands still.

dec'oction (1-5-shn) liquid obtained by boiling something for a long time in water.

d'ec'ode (11-67) change a secret or shortened message into common language.

déc'olleté (2-5-21) wearing a dress cut low at the neck; (of a dress) having a low neck.

d'ecomp'ose (11-9-67z) break up and separate into simple parts; to decay.

decorate (2-9-21) add ornaments to; make beautiful; give a mark of honour to; paint and paper a house.

decorous (2-9-9) fitting and polite; **dec'orum** (1-55) correct dress and behaviour.

dec'oy (1-51) figure of a bird used to bring birds within range of guns; a trick; **to dec'oy**, deceive a person into coming into danger.

decr'ease (1-11s) become less, make less; n. **d'ecrease** (11-11s).

decr'ee (1-11) command of a king or government; judgment of a court of law.

decr'epit (1-2-1) weak from old age; n. **decr'epitude** (——177).

decr'y (1-41) speak ill of; say bad things about.

dedicate (2-1-21) to set apart for some good or holy purpose; give to God; to set apart for some special purpose, e.g. *I dedicate all my spare time to writing*; print a person's name at the front of a book (e.g. *Dedicated to Sir William Bunkum*) to show that the book is written in his honour.

ded'uce (1-177s) reach an idea as a result of considering accepted facts or rules, e.g. *All insects have 6 legs; this creature has 8 legs; therefore I deduce that it is not an insect*; **ded'uction** (1-8-shn) idea so reached; this sort of reasoning.

ded'uct (1-8) take off, e.g. some amount from a bill.

deed (11) an act, e.g. *A brave deed*; paper showing ownership of land; written agreement.

deem (11) e.g. *I deem it wise to* = I think —.

deep (11) going far down, e.g. a hole, water; far in, e.g. *Deep in the water*; *A deep book* = very learned and difficult to understand; *A deep .red* = dark rich red; *The deep* = the ocean.

deep freeze (11 + 11) box in which food is frozen hard and kept for a long time.

deer (19) beautiful wild animal (the males have wide branching horns).

def'ace (1-21s) destroy the surface of, e.g. of a picture by writing across it.

d'e f'acto (11 + 3-67) in actual fact, though not perhaps justly or according to law, e.g. *De facto owner*.

defalcate (11-3-21) use other people's money for one's own purposes; n. **d'efalc'ation**.

def'ame (1-21) try to damage the fame or good name of a person; n. **defam'ation** (2-9-21shn).

def'ault (1-5) fail to do a duty, fail to pay a debt; *A judgment in default* = judgment in a court of law when one fails to come and defend oneself.

def'eat (1-11) beat; win a battle against; cause to fail.

def'ect (1-2) fault; adj. **def'ective** (——1) having faults, not complete; *Mentally defective* = not possessing the usual powers of mind like other people.

def'ection (1-2-shn) deserting a leader; failing to do one's duty.

def'end (1-2) protect from harm; give reasons in support of one's ideas; n. **def'ence** (1-2-s); adj. **def'ensive** (——1) protecting; *On the defensive* = protecting oneself, not attacking.

def'er (1-99) put off to a later time; yield to another's opinion; n. **d'eference** (2-9-s).

def'iant (1-41s) showing no fear or respect; fearlessly refusing to obey.

def'icient (1-1shnt) not perfect; lacking something; *Deficiency disease* = illness caused by not having some substance (e.g. one contained in fresh fruit) which the body must have.

deficit (2-1s1) amount of money owed beyond what one can pay.

def'ile (1-41) make unclean.

defile (11-41) narrow valley between mountains; **to def'ile from,** march out in narrow line.

def'ine (1-41) mark out the edges of; explain the exact meaning of; **a defin'ition** (2-1-1shn) act of defining, *explanation* (n. of Explain) of the meaning of a word.

definite (2-1-1) clear and exact in meaning; having clear or exact edges; **defin'ition** (2-1-1shn) clearness; sharpness of line in a photograph.

defl'ate (1-21) let the air or gas out; cause paper-money to have less value than that printed on it.

defl'ect (1-2) turn a thing (e.g. beam of light) away from a straight path.

def'orm (1-55) make ugly or useless by changing from the natural form.

defr'aud (1-55) obtain money by deceiving.

defr'ay (1-21) to pay.

deft (2) skilful.

def'unct (1-8ngk) dead.

def'y (1-41) be ready to fight against; show no fear of nor respect for; *To defy the law* = do wrong caring nothing for the law; *It defies description* = cannot possibly be described.

deg'enerate (1j2-9-21) become worse; **a deg'enerate** (1j2-9-1) person of very bad character.

degr'ade (1-21) move down to a lower rank or class; n. **d'egrad'ation** (2-9-21shn).

degr'ee (1-11) a step; a measure, e.g. degrees of heat; a rank; title given for learning in a university, e.g. *M.A., B.A.,* etc.; *By degrees* = slowly; *Third degree* = fierce questioning by the police.

d'ehydr'ation (11-41-21shn) drying food so as to preserve it; loss of water from the body in great thirst.

deify (11·1·41) make a god of; regard as a god.

deign to (21) be not too proud to.

deity (11·1·1) having the nature of God; *The Deity* = God.

dej'ected (1-2-1) having low spirits, sad.

del'ay (1-21) cause to be late; wait; act slowly on purpose.

del'ectable (1-2-9) very pleasing, causing great enjoyment.

delegate (2-1-21) give power to a person to carry out a certain piece of work; **a delegate** (2-1-1) person sent (e.g. by government) to do a certain duty or to express its opinions on a certain subject; **deleg'ation** (2-1-21shn) act of *delegating*; group of *delegates*.

del'ete (1-11) strike out part of something written or printed.
delet'erious (2-1-19-19) harmful.
del'iberate (1-1-9-21) consider; adj. **del'iberate** (1-1-9-1) done carefully and purposefully.
delicate (2-1-1) tender, beautiful and easily harmed, e.g. a flower; pleasant and not easily known by the senses, e.g. a taste, a colour, a smell; *A delicate instrument* = one which can show the effect of very small forces and is itself easily damaged; *A delicate child* = of weak health; **delicacy** (2-1-9s1) state of being *delicate*; *A delicacy* = specially nice food.
delicat'essen (2-1-9-2) very nice-tasting foods (especially meats and fish ready for eating).
del'icious (1-1sh9) very nice (usually of taste or smell).
del'ight (1-41) great pleasure; cause great pleasure.
del'imit (11-1-1) mark the outside or farthest edges of a thing (e.g. of land) so as to show how far it reaches, and to fix the exact size.
del'ineate (1-1-121) mark out with lines; draw a picture of; describe a person carefully.
del'inquency (1-1ngkw9ns1) *failure* (= n. of Fail) to do one's duty; *A juvenile delinquent* = young person who has broken the law.
del'irious (1-1-19) wandering in the mind and saying meaningless things because of serious illness; n. **del'irium** (1-1-19).
del'iver (1-1-9) save from danger; carry and give (e.g. a letter) to the owner; *To deliver a speech* = make a speech; aim and throw a ball; *She was delivered of a child* = gave birth to —; *He has a good delivery* = good way of speaking.
dell (2) small valley with trees.
delta (2-9) Greek letter Δ; anything of this shape, e.g. land through which a river flows by many *outlets* (= mouths) to the sea.
del'ude (1-177) deceive.
deluge (2-177j) heavy down-pour of water; rush of words, questions, etc.
del'usion (1-773n) wrong untrue idea.
de l'uxe (9 + 7) specially good and intended for the wealthy.
delve (2) dig; *To delve into old books*, — *into the secrets of nature* = search deeply into —.
demagogue (2-9-5) leader of the common people, who trusts to moving their feelings rather than to reason.
dem'and (1-44) to claim as a right; to want; *Fresh flowers are in demand* = everybody is wanting to buy —; *The law of supply and demand* = the law "Plenty makes prices less: lack makes prices higher."
demarcate (11-44-21) mark and fix the exact outer edge, e.g. of land.
dem'ean (oneself) (1-11) lower oneself; to behave in a way that shows lack of self-respect.
dem'eanour (1-11-9) behaviour.
dem'ented (1-2-1) mad; **dem'entia** (1-2-sh19) madness.

d'em'erit (11-2-1) bad point of character; a fault.
dem'esne (1-21) land round a great house or owned and used by a lord or king.
demi- (2-1) half, e.g. **demi-god** (+ 5).
dem'ise (1-41z) (1) giving up land, money, etc., to somebody else; (2) death.
dem'ob (11-5) Sl. demobilize.
dem'obilize (11-67-1-41) send men back from the army to peace-time work.
dem'ocracy (1-5-9s1) government in which the people elect those who govern; a country so governed; **a d'emocrat** (2-9-3) one who believes in the right of the people to govern themselves.
dem'olish (1-5-1) destroy, e.g. a building; Sl. eat; n. **demol'ition** (11-9-1shn).
demon (11-9) devil; cruel person; adj. **dem'oniac** (1-67-13).
demonstrate (2-9-21) to show; prove clearly; make a show of force or of public feeling.
dem'oralize (1-5-9-41) ruin the character of a person; ruin the spirit and courage of (an army).
d'em'ote (11-67) Am. move down into a lower class.
dem'ur (1-99) to delay; draw back from an action and give reasons against doing it.
dem'ure (1-1779) (of a girl) quiet and serious in manner.
dem'urrage (1-8-1j) keeping a ship or train beyond the agreed time; money paid for so keeping it.
den (2) hole in which an animal lives; hiding-place, usually for thieves; small comfortable sitting-room.
d'en'atured (spirit) (11-21tsh9) *alcohol* (see Alcohol) made unfit to drink.
dengue (2ngg1) illness found in hot countries which causes great pain in the limbs.
den'ial (1-419) act of saying that a thing is not true; act of refusing.
denier (2-19) measure of fineness of thread; in *100 denier yarn* (= thread) 9,000 yards weigh 100 grammes.
denizen (2-1) one who lives in a place.
denom'ination (1-5-1-21shn) name of a particular class or kind; group of people holding certain special beliefs about God and religion.
denom'inator (1-5-1-21-9), e.g. 4 is the denominator in ¾; 3 is the *numerator*).
den'ote (1-67) be a sign of; mean; **denot'ation** (11-67-21shn) act of denoting; exact meaning of a word, e.g. "Pig" denotes a certain animal (it *connotes* (= carries with it) the idea of dirtiness).
dén'ouement (21-77-44ⁿ) untying a knot; end of a story when everything comes out right or is explained.
den'ounce (1-47-s) speak against; put an end to an agreement, especially one between nations.
dense (2) crowded; thick; slow of understanding.

dent (2) cause a bend or hollow place in the surface.

dental (2) having to do with the teeth; **dentifrice** (2-1-1s) powder or other material used for cleaning the teeth; **dentist** (2-1) person who repairs teeth or pulls out teeth and makes **dentures** (2-tshgz) = sets of teeth made to take the place of those which have been pulled out.

den'ude (1-177) uncover; cause to be uncovered; *A land denuded of trees* = having no trees; *Denuded of all his money* = having lost —.

den'unci'ation (1-8-s121shn) act of *denouncing* (see 5th above).

deny (1-41) say that something is not true; refuse to give, e.g. *To deny oneself the pleasure*.

de'odorant (1167-9-9) liquid or powder which takes away bad smells.

depart (1-44) go away.

dep'artment (1-44-9) branch of a business, shop, school, government, etc.; any part of a whole, e.g. one of the parts into which France is divided; Am. **D'epartm'ental st'ore** (11-44-2 + 55) = a large shop selling many different kinds of goods.

dep'arture (1-44tshg) act of going away.

dep'end on (1-2) (= hang from); be supported by; trust to the support of; to be partly caused or controlled by, e.g. *Victory depends on strength and courage; Good temper depends largely on health; It all depends* = it is uncertain, until I know (certain other facts); **dep'endable** (1-2-9) trustworthy; **dep'endency** (1-2-9-sI) country which is controlled by another country.

dep'ict (1-1) show by a picture; describe carefully.

dep'ilatory (1-1-9-9-1) liquid used for taking away hair from the body, for making the skin hairless.

depl'ete (1-11) to empty; to use until little or none is left.

depl'ore (1-55) be sorry that a certain event happened.

depl'oy (1-51) spread out an army in line.

dep'onent (1-67-9) one who says certain facts in a court of law, declaring them to be true.

d'ep'opulate (11-5-17-21) take away the people from a country.

dep'ort (1-55) send a person out of a country as a punishment; send back a foreigner to his own country; *Deport oneself* = to behave; **dep'ortment** (——9) graceful movement and behaviour.

dep'ose (1-67z) put down from some high office, e.g. from being king; declare as true in a court of law.

dep'osit (1-5z1) (put down); leave behind; give for safe-keeping; **a dep'osit**, solid matter which sinks to the bottom of a liquid; money paid into a bank for safe-keeping; part of the price of a thing paid at the time of giving the order to supply it.

d'epos'ition (11-9z1shn) statement made by a *deponent* (see 5th above).

depôt (2-67) store-house for goods; place where soldiers' stores are kept, and where new soldiers are trained; Am. railway station.

depr'ave (1-21) make bad in character.

deprecate (2-1-21) ask that a certain thing be not done; say that one wishes that a thing had not happened, e.g. *I deprecate his rudeness* = I wish he had not been —, I am sorry that he was —.

depr'eciate (1-11shI21) make or become less in value.

d'epred'ation (2-1-21shn) stealing.

depr'ess (1-2) make lower; push down; make sad or low in spirits; **depr'ession** (1-2shn) sadness, loss of hope; bad state of trade.

depr'ive (1-41) take away from; prevent from using.

dept. = department—part of an office, government, business.

depth (2) deep-ness; state of being difficult to understand; *I am out of my depth* = in water too deep for me to stand, unable to understand this subject; strength (of feeling); darkness (of colour); *In the depths of winter* = in the middle of —; *In the depths of despair* = having lost all hope.

d'eput'ation (2-17-21shn) giving of power to another to do one's business; small group which is given power to act or speak for a larger group; **dep'ute** (1-177) give such power; **d'eputy** (2-17-1) one who is given such power.

der'ail (1-21) cause a train to go off the line.

der'ange (1-21nj) put out of order; *He is deranged* = mad.

Derby (the) (44-1) famous horse-race in England; hard hat with a round top.

derelict (2-1-1) left to decay; broken ship with no one on it.

derel'iction (of duty) (2-1-1-shn) failing to do a certain duty.

der'ide (1-41) laugh at as of no value; n. **de'rision** (1-13n).

der'ive (1-41) obtain from, e.g. the word "Deride" is derived from the Latin *De* = down and *ridere* = to laugh; n. **deriv'ation** (2-1-21shn).

derm-, -derm, having to do with the skin.

d'ernier cr'i (29-121 + 11) latest newest thing, e.g. a new kind of hat for ladies.

der'ogatory (1-5-9-9-1) causing loss of respect.

derrick (2-1) high frame with ropes and wheels for lifting heavy weights.

DERRICK

dervish (99-1) follower of Muhammad who gives himself completely to the service of *Allah* (God).

desc'ant (1-3) sing; talk at great length; n. **d'escant** (2-3).

desc'end (1-2) go down; *He is descended from (is a descendant of) William the Conqueror* = is great-great- ... grandson of —; *Descend upon* = attack suddenly.

descr'ibe (1-41) tell what a thing is like, give a picture in words; n. **a descr'iption** (1-1-shn), account or report; *A man of that description* = — that kind.

descr'y (1-41) be able to see something a long way off.

desecrate (2-1-21) use a holy thing (e.g. church) for purposes which are not holy; put to a bad or improper use.

des'ert (1z99) to leave; leave one's duty or one's leader; leave the army without being permitted.

desert (2z9) large sandy piece of land where nothing grows because there is no rain.

des'erts (1z99) *He has got his deserts* = what he deserved, e.g. punishment.

des'erve (1z99) be worthy of.

déshabillé, (en —) (21z3-11·121) (44ⁿ) not fully dressed; **in dishabille** (1 + 1-3-1).

desiccate (2-1-21) to dry.

desider'atum (1z1-9-21-9) very necessary thing.

des'ign (1z41) to plan; mean to do; *A designing person* = one who plans to deceive; **a des'ign,** plan, drawing of something which is to be made.

designate (2z1-21) appoint for special work; point out or call by a special name.

des'ire (1z419) to wish, want very much.

des'ist (1z1) cease doing, not do any more.

desk (2) table at which one reads, writes or does business.

desolate (2-9-9) (place) sad and without people in it; (person) sad and deserted by friends; **to desolate** (2-9-21) make like a desert.

desp'air (1-z9) be without hope; state of being without hope.

desp'atch (1-3) see Dispatch.

desper'ado (2-9-44-67) *desperate* (see below) wrong-doer.

desperate (3-9-1) (of a person) ready for any wild act because of loss of hope; (of an action) wild or dangerous, done as a last attempt.

despi'se (1-41z) look down on as low or worthless; adj. **despicable** (2-1-9).

desp'ite (1-41) in spite of.

desp'oil (1-51) steal, take away by force.

desp'ondent (1-5-9) having lost hope.

despot (2-5) one who has all the power of government and uses it unjustly or cruelly.

dess'ert (1z99) fruit, nuts and sweets eaten at the end of a meal; Am. sweet dish served at the end of a meal.

d'estin'ation (2-1-21shn) place to which one is going or to which a letter is to be sent.

destined (2-1) fated; intended by God; **destiny** (2-1-1) fate.

destitute of (2-1-177) not having, without.

destr'oy (1-51) pull or break to pieces; ruin; kill; n. **destr'uction** (1-8-shn).

des'uetude (1-171-177) *That law or custom is in desuetude* = has gone out of use, is not now obeyed.

desultory (2-9-1) passing from one piece of work to another without plan or purpose.

det'ach (1-3) take apart; **detached** (——t) separate, e.g. a house; (of a person) not moved by other people's opinions.

det'ail (1-21) (1) tell every smallest point about; **detail(s)** (11-21-z) small points of a story, small parts of things; (2) appoint to do some special duty; *A detail of (soldiers)* = small number for a special duty.

det'ain (1-21) prevent a person going away; to delay.

det'ect (1-2) find out; **a det'ective** (——1) special officer of the law who finds and catches thieves, murderers and other law-breakers; **a det'ector** (1-2-9) any instrument used for finding out the presence of a thing.

det'ention (1-2-shn) act of preventing a person from going away; state of being *detained* (see 2nd above); state of being kept in school after school-hours as a punishment.

det'er (1-99) keep from an act by fear, punishment, etc.

det'eriorate (1-19-19-21) become worse.

det'ermine (1-99-1) fix; be the cause of; control; *The quality of a man's clothes is determined by how much he can pay* = is controlled by; to decide; find out and fix, e.g. *He determined how much he had to pay*; make up one's mind; *A determined man* = firm, having a strong will; n. **determin'ation** (1-99-1-21shn).

det'errent (1-2) thing which *deters* (see 3rd above).

det'est (1-2) to hate.

dethr'one (1-67) cause to cease being king.

detonate (2-9-21) cause to explode.

detour (21-779) way round.

detr'act (1-3) take away from; lessen the value; say evil against.

detr'ain (11-21) get off a train.

detriment (2-1-9) loss or harm.

detr'itus (1-41-9) stones brought down by ice from a mountain-side.

de tr'op (9 + 67) too many; unwelcome.

deuce (177s) card of the value of two; 40-40 in *tennis* (a game); *The deuce!* = the devil!—cry of surprise; *To play the deuce* = cause great trouble or disorder; *Deuce of a —, Deuced* = meaningless words used to give force to a saying, e.g. *Deuce of a lot* = very many, very much.

deut'erium (177-19-19) see Heavy water.

devastate (2-9-21) destroy everything in a country.

dev'elop (1-2-9) (1) grow up, become larger or more complete, e.g. *A plant develops from a seed*; (2) cause to grow, e.g. *To develop a* *business*; study or think out fully, e.g. *Develop an idea*; (3) make a picture appear on a film (used in photography).

deviate (11-121) move away from the straight or correct path.

dev′ice (1-41s) (1) a plan; *Leave him to his own devices* = — alone, give him no help; (2) cleverly thought-out instrument, e.g. *A device for sharpening pencils*; (3) drawing or picture, e.g. *The device painted on a knight's shield*.

devil (2) (1) the spirit of evil, Satan; *Between the devil and the deep sea* = having two choices, both of which are bad; *Give the devil his due* = be just even to a bad person; *To go to the devil* = be ruined; *Play the devil with*. = do much harm to; *It's the very devil* = very difficult or painful; *Devil a one* = not one; *Devil-may-care* = careless and wild in behaviour; (2) person who does work for another, e.g. a young beginner working for an experienced lawyer; *A printer's devil* = beginner in the office of a printer; (3) fellow, e.g. *Poor devil* = poor fellow; *A devil of a fellow* = full of spirits, very brave; **to devil**, work for another; cook food in a very hot-tasting liquid.

devious (11-19) indirect; going round about.

dev′ise (1-41z) make a plan; leave money, land, etc., to someone after death.

dev′italize (11-41-9-41) take away the life and power.

dev′oid (1-51) empty of; lacking.

dev′olve (1-5) pass on work to someone else to do; e.g. *The business devolved upon him*; **devol′ution** (11-6-9-77shn) act of devolving.

dev′ote (1-67) set apart for; give wholly (completely) to, e.g. *He devotes himself to his work*; **dev′oted** (——1) very loving, e.g. *A devoted husband*; **devot′ee** (2-9-11) person wholly given over to the service of God—or to other good work; **dev′otions** (——shnz) prayers; **dev′otional** (——sh9) having to do with prayers.

dev′our (1-479) eat up quickly; read quickly; look at eagerly.

dev′out (1-47) given to prayer and holy thoughts.

dew (177) water which forms on plants, etc., after the sun goes down.

dewlap (177-3) loose skin on the throats of cows, dogs, etc.

dexterous (2-9-9) clever with the hands; n. **dext′erity** (2-2-1-1).

di- apart; away from, down from, e.g. **div′ert** (41-99), **dil′ate** (41-21).

di- two, apart, e.g. **dich′otomy** (41k5-9-1) = dividing into two parts.

dia- across; through; apart; completely.

diab′etes (419-11-11z) disease causing too much sugar in the blood.

diab′olic (419-5-1) coming from the devil; evil; cruel.

diadem (419-2) band of precious stones worn on the head.

d′iagn′ose (419-67z) find out the cause or nature of a disease; n. **diagn′osis** (419-67s1).

di′agonal (413-9) going across from corner to corner.

diagram (419-3) figure drawn with lines to show or prove an idea.

dial (419) instrument with a flat surface and an upright for showing the time by means of the shadow thrown by the sun; face of a clock; any round instrument for measuring; numbered circle on a telephone, used in calling a person to speak on the telephone; *To dial* = to call on the telephone.

DIAL (TELEPHONE)

dialect (419-2) peculiar way of speaking a language used by those in some particular part of the country.

dial′ectic(s) (419-2-1) art of reasoning and *debate* (= talking about a subject in public).

dialogue (419-5) talk between two or more people.

di′ameter (413-1-9) line going through the centre of a circle and touching the edges; length of this line.

diamond (419-9) precious stone, usually colourless, of great value and hardness; a shape; playing-card with this figure printed on it; *Diamond wedding* = 60th year of being married; *A rough diamond* = person good at heart though rough in manner; *Diamond cut diamond* = two persons, both clever, trying to deceive each other; *Black diamonds* = coal.

DIAMOND

diap′ason (419-21z) measure of a voice or musical instrument from the highest to the lowest note; grand burst of music; part of an *organ* (= instrument of music made up of many pipes, often seen in churches).

diaper (419-9) fine cotton cloth with raised lines in diamond shape, used (e.g.) to put round young babies.

di′aphanous (413-9-9) (e.g. cloth) so fine that it can be seen through.

diaphragm (419-3) (dividing wall); the muscle which separates the *lungs* (= that part of the body with which we breathe) from the stomach; any thin plate (in various machines and instruments).

diarrh′oea (419-19) illness (caused by eating wrong food) in which waste matter passes *frequently* (= often) from the bowels.

diary (419-1) book in which notes are written every day, e.g. of things done or of things to be done.

diatom (419-9) very small creature or plant living in water.

diatribe (419-41) fierce speech attacking a person or thing.

dibble (1) pointed gardening instrument used for making holes in the earth.
dice (pl.) (41s) small six-sided pieces of bone or wood with one to six spots on each side, used for games of chance; **to dice**, cut into small squares for cooking.
dich′otomy (41k5-9-1) division into two parts.
dicky, dickey (1-1) extra seat at the back in a two-seated motor-car; child's word for a bird.
dict- having to do with speech.
dictaphone (1-9-67) instrument used in business offices for setting down the sounds of the voice on wax and producing them again later so that the words spoken into the machine may be written down on paper.
dict′ate (1-21) read or speak while another person writes it down; give orders and force people to obey; **dict′ator** (——9) ruler who has all the power of government in his own hands; **dictat′orial** (1-9-55-19) behaving like a dictator; rude and commanding in manner.
diction (1ksh9) way in which one chooses and uses words.
dictionary (1ksh9-1) book containing a list of words in A.B.C. order, with their meanings (this book is a dictionary).
dictum (1-9) opinion expressed very strongly.
did (1) p.t. of Do.
did′actic (41-3-1) teaching a lesson; in the manner of a teacher; *He was too didactic* = he was too sure of his own opinion and did not listen to others.
die (41) cease to live; *A die-hard* = one who refuses to give up opinions formed a long time ago and now proved wrong.
die (41) (pl. **dice**, 41s) see Dice; *The die is cast* = the matter is now decided.
die (41) metal block used for pressing metal, etc., into shape; an instrument used for cutting a screw on a bar.
D′iesel ′engine (11z + 2nj1) engine which works by burning heavy oil.
diet (419) food and drink; **to diet**, eat only certain foods for reasons of health; **a diet**, special foods, etc., so ordered; **diet′itian** (419-1shn) one who plans food so that the right amount of each kind is eaten.
diet (419) group of persons who rule a country (e.g. Denmark); meeting of persons to decide certain questions.
differ (1-9) be unlike; disagree with; quarrel; **difference** (1-s) unlikeness; that which makes things unlike; a quarrel; **different** (1) unlike; various; **differ′ential gear** (1-9-2-shl + 19) round box between the back wheels of a motor-car which makes it possible for each back wheel to turn at a different speed, e.g. when going round a corner; **differ′entiate** (1-9-2-shl21) make different; see the difference between.
difficult (1-1) hard to do; not easy; *A difficult person* = one who is hard to please.

diffident (1-1) without belief in one's own powers.
diff′use (1-177z) to spread in every direction, e.g. a smell through air.
dig (1) make a hole in the earth; search into books; *Give him a dig* = give a quick push to make him attend; **diggings** (1-1) **digs** = (1) Sl. lodgings; (2) land where people dig for gold.
dig′est (1j2) change food into a state in which it can be taken into the blood; take the meaning into the mind, e.g. *Digest a book*; **a d′igest** (41j2) short account of a book or other writing.
digit (1j1) finger or *toe* (*toes* = finger-like things on the feet); number, 0, 1, 2, 3, etc., up to 9.
digit′alis (1j1-21-1), **d′igit′alin** (1j1-21-1) medicine which makes the heart beat more slowly.
dignify (1-1-41) show honour to; cause to appear worthy of honour.
dignitary (1-1-9-1) person holding high office.
dignity (1-1-1) calm and grand manner; noble quality of character; rank and honour; person of high rank, e.g. in the Church.
digr′ess (41-2) wander from the subject in speaking or writing.
dike, dyke (41) thick wall built to keep a river or sea from flowing on to low land.
dil′apidated (1-3-1-21-1) in a state of decay or ruin.
dil′ate (41-21) make larger by stretching; *Dilate upon a subject* = speak for a long time about, write a lot about.
dilatory (1-9-9-1) causing delay.
dil′emma (41-2-9) choice of two answers or actions, both of which seem difficult or bad.
dilett′ante (1-1-3-1) one who studies a serious subject in a careless and *irregular* (= not regular) way; adj. (used of such study).
diligent (1-1j9) working with care and not wasting time.
dilly-dally (1-1 + 3-1) to waste time.
dil′ute (41-177) weaken by mixing—usually with water.
dim (1) not bright; (of an idea) not clear; Sl. *To take a dim view of* = think badly of.
dime (41) ten *cents* (= $\frac{1}{100}$ of a *dollar*) in American money.
dim′ension (1-2nshn) size; measure—of length, width, or height; *The Fourth Dimension* = time (as having an effect on the other three measures).
dim′inish (1-1-1) make or become less; n. **diminution** (1-1-177shn).
dim′inu′endo (1-1-172-67) (music) becoming quieter and quieter.
dimple (1) little hollow in the skin, e.g. of the face.
din (1) loud noise; *To din into the ears of* = continue saying the same thing again and again.
dine (41) eat at dinner; **diner** (41-9) a carriage on a train where meals are served; one who eats dinner; Am. small wooden hut by the roadside where food and meals are sold.

d'ing-d'ong (1 + 5) noise made by a bell.
dinghy (1ngg1) small boat.
dingle (1nggl) small valley.
dingo (1ngg67) Australian wild dog.
dingy (1nj1) dirty, faded.
dinky (1ngk1) (e.g. room, dress) made to look pretty in a foolish way.
dinner (1-9) largest meal of the day, in some countries eaten in the middle of the day, in others in the evening.
dinosaur (41-9-55) very large animal of very ancient times.
dint (1) hollow mark in a surface caused by striking; *By dint of* = by means of.
diocese (419s1s) part of the country in the charge of a *bishop* (= high officer of the Church).
dip (1) take a little water with a *dipper* (see 5th below); to let down into a liquid for a short time; to lower for a short time, e.g. *Dip the flag; To dip into a book* = read a little of —; *a dip,* short swim; a quick bath.
diphth'eria (1-19-19) serious and easily spread disease of the throat.
diphthong (1-5) joining of two *vowels* (= a, e, i, o, u) and making one, e.g. bo-il = boil.
dipl'oma (1-67-9) printed paper showing that one has successfully finished a course of study.
dipl'omacy (1-67-9s1) making of agreements with foreign governments; cleverness in making such agreements; **d'iplomat** (1-9-3) one who acts for his government in such matters; **diplom'atic** (1-9-3-1) clever in dealing with other people so as to get them to agree.
dipper (1-9) cup-like vessel on a handle for taking up liquid.
dipsom'ania (1-9-21-19) mad desire for strong drink.
dire (419) fearful, very bad.
dir'ect (1-2) straight, not going round about, e.g. *The direct road; A direct descendant*—from father to son; *Direct current* = electricity flowing one way along a wire, not to and fro (= Alternating current); **to dir'ect**, to guide; control, e.g. a business; cause to turn, e.g. *Direct your eyes towards;* aim at, or send to, e.g. *To direct a letter;* tell a person the way to a place, e.g. *Please direct me to the post-office;* **dir'ectly** (——1) very soon; **a dir'ectory** (1-2-9-1) list of names of people with their addresses, etc.
dirge (99j) sad song sung over a dead person.
dir'igible (1-1j9) adj. which can be guided; n. airship.
dirk (99) short sword.
dirndl (99ndl) cloth and dress worn by village people in Switzerland.
dirt (99) unclean matter; *Dirt road* = — made of earth; *Dirt-track* = path of rolled earth used for racing.

dis- away or separate; not.
d'isab'ility (1-9-1-1-1) state of not being able; weakness; **to dis'able** (1-21) make unable; wound.
disab'use (1-9-177z) to free from wrong ideas.
disaff'ect (1-9-2) make discontented.
disagr'ee (1-9-11) not to agree; to quarrel.
disapp'ear (1-9-19) go out of sight; be seen no more.
disapp'oint (1-9-51) cause sorrow because of failing to do what is expected; **disapp'ointed** (——1) sad at not seeing one's hopes come true.
disappr'ove (1-9-77) hold a bad opinion of; not to be in favour of.
dis'arm (1-44) give up arms, armies, warships, etc.; take away arms from; drive away anger by friendliness.
disarr'ange (1-9-21nj) put out of order.
disarr'ay (1-9-21) throw into disorder; state of disorder.
dis'aster (1z44-9) sudden great misfortune.
disav'ow (1-9-47) say that one has no concern with or knows nothing of —.
disb'and (1-3) let soldiers out of the army; break up an army; separate and go in different directions.
disb'urse (1-99) pay out money.
disc (1) see Disk.
disc'ard (1-44) throw away as useless.
disç'ern (1z99) see or feel—with some difficulty, e.g. a distant object, a fine difference, a faint smell.
disch'arge (1-44j) do (a duty); send away (a person from employment); unload goods from a ship; to fire (a gun); pay (a debt) completely; n. **discharge**, act of discharging; poisonous matter which comes out of a wound.
disç'iple (1-41) follower of a great teacher.
disçipline (1-1-1) training which produces *obedience* (n. of Obey); teaching which produces good qualities of mind or character; *A good* **disçiplin'arian** (1-1-1-29-19) = teacher (or other person in control of a group) who keeps good order in his class.
discl'aim (1-21) say that one has nothing to do with, is not concerned with, does not own or make any claim upon.
discl'ose (1-67z) make known what has been secret; n. **discl'osure** (1-6739).
disc'olour (1-8-9) change or destroy the natural or right colour.
disc'omfit (1-8-1) cause a person's plans to fail; give an unpleasant shock.
disconc'ert (1-9-s99) give a shock to a person, e.g. by ruining his plans.
disc'onsolate (1-5-9-1) sad, hopeless.
discont'ented (1-9-2-1) not satisfied; unhappy.
discont'inue (1-9-1-17) to stop.
discord (1-55) disagreement; notes of music which do not sound well together.
disc'ount (1-47) take off a certain amount from the price or value; *To discount a story* =

discountenance   93   **dispatch**

believe only part of it; n. **d'iscount**, a certain amount taken off.

disc'ountenance (1-47-1-9-s) show dislike for a plan.

disc'ourage (1-8-1j) cause one to lose courage; try to stop what one does not like.

disc'ourse (1-55) a speech.

disc'ourteous (1-99-19) not polite.

disc'over (1-8-9) find for the first time; (in old books) make known.

discr'edit (1-2-1) cause a loss of belief in the goodness or truth of; **discr'editable** (——9) causing harm to one's good name.

discr'eet (1-11) careful and showing good judgment.

discr'epancy (1-2-9-s1) failing to agree; two things said or written by a person which do not agree, e.g. *Born in the year 1900, he was 35 years old in 1930*.

discr'ete (1-11) separate.

discr'etion (1-2shn) carefulness and good judgment.

discr'iminate (1-1-1-21) see the difference between; choose with judgment; *Discriminate against* = treat unfairly.

disc'ursive (1-99-1) wandering, without a fixed plan (e.g. book or speech).

discus (1-9) flat round object used for throwing.

disc'uss (1-8) to talk about; to reason together; Sl. *Discuss a bottle of wine* = share ——.

disd'ain (1-21) look down upon as not worthy of respect; n. feeling of disrespect for.

dis'ease (1z11z) illness.

d'isemb'ark (1-1-44) get off a boat.

d'isemb'ody (1-1-5-1) set free from the body.

d'isemb'owel (1-2-479) cut out the bowels from the body.

d'isench'ant (1-1-44) set free from the effects of magic; show that a thing loved or believed in is unworthy.

d'isent'angle (1-1-3) untie and straighten out a string which is knotted up; set in order and make clear a matter which is mixed up or in disorder.

disf'igure (1-1-9) harm the beauty or shape of.

disfr'anchise (1-3-41z) take away the right to elect people to the government.

disg'orge (1-55j) bring out from the throat what has been eaten; give up, e.g. stolen goods.

disgr'ace (1-21s) loss of respect because of wrong-doing; **to disgr'ace**, bring shame or dishonour upon.

disgr'untled (1-8) in a bad temper through not having got what was expected.

disg'uise (1-41z) change the appearance of (oneself or another) in order to deceive; dress, paints, hair, etc., worn by an actor or dishonest person to hide the real appearance.

disg'ust (1-8) strong feeling of dislike such as is caused by a very bad smell or unpleasant sight.

dish (1) large flat plate, or bowl or other container, e.g. one used to contain food; food cooked and ready for serving; *To dish up* = put food in a dish and bring it to the table; Sl. to ruin.

dishab'ille (1s9-11) not fully dressed.

dish'earten (1s·h44) cause to lose hope.

dish'evel (1-2) disarrange (clothes or hair).

dish'onour (1-5-9) cause shame; treat rudely; refuse to pay.

disill'usion (1-1-7739n) to free from a wrong idea.

disinf'ect (1-1-2) make clean and free from all seeds of disease.

disinh'erit (1-1-2-1) say that one's son or daughter shall not have one's money, etc., after one's death.

dis'integrate (1-1-1-21) break into pieces; change slowly into a powder; to decay.

disint'er (1-1-99) take out of a grave.

dis'interested (1-1-1-1) just and fair because not gaining anything for oneself.

disk, disc (1) round flat object; *Disk-jockey* = person who puts records on the gramophone for radio.

dislocate (1-9-21) put out of its proper place, e.g. a bone in the body; *Traffic was dislocated* = the service of trains, street cars, etc., was thrown into disorder; n. **disloc'ation** (1-9-21shn).

disl'odge (1-5j) move from its place.

dismal (1z) cheerless; sorrowful.

dism'antle (1-3) take away all the sails and *fittings* (= things fixed on) from a ship, all the guns from a fort, machinery from a workshop, etc.

dism'asted (1-44-1) (of a ship) having lost its *masts* (= upright poles which carry the sails).

dism'ay (1-21) loss of courage because of fear or great difficulty; to cause this.

dism'ember (1-2-9) cut the limbs off a body; cut or take to pieces.

dism'iss (1-1) send away; send away from employment.

dism'ount (1-47) get down from a horse, carriage, etc.; take down a thing (e.g. gun) from that upon which it was *mounted* (= fixed, set up).

dis'organize (1-55-9-41) put out of working order.

dis'own (1-67) refuse to accept as being one's own.

disp'arage (1-3-1j) speak ill against; say bad things about; say that a thing is valueless.

disp'arity (1-3-1-1) state of not being equal.

disp'assionate (1-3sh9-1) free from strong feeling; just, because not feeling favour for either side.

disp'atch, desp'atch (1-3) send off quickly; kill; finish quickly; n. quickness of action; quick message; government letter, e.g. *to some foreign country*; *Mentioned in despatches* (of a soldier) = having his name printed in the account of a battle as having fought specially well.

disp'el (1-2) drive away, e.g. *The sun dispels the clouds.*

disp'ensary (1-2-9-1) place where medicines are mixed and given out.

dispensa'tion (1-2-2ɪshn) special act of God; *A special dispensation* = allowing some special action, which usually is not allowed.

disp'ense (1-2) give out; measure out (medicine); *To dispense with* = do without.

disp'erse (1-99) scatter.

disp'irited (1-1-1-1) sad and without hope.

displ'ace (1-2ɪs) put out of place; **displ'acement** (1-2ɪs-9) (of a ship) the weight of water *displaced* (= pushed aside) by a ship—the depth to which the ship sinks into the water; *Displaced person* = one driven out from his own country.

displ'ay (1-2ɪ) to show.

disp'ort (1-55) amuse oneself.

disp'ose (1-67z) arrange; cause one to feel in a certain way; *I am well disposed towards him* = I like him and am willing to help him; *Disposed to help him* = willing to —; *Dispose of* = set oneself free from; — (of goods) = sell or give away; — (of work to be done) = finish; (of an enemy) drive away, make harmless.

dispos'ition (1-9zɪshn) person's natural way of feeling and acting; arrangement, e.g. of an army for battle.

disposs'ess (1-9zz) take away what a person *possesses* (= owns); turn a person out of a place.

disprop'ortionate (1-9-55sh9-1) unequal, too much on one side and too little on the other.

disp'ute (1-177) talk about and disagree; to quarrel; say that an opinion is not true.

disqu'alify (1-5-1-41) make unfit or unable to act.

disqu'iet (1-419) make anxious.

disquis'ition (1-1zɪshn) long speech or written report about some subject.

disr'eputable (1-2-17-9) having a bad character or bad name.

disr'obe (1-67) take off the clothes.

disr'upt (1-8) tear apart.

diss'ect (1-2) cut up into pieces in order to examine, e.g. a dead body; study a book very carefully.

diss'emble (1-2) pretend not to be what one really is; hide one's feelings.

diss'eminate (1-2-1-2ɪ) (to scatter like seed); to spread around; to send reports everywhere.

diss'ent (1-2) disagree; quarrel; n. **diss'ension** (1-2-shn) quarrelling; adj. **diss'entient** (1-2-shɪ9) not agreeing; **a diss'enter** (1-2-9) one who does not agree with the teachings of the Church of England.

d'issertation (1-99-2ɪshn) long report or speech.

diss'ervice (1-99-ɪs) harmful action.

diss'ever (1-2-9) to cut apart.

diss'imulate (1-1-17-2ɪ) hide one's feelings.

dissipate (1-1-2ɪ) scatter; waste by foolish spending; n. **dissip'ation** (1-1-2ɪshn) waste of health and money by wild living.

diss'ociate (1-67shɪ2ɪ) to separate from; think of as separate; say that one has nothing to do with a person or idea.

dissolute (1-9-77) living an evil life.

diss'olve (125) make a solid or a gas liquid by putting it into liquid, e.g. *Sugar dissolves in water*; *Dissolved in tears* = weeping; break up; send away, e.g. *To dissolve a meeting*; melt away, to be seen no more.

dissonant (1-9-9) not agreeing in sound.

dissu'ade (1sw2ɪ) reason with a person and prevent him from taking certain action.

distaff (1-44) stick from which the wool is pulled in *spinning* (= making thread); *On the distaff side* = on the woman's side of the family.

distance (1-s) amount of space between two points; *To keep one's distance* = not to go too near, not be too friendly; **distant**, far away from; a long time ago; *Distant in manner* = not friendly.

dist'asteful (1-2ɪ) disliked; unpleasant.

dist'emper (1-2-9) water-paint for walls; disease of dogs.

dist'end (1-2) cause to swell.

dist'il(l) (1-1) (1) get the liquid from a material by heating it so that the liquid comes off in a gaseous form; the gas is then cooled and becomes pure liquid; (2) come drop by drop.

dist'illery (1-1-9-1) place where *whisky* or other such drinks are made.

dist'inct (1-ɪngk) separate; clear; with each part well marked; **dist'inction** (1-ɪngkshn) special mark of honour; difference between; **dist'inguish** (1-ɪnggwɪ) notice carefully the difference between; *Distinguish oneself* = make oneself noticed by all, or famous.

dist'ort (1-55) change the natural appearance of; turn from the true meaning.

distr'act (1-3) cause one's mind to wander in many directions; **distr'acted** (———1) made anxious by being troubled about many things.

distr'ain (1-2ɪ) seize goods for debt; n. **distr'aint**.

distr'ait (1-2ɪ) thinking of other things, not of the present business.

distr'aught (1-55) see Distracted (3rd above).

distr'ess (1-2) pain or difficulty of any kind.

distr'ibute (1-1-17) give out, or scatter, among many people, or in different places.

district (1-1) part of a country, etc.; part of a country marked out for some special purpose, e.g. government, school, etc.

distr'ust (1-8) not to have faith in.

dist'urb (1-99) to change the usual or natural condition, e.g. *A wind disturbed the surface of the water*; break in upon a person who is working; cause a person to become anxious; break one's peace of mind, sleep, etc.; *To cause a disturbance* = make a noise, start a fight.

dis'use (1-177s) state of not being used.

ditch (1) deep water *channel* (= deep, narrow way in which water runs) for carrying off water, e.g. at the side of a road; *To die in the last ditch* = fight to the very end; *To ditch an aeroplane* = bring it down on or into the sea.

ditto (1-67) the same; a mark (,, ,, ,,) meaning the same.

ditty (1-1) simple song.

di'urnal (4199) having to do with the daytime; happening each day.

div'an (1-3) long, low soft seat; room with long seats in it, e.g. smoking-room in a hotel.

dive (41) jump head first into the water; go down quickly, as a rabbit into its hole; *a dive*, place where bad men live or plan evil deeds; *diver* (——9) man who works at the bottom of the sea in a special dress with a supply of air.

div'erge (41-99j) go out in a different direction from.

divers (41-9z) many different; **div'erse** (41-99) different; various; **div'ersion** (——shn) act of turning from a regular course; any act which amuses and makes one forget one's regular work for a short time; **to div'ert** (41-99) turn from a regular course; amuse; cause to forget one's regular work; **div'erting**, amusing.

div'est (41-2) take off the clothes or coverings.

div'ide (1-41) separate into parts; divide one number by another, e.g. $6 \div 3 = 2$, 6 divided by 3 equals 2.

dividend (1-1-2) share of the money which has been made by a business, divided among those who own the business.

divin'ation (1-1-21shn) act of telling the unknown or the future.

div'ine (1-41) having to do with God; **divinely** (——1) by God; *To sing divinely* = very well; *a div'ine* = priest.

div'ine (1-41) guess what is hidden; *A waterdiviner* = one who finds underground streams with the help of a Y-shaped stick.

div'inity (1-1-1-1) a god; study of the nature of God.

div'isible (1-1z1) which can be divided.

div'ision (1-13n) act of dividing; part divided off; part of an army, about 20,000 men.

div'orce (1-55s) act of separating a man and wife by a court of law; separate that which should be joined together, e.g. *His talk is divorced from reason.*

div'ulge (1-8-j) tell what has been secret.

dizziness (1-1-1) unpleasant feeling in the head, e.g. after turning round many times.

do (did, done) (77) (1, 8) *Do the flowers* = arrange; *Do one's hair* = brush; *Do the meat well* = cook; *Done to a turn* = perfectly cooked; *To do Oxford* = see all places of interest in —; Sl. *Done in the eye* = deceived, tricked; *Will this do you?* = suit; *Do oneself well, proud* = live in great comfort; *Have to do with* = be concerned with; *Have nothing to do with him* = not deal with, not meet or talk to; *It doesn't do to be* = is not wise —; *That will do* = is enough; *Do away with* = kill, destroy, put an end to; *Do for* = kill, ruin; *Do out a room* = clean; *Do up a (house)* = paint and repair; *Do up a (shoe, dress)* = tie up, fasten; Sl. **a do**, trick, feast or party of guests; Sl. *Fair do's* = share equally.

docile (67s41) easily taught or led.

dock (5) common plant which grows by the road-side in England.

dock (5) a place where ships stay while loading; a place where ships are built or repaired.

dock (5) to cut off a part. DOCK

dock (5) place in a court of law where the prisoner stands.

docket (5-1) list of things to be done; **to docket**, write on the back of a long report a short description of what it contains; set of papers tied together and so described.

dockyard (5-44) yard where ships are built or repaired.

doctor (5-9) one who attends to people when they are ill; highest title given by a university; *To doctor a thing* = repair it; *To doctor food* = mix with other things of bad quality; *To doctor accounts* = make them seem true.

d'octrin'aire (5-1-29) person who has strong beliefs which he is always wishing to put into practice even in matters where they are unsuitable or impossible.

doctrine (5-1) what is taught, e.g. by the Church, a set of beliefs.

document (5-17-9) written or printed paper.

d'ocum'entary film (5-17-2-9-1 + 1) a cinema film about real things or events.

dodder (5-9) shake and be unsteady like an old man.

dodge (5j) move suddenly in order to escape something; escape (one's duty) by a trick; *A clever dodge* = clever trick.

doe (67) female deer or rabbit.

doff (5) take off, e.g. one's hat.

dog (5) common animal; iron frame for supporting burning wood in a fireplace; *A gay dog* = person who is always seeking amusement; *You dog!* = low, bad person; *To lead a dog's life* = have many troubles; *To go to the dogs* = become ruined in character; *Dog in the manger* = one who does not wish to use a thing, yet will not allow others to use it; *Let sleeping dogs lie* = leave alone things which may cause trouble; **to dog**, follow closely.

d'ogcart (5-44) two-wheeled cart.

d'og-days (+ 21z) very hot days in July and August.

d'og-eared (book) (+ 19) having the corners of the pages turned down.

dogged (5-1) having a character which refuses to yield or give up in the face of difficulty.

doggerel (5-9) rough, foolish poetry.

dogma (5-9) fixed teaching which must be accepted without reasoning; adj. **dogm'atic** (5-3-1).

d'og-rose (+ 67z) wild rose.

d'og-star (+ 44) brightest star in the heavens, Sirius.

d'og-t'ired (+ 419) very tired.

dog-tooth, dog's tooth, (+ 77) ornament on stone as shown.

d'og-watch (+5) shortest *watch* (= time during which a seaman is on duty —working or guarding the ship) in a ship from 4 to 6 o'clock in the afternoon.

DOG-TOOTH ORNAMENT

doily (51-1) small ornamental cloth put under a dish or other vessel on the table.

doldrums (5-9) place on the ocean where ships cannot move because there is no wind; *In the doldrums* = in a low and sad state of mind.

dole (67) a share; *To dole out* = give out a small part at a time.

doll (5) small play-thing made like a human figure; Sl. *To doll up* = dress up in fine clothes.

dollar (5-9) piece of money used in America, China, etc.

dolorous (5-9-9) sorrowful; n. **dolour** (67-9) sorrow.

dolphin (5-1) sea animal, 6-8 feet long, which swims very quickly moving in and out of the water in curves.

DOLPHIN

dolt (67) fool.

-dom, used to express rank or country ruled, e.g. **dukedom** (177-9) = rank of duke; **kingdom** (1-9) the country ruled by a king.

dom'ain (9-21) land; right to rule over a land; *The domain of science* = those studies which are dealt with by scientists.

dome (67) rounded top on a building; any rounded top or cover.

dom'estic (9-2-1) having to do with the home; *A domestic* = servant in a home.

domicile (5-1s41) home; country in which one's home is.

dominate (5-1-21) to rule; be the most important; rise above, e.g. *This tall building dominates the city.*

domin'eer (5-1-19) rule by force; force others to let one have one's own way.

dominie (5-1-1) schoolmaster (in Scotland).

dom'inion (9-1-19) right to rule; country ruled by one government.

domino (5-1-67) loose garment and covering for the face worn at special parties when one wishes to be unknown; flat piece of wood with white spots on it used for playing a game.

don (5) teacher in a university; title of a gentleman or nobleman in Spain; "Sir" or "Mr." in Spain; **doña** (5ny4) = Mrs., Madam, in Spain (Italy: **donna** (5-4)).

don (5) put on clothes.

don'ate (67-21) give.

done (8) p.p. of Do.

donkey (5ngkr) ass.

donor (67-9) one who gives something.

don't (67) do not.

doodle (77) make meaningless marks on paper.

doom (77) fate; ruin.

doomsday (77-z-21) day of judgment when the world ends.

door (55) that through which one enters a house or room; *Next door* = in the next house; *Out of doors* = in the open air; *Lay at a person's door* = blame him for; **doorway** (55-21) a door, an opening.

dope (67) paint used on the wings of aeroplanes; medicine not ordered by a doctor but taken because of a pleasant effect on the body (bad in its effects on character) e.g. morphia.

dormant (55-9) sleeping; not active.

dormer-window (55-9 + 1-67) upright window in a sloping roof.

dormitory (55-1-1) large sleeping-room for a number of persons.

DORMER-WINDOW

dormouse (55-47s) small, mouse-like animal with a long furry tail.

dorsal (55) having to do with the back.

dory (55-1) flat-bottomed boat; sea fish (John Dory).

dose (67) amount of medicine taken at one time; anything unpleasant which has to be taken.

doss-house (5 + 47) sleeping-place for the very poor.

dossier (5-121) collection of papers about a person.

dost (8) *Thou dost* = you do.

dot (5) any small round mark; Sl. *On the dot* = at the exact time; Sl. *To dot him one* = hit; *Dotted with houses* = with houses scattered over it.

dot (5) money a woman brings with her at marriage.

dotage (67-1j) state of old age when one only remembers past events and does not notice present happenings; **dotard** (67-9) very old man.

dote upon (67 + 9-5) love in a foolish way.

doth (8) *He doth* = he does.

dotty (5-1) Sl. mad.

double (8) twice; meant for two persons, e.g. *A double bed; A double door* = one having two parts; *Advance at the double* = run (of soldiers); *One's double* = person who looks just like oneself; **to double,** make double, or become double; fold a thing over on itself, e.g. a cloth;

double-cross   97   **dram**

Double up = fold up; Sl. sit closer; run faster; *Double back* = bend back, run back.

d'ouble-cr'oss (+ 5) deceive.

d'ouble-d'ealing (+ 11-1) dishonest, dishonesty.

d'ouble-ent'endre (77 + 44ⁿ-44ⁿ) words which have two meanings, one good and the other improper.

d'ouble 'entry (8 + 2-1) way of keeping accounts in which everything is written twice, once as an outgoing and once as an incoming amount.

d'ouble-faced (+ 21st) friendly in one's presence but secretly unfriendly.

d'ouble-quick (+ 1) very quickly.

doublet (8-1) tight garment worn on the upper half of the body.

doubl'oon (8-77) gold piece of money once used in Spain.

doubt (47) question the truth of; be uncertain.

douche (77sh) instrument for forcing a stream of water into or on to any part of the body to wash it.

dough (67) flour mixed with water ready for baking; Sl. money; **doughnut** (67-8) small soft round cake cooked in boiling fat.

doughty (47-1) brave.

dour (779) silent and unwilling to change an idea.

douse (47s) put into water; throw water on; put out a light.

dove (8) soft-voiced bird often used as a sign of peace; **dovecot, dovecote** (8-9) box or house built for *doves* to live in.

dovetail (18-21) join wood together tightly in a special way; *Their plans dovetailed* = their plans fitted very well together.   DOVETAIL

dowager (479j9) e.g. *The Dowager Queen of X* = the wife of the dead king of X, not the wife of the present king.

dowdy (47-1) badly-dressed.

dower (479) money, lands, etc., which a woman gets on her husband's death (or brings at her marriage); natural powers which one has at birth.

down (47) opposite to up; *To do down* = deceive; *To down a person* = beat or conquer; *To be down on, To have a down on* = dislike especially; *To be down with* = be in bed with (illness); *To be sent down* = be sent away from a university for bad behaviour; *Ups and downs* = good and bad fortune; *He is down for a speech* = he is on the list of speakers; *Down and out* = man without money, employment or hope.

down (47) soft feathers on a bird; any fine soft wool.

downcast (47-44) very low in spirits.

downright (47-41) saying one's meaning plainly and with force.

downs (47-z) low hills covered with grass.

d'ownst'airs (47-29z) not in the upper part of the house.

d'owntr'odden (47-5) not getting just treatment; pushed down by a stronger power.

dowry (47-1) money, land, etc., which a woman brings when she is married.

dowser (47s9) man who finds underground streams with the help of a Y-shaped stick.

d'ox'ology (5-5-9j1) short song of praise to God.

doyen (dw412n) oldest member of.

doze (67) be half asleep.

dozen (8) twelve; *A baker's dozen* = thirteen.

D.P. (11 + 11) displaced person; see Displace.

Dr. doctor.

dr. debtor (= one who owes money).

drab (3) without pleasant colours; uninteresting.

drachm (3) (1) 1/16 of an ounce (*avoirdupois*), (2) 1/8 ounce (*apothecaries*).

draft (44) first rough writing of anything; rough plan; written order to pay money, used in sending money to distant places; number of soldiers chosen to be sent to another place; **to draft**, write or draw roughly; send soldiers; **draftsman** (——9) man who draws plans, e.g. of machines or buildings, or draws up (writes) laws.

draft (44) group of men called up into the U.S. army; **to draft**.

drag (3) pull a heavy object; be slow and uninteresting; **a drag**, thing which is dragged; large horse-carriage; *A drag on the party* = one who prevents a gathering of friends from being enjoyable; *To drag the lake* = pull nets along the bottom, e.g. in order to get out a dead body.

drag'ée (44321) small ball of medicine; small sweet, e.g. a sugar-coated nut.

draggled (3) dirty and wet and with clothes in disorder.

dragoman (3-9-9) one who speaks the language of foreigners and leads them round to see places in Eastern countries.

dragon (3-9) imaginary fire-breathing animal in children's stories.

dragon-fly (+ 41) flying insect.

drag'oon (9-77) horse-soldier; **to drag'oon**, treat persons fiercely and make them obey very quickly and exactly.   DRAGON-FLY

drain (21) make dry by running the water out of; (of liquid) flow; **a drain**, pipe or *channel* (= narrow water-way) for dirty water; continued loss, e.g. of blood, money, etc.; **drainage** (——1j) water or waste carried away; pipes, etc., which carry away waste water.

drake (21) male duck.

dram (3) small measure of weight; small drink of strong drink (e.g. whisky).

drama (44-9) a play; exciting events like those in a play; adj. **dram'atic** (9-3-1) having to do with plays; sudden and surprising, as if it were an event in a play.

dr'amatis pers'onae (3-9-1 + 99-67-11) persons in a play.

drape (21) cover loosely with cloth.

draper (21-9) one who sells women's clothes, cloth, curtains, etc.

drastic (3-1) done completely and with force.

draught (44ft) stream of air blowing through a room; measure of how deep a ship is in the water; plan or drawing; amount taken at one time, e.g. *Draught of fishes* = number caught in the net; *Draught of wine* = one large mouthful; *A draught-horse* = strong horse for pulling heavy things.

draughts (44fts) game played by two people, each with twelve round pieces on a board of sixty-four squares.

draughtsman (44ft-9) see Draftsman; piece used in *draughts* (above).

draw (55) (1) pull, e.g. *A horse draws a load*; *To draw teeth* = pull out; (2) *To draw one's pay* = receive; *To draw a glass of wine from a barrel*, *To draw blood* = cause to flow; (3) sink to a certain depth, e.g. *The ship draws 30 feet*; (4) finish a race or fight, neither side having won, e.g. *A drawn game*; (5) *To draw a line, Draw a picture* = make with pencil or pen; *To draw the line at (murder)* = be unwilling to go so far as —; *Draw for places* = take out a marked piece of paper showing which is one's place, thus settling the matter by chance; *The chimney draws well* = air passes up it making the fire burn; *Draw back, near, away* = go; *Draw on, — round* = come; *The play is a great draw* = success.

dr'awback (55-3) (1) difficulty; thing which causes trouble; (2) repayment of duty (= money paid on foreign goods brought into a country) on goods.

dr'awbridge (55-1j) bridge which can be pulled up, e.g. to let ships pass, or when a castle is attacked.

drawer (559) one who makes pictures with pen or pencil; one who writes; box-like container in a piece of furniture which can be pulled out or pushed in.

drawers (55z) undergarment covering the lower part of the body and upper part of the legs.

drawing (551) a picture.

drawing-room (+ 7) sitting-room used in the afternoon and evening.

drawl (55) speak slowly, making each word long.

drawn (55) p.p. of Draw.

dray (21) heavy four-wheeled cart.

dread (2) fear greatly.

dreadnought (2-55) one who fears nothing; large warship.

dream (11) thoughts passing through the mind when asleep; *I shouldn't dream of doing that* = will certainly not —.

dreary (19-1) cheerless, sad.

dredger (2j9) boat with a machine for taking up mud from the bottom of a river or harbour; **to dredge** (2j) clear a river, etc., by such means.

dredger (2j9) pot with holes in the top used for scattering sugar, salt, etc., over food, also for flour in the kitchen; **to dredge** (2j) scatter (sugar) over.

dregs (2-z) muddy matter at the bottom of a liquid, e.g. of wine.

drench (2-tsh) make thoroughly wet.

dress (3) put clothes on; wash and bind up (a wound); prepare for use, e.g. food, leather, etc.; *To dress up* = put on special clothes as for a play; *To dress ship* = put up many flags on a —; *Don't dress* = do not put on evening (ceremonial) clothes; *To dress on £12 a year* = not spend more than £12 a year for one's clothes; *Dress by the right* = look to the right and get into line; *Dress down* = scold; a **dress**, garment; a woman's outer garment; *Full dress* = evening (ceremonial) clothes.

dress'age (2-443) art of controlling a horse.

dr'ess c'ircle (+ s99) raised seats in a theatre just above the lowest floor.

dresser (2-9) one who dresses (3rd above); a fitting in a kitchen with open shelves above and closed places below for pots, etc.

dressing (3-1) act of putting on clothes; mixture of oil and other matter served with some foods; material which is put on a wound.

dressing-gown (+ 47) long garment used when one is undressed.

dressy (2-1) wearing fine clothes; always well-dressed.

drew (77) p.t. of Draw.

dribble (1) let fall drop by drop; give short quick kicks to a ball while running with it;

driblet (1-1) small amount, e.g. of liquid.

dried (41) p.t. of Dry.

drier (419) see Dryer (which is correct); more dry.

drift (1) float along slowly; go along having no plan or fixed idea; *A snow-drift* = snow blown by the wind to form a small hill; *The drift of a speech* = general meaning.

driftwood (1-7) wood blown on to the shore by wind.

drill (1) make a hole through or into; **a drill**, machine or instrument used for making holes.

drill (1) plant seeds with a machine; the machine used.

drill (1) train soldiers in correct movements; train by giving much practice; n. **drill**, correct movements as ordered.

drill (1) heavy, cotton cloth.

drily (41-1) Dry + ly (Dryly is correct).

drink (1ngk) take in liquid with the mouth; take too much wine, etc.; *Drink like a fish* = take too much wine; n. **drink**, any liquid used

drip for drinking, especially wine and strong drinks; *To take to drink* = begin to drink too much wine or strong drink.

drip (1) small drop of liquid; fall in drops.

dripping (1-1) fat used in cooking.

drive (41) force to go in a certain direction; ride in a carriage or car; control a horse-carriage or motor-car; *To drive a nail* = hit it in; *To drive a hard bargain* = make an agreement in which the other person gains little or nothing; *To drive a ball* = hit it a long way; *Let drive at* = aim a blow at; *What are you driving at?* = what is your meaning or intention?; *a drive*, short journey in a carriage or motor-car; distance a ball is hit; hitting of a ball; a road up to the door of a house.

drivel (1) foolish talk.

driven (1) p.p. of Drive.

drizzle (1) fine rain.

drogue (67) thing pulled by a ship to keep it pointing into the wind; a bag pulled behind an aeroplane to be shot at.

DROGUE

droll (67) peculiar, causing laughter.

dromedary (8-1-9-1) animal with a raised place on its back, used in dry sandy countries.

drone (67) male bee; lazy person; low sound as of bees.

droop (77) bend downwards like a half-dead plant; lose one's spirits.

drop (5) (1) allow to fall; *To drop a brick* = say or do something very foolish when in company; *Drop money* = lose; *I'll drop you at your house* = let you get down from my car at —; *To drop a person* = cease to be friendly to; (2) to fall, e.g. *To drop down dead*; become less, e.g. *Prices have dropped*; *Drop behind* = be left behind; *Drop in* = make an unexpected visit to a friend.

DROMEDARY

drop (5) small amount of liquid; *Take a drop too much* = take too much wine; *A drop of 10 feet* = fall of —.

dropsy (5-1) collection of liquid in the body, especially in the legs, as a result of disease.

droshky (5-1) light four-wheeled horse-carriage as used in Russia.

dross (5) worthless matter taken off the surface when metal is melted.

drought, drouth (47) lack of rain.

drove (67) p.t. of Drive.

drove (67) number of animals, e.g. sheep being driven along together.

drover (67-9) one who drives cattle.

drown (47) die by being under water for a long time; kill in this way; *To drown a voice* = make so much noise that it cannot be heard.

drowsy (47z1) sleepy.

drub (8) beat with a stick.

drudge (8j) one who does hard unpleasant work for little pay.

drug (8) (1) medicine, or material of which medicines are mixed; (2) medicine which takes away feeling and causes sleep; *A drug in the market* = goods which no one wants to buy; **to drug**, give drugs to; **druggist** (——1) one who sells medicines.

drugget (8-1) woollen floor-covering.

drum (8) musical instrument with a tight skin over a round, hollow box, beaten with sticks to make a loud sound; **eardrum** (19-8), that part of the ear which receives sounds; *To drum a thing into a boy's head* = cause him to remember by saying it over again and again.

drunk (8ngk) p.p. of Drink; *He is drunk* = he has taken too much wine and has lost control of himself; **drunkard** (8ngk9) one who often drinks too much wine or strong drink.

drupe (77) fruit with a stone, e.g. plum.

dry (41) not wet; not interesting, e.g. *A dry book*; **to dry**, make dry; take out all the water from; *To dry up* = become dry; Sl. *Dry up!* = stop talking; **dryer** (419) more dry; an instrument or machine used for drying.

dryad (419) a spirit of the forest.

dry-dock (+ 5) a place in which a ship is taken out of the water for repair.

dry-goods (+ 7-z) Am. cloth, etc., sold in a shop.

dry-rot (+ 5) diseased growth in wood (e.g. wooden floors) which turns wood into powder.

D.T.(s) (11 + 11z) *Delirium Tremens* (1-1-19 + 11-2-z) illness caused by drinking too much wine or strong drink.

dual (179) having to do with two.

dub (8) make a man a knight by touching him on the shoulder with a sword; to name; Am. *A dub* = a foolish fellow.

dub (a film) (8) put English speech on to a French-speaking film, or French, etc. on to English, etc.

dubbin(g) (8-1) oily matter used to make leather soft.

dubious (177-19) doubtful.

ducal (177) having to do with a *duke* (= nobleman).

ducat (8-9) piece of money used in old times in Europe, worth about 90 pence (gold ducat), 30 pence (silver ducat).

duchess (8-1) wife of a *duke* (= nobleman).

duchy (8-1) part of a country controlled by a *duke* (= nobleman).

duck (8) common water-bird; *Like water off a duck's back* = having no effect; *Take to it like a duck to water.* = learn naturally and very easily; *Ducks and drakes* = game in which one makes stones jump along the surface of water; *Play ducks and drakes with one's money* = waste money wildly; *A lame duck* = person or ship which cannot move properly; *She's a perfect duck* = very nice; *A duck's egg (A duck)* = 0 (e.g. in *cricket* and other games).

duck (8) push under water; move the body down quickly so as to save the head from a blow.

duck (8) heavy cloth used (e.g.) for sails and seamen's clothes.
duckling (8-1) young duck.
duct (8) any pipe, e.g. in the body.
ductile (8-41) which can easily be pulled out into a thread.
dud (8) useless person or thing.
dude (177) Am. Sl. a man who loves to wear fine clothes.
dudgeon (8j9) anger.
duds (8-z) Sl. garments.
due (177) (1) owed, e.g. *The debt is due on April 15th* = should be paid on —; *To give a man his due* = give what is right; *Give the devil his due* = be just even to a bad person; (2) proper, e.g. *With due respect*; *In due time, in due course* = at the proper time; (3) caused by, e.g. *Death due to an accident*; *Due east* = straight towards the —.
duel (1779) a fight with *pistols* (= small gun held in one hand) or swords arranged between two people because of a quarrel.
duet (1772) piece of music performed by two people.
duffer (8-9) foolish fellow; slow learner.
duffel-coat (8 + 67) coat as shown, with wooden fasteners.
duffle-coat, see Duffel-coat.

DUFFEL-COAT

dug (8) p.t. and p.p. of Dig; (of animals), point where the young gets milk from the mother.
dugong (77-5) large fish-like creature found in the sea, also called a "sea-cow".

DUGONG

dugout (8-47) (1) boat made by hollowing out a tree; (2) an underground room used as a shelter in war-time; (3) old army officer called up again to serve in a war.
duke (177) highest rank in England below a prince.
dulcet (8-s1) soft and pleasant sounding.
dulcimer (8-s1-9) musical instrument with strings hit with a small hammer.
dull (8) (1) slow in understanding; (2) uninteresting; (3) not keen (of sight or other senses); (4) not bright or clear (of light, sounds, pain); (5) not sharp, e.g. a knife; (6) not active, e.g. trade.
dullard (8-9) one who is slow of understanding.
duly (177-1) at the proper time; according to what is right.
dumb (8) (1) unable to speak; (2) not speaking; *Dumb show* = giving ideas by means of the hands without speaking; Am. slow of understanding, foolish.
dumb-bell (+ 2) wood or iron weight used in exercising the arms; Am. fool.
dumbf'ound (8-47) cause one to lose the power of speech, e.g. because of surprise.
d'umb -w'aiter (+ 21-9) movable table used for serving food; Am. two doors in a wall used for passing food from one room to another, or pulling it up from the kitchen.
dummy (8-1) object made to look like and take the place of a real thing, e.g. *A dummy gun made of wood*; human figure made of wood or wax used to show off clothes; rubber thing put in a baby's mouth to keep it quiet; the cards on the table in playing *Bridge* (= a card game); Am. fool.
dump (8) place in the open for storing goods, especially in war; place for throwing unwanted matter; *To be in the dumps* = to be sad and spiritless; **to dump**, throw down in mass; to set down carelessly; to sell goods in a foreign country at a very low price.
dumpling (8-1) round mass of boiled food made of flour, fat, etc., sometimes with meat or fruit in the middle.
dumpy (8-1) short and thick.
dun (8) dark-brown colour.
dun (8) demand payment of a debt.
dunce (8-s) slow learner.
dunderhead (8-9-2) fool.
dune (177) sandhill.
dung (8) waste matter passed from the bodies of animals, often mixed with soil to make the soil produce more plants.
d'ungar'ee(s) (8ngg9-11z) outer garments worn by men who look after trains, engines, etc., to protect their clothes.
dungeon (8nj9) dark, underground prison.
dunk (8ngk) dip bread in a liquid, e.g. coffee, before eating it.
dunnage (8-1j) pieces of wood used to prevent goods in a ship from moving about when the ship rolls.

DUNGAREES

duo- having to do with two.
d'uod'enum (17767-11-9) first (highest) 12 inches of the bowel.
dupe (177) one who is deceived; one who is unknowingly used by another for a wrong purpose.
duplex (177-2) two in one; Am. house divided into two homes, one above the other.
duplicate (177-1-21) make an exact copy; n. **duplicate** (177-1-1); **duplicator** (—21-9) machine used for making many copies of a letter.
dupl'icity (177-1s1-1) act of being dishonest.
durable (177-9) lasting a long time, e.g. *Durable shoes, cloth*.
durance (177-9-s) state of being kept a prisoner.
dur'ation (177-21shn) time during which anything continues.
durbar (99-44) special meeting of a ruler and the important men of his government in India.
dur'ess(e) (177-2) state of being in prison; *A promise made under duress* = made, not willingly, but because of force, and so not binding.

during (177-1) e.g. *During dinner* = while dinner was going on.

durst (99) dared.

dusk (8) time when daylight is fading; *A dusky skin* = a dark skin.

dust (8) powder made up of very small pieces of waste matter; finely powdered earth; *To bite the dust* = to die; *Throw dust in his eyes* = deceive; *Shake the dust off one's feet* = go away in anger; **to dust**, cover with dust, e.g. *Dust with sugar*; take the dust off, e.g. *Dust a room*.

duster (8-9) cloth used to clean away dust.

duteous (17-19) **dutiful** (17-1) obeying regularly and willingly.

duty (177-1) that which one ought to do; *To do duty for* = do a person's work for him; money which must be paid to the government before goods can come into the country; adj. **dutiable** (177-19) (goods) on which one must pay duty.

D.V. (11 + 11) (Latin) *D'eo vol'ente* (1167 + 67-2-1) = if God is willing.

dwarf (55) man who is very much smaller than the natural size; anything unusually small; cause to appear small.

dwell (2) live in a place; *To dwell on (a subject)* = think or talk much about; a **dwelling** (———1) a house; dwelt, p.t. of Dwell.

dwindle (1) become less and less.

dye (41) cause to become of a certain colour, e.g. to colour cloth; material used to make colour; *Of the deepest dye* = of the worst kind; **dyeing** (41·1) **dyed** (41).

dying (41·1) nearing death; becoming useless.

dyke (41) see Dike.

dyn'amic (41-3-1) having to do with or producing force or power; (of a person) having great strength of character.

dynamite (41-9-41) powerful explosive, used to break up rocks.

dynamo (41-9-67) machine which produces electric power.

dynasty (1-9-1) line of kings all of the same family; time during which a number of kings of the same family rule a country.

dysentery (1-1) disease of the bowel.

dysp'epsia (1-2-19) difficulty in changing food in the stomach into a form in which it can be built into the body.

E

each (11) every one taken separately.

eager (11-9) full of desire; very anxious to (do).

eagle (11) large meat-eating bird; *Eagle-eyed* = able to see very clearly like the eagle.

ear (19) that part of the body with which we hear; *An ear for music* = power of hearing music clearly and enjoying it; *Give ear to* = listen; *He was all ears* = eager to hear; *Set people by the ears* = cause a quarrel.

ear (19) head of a grain-producing plant.

'ear-drum (19 + 8) tight thin skin in the ear which causes one to hear the sound waves which beat against it.

earl (99) title of an English nobleman, 3rd below prince.

early (99-1) near the beginning of (the day, etc.); *An early bird* = a person who gets out of bed early.

earmark (19-44) mark made on the ear of a sheep, pig, etc., so that its owner may know it; any special mark by which a thing may be known; **to earmark**, to set something (e.g. money) on one side for a special purpose.

earn (99) obtain as payment for work; be worthy of.

earnest (99-1) eager and serious; *I am in earnest* = serious of purpose, I mean what I say; n. **earnest**, promise of something to be done; money given to make an agreement sure and unchangeable.

earshot (19-5) *Within earshot* = near enough to hear.

earth (99) (1) world on which we live; *How on earth — ?* = in what possible way?; *To move heaven and earth* = do everything possible to gain some aim; *Come back to earth* = not dream, think of the facts; (2) the surface of the ground; *To run to earth* = drive an animal into its hole, discover something after a long search; *Earth-wire* = wire leading electricity from radio (etc.) to earth.

earthbound (99-47) not caring for the higher things of life.

earthenware (99-29) dishes made of baked earth.

earthquake (99-21) shaking of the earth which often destroys buildings.

earwig (19-1) small insect with two curved tooth-like things on its tail.

EARWIG

ease (11z) state of freedom from difficulty; state of being comfortable, rich or without any cause to be anxious; *To ease the pain* = make less; *To ease a coat* = make larger.

easel (11z) frame for holding a picture while it is being painted.

east (11) direction in which the sun rises; *The Middle East* = the countries of Turkey, Syria, Jordan and neighbouring countries; *The Far East* = China, Japan, etc.

Easter (11-9) feast-day in memory of Christ's rising from the dead.

eastern (11-9) towards the east or having to do with the east; **easterly** (11-9-1) in or coming from the east.

easy (11z1) not difficult; free from care or pain; comfortable; *Easy! Easy!* = go slowly or gently; *An easy-going person* = one who does not trouble himself or other people; *Easy money* = money obtained for little work; **'easy-ch'air** (+ 29) large comfortable chair.

eat (11) take in food through the mouth; *Eat one's words* = take back —, say that one is sorry for having said —; *Eat one's heart out* = be very sad; *Eating its head off* (of a horse) = costing more to feed than it is worth; *The acid is eating away the metal* = destroying; *Eat into* = destroy part of; *Eaten up with pride* (n. of proud) = very proud and unpleasant; **eatables** (11-9-z) food.

eaves (11-z) edge of a roof which comes out beyond the wall.

eavesdrop (11-z-5) listen secretly to other people talking.

ebb (2) flow back; become lower and lower slowly; *Ebb-tide* = flow of the sea back from the shore.

ebony (2-9-1) very hard heavy wood; **ebon**, like ebony, very black; **ebonite** (2-9-41) hard, black form of rubber.

eb'ullient (1-8-19) overflowing with (very full of) high spirits and excitement; in a state of boiling.

ecc'entric (1ks2-1) (circles) not drawn round the same centre; (movement) not moving in a regular circle; (behaviour) unusual, peculiar; (person) rather mad; n. **eccentr'icity** (2-2-1s1-1).

ecclesi'astic (1-11z13-1) having to do with the government of the Church; officer of the Church.

echelon (2sh9-5) arrangement, e.g. of soldiers, in lines as shown.

echo (2k67) the same sound coming back again, as when one shouts in a large hall; *He is an echo of his master* = he says the same things as his master.

ECHELON

éclair (21-29) finger-shaped cake filled with *cream* (= the fat of milk).

éclat (21-4) great success and praise.

ecl'ectic (2-2-1) not following one opinion but choosing ideas here and there.

ecl'ipse (1-1) shutting off of the sun's light by the moon coming between the sun and the earth (or of the moon's light by the earth); *She is quite eclipsed by her sister* = is far less beautiful (amusing or clever) than her sister.

ec'ology (11-5-6-1) study of living things in their surroundings.

econ'omic (11-9-5-1) having to do with *economy* (see below); **econ'omics**, scientific study of the laws which govern the *production* (= producing) of wealth; **econ'omical**, careful and saving (money).

ec'onomy (11-5-9-1) careful saving of money or materials; planning or doing of any business; study of how wealth is obtained.

ecstasy (2-9-1) state of very strong feeling, especially happiness.

eczema (2-s1-9) disease of the skin.

eddy (2-1) movement of water or air in a circle.

edge (2j) thin sharp cutting part of a knife; border of anything; *Put an edge on* = sharpen; *To be on edge* = very easily excited; *It set my teeth on edge* = was very sharp in sound, or very acid in taste; **to edge**—away, into, off = move sideways and in such a way as not to be noticed; **'edgeways**, in the direction of the edge; *Can't get a word in edgeways* = have no chance to speak.

edible (2-1) fit to be eaten.

edict (11-1) an order, e.g. of the king or government.

edifice (2-1-1s) a building.

edify (2-1-41) improve one's thoughts; teach good thoughts.

edit (2-1) prepare matter for printing; **ed'ition** (1-1shn) one printing of a book, paper, etc.; form in which a book is printed; **editor** (2-1-9) one who prepares books, papers, etc., for printing; **an edit'orial** (2-1-55-19) part of a newspaper written by the editor giving an opinion on some question of the day.

educate (2-17-21) teach; cause to have knowledge, good character and manners, and power to make a living.

ed'uce (11-177s) draw or lead out, e.g. a hidden power; form some judgment from facts.

eel (11) fish shaped like a snake.

e'en (11) even.

e'er (29) ever.

eerie, eery (19-1) strange and fearful.

eff'ace (1-21s) rub (writing) off the surface; *To efface the memory of* = cause to forget.

eff'ect (1-2) result of a cause; result produced on the mind; *To talk for effect* = talk so as to make people think how clever one is; *My effects* = my goods, things belonging to me; adj. **eff'ective** (1-2-1), **eff'ectual** (1-2-179).

eff'eminate (1-2-1-1) (of men) behaving like a woman, soft, lacking courage.

eff'endi (2-2-11) title given in Turkey or Egypt to an officer of government, or used as a polite way of speaking to a gentleman.

efferent (2-9) (nerve) leading away or outwards (from the brain).

efferv'esce (2-9-2) (of a liquid) give off gas; (of a person) be gay, in high spirits.

eff'ete (2-11) worn out, useless.

effic'acious (2-1-21shqs) having power to produce a desired result; n. **'efficacy** (2-1k9s1).

eff'icient (1-1shnt) performing a duty well; producing a desired result.

effigy (2-1j1) shape of a person cut in wood or stone, or painted; *To be burnt in effigy* = to have some figure of oneself (e.g. of wood dressed in old clothes) burnt by the people as a sign of anger and hatred.

efflor'esce (5-5-2) be covered with flowers; become hard and powdery on the surface.

effluent (2-79) flowing out.

effl'uvium (2-77-19) unpleasant smell.

effort (2-9) using strength; *It was a great effort to* — = was difficult; Sl. *It was a good effort* = was well done.

effr'ontery (1-8-9-1) daring rudeness, without sense of shame.

eff'ulgence (1-8-j9-s) stream of brightness.

eff'usion (1-1773n) act of pouring out or sending out; outburst of excited writing.

eff'usive (1-177s1) expressing feeling very freely.

e.g. (11 + j11) (Latin), *ex'empli gr'atia* (2gz2-1 + 44s1114) for example.

eg'alit'arian (1-3-1-29-19) person who thinks that all men should be equal.

egg (2) rounded object containing new life, laid by female birds, fishes, snakes, etc.; seed of life in a mother animal; Sl. *He is a bad egg* =, he is a wrong-doer; *To teach one's grandmother to suck eggs* = teach a person who knows more than oneself; *Put all one's eggs in one basket* = risk all in one attempt, put all one's money into shares in one company; **to egg on**, urge on.

egg-nog (+ 5) drink of eggs mixed with milk and wine.

eglantine (2-9-11) wild rose-bush.

ego (2-67) the self; **egoism** (2-671z) thinking too much about one's self; **egoist** (2-671) one who thinks always about himself; **egotism** (2-67-1z) talking too much about oneself; **egotist** (2-67-1) one who talks too much about himself; adj. **egoistic(al)**.

egr'egious (1-11j19) (chosen out of the rest of the group); especially bad in some way, e.g. *An egregious ass* = a person who is most unusually foolish.

egress (11-2) act or power of going out; way out.

egret (11-2) white bird with a long white tail and back feathers.

eider (41-9) large black and white duck with *down* (= very soft feathers) on the breast; **eiderdown** (41-9-47) thick covering for a bed filled with the fine feathers of the eider duck.

eikon (41-5) see Icon.
Eist'eddfod (21-2-5) meeting of Welsh singers and poets.
either (41ð9) one or the other of two; *He will not go, and I shall not either* = I also shall not.
ej'aculate (1-3-17-21) cry out suddenly; throw out (liquid) with force.
ej'ect (1-2) throw out with force.
eke (out) (11) cause a small supply to last a long time by being careful, or by obtaining small amounts to add to it.
eke (11) (in old books) also.
el'aborate (1-3-9-1) worked out with great care; having many different parts, e.g. *An elaborate machine*; **to el'aborate** (1-3-9-21) do more work upon and improve.
el'an (21-44ⁿ) forward rush; eagerness.
eland (11-9) large South African deer.
el'apse (1-3-s) (of time) pass away.
el'astic (1-3-1) An *elastic* material can be stretched, and afterwards springs back into its first or natural shape; *A piece of elastic* = rubber covered with silk or cotton; *An elastic rule* = not stiff, able to fit all *cases* (= examples, needs).

ELAND

el'ated (1-21-1) full of joy.
elbow (2-67) place where the arm bends; anything L-shaped, e.g. bend in a pipe; *Out at elbows* = badly dressed, poor-looking; *To elbow one's way through a crowd* = push; *Elbow-grease* = hard work; *To have elbow-room* = enough room.
elder (2-9) flowering tree.
elder (2-9) older; officer in the Church having years and wisdom; **eldest** (2-1) oldest.
El Dor'ado (2 + 5-44-67) imaginary country or city in which there is much gold.
el'ect (1-2) choose, e.g. choose a member for the government of the country; *Headmaster elect* = chosen but not yet in office; *He elected to stay* = he decided to —; *The elect* = the chosen, e.g. specially chosen by God; **el'ection'eer** (1-2-sh9-19) one who works to get someone else elected by the people for an office; **el'ectorate** (1-2-9-1) all those persons who have the right to join in electing a person for an office.
el'ectric, el'ectrical (1-2-1) adj. of *electricity* (see below); *Electric chair* = thing used for killing murderers in U.S.A.; **electr'ician** (1-2-1shn) man who makes or works with electrical instruments; **el'ectrify** (1-2-1-41) put electricity into; surprise greatly; **electr'icity** (1-2-1s1-1) power used to produce heat, light, etc.
el'ectro- having to do with electricity; **el'ectrocute** (1-2-9-177) kill with electricity; **el'ectro-pl'ate** (1-2-67 + 21) put a thin covering of metal on another metal object by means of electricity.
electr'olysis (1-2-5-1-1) breaking up chemical substances by means of electricity, e.g. in electro-plating.
el'ectrom'agnet (1-2-6-3-1) *magnet* (= bar which draws pieces of iron to it) made by passing electricity round a soft iron bar.
el'ectron (1-2-5) *Atoms* were thought to be the smallest pieces into which any matter ELECTROMAGNET can be divided; but an atom is made up of *electrons* (=small "bits" of *negative* electricity) moving quickly round a *proton* (= a small "bit" of *positive* electricity); (*positive*, +, *plus*; *negative*, —, *minus*).
el'ectr'onics (1-2-5-1) the study of instruments in which electrons move, e.g. radio, television, radar.
eleem'osynary (2-1-11-5z1-9-1) having to do with work done without pay for others; kindness shown to or received by the poor, e.g. money help.
elegant (2-1) (person) having grace or good manners; (things) graceful, neat and beautiful.
elegy (2-1j1) poem expressing sorrow for the dead; adj. **eleg'iac** (2-1j419).
element (2-1-9) simple thing of which other things are made up; *The four elements* = earth, air, fire, water; material which scientists cannot break up or separate into other materials different from itself; *To learn the elements of a subject* = the simplest beginnings of —; *There is an element of truth in it* = some truth —; adj. **elem'entary** (2-1-2-9-1); *An elementary school* = school where learning begins.
elephant (2-1-9) very large animal with a *trunk* (= long nose which hangs down) and two *tusks* (= long teeth); *A white elephant* = useless possession of which one would gladly be free, e.g. a very large piece of furniture.

ELEPHANT

elephant'iasis (2-1-9-419-1) disease which causes a part of the body (usually the legs) to swell up and grow very large.
elevate (2-1-21) lift up to a higher level or rank; **elevated** (——1) (thoughts, way of writing), fine, noble; **elev'ation** (——shn) act of lifting up; hill; plan showing one side of a building; **elevator** (——9) machine for lifting people or goods from one floor of a house to another; *A grain elevator* = machine used for loading corn (wheat) or other grain on to ships, or for unloading it from ships.
el'evenses (1-2-9-z1z) tea, coffee or a light meal taken by workers at 11 a.m.
elf (2) small fairy; adj. **elfin**.

el'icit (1-1s1) draw out, e.g. a teacher elicits knowledge from a child by questioning.

el'ide (1-41) leave out a letter or sound, e.g. *He's, They're*; n. **el'ision** (1-13n).

eligible (2-1j9) fit to be chosen; desirable, e.g. as a husband.

el'iminate (1-1-1-21) take out, e.g. unfit persons from a group; pass poison from the body; *We may eliminate the possibility of* = need not think of that as possible.

el'ision (1-13n) n. of Elide (3rd above).

él'ite (21-11) best people in any group.

el'ixir (1-1-9) imaginary liquid able to turn metals into gold—or to make life last for ever.

elk (2) large deer with broad flat horns.

ell (2) 1¼ yards; *Give him an inch and he'll take an ell* = if you give a little, he will demand more.

ell'ipse (1-1) curve seen when you look at a circle sideways.

elm (2) large tree.

ELLIPSE

elocu'tion (2-9-177shn) art of public speaking—especially the proper use of the voice.

elongate (11-5ngg21) make longer.

el'ope (1-67) run away from home and marry secretly.

eloquent (2-9-9) able to make good speeches; n. **eloquence** (2-9-9-s).

else (2) *No one else* = no other person; *Come or else you will be sorry* = if you do not come you will —; **'elsewh'ere** (2-29) in some other place.

el'ucidate (1-177s1-21) make the meaning clear.

el'ude (1-177) to escape—especially by means of a trick; adj. **el'usive** (1-177-1) such as escapes, e.g. *An elusive person* = one who is difficult to catch; *An elusive word* = word which escapes the memory, is difficult to remember; **el'usory** (1-177-9-1) elusive.

elver (2-9) young of an *eel* (= fish shaped like a snake).

elves (2-z) fairies (pl. of Elf).

El'ysium (1-1z19) heaven; adj. **El'ysian**.

em-, en-, (1) in, into, e.g. **emb'ed** (1-2) put into a bed; **encl'ose** (1-67z) to close in, shut in; (2) make, e.g. **end'ear** (1-19) make dear.

em'aciate (1-21s121) cause to become very thin.

emanate (11-9-21) come from; be made or caused by; *This offer emanates from Mr. X* = comes from, was made by; (of gas, light, etc.) to come out from.

em'ancipate (1-3-s1-21) make free, e.g. slaves; *An emancipated woman* = one who does not obey the usual customs.

em'asculate (11-3-17-21) take away the strength of; take away the power of becoming a father.

emb'alm (2-44) preserve a dead body so that it does not decay.

emb'ankment (1-3ngk-9) wide wall of stones and earth, e.g. one built to keep a river in its course.

emb'argo (2-44-67) order forbidding movement of ships or trade; any order forbidding any action.

emb'ark (1-44) go on to a ship; *To embark upon an action* = start.

emb'arrass (1-3-9) make movement difficult; *Embarrassed* = feeling uncomfortable and in doubt what to say; *Embarras de richesses* (44ⁿ-4-4 + 9 + 11sh2) = having too many good things.

embassy (2-9-1) officers sent by a government to do its business with the government of another country; place where these people live in a foreign country.

emb'ed (1-2) put into, as in a bed; set firmly in, e.g. *Precious stones embedded in rocks*.

emb'ellish (1-2-1) make beautiful with ornaments.

ember (2-9) red-hot piece of wood or coal.

emb'ezzle (1-2) use for oneself money entrusted to one for some other purpose.

emb'itter (1-1-9) make hatred or anger worse; *Embittered* = sad and angry.

embl'azon (1-21) to set out in beautiful colours—e.g. upon a shield.

emblem (2-1) object which is a sign of something, e.g. *A crown is the emblem of the King*; adj. **emblem'atical** (2-1-3-1).

emb'ody (1-5-1) to give form to, e.g. *Words embody thought*; to collect together, e.g. *This book embodies all the rules of —*.

embolism (2-9-1z) hard mass of blood blocking up a blood-vessel in the body.

embonp'oint (44ⁿ-5ⁿ-74ⁿ) fatness, largeness round the waist.

emb'oss (1-5) make raised figures or letters (etc.) on metal or other material by pressing this material up from the back.

embr'ace (1-21s) (a person) to hold in the arms; (a chance) make use of; (a belief) become a believer in; *This book embraces many subjects* = contains, deals with.

embr'asure (1-21z9) opening in a wall of a fort through which the defenders may shoot.

embroc'ation (2-9-21shn) medicine used for rubbing.

embr'oider (1-51-9) ornament cloth with a needle and thread; (a story) improve by adding something from the imagination.

embr'oil (1-51) *To embroil in a quarrel* = draw a person into —.

embryo (2-167) young of any creature in its first state before birth; adj. **'embry'onic** (2-15-1) anything in a very early stage of growth.

em'end (11-2) to correct; improve and make free from faults; n. **emend'ation** (11-2-21 shn).

emerald (2-9-9) green precious stone; bluegreen colour; *The Emerald Isle* = Ireland.

em'erge (1-99j) (of a person) come out of, e.g. from water, from a hiding-place; (of things) become known as a result of inquiry.

em'ergency (1-99j-si) sudden happening which makes it necessary to act without delay.

em'eritus (11-2-1-9) (Professor) (= teacher in a university) who is no longer holding office.

em'ersion (11-99shn) act of emerging (3rd above).

emery (2-9-1) very hard material, often made into powder and stuck on paper; used for smoothing wood, metals, etc.; *Emery wheel* = wheel made of emery used for sharpening knives and other cutting instruments.

em'etic (1-2-1) any medicine given to cause one to be sick (throw up what is in the stomach).

emigrate (2-1-21) leave one's own country and go to live in another country; **an emigrant** (2-1-9).

eminent (2-1-9) high in rank or fame; *His Eminence* = way of speaking of a *Cardinal* (= high officer of the Church of Rome).

em'ir (2-19) prince; officer in Turkey; one who is of the family of Muhammad.

emissary (2-1-9-1) one who is sent to carry a message or do some special piece of work, usually of a bad or unpleasant kind, e.g. *An emissary of the Devil*.

em'ission (1-1shn) act of sending out; matter sent out, e.g. smoke from a gun.

em'it (1-1) send out, e.g. a smell, light from the sun.

em'ollient (1-5-19) softening; n. medicine which softens the skin.

em'olument (1-5-17-9) money received by one who holds an office.

em'otion (1-67shn) deep feeling.

emp'anel (1-3) put the name of a person on a list of persons who will serve on a *jury* (= 12 men in a court of law who settle whether the prisoner has or has not done wrong).

emperor (2-9-9) ruler of an empire.

emphasis (2-9-1) special force given to certain words or ideas in speaking or writing so that they will be noticed and remembered; **to emphasize** (2-9-41); adj. **emph'atic** (1-3-1).

empire (2-41g) number of different countries ruled by one chief government.

emp'iric (2-1-1) guided by experience rather than by scientific ideas.

empl'acement (1-21s-9) special place built for guns.

empl'oy (1-51) to use; to use the services of, take on as a paid worker; **employ'ee** (1-51-11) person employed.

emp'orium (2-55-19) place of trade; large shop.

empress (2-1) wife of an *emperor* (= ruler of an empire).

empty (2-1) containing nothing; *On an empty stomach* = when hungry; *Empty promises* = meaningless, unreal.

empyr'ean (2-1-11·9) highest part of the heavens; heaven.

emu (11-177) large Australian running bird about six feet high.

emulate (2-17-21) try to do as well as, or better than.

em'ulsion (1-8-shn) mixture of two liquids which do not really unite, e.g. oil and water.

en- in, or into, e.g. **enc'ircle** (1-s99) put in a circle.

en- make into, or cause to be, e.g. **en'able** (1-21) cause to be able.

EMU

-en, make, e.g. *Blacken* = to make black; *Sharpen* = make sharp.

-en, made of, e.g. *Wooden*.

en'act (1-3) make into a law; perform, e.g. a part in a play.

en'amel (1-3) glassy material melted at great heat and put on metals as an ornament; paint which has a very *shiny* (= polished, shining) appearance when it dries; hard outer covering of the teeth.

en'amour (1-3-9) cause to be filled with love; *To be enamoured of* = be in love with.

enc'amp (1-3) make a camp; be in a camp.

enc'ase (1-21) to put in a case, to shut up within some material, e.g. *Encased in gold*.

ench'ant (1-44) put a magic charm on; to please greatly.

en clair (5ⁿ + 29) in clear, not in secret, writing (cipher).

encl'ose (1-67z) to close in and shut off from things outside; put something inside a letter; n. **encl'osure** (1-6739) a thing enclosed, e.g. piece of ground with a fence round; thing put in with a letter.

enc'omium (2-67-19) expression of praise.

enc'ompass (1-8-9) encircle.

enc'ore (44ᵏk55) word said by listeners who are pleased by a song or other performance; *Encore!* = please do it again; the song, etc., given in reply to an *encore*.

enc'ounter (1-47-9) meet with, e.g. an enemy or a great difficulty.

enc'ourage (1-8-1j) give courage to; urge on; help on.

encr'oach (1-67) go beyond one's own (land) and take part of the (land) of another person; *The sea is encroaching upon the land* = is cutting into; *Encroach upon a person's time* = use too much of —.

encr'ust (1-8) to cover with a thin hard outer covering.

enc'umber (1-8-9) make it difficult for a person to act freely, e.g. *Encumbered with boxes, with a large family, with debts*; n. **an enc'umbrance** (1-8-9-s) thing which prevents free action; debt; *Wanted, man and wife for housework, no encumbrances* = with no children.

enc'yclical (2-s1-1) letter sent round by the *Pope* (= head of the Church of Rome) to all his churches.

encyclop'aedia (2-s4I-9-II-I9) book or set of books in which all branches of knowledge are dealt with in order from A to Z.

end (2) (1) farthest or last point; *At a loose end* = having nothing to do; *To make both ends meet* = get just enough money for one's needs; *At the end of one's tether* = unable to suffer any more; *At one's wit's end* = very anxious, not knowing what to do; *Odds and ends* = small useless pieces; *Got hold of the wrong end of the stick* = get a wrong idea exactly opposite to the right idea; *Put an end to, Make an end of* = stop, destroy; *He is near his end* = near death; (2) purpose, e.g. *To gain one's ends*; *The end justifies the means* = wrong-doing may be allowed if the purpose is good; **to end**, finish; *End in smoke* = have no result.

end'ear (1-19) cause to be loved; **end'earments** (1-19-9) loving words or acts.

end'eavour (1-2-9) to try.

end'emic (disease) (2-2-1) always present in certain people or places.

endive (2-1) bitter plant used for food.

endocrine (gland) (2-67-41) part of the body which puts into the blood liquid which has a general effect on the whole body, e.g. upon growth; so also the changes in the body in fear or anger are caused by action of an endocrine gland, also the special characters (e.g. hair on face, deep voice) of male and female.

end'orse (1-55s) agree with what has been said or done; write one's name on the back of a written or printed paper.

end'ow (1-47) give (e.g. to a school) a large amount of money which brings in a yearly amount for use; *Well endowed by nature* = clever, beautiful (etc.) by birth.

end'ue (1-177) clothe with; give, e.g. *Endue him with grace*.

end'ure (1-179) suffer bravely and without complaining; *I can't endure him* = I hate him; *Will endure for ever* = will remain —.

enemy (2-1-1) person who is hated, who is trying to do harm to one; nation at war with us; the army of (or the ships of) a nation at war with us.

energ'etic (2-9j2-1) full of force, active; **energy** (2-9j1) force, strength, power.

enervate (2-99-21) cause to become weak.

enfil'ade (2-1-21) shoot at a line of men from one end; place on a battle-field which can be shot at from one end to the other.

enf'old (1-67) bend something round an object, e.g. *Enfold in one's arms* = put one's arms round.

enf'orce (1-55s) make people obey (a law).

enfr'anchise (2-3-41z) give the right to elect members to the government; *To enfranchise slaves* = set free.

eng'age (1n·g21j) (1) bind by a promise; *Engage oneself to* = promise; *Miss A is engaged to Mr. B* = has promised to marry; *Can you come on Monday? — No, I'm engaged* = I have promised to go somewhere else; *To engage a room (a seat)* = order a room (seat) to be kept for one; *An engaging manner* = pleasing —; *To engage a servant* = arrange to employ; (2) fill the time of, to be busy, e.g. *Engaged in letter-writing*; (3) join battle, e.g. *To engage the enemy*; (4) fasten on to, e.g. *The wheel x engages with wheel y and turns it*; **eng'agement** (——9) a promise; a promise to marry; a promise to meet or go out with a person; a battle.

eng'orge (1n·g55j) to swallow; *Engorged with blood* = full of —, swollen with —.

engr'ain (1n·g-21) cause to sink deeply into, e.g. colour into wood; *Engrained habits* = things done so often that they have become part of one's character.

engr'ave (1n·g-21) cut names, pictures, etc., on metal or stone or wood; make special plates of metal from which pictures are printed.

engr'oss (1n·g-67s) fill all one's time; fill one's mind; *Engrossed in a book* = giving his whole mind to reading; *An engrossing story* = very interesting; to write in a large clear way, as on a law paper.

eng'ulf (1n·g8) to swallow up, e.g. *The waves engulfed the ship.*

enh'ance (1-44-s) increase the value, beauty, etc., of a thing.

en'igma (2-1-9) thing that is difficult to understand—also a person who is —; adj. **'enigm'atic** (2-1-3-1).

enj'oin (1-51) to command; *To enjoin silence upon* = order to be silent.

enj'oy (1-51) (1) have delight in; (2) possess or have the use of.

enl'ace (1-21s) bind or twist together.

enl'arge (1-44j) make larger; speak for a long time on some subject; **an enl'argement** (——9) larger copy of a small picture.

enl'ighten (1-41) cause to understand.

enl'ist (1-1) to put on a list for service; join the army; *To enlist his help* = get him to help.

enl'iven (1-41) make bright and full of action.

en masse ($44^n + 4$) in a mass, in a crowd.

enm'esh (1-2) catch in a net.

enmity (2-1-1) state or feeling of being an enemy.

ennui (44^n-711) tiredness caused by lack of interest.

en'ormity (1-55-1-1) *An enormity* = very bad act; *The enormity of the offence* = very great badness of the wrong act.

en'ormous (1-55-9) very large.

en'ough (1-8f) as much as is needed.

en passant ($44^n + 4$-44^n) in passing.

enqu'ire (1-419) see Inquire.
enr'age (1-21j) make very angry.
enr'apture (1-3-tsh9) cause a state of great delight.
enr'ol, enr'oll (1-67) write on a list; make a person a member of a group.
en route (44ⁿ + 77) on the way; let us start.
ensc'once (1-5-s) put in a comfortable or safe place.
'ens'emble (44ⁿ-44ⁿ) all the parts brought together; *Tout ensemble* (77 +) the whole effect.
enshr'ine (1-41) put in a holy place; *His name is enshrined in our memory* = we shall remember him always with love.
enshr'oud (1-47) to cover, as a dead body is covered with fine cloth.
ensign (2-41) flag; serving as a special sign, e.g. the red ensign is the flag of British *merchant-ships* (= ships used for trade).
ensilage (2-1-1j) green food for cattle preserved in a container into which no air can get, and used during the winter.
ensn'are (1-29) get a person or creature into a trap.
ens'ue (1-177) come after, usually as a result of.
ens'ure (1-sh779) make certain.
ent'ail (1-21) leave land, money, etc., so that it can pass only from father to son (or as arranged), but cannot be sold to a stranger; make necessary, e.g. *Writing this book has entailed much work.*
ent'angle (1-3ngg) get a person tied up as in a net; put a person into difficulties; get a person into one's power; **an ent'anglement,** as above—also wire arranged so as to stop the enemy in war.
ent'ente (44ⁿ-44ⁿ), entente cordiale (+ k55-144) a friendly understanding between nations.
enter (2-9) (1) go into, e.g. *To enter the room;* (2) become a member of, e.g. *Enter the army;* (3) put a name on to a list, e.g. *Enter a boy for an examination;* write down a thing in a book, e.g. *Enter this amount in the account book; To enter into details* = tell all the small points about; *Enter into the composition of* = be a part of; *He entered into the game with great spirit* = took part in; *Enter into a person's feelings, Enter into the spirit of* = understand; *Enter into an agreement* = make —; *Enter upon a new life* = begin —.
ent'eric (fever) (2-2-1) dangerous disease of the bowels.
enterprise (2-9-41z) courage; daring plan; carrying out of a daring plan; *A business enterprise* = an attempt to start a new business; **enterprising** (——1) willing to do daring things.
entert'ain (2-9-21) receive as a guest; give food and drink to; amuse; *To entertain an idea* = have—in mind; **entert'aining** (——1) amusing; **an entert'ainment** (——9) an amusement, e.g. a play, singing, etc.
enthr'al(l) (1-55) make a slave of; hold by magic charm and have power over; **enthr'alling** (——1) very interesting.
enthr'one (1-67) put a king on a *throne* (= seat of a king); make a person king; *Enthroned in our hearts* = much loved and respected.
enth'usiasm (2-177z13z) strong feeling of admiration (n. of Admire) for someone or something; outward signs of such admiration, e.g. shouting; **an enth'usiast** (1-177z13) one who is very eager and interested in some idea.
ent'ice (1-41s) draw away, usually for evil purposes; draw over to one's side by an offer of some desirable thing.
ent'ire (2-419) whole, complete, unbroken, undamaged; (as a sign on an inn) *Murray's Entire* = this inn sells drinks supplied by Murray & Co.
ent'itle (1-41) give a right to; give a name to.
entity (2-1-1) any real thing.
entom'ology (2-9-5-9j1) study of insects.
entr'acte (55ⁿ-4) time between the acts of a play.
entrails (2-21-z) inside parts of an animal.
entr'ain (1-21) put (soldiers) into a train.
entr'ammel (1-3) tie up as in a net.
entrance (2-9-s) act, power or means of entering; *Entrance fee* = money paid to go in (e.g. for an examination), etc.; large front door of a building.
entr'ance (1-44-s) cause to be in a state of great wonder and delight.
entrant (2-9) one who goes in; one who takes part in a race, examination, etc.
entr'eat (1-11) pray, beg; n. **entr'eaty** (——1).
entrée (44ⁿ-21) (1) right of entering, e.g. a person's house; (2) small carefully prepared meatdish served after the fish and before the main dish of meat in a dinner.
entr'ench (1-2) protect a place or army with *trenches* (= long holes in the ground dug by soldiers as a shelter).
entre nous (44ⁿ-9 + 77) as a secret between ourselves.
'entrepren'eur (44ⁿ-9-2-99) one who makes the plans for a business and arranges to get it going—especially one who arranges for the performance of plays or musical shows.
entr'ust, intr'ust (1-8) give into another's care; give a person a duty to do.
entry (2-1) act of coming in; right to enter; something written down, e.g. in an account of money; names on a list of those who will run in a race.
entw'ine, intw'ine (1-41) twist round and round; grow round and round, e.g. a plant round a tree.
en'umerate (2-177-9-21) to count; to name one by one.
en'unciate (1-8-s121) say solemnly or clearly; form one's words clearly in speaking.
env'elop (1-2-9) bind round or cover, e.g. in a garment, in flames, in clouds.

envelope (2-9-67) cover for a letter; any covering which contains something.

env'enom (1-2) cause to be poisonous; fill with hatred.

enviable, envious (2-19), see Envy (4th below).

env'irons (1-419-9-z) those parts of a town which lie outside, and are more distant from the centre; **env'ironment** (——9) all the conditions which have an effect on growth and character.

env'isage (1-1z1j) to see; form a picture in the mind.

envoy (2-51) special *messenger* (= carrier of a message) of high rank sent from one government to another.

envy (2-1) feeling of hate or ill-will caused by the sight of another's success or wealth; **to envy**, desire something owned by another, and hate the owner for possessing it.

enzyme (2-41) substance produced by living matter which causes chemical changes, e.g. the enzymes of yeast change sugar into alcohol.

epaulet(te) (2-67-2) ornament worn on the shoulders by soldiers, ship's officers and others.

eph'emeral (1-2-9) living only for a day; short-lived.

epi- upon or over, outer, e.g. *epidermis* (2-1-99-1) (4th below).

epic (2-1) long poem telling a story of great deeds.

epicure (2-1-1779) one who takes great interest in the pleasures of eating, drinking; **epicur'ean** (2-1-179-11·9) having to do with the teaching which holds that what gives pleasure is good and what gives pain is evil.

epid'emic (disease) (2-1-2-1) disease which passes from one person to another very quickly.

'epid'ermis (2-1-99-1) outside part of the skin.

epigram (2-1-3) a few words expressing a clever or amusing thought; adj. **epigramm'atic** (2-1-9-3-1).

epilepsy (2-1-2-1) disease causing one to fall down because of sudden loss of thought and feeling.

epilogue (2-1-5) short speech given at the end of a play; end or finishing-off of a speech or book.

Ep'iphany (1-1-9-1) feast on January 6th remembering the coming of the Wise Men to the child Jesus.

ep'iscopal (1-1-9) having to do with *bishops* (= high officers of the Church).

episode (2-1-67) account of one separate set of events in a play or *novel* (= story-book); one separate event (usually important) in a set of events.

ep'istle (1-1) letter, usually long and important; adj. **ep'istolary** (1-1-9-9-1).

epitaph (2-1-44) that which is written on a stone above a grave.

epithet (2-1-2) word expressing some quality of a thing.

ep'itome (1-1-9-1) short account of a book or speech.

epoch (11-5k) certain length of time during which a set of important events happened, such as would all be told together in one part of a history book, e.g. *The Great War begins a new epoch in history*; **'epoch-making,** very important.

equable (2-9) steady; not changing suddenly; (of the weather in some place) never very hot nor very cold.

equal (11-9) same in value, weight, size, etc.; *Equal to his work* = able to do —; *Equal to the occasion* = able to meet or deal with whatever happens; *He treated us equally* = treated both alike; *One's equals* = persons of the same rank.

equan'imity (11-9-1-1-1) calmness of mind.

equ'ate (1-21) to make equal.

equ'ation (1-21shn) e.g. $x + 3y = 7$.

equ'ator (1-21-9) imaginary line round the middle of the earth half-way between the north and south *poles* (= points, ends).

equerry (2-9-1) officer in a king's court, in ancient times in charge of the king's horsemen.

equ'estrian (1-2-19) having to do with riding horses.

equil'ateral (11-1-3-9) having all sides equal.

equil'ibrium (11-1-1-19) state in which a thing is held level or steady because there is equal weight on each side.

equine (11-41) having to do with horses.

equinox (11-1-5) those times in each year (about March 21st and September 22nd) when day and night are of equal length.

equ'ip (1-1) supply with the necessary knowledge or instruments for doing certain special work.

equipage (2-1-1j) carriage, horses, and servants riding on or beside the carriage.

equipoise (2-1-51z) state in which there is no change or movement because the forces on each side are exactly equal (used often of the mind).

equitable (2-1-9) just; fair; **equity** (2-1-1) justice; fairness; *Equity* = union of actors and musicians to get fair pay.

equit'ation (2-1-21shn) art of horse-riding.

equ'ivalent (1-1-9-9) equal in value to.

equ'ivocal (1-1-9) of doubtful meaning; (of a person) of doubtful character; **to equ'ivocate** (1-1-9-21).

era (19-9) time in history usually begun from some important event, e.g. the Christian era began from the birth of Christ.

er'adicate (1-3-1-21) take out with its roots; destroy completely.

er'ase (1-21z) rub out, e.g. pencil marks; n. **er'asure** (1-21 39) word rubbed out.

ere (29) before; sooner than.

er'ect (1-2) upright; standing up on end; **to er'ect**, set up on end; build; **er'ectile** (1-2-41) which can be made to stand up straight, e.g.

hairs on a dog's back; **an er'ection** (1-2-shn) a building.

erg (99) measure of work, e.g. lifting one pin one inch = about 350 ergs.

ergo (99-67) (Latin) therefore.

ergot (99-5) substance from diseased grasses used to stop bleeding and help child-birth.

ermine (99-1) small animal which has thick white fur in winter, with a black end to its tail; fur of this animal— worn as a sign of office by judges in England.

ERMINE

er'ode (1-67) wear away slowly, e.g. *The sea is eroding the land*; n. **er'osion** (1-637n).

Eros (2-5) god of love; statue as shown, in Piccadilly Circus, London.

er'otic (1-5-1) having to do with love.

err (99) make a mistake; do what is wrong.

errand (2) journey made to carry a message.

errant (2) wandering.

err'atic (1-3-1) not regular in movement; (of behaviour) one can never tell what an erratic person will do next.

EROS

err'atum (2-21-9) mistake in printing or writing; pl. **err'ata** (2-21-9).

err'oneous (2-67-19) mistaken; not correct.

error (2-9) mistake; wrong idea.

erst- (99), **erstwhile** (99-41) former, formerly.

eruct'ation (11-8-21shn) sending gas from the stomach up through the mouth.

erudite (2-7-41) full of learning.

er'upt (1-8) break out or through, e.g. teeth through the skin inside the mouth, fire and smoke out of a mountain.

-ery (9-1) —added to the end of a word to show place of business, e.g. *Fishery*; or to show quality or behaviour, e.g. *Trickery*; also an art, or way of working, e.g. *Archery* = the art of shooting arrows; *Witchery* = the art of *bewitching* (= charming, doing magic).

erys'ipelas (2-1-1-1-9) serious disease of the skin.

'escal'ade (2-9-21) act of getting up a wall by the use of *ladders* (= steps made by fixing cross-pieces between two long pieces).

escalator (2-9-21-9) set of stairs moved by a machine to save the trouble of walking up.

'escap'ade (2-9-21) wild and exciting act; daring disobeying of rules.

esc'ape (1-21) get free from prison or from anything which takes away one's freedom; *This matter escaped my notice* = I did not notice this matter; *Gas escapes from an open bottle* = gets out —; *He escaped being hurt* = he was fortunate not to be hurt.

esc'apement (1-21-9) that part of a clock which makes the noise "tick-tick" and keeps the clock running true to time.

esc'apist (2-21-1) person who tries not to face reality.

esc'arpment (1-44-9) steep slope just below the wall of a fort.

esch'eated (1-11-1) (of land) seized by the king as a punishment or because the owner had no descendants.

esch'ew (1-77) keep away from (an evil thing).

esc'ort (1-55) go along with to protect or in order to show the way; **an 'escort** (2-55) a person who *esc'orts* another (as above); group of armed men or of warships protecting the journey of an unarmed group or ship.

escritoire (2-1tw44) small writing-table with a top which opens downwards for writing, and is closed when not in use.

esc'utcheon (1-8-9) shield on which the signs of families are painted.

esot'eric (2-67-2-1) having deep or secret meanings which can only be understood by some special group of persons.

esp'ecial (1-2shl) worthy of particular notice; particular.

Esper'anto (2-9-3-67) specially made easily learnt language by means of which peoples of all nations may talk to each other.

espion'age (2-19-443) act of using secret *agents* (= paid workers) to find out about the war-plans, armies, etc., of foreign governments.

'esplan'ade (2-9-21) level place for walking, usually beside the sea.

esp'ouse (1-47z) marry; decide to support some idea or work.

esprit de corps (2-11 + 9 + 55) loyalty among the members of a group.

espy (1-41) see, usually from a distance—or something hidden.

esqu'ire (1-419) one who looks after a knight; polite way of addressing a gentleman on a letter: *G. Smith, Esq.*

essay (2-21) an attempt; short piece of writing on one subject; **to ess'ay**, make an attempt.

essence (2-9-s) that which contains or shows the real nature of a thing; best of a thing with all the unnecessary parts taken away; *Fruit essence* = liquid containing the taste and smell only of the fruit; **ess'ential** (1-2nshl) having to do with the real nature of; very necessary.

est'ablish (1-3-1) make firm; build up; prove; **an est'ablishment** (——9) set of persons kept together for a certain purpose, e.g. the servants in a house; all the men and offices of a certain part of the government, e.g. the army; *The Peace establishment of an army* = those men employed in the army in time of peace.

est'aminet (2-3-1-21) small drinking-shop in France.

est'ate (1-21) rank; place in life; all the money, goods, etc., which a man owns; *An estate in the country* = land and a house in —; **an estate agent** (+ 21j) man who arranges the buying and selling of houses; *Real estate*, houses and land.

est'eem (1-11) set a high value on; have a high opinion of.

estimable (2-1-9) worthy of respect.

estimate (2-1-21) form an opinion about the value, cost, size of, etc.; **an estimate** (2-1-1) account of the probable cost of doing a certain piece of work; *In my estimation* = in my opinion.

estr'ange (1-21nj) cause to become unfriendly.

estuary (2-179-1) broad mouth of a river into which the sea flows.

-et, added to a word to show smallness, e.g. *Islet* (41-1) = small *isle* (= island).

etc. (1ts2tr9) *et cetera* = and the rest, and other things of the same kind.

etch (2) with the help of acid to cut a picture into the surface of a metal plate so as to print from it; **an etching**, picture so printed.

et'ernal (1-99) without beginning or end, lasting for ever; **et'ernity** (1-99-1-1) time without end; life after death.

ether (11-9) (1) very fine matter (finer than air) supposed to fill all space; (2) upper air; (3) medicine used to make people sleep and lose all feeling.

eth'ereal (1-19-19) very light, like air; like a spirit or fairy.

ethics (2-1) study of right and wrong in human behaviour; adj. **ethical** (*Not ethical* is often incorrectly used as "Not right, not honest").

ethnic (2-1) having to do with a race of people; **ethn'ology** (2-5-9j1) study of the races of man.

'etiqu'ette (1-1k2) rules of good behaviour.

Eton (11) very old school for boys in England; *Eton jacket* = a short coat reaching only as far as the waist; *Eton crop* = cutting a woman's hair short like a boy's.

-ette (1) small, e.g. **statu'ette** (3-172) small *statue* (= stone or metal figure of a man or animal); (2) made to look like, e.g. **l'eather'ette** (2ð9-2) material made to look like leather.

etym'ology (2-1-5-9j1) study of the history of words.

eucal'yptus (177-9-1-9) tree which produces a strong-smelling oil used in medicine, e.g. for a *cold* (= illness with running nose, painful throat, etc.).

euchre (177k9) card game.

Euclid (177-1) form of *geometry* (= the study of lines, angles, surfaces and solids).

eug'enics (177j2-1) science of improving the human race or the quality of animals by care in choosing the fathers and mothers.

eulogy (177-9j1) speech or writing praising some person or thing.

eunuch (177-9k) man so treated that he cannot become a father; such a man employed as servant for wives.

euphemism (177-1-1z) pleasant way of saying an unpleasant truth, e.g. *He is rather excited*—meaning that he has taken too much wine.

euph'onious (177-67-19) sounding well; **euph'onium** (177-67-19) brass instrument of music.

Eur'asian (177-21319) person of mixed European and Asian birth.

eur'eka (177-11-9) expression of joy at discovery, meaning "I have found it!"

eurh'ythmics (177-1ð-1) art of expressing music by movements of the body.

euthan'asia (177-9-21z19) any painless way of dying.

ev'acuate (1-3-1721) to leave, e.g. *The army evacuated the city*; to make empty, e.g. *To evacuate the bowels* = cause them to be empty.

ev'acu'ees (1-3-17-11) people taken away from a city in time of war.

ev'ade (1-21) to escape; try not to meet; try not to answer a question; *To evade the law* = act dishonestly yet just not breaking the law.

evan'escent (11-9-2) quickly disappearing.

ev'angelist (1-3nj9-1) teacher of good news; writer of one of the four books of the Bible which tell the life of Christ.

ev'aporate (1-3-9-21) change a liquid into a gas; drive out the water and make dry.

ev'asion (1-213n) act of *evading* (4th above).

eve (11) evening; *Christmas Eve* = evening (or day) before —; time just before an important event, e.g. *On the eve of a great discovery*.

even (11) (1) not rough, e.g. *An even surface*; *Even with the ground* = level with; *I'll get even with him* = will do as much harm to him as he has done to me; (2) regular, not changing; *Even-tempered* = calm, not easily made angry; (3) *An even number* = number which can be divided by 2; *Even money on a horse* = £1 put on a horse gets £1 + £1 if it wins.

even (11) just at the moment, e.g. *Even as I spoke*; *I even gave him my own shoes*—here "even" shows that one did more than might be expected; *Even if* = although.

evening (11-1) first few hours of darkness.

ev'ent (1-2) anything which happens; important happening; *In the event of his death* = if he dies; *At all events* = whatever happens.

eventide (11-4I) evening.

ev'entual (1-2-179) happening as a result; last.

ever (2-9) at any time; *Ever and anon* = from time to time; *For ever, For evermore* = always; *Ever* gives force to a word or group of words, e.g. *Ever so much* = very much; *Whatever do you mean?* = I cannot imagine what —.

-ever (2-9) e.g. *Whoever, Whatever* = it does not matter who, what —.

evergreen (2-9-11) any tree or plant which does not lose its leaves in winter.

every (2-1) all, counted one by one; *After every three days* = on every fourth day; *Every now and again* = from time to time; **everywhere** (2-1-29) in all places.

ev'ict (1-1) make a person go out of a house (or off land) by using the power of the law.

evidence (2-1-s) anything which helps to prove a fact.

evident (2-1) plain and clear to the mind.

evil (11) bad; harmful, unfortunate; *The Evil One* = the Devil, Satan; *The evil eye* = one who is imagined to bring bad fortune on any- one he looks at.

ev'ince (1-1-s) show (feeling).

ev'iscerate (1-1-9-21) cut out the inner parts of the body.

ev'oke (1-67) call forth (out), e.g. *To evoke spirits of the dead* = call up; *To evoke a feeling* = to produce.

evolu'tion (11-9-77shn) (the opening out of something which is rolled up); way in which simple forms of life, by slow changes, grow into other higher forms of life; e.g. man is said to have evolved from a kind of monkey; so also of things, e.g. the evolution of the motor-car of to-day from the simple machines of 20 years ago; *Evolutions of a dance* = movements; *Evolution of a story* = unfolding of a story, so that the reader slowly comes to know the events told.

ev'olve (1-5) grow out of; change into slowly (see Evolution).

ewe (177) female sheep.

ewer (1779) large water-pot with a handle.

ex- out, e.g. exit (2-1), door leading out; beyond, e.g. exc'el (1-s2) go beyond, be better than; **ex-**, formerly but not now, e.g. **'ex-k'ing** (2 + 1) one who has ceased to be a king.

ex'acerbate (2-3s9-21) cause bitterness of feeling to increase.

ex'act (1gz3) correct; **to ex'act**, make someone pay (money); **ex'acting** (1——) demanding much work or care; *Exactly!* = that is just what I think; **ex'actitude** (1gz3-1-177) great care in being correct.

ex'aggerate (1gz3j9-21) say that something is larger (better, etc.) than it is; add to the true facts; *To exaggerate an illness* (*an evil*) = make worse.

ex'alt (1gz55) raise in rank; to praise; **exalt-a'tion** (2gz55-21shn) state of great excite- ment and of pleasure at one's own skill, cleverness or good fortune; **ex'alted** (1gz55-1) high, noble.

ex'amine (1gz3-1) look at and consider care- fully; question, e.g. a school-child; question a man in a court of law; **examin'ee** (1gz3-1-11) person being examined, e.g. in a school or university.

ex'ample (1gz44) (1) particular event or thing which shows the meaning of some general rule; (2) one thing which shows what others are like, e.g. *An example of his painting*; (3) thing to be copied; *To set a good example* = behave so well that others may perhaps do the same; *To make an example of him* = punish him so that others may be afraid to behave as he did.

ex'asperate (1gz44-9-21) excite anger in a person; make an illness (or any other evil) worse.

excavate (2-9-21) dig; uncover what has been covered by earth, e.g. an ancient city.

exc'eed (1-11) go beyond what is necessary or allowed; be greater, faster, better than; **exc'eedingly** (1-11-1-1) very greatly.

exc'el (1-2) be better than others; have the highest qualities; **'excellence** (2-9-9-s) state of being very good; **Your 'Excellency** (——s1), form of address to high officers of government, e.g. the Governor; **'excellent** (2-9-9) very good.

exc'elsior (1-2-155) let us try to go higher or do better.

exc'ept (1-2) to leave out; *All except John* = all, but not John; **exc'eption** (1-2-shn) act of not counting something; a thing that is not counted or not covered by the rule; *To take exception to* = disagree with, to be angry at; **exc'eptional** (1-2-sh9) unusual; better than usual.

excerpt (2-99) short interesting piece of writing taken out of a book.

ex'cess (1-2) n. too much, the amount beyond what is right or necessary; *Excess baggage* = that weight of bags, boxes, etc., beyond what is allowed free to a traveller by train, etc., on which he has to pay; **exc'esses** (——1z) too much eating and drinking.

exch'ange (1-21nj) give something and receive something else for it; *The Exchange* = place where money, shares in businesses, companies, etc., are bought and sold; central place where all the telephone wires are joined so that people may speak to each other.

exch'equer (1-2k9) that part of the govern- ment which deals with public money.

exc'ise (2-41z) money which must be paid to the government on certain goods produced in the country, e.g. wine and strong drink.

exc'ise (2-41) cut out or off; **exc'ision** (2-13n) act of cutting out or off; a part cut out.

exc'ite (1-41) make active; cause strong feeling.

excl'aim (1-21) cry out suddenly; speak with strong feelings; **an exclama'tion** (2-9-21shn) act of crying out; word or words spoken suddenly with strong feeling, e.g. "*Oh, how terrible!*"

excl'ude (1-77) to shut out; n. **excl'usion** (——3n); adj. **excl'usive** (——s1) shutting out; kept for a special class; *An exclusive school* = one which takes in only the children of well-known or rich people.

exc'ogitate (1-5j1-21) think out.

excomm'unicate (2-9-177-1-21) put out of a group; take away the special rights of a member of the Christian Church.

exc'oriate (2-5-121) rub or cut the outer skin off.

excrement (2-1-9) waste matter passed out of the body.

excr'escence (1-2-s) out-growth; unnatural growth on the surface.

excr'ete (2-11) separate and pass out, e.g. *The body excretes waste matter*; **excr'eta** (2-11-9) *excrement* (2nd above).

excr'uciating (pain) (1-77sh121-1) very great (pain).

exculpate (2-8-21) to free from blame.

exc'ursion (1-99shn) short journey made for pleasure; *An excursion train*, special train on which the price of a ticket is less than usual.

exc'use (1-177z) make free from blame or duty; forgive; **an exc'use** (1-177s) reason given when asking to be forgiven.

execrable (2-1-9) very bad; worthy of being cursed; **to excrate** (2-1-21) curse.

execute (2-1-177) (1) carry out orders; carry out a plan; (2) put to death by order of the law; n. **exec'ution** (2-1-177shn) way in which work is carried out; act of putting to death; **exec'utioner** (2-1-177shən9) man who kills people by order of the law; adj. **ex'ecutive** (1gz2-17-1) carrying into effect; doing; *Executive ability* = power of getting things done; **an ex'ecutive** (1gz2-17-1) man who has charge of a business; **ex'ecutor** (1gz2-17-9) person appointed to do what has been written in a dead person's *will* (= paper telling what a person wants done with his goods, money, etc.; after he is dead); **ex'ecutrix** (1gz2-17-1) woman *executor*.

ex'emplary (1gz2-9-1) worthy of being copied, e.g. *Exemplary conduct* (= behaviour); *An exemplary punishment* = — which should serve as a warning to others.

ex'emplify (1gz2-1-41) show by example.

ex'empt (1gz2) make free from, e.g. *To exempt from service in the army.*

exercise (2-9s41z) use of any part of the body in order to strengthen it, e.g. *Voice exercises*; also such use of the mind, e.g. *An exercise in clear thinking*; a piece of work set to a learner or school-child, e.g. *A French exercise*; **to exercise**, use; make stronger or better by use; *To exercise patience* = be *patient* (= suffer without complaining); *Greatly exercised about* = anxious.

ex'ert (1gz99) put forth strength or force of character; *To exert oneself* = try hard.

exeunt (2-18) (in a written play)—they go out.

exh'ale (2-21) breathe out; **exhal'ation** (2-9-21shn) act of breathing out; air breathed out; mist or steam.

exh'aust (1gz55) use up completely; finish; come to the end of one's strength; make very weak; **the exh'aust**, burnt gas which is passed out of an engine; adj. **exh'austive** (——1) complete, leaving no part unfinished, e.g. *An exhaustive book on* — = covering the whole subject.

exh'ibit (1gz1-1) to show; put in a public place for people to look at; **exhib'ition** (2-1-1shn) act of showing; **an exhib'ition**, collection of things (e.g. pictures) set out for people to see; *To make an exhibition of oneself* = to make oneself appear very foolish.

'exhib'itionist (2-1-1sh9-1) person who tries to make other people look at him (her), e.g. by showy or strange dress or behaviour.

exh'ilarate (1gz1-9-21) cause joyful feelings; make one feel fresh and strong.

exh'ort (1gz55) urge; advise strongly, e.g. **to** do good.

exh'ume (2-177) take a body out of a grave.

ex'igency (2-1j9-s1) (1) such a state of things as demands that some action be taken at once, e.g. some great danger; (2) state of being very poor; *Reduced to exigency* = having become very poor.

ex'iguous (2gz1-179) small in amount, not enough.

exile (2-41) send a person out of his own country as a punishment; **exile**, this form of punishment; person so punished.

ex'ist (1gz1) be; have life.

exit (2-1) door for going out; in a written play *Exit Smith* = Smith goes out.

'ex l'ibris (2 + 41-1) (from the books), this book belongs to —.

exo- outside.

exodus (2-9-9ʃ) an outward march of many people, e.g. of the Jews from Egypt.

'ex off'icio (2 + 5-1sh167) because of one's office.

ex'ogamy (2-5-9-1) custom of marrying persons outside the *tribe* (= group, small nation).

ex'onerate (1gz5-9-21) to free from blame.

ex'orbitant (1gz55-1) (price, demand) far too great.

exorcize (2-55s41z) drive out evil spirits.

ex'ordium (2-55-19) beginning of a speech or writing telling the subject, etc.

ex'otic (2gz5-1) strange; foreign.

exp'and (1-3) become larger; make larger; spread out, e.g. *The bird expanded its wings*; *Iron expands when heated*; **exp'anse**, wide stretch of land, water, etc.; **expansive** (——1) large; (of a person) expressing his thoughts and feelings freely.

'ex p'arte (2 + 44-1) expressing only one side of a question, not fair to both sides.

exp'atiate (1-21sh121) speak or write at length about something.

exp'atriate (2-21-121) drive a person from his own country.

exp'ect (1-2) think that an event will probably happen; think that a person will come; n. **expect'ation** (2-2-21shn); *He has expectations* = he believes that someone will leave money to him at death.

exp'ectorate (2-2-9-21) to *spit* (= force liquid suddenly from the mouth).

exp'edient (1-11-19) (action) well fitted to a certain state of things, or wise at a certain time; not right, but useful; n. **exp'ediency**

(——sɪ) thinking of what is useful or helpful, rather than of what is right.

expedite (2-1-4ɪ) make go faster; send quickly.

exped'ition (2-1-ɪshn) march of a body of soldiers to make war in some place; journey for the purpose of discovery, etc.; *With expedition* = quickly; **exped'itious** (2-1-ɪshgs) quick.

exp'el (1-2) drive out; *To expel from a school* = make a pupil leave a school because of bad behaviour.

exp'end (1-2) spend time, money, etc.; use up —in doing something; **exp'enditure** (1-2-ɪtsh9) spending of money, money spent; **exp'ense** (1-2) money spent; cost; *At the expense of* = with the loss of, causing the loss of; **exp'ensive** (——ɪ) costing much money.

exp'erience (1-19-19-s) knowledge or skill gained by practice or by living; events which have given one such knowledge or skill.

exp'eriment (1-2-1-9) *To experiment, to make an experiment* = to do something in order to discover whether an (e.g. scientific) idea is in fact true; n. a trial.

expert (an ——) (2-99) one who has special knowledge or power obtained by practice; adj. skilful, practised.

'expert'ise (2-9-11z) special knowledge and judgment about a certain form of art or work.

expiate (2-1-21) pay for a wrong act by suffering the full punishment.

exp'ire (1-419) (breathe out); die; come to an end, e.g. *My holiday expires to-day*; *At the expiry of* = at the end of.

expl'ain (1-2ɪ) tell the meaning of; give reasons for; *Explain yourself* = tell why you have done this, tell what you mean; adj. **expl'anatory** (1-3-9-9-1).

expl'etive (2-11-1) meaningless bad word spoken in anger.

expl'icit (1-15ɪ) clearly and fully expressed.

expl'ode (1-67) burst with a loud noise, e.g. gunpowder explodes; *To explode with rage* = become suddenly very angry; *To explode an idea* = show that it is not true.

exploit (2-5ɪ) great deed; **to expl'oit** (1-5ɪ) make full use of, e.g. *To exploit the coal and iron fields*; make unfair use of, e.g. *To exploit the poor and helpless by making them work for very low pay*.

expl'ore (1-55) to search into; to travel through a strange country and learn about it.

expl'osion (1-673n) act of *exploding* (3rd above); adj. **expl'osive** (1-67sɪ); **an expl'osive**, e.g. gunpowder.

exp'onent (2-67-9) one who explains the meaning; example; sign, e.g. 5^3, 3 is the *exponent* and means $5 \times 5 \times 5$.

exp'ort (2-55) send goods to other countries; **exports**, goods so sent.

exp'ose (1-67z) uncover; lay open to the effects of, e.g. *To expose one's skin to the sunlight*; show the true character of; make known secret evil deeds.

exp'osé (2-67z2ɪ) making known a secret wrongdoing.

expos'ition (2-9zɪshn) explaining of a thing; act of putting goods out for the public to see; collection of things so shown.

exp'ostulate (1-5-17-2ɪ) reason with a person and urge a different idea.

exp'osure (1-6739) act or state of being *exposed* (4th above); *To die of exposure* = from being left out in the cold air.

exp'ound (1-47) explain clearly.

expr'ess (1-2) (press out) (1) say or show clearly; (2) send quickly; adj. clearly said, e.g. *He did it for this express purpose* = for this reason, and he said clearly that this was the reason; fast, e.g. *An express train*; **expr'ession** (1-2shn) act of expressing; particular set of words, e.g. *He used some very rude expressions*; use of the voice in showing feelings, e.g. *She sang with great expression* = showing great feeling in her voice; appearance or look of the face as showing feelings; **expr'essive** (1-2-1) e.g. *A look expressive of great joy* = showing —; *An expressive look* = full of secret meaning.

expr'opriate (2-67-12ɪ) take away a thing possessed.

exp'ulsion (1-8-shn) act of driving out, e.g. a bad child from school.

exp'unge (2-8nj) rub out (a word).

expurgate (2-99-2ɪ) take out what is bad or dirty from a book so as to make the book fit for children.

exquisite (2-ɪzɪ) carefully chosen; very fine and beautiful; **exquisitely (1)** very beautifully; **(2)** very, e.g. *Exquisitely painful* = very painful.

exsc'ind (2-1) to cut out.

ext'ant (2-3) still standing, still living, not destroyed.

ext'empore (2-2-9-1) *To speak extempore* = speak without preparing a speech before the meeting; adj. **extempor'aneous** (2-2-9-21-19).

ext'end (1-2) stretch out; make longer or larger; offer; *To extend kindness to* = be kind to; n. **ext'ension** (1-2-shn) an *extending*; part built on to a house; *An extension course* = course of study given by a university to persons who are not members of the university; **ext'ensive** (——sɪ) stretching a long way; wide; *Extensive repairs* = large and thorough repairs; **ext'ent** (1-2) size; distance a thing stretches.

ext'enuate (1-2-172ɪ) weaken; make (a fault) seem less bad.

ext'erior (2-19-19) outside.

ext'erminate (2-99-1-2ɪ) destroy all, e.g. animals of a certain kind.

ext'ernal (2-99) having to do with the outside; foreign.

ext'inct (1-ɪngk) dead; no longer found alive, e.g. *Extinct animals* = animals of ancient times.

ext'inguish (1-1nggw1) put out, e.g. fire with water; **ext'inguisher**, instrument for putting out fire; metal cap used to put out a candle.

extirpate (2-99-21) tear up by the roots; destroy.

ext'ol (1-5) praise very highly.

ext'ort (1-55) obtain unjustly or by force, e.g. *He extorted a promise from me; The king extorted money from his people;* **ext'ortionate** (——shqn1t) demanding too much (money).

extra (2-9) something added; more than usual.

extra- (2-9) outside, e.g. *extra-mural* = outside the walls.

extr'act (1-3) pull or draw out; take out part of a book as an example of what the book contains; **an extract** (2-3) part taken out; the purest form of anything, e.g. *Extract of meat* = best part of meat obtained by boiling it down to a liquid.

extradite (2-9-41) send back to his own country a law-breaker who has escaped to a foreign country.

extr'aneous (2-21-19) foreign; not belonging to the special group being studied, spoken of, etc.

extra'ordinary (1-55-1) unusual; causing wonder because greater (better, etc.) than usual.

extr'avagant (1-3-9) wasteful; spending money foolishly; foolish and uncontrolled, e.g. *Extravagant behaviour; Extravagant praise* = far too great, wild and foolish praise.

extravag'anza (2-3-9-3-9) book, play, piece of music, etc., which is full of strange ideas and does not follow common rules.

extr'eme (1-11) the very end of anything, e.g. farthest, lowest, best, worst, least, etc.; *Extreme ideas* = very different from the ideas of most people; **an extr'emist** (1-11-1) one who holds *extreme* (unusually strong) opinions;

extr'emity (1-2-1-1) last or farthest point, e.g. *Extremities of the body* = hands, feet, fingers, etc.

extricate (2-1-21) to set free from a difficulty.

extrovert (2-67-99) person who does not turn his thoughts inwards and think about himself, but thinks only of the world outside.

extr'ude (2-77) push out.

ex'uberant (1gz177-9) full of life and high spirits; (of plants) growing freely and richly; (of painting or ornament) uncontrolled, having too much ornament.

ex'ude (1gz177) come out slowly as the liquid through the skin when one is hot.

ex'ult (1gz8) show great joy; feel proud of having done something.

eye (41) (1) that part of the body with which we see; (2) any small hole; (3) power of knowing the value of, e.g. *An eye for beauty;* spot, e.g. on some vegetable roots; *Have an eye for manners* = have a regard for them; *Up to the eyes in work* = very busy; *Keep an eye on him* = watch him; *To have an eye on someone's goods* = have a desire to obtain them; *To see eye to eye* = agree on all points; *Make him open his eyes* = surprise him; Sl. *To do him in the eye* = deceive; *To make eyes at* = look lovingly at; *Sheep's eyes* = loving looks; *Oh my eye!* (cry of surprise); *It's all my eye* = it is a foolish attempt to deceive; **to eye**, look at angrily or with desire; **eyebrow** (41-47) the hair above the eye; **eye-lashes** (+ 3-1z) hairs on the edge of the cover of the eye.

eyelet (41-1) hole with a metal ring round it, e.g. in a shoe; any small hole, e.g. in cloth.

eyelid (41-1) cover which comes down over the eye.

eye-opener (+ 67-9) anything which causes great surprise.

eyesight (41-41) power of seeing; *Within eyesight* = near enough to be seen.

eyesore (41-55) any very ugly or unpleasant thing.

eye-tooth (+77) long tooth just below the eye.

eyewash (41-5) Sl. things done to deceive a person into thinking that the work done (e.g. in a school or company of soldiers) is good.

eye-witness (+ 1-1) one who himself saw an event happen.

eyrie (29-1) see Aerie.

F

f. (2) (in music) = loud.

fable (21) story with a *moral* (= a teaching about good behaviour); fanciful story of something which could not happen, e.g. fairy-story.

fabric (3-1) material made into cloth; material used for making or building things.

fabricate (3-1-21) make or put together, e.g. *To fabricate an untrue story; To fabricate a document* (= written paper).

fabulous (3-17-9) concerned with *fables* (3rd above); impossible to believe; unbelievably large.

façade (9s44) outside face of a building.

face (21s) front of the head containing eyes, mouth, etc.; front of anything; *To have the face to say* = dare to say; *In the face of danger* = when about to meet danger; *On the face of it* = judging by outward appearances only; *To fly in the face of good fortune* = make no use of one's chances; *To put a brave face on* = pretend not to be afraid; *Make a face* or *Pull a face* = cause one's face to become ugly by moving the mouth, eyes, etc.; *To save one's face* = pretend that one has succeeded when one has failed; *To set one's face against* = not be in favour of; **to face**, look towards; stand opposite to; stand bravely against; *To face the music* = be ready to suffer punishment; *Face up to* = accept an unpleasant fact, not pretend that it is not so; **face value** (+ 3-177) value marked on a piece of money, stamp, etc., not always its real value.

facet (3s2) small flat side; e.g. on a precious stone.

facetious (9s11sh9) amusing; trying to be amusing.

facial (21sh19) of the face; *Facial massage, A facial* = rubbing and pressing the face so as to make it look fresher and more beautiful.

facile (3s41) easy; (of work) seeming to have been done easily; too easily done, careless; (of a person) able to do things easily; very ready to do as asked.

f'acile pr'inceps (3s1-1 + 1ns2) easily the best or first.

facilitate (9s1-1-21) to help, or make work easier to do.

facility (9s1-1-1) (1) easiness; special skill; (2) chance; *In the country one has no facilities for study* = has no books and other things needed for —.

facsimile (3-1-1-1) exact copy.

fact (3) something done, e.g. *Before or after the fact*; something which has really happened, or which is really true; *In fact* or *In point of fact* = according to the truth, really; *As a matter of fact* = to tell you the truth.

faction (3-shn) group which quarrels with, and will not work with others; a quarrel; adj. **factious** (3-sh9).

fact'itious (3-1sh9) not natural but made by man; untrue; unnatural (of behaviour).

factor (3-9) one who acts for another; that which helps to produce a result, e.g. *Rain and heat are factors in growing food;* $2 \times 3 = 6$, *2 and 3 are factors of 6*.

factory (3-9-1) trading station in a foreign country; building in which things are made, usually by machines.

fact'otum (3-67-9) one who does all kinds of business; man of all work.

factual (3-179) adj. of Fact.

faculty (3-1) power of doing anything; *A person's faculties* = powers of hearing, seeing, thinking, etc.; *The Faculty of Medicine* = those teachers in a university who teach medicine; in England students also.

fad (3) custom or interest which lasts only a short time; foolish or unreasonable practice.

fade (21) lose colour, brightness, or strength.

fag (3) Sl. make tired; work hard; (in a school) make a small boy do work for a larger boy; small boy so made to work; Sl. cigarette; **f'ag-'end**, last part of anything, usually worthless or worn-out.

faggot (3-9) number of small sticks tied together for burning.

Fahrenheit (3-9-41) way of measuring heat; 32° = freezing, 212° = boiling water.

fail (21) not to succeed; lose power or health; lose all one's money in business; *Do not fail me* = keep your promise to me, do not deceive me; **failing**, weakness, e.g. *A failing for drink* = desire to drink too much wine; **failure** (21-19) act of not succeeding; *Failure to report* = not reporting when one ought.

fain (21) glad, willing; *I fain would help him* = I would help him with pleasure.

faint (21) adj. lacking in strength; not bright; difficult to hear, see, etc.; n. sudden loss of all feeling caused by illness or shock; **f'aint-h'earted** (+ 44-1) having little courage.

fair (29) (1) beautiful; *The fair sex* = women; (2) clean, e.g. *A fair copy; One's fair name* = honour, good name; (3) just; *Fair play* = honest behaviour; *Fair and square* = just and right; (4) good, but not very good, e.g. *A fair chance of success; A fair amount* = some but not a lot; (5) fine, calm, e.g. *Fair weather*; (6) light coloured, e.g. *Fair hair*; (7) *Hit the nail fair on the head, fair and square on the head* = exactly on —; **fairly** (——1), e.g. *Fairly well* = well, but not very well.

fair (29) gathering of people at a special time

fair-spoken and place to buy and sell or to see strange things and amuse themselves.

fair-spoken (+ 67) speaking politely.

fairway (29-21) that part of a road or river which is open for travel; wide path on which the grass is cut short, e.g. for a game.

fairy (29-1) imaginary small beautiful creature supposed to have more than human powers.

faith (21) act of believing something; that which is taught and believed by any group; trust in God; *He did it in good faith* = meaning to be honest; **faith-healing** (+ 11-1) teaching people to become well by making them believe that they are well; *To keep faith* = be true to a promise, loyal; **faithful**, believing; honest and loyal in serving; *The faithful* = those who believe in and obey a certain god.

fake (21) change a thing so as to make it look like the real thing; thing so changed; man who pretends to be what he is not.

fakir (9-19) holy man in the East.

falchion (55lshn) broad, curved sword.

falcon (55) meat-eating bird used to catch other birds for a hunter; **falconry** (——1) hunting birds with falcons.

fall (55) (p.t. **fell**) (1) to drop from a higher to a lower level; (2) become less; *The river is falling* = the water in it is becoming lower; *Prices are falling* = are becoming lower; (3) to yield, e.g. *The Greeks attacked Troy and the city fell*; Sl. *To fall for* = be charmed by and yield; *To fall back* = go back; *The soldiers fell in* = got into line; — *fell out* = got out of line; *Mr. A and T fell out* = quarrelled; *To fall short of one's hopes* = be less than —; Sl. *Fall for him* = fall in love with him; *The plan fell through* = failed; *To fall on one's feet* = have good fortune; n. a **fall** (all the above meanings).

fallacy (3-9s1) untrue idea; that which deceives the eye or mind; *A popular fallacy* = idea believed by many people but really untrue; adj. **fallacious** (9-21sh9).

fallen (55) p.p. of Fall; *The fallen* = those killed in battle.

fallibility (3-1-1-1-1) state of being able to make mistakes.

fallow (3-67) light brown; land which has been prepared for seed and left for a year; *To lie fallow* = to rest.

false (5) wrong; not true; not faithful or loyal; *Sailing under false colours* = acting so as to deceive, e.g. as *pirates* (= thieves who attacked ships at sea) used flags of different nations; *A false note* = wrong note in music, or something which is not in good taste; a **falsehood** (5-7) untruth.

falsetto (5-2-67) high voice such as a man uses when trying to sing like a woman.

falsify (5-1-41) make untrue; *My hopes have been falsified* = proved untrue.

falter (5-9) speak unsteadily, as if afraid; walk unsteadily.

fame (21) good name; state of being known by all; *Ill fame* = bad name, state of being known as bad.

familiar (9-1-19) well-known; seen often; friendly; *To familiarize oneself with* = to accustom oneself to.

family (3-1-1) father, mother and children; children of two parents; group of people having a common parent in the past; *A family tree* = plan of a family showing all the births, marriages and deaths.

famine (21) state of having no food.

famished (3-1-t) *I am famished* = very hungry.

famous (21-9) well-known, e.g. because of having done great things; Sl. very good.

fan (3) instrument for moving the air, or for sending a stream of air in a certain direction; **to fan**, drive air on to; Sl. *A film fan* = one who loves going to the cinema (= moving pictures); here "fan" is perhaps short for *fanatic* (below); adj. shaped like a fan, e.g. *Fantail pigeon* = kind of bird; *A fan-light* = window shaped like a fan, usually above a door.

FAN   FAN (ELECTRIC)

fanatic (9-3-1) one who has a fierce belief in some opinion, and is unable to understand reason or common sense on that subject; **fanatic**, adj. having such beliefs, etc.

fancier (3-s19) one who keeps special kinds of animals for amusement or to sell; good judge of certain kinds of animals or things.

fancy (3-s1) (1) the power of forming in the mind pictures of things not present; (2) picture in the mind, or an idea; something imagined; (3) opinion not formed by reasoning, e.g. *These are mere fancies—you have no proof*; *To take a fancy to* = to like; *I have a fancy for* = would like; adj. ornamented, e.g. *Fancy cakes*; *Fancy dress* = special and unusual dress for dancing; **to fancy**, imagine; to like; *To fancy oneself* = have a high opinion of —.

fancy-free (+ 11) not loving or wanting to marry anyone.

fancy-work (+ 99) needle-work done for ornament.

fane (21) holy building, e.g. a church.

fanfare (3-29) noise of blowing *trumpets* (= brass instruments of music), e.g. when an important person arrives.

fang (3) long sharp pointed tooth.

fantastic (3-3-1) strange; unreal and impossible.

fantasy (3-9z1) strange idea; strange and

far 118 **favour**

unusual piece of writing, or music—sometimes called a **fant'asia** (3-21z19).

far (44) (1) not near, at a distance; *How far can you go?* = to what distance?; *Far be it from me to — —* = I would not dare to; *He will go far* = be very successful; (2) very much (better, etc.); *Far stronger* = much stronger; *Far and away better* = very much better; adj. distant; *It is a far cry to —* = a long way; *Few and far between* = not often found.

farce (44s) play meant only to make people laugh; anything very foolish causing laughter; *His plans were a farce* = his plans were useless and foolish; adj. **farcical** (44sl).

fare (29) (1) (in poetry) go; *He fared forth* = went out; (2) be successful; *It fared ill with him* = he was unsuccessful; *You may go farther and fare worse* = be content with what you have; n. food; *A Bill of Fare* = list of foods in a hotel; the cost of a journey, e.g. *The fare from London to Paris is £—*.

f'arewe'll (29-2) good-bye.

f'ar-f'etched (44 + 2-t) unreasonable; foolish.

farin'aceous (food) (3-1-21sh9) food made of flour, e.g. bread.

farm (44) piece of land used for growing corn, vegetables, feeding cattle, etc.; **to farm**, keep and use a farm; *To farm out the work* = give it to several people to do; a **farmer**, one who owns or works a farm; **farmstead** (44-2) farmhouse and buildings near it.

farr'ago (of nonsense) (9-44-67) mixture of foolish talk or ideas.

farrier (3-19) one who makes and fixes *horseshoes* (= pieces of curved iron on horses' feet); horse-doctor.

f'ar-s'eeing (+ 11·1), **f'ar-s'ighted** (41-1) wise and thinking of the future.

farther (44ð9) more distant; **farthermost** (44ð9-67) the most distant.

farthing (44ð9) Obs. ¼ of a penny.

farthingale (44ðɪngg2I) frame put under women's skirts in old days to make them stand out.

fas̟cinate (3-1-21) to charm; fix with the eyes as a snake does a small animal; hold the interest of.

Fascist (3shɪ) member of a group which does not believe in government by elected persons, but would have the country ruled by one leader.

fashion (3shn) (1) way in which a thing is made; manner; *To act in a strange fashion* = in a strange way; *After a fashion* = not very well; *After the fashion of* = like; (2) that way of dressing or behaving which is considered the best at a certain time, e.g. *Short skirts were the fashion in 1919*; *To be the fashion* = be admired and copied by all; *It is not the fashion to — —* = not the present custom; **to fashion**, to shape, make; **fashionable** (3-9-9) according to the present custom (especially of women's clothes); **a fashion-plate** (+ 21) picture showing different kinds of dress.

fast (44) moving quickly; acting quickly; *The fast set* = group of people who seek pleasure and spend money quickly; *A fast woman* = foolish and bad —; *To lead a fast life* = live for pleasure.

fast (44) eat no food.

fast (44) firmly fixed; *A fast friend.* = true, loyal —; *To hold fast* = hold tight; *Fast asleep* = in a deep sleep; *To play fast and loose* = keep changing one's way of behaviour.

fas̟ten (44) make firm; fix on to; **fas̟tening**, act of making firm; thing which makes firm, which holds things firmly together, e.g. the fastening of a shoe, coat, bag.

fast'idious (3-1-19) difficult to please; too careful about small and unimportant things.

fastness (44-1) fort.

fat (3) well-fed; having a great deal of fat on the body; short and broad; Sl. *A fat-head* = foolish fellow; Sl. *A fat lot you care* = you do not care at all; n. oily part of meat; *To live on the fat of the land* = live in great comfort; *The fat is in the fire* = you have done something which will cause great trouble.

fatal (21-9) caused by fate; causing death or ruin; **fatalism** (21-9-1z) teaching that all things happen according to fate and one's acts have no effect on the future; **a fat'ality** (9-3-1-1) a death; a misfortune.

fate (21) imaginary power which has settled everything which is to happen; future events so settled; **fateful**, full of the possibility of good or evil; very important.

father (44ð9) male parent; title of respect; *To father a plan* = think of it or help to put it in practice; *The fathers of their country* = wise men who planned it and governed it; **f'ather-in-law**, father of one's wife (or husband).

fathom (3ð) measure of six feet in length used in measuring depth of water; **to fathom**, find out and understand; **fathomless** (——1) so deep that it cannot be measured.

fat'igue (9-11) tiredness; tiring task; *To do fatigue duty in the army* = do the task of cleaning, washing, cooking, etc.

fat'uity (9-177-1) foolishness; adj. **fatuous** (3-1779).

faucet (55sl) American word for tap (see Tap).

fault (5) mistake or failing; bad part in any material; weak place in one's character; *It's my fault* = I am to be blamed; *Kind to a fault* = much too kind; *To be at fault* = not to know what to do next; **a fault-finder** (+ 41-9) one who finds unnecessary faults.

faun (55) spirit of the woods, with the body of a man and the feet of a goat.

fauna (55-9) all the animals found in a certain place.

faux̟ pas (67 + 4) mistake, e.g. saying something which causes pain or anger when one does not mean to do so.

favour (21-9) feeling of kindness towards; **to favour**, show kindness to; special kindness

fawn (55) young deer; **to fawn on** (of an animal) *lick* (= pass the tongue over) one's hands as a sign of love; (of a man) try to get favour by doing things which cause loss of self-respect; adj. yellow-brown.

fay (21) a fairy.

F.B.I. (2f-b11-41) (1) Federal Bureau of Investigation, officers of the central government in U.S.A. who look into special cases of wrongdoing against the whole nation; (2) Federation of British Industries (*federation* = union; *industries* = manufactories, etc.).

fealty (119-1) loyalty to a king, ruler, or those above one.

fear (19) feeling which one has when in danger; state of being very anxious; *To fear God* = have great respect for God; *There is no fear of rain* = it certainly will not rain; *I fear it is too late* = I think it is too late and I am sorry; *Never fear* = do not be anxious; Sl. *No fear!* = certainly not; **fearful,** afraid; causing fear; Sl. very great, unusual; **fearsome** (——9) causing fear.

feasible (1129) able to be done.

feast (11) day of special joy in honour of some past event; specially large meal; **to feast,** eat a feast; *To feast one's eyes on* = enjoy looking at.

feat (11) act worthy of notice because of special difficulty, courage, etc.

feather(s) (2ð9z) the light coverings which grow on a bird's body; any very light object like those on a bird's wing; *Birds of a feather* = people of the same kind; *That's a feather in his cap* = an honour for him; *To be in high feather* = be in high spirits; *To feather one's nest* = get enough money to make oneself comfortable, get money dishonestly; *To show the white feather* = have no courage; *Fur and feather* = those animals and birds which are shot for amusement and food; *Feather an oar* = make the blade lie flat on the water.

feature (11tsh9) one part of the face, e.g. nose, mouth, etc.; important or noticeable part of anything; *To feature anything* = give it an important place; *Feature film* = the long important film in a cinema-show.

febrile (2-41) having to do with fever.

feckless (2-1) thoughtless, careless.

fecund (2-9) fruitful; producing many young.

fed (2) p.t. and p.p. of Feed; *Fed up* = tired of and angry with.

feder'ation (2-9-21shn) joining together of separate *states* (= self-governing parts of a country) to form one government, each state keeping control of some matters; so also business companies; adj. **federal;** *The Federal Government* = — of all the states as a unity.

fee (11) payment made for special services of any kind, e.g. doctor's fee, school fees.

feeble (11) having no strength; **f'eeble-m'inded** (+ 41-1) born with weak powers of understanding.

feed (11) give food to; supply with what is necessary; *Feed the flames* = put (coal) on the fire; n. food given, e.g. to an animal; instrument which carries material to a machine.

feel (11) (1) e.g. *To feel cold* = know that one is cold; (2) to touch; (3) suffer, e.g. *I feel the cold* = I suffer from the cold weather; (4) understand or be moved by, e.g. *I feel the truth of what he says; I feel the beauty of his poem;* (5) have an opinion, e.g. *I feel that you are right; To feel one's way* = find one's way by touching things, go forward very carefully; *I feel like a drink* = I wish to have a —; **feelers** (——9z) long thread-like things on the front of an insect's head; **feelings** (11-1-z) e.g. anger, sorrow, love, etc.; *He hurt my feelings* = he caused me pain (of mind); *Good feelings* = friendship.

feign (21) pretend.

feint (21) pretended blow or attack; **to feint,** pretend to attack.

feldspar, felspar (2-44), glassy white or red rock.

fel'icitate (1-1s1-21) wish happiness to; show that one is pleased by another's good fortune.

fel'icitous (speech) (1-1s1-9) well expressed and suited to that special time.

fel'icity (1-1s1-1) state of being happy; *He expresses himself with great felicity* = using just the right words.

feline (11-41) like a cat; of cats.

fell (2) p.t. of Fall.

fell (2) cut down (a tree); knock down (a man or animal).

fell (2) rocky hill.

fell (2) fierce; cruel; terrible.

fellah (2-9) worker on the land in Egypt or Syria; **fellah'in** (pl.) (——h11).

felloe (2-67) outer edge of a wheel.

fellow (2-67) one who works, plays or studies (etc.) with another; an equal; member of any special group; *Old fellow* = way of addressing a friend of any age; *Our fellow workers* = those who work with us; *Our fellow creatures* = human beings; *F'ellow-f'eeling* = feeling shared with another; *The fellow of this shoe* = shoe for the other foot; *Fellow-traveller* = person who believes in and works for Russian communism.

f'elo-de-s'e (11-67 + 11 + 11) one who kills himself.

felony (2-9-1) serious breaking of the law, e.g. murder, burning a house, etc.; **a felon,** one who does such an act.

felspar (2-44) see Feldspar.

felt (2) p.t. of Feel.

felt (2) material like thick cloth, made by pressing and sticking hair together, used to make hats.

female (11-21) woman; a human, animal or bird which is able to produce eggs or young.

feminine (2-1-1) belonging to women; like a woman.

feminist (2-1-1) one who believes in equal rights for women and men.

femur (11-9) long upper bone of the leg; adj. **femoral** (2-9).

fen (2) flat low wet land.

fence (2-s) practise fighting with swords; try not to give a straight answer to a question, turn a question aside.

fence (2-s) light wall of wood, or of wire stretched between poles, used to keep men and animals in (or out of) a field; **to fence,** put up a fence round.

fence (2-s) person who buys and sells stolen goods.

fend (2) to care for; protect; *To fend off a blow* = protect oneself from.

fender (2-9) anything used to prevent damage caused by striking against another thing, e.g. mass of rope or wood put between a ship and the wall of the harbour; guard round the fireplace in a room; Am. mud-guard above the wheels of a motor-car.

ferm'ent (9-2) change the liquid of fruits into wine; a **f'erment** (99-2) material which causes this change; *In a ferment* = very excited.

fern (99) flowerless plant with leaves; its seeds are found on the backs of the leaves.

FERN

fer'ocious (9-67sh9) fierce, cruel.

-ferous (9-9) containing, e.g. *Carboniferous* = containing *carbon* (e.g. coal).

ferret (2-1) cat-like creature used to hunt rabbits by going into their holes and driving them out; *To ferret out* = make a careful search into hidden or secret things.

FERRET

ferric (2-1) **ferrous** (2-9) having to do with iron; *Ferrous metals* = metals containing iron; *Non-ferrous* = not —.

ferrule (2-77) metal cap on the end of a stick, e.g. a walking-stick; metal ring used to strengthen any joint.

ferry (2-1) boat which carries people across a river; place where this boat works; **to ferry,** take across a river in a boat.

fertile (99-41) producing much; fruitful; *A fertile mind* = mind able to think of many plans and ideas; **fertilize** (99-1-41) cause to bear fruit; **fertilizer** (——9) any material scattered on the earth in order to make it produce larger crops.

fervent (99) eager; (of feeling) strong, e.g. *Fervent desire*.

fervid (99-1) burning; very keen (mind); n. **fervour** (99-9).

festal (2) having to do with a feast; gay.

fester (2-9) (of a wound) become poisoned, decay; (of the feelings) become bitter and angry from a continued sense of wrong.

festival (2-1) feast-day; day of rejoicing; adj. **festive.**

fest'oon (2-77) ornament fixed at both ends and hanging in a curve, e.g. a paper chain or string of flags hung from one side of a room to the other.

fetch (2) go to another place and bring a thing from it; *To fetch a man a blow on the nose* = give —; *The picture fetched £100* = was sold for —; **fetching,** pleasing.

fête (21) feast-day; outdoor gathering for amusement; **to fête,** give feasts in honour of.

fetid, foetid (11-1) having a very bad smell.

fetish (11-1) charm having magical powers; any object loved, or regarded as holy, in a foolish or unreasonable manner.

fetlock (2-5) part of a horse's leg just above the foot.

fetter (2-9) chain for the feet, used on prisoners; anything which takes away one's freedom.

fettle (2) *In fine fettle* = in very good spirits.

feud (177) long-continued quarrel between persons, families, or groups, usually resulting in killing.

feudal (system) (177) *The Feudal System* settled the duties of landowner and *tenant* (= person who rents land) in ancient times—the tenant had to fight for the landowner in time of war.

fever (11-9) great heat in the body caused by disease; state of excitement; adj. **feverish.**

few (177) not many; *A few* = not many, but more than one would expect; *Every few (days)* = once in a group of a few —; *A good few* = rather large number.

fey (21) fated to die soon; excited state supposed to come just before sudden death.

fez (2) red cap with black threads hanging from the top as worn by many Muslims.

fi'ancé (14ˢs21) man who is promised in marriage; **fi'ancée,** woman who is —.

fiasco (13-67) foolish laughable *failure* (= n. of Fail).

fiat (413) a command.

fib (1) Sl. unimportant untruth.

fibre (41-9) thread-like part of anything, e.g. wood, muscles, etc.; that which gives strength to any material; *A man of coarse fibre* = of rough character; adj. **fibrous** (41-9) **fibroid** (41-51); *A fibroid* = diseased growth in the body.

fibula (1-17-9) thin outer bone between the knee and the foot.

fichu (11sh77) piece of fine cloth worn round a lady's neck and shoulders.

fickle (1) changeable; weak in character; having no quality of faithfulness.

fiction (1-shn) anything which is only imagined, not a fact; story; art of writing stories; adj. **fict′itious** (1-1sh9).

fiddle (1) a *violin* (= musical instrument with four strings played by rubbing with a *fiddlestick*—see below); *With a face as long as a fiddle* = looking very sad; *To play second fiddle* = be led or ruled by another; *Fit as a fiddle* = in perfect condition; **a fiddler** (1-9) (bad) player on the fiddle; **to fiddle**, play the fiddle; waste time doing useless things; play with any small object in a thoughtless (unthinking) way; Sl. to cheat; to steal.

f′iddle-dee-d′ee (1 + 1 + 11) foolishness; *nonsense* (= not good sense).

fiddlestick (1-1) curved stick with horse-hair joining the two ends used for playing the *fiddle* (2nd above); *Fiddlesticks!* = foolishness, *nonsense* (= not good sense).

fid′elity (41-2-1-1) faithfulness; (of a copy) exactness.

fidget (1j1) be unable to sit or stand still; move restlessly.

fidu′ciary (1-177s19-1) having to do with a trust, e.g. taking care of the money left to children until they are grown up; (of paper money) getting its value from the trust people have in it, not because it can be changed for gold.

fie (41) e.g. *Fie upon you!* = you ought to be ashamed of yourself.

fief (11) land held under the *feudal system* (see Feudal).

field (11) (1) open country, e.g. *Beasts of the field*; (2) any large open space, e.g. *A snow-field*; *The field of my work* = the part of the subject which I am studying; *My field of vision* = the space I can see; *The flag showed golden lions on a red field* = main part of the flag was red and the lions were painted or fixed on to it; (3) enclosed piece of land used for growing crops or keeping animals; *A battlefield* = the place of a battle; *Army in the field* = fighting against the enemy; *To take the field* = begin fighting a war; *To hold the field* = keep one's place against all others; (of horses) *To beat the field* = win against all the rest; *To field a ball* = stop a ball in a game, e.g. in *cricket*; **a f′ield-day** (+ 21) day on which soldiers go into the country and practise fighting; short journey into the country.

f′ield-glass (+ 44) instrument put to both eyes for seeing distant things; **a f′ield-gun** (+ 8) **f′ield-piece** (+ 11s) a gun on wheels; **F′ield M′arshal** (+ 44) the highest officer in the army.

fiend (11) evil spirit; very cruel person; Sl. *Fresh air fiend* = person who is troublesomely interested in —.

fierce (19s) cruel; wild; uncontrolled; eager.

fiery (419-1) having to do with fire; hot; quick-tempered.

fife (41) small musical instrument for blowing (a kind of whistle).

fifth (1) **Fifth column** (+ 5-9) people in a city or country who are ready to help an enemy attacking it.

fig (1) small fruit with many very small seeds in it; *I don't care a fig* = I do not care at all; *A fig for Mr. — —* = he deserves no notice.

FIG

fight (41) struggle against; try to get control of; *To fight out a thing* = decide by fighting; *To fight shy of* = keep away from; *A free fight* = everyone fighting against everyone else.

figment (1) something imagined or pretended.

figurative (1-17-9-1) (1) (of a word or saying) not to be understood in its exact meaning, e.g. *Brave as a lion* means, not perhaps quite as brave as a lion, but very brave; (2) having in it many such figures of speech.

figure (1-9) (1) form of the human body, e.g. *She has a beautiful figure, A fine figure of a man*; general appearance, e.g. *To cut a poor figure* = look foolish; (2) stone, wood or metal cut into the shape of a man or animal; (3) picture or drawing, e.g. *A curtain ornamented with beautiful figures*; *A figure of speech* = a *figurative* (see above) way of speaking; (4) a shape, e.g. one drawn for ornament in a book; (5) fixed set of steps in a dance; (6) written number, e.g. *1, 2, 3*; **to figure**, *To figure in a play* = act in —; *To figure out* = work out the answer to a question of figures; to add.

figurehead (1-9-2) likeness of something (e.g. the wooden form of a man or woman) fixed on the front of a ship; one whose name is used in a business but who has no power.

filament (1-9-9) very thin thread; thin metal thread used in an electric light.

filbert (1-9) small *nut* (= hard-shelled fruit of a tree).

filch (1) steal.

file (41) (1) arrange in order, e.g. letters, papers, etc.; **a file**, box or paper-cover in which letters, papers, etc., are kept in order; (2) straight line of people or objects; (in the army) two lines of men walking each behind the other; *Single file* = one line of men walking one behind another; *The rank and file* = common soldiers and *corporals* (= lowest rank above a common soldier).

file (41) metal instrument with rough points on it used for making metals or wood smooth by rubbing; wear a thing away by rubbing.

filial (1-19) having to do with sons or daughters;

filibuster — 122 — **fire-arm**

Filial piety = love and duty one ought to give to one's parents.

filibuster (1-1-8-9) person who makes war against a foreign nation, acting for his own gain only; person who delays the passing of a law by endless talking.

filigree (1-1-11) ornamental work made of fine gold or silver wire; any fine work which is open, so that one can see through it.

filings (41-1-z) fine dust made when rubbing or cutting a piece of metal.

fill (1) put into any container all that it will hold; make full; satisfy; *To fill the bill* = satisfy the need; *To fill the office* = do the work needed in the position; *To fill out* = become fat; *To fill out (or fill in) a form* = write what is necessary in all the empty spaces in a printed paper.

fillet (1-1) thin band worn round the hair; thin band of wood or metal used as an ornament or to give strength; thin piece of meat or fish without any bones in it.

fillip (1-1) urge on or *encourage* (= give courage to); strike with the finger; *This medicine gives one a fillip* = makes one feel fresh and strong.

filly (1-1) young female horse.

film (1) thin skin or covering of any kind; thin band used for making photographs; long band of pictures used to show moving pictures in the *cinema* (= moving pictures); *A film-actor* = actor for the *cinema*.

filter (1-9) instrument used to take all solid or impure matter out of liquids; **to filter**, flow in or out very slowly, e.g. *New ideas filter into people's minds.*

filth (1) dirty matter.

filtrate (1-21) to *filter* (2nd above); liquid obtained by filtering.

fin(s) (1-z) wing-like parts on the backs and sides of sea animals, fish, etc., with which they swim.

final (41) last; settling a question, e.g. *The final game* = that which shows who really wins; settled, fixed, e.g. *My judgment is final* = I shall not change it; **fin'ale** (1-44-1) ending of a play, piece of music, etc.; **fin'ality** (41-3-1-1) state of being settled and complete.

fin'ance (1-3-6) science of controlling money, e.g. public money; **to fin'ance** (a plan) find the money for it; **fin'ancial** (1-3-shl) having to do with money matters; **fin'ancier** (1-3-s19) one who understands money matters; one who controls a large amount of money.

finch (1) small singing bird.

find (41) p.t. Found; **(1)** discover after search, e.g. *He found gold in Australia*; **(2)** get back a thing lost, e.g. *I found my pen in the bedroom*; **(3)** provide, e.g. *Find the money for starting a new school*; *The ship is well found* = well provided with stores; **(4)** decide, to judge, e.g. *The court found the prisoner guilty* = decided that he had really done the wrong act; *To find oneself* = discover one's powers, get a chance of using one's powers; *Find one's feet* = get a chance of doing well; *How did you find the weather?* = like —; *I found him out* = discovered that he was not honest; **a find**, valuable discovery; **a finding**, judgment, e.g. of a court.

fine (41) amount of money paid to a court of law as a punishment for breaking the law; so also elsewhere.

fine (41) pure, e.g. *Fine gold*; good, beautiful, e.g. *A fine day* = good weather; thin, e.g. *A fine line, Fine dust, Fine cloth.*

finery (41-9-1) beautiful clothes and ornaments.

fin'esse (1-2) clever way of dealing with a difficult matter so that the purpose is gained without making anyone angry.

finger (1ngg9) **(1)** there are five fingers on each hand; **(2)** anything that can be used as a finger; *To finger a thing* = touch and rub with the fingers; *To have the business at one's finger-tips* (= finger-ends) = know every little thing about it; *A light-fingered person* = thief; *I can twist him round my little finger* = make him do anything I want; **fingered**, marked to show how to use the fingers, e.g. a piece of music; having fingers; **fin'ger-post** (+ 67) post by the road-side showing which way to go; **f'inger-stall** (+ 55) small cover for a damaged finger.

finical (1-1), **finickin** (1-1-1), **finicking** (1-1-1), **finicky** (1-1-1) taking too much trouble about small unimportant matters; (of a thing) having many small parts, troublesome and difficult to use.

finis (41-1) the end.

finish (1-1) bring to an end; make perfect; *It nearly finished me* (*off*) = nearly killed; *The table has a good finish* = is well polished.

finite (41-41) having a beginning and an end; able to be counted, measured, etc.

finny (1-1) having *fins* (= the wing-like parts on the backs and sides of fish).

fi'ord, fjord (155) long opening from the sea with hills on each side.

fir (99) tree which has needle-like leaves and long hard egg-shaped containers for seeds.

fire (419) that which burns, giving out heat and light; **to fire** (a gun), shoot; *He is full of fire* = has great force of character; *The speaker fired his listeners* = made them feel strongly, made them eager to act; *He won't set the Thames on fire* = will not do anything great; Sl. *Tell him to fire away* = tell him to start, or continue; *To keep up a running fire of words* = continue speaking quickly without stopping; *Under fire* = being shot at; Sl. *To fire an employee* = send away, not employ any more.

FIR

f'ire-arm (+ 44) any gun which can be carried.

firebrand (419-3) one who urges others to change conditions, e.g. of government, by the use of force.

f′ire-brigade (+ 1-21) special group of men, having necessary machines, who put out fires (e.g. burning houses) in a city.

firecracker (419-3-9) paper object containing a small amount of gun-powder which bursts with a loud noise, much used on feast-days.

firedamp (419-3) dangerous gas found in coal *mines* (= deep holes in the ground from which coal is obtained).

f′ire-dog (+ 5) iron supports for wood in an open fire-place.

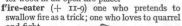
FIRE-DOG

f′ire-eater (+ 11-9) one who pretends to swallow fire as a trick; one who loves to quarrel and fight.

f′ire-engine (+ 2nji) machine for forcing water through a pipe to throw it on a burning building.

FIRE-ENGINE

f′ire-escape (+ 1-21) *ladders* (= two long pieces of wood or iron joined together by bars used as steps) used for escaping from a burning building; iron stairs on outside of a building for use if there is a fire.

firefly (419-41) insect which gives out light from its body.

fireproof (419-77) which cannot be burned.

firetrap (419-3) dangerous place if there is a fire, e.g. a badly planned building.

fireworks (419-99) things made from gunpowder and other materials, which burn with beautiful colours, or burst with a loud noise—or do both.

firm (99) solid; strong; steady; *To be firm with children* = make them obey.

firm (99) business company; number of people who join together for business purposes.

firmament (99-9-9) sky.

first (99) Number 1 in order; at the beginning; earliest; most important; *From the first* = from the beginning; *I will come first thing* = early in the morning; *I′ll see him hanged first* = I will not do what he asks; *The first Cause* = beginning of everything, God; **f′irst-′aid** (+ 21) help given to one who is wounded, before the doctor arrives; **f′irst-cl′ass** (+ 44) of the best quality; **f′irst c′ost** (+ 5) the money it costs to produce a thing; **f′irst fl′oor** (+ 55) in America the floor level with the ground, in Europe first floor above the ground; **f′irst-h′and** (knowledge) (+ 3) knowledge which one has obtained by one's own ears, eyes, etc., not by being told by someone else; **f′irst-rate** (+ 21) of the best kind.

firth (99) arm of the sea; mouth of a river.

fiscal (1) having to do with money, especially the money of governments.

fish (1) cold-blooded creature which lives in water; *Feeling like a fish out of water* = uncomfortable among strangers; Sl. *A poor fish* = foolish, worthless person; *I have other fish to fry* = other more important things to do; *A pretty kettle of fish* = this is a bad business, a difficult matter; *Cry stinking fish* = say bad things about what one is trying to sell; **to fish**, catch fish; *To fish in troubled waters* = get *profit* (= gain) from troubled conditions; *To fish for —* = try to make a person give something without actually asking for it; **f′ish-monger** (+ 8ngg9) seller of fish; **f′ishwife** (1-41) woman who sells fish; **fishy** (——-1) having to do with fish; *That sounds fishy* = is probably untrue or dishonest.

fissile (1-41) which can be broken by *fission*.

fission (1sh9) breaking into two parts; *Nuclear fission* = breaking the *nucleus* (= centre part) of an atom as in the explosion of an atom-bomb.

fissure (1sh9) a crack.

fist (1) hand when closed tight; *Close fisted, Tight fisted* = very unwilling to spend money; **fisticuffs** (1-1-8) a fight with fists.

fistula (1-17-9) opening in the surface of the body caused by disease, through which poisonous liquid flows out.

fit (1) sudden illness; sudden loss of feeling; sudden state of strong feeling, e.g. *A fit of anger*; *To do things by fits and starts* = do a little, then stop, then begin again, etc.

fit (1) proper, *suitable* (= which suits); *Fit time and place* = right, proper —; *Law of survival of the fittest* = scientific law that those animals which are best suited to their conditions, live and increase—the others are killed off and become less, or die out; *Fit to drop* = very tired; Sl. *Laughed fit to bust* = uncontrolledly; *To think fit* = decide; *To feel fit, To be as fit as a fiddle* = be in good health; **to fit**, be right for, be large enough, not too large (or small) for, e.g. *This coat fits me*; cause to fit, e.g. *To fit a key to a lock*; *To fit in* = find a place for, press into a small space; *To fit out* = provide with all necessary things; *To fit up* = get ready for use; **a fitter**, man who fits clothes on one; a man who puts together parts of a machine and sees that they fit properly; **fitting**, right, proper; thing fitted on to another thing, e.g. *The inside fittings of a motor-car* = clock, little boxes, lamps, etc.

fitful (1) not regular, unsteady.

fiver (41-9) Sl. *£5 note* (= paper money).

fives (41-z) game played by hitting a ball against a wall.

fix (1) make firm; prevent from being moved or changed; settle; join firmly on to; *I′ll fix you up* = take you in as a guest; *To fix up to go to the play* = arrange; *Fix up a quarrel* = settle; *I′ll fix him!* = punish; Am. **to fix**, e.g. *Fix these shoes for me* = repair; n. *In a bad fix* =

in a difficulty; *Take a fix* = look at the sun (or stars) with an instrument to find out where the ship is.

fixture (1-tsh9) things which are fixed into a house and are not taken away when one leaves the house, e.g. pipes, fire-place, built-in shelves, etc.; *A football fixture* = game arranged on a certain future date; *I'm a fixture here* = I shall not leave this place.

fizz (1) make a noise as of gas coming out of liquid; Sl. *champagne* (= gaseous yellow wine).

fizzle (1) make a noise like water on the fire; Sl. *Fizzle out* = come to a foolish end.

fjord (155) see Fiord.

flabbergast (3-9-44) cause such surprise as takes one's breath away (makes one unable to breathe for a few moments).

flabby (3-1) soft; not firm; lacking in strength of character.

flaccid (3ksi) weak; soft.

flag (3) piece of coloured cloth, usually with special marks on it, used as the sign of some group or nation; *The white flag* = sign that one yields; *The flag-ship* = ship on which the commander sails; **to flag**, use a flag to send a message.

FLAG

flag (3) tall stiff, flowering plant which grows near water.

flag (3) become tired; lose strength.

flagellate (3j1-21) hit the body with a *scourge* (= knotted strings).

flageolet (3j67-2) wind instrument of music, which makes a whistling sound.   FLAGEOLET

flag'itious (9j1sh9) shameful; very wrong.

flagon (3) vessel with a narrow mouth (opening) used for containing liquids.

flagrant (21) clearly wrong; *A flagrant wrong-doer* = one who does wrong openly and without shame.

flagstone (3-67) large flat stone used in making a path or floor.

flail (21) wooden instrument used for beating the grain out of a plant.

flair (29) natural liking for a thing; natural power of doing anything.

flak (3) gun-fire to bring down attacking aeroplanes.

flake (21) small thin piece of anything.

flambeau (3-67) burning stick carried in the hand when marching at night.

flamb'oyant (3-519) highly coloured; richly ornamented.

flame (21) mass of burning gas rising from a fire; *She is a flame of his* = is loved by him; — *an old flame* = was once loved by him; **to flame**, burn brightly, be bright, e.g. *Flaming eyes* = bright with anger; *Flaming cheeks* = red —.

flam'ingo (9-1ngg67) water-bird having long legs, and bright red wings.

flan (3) a flat open pastry container filled with fruit.

flange (3nj) edge of a wheel so made as to keep it from running off the line.

flank (3ngk) side of the body; the right or left side of an army.

flannel (3) soft woollen cloth; *Flannels* = clothes made of flannel used when playing outdoor games.

fl'annel'ette (3-2) cotton cloth made to look like *flannel* (see above).

flap (3) move up and down, as a bird moves its wings; (of any wide flat object) to move—especially with a sound "flap! flap!" e.g. *A sail (flag) flaps in the wind*; Sl. *In a flap* = excited.

flap (3) piece of cloth, leather, etc., fixed at one edge and hanging down over an opening, e.g. *The flap of a pocket*; any flat part made to hang down, e.g. *The flap of a folding table*.

flapjack (3-3) Am. thin flat cake.

flapper (3-9) young girl of about sixteen years.

flare (29) burn; shine; burn with a sudden unsteady light; *The flare of a dress* = lower edge which stretches or spreads out in a bell-shape; *A flare-up* = sudden fierce quarrel; *Flare-path* = line of lights to guide an aeroplane in to land on an air-field.

flash (3) appear with sudden brightness; move very quickly; *To flash a message* = send a message with a bright lamp; **a flash,** sudden bright light; *A flash in the pan* = something which has a great effect for a short time, but soon fails; *In a flash* = very suddenly and quickly; *Flash-back* = going back in a story or cinema film to tell something which had happened earlier.

flashlight (3-4I) small electric handlamp.

flashy (3-1) looking very bright and good but really worthless, e.g. cheap clothes or jewelled ornaments which are not real.

flask (44) flat bottle.

flat (3) smooth; level; without interest; (in music) below the true note; *Life is flat* = without interest; *The story fell flat* = nobody thought it amusing; *And that's flat* = and I shall not change this opinion; *To give a flat rate* = sell a number of different things all at the same price; *I told him flat* = plainly; *A flat spin, Go into a flat spin*—An aeroplane goes into a flat spin when it goes straight down, out of control, turning round and round; Sl. (Of a man) become very excited and unable to think; **a flat,** set of rooms all on one floor of a house, used as a home for one person or family; **a flat, a r'iver flat, flats,** low flat land near a river.

flat-iron (3 + 4I9) heavy iron instrument used for pressing cloth smooth.

flatter (3-9) please by praising greatly without

flatulence (3-17-9-s) gas in the stomach.

flaunt (55) wave a thing about proudly and more than is necessary; make a great show of something of which one is very proud.

flautist (55-1) one who plays a *flute* (= a wind instrument of music like a whistle).

flavour (21-9) that quality which gives a thing taste or smell; a quality which has an effect on the feelings, e.g. *There is a flavour of dishonesty about the business.*

flaw (55) a crack; imperfect part in anything, likely to cause it to break or fail.

flax (3) plant used for making fine cloth; the thread made from this; **flaxen**, having to do with flax; light yellow coloured.

flay (21) take the skin off; *To flay him alive* = pull the skin off while living; to say very strong words so as to make a wrong-doer feel ashamed.

FLAX

flea (11) very small jumping insect which bites animals in order to get blood.

fl'ea-bite (+ 41) bite of a flea; something very small and unimportant.

fleck (2) spot of colour; to mark with spots.

flection (2kshn) see Flexion.

fled (2) p.t. of Flee.

fledge (2j) grow feathers; **fledgeling, fledgling** (2j-1) young bird with just enough feathers to fly; *A newly-fledged doctor* = one who has just obtained the right to practise; *Full fledged* = one who has full powers, full right, e.g. to act as a doctor.

flee (11) run away from, e.g. danger.

fleece (11s) the woolly covering of a sheep's body; any soft warm material which feels like wool; *Fleecy clouds* = clouds which look like wool; *To fleece a man* = steal all his money by deceiving him.

fleet (11) fast; **fl'eet-f'ooted** (+ 7-1) able to run very fast.

fleet (11) number of ships together; large group of warships under one commander.

fleeting (11-1) moving quickly and silently away, e.g. *Life is fleeting.*

Fleet Street (11 + 11) street in London where most of the newspapers are prepared.

flesh (2) meat on a body; *One's own flesh and blood* = members of one's family; *The flesh* = desires or weaknesses of the body, e.g. *The spirit is willing but the flesh is weak*; *Appear in the flesh* = come oneself; *To put on flesh* = become fat; *To lose flesh* = become thin; *Have one's pound of flesh* = demand payment of the whole amount of a debt; *Go the way of all flesh* = die; *Proud flesh* = hard red skin round a wound; *The flesh-pots (of Egypt)* = good food and comfort.

fleur-de-lis (99 + 9 + 11) sign used by the Kings of France.

flex (2) bend or cause to bend; n. easily bent electric wire; **flexion** (2kshn) act of bending or the state of being bent; **flexible** (2-9) able to be bent, easily made to obey; n. **flexib'ility** (2-9-1-1-1).

FLEUR-DE-LIS

fl'ibbertig'ibbet (1-9-1j1-1) person who has no steadiness of character.

flick (1) strike lightly with a quick small movement, e.g. *To flick a horse with the whip* (= string tied on the end of a stick).

flicker (1-9) burn unsteadily; give an unsteady light—as a lamp about to go out.

flight (41) act of flying through the air; distance flown; *The flight of time* = passing of —; *A flight of birds, — of arrows* = number of — flying together; *A flight of stairs* = set of steps up; *Two flights up* = up two sets of stairs.

flight (41) act of running away; *Put to flight* = cause to run away.

flighty (41-1) unsteady in character, not to be trusted.

flimsy (1-21) thin; weak; easily destroyed.

flinch (1) draw back in pain or fear.

flinders (1-9z) little bits, e.g. *Broken into* —.

fling (1) throw with great force; throw hurriedly (= in a hurry), e.g. *To fling one's clothes on* = dress quickly; *She flung out of doors* = went out quickly, in anger; *Have a fling at* = make an attempt; *I've had my fling* = have had my chance or have had my time of foolish pleasure; *The Highland Fling* = a Scottish dance.

flint (1) very hard stone which can be struck to make fire; a small bar of metal rubbed by a wheel in a cigarette-lighter; *A flint-lock* = old kind of gun.

flip (1) strike with a light quick blow of the first finger pressed outward from the inner side of the thumb.

flippant (1) speaking lightly about serious matters.

flipper (1-9) limb of a water-creature (other than a fish) used in swimming.

flirt (99) (1) move or shake quickly, e.g. wings, a bird's tail; (2) to play at love-making; **a flirt**, man or woman (especially woman) who plays at love-making; **a flirt'ation** (99-21shn) love-making (not serious); adj. **flirt'atious** (99-21shg).

flit (1) move quickly from place to place as a small bird from tree to tree; *Do a moonlight flit* = leave one's house secretly to escape paying debts.

flitch (1) side of *bacon* (= pig's meat salted and smoked).

float (67) to rest on the surface of a liquid, e.g. *Wood floats in water*; move without effort, e.g.

Clouds float across the sky; *To float a company* = find the necessary money and start a business company; **a float**, thing which floats, e.g. piece of wood from which a fishing-hook or net hangs.

flock (5) group of animals or birds; crowd; people under the care of a priest; *Flower of the flock* = best child in a family.

floe (67) large piece of floating ice.

flog (5) punish by beating; *To flog oneself on* = force oneself to go when tired; *To flog a dead horse* = go on with a thing after everyone has lost interest in it.

flood (8) great amount of water covering land which is usually dry; *A flood of tears, of words, of people* = sudden flow, rush of —; **fl′oodgates** (+ 21) doors in a *dam* (= a wall built across a river, lake, etc., in order to keep the water from flowing away) which let the water out; **fl′oodlights** (8-41) very powerful lamps used to light up the outside of a beautiful building at night; **fl′ood-t′ide** (+ 41) highest point of the *tide* (= flowing up of the sea on to the land, caused by the moon).

floor (55) bottom part of a room on which one walks; any smooth level bottom; (in England) *Ground floor* = floor level with the street; *First floor* = floor above the ground floor; (in America) *First, Main or Ground floor* = floor level with the street; *He was floored* = he could not answer the question; *He has the floor* = it is his turn to speak.

fl′oor-w′alker (+ 55-9) man in a shop who walks about to see that everything is going on as it should.

flop (5) fall heavily; *Flop-eared dog* = dog with large hanging ears; Sl. *The play was a flop* = failed badly.

flora (55-9) plant life of place, country, etc.; *Flora and fauna* = plants and animals; adj. **floral**, of flowers.

flor′escent (5-2) in a state of putting forth flowers.

florid (5-1) flowery; richly ornamented; *Florid speech* = speech with many (or too many) long words and high-sounding expressions.

florin (5-1) piece of English money worth ten pence.

florist (5-1) grower or seller of flowers.

floss (5) short threads of natural silk.

flot′illa (67-1-9) group of warships, usually all of the same kind.

flotsam (5-9) goods floating on the water, e.g. from a wreck; *Flotsam and jetsam* = goods floating on the water, or thrown up on the shore.

flounce (47-s) ornamental piece joined to the lower edge of a woman's dress; *To flounce out of a room* = go out quickly and angrily.

flounder (47-9) make strong but useless movements as in trying to get out of water; roll about helplessly; become mixed up in speaking, and talk foolishly; **a flounder**, a flat sea-fish.

flour (479) fine white powder made from grain and used to make bread.

flourish (8-1) grow in a healthy way; wave something so that others can see it; short burst of music; *A flourishing business man* = very successful —.

flout (47) treat with great lack of respect; laugh at.

flow (67) run or spread like water; *The flow of a river* = the running water in a river; *The wine flowed freely* = they drank much wine; *The flowing lines of a dress* = dress which has beautiful curves.

flower (479) beautiful part of a plant which will produce seed; any flower-like shape; best or most perfect of any set of things; *The flower of life* = time when one's powers are at their best; *Flower of the flock* = best child in the family; *A flower of speech* = a *poetical* (= as in poetry) way of speaking.

flu (77) short for *influenza* (see Influenza).

fluctuate (8-1721) to rise and fall, e.g. *Fluctuating prices*.

flue (77) pipe for leading away smoke from a fire or leading air to a fire.

flue (77) loose bits of wool, cotton, etc., as found on the floor of a dirty room.

fluent (779) having a ready flow of words and ideas; n. **fluency** (779-sI).

fluff (8) fine soft feathery material; Sl. **to fluff**, forget one's words when acting in the theatre; *To fluff out* = shake out, to make loose, e.g. as a bird fluffs out its feathers.

fluid (771) able to flow like water; not settled and firm; **a fluid**, liquid.

fluke (77) unexpected fortune; *He did it by a fluke* = by chance, not by good play or good judgment.

fluke (77) small flat creature found in the *liver* (= part of the body which makes the blood pure and stores up sugar) of diseased sheep; flat sea fish.

fluke (77) broad flattened end of a fish's tail; flat part of a weapon used for killing large fish; flat point of an *anchor* (= heavy hook let down to the bottom of the sea by a ship).

flummery (8-9-1) foolish talk; sweet dish of flour, milk, fruit, etc.

flummox (8-9) Sl. make *speechless* (= unable to speak) — with surprise, or because one cannot answer the question asked.

flung (8) p.t. and p.p. of Fling.

flunkey (8ngkI) male servant in special clothes; one who serves another for the purpose of getting favours.

fl′uor′escent (779-2-9) — electric rays, or light which cannot be seen by the human eye causes fluorescent substances to give out light which we can see, e.g. television screen.

FLUNKEY

flu′oroscope (75-9-67) instrument used for

fl'uor-spar (779 + 44) glass-like rock of various colours.

flurry (8-1) sudden light fall of snow or rain with high wind; state of great excitement.

flush (8) wash clean with a flow of water; flow quickly; become red because of a rush of blood to the face; adj. full; level, e.g. *Flush with the edge of the table* = level with —; *The flush of victory* = first great joy of having won; *Being flush* = having plenty of money; *The flush of youth* = fresh eagerness of youth; *A flush (of cards)* = 5 cards of the same *suit* (= set, e.g. Hearts, etc.).

fluster (8-9) excite; make a person too excited or anxious to be able to work or act.

flute (77) musical instrument (kind of whistle).

FLUTE

fluting (77-1) long narrow hollows cut up and down on the surface of a pillar, as ornament.

flutist (77-1) flautist (55-1) one who plays the *flute* (see 2nd above).

flutter (8-9) move the wings quickly, as a bird does; move about quickly in excitement; *To be all in a flutter* = be in a state of great excitement.

fluvial (77-19) having to do with a river.

flux (8) state of flowing; state of continued movement and change; *To be in a state of flux* = be in a state of change; **to flux**, make liquid with heat, e.g. a metal.

FLUTING

fly (41) (1) small flying insect; *A fly in the ointment* = small thing which *decreases* (= makes less) the value of something; *A fly on the wheel* = unimportant person who thinks himself important in some great business; (2) one-horse public carriage; (3) loose cloth which acts as door of a tent.

fly (41) **flew** (77) **flown** (67) (1) move through the air like a bird; *As the crow flies* = in a straight line across country; *To fly high* = have high aims; *To let fly at* = shoot at, speak angrily to; *To fly a flag* = put up —; *Return with flying colours* = as winner, after a great success; (2) move quickly; *Time flies* = passes away quickly; *To fly in the face of Providence* = do a very dangerous thing; *The door flew open* = opened suddenly; *A flying visit* = a short hurried visit; *To fly into a rage* = become suddenly angry; *Fly off at a tangent* = suddenly start talking about something different; *Fly at* = attack suddenly; (3) run away from danger.

fly (41) quick, clever, *wide-awake* (= fully, completely awake).

N.M E.D.—5

flyblown (41-67) covered with dirt and eggs of flies.

flybuttons (41-8-z) *buttons* (= round pieces of bone or metal) used to close the front of a man's trousers.

fl'ying-f'ox (41·1 + 5) flying creature with skin-covered wings and a red hairy body.

FLYING-FOX

flyleaf (41-11) unprinted page at the beginning or end of a book.

flywheel (41-11) heavy wheel which, by its weight, keeps a machine running at a regular speed.

F.O. (2 + 67) *Foreign Office* (= that part of the government which deals with foreign countries).

foal (67) very young horse; give birth to a horse.

foam (67) mass of *bubbles* (= small round balls of liquid filled with air); *To foam at the mouth* = be very angry.

f.o.b. (2 + 67 + 11) Free on board, e.g. *Price £100 f.o.b.* = £100 without any more to pay for taking it to and putting it on the ship.

fob (5) ornamented chain put on a *watch* (= pocket clock); *To fob a person off with* = deceive a person into taking (some worthless thing).

fo'c'sle (67ksl) see Forecastle.

focus (67-9) point where lines, e.g. of light, come together; cause the picture thrown by light on a glass or white sheet to become clear; any central point; *To focus one's attention on* = turn one's whole mind to; adj. **focal**.

fodder (5-9) food for cattle.

foe (67) enemy.

foetid, **fetid** (11-1) having a very bad smell.

fog (5) thick cloud-like condition of the air which makes it impossible to see clearly; *To be fogged* = have no clear ideas.

fogey (67-1) *An old fogey* = person with old ideas which he is unwilling to change.

foible (51) weak or foolish point in one's character.

foil (51) cause an enemy to fail in an attempt.

foil (51) metal rolled into very thin sheets; *Mr. A used Mr. B as a foil* = clever Mr. A made use of the foolishness of Mr. B to show up his own cleverness.

foil (51) thin sword without any point, used for practice.

foist (51) secretly or by a trick to cause a person to accept something bad, e.g. *To foist off bad money on a person*.

fold (67) bend and press one part of a thing on another part; close up tightly in, e.g. *He folded the child in his arms*; **a folder**, anything which folds or is used for folding; stiff sheet of paper bent in two and used for holding letters, papers, etc.

fold (67) place where sheep are kept; group of sheep; *To return to the fold* = come home (e.g. a sheep back to the other sheep).

-fold (67) e.g. *fourfold* = four times.

f'older'ol (5-1-5) meaningless word used in old songs.

foliage (67-1-1j) leaves (of a tree).

folio (67-167) sheet of paper folded over to make two pages; large book; (in paying for copying written papers) 72 words:

folk (67) people, e.g. *Young folk(s)*; *One's folks*, *My ain folk* = one's family and relations; **folk-dances** (+ 44-siz) ancient dances of the country people; **folklore** (67-55) study of the stories, beliefs and customs of people in early times.

follicle (5-1) small hole in the skin out of which the hair grows; (in a plant) little bag containing a seed.

follow (5-67) go or come after; be next in rank or importance; agree with; understand, e.g. *Do you follow me?*; *To follow the business of the law-courts* = watch it with interest; *He is good, but it does not follow that he is wise* = you cannot reason from this that he is wise; *To follow the sea* = be a seaman; *Follow your nose* = go straight on; *As follows* = as written below; *The following* = those things named in the list below.

folly (5-1) foolishness.

fom'ent (67-2) put hot cloth or hot medicines on the skin in order to bring much blood to one place, so as to get poison out or to lessen pain; cause excitement or trouble.

foment'ation (67-9-21shn) hot material put on a diseased part.

fond (5) loving; *A fond mother* = one who may harm her children by loving them too much; *A fond belief* = thing which is strongly but foolishly believed.

fondle (5) touch in a loving way.

font (5) large stone container for the water which is put on a child when he is *baptized* (= named and accepted as a member of the Church).

font (5) see Fount.

food (77) anything which one eats or drinks; *Food for thought* = matter which should be thought about.

fool (77) person without good sense; **to fool**, deceive; *The king's fool* = person in the court of a king or great lord whose special work is to do and say amusing things; *To fool away one's time* = waste one's time; *To fool with a gun* = play with a gun in a way that may cause harm; *A fool's paradise* = state of being joyful or satisfied when there is no reason to be so; *To go on a fool's errand* = do some business which proves to be foolish or useless; *All Fools' Day* = April 1st, when anyone may say untrue things for amusement; *April fool* = one who believes such things; *Fool's cap* = cap of white paper put on a child in a class who will not learn; **foolscap** (77-z-3) large size of paper, 13 × 8 inches; **foolery** (77-9-1) amusing play; **foolhardy** (77-44-1) going into unnecessary danger; **foolproof** (77-77) so simple and easy that no one can make a mistake.

foot (7) 12 inches, ⅓ of a yard; 30·5 centimetres.

foot (**feet**). (7) (11) lowest part of the leg on which one walks; lowest part of anything; group of sounds in a line of poetry; *To set a plan on foot* = start it going; *To stand on your own feet* = trust your own powers; *Carried them off their feet* = made them so excited that they lost their power of judgment; *To fall on one's feet* = have good fortune; *To foot the bill* = pay the cost; *To put one's foot down* = give clear and firm orders that a certain thing is to be stopped; *To put one's foot in it* = make a serious or amusing mistake; *Horse and foot* = soldiers of both kinds; **footfall** (7-44) sound of a step; **foothills** (7-1-z) low hills at the bottom of high mountains; **foothold** (7-67) place for the foot in climbing; a beginning from which one may go on; **footing** (7-1) place, e.g. *To get a footing in a group of persons* = be accepted as a member; *The army is on a war footing* = the army is *enlarged* (= made larger) and prepared for war; *To be on a friendly footing* = be friendly with; **footlights** (7-41) lights on the floor of the *stage* (= raised place for actors in a theatre); **footman** (7-9) manservant; **footnote** (7-67) note at the bottom of a page; **footpad** (7-3) thief who walking (not riding a horse) attacks travellers; **footprint** (7-1) the mark made by a foot, e.g. in sand; **footstep** (7-2) sound or mark made when walking.

football pool (7-55 + 77) see Pool.

footling (77-1) Sl. small and worthless; foolish.

foozle (77) Sl. fail to hit the ball properly; do a piece of work badly.

fop (5) man who has too great a love for fine clothes.

f.o.r. (2f + 67 + 44) Free on rail, e.g. *Price £100 f.o.r.* = £100 without more to pay for putting the goods on the train.

forage (5-1j) food for cattle; go out and seek food, as soldiers do in war.

forasm'uch as (9-9z-8 + 9z) because.

foray (5-21) sudden attack made in order to take away goods or cattle by force.

forb'ade (9-3) p.t. of forbid.

forb'ear (9-29) keep oneself from doing, e.g. *To forbear from hitting an enemy*.

forb'id (9-1) order a person not to do something; *God forbid* = may that not happen; *A forbidding manner* = bad-tempered, unpleasant.

f'orb'ore (55-55) p.t. of Forbear.

force (55s) strength; power; *The force of a reason* = power it has to cause agreement; *To see the force of an expression* = the meaning; *Turn out in force* = in great numbers; *The police force* = all the men and officers of the police; *Our forces* = our army, warships, aeroplanes, etc.; **to force**, use force to produce an effect; *To force plants* = cause them to produce flowers or fruit earlier than usual; *To force one's hand* = make one to act when one does not wish to do so; *A forced laugh* = laugh when one is really not pleased or amused; **forcemeat** (55s-11) meat and pleasant-tasting vegetables cut small and mixed.

forceps (55s2) instrument used by doctors for getting a tight hold, e.g. on a tooth.

forcible (55s9) having force.

ford (55) part of a river, where the water is not deep, used as a crossing.

fore- (55) before; in the front part; *Fore and aft* = in front and behind, from the front to the back of a ship.

forearm (55-44) lower part of the arm.

f'ore'arm (55-44) prepare for an attack; *Forewarned is forearmed* = if one knows that a thing is going to happen, one can be prepared against it.

forebear (55-29) e.g. *My forebears* = those relations from whom I am descended.

foreb'ode (55-67) tell or be a sign of some future event; have a feeling that some evil is about to happen.

forecast (55-44) tell future events, e.g. *The weather forecast* = account of the weather which is to be expected during the next few days.

forecastle (67ksl) raised part at the front of a ship.

forecl'ose (55-57z) *To foreclose a mortgage* = seize and sell land or buildings in order to get back money lent to their owner.

fored'oom (55-77) *Foredoomed to failure* = sure (from the very beginning) to fail.

forefather (55-44ðg) person from whom one is descended.

forefront (55-8) (in the —) right in the front, not a little way behind it.

foreg'oing (55-67I) earlier; **foregone** (conclusion) (55-5) result which was never in doubt.

foreground (55-47) front part of a picture; *To keep oneself in the foreground* = to make sure of being seen.

forehand (stroke) (55-3) (Lawn-tennis) hit the ball in the usual way (not *backhand* when the back of the hand is turned away from the face).

forehead (5-1) front part of the head above the eyes.

foreign (5-1) not belonging to one's own country; *Foreign matter* = matter out of proper place, e.g. grain of sand in the eye; *Foreign to his nature* = not the sort of thing he would do.

forelock (55-5) curl of hair on the front of the head; *To seize time by the forelock* = be ready to make use of any chance when it first appears.

foreman (55-9) man in charge of a number of workmen.

foremost (55-67) first in time, place, rank, or importance.

forenoon (55-77) the morning before 12 o'clock.

for'ensic (5-2-s1) having to do with the law.

f'oreord'ained (55-55-21) fated; fixed as a thing which must happen.

fores'ee (55-11) see what will happen in the future.

foresh'adow (55-3-67) be a sign of future events.

foreshore (55-55) that part of the shore near the water.

foresh'ortening (55-55-1) way of drawing used to show an object coming forward out of the picture, e.g. a picture of a man lying down, the eye of the person drawing being near the feet and looking towards the head.

foresight (55-41) power to see the future and care in preparing for it.

forest (5-1) large piece of land covered with trees.

forest'all (55-55) prevent a person from doing something by doing it first.

forestry (5-1-1) art of taking care of forests.

for'ever (9-2-9) for all time, without end.

foreword (55-99) a few words at the beginning of a book to explain its purpose.

forfeit (55-1) payment which has to be made as a punishment; loss because of not keeping a promise; lose any right as a punishment.

forf'end (55-2) *God forfend* = may God prevent it from happening.

forg'ather (55-3ðg) meet together.

forge (55j) fire in the shop of a man who works with iron; make or shape an iron instrument in a fire; *To forge ahead* = push forward through difficulties.

forge (55j) make or change a written paper in order to deceive; copy another person's handwriting; n. **forgery** (55j9-1).

forg'et (9-2) not to remember.

forg'et-me-not (9-2 + 1 + 5) small light-blue flower.

forg'ive (9-1) forget a wrong, not to punish nor be angry at a wrong.

forg'o (55-67) do without; give up.

forg'otten (9-5) p.p. of Forget.

fork (55) instrument with a handle and two or more points used for picking up food, also for loosening or turning over soil; anything of this shape—Y-shaped, *A fork in the road* = place where the road divides into two roads; *A tuning-fork* = instrument which gives a true note in music; Sl. *Fork out* = pay money.

forl'orn (9-55) cheerless, deserted; *A forlorn hope* = plan which has very little chance of succeeding.

form (55) long seat with no back.

form (55) class in a school.

form (55) shape; plan; make; *A diamond* (= hard white jewel) *is a form of coal* = made of the same matter but changed and of a different appearance; *A telegraph form* = special paper

formal   130   **fountain**

on which to write a message to be sent by electricity; *Good form* = good taste and manners; *It is a matter of form* = it must be done because of a rule but it is not important; **to form**, make, shape; *Form a class* = get together —; *Plans are being formed* = made; *To form an idea* = think out in the mind; go into a certain shape, e.g. *The soldiers formed line; Clouds formed in the sky.*

formal (55) careful of all the correct rules and customs; *Formal manners* = manners according to rules, not showing any feelings; *Formal dress* = correct dress for certain important occasions; n. **form′ality** (55-3-1-1) *A mere formality* = something unnecessary, done only because of a rule.

formalin (55-9-1) liquid used to destroy smells and to clean wounds.

form′ation (55-21shn) act or state of being shaped or planned; manner in which anything, e.g. an army, is set in order.

former (55-9) earlier in time; *The former* = the person or thing first spoken of, e.g. *Mr. A and Mr. B are here; the former —* (= Mr. A)

formidable (55-1-9) causing fear; *A formidable task* = very difficult —.

formula (55-17-9) fixed form of words to be used at the proper time and place; any truth which has been written out in a short form; **to formulate** (55-17-21) set out in a short and clear form.

forsake (9-21) give up, leave, e.g. one's old friends, a former way of living; p.t. **fors′ook** (9-7), p.p. **fors′aken** (9-21).

fors′ooth (9-77) (in truth)—word used to show disbelief.

forsw′ear (55-29) to promise not to use any more; declare as true that which one knows to be untrue; p.p. **forsw′orn** (55-55).

fort (55) castle or strong place which may be defended against an enemy.

forte (55-1) (music) loud.

forte (55) *Dancing is not my forte* = is not one of the things at which I am specially clever.

forth (55) forward; out; **forthc′oming** (55-8-1) which will soon come; *The promised money was not forthcoming* = could not be had when needed.

f′orthr′ight (55-41) honest; saying what is in one's mind.

f′orthw′ith (55-1ð) immediately.

fortify (55-1-41) make a place strong against the attack of an enemy.

fort′issimo (55-1-1-67) very loud (in music).

fortitude (55-1-177) that courage and self-control which makes one able to suffer pain without complaining and to meet danger calmly.

fortnight (55-41) two weeks.

fortress (55-1) large fort.

fort′uitous (55-1771-9) happening by chance.

fortunate (55-17-9) succeeding by chance.

fortune (55-17) chance; the good and evil which happens to a man; great wealth; *To make a fortune* = gain much money; *A soldier of fortune* = one who is willing to fight for anyone; *To tell fortunes* = tell what one's future will be; *A fortune-hunter* = one who tries to get money by marrying a wealthy person.

forum (55-9) market-place in a Roman town; any place in which questions of public interest are talked about.

forward (55-9) front part; onward; too eager; not polite; *Carriage forward* = the cost of sending the goods will be paid by the receiver; *Look forward to* = expect with feelings of pleasure; **to forward**, send; *Please forward* = please address this letter again and send it on to where Mr. X is now staying; *To forward a plan* = to help on; **forwards** (——z) in a forward direction.

fosse (5) *ditch* (= long deep hole dug in the ground, e.g. at the side of a road) especially one round a fort.

fossil (5) ancient plants or animals changed to stone and found in rocks or in the earth; *An old fossil* = old man who will not change his ideas.'

foster (5-9) to nurse; *A foster mother* = woman who nurses and brings up a child instead of the real mother; *Foster brother, sister* = one of two children nursed as above; to help; *To foster evil thoughts* = keep — in the mind.

fought (55) p.t. of Fight.

foul (47) dirty; unpleasant, e.g. — temper, language; **a foul** (in a game) act which is against the rules; *Foul play* = evil deed; *Fall foul of* = quarrel with; *The ship fouled another ship* = ran against.

foulard (77-44) soft, silk material.

found (47) p.t. and p.p. of Find.

found (47) (1) begin the building of a house; *Founded upon a rock* = built on —; *His opinion is not founded on facts,* — *is unfounded,* = is not proved to be true, nor according to the facts; (2) set up or start, e.g. *To found a school*; **found′ation** (47-21shn) that part of a building below the ground on which the walls stand; strongest or most necessary part of anything; amount of money given for the support, e.g. of a school.

founder (47-9) fill with water and sink, e.g. a ship at sea; be unable to go on running.

foundling (47-1) child left by its parents and found by other persons.

foundry (47-1) place where metals, etc., are melted and made into things.

fount (47) water coming up out of the ground; cause or beginning of anything.

fount (47) all the letters of one size used in printing books.

fountain (47-1) water coming up out of the ground; water thrown high into the air from a pipe; *Fountain pen* = pen containing a supply of ink; **f′ountain-h′ead** (+ 2) place from

four-in-hand   131   **freelance**

which a river flows; the beginning of anything.
f'our-in-h'and (55 + 1 + 3) carriage with four horses.
foursome (55) game between two pairs of players.
f'our-wh'eeler (55 + 11-9) closed horse-carriage with four wheels.
fowl (47) bird, usually large enough to be eaten; hen or *cock* (= male form of hen); meat of these; fowler (——9) one who shoots or catches birds for eating.
fox (5) small wild dog-like animal — usually red, with a bushy tail; clever, dishonest person.

FOX

fox-glove (+ 8) flower.
fox-t'errier (+ 2-19) a small white dog.
fox-trot (+ 5) kind of dance.
foxy (5-1) clever and deceiving; (hair) red.
foyer (5121) large public room at the entrance of a hotel or theatre.
fracas (3-44) noisy quarrel or fight.
fraction (3-shn) a part, e.g. ½, ⅓, ¾; *A fraction of a second* = very short time.
fractious (3kshg) in a bad temper, e.g. *A fractious child*.

FOX-GLOVE

fracture (3-tshg) a break—especially of a limb.
fragile (3j41) very fine and easily broken; easily harmed, e.g. *Old and fragile people*.
fragment (3-9) small part broken off.
fragrance (21-9-s) pleasant smell.
frail (21) weak; easily broken; easily led to do wrong; frailty (——1) state of being frail.

FOX-TERRIER

frame (21) (1) most important bars or poles, posts, etc., on which the rest of a thing is built, e.g. *The frame of a house* = upright supports and cross-bars; *He has a strong frame* = strong body; (2) any form made up of bars with the spaces not filled in; open square (or other shape) of metal or wood into which a picture is put; box with a glass top used to grow plants quickly; *A happy frame of mind* = state of mind; **to frame** (1) to put together, make, e.g. *To frame a plan*; *His lips could not frame the words* = say —; (2) to set in a frame, e.g. *To frame a picture*; Sl. *To frame a person* = make it appear that he has done some wrong act; framework (21-99) = frame on which, or round which, something will be made.
franc (3ngk) piece of French money.
franchise (3-41z) right to elect people to the government.
frank (3ngk) freely saying one's real thoughts; honest.

frank (3ngk) mark a letter so that it may be sent through the post free of postage.
frankincense (3ngk1-s2) matter obtained from a tree, burned to give a sweet-smelling smoke.
frantic (3-1) wildly excited or uncontrolled with joy, fear, pain, etc.
frat'ernal (9-99) having to do with brothers; like a brother.
frat'ernity (9-99-1-1) state of being brothers; group united for a certain purpose; Am. group of young men at a university having secret signs and usually sharing the same lodging-house.
fraternize (3-9-41) meet together in a friendly way; behave towards each other as brothers.
fratricide (21-1s41) act of killing a brother.
frau (47) (German) Mrs., Madam; fräulein (51-41) = Miss.
fraud (55) a trick; dishonesty; *He is a fraud* = not what he pretends to be; adj. fraudulent (55-17-9).
fraught (with danger) (55) full (of danger).
fray (21) a fight.
fray (21) wear or pull the edge of cloth into loose threads.
frazzle (3) *fray* (1st above); state of being very tired or worn out; Sl. *Beat him to a frazzle* = beat him thoroughly.
freak (11) peculiar and unusual act or thing (e.g. a sheep with five legs).
freckle (2) light brown spot on the skin; to mark with spots.
free (11) (1) able to do what one wishes; not tied; not in prison; not controlled by rules; *Free speech* = the right to say what one thinks; *I made him free of my house* = I said that he might go where he pleased and do what he wished; *The way is free* = open, with nothing to stop one; *The free end of a rope* = not tied down; *To get a free hand* = power to do whatever one wishes; *A free fight* = everyone fighting against everyone else; (2) easy, graceful; *Free and easy* = friendly and simple, not stiff and ceremonious; *Free with his money*, *Free-handed* = generous; (3) not busy; not already being used by someone else; *I am free to-morrow morning* = not busy, can see you; *Have you any rooms free?* = not in use; (4) given without payment, e.g. *Free drinks all round* = give each a glass of drink and I will pay; = *Price 5p post free* = 5p post paid; *Free trade* = allowing foreign goods to come into the country without payment; *Free will* = the idea that one's future and fortune are not fixed by fate.
freebooter (11-77-9) sea-thief, or soldier who makes war in order to steal.
freedom (11-9) state of being free.
freehand (11-3) (drawing) done by hand without any drawing instrument.
freehold (11-67) complete ownership of land.
freelance (11-44-s) writer who belongs to no one newspaper but writes, as he pleases, for any.

freem'ason (11-21) member of an ancient *brotherhood* (= group of persons who behave like brothers) which holds secret meetings and has secret signs by which the members may know each other.

fr'eeth'inker (11-1ngk9) one who forms his own ideas about God without following the teaching of others.

freeze (11) p.t. froze, p.p. frozen (67) (1) become solid because of cold; be very cold; (2) (of an animal or soldier) suddenly to keep quite still so as not to be seen; *His face froze* = became stiff and without sign of his feelings; *To freeze on to* = seize and hold tightly; *Freeze out* = drive away a person by making things difficult for him; *To freeze prices* = cause prices to stay the same.

freight (21) load of any kind; money paid for carrying goods; Am. *A freight train* = train used to carry goods, not people; **freighter** (——9) ship which carries goods only.

Fr'ench l'eave (2-sh + 11) (to take —) go away without having asked to be allowed to go.

fren'etic (2-2-1) see Phrenetic.

frenzy (2-1) state of wild feeling; madness.

frequency (11-9-s1) number of times anything happens; **frequent**, happening very often.

fresco (2-67) painting on a wall, e.g. of a church.

fresh (2) (1) newly grown, newly made, e.g. *Fresh green grass; Fresh milk*; (2) smelling, tasting or looking clean and new, e.g. *Fresh air; Fresh paint*; (3) not experienced, e.g. *A freshman* = one in his first year at the university; (4) not seen or heard before, e.g. *Have you any fresh news?*; (5) not tired; (6) (of water or meat) not salt; Am. Sl. not respectful, e.g. treating a stranger as if he were an old friend; **fresher** (——9) *freshman* (see above).

freshet (2-1) sudden rush of water down a river; narrow stream of fresh (not salt) water flowing into the sea.

fret (2) be anxious; wear away by rubbing; *Sick people are often fretful* = bad-tempered and difficult to please.

fretsaw (2-55) very narrow *saw* (= blade with teeth) used for cutting out pieces from a thin piece of wood so as to make an ornament; **fretwork** (2-99) art of making wooden ornaments in this way.

friable (419) easily broken into powder.

friar (419) member of a religious group.

fr'icass'ee (1-9-11) cook small pieces of meat in a pleasant-tasting liquid; meat so cooked.

friction (1-shn) rubbing; waste of power caused by rubbing together of parts of a machine; *There is friction in the group* = quarrelling.

fridge (1j) short for Refrigerator.

fried (41) p.t. of Fry.

friend (2) one who loves another person, has the same purposes, etc.; helper; **a Friend**, member of a certain religious group called Quakers (Quakers are very simple in dress and speech, and very strongly against war).

frieze (11) ornamented band along the top of a wall just below the roof.

frig (1j) short for Refrigerator.

frigate (1-9) fast warship.

fright (41) state of being greatly afraid; *She looks a fright* = very peculiar and ugly; **frightful**, causing great fear; Sl. very bad, ugly; **frightfully** (——1) Sl. very.

frill (1) loose ornamental edge on a garment; ring of long feathers or hairs growing on a bird or animal; unnecessary ornament of any kind.

fringe (1nj) ornamental edge of loose threads; outside edge; *The river is fringed with trees* = the river has trees on its edges.

frippery (1-9-1) unnecessary ornament, especially on a dress.

frisk (1) to jump and run about; behave in a joyful way; **frisky** (——1) playful.

fritter (1-9) piece of fruit enclosed in a mixture of egg and flour, cooked in hot fat.

fritter (1-9) cut or break into small pieces; *To fritter away one's time* = waste time.

frivolous (1-9-9) not serious; foolish; too interested in light and amusing things; n. **friv'olity** (1-5-1-1).

frizz, friz (1) to curl (the hair).

frizzle (1) cause to curl by heat, e.g. while cooking; burn slightly in cooking.

fro (67) e.g. *To and fro* = forward and back again.

frock (5) long outer garment; woman's dress; *To unfrock a priest* = to take away his right to act as a priest; **fr'ock-c'oat** (+ 67) long black coat worn by men.

frog (5) green and brown jumping creature which lives both on land and in the water; *A frog in his throat* = uncomfortable feeling in the throat which causes difficulty in speaking; *To frog-march* = carry a person face downwards, one man holding each of his limbs.

frog (5) soft part of a horse's foot.

frog (5) ornamental fastening on a garment; leather ring for a sword.

FROG

frogman (5-9) man dressed as someone to swim for a long time under water. An instrument enabling him to breathe is carried on his back.

frolic (5-1) to play happily.

from (5 or 9) ....; *Paint from nature* = to paint looking at the actual scene; *Die from weakness* = because of —; *Act from pity* = because of —.

FROGMAN

frond (5) long leaf-like part of a plant.

front (8) the face; the forward part; *In front of* = before; *Come to the front* = become famous; *The sea-front* = road along the edge of the sea; *To go to the front* = go into the fighting line; *Put on a bold front* = pretend that one is not afraid; *Cold front* = a mass of cold air pushing warm air up and so causing a change in weather; **to front**, to face, e.g. *The house fronts the sea.*

frontage (8-1j) front of a building; that part of a piece of land which is on the edge of a street, river, etc.

frontier (8-19) farthest edge of a country; new country in which people are beginning to settle.

frontispiece (8-1-11s) picture in the front of a book.

frost (5) act or state of freezing; Sl. *It was a frost* = it failed completely; **fr'ost-bite** (+ 41) damage caused by cold to a part of the body; **to frost**, cover a cake with white sugar; make glass so that one cannot see through it.

froth (5) mass of small *bubbles* (small round balls of any liquid filled with air or gas).

froward (67-9) unwilling to obey or be controlled.

frown (47) draw the skin above the eyes into folds as when displeased, or when thinking deeply.

frowzy (47-1) smelling unpleasant because unwashed.

froze (67) p.t. of Freeze.

fructify (8-1-41) cause to produce fruit.

frugal (77) careful not to waste, e.g. money, food; *A frugal meal* = simple meal not costing much.

fruit (77) (1) anything produced from the earth, e.g. grain, apples, eatable leaves, etc.; (2) sweet eatable part of a plant which contains the seed; (3) anything produced, e.g. *The fruit of his labours* = result of —; *The fruit of his body* = children; **fruiterer** (77-9-9) one who sells fruit; **fru'ition** (77Ishn) enjoyment of the fruit or result; *Came to fruition* = succeeded; **fruitless** (77-1) without result, unsuccessful; **fruity** (77-1) like fruit, having a strong taste or smell.

frump (8) badly dressed woman.

frustr'ate (8-21) bring one's plans to nothing; prevent from doing.

fry (41) cook in hot fat; *Out of the frying-pan into the fire* = going from one danger or difficulty into a worse one.

fry (41) small young fish; *He is very small fry* = person of no importance.

fuchsia (177shI9) garden plant with hanging flowers.

fuddled (8) not able to think clearly because one has drunk too much wine.

fudge (8j) kind of soft sweet; expression of disagreement.

FUCHSIA

fuel (1779) material for burning, e.g. wood, coal, oil.

fug (8) Sl. hot air which is not fresh; adj. **fuggy** (——1); *To fug indoors* = stay in a hot room.

fugitive (177j1-1) one who is running away from the law; escaping; not lasting very long.

fugue (177) piece of music in which the *melody* (= pleasing set of notes, one following another) is immediately repeated on higher or lower notes.

-ful, having a certain quality, e.g. **graceful** (21s), **masterful** (44-9); amount that will fill, e.g. **cupful** (8-7).

fulcrum (8-9) support on which a *lever* (= bar supported at one point used for lifting or moving heavy things) moves.

FULCRUM

fulfil (7-1) to complete, e.g. a promise; *To fulfil his expectations* = be as good as he hoped.

full (7) having in it as much as it will contain; *Full house* = no more room in a theatre; complete, e.g. *A full report*; *My heart is too full for words* = I have such deep feeling I cannot express it; *Full speed* = as fast as possible; *Full face* = face seen from the front, not from the side; *I ran full tilt into him* = I ran against him very hard; *Full dress* = clothes as worn at a ceremony; *In full swing* = going on very actively; *Fully-fashioned* (*stockings*) = made the same shape as the leg.

fuller (7-9) one who makes cloth thick and tight by wetting and pressing; **f'uller's 'earth** (——z + 99) soft yellow earth used to get the fat or oil out of newly made cloth—used also in making soap.

fulminate (8-1-21) to thunder; speak loudly and angrily against someone or something; material which explodes when hit.

fulsome (7-9) *A fulsome compliment* = praising too much and not meaning all of it.

fumble (8) lack skill in using one's hands; fail in doing something.

fume (177) smoke or gas coming from burning material or from a strong acid; **to fume**, give off fumes; show signs of anger; *Fret and fume* = be very anxious and angry.

fumigate (177-1-21) make a room free from disease by burning some medicine which gives off a heavy smoke.

fun (8) amusement; play; *To do a thing in fun* = without any serious purpose; *To poke fun at* = cause others to laugh at a person.

function (8ngkshn) any natural action, e.g. *The function of the eye is to see*; special work or duty, e.g. *The function of a judge is to decide questions of law*; *A social function* = meeting of people for pleasure or in honour of some great person; **a functionary** (8ngksh9-9-1) officer with certain special duties to perform.

fund (8) amount of money set apart for some special purpose; a supply of; *He has a fund of humour* = has many amusing ideas.

fundamental (8-9-2) at the bottom of, as that upon which all else is built up; of first importance; most necessary.

funeral (177-9) all those customs and acts which have to do with putting a dead person in the grave; adj. **fun'ereal** (177-19-19) of a funeral; sad and solemn.

fungus (8ngg9) (pl. **fungi** (8ngg41)) kind of plant which has no green leaves but gets its food from decayed vegetable matter, e.g. dead wood on which it grows (e.g. a mushroom is a fungus). FUNGUS

funk (8ngk) Sl. feeling of fear; one who is afraid; fail because of fear; *A blue funk* = great fear.

funnel (8) vessel round at the top and becoming small at the bottom, used in pouring liquids into a small opening; smoke-pipe of a steamship.

funny (8-1) amusing; strange; **funny-bone** (+ 67) pointed bone at the outside of the bend of the arm.

fur (99) thick soft hair on some animals, e.g. cats; **a fur**, skin of an animal with the hair still on, e.g. used as a garment; *To make the fur fly* = to quarrel and fight; *Fur and feather*, see Feather; *A furred tongue* = tongue covered with white matter because of illness.

furbelow (99-1-67) *Frills and furbelows* = pieces of ornamental cloth put on women's dresses.

furbish (99-1) to cause to shine and look like new.

furious (177-19) (of any feeling or force) strong and uncontrolled; very angry; *At a furious pace* = at great speed.

furl (99) roll up, e.g. a sail; take down a flag and put it away.

furlong (99-5) ⅛ of one mile.

furlough (99-67) time of rest from one's work, e.g. such as is given to a man working in a foreign country so that he may return home.

furnace (99-1s) large enclosed fire, e.g. as part of a steam-engine.

furnish (99-1) to supply, especially the things of daily use in a home, e.g. chairs, tables, curtains, etc.; **furniture** (99-1tsh9) things of daily use in a home, e.g. tables, chairs, etc.

fur'ore (177-55-1) great excitement and *admiration* (n. of Admire).

furrier (8-19) one who buys and sells furs.

furrow (8-67) long line cut in the earth by a *plough* (= instrument for cutting and turning over the earth before putting in the seed).

furry (99-1) like fur or having fur.

further (99ð9) more forward; more, e.g. *I have no further orders* = no more; *To further one's plans* = help on one's plans; **furtherance** (99ð9-9-s) act of helping on a plan or work.

furtive (99-1) done secretly.

fury (177-1) great anger; great uncontrolled force; *To rain like fury* = heavily; **the Furies** (——z) *goddesses* (= female gods) who were believed to punish men for their wrong acts.

furze (99) low-growing evergreen bush.

FURZE

fuse (177z) melt; change into liquid by heat; join two metals by heating them together; **a fuse**, piece of special metal which melts if more than a certain amount of electricity flows through it (when the fuse melts the electricity is cut off, thus preventing damage by fire).

fuse (177z) long pipe-like container with gunpowder in it which is used for setting fire to large amounts of powder, while giving the people who light it time to get out of danger.

fuselage (177z1-1j) frame of the body of an aeroplane.

fusel oil (177z + 5l) poison found in strong drink which has not been properly made.

fusillade (177z1-21) continued and rapid firing of guns.

f'usil'ier (177z1-19) soldier (A.D. 1700) who carried a light gun called a fusil.

fusion (1773n) act of melting by heat; act of mixing materials together when melted.

fuss (8) excited and anxious state of mind; Sl. *Fuss-pot* = person who often makes a fuss; **to fuss**, be excited and anxious.

fustian (8-19) heavy cotton cloth; empty high-sounding language.

fusty (8-1) having a bad, not fresh, smell.

futile (177-41) worthless, having no effect.

future (177tsh9) that which is going to come or happen; *To deal in futures* = buy crops (or other things) before they are produced, in the hope of selling at a higher price; *He has a future* = he will become great.

futurist (177tsh9-1) one whose ideas of art are not accepted by those living now—but who hopes the people of the future will like them.

fuzzy (8-1) very curly (hair).

-fy (41) make ——, become ——, e.g. **sol'idify** (9-1-1-41) = make into a solid, to become solid.

G

gab (3) *The gift of the gab* = power of speaking well—or much.

gabardine (3-9-11) kind of thin cloth; **gaberdine** (3-9-11) long loose garment as of Jews.

gabble (3) talk quickly and foolishly.

gable (21) pointed part of a wall between the two sloping sides of a roof; small roof over a window.

gad (3) wander without purpose; go from place to place looking for amusement; **gadabout** (3-9-47) person (usually a woman) who loves to go visiting rather than work at home.

gadfly (3-41) fly which bites cattle.

gadget (3j1) any useful instrument.

Gaelic (21-1) language of the *Highlands* (= mountainous part) of Scotland.

gaff (3) (1) hook used for pulling a fish up on to the land; (2) pole at the upper edge of certain kinds of sail; Sl. *To blow the gaff* = tell a secret.

gaffe (3) mistake; *To commit a gaffe* = say or do by accident something which is very displeasing to others.

gaffer (3-9) old man—especially one in a village; grandfather.

gag (3) stop the mouth by force; Sl. add to one's part when acting in a play; n. something put in the mouth to keep it open and prevent speech; to make the noise of being sick (vomiting).

gaga (3-44) Sl. silly, mad.

gage (21j) something of value given to make the fulfilment of a promise sure; *To throw down the gage* = throw down the *glove* (= garment worn on the hand)—the way in which an ancient knight called upon another knight to fight him.

gaiety (21-1-1) state of being very happy and light-hearted; **gaily** (21-1) happily; *Gaily dressed* = in bright colours.

gain (21) get by working; make money; *To gain ground* = go forward, be successful; *To gain on (a runner)* = come nearer to him; *To gain time* = save time, get something done more quickly; *Gain the upper hand* = get power over, win.

g'ains'ay (21-21) say that something is wrong or untrue.

gait (21) manner of walking.

gaiter (21-9) covering (usually of leather) for the lower part of the leg.

gala (21-9 or 44-9) time of feasting and general happiness; *Gala night* = night on which there will be a specially good show at a place of amusement.

GAITER

galaxy (3-9-1) that part of the sky which is brightest with stars; group of beautiful women or famous men.

gale (21) strong wind.

gall (55) swelling on plants caused by an insect; painful place on the skin of an animal caused by rubbing.

gall (55) bitter liquid which mixes with food after it leaves the stomach and changes the fats into liquids which can be built into the body; feeling of bitterness or hatred; Am. Sl. shameless boldness; *A galling fire* = very harmful fire from the enemy's guns.

gallant (3-9) brave; attending ladies in a polite way; **a gallant**, or **gall'ant** (9-3) well-dressed man with fine manners; lover.

galleon (3-19) large sailing-ship of ancient times, e.g. about A.D. 1600.

gallery (3-9-1) (1) long narrow hall, e.g. one in which pictures are hung; (2) upper floor at the back of a large hall or theatre in which people sit to see a show or hear music; *To play to the gallery* = seek the praise of the common people.

galley (3-1) ancient warship; **a galley-slave** (+ 21) one sent to be a slave on a warship; **galley proofs** (+ 77) long pieces of paper containing the first printing of a book to be corrected; **ship's galley**, ship's kitchen.

g'alliv'ant (3-1-3) go about seeking pleasure.

gallon (3-9) measure for liquids or grain = 4½ litres.

gallop (3-9) ride a horse at its fastest speed; (of a horse) run its fastest; *Galloping consumption* = disease of the *lungs* (= that part of the body with which we breathe) which is rapidly getting worse.

gallows (3-67z) wooden framework for killing wrong-doers by hanging them by the neck; *Gallows-bird* = person who ought to be hanged.

gall-stone (55 + 67) hard diseased mass formed in that part of the body which produces *gall* (see Gall).

Gallup poll (3-9 + 67) finding the general opinion of the nation or any large group by questioning a number of people of different ages, men/women, rich/poor, etc.

gal'ore (9-55) in plenty.

gal'oshes, gol'oshes (9-5-1z) rubber overshoes to keep the feet dry.

galv'anic (3-3-1) having to do with producing electricity by the action of an acid on metal; *He produced a galvanic effect* = excited people as if by an electric shock.

galvanize (3-9-41) put on a coat of metal by electricity; treat disease by means of electricity; *To galvanize into action* = cause sudden action—as by giving an electric shock.

gambit (3-1) certain way of beginning the game of *chess* (= game played with King, Queen and other wooden pieces on a squared board).

gamble (3) play cards or other games for money; risk money on a future event or possible happening.

gamb'oge (3-773) yellow-brown colouring matter.

gambol (3) playful jumping about.

game (21) (1) any form of play; certain form of play with special rules, e.g. football; *Play the game* = be fair, keep the rules; *To have the game in one's hands* = be sure of success; *To make game of* = cause people to laugh at; *The game is up* = the plan has failed; *Don't try any of your games* = of your tricks; *A game leg* = a hurt leg; (2) wild birds or animals which may be shot or hunted; *He is fair game* = it is not unfair to try to attack or deceive him; a **g'amekeeper** (21-11-9) one who prevents outsiders from shooting birds and animals, e.g. on the lands of a lord; a **g'amecock** (+ 5) fighting male bird; *A game person* = person with a fighting spirit; *To die gamely* = die with courage; *Game for anything* = ready and eager to do anything; a **gamester** (21-9) one who plays cards or other games for money.

gamin (3-3ⁿ) a street boy usually bad-mannered.

gamma (3-9) third Greek letter; of third-class quality; *Gamma plus* = just above third-class (examination mark); *Gamma minus* = below third-class.

gammon (3-9) part of a pig salted and prepared for food; senseless talk; a trick to deceive.

gamut (3-9) from the lowest note to the highest; *The whole gamut of (pleasure)* = all kinds —.

gander (3-9) male *goose* (= large white bird like a duck).

gang (3) number of men working together; group of law-breakers; Sl. group of friends.

gang agley (3 + 9-21) go wrong.

ganglion (3ngg-19) group or meeting-place of nerves; painful growth on the body usually containing liquid.

g'ang-plank (3 + 3ngk) movable bridge between a ship and the shore.

gangrene (3ngg-11) decay of a part of the body caused by lack of blood-supply or damage.

gangster (3-9) member of a group of law-breakers—especially in America (U.S.A.).

gangway (3-21) way (path) between rows of seats; movable bridge from a ship to the shore.

gannet (3-1) duck-like water-bird.

gaol, jail (j21) prison; *A gaol-bird* = person who is often in prison; **gaoler** (——9) prison-guard.

gap (3) space between; hole, e.g. in a wall; deep valley.

gape (21) look at in a foolish way without understanding; open the mouth wide; *To make people gape* = cause great surprise; **the gapes,** disease of birds causing death with wide-open mouth.

garage (3-443) building in which a motor-car is stored; shop in which things needed for motor-cars are sold and cars are repaired.

garb (44) clothes; *In the garb of* = dressed like.

garbage (44-1j) waste food, etc., thrown outside the house.

garble (44) change a story so as to cause it to be untrue, e.g. *A garbled report of a meeting*; change and destroy the value of (a book).

garden (44) place for growing vegetables or flowers; *(Kensington) Gardens*, houses built round an open space in a city; **to garden,** to work in a garden.

garg'antuan (44-3-179) very large; eating a great deal of food.

gargle (44) wash the throat by holding the head back and singing with liquid medicine in the mouth; n. liquid medicine for the throat.

gargoyle (44-51) stone figure of a man, animal or strange creature, cut hollow on the walls and corners of a building, e.g. a church, to carry off water from the roof.

GARGOYLE

garish (29-1) bright; showy.

garland (44-9) circle of leaves or flowers, often used as a sign of victory.

garlic (44-1) very strong-smelling vegetable.

garment (44-9) any article of dress.

garner (44-9) gather in; store-house.

garnet (44-1) precious stone, usually dark red.

garnish (44-1) put on ornaments; (in law) warn.

garniture (44-1tsh9) ornament.

garret (3-9) small room just under the roof of a house.

garrison (3-1) soldiers who live in and guard a town; **to garrison** (a town) put soldiers in —; *Garrison artillery* = heavy guns used to defend a city.

garr'otte (9-5) kill by putting a tight band round the throat.

garrulous (3-7-9) talking much about unimportant matters.

garter (44-9) band worn round the leg; *Knight of the Garter* = a knight of the highest rank in England.

gas (3) air is a mixture of gases; steam is the gaseous form of water; **c'oal-gas** (67 + 3) air-like matter obtained by heating coal in a closed vessel; *A gas-bag* = one who loves to talk; Sl. *Step on the gas* = increase the speed; **g'as-mask** (+ 44) covering for the face which enables one to breathe when in poisonous gas.

gas (3) Am. = *gasolene* (3rd below).

gash (3) deep cut in the body.

gasket (3-1) rope for fastening a sail; any thin material put between metal surfaces in an engine to prevent oil from running out, or to make the joint tight.

gasolene, -ine (3-9-11) Am. light easily burnt oil used for driving motor-cars (in England called *Petrol*).

gas'ometer (3-5-1-9) large container in which gas is stored for the use of a city.

gasp (44) struggle for breath, take short quick breaths, e.g. when very surprised.

gastric (3-1) having to do with the stomach; **gastr'itis** (3-41-1) disease of the stomach; **gastr'onomy** (3-5-9-1) art of cooking and choosing food.

gate (21) entrance in a wall, fence, etc.; *The game had a good gate* = many people paid to see the game; *This is between you, me and the gate-post* = is a secret; **g'ate-crasher** (+ 3-9) uninvited guest.

gather (3ðg) bring or come together; to pick (flowers); *I gather he is ill* = I understand, from what I hear, that —; *Gathered to his fathers* = dead; *To gather oneself together* = control oneself and use one's powers when in danger; a **gathering** (——1) meeting of people; **to gather** (cloth) draw together into small folds; (of a wound) become poisoned and swollen.

gauche (67sh) unable to behave gracefully or politely in company.

gaudy (55-1) worthless and showy (ornaments).

gauge (21j) measure the size, power, value, etc.; a **gauge**, instrument for measuring, e.g. *a wind-gauge*; *Broad gauge* = railway lines which are more than 56½ inches apart.

gaunt (55) thin, looking ill or death-like.

gauntlet (55-1) metal or leather covering for the hand; *To throw down the gauntlet* = show that one is ready to fight; *To run the gauntlet* = to pass between two rows of people who strike as one passes.

gauze (55) fine cloth through which one can see.

gave (21) p.t. of Give.

gavel (3) small hammer used by the chief man at a meeting for hitting the table to get attention.

gav'otte (9-5) a dance; music for this dance.

gawk (55) very unskilful person; tall overgrown youth.

gay (21) merry; (of colours) bright.

gaze (21) look at, usually for a long time, e.g. with wonder or desire.

gaz'elle (9-2) graceful deer-like animal.

gaz'ette (9-2) newspaper, especially one printed by the government or a university giving notices of public matters; **g'azett'eer** (3-9-19) list of place-names in ABC order showing where they are to be found on a map.

gear (19) all the things used in controlling or working a machine, ship, etc.; arrangement of toothed wheels which makes a machine go faster or slower while the engine runs at the same speed; *All one's worldly gear* = all the things which one owns; *To be out of gear* = be not working well.

gee (j11) Am. expression of surprise; **g'ee-'up** (+ 8) (to a horse) go faster!; **g'ee-gee** child's word for a horse.

geese (11) pl. of Goose.

Geh'enna (1-2-9) place of punishment after death.

Geiger counter (41-9 + 47-9) instrument used to find and measure the strength of *radioactive substances* (= which send out particles of electricity like radium).

geisha (21-9) girl in Japan who sings and dances to amuse the public.

gelatin (j2-9-1) **gelatine** (j2-9-11) clear material which melts in water and thickens to a jelly when cold; **gel'atinous** (j2-3-1-9) like gelatine, jelly-like.

gelding (2-1) male horse which cannot become a father.

gelid (j2-1) cold.

gem (j2) jewel; Sl. *She is a gem* = a very good person.

gen (j2) Sl. *Give him the gen* = tell him the facts.

gendarme (344ⁿ-44) armed officer of the law in France.

gender (of words) (j2-9) quality of being male or female or neither, e.g. the word "Man" is of *masculine* (= male) gender; the word "Woman" is of *feminine* (= female) gender; the word "Stone" is of *neuter* (= neither) gender.

gene (j11) — The character and nature of a baby (or young of any animal) is fixed by genes from the mother or father. Each gene carries one character (e.g. colour of hair, shape of a certain part, and whether boy or girl, etc.).

gene'alogy (j11-13-9j1) plan or history of the descendants of a family; the study of family history; adj. **geneal'ogical** (j11-19-5j1).

general (j2) (1) having to do with all or the whole; common; (2) high officer of the army; *A general experience* = some experience which all people have felt or known; *A general dealer* = one who buys and sells many kinds of goods; *A general servant* = one who does all kinds of work; n. **gener'ality** (j2-9-3-1-1); **generally** (j2-9-1) in a general way; usually; **generalize** (j2-9-4l) make very wide in meaning; make widespread; say something which is true of all persons or things.

generate (j2-9-21) produce young; produce power, heat, electricity; cause to happen, e.g. *Unhappiness generates wrong-doing*; **gener'ation**, act of producing; all the people of the same time or age, e.g. a son, father and grandfather are three generations; **generator** (——9) machine for producing electricity, gas, etc.; **gen'eric** (j1-2-1) having to do with a class as a whole; of wide use or meaning.

generous (j2-9-9) giving freely; kind, noble-minded; n. **gener'osity** (j2-9-5-1-1).

genesis (j2-1-1) the beginning; act of producing; **Genesis**, book of the Bible telling how the earth and man were first made.

gen'etic (j1-2-1) having to do with the producing or beginning of anything.

genial (j11-19) pleasant and cheerful in manner.

genie (j11-1) good or evil spirit in Eastern stories; pl. **genii** (j11-141).

genital (j2-1) having to do with the producing of young; **genitals** (——z) those parts of the body which have to do with——.

genitive (j2-1-1) (in the study of a language) word or sign showing ownership, e.g. *Man's* (= of man) is the genitive of *Man*.

genius (j11-19) person of wonderful power and skill; *One's evil genius* = any person who has a bad effect upon one; *The genius of a nation* = that in-born character and special power which makes it different from other nations.

genocide (j2-6s41) killing off a whole race of people.

genre (344ⁿr9) kind, sort.

gent (j2) Sl. gentleman.

genteel (j2-11) unkind word for people who are too polite.

gentian (j2-tsh19) flowering plant from which a bitter medicine is obtained.

gentile (j2-41) not a Jew.

gentility (j2-1-1-1) state of having good manners or of being well-born.

gentle (j2) kind, not rough; slow and soft; *Of gentle breeding* = of good birth; *A gentle blow* = not a hard blow; *A gentle slope* = not a steep hill; *A gentle wind* = not strong——.

gentle (j2) young of a house-fly, used in catching fish.

gentleman (j2-9) man born of a good family and (usually) having enough money to live as one of the upper classes; man of good taste and manners; *Gentleman of fortune* = a soldier who offers his services to any employer;

gentlewoman (j2-7-9) a lady of good birth and manners.

gentry (j2-1) people of high rank below the titled people; *Light-fingered gentry* = thieves.

genufl'ection (j2-17-2-shn) act of bending the knee as a sign of respect.

genuine (j2-171) real; true.

genus (j11-9) group of living things which are all alike, e.g. the genus Felis (cat) is divided into species, Lion, Tiger, House-cat, etc.

geo- having to do with the earth on which we live, e.g. **geoc'entric** (j167s2-1) considering the earth as the centre (an ancient mistaken form of *astronomy* = scientific study of the stars).

ge'ography (j1·5-9-1) study of the earth, its peoples, seas and mountains, weather, etc.; adj. **geogr'aphical** (j1-9-3-1).

ge'ology (j15-9j1) study of rocks and the surface of the earth so as to learn its history and how it was formed; **ge'ologist**, one who studies——; adj. **geol'ogical** (j19-5j1).

ge'ometry (j15-5-1-1) science of lines and figures; **geom'etrical** (j19-2-1) *progression* = 3, 9, 27, 81, etc., each result increased the same number of times.

georgette (j55j2) very thin silk material used in ladies' dresses.

ger'anium (j9-21-19) flower, usually red, often grown in pots in the windows of houses.

g'eri'atrics (g2-13-1) medical treatment of old people.

GERANIUM

germ (j99) very small piece of living matter from which a plant or animal grows; seed of disease; the first beginning from which anything grows.

german (j99-9) of the same parents or grandparents.

germ'ane (j99-21) *What he said was germane to the question* = had something to do with the question and was not out of place.

germicide (j99-1s41) any cleaning material which kills the seeds of disease.

germinal (j99-1) adj. of *germ* (4th above).

germinate (j99-1-21) start to grow; cause to grow.

ger'ont'ology (g2-5-5-9j1) scientific study of old age.

gerrym'ander (j2-1-3-9) Am. use unfair tricks, especially in electing persons to the government.

Gest'apo (g2-44-67) German secret police; any secret police.

gest'ation (j2-21shn) act or condition of producing young in the body.

gest'iculate (j2-1-17-21) to express ideas or feelings by movements of the hands and face.

gesture (j2-tsh9) deed, or movement of the face, hands, etc., used to express feelings.

get (2) (1) obtain; *Get me a chair* = bring ——; *Get a new hat* = buy; *Get singing lessons* = be taught to sing; *To get an illness* = catch an illness, become ill; *Get one's own back* = punish a person for doing harm to one; *I have got* = I own, e.g. *I've got no money*, *She's got a lovely voice*; (2) cause to be done; *I got my hair cut* = caused it to be cut; *Get the child to bed* = make him go to bed, put him in ——; *Get the tea ready* = prepare; *I can't get the door to shut* = force it to ——; *Can you get him to come?* = reason with him so that he may ——; *The lawyer got him off* = proved that he had not done wrong, or arranged that he might not be punished; *To get up* = stand up, prepare, to get out of bed and to dress; *To get up a play* = prepare, train actors in, etc.; *To get up a shirt* = make a rough-washed shirt ready for wear; *A well-got-up book* = well printed and having a good cover; (3) arrive, e.g. *We cannot get home to-night*; *You'll get nowhere if you speak like that* = not produce any result, not succeed; *The story got about* = reached people's ears, became known; Sl. *I don't get you* = do not understand; *He's been got at* = has been given

get-'at-able

money to do something dishonest; *She got round him* = pleased him and made him do what she wanted done; *She'll soon get over (the loss of her friend)* = be comforted; *You'll get to like it in time* = learn to —, begin to —; (4) become, e.g. *The days are getting warmer*; *You'll get hurt* = be hurt; *Get tired* = become —; Sl. *Get left, get left behind* = others will be more successful than you; (5) go; *Get out!* = go out of the room; *Get along with you!* = go away and do not trouble me; *Get on with your work* = go on with, continue.

get-'at-able (2 + 3 + 9) *He is very un-get-at-able* = it is difficult to see or meet him.

gewgaw (gi77-55) plaything or unimportant ornament.

geyser (41z9) natural spring of hot water which shoots up into the air; **geyser** (11z9) an instrument for heating water quickly by running it over plates heated by gas.

ghastly (44-1) death-like; terrible.

gherkin (99-1) small, long and round green vegetable used for making *pickles* (= vegetables boiled in very sour liquid (*vinegar*)).

ghetto (2-67) part of a city where poor Jews live.

ghost (67) (1) spirit of a dead person appearing to the living; shadowy likeness of a thing; *A ghost of a smile* = very faint smile; *Give up the ghost* = die; *Haven't a ghost of a chance* = no chance; (2) person who writes a book for a well-known man and lets the other pretend that he has written it.

ghoul (77) evil spirit which feeds on the dead; person who delights in terrible things.

G.I. (j11 + 41) Sl. soldier of the U.S. army. (The letters stand for Government Issue = thing supplied by the government.)

giant (j419) person of more than ordinary, or human, size; very large powerful person in fairy stories.

gibber (j1-9) make quick meaningless word-like noises; **gibberish** (g1-9-1) such noises.

gibbet (j1-1) wooden frame like the figure Γ used for hanging law-breakers; speak or write against a person and cause him to appear foolish.

gibbon (1) man-like monkey.

gibbous (g1-9) (moon) more curved on one side.

gibe (j41) laugh at, intending to hurt the feelings.

giblets (j1-1) those inside parts of a bird which can be cooked and eaten.

giddy (1-1) feeling as if the head were turning round; not steady or serious in character; loving amusement too much.

gift (1) that which is given; natural in-born power, e.g. *A gift for poetry*; *Gift of the gab* = power of speaking well; *Gifted with* = having a natural power.

gig (1) light two-wheeled carriage; small boat.

gig'antic (j41g3-1) very large; like a *giant* (= person of more than ordinary size).

giggle (1) laugh in a silly way but not loudly.

gigolo (j11g9-67) man who dances with ladies for payment.

gild (1) cover thinly with gold; *Gilded youth* = wealthy young people; *To gild the pill* = make an unpleasant thing seem pleasant; **gilding**, thin leaves of gold used to cover over other material; material so covered.

gill (1) that part of a fish's body with which it breathes; *Green (or white) about the gills* = looking ill or afraid.

gill (j1) one quarter of a *pint* (= about $\tfrac{1}{10}$ litre).

gillie (1-1) helper in fishing or hunting in Scotland.

gilt (1) covered with gold or gold paint.

gilt (1) young *sow* (= female pig).

gimcrack (j1-3) pretty but useless thing.

gimlet (1-1) small T-shaped instrument used for making holes in wood.

gin (j1) colourless strong drink.

gin (j1) instrument used for pulling up heavy weights; machine for cleaning cotton; instrument for catching animals.

ginger (j1nj9) hot-tasting root of a plant; red-brown colour; *To do a thing gingerly* = carefully for fear of a mistake or of getting hurt; *To ginger up* = cause to be more active; **gingerbread** (j1nj9-2) cake with ginger in it; *To take the gilt off the gingerbread* = show that a thing is not so pleasing as was imagined; **gingernut** (j1nj9-8) a small hard cake with ginger in it.

gingham (1-9) coloured cotton cloth.

gipsy, gypsy (j1-1) member of a wandering race which lives in covered carts and is always moving about.

gir'affe (j1-44) animal as shown.

gird (99) tie on firmly, e.g. a sword; *Gird up one's loins* = get ready, e.g. for battle; **to gird at**, to complain against.

girder (99-9) large support, usually made of iron, used in building bridges and roofs.

girdle (99) band worn round the waist.

GIRAFFE

girl (99) young female; young female servant.

girt (99) p.t. and p.p. of Gird.

girth (99) distance round the middle; band round the middle of a horse to keep the *saddle* (= leather seat on horse) firm.

gist (j1) most necessary or most important part.

give (1) (p.t. **gave**) (21) (1) cause to have without payment; Sl. *Give it him hot* = punish him; *Give me — every time!* = I like — the best of all; (2) allow one to have the use of; *give him a hand* = help him; *To give one's life to science* = use all one's time in working for —; (3) to cause or produce; *To give out news* = to make the news public; *His voice gave him away* = showed what he wished to keep secret; *I give you joy of it* = I hope you will enjoy it (but fear you will not); (4) yield or stretch, e.g. *A soft chair gives when one sits in it*; *To give up* = stop trying, believing, etc.; *To give in* = yield; *To give way to tears* = allow the tears to come; *The water has given out* = there is no more (water); *There must be give and take* = both sides must yield a little; *The rope gave way* = broke; Sl. *Give over* = stop; *The door gives upon the street* = the door opens on to the street; n. **give**, power of yielding, state of not being quite stiff; p.p. **given** (1) already fixed or agreed upon, e.g. *Within a given time*; *Given that* — = supposing that —; *He is given to stealing* = he often steals.

gizzard (1-9) second stomach of a bird in which the food is broken into very small pieces.

glacier (3s19) very large slow-moving river or mass of ice; **glacial** (21s19) having to do with glaciers; like ice.

glad (3) happy; Sl. *Give the glad eye to* = look lovingly at.

glade (21) open space between trees.

gladiator (3-121-9) trained fighter of ancient Rome who fought with men or wild animals for public amusement.

gladi′olus (3-167-9) bright-coloured flower with sword-shaped leaves.

gladsome (3) happy.

glamour (3-9) such charm or beauty as deceives one and causes things to appear different from what they really are.

GLADIATOR

glance (44-s) give a quick look at; (of a blow or sword) *To glance off* = hit and slip off a hard surface.

gland (3) small part of the body which produces a liquid which, poured into the bloodstream, produces certain effects on the body as a whole or on large parts of it, e.g. the *adrenal* gland causes all the signs and feelings of fear; the *pituitary* gland controls growth (see also Thyroid). Certain glands produce liquids which are sent out of the body, e.g. the poison glands of a snake; adj. **glandular** (3-17-9).

glanders (3-9z) disease of the mouth and throat in horses.

glare (29) shine with a very bright light; look at angrily; *Glaring colours* = very bright —; *A glaring mistake* = bad mistake which everyone will notice.

glass (44) hard clear material which lets light in through windows; drinking vessel; *A glass, a spy-glass* = instrument which enables one to see distant objects; *A looking-glass* = glass in which one may see one's own face; *He's fond of his glass* = he likes drinking wine; *The glass is falling* = the *barometer* (= instrument which measures the weight of air) shows that there will be bad weather; **glasses** (44-1z) pieces of specially shaped glass held in a frame in front of the eyes to correct weak eyesight; *A glassy stare* = fixed look showing no *recognition* (n. of Recognize); **gl′ass-paper** (+ 21-9) paper covered with powdered glass, used for making a surface smooth.

glaze (21) any paint-like liquid used to give a glassy surface; **to glaze**, cover with a shining surface like glass; to become glassy, e.g. *His eyes were glazed in death*; **to glaze**, fix glass into; **glazier** (——19) one who fixes glass into windows.

gleam (11) send out light; narrow beam of light; *A gleam of humour* = slight sign of amusement.

glean (11) gather what is left when the grain has been cut and taken away; gather slowly.

glebe (11) land belonging to a church.

glee (11) state of being very happy or merry; song sung by a number of persons all taking different parts in the music.

glen (2) narrow valley.

glib (1) easy-flowing (in speech), but having no deep thought, or not speaking the truth.

glide (41) move gently and quietly over a smooth surface or through the air; pass from one note of music to another without a stop; **glider**, airplane which has no engine.

glim (1) gleam.

glimmer (1-9) give a weak, unsteady light.

glimpse (1) quick imperfect or passing view of anything.

glint (1) flash of light, e.g. from polished metal in the sun.

glisten (1) throw back light from a smooth surface, shine, e.g. well-oiled hair glistens.

glitter (1-9) shine with a bright unsteady light, e.g. jewels glitter.

gloaming (67-1) time between light and dark in the evening.

gloat (67) enjoy the sight or thought of, e.g. *To gloat over one's wealth*.

globe (67) anything shaped like a ball; *The globe* = the earth; **gl′obe-trotter** (+ 5-9) one who is always travelling to foreign countries; adj. **globular** (5-17-9) shaped like the globe; **globule** (5-177) very small ball of matter; drop of liquid.

gloom (77) darkness; low spirits.

glorious (55-19) beautiful, heavenly; very fine; *To have a glorious time* = a very happy time; Sl. *He made a glorious mess of the room* = put the room in complete disorder.

glory (55-1) state in which God lives; fame and honour; *To go to glory* = die; *To be in one's glory* = be doing that which one enjoys most; *Old Glory* = the American flag; **glory-hole** (+ 67) small store-room.

gloss (5) brightness; bright shining surface; **to gloss over,** cover over a mistake.

glossary (5-9-1) list of difficult words with notes explaining them.

glove (8) covering for the hand; *To be hand in glove* = be very friendly and work together; *To handle without gloves* = treat a person very firmly and not very politely; *To throw down the glove* = declare war (see Gage).

glow (67) give out heat without fire; to feel warm and comfortable, e.g. after exercise; show strong feeling, e.g. *To glow with anger*; *To speak in glowing terms* = use words of great praise.

glower (479) give a fierce, angry look.

glucose (77-67) natural sugar found in fruits and plants.

glue (77) material used for sticking things (e.g. pieces of wood) together.

glum (8) silent and low in spirits.

glut (8) fill too full; supply too much, e.g. *To glut the market* = produce more than can be sold; *a glut,* too great a supply.

glutinous (77-1-9) sticky, like glue.

glutton (8) one who eats too much.

gl'ycer'ine (1s9-11) sweet clear liquid obtained from animal and plant fats, used for medicine and in science.

G-man (j11 +3) one of the armed police of the central (not State) government of U.S.

gnarled (44) having a rough surface like that of an old tree.

gnash (3) *To gnash the teeth* = strike or press the teeth together in anger.

gnat (3) small flying insect which bites and draws blood.

gnaw (55) keep in the mouth and continue to bite, especially with the back teeth, e.g. *A dog gnaws a bone.*

gnome (67) small ugly fairy supposed to guard hidden gold and jewels.

gnu (177) an African deer.

go (67) (p.t. **went**) (1) move from place to place, e.g. *To go to France;* (2) leave or pass away, e.g. *It is time to go; The spring is going;* (3) be carried away or broken off, e.g. *I thought the tree would go in the wind* = be thrown down; (4) be guided or worked by, e.g. *To go by one's feelings; This engine goes by electricity; I have nothing to go by* = nothing to guide me; (5) become, e.g. *To go black in the face (with anger); To go to pieces* = become sick in body or mind, or to learn bad ways of living; *It has just gone six* = the bell of the clock has just sounded six o'clock; (7) sell for, e.g. *This goes for (at) five pence; Going like hot cakes* = selling well; (8) agree, suit, be useful or possible; *I can't go with you in what you say* = can't agree —; Sl. *It's a go* = it is agreed; *It's no go* = is useless or impossible; *Her dress does not go with her hair* = the colour of the dress is wrong for the hair; *That won't go down with me* = I won't agree or I won't believe it; *The play went down well* = was liked by the people. Special uses: *To go about it the right way* = begin work in —; *The speaker went for the rich* = said bad things about —; *To go in for music* = give time to; *He will go you one better* = will offer more than you have offered; *Oh, go on! Go along with you!* = don't be foolish; *To go back on a person* = not help after having promised to help; *The party is going off well* = is a success; *Let's have a go at it* = try to do it; *He's been on the go since 10 a.m.* = has been very busy —; *Big hats have gone out* = nobody likes — any more; *The fire has gone out* = stopped burning; *A going concern* = successful business; *All my work goes for nothing* = has no result; *To give him the g'o-by* = pass him without seeing him because of unfriendly feeling.

goad (67) pointed stick used to drive cattle; to drive, urge.

goal (67) place or effect aimed at; that which marks the end of a race; *To score a goal in football* = get one point by kicking the ball between the two posts guarded by the other players.

goat (67) animal like a sheep, having long hair and horns; *To play the giddy goat* = behave foolishly; *Separate the sheep from the goats* = the good persons from the bad; Sl. *This gets my goat* = makes me angry.

GOAT

goat'ee (67-11) beard like that of a goat.

gob (5) any large piece of soft wet material; Am. Sl. seaman on a warship; Sl. *Stop your gob* = put something in your mouth, stop talking; *A gob-stopper* = a large sweet.

gobble (5) swallow food in a hasty bad-mannered way; make a noise in the throat like a **gobbler** (5-9) (= male *turkey,* see Turkey).

g'o-betw'een (67 + 1-11) one who makes arrangements for matters between people who do not meet.

goblet (5-1) drinking vessel.

goblin (5-1) fairy that plays tricks on people.

g'o-by (67 + 41) see Go.

go-cart (67 + 44) small carriage for a baby, pushed by hand.

god (5) one of a number of beings believed to have power over man; **goddess** (5-1) female god; *He's a little tin god* = unimportant person with a high opinion of himself.

God (5) a single being thought of as having measureless power; the ruler of heaven; *God forbid!* = I hope not; **godchild** (5-41) When a Christian child is given a name, people other than the real father and mother (called the **godfather** (5-44ð9) and **godmother** (5-8ð9)) agree to help their godchild to grow up well and become a good person; *A* **godly** (——1) *person* = one who loves God and lives a good

life; **godsend** (5-2) any great help which comes unexpectedly; *I wish you* **g'od-sp'eed** (5 + 11) = a safe journey.
godown (67-47) large building for storing goods (in India and China).
go-getter (67 + 2-9) Sl. person who gets what he wants at whatever cost to other people.
goggle (5) open the eyes very wide; **goggles** (——z) glasses to protect the eyes from dust.
goitre (51-9) swelling in the neck caused by disease.
gold (67) precious yellow metal.
gold-digger (67 + 1-9) Sl. woman who uses her charms to get money from rich men.
golden (67) made of gold, like gold; *The golden age* = the age of great writings, paintings, etc.; *Worship the golden calf* = think only of getting wealth; **g'olden-r'od** (+ 5) a yellow flower; **g'olden r'ule** (+ 77) the rule "Treat others as you wish them to treat you"; any very good rule of behaviour; **g'olden s'yrup** (+ 1-9) thick yellow liquid form of sugar; **g'olden w'edding** (+ 2-1) fiftieth return of the day on which one was married; **g'oldfinch** (67-1) bird; **g'old l'eaf** (+ 11) very thin sheet of gold used for ornamenting things, e.g. the edges of books; **g'oldsmith** (67-1) one who makes things of gold.
golf (5) game in which a small ball is hit into each of 18 holes arranged in a large open piece of land — the winner is he who takes least strokes to put his ball into all the holes.
golliwog (5-1-5) ugly black *doll* (see Doll) with large eyes.
gol'oshes (9-5-1z) rubber over-shoes to keep the feet dry.
gondola (5-9-9) long narrow boat with high ends used in Venice; **g'ondol'ier** (——19) one who rows a gondola.

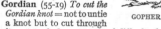
GOLDFINCH

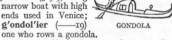
GONDOLA

gone (5) p.p. of **go**; *Gone case, Gone man, Gone coon* = ruined; Sl. *Gone on* = in love with.
gong (5) flat metal instrument which makes a bell-like sound when struck—used to give warning that a meal is ready.
good (7) of fine quality; *All in good time* = at the proper time; *Good works* = acts of helpfulness and service; *A good scolding* = thorough —; *A good while, a good distance* = a long (time); *A good deal* = much; *He is good for a hundred pounds* = we can be sure he will pay —; **good-b'ye** (+ 41) expression used when going away; **Good Friday** (+ 41-1) holy day in memory of the death of Christ; **goodly** (7-1) good; *A goodly share* = large share; **goods** (7-z) any materials, articles, etc.; *Goods and chattels* = all one's possessions;

g'oody-g'oody (7-1) pretending to be very holy.
goose (77s) pl. **geese** (g11s) large duck-like bird, used for food; foolish person; *Cook his goose* = cause him to fail; *All his geese are swans* = he thinks that all his friends or children are wonderful; *Can't say boo to a goose* = is afraid of everything; **a tailor's goose,** iron instrument used by a maker of clothes to flatten and smooth cloth.

GOOSE

gooseberry (7z-9-1) small round fruit which grows on a bush; Sl. unwanted third person walking or sitting with two lovers.
g'oose-flesh (77s + 2) rough appearance of the skin when one is made suddenly very cold or afraid.
g'oose-step (77s + 2) way of marching without bending the knees.
gopher (67-9) North American rat-like animal which lives in the ground.
Gordian (55-19) *To cut the Gordian knot* = not to untie a knot but to cut through it, not to find a way out of difficulty but to settle the question by force.

GOPHER

gore (55) blood.
gore (55) to wound with the horns, as a cow does.
gorge (55j) food-passage to the stomach; deep narrow passage between hills; **to gorge,** eat too quickly and more than is necessary; *To make one's gorge rise* = cause one to feel ill with dislike or hate.
gorgeous (55j9) very fine and beautiful.
gorget (55-1) thing (e.g. armour or soldier's ornament) worn round or on the neck.
gor'illa (9-1-9) large man-like monkey.
gormandize (55-9-41) eat a lot of food.
gorse (55) low bush with sharp points on its branches and sweet-smelling yellow flowers.
gosling (5z-1) young *goose* (= large duck-like bird used for food).

GORILLA

gospel (5) *The Gospels* = story of the life of Christ as written by Matthew, Mark, Luke and John in the Bible; teachings of the Church as to how man may be saved from wrong-doing; *Gospel truth* = pure truth.
gossamer (5-9-9) fine silky threads.
gossip (5-1) worthless talk, usually about the faults and mistakes of others; news which is spread by word of mouth; **a gossip,** person who talks thus.
got (5) p.t. of Get.
Gothic (5-1) (architecture) way of building with pointed arches.

gouge (47j) curved sharp instrument for hollowing wood; **to gouge,** make hollow by cutting out.

goulash (77-3) meat and vegetables boiled with a red substance (paprika).

gourd (79) very large fruit usually grown on the ground; vessel made from this fruit when dried and made hollow. GOURD

gourmand (79-9) one who eats too much;

gourmet (79-21) one who takes great interest in food and chooses his food very carefully.

gout (47) disease caused by too much acid in the blood, resulting in swelling and pain in the joints, e.g. knee, foot, fingers.

govern (8) to direct or control or rule; **government** (——9) that body of people which rules a country; **governor** (8-9-9) man appointed by a government to rule any part of a country; instrument in an engine which controls the speed.

governess (8-9-1) woman who teaches and takes charge of young children.

gown (47) long indoor garment; woman's dress; long black garment worn by teachers in a college.

grab (3) seize quickly; take by force, e.g. the land of another country.

grace (21s) (1) beauty; (2) pleasant way of moving, of writing; *Did it with a good grace* = as if he liked doing it; (3) kindness; *Have the grace to* = be so kind as to; *To be in a person's good graces* = be liked by him; *To grant a week's grace* = allow a person one week in which to pay a debt which really ought to be paid now; (4) the kindness of God; *A state of grace* = state in which one is doing God's will; *This year of grace* = after the death of Christ; *To say grace* = give thanks to God before or after a meal; *The Three Graces* = goddesses (= female gods) of beauty; **grace,** give beauty to, make pleasant; *Your Grace* = way of addressing an *Archbishop* (= highest officer of the Church), or a *Duke* (= nobleman just below Prince).

gracious (21shg) pleasant in manner, kind; gentle; *Good gracious!* — a cry of surprise.

grad'ate (9-21) arrange in order so that the difference between one thing and the next is not very noticeable.

grade (21) a step; class; a slope; *On the upgrade* = getting better; Sl. *Make the grade* = reach a certain class in school; be good enough for certain work; **to grade,** to arrange in groups according to size or kind, etc.; **gradient** (21-19) steepness of a road.

gradual (3-179) step by step, little by little, slowly.

graduate (3-171) one who has finished a course of study at a university (Am. at any school).

graduated (3-1721-1) marked with lines for measuring, e.g. *A graduated glass.*

graft (44) to cut off a small part of a plant (= a graft) and tie it on to another plant so that it grows on the other plant.

graft (44) get money secretly and dishonestly, usually from the government; n. dishonesty; money got dishonestly.

grain (21) (1) any small piece of matter; *To take it with a grain of salt* = not to believe all of it; (2) single seed of wheat, corn, etc. mass of corn, etc., spoken of generally; (3) small measure of weight (·0648 gramme); (4) lines of growth in wood; *It went against the grain* = was particularly unpleasant to a person of my character; *An ingrained habit* = thing done so often that it has become part of one's nature to do it.

grammar (3-9) science of the use of language; **gr'ammar school** (+ 77) school for children aged 11 to 18, leading to a university or learned employment; adj. **gramm'atical** (9-3-1).

gramme, gram (3) measure of weight = 0·035 ounce (*avoirdupois*).

gramophone (3-9-67) machine which produces music from a flat black plate on which sound-waves are written in a fine wavy line.

grampus (3-9) large fierce sea animal; *Puffing like a grampus* = breathing in a loud, quick way.

granary (3-9-1) store-house for grain.

grand (3) (1) very fine and noble, e.g. *A grand sight; A grand character; We had a grand time* = enjoyed ourselves very much; (2) large and fine-looking, e.g. *A grand house;* (3) (of persons) proud, thinking oneself very important, e.g. *He is too grand to speak to us;* (4) largest, most important, e.g. *The grand stairway.*

grand- (3), **gr'andfather** (3-44ð9) one's father's or mother's father; **gr'andson** (3-8) one's son's son, one's daughter's son.

Grand Duke (+ 177) ruler of certain small countries.

grand'ee (3-11) nobleman of high rank.

grandeur (3-19) state of being great or beautiful in appearance, character, etc.

grand'iloquent (3-1-9-9) using high-sounding long words.

grandiose (3-167) having a grand effect; pretending to be grand, but not really so.

gr'andstand (3-3) long rows of seats built up one above the other for people to sit and watch a game or horse-races.

grange (21nj) farm-house with all the small outside buildings.

granite (3-1) very hard rock.

granny (3-1) old woman; one's father's (or mother's) mother.

grant (44) give; allow; an amount of money given for a purpose; *To take for granted* = to accept as true without reason or proof being given.

granule (3-177) small grain of matter; **granulate** (3-17-21) make into small grains.

grape (21) fruit from which wine is made; *Sour grapes* = that which one says is worthless because one cannot obtain it.

grapefruit (21-77) fruit like a very large light-coloured orange.

grapevine (21-41) plant on which grapes grow; secret spreading of news in a country.

graph (3) straight line or curve drawn on squared paper to show the relation between two changing quantities, e.g. my age and height.

-graph (3) having to do with writing.

graphic (3-1) written; very clear and like the real thing, e.g. *A graphic account of a fight*; *The graphic arts* = drawing, painting, printing.

graphite (3-41) black material used inside pencils.

grapnel (3) hooked instrument used for holding an enemy's ship during a fight, or for holding a small boat from being carried away.

grapple (3) seize and hold; hold and fight with an enemy.

grasp (44) seize and hold with the hand; understand (an idea); *He is a grasping fellow* = he gets all the money he can for himself and is never generous.

grass (44) that very low-growing plant which covers fields, hills, etc.; *To go to grass* = take a time of rest; *Not let the grass grow under one's feet* = waste no time; **grasshopper** (44s·h5-9) a jumping insect which lives among grass; **gr'ass w'idow** (44 + 1-67) wife whose husband is away.

grate (21) iron frame used to hold wood or coal in a fire-place.

grate (21) break in pieces by rubbing on a rough, hard surface; make a hard unpleasant noise; *Such expressions grate on me* = I dislike — very much.

grateful (21) (1) thankful; (2) pleasing, e.g. *Grateful shade after the heat*.

graticule (3-1-177) network of fine lines, e.g. in a scientific instrument.

gratify (3-1-41) please or satisfy.

grating (21-1) frame with small openings.

gratis (21-1) free, without payment of money.

gratitude (3-1-177) thankfulness.

grat'uitous (9-1771-9) free, without payment; not asked for; unwanted; *A gratuitous insult* = rude words (or actions) when one has done nothing to deserve them.

grat'uity (9-1771-1) small gift of money to a servant.

grave (21) hole in the earth in which a dead body is put.

grave (21) serious, important.

gravel (3) mixture of yellow earth and small stones used for roads and paths; small solid pieces formed in the body and passed out with the *urine* (= waste water of the body).

graven (21) cut, as a figure in stone.

gravitate (3-1-21) move in any direction as if pulled by some force; feel a desire to go, e.g. *In summer people gravitate to the seaside*.

gravity (3-1-1) weight; force which pulls objects to the ground; seriousness of manner or character, of an act.

gravy (21-1) liquid which comes out of cooked meat; liquid made to be poured over cooked meat.

gray (21) see Grey.

grayling (21-1) kind of fresh-water fish.

graze (21) feed on grass, as sheep do; **grazier** (——19) man in charge of cattle in the field; one who keeps cattle.

graze (21) pass or rub lightly along a surface.

grease (11) oily matter; **to grease**, put oil on the parts of a machine; *To grease the palm* = give money to a person so that he may help or favour one dishonestly or unfairly.

great (21) big; extending far and wide; *A great talker* = one who talks much; *That's great* = is very good; *He's great on history* = very interested in —.

great- e.g. **gr'eat-gr'andmother**, mother's mother's mother, or father's — —; so also **great-grandfather**, etc.

gr'eatcoat (21-67) coat worn outside one's usual indoor clothes.

greave (11) armour for the lower part of the leg.

greed (11) great desire to get for oneself only; too great an interest in food.

green (11) colour of grass; fresh; (of fruit) not ready to be eaten; *A greenhorn* = inexperienced person; **a v'illage gr'een** (1-1j + 11) open piece of grass-land in the middle of a village.

greenback(s) (11-3) American paper money.

greenfinch (11-1) small bird.

greengage (11-21j) small green fruit with a large stone in it.

greengrocer (11-67s9) one who sells fruit and vegetables.

gr'eenhouse (11-47) house, made of glass, in which plants are grown.

gr'eenroom (11-7) actors' resting-room in a theatre.

greens (11-z) green vegetables used for food.

greet (11) express welcome or pleasure at meeting a person.

greg'arious (2-29-19) living in large groups; liking to live in a group.

gremlin (2-1) Sl. evil spirit supposed to cause trouble in aeroplanes.

gren'ade (1-21) iron shell filled with powder which bursts when it strikes anything—or after a fixed time; **grenad'ier** (2-9-19) soldier who threw grenades, now soldier in the Grenadier Guards.

grenadine (2-9-11) a dark-red drink made from *pomegranates* (see Pomegranate).

grew (77) p.t. of Grow.

grey (21) colour obtained by mixing black and white; *Grey matter* = part of the brain; *The* *future looks grey* = is without hope; **gr'ey-beard** (21-19) old man; **gr'eyhound** (21-47) large fast-running dog.

grid (1) iron framework; frame of fine wires in an electrical instrument.

griddle (1) round iron plate for cooking cakes.

gridiron (1-419) framework of iron bars used in cooking; any arrangement of things in lines like a gridiron.

GRIDIRON

grief (11) great sorrow; *To come to grief* = fail, have an accident.

grievance (11-s) cause for complaint.

grieve (11) feel sorrow; cause sorrow to others.

griffin (1-1) animal with the body of a lion and the wings of a bird told of in fairy stories.

grill (1) cook over a hot fire on iron bars (= the grill); eating-house where food is so cooked; meat or fish so cooked.

grille (1) iron bars across an opening in a wall.

grim (1) having a cruel, unpleasant and unyielding appearance.

grim'ace (1-21s) strange or ugly look on the face.

grime (41) dirt, specially that collected on the skin.

grin (1) wide smile.

grind (41) rub into a powder; rub on a hard stone, e.g. to make a knife sharp; study very hard; **gr'indstone** (41-67) hard stone used for sharpening knives and other instruments; *To keep one's nose to the grindstone* = force oneself to work very hard; **grinder** (41-9) tooth used for grinding or breaking food; *An organ-grinder* = one who plays a street-*organ* (= wind instrument of music) by turning a handle.

grip (1) seize or hold firmly in the hand; *A gripping story* = very interesting; n. act or way of seizing or holding; *A good grip of the affair* = understanding —.

gripe(s) (41) pains in the stomach.

grisly (1z-1) causing terror; unpleasant.

grist (1) corn which is to be *ground* (= made into flour); *To bring grist to the mill* = bring in money; *All is grist that comes to his mill* = he is ready to get money by any means.

gristle (1) young bone which has not yet become hard and breakable.

grit (1) small hard pieces of matter, e.g. fine sand; *He has plenty of grit* = courage; *To grit the teeth* = press them firmly together, e.g. when doing something difficult or painful.

grizzle (1) continue to cry and complain.

grizzly-bear (1z-1 + 29) large fierce bear in Canada and U.S.

grizzled (1) grey.

groan (67) make a low sound, as in pain; *The table groaned with food* = was loaded with food.

groat (67) small piece of money in ancient times.

groats (67) inside part of grain when the outer covering has been taken off.

grocer (67s9) one who sells dry and tinned food, soap, candles, etc.; **groceries** (——1z) such goods.

grog (5) strong drink; Sl. **gr'og-blossom** (+ 5) small red swelling on the face, often caused by too much eating or drinking; Sl. **groggy** (——1) unsteady, weak.

groin (51) hollow where the legs join the body; curved line made by the meeting of two *vaults* (= arched roofs).

groom (77) servant in charge of horses; man just about to be married; **to groom** (a horse), brush and clean; *Well groomed* (man) = looking neat and clean.

groove (77) long narrow hollow cut in wood or other material; *His life runs in a groove* = in the same way and never changes.

grope (67) feel for with out-stretched hands, e.g. when looking for something in the dark.

gross (67) big; fat; not fine or polite; *A gross mistake* = very bad mistake; *Gross amount* = whole amount without taking anything off.

gross (67) one gross = 144.

grot (5) see Grotto.

grot'esque (67-2-k) so strange as to appear foolish.

grotto (5-67) small cave.

grouch (47) express bad temper, complain.

ground (47) p.t. and p.p. of Grind; **gr'ound gl'ass** (+ 44) glass with a rough surface so that one cannot see through it.

ground (47) bottom or lowest part of anything; solid surface of the earth; *On what grounds?* = for what reasons?; *To shift one's ground* = change one's line of reasoning in defending an idea; *Flowers on a black ground* = painted on a black surface; *The ship grounded* = ran on to the ground; *He had a good grounding in Latin* = he was taught the beginning part well; **groundless** (47-1) (hopes, fears) without reason or real cause; **gr'ound sw'ell** (+ 2) long rolling waves.

gr'ound nut (47 + 8) peanut, monkey nut; a seed one inch long with a thin white cover and yellow inside skin; it grows under the ground.

grounds (47-z) small bits left at the bottom of a cup or pot of liquid; **the grounds** = garden or land round a house.

group (77) number of persons or objects in one place, or gathered for a special purpose; class or kind.

grouse (47) small wild bird shot for food; Sl. complain.

grove (67) small group of trees.

grovel (5) lie on the ground face down, as a prisoner begging for mercy.

grow (67) become larger; live, e.g. *Roses grow in England*; cause to grow, e.g. *I grow roses in my garden*; to become, e.g. *His hair has grown*

growl   146   **gun**

grey; *This book begins to grow on me* = I begin to like it; *To grow up* = become a man (woman).

growl (47) make a low sound in the throat as wild animals do when angry.

grown (67) p.p. of Grow; *Grown-ups* = persons of full growth, not children.

growth (67) act or amount of growing; that which is produced; *A growth in the body* = diseased mass growing in the body.

grub (8) to search in the earth for food; *To grub up* = dig up out of the ground; *To grub along* = seek a living day by day; Sl. food.

grub (8) form of an insect before it changes into its final form; Sl. any insect.

grubby (8-1) dirty.

grudge (8j) give or allow unwillingly; hate a person because he has something which one has not got; *To owe a person a grudge* = be angry with a person and wish to harm him.

gruel (79) thick liquid food made from powdered grain.

gruesome (77-9) very unpleasant; terrible.

gruff (8) rough and unpleasant in voice or manner.

grumble (8) complain; make a low noise like distant thunder.

grumpy (8-1) bad-tempered.

grunt (8) make a noise like that of a pig.

gu'ano (1744-67) waste matter dropped by sea-birds and used to make plants grow better.

guarant'ee (3-9-11) to promise to see that another person fulfils his promise; *This clock is guaranteed for one year* = we promise it will work well for one year and will give you another or set it right if it does not; Sl. promise, say as being quite certain, e.g. *I guarantee he'll come*.

guard (44) to watch against danger or surprise; defend against attack; a **guard**, person who watches or defends; soldier of the home army; thing which prevents damage, e.g. *A fireguard* = iron frame used to keep children out of the fire; *A guarded answer* = careful —;

guardian (44-19) one who guards; one who has charge of.

gubernat'orial (17-9-9-55-19) having to do with a governor.

gudgeon (8j9) fresh-water fish; pin fixing a moving bar to some other part of a machine.

guerdon (99) *A reward* (= gift given in return for a good deed).

guerr'illa (war) (9-1-9) fighting carried on by men who are not regular soldiers nor members of an army; member of such a company of irregular (= not regular) fighting men.

guess (2) form an idea without real proof or reason; try to get the correct answer to a question by chance, when one does not really know; Am. Sl. suppose.

guest (8) visitor; one who stays for meals or sleeps in the house; any invited person.

guff'aw (9-55) loud laugh.

guide (41) lead or direct in the right way; a **guide**, one who leads or shows the way.

guild (1) group joined together for trade or other purposes.

guile (41) cleverness in deceiving.

guillotine (1-9-11) machine used for cutting off the heads of law-breakers in France; for cutting off the edges of the pages in a book.

GUILLOTINE

guilt (1) fact of having done wrong; *He is guilty* = he has done wrong; *A guilty look* = look which shows that one has done wrong.

guinea (1-1) Obs. worth £1.05.

guinea-fowl (+ 47) large spotted bird used for food.

guinea-pig (+ 1) small animal rather like a rabbit; a person who gets *guineas* (= 21 shillings) for small services, e.g. a priest who works in place of a priest who is ill; person experimented on, e.g. to try out a medicine.

GUINEA-FOWL

guise (41z) general appearance; manner.

guit'ar (1-44) musical instrument having six strings which are picked by the fingers to make the sounds.

gulch (8) Am. rocky valley.

gulf (8) narrow part of the sea with land on all sides except one; deep hole in the earth.

gull (8) large sea-bird.

GUINEA-PIG

gull (8) easily deceived person; deceive.

gullet (8-1) that part of the throat down which food passes when swallowed.

gullible (8-1) easily deceived.

gully (8-1) small valley worn by running water.

gulp (8) swallow quickly in large amounts; make a movement of the throat as if swallowing.

gum (8) red part of the mouth in which the teeth are set.

gum (8) sticky liquid obtained from trees; a form of rubber; *To be up a gum tree* = be in difficulties; Am. **gum, ch'ewing-gum** (77-1 + 8), sweet-tasting wax kept in the mouth and bitten—as a form of pleasure.

gumboil (8-51) painful swelling inside the mouth.

gum-boots (+ 77) high boots made of rubber.

gum-drop (+ 5) small round jelly-like sweet.

gumption (8-shn) common sense.

gun (8) instrument used for shooting; *The wind is blowing great guns* = very strongly; **guncotton** (8-5) explosive made from cotton and acids; **g'unrunning** (+ 8-1) taking guns into a country

GUM-BOOTS

when it is against the law; **gun-room** (+ 7) room in which guns are kept; younger officers' room in a warship; **g'unsmith** (8-1) one who makes or repairs guns.

gunnel (8) see Gunwale.

gunny (8-1) cheap rough cloth used for packing goods.

gunwale (8) upper edge of the side of a boat.

gurgle (99) make a sound like running water.

guru (77-77) teacher; family priest in India.

gush (8) flow out quickly; *A gushing person* = one who gives expression to her feelings too freely and pretends to feel more than she really does; **a gusher** (8-9) oil-*well* from which the oil flows by its own force (*well* = hole in the ground from which water—or oil—is obtained).

gusset (8-1) piece of cloth put into a garment to make it larger.

gust (8) sudden rush of wind.

g'ust'atory (8-21-9-1) having to do with taste.

gusto (8-67) enjoyment.

gut (8) (1) pipe-like part of the body which leads from the stomach and takes away the waste matter; (2) strong string made from the bowel of a sheep and used in musical instruments; (3) narrow water-course or path; Sl. *He has no guts* = has no courage; *Fire gutted the building* = destroyed the inside of —.

g'utta-p'ercha (8-9 + 99-9) form of rubber.

gutter (8-9) hollow pipe along the edge of a roof to carry off water; *channel* (= narrow water-course) along the side of a road for carrying away the water; *Gutter-snipe* = small dirty child which plays in the dirt at the sides of the road and has bad manners.

gutter (8-9) run down as melted wax runs down the side of a candle.

guttural (8-9) (sound) formed in the throat.

guy (41) rope used to fasten something and keep it steady.

guy (41) figure made to look like a man dressed in old clothes and burned on November 5th; badly dressed person; Am. fellow; Sl. **to guy,** make a person look foolish.

guzzle (8) eat and drink quickly, usually with bad manners.

gymkh'ana (j1-44-9) show of games, running, of men and horses, etc.

gymn'asium (j1-21z19) (1) large room in which *gymnastics* (see below) are done; (2) High School in Germany, Holland, etc.;

gymnast (j1-3) one who is good at *gymnastics*;

gymn'astics (j1-3-1) exercises for making the body strong and graceful.

gynae-, gyne- having to do with woman;

gynaec'ology (41-1-5-9j1) study of the diseases of women.

gyp (j1) male servant at Cambridge University; *To give him gyp* = to punish or give pain to; Am. Sl. *I've been gypped* = deceived.

gypsum (j1) chalk-like material used to make soil better and for other purposes.

gypsy (j1-1) see Gipsy.

gyrate (j41-21) turn round and round.

gyroscope (41-9-67) a heavy wheel, usually in a frame, which, when turning quickly, will stay just as it is put; it is used to keep ships and aeroplanes steady; **g'yro-c'ompass** (41-67 + 8-9) a *compass* (= instrument which shows the north) kept steady by a gyroscope.

gyves (j41-z) chains or bars fixed on the hands or feet of a prisoner.

H

ha! (44) expression of surprise or sudden feeling.
h'abeas c'orpus (21-13 + 55-9) paper ordering that a prisoner be brought before a judge to decide whether his imprisonment is according to law.
haberdasher (3-9-3-9) one who sells thread, pins, needles, small ornaments for clothes, hats, etc.
hab'iliments (9-1-1-9) clothes.
habit (3-1) custom; fixed way of doing things; *A riding habit* = correct dress for ladies when horse-riding.
habitable (3-1-9) fit to live in; **habit'ation** (3-1-21shn) place in which one lives.
habitat (3-1-3) natural place of growth of a plant or animal.
hab'itual (9-1-179) fixed by *habit* (= custom).
hack (3) to cut to pieces; Sl. to kick.
hack (3) horse which may be hired; horse used for all kinds of work; person employed to do uninteresting work, e.g. writing the less important parts of a book.
h'acking c'ough (3-1 + 5f) hard dry *cough (to cough* = to force air suddenly from the throat).
h'ackney c'arriage (3-1 + 3-1j) carriage which may be hired.
hackneyed (3-1) *A hackneyed saying* = group of words used too often.
h'ack-saw (3 + 55) narrow blade with teeth on the edge used for cutting metal.

HACK-SAW

had (3) p.t. of Have; *You had better do it* = I advise you —; *To be had-up* = brought before a judge; Sl. *You've been had* = you've been deceived; Sl. *He's had it* = has been killed.
haddock (3-9) sea-fish much used for food.
Hades (21-11z) place of punishment for the souls of wrong-doers after death.
h'aemogl'obin (11-9-67-1) red matter in the blood which takes in *oxygen* (= that gas which is necessary for life and for fire) from the air and carries it to all parts of the body.
h'aemoph'ilia (11-6f1-19) disease in which a wound does not stop bleeding, so that the sufferer may bleed to death from a small cut.
haemopt'ysis (11-5-1-1) coughing up blood (*cough* = drive air suddenly from the throat).
haemorrhage (2-9-1j) sudden and serious loss of blood.
haemorrhoids (2-9-51-z) painful places at the lower end of the bowel.
haft (44) handle of a weapon or other instrument.
hag (3) ugly old woman.
haggard (3-9) having a worn and tired look.
haggis (3-1) meat cut into small pieces, mixed with *oatmeal* (= rough kind of flour), etc., and boiled in a sheep's stomach—much enjoyed by Scotsmen.
haggle (3) to talk about the price of an article; trying to make it less.
ha ha! (44 + 44) sound of laughing; a *ditch* (see Ditch) instead of a fence round a garden.
hail (21) frozen rain falling as little balls of ice, called hailstones (21-67).
hail (21) shout an expression of welcome; *He hails from England* = comes from —; *Hail-fellow-well-met with everyone* = always friendly and pleased to see —.
hair (29) fine thread-like growth on the skin of men and animals; Sl. *To lose one's hair* = become angry; Sl. *Keep your hair on* = do not get angry; *Make one's hair stand on end* = frighten; *Not to turn a hair* = show no fear; *To split hairs* = pretend to see fine differences.
hairdresser (29-2-9) one who cuts and curls hair.
halberd (3-99) battle-axe.
halcyon (days) (3-s19) days of peace and happiness.
hale (21) healthy.
hale (21) bring a person somewhere by force.
half (44) one of the two equal parts of a thing; *My better half* = my wife; *To do a thing by halves* = do it badly or incompletely.
h'alf-bl'ood (+ 8) (relations) having the same mother but a different father (or same father but a different mother).
h'alf-br'eed (+ 11), **h'alf-caste** (+ 44) a person whose parents are of different races, e.g. of a white and a coloured race.
h'alf-cr'own (44 + 47) **h'alf a cr'own** (44 + 9 + 47) Obs. worth 12½ pence.
h'alf-h'earted (+ 44-1) not eager.
h'alf-m'ast (+ 44) *To put the flag at —* = halfway up the *mast* (= pole which carries the sails on a ship) as a sign of respect at the death of a great man.
h'alf-seas-'over (44 + 11z + 67-9) having drunk too much wine.
h'alf-tone (+ 67) way of copying pictures in order to print them in books or newspapers; picture so printed.
h'alf-tr'ack see Track.
h'alf-w'itted (+ 1-1) half mad.
halibut (3-1-9) large flat sea fish.
h'alit'osis (3-1-67-1) bad-smelling breath.
hall (55) (1) large room, e.g. *A dining-hall* = room for eating; (2) entrance hall of a house; (3) large building, e.g. the home of a lord; *The City Hall* = house in which government of the city is carried on; (4) a building used for meetings or amusements; **h'all-m'ark** (+ 44) special mark placed on articles to show that they are made of real silver or gold.

h'allel'ujah (3-1-77y9) expression of praise.

hall'o (8-67) cry of surprise; cry used to get a person's attention; **halloo** = hallo; **to hall'oo** (9-77) urge on dogs in hunting.

hallow (3-67) make holy.

hall'ucin'ation (9-77s1-21shn) thinking that one sees things which are not really there.

halma (3-9) game played on a squared board with wooden pieces which are jumped one over another so as to get them into the opposite corner.

HALMA

halo (21-67) circle of light, e.g. round the head of a holy person in a picture.

halt (55) to stop, e.g. stop marching; cause to stop.

halt (55) walking with difficulty because one leg is damaged; *Halting speech* = speaking in a difficult and uncertain way.

halter (55-9) arrangement of bands put round a horse's head for holding or leading it; rope used for hanging a bad man.

halve (44) divide into two equal parts.

halyard (3-9) rope used for pulling up a sail or flag on a ship.

ham (3) back of the upper part of the leg; upper part of the back leg of a pig salted and ready for cooking; Sl. *Ham actor, A ham* = bad actor; Sl. *Ham-fisted, Ham-handed* = unskilful with his hands.

hamadr'yad (3-9-419) tree fairy; poisonous Indian snake.

hamburger (3-99-9) hot cooked meat cut small and put between two halves of a roll (bread).

hamlet (3-1) few houses in a group in the country.

hammer (3-9) instrument for driving in nails; *To hammer away at it* = work hard and steadily; *To hammer out* = produce as a result of hard work; *To come under the hammer* = be sold in public to the person who offers the most; *To go at it hammer and tongs* = work (or fight) with all one's strength.

hammock (3-9) hanging bed made of thick cloth or string net-work.

hamper (3-9) large closed basket usually shaped like a box—often used to contain food.

hamper (3-9) cause difficulty; prevent natural movement.

hamstring (3-1) thick string-like part at the back of the knee; cut this and destroy the power of walking.

hand (3) end of the arm which has the power of seizing; pointer of a clock; worker; *At hand* = near; *The matter in hand* = now being done; *Live from hand to mouth* = live without making preparation for the future; *To take him in hand* = control him; *Bird in the hand* = something which one has really got (not just hoped for); *In the hands of* = in the power of; *To win hands down* = easily; *Hands up!* = put your hands up as a sign that you yield; if you do not, I shall shoot you; *To keep my hand in* = keep up my skill by practice; *To ask for a lady's hand* = ask for marriage; *To force his hand* = make him do what he did not wish to do; *To lay hands on* = attack, seize; *To get the upper hand* = win or get control of; *Get work off one's hands* = finish; *A hand of cards* = cards given to one player in a game; *An old hand* = experienced person; *On all hands* = on all sides (directions); *To set one's hand to a printed paper* = write one's name on it; *High-handed* = proud and determined to get one's wishes carried out; *Heavy handed,* = rough, using greater force than is necessary; *A cool hand* = daring and shameless; *All hands* (on a ship) = all the seamen.

hand (3) to pass on; give by hand; *A hand-out* = a paper of news or opinion given to a group of newspaper-men.

handbill (3-1) printed paper given out in the street.

handbook (3-7) small book of useful facts or notes.

handcuffs (3-8) iron bands for fastening the hands of a prisoner.

handful (3-7) as much as the hand can contain; *He's a handful* = difficult to control.

handicap (3-1-3) way of making a game equal, by giving a number of points (or other help) to the weaker player, or by making the game more difficult for the stronger player; anything which makes it difficult for one to succeed.

handicraft (3-1-44) skilled work done with the hands, e.g. making pots, cloth, ornaments, etc.

handiwork (3-1-99) work done with the hands.

handkerchief (3ngk9-11) cloth used for keeping the nose clean.

handle (3) touch or feel with the hands; deal with or control; n. the name of anything which is made to be held by the hands; *To have a handle to one's name* = have a title; *Give him a handle against me* = give him a chance to harm me.

handmaid (3-21) female servant.

handrail (3-21) upright framework to support the hand, e.g. when going upstairs.

handsome (3-9) good-looking (of a man); generous, e.g. *Handsome is as handsome does* = a kind heart is more important than beauty of appearance.

handy (3-1) clever with one's hands; near, easy to reach; *It will come in handy* = will be useful.

h'andym'an (3-1-3) man who can do any sort of work with his hands; man who does small repairs and other work in the house.

hang (3) to support from some point above; fix one end leaving the other end free to swing; kill a law-breaker by means of a rope round his neck; *To hang one's head* = allow the head to fall forward on the breast as a sign of shame;

Oh, hang it all! = an expression of anger; *To hang back* = hold back or delay; *To hang fire* = be delayed; *Let it go hang* = it does not matter; *To hang on (his words, her smiles, etc.)* = wait eagerly for —; *To hang together* = to support each other; *His story does not hang together* = can be shown to be untrue; *The children hang about their mother* = stay near to; *To hang on to a thing* = get a tight hold of; *To be hung up* = be delayed; Sl. *Where does he hang out?* = live?; *The tree hangs over the house* = leans over; **hang**, n. way in which a thing hangs, e.g. *The hang of a dress*; *To get (see) the hang of* = understand the general idea.

hangar (3-9) building in which aeroplanes are kept.

h'ang-dog (look) (3 + 5) look of shame.

h'anger-'on (3-9 + 5) one who depends on another, who joins himself to another person in hope of gain.

hangman (3-9) the man who kills law-breakers by hanging them.

h'ang-nail (+ 2I) small piece of loose skin at the side of the finger-nail.

hang-over (+ 67-9) feeling of illness on the morning after drinking too much.

hank (3ngk) amount of silk or woollen thread; iron ring for fastening rope to a pole.

hanker (3ngk9) to desire.

hanky (3ngkI) childish name for Handkerchief.

h'anky-p'anky (3ngkI + 3ngkI) tricks; attempts to deceive.

hansom (3-9) two-wheeled closed carriage.

hap (3) happen; n. chance; **hapless** (——I) unfortunate; **haply** (——I) by chance.

HANSOM

h'aph'azard (3p-h3-9) chance; accident, by chance or without plan.

ha'p'orth (2I-9) Obs. goods worth one halfpenny.

happen (3) e.g. *This event happened in 1066* = was, arrived, took place; *It happened that —* = it chanced that —; *To happen on* = find by chance.

happy (3-I) glad, merry; *A happy idea* = good idea, one that is just right.

h'appy-go-l'ucky (3-I + 67 + 8-I) careless or thoughtless.

h'ara-k'iri (4-4 + I-I) Japanese way of killing oneself by cutting open the stomach.

har'angue (9-3) speech urging people to do something.

harass (3-9) cause difficulty; make anxious.

harbinger (44-InjQ) that which goes before and tells or shows what will happen, e.g. *Birds are harbingers of spring*.

harbour (44-9) place of safety in which ships take shelter; **to harbour** = keep safe; *To harbour evil thoughts* = allow — to remain in the mind.

hard (44) difficult; not soft; unkind, cruel or unjust; *A hard and fast rule* = rule which cannot be changed; *A hard voice* = one which is not musical; *Hard water* = water with much lime in it; *Hard drink, Hard liquor* = strong drinks, e.g. *whisky*; *A hard master* = one who forces those under him to work too much; *To run hard* = fast; *Follow hard upon, Hard by* = very near to; *Hard put to it* = having great difficulty; *Hard of hearing* = not able to hear clearly; *To go hard with* = be painful for; *A hard bargain* = agreement which will bring little gain; *Hard up* = having no money; *Hard cash* = real money, i.e. not just a promise to pay; *Hard currency* = dollars or money which can freely be changed into dollars; *Prices are hard* = are high and will not become lower; *Hard labour* = being kept in prison and made to do hard work; *Hard luck* = bad fortune.

h'ard-b'itten (+ I) Am. having a strong will, not easily guided.

h'ard-boiled (+ 5I) boiled till solid, like an egg; Sl. without a sense of shame.

h'ard-h'eaded (+ 2-I) keen and clever in making money; without the gentler feelings.

hardly (44-I) not quite.

h'ard-m'outhed (+ 47ð) (of a horse) not easily driven or guided; using rough speech.

hardtack (44-3) small cakes of bread made very hard, for soldiers, hunters, etc.

hardware (44-29) articles made of metal used in the house.

hardy (44-I) bold; strong; difficult to kill.

hare (29) large rabbit-like animal; **h'are and h'ounds** (+ :47-z) game in which one set of boys (the hares) run across country, dropping pieces of paper, and the others (the hounds) follow; **h'are-brained** (+ 2I) foolish, thoughtless; **h'are-lip** (+ I) lip divided below the nose.

HARE

harem (29-9) women's part of the house in the East; women in a harem.

haricot (bean) (3-I-67) large seed boiled for food; *Haricot (mutton)* = small pieces of meat boiled with vegetables.

hark (44) listen; *To hark back* = return to what one was saying.

harlequin (44-I-I) fool in a play; foolish fellow; many-coloured dress worn by a harlequin; **h'arlequin'ade** (——2I) scene at the end of a Christmas play in which the actors do many foolish and amusing tricks.

harm (44) to hurt or damage; n. wrong or damage.

harm'onic (44-5-I) producing a right and pleasing mixture of musical sounds; **harm'onious** (44-67-I9) producing pleasant sounds; friendly and agreeing with each other; h'armony (44-9-1) agreement; proper arrangement of musical notes; *To live in harmony* = live together without quarrelling.

harm'onium (44-67-19) musical instrument played by pressing down *keys* (= wooden blocks) with the fingers, while the feet are used to force air through small holes covered with thin metal blades.

harness (44-1) bands, ropes, etc., used to tie a horse to what it is pulling; — *of a knight* = his armour and arms; *To die in harness* = die while working; *To harness a waterfall* = use water to produce electric power.

harp (44) musical instrument having many strings played by touching the strings with the fingers; *Harping on the same string* = saying the same thing again and again.

h'arp'oon (44-77) long spear used for killing *whales* (= the largest sea animals).

harpsichord (44-1k55) large musical instrument of earlier times, played by striking *keys* (= wooden blocks) with the fingers.

harpy (44-1) creature, half bird, half woman, told of in Greek fairy stories; person who tries to get everything for herself; woman of bad character.

harridan (3-1) old woman of bad character.

harrier (3-19) small dog used for hunting rabbits; long-distance runner.

harrow (3-67) instrument with many sharp points pulled over the soil to break up the surface and make it even; *To harrow the feelings* = cause great pain in the mind and heart.

HARROW

harry (3-1) steal by force; destroy (enemy cities).

harsh (44) rough; unpleasant to feel or taste; cruel.

hart (44) male deer.

h'arum-sc'arum (29-9 + 29-9) wild thoughtless person.

harvest (44-1) time for gathering in the crops; that which is produced by the earth; results of work or of one's behaviour.

harvester (44-1-9) man who gathers the crops; machine for cutting and gathering grain (e.g. corn, wheat, etc.); small biting insect.

h'arvest h'ome (44-1 + 67) autumn feast after the wheat, grain and fruits have been gathered.

hash (3) dish of meat cut small and heated up again; *To make a hash of it (work)* = do work badly; Sl. *I'll settle his hash* = deal with him so that he will give no more trouble.

hashish (3-11) preparation made from an Indian plant which causes people to lose their right senses.

hasp (44) fastener for a door.

hassock (3-9) small square cushion on the floor used when kneeling in church.

hast (3) *Thou hast* = you have.

haste (21) hurry; to hurry; hasten, to hurry, cause a thing to act quickly; hasty (21-1) quick-tempered; done without thought.

hat (3) a covering for the head; *To pass the hat* = collect money; Am. *High hat* = proud; Sl. *To talk through one's hat* = talk foolishly; Sl. *My hat!* = cry of surprise.

hatch (3) opening, e.g. in the *deck* (= floor) of a ship; an opening made to let water out but keep fish in.

hatch (3) cause young ones to come out of eggs; *Hatching a plan* = producing a plan in secret.

hatch (3) cut thin lines on stone as an ornament.

hatchery (3-9-1) place where young fish are produced from eggs.

hatchet (3-1) small axe; h'atchet-faced (+ 21st) having a thin narrow face; *To bury the hatchet* = make peace.

hatchway (3-21) opening in the *deck* (= floor) of a ship.

hate (21) have a very strong feeling of dislike; desire to destroy; n. hatred (21-1) hate.

hath (3) *He hath* = he has.

hauberk (55-9) coat of chain-armour.

haughty (55-1) having or expressing a high opinion of oneself and often a low opinion of others.

haul (55) pull by force; amount taken, e.g. *A fine haul* for a thief, or a fisherman; *To haul over the coals* = to scold; *I hauled him up* = stopped him from doing wrong.

haunch (55) thick part of the body and leg where they join together.

haunt (55) visit often; keep coming back to the mind, e.g. a picture, music; *A haunted house* = house in which spirits of the dead appear to the living.

hauteur (67-99) *haughtiness* (see 4th above).

have (55) (1) to own; to keep; (2) suffer, e.g. *To have an illness*; (3) be forced to, e.g. *I have to go to school* = I must —; (4) cause to be done, e.g. *To have a house built*; *To have the matter out* = settle a quarrel by talking fully—or by fighting; *To have to do with* = be concerned with; *To have a baby* = give birth to —; *I won't have it* = won't allow it; *Have at him!* = attack him; *Let him have it!* = punish him; Sl. *To have a person* = deceive.

haven (21) harbour; any place of shelter or rest.

haver (21-9) talk foolishly (also, wrong use, act in an uncertain way).

haversack (3-9-3) bag tied on the back, used by soldiers and travellers.

havoc (3-9) wide-spread waste or *destruction* (n. of Destroy); *Cry Havoc* = give the sign to start destroying a country.

haw (55) fruit of a *hawthorn* (see 7th below).

haw (55) sound made when one is uncertain

hawk and pauses in speaking; *Haw, haw!* = sound of laughing.

hawk (55) meat-eating bird; *Hawk-eyed* = having very good eyesight.

hawk (55) clear the throat noisily.

hawk (55) carry things about the streets on a cart to sell them; **hawker**, street-seller.

hawse (55z) one of the holes in the front part of a ship through which ropes are passed to hold it to the land or to its *anchor* (see Anchor).

hawser (55z9) thick strong rope.

hawthorn (55-55) tree which has small white or red rose-like flowers and a small dark red fruit, often grown round the edges of fields in England.

HAWTHORN

hay (21) grass cut and dried for use as food for cattle; *To make hay of* = throw into disorder; *Make hay while the sun shines* = make full use of one's chances before it is too late.

haycock (21-5) small collection of *hay* (= dried grass) set up on end in a field ready for taking away in a cart.

h'ay-f'ever (21 + 11-9) running of liquid from the nose, pain in the throat, etc., caused by small pieces of foreign matter (e.g. dust from flowers or plants) getting into the throat and nose.

h'ayrick (+ 1), **h'aystack** (21-3) store of hay built up in the shape of a hut.

haywire (21-419) Sl. mad.

hazard (3-9) risk; to risk; dangerous act.

haze (21) mist; lack of clearness in the air.

hazel (21) bush which has eatable nuts; *Hazel eyes* = eyes of a light brown colour.

hazy (21-1) not clear, misty.

H bomb (21 + 5) see Hydrogen bomb.

head (2) **(1)** that part of the body above the neck; *To work one's head off* = work very hard; *Eat one's head off* = do no work and eat

HAZEL

a lot; *Head over ears in love* = completely —; *To turn head over heels* = turn the body right (= completely) over and then stand up again; *I cannot make head or tail of it* = cannot understand it; *Give him his head* (of a horse or person) = allow freedom of action; **(2)** chief or most important part, e.g. *Head of the business*; adj. *The head boy of the school*; **(3)** power of understanding; *We must put our heads together* = take each other's advice; *The speech was above my head* = I could not understand it; *Off his head* = mad; *To lose one's head* = become excited and unable to think; *Keep one's head* = remain calm; *Success turned his head* = made him proud and foolish; **(4)** top; *The head on a glass of beer* (= a bitter drink) = the white wool-like mixture of air and liquid; *Things came to a head* = the matter reached that state when action was necessary; **(5)** one example of a thing, e.g. *50 head of cattle* = 50 beasts; *Dinner at 50p a head* = for each person; **(6)** words written at the top of a page or piece of writing to show the subject; e.g. *I shall divide my speech under five heads.*

head (2) use the head, e.g. *To head a ball* = strike with the head; be at the head of, to lead, e.g. *To head a group of persons*; *I headed him off* = drove him away; *To head straight for* = go direct towards.

h'ead-dress (+ 2) any ornamental covering for the head.

header (2-9) fall on one's head; going into water head first.

heading (2-1) words at the top of a piece of printed matter showing the subject of what follows.

headland (2-9) high piece of land reaching out into the sea.

headlights (2-41) the big lamps in front of a motor-car.

h'eadline (2-41) line of large print at the top of the news in a newspaper.

headlong (2-5) *To fall headlong* = head first; *He rushed headlong* = ran with the head down, not looking where he was going.

h'eadqu'arters (2-55-9z) chief place of business; in the army the place where the commanding officer is.

headsman (2-z-9) one employed to cut off the heads of wrong-doers.

headstrong (2-5) determined to have one's own will.

headway (2-21) forward movement; clear space over one's head, e.g. in a doorway.

heady (2-1) ungovernable; exciting.

heal (11) cause to become well or healthy.

health (2) state of being well; *To drink his health* = lift one's glass and wish him good fortune.

heap (11) amount or number of things put together one on top of the other; put things in this way; *Heaps of times* = often.

hear (19) p.t., p.p. **heard** (99); listen; receive sounds through the ear; *To get a hearing* = get a chance to say what one wishes to say; *I hear from him often* = get a letter from him; *Hear! hear!* = I agree with what you say; **h'earsay** (19-21) news passed by word of mouth and not proved true.

hearken (44) listen.

hearse (99) carriage used for taking the box containing a dead body to the grave.

heart (44) that part of the body which sends the blood through the body; anything of the supposed shape of a heart; the centre of the kindly tender feelings; *To know a thing by heart* = by memory; *Take it*

HEART

to heart = consider it seriously, be greatly grieved by it; *To eat (or cry) one's heart out* = have great sorrow; *To have one's heart in the right place* = be a kind person; *Have a heart!* = have mercy; *An affair of the heart* = experience of love; *To have one's heart in one's mouth* = feel great fear; *To lose heart* = feel that what one is doing is worthless; *To lose one's heart* = fall in love; *Wear one's heart on one's sleeve* = show one's feelings, not hide them; *A change of heart* = change from being bad to good; *A man after my own heart* = just the sort of man I like; *A heart-to-heart talk* = friendly talk in which nothing is hidden; *In the heart of Africa* = in the centre of —.

heart-ache (44-21k) sorrow, unsatisfied desire.

h'eart-beat (+ 11) movement of the heart (about 72 times a minute).

h'eartbreak (44-21) great sorrow; that which causes great sorrow.

h'eartburn (44-99) discomfort in the stomach after a meal.

hearten (44) give courage and hope to.

heartfelt (44-2) deeply felt.

h'eart-free (44 + 11) not loving anyone (not wanting to marry).

hearth (44) large flat stone before an open fireplace; *A man's hearth* = home.

heartless (44-1) cruel; without tender feelings.

h'eart-rending (+ 2-1) causing sorrow or pain in the mind.

h'eart-stricken (+ 1) full of deep sorrow.

h'eart-string (+ 1) *To pull at one's heartstrings* = touch one's deepest feelings.

h'eart-whole (+ 67) not in love, not wanting to marry.

hearty (44-1) high-spirited; healthy; full of deep true feeling; *To have a hearty meal* = eat much with great enjoyment.

heat (11) opposite of cold; *He spoke with heat* = with strong feeling or anger; *The first heat is taking place* = first part of a race; *(On) heat* = seasonal excitement of an animal, e.g. dog.

heath (11) stretch of waste land.

heathen (11ð) person having no true knowledge of God; *Those children are young heathens* = are wild and bad-mannered.

heather (2ðŋ) rough wild plant with very small red-blue flowers found on waste land, mountain sides, etc.

heave (11) lift or move any heavy object; pull hard at a rope; breathe deeply; move up and down like waves; *To heave to* (of a ship) = stop; *To heave a sigh* = give out a deep breath.

heaven (2) place of complete happiness after death; *The heavens* = sky.

heavy (2-1) having weight; difficult to lift; serious; *Heavy seas* = big waves; *A heavy line* = thick line; *Heavy handed* = using greater force than is necessary or than one means to.

h'eavy w'ater (+ 55-9) Hydrogen is a gas. An atom is the smallest possible piece of any substance. Water = 2 atoms of hydrogen + 1 atom of oxygen, H_2O. There are two sorts of hydrogen atom, a lighter atom (the common sort) and a heavy hydrogen (Deuterium) atom. Heavy water is water in which the H atoms are heavy hydrogen.

hecatomb (2-9-67) killing of 100 cattle as an offering to a god; great killing.

heckle (2) to trouble, e.g. a public speaker by asking many questions.

hectic (2-1) having to do with a slow wasting disease; having a red colour; Sl. *A hectic time* = very exciting time.

hecto- one hundred, e.g. **h'ectogram** (2-9-3) = *100 grams* (= a measure of weight).

hector (2-9) behave roughly and fiercely to a weaker person.

hedge (2j) row of bushes used as a wall or fence; protect as with a hedge; to shelter; *To hedge on a question* = not to give a straight, honest answer.

hedgehog (2jh5) animal covered with long prickles which protect it from enemies — when frightened it rolls itself into a prickly ball.

hedgerow (2j-67) see Hedge (2nd above).

hedonist (11-9-1) one who believes that pleasure is the chief good.

heed (1) give attention to; take notice of; **heedless** (——1) careless.

h'ee-h'aw (11-55) sound made by a donkey (ass).

heel (11) (**1**) the back part of the foot; Sl. a lowdown, dishonest person; *To cool (kick) one's heels* = to be kept waiting; *Down at heel, Out at heel* = having worn-out shoes, badly dressed, poor-looking; *To come to heel* = obey like a dog; *To show one's (a clean pair of) heels* = run away; *Kick up one's heels* = be merry, show joy at being free; *Under the heel of* = in the power of, being ill-treated by; (**2**) part of a shoe under the heel of the foot; *No heel taps* = drink down to the last drop in the glass; **to heel,** strike with the heel.

h'eel 'over (+ 67-9) (of a ship) lean over to one side.

hefty (2-1) Sl. strong.

heg'emony (1-2-9-1) leadership among a group of nations.

heifer (2-9) young cow which has not yet produced a young one.

heigh (21) expression of surprise or questioning.

h'eigh-h'o (21 + 67) expression of sadness or tiredness.

height (41) state of being high; distance from the top to the bottom; high place; *At the height of his power* = when he had greatest power.

heinous (offence) (21-9) very bad (unlawful act).

heir (29) person who will get certain money, lands, or power when another person dies;

heirloom (29-77) any valuable thing which is passed on to an heir and may not be sold out of the family.

held (2) p.t. and p.p. of Hold.

helical (spring) (11-1-9) screw-shaped, not *spiral*, which is flat.

helicopter (2-1-5-9) flying-machine as shown, able to go straight up from the ground, stay still in the air, or move forward.

helio- having to do with the sun, e.g. **heliograph** (11-167-44) instrument used for sending messages by means of sunlight.

heliotrope (2-19-67) flower; light red-blue colour.

helium (11-19) very light gas which will not burn.

hell (2) place where the souls of wrong-doers are punished after death; *A gambling hell* = house where people play cards for money; Sl. *A hell of a —* = a very unpleasant, e.g. *time, noise, life,* etc.; *Go hell for leather* = as fast as possible.

Hell'enic (2-11-1) Greek.

hell'o (2-67) expression of greeting or surprise; also used in calling a person on the telephone.

helm (2) (1) handle of the *rudder* (= blade at back of a boat which makes it move in various directions); the rudder and handle or wheel by which a boat is guided; (2) in poetry a *helmet* (see below).

helmet (2-1) iron covering to protect the head when fighting.

helot (2-9) slave in ancient Greece.

help (2) do part of another person's work; do something for another person; save from danger; *He helped me to some vegetables* = put some vegetables on my plate at the table; *Help yourself* = take what you want; *I can't help it* = I can do nothing to prevent it; *Don't do more than you can help* = do as little as possible; *There's no help for it* = nothing can be done to prevent it; *a help,* servant; *a helping,* food put on one's plate.

helpmate (2-21), **helpmeet** (2-11) helper; wife.

h'elter-sk'elter (2-9 + 2-9) in a hurry, in disorder.

hem (2) to fold over the edge of cloth and fasten it down with needle and thread; *The trees hem in the house* = enclose it on all sides; n. **hem,** edge of cloth so fastened.

hemi- half, e.g. **h'emisphere** (2-1-19) half of a ball; *The northern hemisphere* = northern half of the earth.

hemlock (2-5) poisonous plant.

hemorrhage (2-9-1j), **hemorrhoids** (2-9-51-z) see Haem-.

hemp (2) plant used for making rope and heavy cloth; threads prepared from the plant of which rope, etc., is made; *Indian hemp* = plant from which a medicine is made which produces sleep and strange dreams (see Hashish).

hemstitch (2-1) ornamental work done with needle and thread, usually at the edge of cloth.

hen (2) bird used as food and for laying eggs; any female bird.

henbane (2-21) poisonous plant from which *hyoscine* (= the most powerful medicine for producing sleep) is obtained.

hence (2-s) from here; for this reason; *A year hence* = a year from now.

HENBANE

h'encef'orth (2-s-55) from now on.

henchman (2-9) servant.

henna (2-9) red-brown colour made from the leaves of a plant, used to colour finger-nails and hair.

henpecked (husband) (2-2-t) one ruled by his wife.

hep'atic (1-3-1) having to do with the *liver* (= that part of the body which makes the blood pure and stores up sugar).

hepta- seven-, e.g. **heptagon** (2-9-9) figure with seven sides.

herald (2) officer who declares important news to the public, e.g. war; officer who has to do with the signs painted on shields; any person who carries news; person or thing which acts as a sign of some future event, e.g. *Birds are heralds of spring.*

heraldry (2-1-ri) having to do with the special signs painted on shields, etc., as the family sign of noble persons; adj. **her'aldic** (2-3-1).

herb (99) any plant which dies down to the roots in winter; plant used for medicine or for giving a special taste; **herb'aceous** (99-21shj) having to do with plants; **herbage** (99-1j) grass and other field plants; **herbalist** (99-9-1) one who studies plants and uses them as medicines.

H'ercul'ean (task) (99-17-11·9) piece of work which needs more than human strength.

herd (99) number of beasts together; all the cattle of one kind on a farm; *The common herd* = common people; **to herd,** collect together; *To herd sheep* = take care of, be in charge of, sheep; **a cowherd** (47-99), **a herdsman** (——z-9) man who takes care of, is in charge of, cattle; to herd, to act as a herdsman; move in a group, to drive together into a group.

here (19) in this place; *Here!* = a cry of surprise or complaint, also to get attention; *Here below* = on this earth; *That's neither here nor there* = has nothing to do with the subject; *Here's to you* = I drink in your honour, to your good fortune.

HELICOPTER

here- (19) -after, -at, -by, -in, -of, -on —In these words Here means this, this place, this time, e.g. her**e**after = after this.

here**about(s)** (19-9-47) near here.

her'edita**ry** (1-2-1-1) which is passed down from parents to children; *Hereditary powers* = in-born powers—obtained at birth; *The study of* **her'edity** (1-2-1-1) = study of the passing on of powers and character from parents to their children.

heresy (2-9-1) any teaching which is not according to what has been settled as true by the Church; teaching not in agreement with what is believed by most people; **heretic** (2-9-1) one who teaches heresy.

h'eretof'ore (19-7-55) up to this time.

heritage (2-1-1j) that which is passed on to a child by his or her parents.

herm'etic (99-2-1) fitting so closely as to keep out all air.

hermit (99-1) man who lives apart from all people in order to live a holy life.

hernia (99-19) breaking or separating of the covering muscles in front of the body, allowing part of the bowel to come through or move from its natural place.

hero (19-67) (1) great man in the early history of any people; (2) very brave person; chief *character* (= person) in a story-book, poem; adj. **her'oic** (1-671) like a hero, very brave; **her'oics** (1-671) loud and foolish talk, as when pretending to be very brave; **heroism** (2-671z) great courage.

heroin (2-671) medicine which stops the feeling of pain and causes one to sleep.

heroine (2-671) female *hero* (2nd above).

heron (2) large bird with very long legs and neck.

herpes (99-11z) disease of the skin.

Herr (29) (German) Mr.

herring (2-1) small fish used for food; *Neither fish, flesh nor good red herring* = thing which one cannot put into any one class; *To draw a red herring across the path* = draw people's attention away from a subject; Sl. *The herring-pond* = the Atlantic Ocean; **herring-bone** (+ 67) adj. any ornamental work shaped like the back-bone of a fish.

hesitate (2z1-21) to pause because one is undecided.

hessian (2-19) rough stiff cloth; *Hessian boots*, *Hessians* = foot coverings which come below the knee, as worn by soldiers.

hetero- different; **heterodox** (2-9-5) not according to the opinion held by other people; **heterog'eneous** (2-9j11-19) of many different kinds.

hew (177) to cut with heavy blows.

hexa- having to do with six, e.g. **hexagon** (2-9-9) six-sided figure.

hey (21) expression of surprise or questioning; **hey presto** (+ 2-67) words said at the moment of doing a magic trick.

h'ey-d'ay (21 + 21) time of greatest strength, high spirits and joy of living.

hi'atus (41z1-9) break in a written paper where some words are lost; two open sounds coming together, e.g. India Office.

hibernate (41-9-21) go into a state of sleep for the winter.

hib'iscus (1-1-9) flowering plant as shown.

HIBISCUS

h'ic j'acet (1 + 21s1) "Here lies" (in this grave) the body of —.

hiccup (1-9) sudden catching of the breath—sometimes caused by eating or drinking too much or too quickly.

hickory (1-9-1) American tree with very hard wood.

hid (1) p.t. of Hide.

hid'algo (1-3-67) person of high rank in Spain.

hide (41) to cover up; keep out of sight or keep secret.

hide (41) the skin of an animal; *To save one's hide* = save oneself from punishment or death; *Give him a hiding* = give him a beating.

hide-bound (+ 47) very narrow-minded; unable to receive a new idea.

hideous (1-19) very ugly; very unpleasant.

hie (41) to hurry.

hierarchy (419-44k1) order of ranks of priests or holy persons; any order of rank one above another; **hieratic** (419-3-1) adj.

h'ierogl'yphic (writing) (419-67-1-1) picture writing as in ancient Egypt.

h'iggledy-p'iggledy (1-1 + 1-1) in complete disorder.

high (41) raised up; *To ride the high horse* = be proud; *A high (old) time, High jinks* = merry time; *High living* = living in great comfort; *High wind* = strong —; *High colour* = red face; *It is high time you were gone* = you are late in going; *To play high* = for much money; *High seas* = rough —; *The high seas* = open sea far from land; *High school* = school for children aged 12 or 13 upwards.

highball (41-55) mixture of *whisky and soda* (= strong drink and water with gas in it).

highbred (41-2) born of a good family and well trained.

highbrow (41-47) (person) one who puts on an appearance of great learning; (music, etc.) too difficult to be understood by the general public.

h'ighfal'utin (47-9-77-1) full of high-sounding words but really foolish.

h'igh-fl'own (+ 67) (language) sounding fine but meaning little.

hi'gh-h'anded (+ 3-1) using one's powers in a way which hurts other people's feelings.

hi'gh-h'atted (+ 3-1) Am. pretending to be a great person; proud.

Highlander (41-9-9) one who lives in the mountains—especially in Scotland.

highlight (41-41) *It was the highlight of the show* = was the best (most noticed) thing in the show.

high-minded (+ 41-1) very good and honest.

highness (41-1) state of being high; *Your Highness*—way of addressing princes and members of the king's family.

highroad (41-67) large wide road through the country.

high-strung (+ 8) easily excited.

highway (41-21) see Highroad, 2nd above.

highwayman (41-21-9) thief who uses a gun and steals from travellers.

hike (41) long walk taken for amusement.

hil'arious (1-29-19) very merry.

hill (1) small mountain; **hillock** (1-9) small hill.

hilt (1) handle of a sword; *Up to the hilt* = completely.

hind (41) female deer.

hind (41) servant on a farm.

hind (legs) (41) at the back of an animal.

hinder (41-9) back (parts).

hinder (1-9) prevent, try to stop a person doing what he wants to; **hindrance** (1-9-s) anything which causes trouble or difficulty.

hindermost (41-9-67) farthest behind the others.

Hindi (1-11) a language spoken in India.

Hinduism (1-71z) beliefs in God held by many peoples of India; **a Hind'u** (1-77) one who holds these beliefs.

Hindust'ani (1-7-44-1) mixed language spoken in most parts of India and Pakistan.

hinge (1nj) instrument for joining two parts so that one of them can move (e.g. a door and its door-post, or a box and its top); *To hinge upon* = depend on; *His mind is off its hinges (or unhinged)* = he is mad.

hint (1) say something indirectly; *To take a hint from* = get an idea from; *There is a hint of trouble* = a slight appearance —; *He can't take a hint* = he must be told directly or he won't understand.

hinterland (1-9-3) inner part of a country a long way from the coast or from a large river or cities.

hip (1) upper part of the leg where it joins the body; *To have him on the hip* = to beat or get control of; *Smite hip and thigh* = win a complete victory.

hip (1) seed-container of the wild *rose* (= a common sweet-smelling flower).

hip (1) *Hip! hip! hurr'ah!* (+ 7-44) = shout of joy.

hipped (1-t) Sl. sad.

HIPPOPOTAMUS

hippodrome (1-9-67) place for racing, place of amusement.

hippop'otamus (1-9-5-9-9) very large wild animal found in Africa.

hire (419) price paid for a person's service or for the use of things; pay for the use of a thing; *To hire out* = let persons have the use of a thing on payment; **hireling** (419-1) one who gives service for money; **hire purchase** (+ 99-9) buying a thing by small payments made while using it.

hirsute (99-177) hairy.

hiss (1) make a sound like the letter "s"—e.g. as an expression of great dislike.

hist! (1) silence! listen!

histamine (1-9-11) substance produced in the body which makes the small blood-vessels open, so causing the red mark when one is hit.

hist'ology (1-5-9j1) study of the way in which living matter is built up.

hist'oric (1-5-1) having to do with history; *A historic event* = great and important event; **hist'orian** (1-55-19) one who studies and writes history.

history (1-9-1) study and story of past events, conditions, or thought; *To make history* = do important deeds.

histri'onic (1-15-1) having to do with acting plays; like an actor; not real or honest.

hit (1) to strike; *To hit upon* = find by chance; *To make a hit* = make a great success; *To be hard hit* = lose a lot of money or be seriously harmed; *You've hit the nail on the head* = said the exact truth; *You've hit it* = you've said just the right thing; *They hit it off well* = are great friends.

hitch, h'itch 'up (1), pull up; **h'itch 'on to,** fasten or tie on to.

hitch (1) simple knot; difficulty or cause of delay, e.g. *A hitch in one's plans*.

h'itch-h'iker (1 + 41-9) Am. one who gets about the country by stopping strangers on the road and asking to be taken along in their motor-cars.

hither (1ð9) in this direction; **h'ithert'o** (1ð9-77) up to this time.

hive (41) hut-shaped container in which bees live; *A hive of industry* = place of busy work.

hives (41-z) (1) skin disease; (2) disease of the throat.

ho (67) call to get attention; *Ho! ho!* = expression of amusement; *Westward ho!* = we are starting on a journey towards the west.

hoar(y) (55) (55-1) grey or white from age; very old; **h'oar frost** (+ 5) white *frost* (= frozen drops of water on the ground, trees, etc.).

hoard (55) store of hidden money; store up anything secretly for one's own use.

hoarding (55-1) wooden frame or wall on which are stuck *advertisements* (= public notices to make people buy).

hoarse (55) (of the voice) rough-sounding, e.g. after shouting too much.

hoax (67) deceive a person in order to be able to laugh at him; trick of this kind.

hob (5) shelf at the side of a fire on which pots are kept warm.

hobble (5) walk putting more weight on one leg than on the other because of pain, a damaged leg, etc.; tie the legs of a horse so that he can only move very slowly.

h'obbledeh'oy (5-1-51) young person of careless manners and unskilful movements.

hobby (5-1) subject which one studies for amusement; *To ride a hobby to death* = give too much time to what is studied only for amusement.

h'obby-horse (+ 55) wooden horse as a plaything for children.

hobg'oblin (5-5-1) fairy which does harmful tricks.

hobnail (5-21) short nail with a large head fixed in the bottoms of shoes.

hobnob (5-5) be friendly with.

hobo (67-67) Am. Sl. unemployed person who wanders from place to place.

Hobson's choice (5-z + 51s) no chance of choosing.

hock (5) joint in the middle of the back legs of a horse; light white wine; Sl. to borrow money on something (e.g. a watch).

hockey (5-1) game played on grass or ice, using curved sticks and a ball or round object which must be pushed or hit between two upright posts.

h'ocus-p'ocus (67-9 + 67-9) talk or action for the purpose of deceiving.

HOCKEY

hod (5) wooden container used for carrying bricks.

hodgepodge (5j-5j) see Hotchpotch.

hoe (67) instrument used in the garden for loosening the soil and getting unwanted plants out.

hog (5) pig; dirty person; *to hog*, seize food in an eager and rude way; *To go the whole hog* = do something completely and thoroughly.

Hogmanay (5-9-21) the last day of the year, a feast-day in Scotland.

hogshead (5-z-2) large round wooden container for wine or strong drink; a measure for liquids (52½ or 54 gallons, about 239–246 litres).

hoist (51) lift up to a higher position; *Hoist with his own petard* = caught by his own trick; *a hoist*, machine used for lifting up goods.

hoity-toity (51-1 + 51-1) expression used when another person talks crossly and loudly and behaves as if more important than he is.

hold (67) place in a ship which contains the goods; control or power, e.g. *I have a hold on him* = have power over him; *To lay hold on* = seize.

hold (67) (1) keep in the hand; *To hold in the hollow of one's hand* = have complete power over; (2) to support, as a post holds up a roof; remain firm or not break, e.g. a rope or nail; *The cold weather holds* = continues; *To hold a meeting* = arrange and have charge of; (3) keep oneself in any condition, e.g. *Hold oneself ready to go*; (4) to own, e.g. *To hold a piece of land*; *To hold a fort* = defend; (5) contain e.g. *This box holds four pounds*; *That reason won't hold water* = can be proved to be untrue; (6) have an opinion, e.g. *I hold him to be a fool*; (7) to control; *Hold one's breath* = stop breathing for a short time; *Hold a man to his promise* = force him to do what has been promised; *Hold your tongue* = stop talking; (8) agree with or be loyal to, e.g. *I hold by the government*; *To hold back* = to delay; *To hold off* = prevent from coming or attacking; *To hold up* = stop a traveller and steal from him by force; *To hold forth* = make a long speech; *I don't hold with* = am not in favour of; *Hold hard!* = stop!

holdings (67-1-z) amount which one owns, e.g. in a business.

hole (67) opening or empty space in anything; *I'm in a hole* = in great difficulty; *Like a rat in a hole* = in a place from which there is no escape; Sl. *He lives in a rotten hole* = a nasty, dirty, little place; *To pick holes in* = find fault with; *Hole and corner methods* = secret dishonest ways of doing things.

holiday (5-1-21) feast-day; day of rejoicing, day free from work.

holland (5-9) stiff linen (see Linen) cloth made with thick threads; **Hollands** (———z) a strong drink.

hollow (5-67) having an empty space inside; *a hollow*, that is wide but not deep; small valley; *Hollow cheeks* = very thin cheeks which sink back into the face; *A hollow victory* = worthless or unreal victory; *A hollow sound* = sound like that which is made in large empty spaces; *To beat him hollow* = completely.

holly (5-1) evergreen tree with a small red fruit and leaves which have sharp points.

hollyhock (5-1-5) tall plant having many flowers.

holocaust (5-9-55) any terrible event which completely destroys something, e.g. the burning of many houses.

holster (67-9) leather case for carrying a *pistol* (= small gun fired with one hand).

HOLLYHOCK

holy (67-1) having to do with God; respected as being very good and pure; *He is in holy orders* = a priest; Sl. *A holy terror* = very unpleasant, bad-mannered person.

holystone (67-1-67) soft stone used for cleaning the *deck* (= floor) of a ship.

homage (5-1j) act (in old days) of declaring oneself to be the loyal servant of one's lord or king; act of showing great respect and readiness to serve.

Homburg hat (5-99 + 3) man's soft hat as shown.

home (67) place where one lives; one's native place or country; *To drive a nail home* = hit hard and make it firm; *His words went home* = touched the deepest feelings of his hearers; *Not at home* = not wishing to receive visitors; *Bring it home to him* = prove that he did the wrong act; *An at-home* = party; *Home-rule* = self-government; *Home-sick* = having a great desire to be at home. — HOMBURG HAT

homely (67-1) homelike or causing one to remember home; *Homely speech* = simple common speech; *Homely fare* = simple food; Am. not good-looking; (in Australia) friendly and very kind to guests.

h'ome'opathy (67-15-9-1) see Homoeopathy.

homestead (67-1) farm or home with the land round it.

homicide (5-1s41) act of killing another person.

homily (5-1-1) speech about God, being good, etc.; long uninteresting speech about goodness; adj. **homil'etic** (5-1-2-1).

homing (67-1) coming home; **homing pigeon** (67-1 + 1j1) bird (see Pigeon) which flies back to its home over very long distances.

hominy (5-1-1) flour made from *Indian corn* (= large yellow grain, also called Maize in England).

homo (67-67) Latin word for " man."

homo-, having likeness, of the same nature.

homoe'opathy (67-15-9-1) way of treating illness in which very small amounts of medicine are given, these medicines being such as produce results like those of the disease; **homoeopath** (67-19-3) man who treats illness in this way.

homog'eneous (5-9j11-19) of the same nature in all parts.

homonym (5-6-1) one of two or more words having the same sound but different meaning, e.g. Spring (of water; to jump).

h'omos'exual (5-6-2-179) person who falls in love with persons of the same sex.

hone (67) small smooth stone used for giving a sharp edge to cutting instruments.

honest (5-1) true; free from anything which deceives; fair.

honey (8-1) sweet liquid made by bees; sweetness; *My honey* = my dearest one; **h'oneycomb** (8-1-67) six-sided wax framework made by bees for storing their honey; **honeyed** (8-1) (words) = pleasant words intended to gain friendship.

honeymoon (8-1-77) time between marriage and settling in a new home, often spent in travel.

honeysuckle (8-1-8) sweet-smelling flower.

honk (5ngk) noise made by the horn of a motor-car.

honorary (5-9-9-1) working without pay, e.g. *Honorary Magistrate* = judge having the rank and title, but not the pay.

honor'arium (5-9-29-19) money given for services for which it is not usual to fix a price.

honour (5-9) good name; self-respect; *I promise on my honour* = may I lose my good name if I do not —!; *I put him on his honour* = I told him that I trusted him to do it; *A debt of honour* = what one is forced to pay, not by law, but by one's self-respect and good name; *Maid of honour* = lady serving a queen or princess; *Birthday honours* = list of high ranks and titles declared on the king's birthday; *I did honour to the meal* = it was a good meal and I ate a lot; *Do the honours of the house* = act as host; *Your Honour* = a way of speaking to a judge; **to honour**, do honour to; *To honour a promise* = fulfil —; *Honour a debt* = pay —;

honourable (5-9-9) honest, respected.

hooch (77) Sl. bad spirits for drinking.

hood (7) covering for the head, neck and shoulders; piece of bright coloured silk worn round the neck and on the back, as a part of university dress; top of a car which can be folded back.

hoodlum (77-9) Am. rough, noisy, bad-mannered fellow.

h'ood'oo (77-77) that which causes bad fortune.

hoodwink (7-1ngk) cover the eyes of (an animal); deceive (a person).

hoof (77) solid part of some animals' feet, e.g. horses; *He showed the cloven hoof* = he showed the badness in his nature; Sl. **to hoof**, kick, walk.

hook (7) piece of wire bent in the shape of a J; *Bill hook* = a curved knife; *Hook and eye* = a way of fastening clothes by putting a hook into a U-shaped fastener on the other side; *I'll do it by hook or by crook* = I mean to succeed by one way or another; Sl. *Do it on my own hook* = alone, without help.

hookah (7-9) pipe for smoking in which the smoke is drawn through water.

hook-up (7 + 8) joining together radio-stations so that many hear the same thing.

hookworm (7-99) small creature which enters the body, hooks on to the inside of the bowel, and sucks blood, so causing illness and loss of strength.

hooligan (77-1) rough person who fights and makes a noise in the streets.

hoop (77) ring of thin metal, wire or wood.

hoor'ay (7-21) shout of joy.

hoot (77) shout showing anger or dislike; noise made by an *owl* (= night-flying bird with big eyes); **hooter** (——9) steam instrument which makes a deep sound.

Hoover (77-9) machine which brushes the floor and draws up the dust into a bag (Trade name).

hop (5) to move by short jumps; to jump on one

hop (5) leg; Sl. *Hop it!* = go away; *Catch him on the hop* = when unprepared; **a hop,** short jump; small dance.

hop (5) tall, climbing plant, the fruit of which is used in making *beer* (= a bitter strong drink).

HOP

hope (67) to desire and expect; **a hope,** feeling of hope, thing hoped for; *Hoping against hope* = hoping when there is no more reason for hope; *A hopeless* (——1) *fool* = a complete —

hopper (5-9) (1) box with a wide opening in the top, sloping sides, and a small hole in the bottom through which material is poured into a machine; (2) any small insect which jumps.

hopscotch (5-5) game in which a child jumps on one foot and at the same time kicks a small stone.

horde (55) large disorderly crowd.

horizon (9-41) circular line where the earth and sky appear to meet; width of one's ideas or experiences.

h'oriz'ontal (5-1-5) level or flat.

hormone (55-67) material carried by the blood to different parts of the body which excites those parts to increased action.

horn (55) (1) hard bone-like material that covers the upper ends of the fingers, and the feet of some animals; (2) long pointed objects on the head of a cow, deer, etc.; *To draw in one's horns* = become less active; *Take the bull by the horns* = deal with a danger or difficulty in a fearless way.

horn (55) musical instrument played by blowing; instrument on a motor-car which makes warning sounds.

hornbill (55-1) bird with a very large beak.

hornet (55-1) large bee-like insect with a poisonous *sting* (= needle at the back of the body); *To stir up a hornet's nest* = make trouble by causing many persons to become angry.

hornpipe (55-41) dance usually performed by seamen.

hor'ology (55-5-9j1) art of making clocks.

horoscope (5-9-67) plan of the stars at the moment of a person's birth (or other time) and an account of future events said to be made probable by the stars.

horrible (5-1) causing great fear or dislike.

horrid (5-1) very unpleasant.

horrify (5-1-41) cause *horror* (see below).

horror (5-9) great fear and dislike.

h'ors de c'ombat (55 + 9 + 5-44) not taking part in the battle; unable to join in the work.

hors d''oeuvre (55 + 99-1-9) collection of various strong-tasting foods served at the beginning of a dinner.

horse (55) (1) four-footed animal used for riding; (2) any frame shaped like a horse; *A horse breaker* = one who trains young horses; *Horse and foot* = horse soldiers and foot soldiers; *To ride the high horse* = be proud; *A dark horse* = unknown and unexpected winner; *To flog a dead horse* = continue speaking of something which is finished or agreed on; *To put the cart before the horse* = do things in the wrong order; *To look a gift horse in the mouth* = find fault with a thing received as a gift; *A horse laugh* = noisy laugh; *Horse sense* = good common sense; *Horse-play* = rough noisy play; *Tell it to the horse marines* (= horse soldiers on a warship; there are none) = no one will believe it.

horseman (55-9) man riding a horse; horse soldier.

horse-power (55 + 479) measure of power, equal to that which is necessary to lift 550 pounds to a height of one foot in one *second* (= $\frac{1}{60}$ minute).

horse-radish (55 + 3-1) plant with a white hot-tasting root eaten with meat.

hortative (55-9-1) **hortatory** (55-9-9-1) giving advice, urging on.

horticulture (55-1-8-tsh9) science of gardening.

hosanna (67z3-9) cry of praise.

hose (67z) pipe (usually made of rubber) used for throwing a stream of water, e.g. on a fire, garden, etc.

hose (67z) coverings for the legs, made of silk, wool, or cotton (e.g. *socks, stockings,* etc.); **hosiery** (67z19-1) (1) hose; (2) men's underclothes; **hosier** (67z19) seller of men's underclothes.

hospice (5-1s) house of rest for travellers.

hospitable (5s-1-9) friendly and kind to guests.

hospital (5-1) building used for the care of sick people.

hospit'ality (5-1-3-1-1) act of serving guests.

host (67) man who receives guests; **hostess** (——1) woman acting as host; the wife of one's host.

host (67) great crowd; army.

host (67) holy bread in that ceremony of the Church which calls to memory the last supper of Jesus Christ.

hostage (5-1j) person held prisoner until some promise has been fulfilled.

hostel (5) place of rest for travellers; livinghouse for persons studying at a school or university away from home; **hostelry** (——1) inn.

hostile (5-41) acting like an enemy.

hostler (5-9) man who looks after horses (more often written **ostler** (5-9)).

hot (5) (1) having much heat; Sl. *Hot air* = foolish talk; Sl. *Hot money* = stolen papermoney which cannot safely be used; *Give it to him hot* = punish him thoroughly; *He is hot on the scent (or trail)* = he is close to finding what he wishes to find; *This place is too hot for* *him* = he has behaved very badly and must leave; (2) having a strong burning taste; **hot dog** (+ 5) hot *sausage* (= meat inside a pipelike skin) between pieces of bread.

h'ot-bed (+ 2) place where plants are kept warm and grow quickly; *A hot-bed of crime* = place which produces much wrong-doing.

hotchpotch (5-5) disorderly mixture.

hot'el (67-2) place where travellers may find rooms and food.

hot'elier (6-2-12I) hotel-keeper.

h'ot-foot (5 + 7) in great haste.

hothouse (5t·h47) glasshouse for growing plants out of the proper season.

Hottentots (5-5) yellow-brown wandering people who once covered much of South Africa but have now nearly died out.

hound (47) large hunting dog; (of a person) bad worthless fellow; *To hound out* = drive out.

hour (479) measure of time, 1/24 of a day and night; *The eleventh hour* = latest possible time for doing something; *His hour has come* = the time for his death (or, his great chance) has come; *The question of the hour* = most important question at the present time; *In an evil hour* = unfortunately; *After hours* = after the proper time of business.

h'our-glass (+ 44) glass containing sand used for measuring hours of time.

houri (779-1) beautiful woman (Persian and Arabic word).

house (47) building made to live in; place of business; *To keep house* = stay at home, to have charge of the work in a house; *House of God* = church; *The Upper (Lower) House* = meeting of law-givers who govern a country (*Upper* = of noblemen); *It went like a house on fire* = very quickly, very successfully; *A full house* = full theatre; *To bring down the house* = delight everyone and cause them to shout loud praises in a theatre; *Son of a noble house* = — family; **to house** (47z) give room in a house to, to receive in one's house.

housebreaker (47-2I-9) thief who breaks into houses in the daytime; man employed to pull down useless houses (Am. house-wrecker).

household (47-67) family; all those living in one house; *A household word* = something known and talked of by everybody.

housewarming (47-55-1) feast given after entering a new house.

housewife (47-41) (1) lady in charge of a house; (2) (h8zIf) small container for needles, thread, etc.

hove (67) p.t. of Heave.

hovel (5) poor dirty home.

hover (5-9) (of a bird) remain in one place in the air; (of a person) wait about near a person or thing in an uncertain manner.

howdah (47-9) box in which one rides on the back of an elephant.

howitzer (47-1-s9) short gun used for dropping heavy *shells* (= explosive shots) straight down on the enemy.

howl (47) cry of dogs and such animals; noise made by a strong wind; *A howler* = very laughable mistake; *A howling success* = great success.

howso'ever (47-672-9) in whatever manner.

hoyden (5I) rough-mannered girl.

hub (8) centre of a wheel.

hubble-bubble (8 + 8) a kind of tobacco pipe (smoke is drawn through water in the lower part).

hubbub (8-8) great noise.

hubby (8-1) Sl. husband.

huckleberry (8-9-1) small dark-blue fruit.

huckster (8-9) seller of small unimportant things.

HUBBLE-BUBBLE

huddle (8) to crowd together, e.g. when cold, or in fear; put together without order.

hue (177) colour; darkness or lightness of colour; particular kind of a colour.

hue and cry (177 + 41) cry raised by one who has had something stolen and wishes all people to help catch the thief.

huffed (8-t) angry; **huffy** (8-1) easily made angry.

hug (8) press close to the body with one's arms, as a mother does a child; (of a ship) *To hug the shore* = stay close to —; *To hug oneself* = have a secret feeling of joy.

huge (177j) very large.

hugger-mugger (8-9 + 8-9) disorder; mixed and disorderly (way).

hulk (8) body of an old ship no longer in use; any large ungraceful person or thing difficult to move; **hulking**, large and ungraceful.

hull (8) outer covering of a grain.

hull (8) body of the ship without the *masts* (= poles which carry the sails), ropes, etc.

h'ullabal'oo (8-9-9-77) great noise.

hull'o (8-67) expression of greeting or surprise.

hum (8) make a noise like a bee; sing with the lips closed; *To hum and haw* = make sounds like these words when in difficulty during a speech; *To make things hum* = cause a business to go on quickly.

human (177-9) having to do with man; having the qualities of man; *Humanly speaking* = speaking like man, therefore perhaps mistaken.

hum'ane (177-21) kind and gentle; *Humane learning* = study of man and the arts.

humanism (177-9-1z) form of thought which regards man as the most important object of study—not God or nature.

humanit'arian (177-3-1-29-19) having kindness and mercy; trying to make pain and suffering less.

hum'anity (177-3-1-1) the whole human race; *The humanities* = study of Latin and Greek and the writings of the past.

humble (8) not proud; not trying to bring oneself to the notice of others; *Of humble birth* = born of common, poor people; *My humble task* = simple and unimportant; **h'umble-b'ee** (8 + 11) see Bumble-bee.

h'umble p'ie (8 + 4I) *To eat humble pie* = go and say that one is sorry for what one has done.

humbug (8-8) act done for the purpose of deceiving; (of speech) dishonest or untrue; foolish, empty talk; **a humbug,** person who pretends to do more than he can; **to humbug,** deceive.

humdrum (8-8) uninteresting, unchanging.

humerus (177-9-9) bone of the upper part of the arm.

humid (177-1) slightly wet; **hum'idity** (177-1-1-1) wetness; amount of water in the air.

hum'iliate (177-1-121) lower the *pride* (n. of proud), of, make ashamed.

hum'ility (177-1-1-1) *humble* (= not proud) state of mind.

humming bird (8-1 + 99) very small brightly coloured bird which makes a *humming* (= noise like that of a bee) noise with the speed of its wings.

hummock (8-9) little hill.

humour (177-9) **(1)** (in old books) any liquid; certain liquids found in the body; **(2)** liquid inside the eye; **(3)** quality of mind which causes one to see and tell the amusing side of things, e.g. *He has a sense of humour*; **(4)** state of feeling, e.g. *Good-humoured* = kind, pleased, never angry; *To humour a child* = make him happy by giving him all he wants.

hump (8) rounded raised-up part, e.g. on a person's or animal's back.

humph (8) sound made to show dislike or disbelief.

humus (177-9) earth made by decayed leaves.

hunch (8) rounded raised-up part; curve the back as a cat does when angry; **hunchback (-ed)** (8-3) having the back so curved; Sl. *I have a hunch that* = I believe (though without reason) that —.

hung (8) p.t. of Hang.

hunger (8ngg9) desire for food; any strong desire; *To go on a hunger strike* = to refuse to eat when in prison; adj. **hungry** (8ngg-1).

hunk (8ngk) large piece.

hunkers (8ngkgz) *On one's hunkers* = sitting down on one's heels.

hunt (8) go after wild animals and try to catch or kill them; look for that which is lost; *To hunt up, To hunt out* = look for something which is difficult to find; **hunter** (8-9) man who hunts animals; horse used in *hunting* (= riding after) foxes.

hurdle (99) movable frame over which men or horses jump.

hurdy-gurdy (99-1 + 99-1) musical instrument played by turning a handle.

hurl (99) throw with great force.

hurly-burly (99-1 + 99-1) great noise and action.

hurrah (7-44) shout of joy.

hurricane (8-1-9) very strong wind blowing in a circle; any strong wind; **hurricane lamp,** lamp, as shown, which is not blown out by the wind.

HURRICANE LAMP

hurry (8-1) cause to move or act quickly; increase speed; **hurry-scurry** (8-1 + 8-1) (in) a state of hurry.

hurt (99) cause pain of body or mind; *It won't hurt if* = will do no harm if.

hurtle (99) rush with great force or speed.

husband (8z-9) the man to whom a woman is married; *To husband one's money* = save one's money and use it very carefully.

husbandman (8z-9-9) farmer; **husbandry** (——1) work of farming.

hush (8) make silent; *Hush!* = be silent; *To hush up the affair* = keep secret, prevent talk about; *Hush-money* = money paid to one who knows of wrong-doing so that he may be silent.

husk (8) dry outer covering of a grain.

husky (8-1) (of the voice) rough, not clear—because the throat is dry or tired.

huss'ar (7244) horse-soldier.

hussy (8z1) troublesome girl.

hustings (8-1-z) places where those who wished to be elected to the government held meetings and made speeches formerly.

hustle (8) to hurry; push roughly against; Sl. *He is a hustler* = is very active and gets things done.

hut (8) small roughly-built house.

hutch (8) box with bars across the front used for keeping rabbits or other small animals.

huzz'a (77-44) shout of joy or agreement.

hyacinth (419s1) sweet-smelling spring flower.

HYACINTH

hyaena (41·11-9) see Hyena.

hybrid (41-1) having parents of different kinds.

hydr'angea (41-1nj9) bush having large round balls of flowers.

hydrant (41-9) large pipe in the street from which water may be drawn, e.g. to put out the fire in a burning house.

hydrate (41-21) mixture of water with other materials.

HYDRANGEA

hydr'aulic (41-55-1) worked by water-power.

hydro- having to do with water, e.g. *Hydro-electric Company* = business company which makes electricity by water-power; **a Hydro** (41-67) hotel in which medical treatment may be had.

hydrogen (41-9j9) lightest known gas; joined with another gas, *oxygen*, it forms water.

hydrogen bomb (+ 5) *Hydrogen* = a very

hydrophobia   162   **hysteria**

light gas. *Bomb* = thing which explodes when dropped from an aeroplane (etc.). In the hydrogen bomb, *atoms* (= smallest possible pieces) of hydrogen break up and form another gas, helium, so causing the most powerful of all explosions.

hydroph'obia (41-9-67-19) disease caused by the bite of a mad dog.

hydroplane (41-9-21) motor-boat which travels at great speed on the surface of water.

h'ydrop'onics (41-9-5-1) growing plants in a chemical liquid.

hydroth'erapy (41-67-2-9-1) science of treating disease by the use of water.

hy'ena (41·11·9) dog-like wild animal which makes a strange laughing sound and eats dead bodies.

hygiene (41j11) science of keeping people healthy in body and mind.

hygro- having to do with wetness, e.g. **hygroscope** (41-9-67) instrument for measuring the wetness of the air.

h'ygrosc'opic (41-9-5-1) taking in water, e.g. salt on a rainy day takes water from the air and becomes liquid.

hymen'eal (41-2-119) having to do with marriage.

hymen'optera (41-2-5-9-9) insects (such as bees, ants, etc.) which have four wings.

hymn (1) song of praise, usually used in church; **hymnal**, book of hymns.

hyper- over, above, too much.

hyp'erbola (41-99-9-9) track followed by a moving mass passing an object which *attracts* (= pulls it towards itself) it; Example: A star comes from *Infinity* (= measureless distance) and, as it gets nearer to the earth, is drawn in towards the earth more and more strongly. It passes the earth; then, as HYPERBOLA it moves away, it is pulled less and less strongly by the earth as it goes into Infinity again. A hyperbola is the curve so produced.

hyp'erbole (41-99-9-1) way of speaking which says more than the truth, e.g. to say that the boys in the class are all asleep when only half are asleep.

hyp'ertrophy (41-99-9-1) too great growth of some part of the body.

hyphen (41) mark (-) used to join or separate words, e.g. self-praise.

hypnotism (1-9-1z) art of producing a state of sleep during which a person will do whatever is ordered; **hypnotize** (1-9-41) cause one to fall into this state; n. **hypn'osis** (1-67-1).

hypo (41-67) white powder used in making photographs.

hypo- less than, under.

hypoch'ondriac (41-67k5-13) having low spirits and being too anxious about one's health.

hyp'ocrisy (1-5-9-1) act of pretending to have goodness and strength of character which one does not possess; **h'ypocrite** (1-9-1) one who does this.

h'ypod'ermic (41-9-99-1) having to do with parts just under the skin; medicine put just under the skin by a needle.

hyp'otenuse (41-5-1-177) longest side in a *right-angled* triangle; *right angle* = such an angle as is formed by the letter L. AC is the hypotenuse.

hyp'othecate (41-5-1-21) give some object of value which may be kept or sold if a debt is not HYPOTENUSE paid.

hyp'othesis (41-5-1-1) that which is supposed in order to explain certain facts.

hyssop (1-9) bushy plant having blue flowers, a strong smell, and a hot taste.

hyst'eria (1-19-19) **hyst'erics** (1-2-1) disorder of the feelings, causing one to cry or laugh without cause; state in which one's feelings cannot be controlled; uncontrolled excitement.

I

ib., short for Ibidem (2nd below).
ibex (41-2) wild goat.
ibid., ib'idem (1-41-2) in the same place in the book.
ibis (41-1) large long-legged water-bird.
-ible, -able, which can be, e.g. **reduc-ible** (1-177s9) = which can be *reduced* (= made less).
ice (41s) water which has become solid with cold; frozen food—see Ice-cream below; *To break the ice* = start being friendly, take the first step in a difficult matter; *To cut no ice* = be of no importance or have no effect; *On thin ice* = in a dangerous or difficult place; *To ice* = make food cold; to cover with sugar, e.g. *To ice a cake;* **'ice-berg** (+ 99) mountain of ice floating in the sea; **'ice-boat** (+ 67) light boat for going over ice; **'ice-cream** (+ 11) cream (= fat part of milk) with other materials frozen as a sweet food; **'ice-pack** (+ 3) mass of broken ice in the Far North or Far South; bag of ice laid on the head of a sick person.

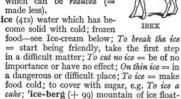

IBEX

ich'neumon (1k-177-9) small cat-like animal which kills snakes; — **fly** (+ 41) insect which lays its eggs in the bodies of other insects.
ichthyo- (1k-19) having to do with fish.
'ichthyos'aurus (1k-19-55-9) animal of very ancient times, having a very long mouth and fish-like body.

ICHTHYOSAURUS

icicle (41s1) long hanging piece of ice caused by the freezing of water which is dropping slowly, e.g. from a roof.
icing (41s1) covering of sugar on cakes.
icon (41-5) holy object, e.g. picture of a holy person.
ic'onoclast (41-5-9-44) breaker of holy objects; one who tries to destroy old beliefs or customs.
ic'onoscope (41-5-9-67) instrument used for sending pictures by television (radio-pictures).
icy (41s1) covered with ice; like ice; very cold.
id'ea (41-19) thought or picture in the mind; *The idea of such a thing!* = how can you say such a thing!
id'eal (41-19) according to one's highest idea, e.g. *An ideal day* = perfect; which is an idea only, not real; **id'ealism** (——1zm) (in art) making pictures, not of things as they are, but as they are imagined; (in character) forming high *ideals* (= plans and ideas as to what things ought to be done); (in thought) teaching that all we know of the world is the ideas in our own minds, and that ideas are the only *realities* (= real things); **id'ealize**
(——41) form ideals; think of a person or thing as perfect not noticing the faults.
id'ée f'ixe (11-21 + 1) idea filling the mind and keeping out all other thought.
idem (1-2) the same (writer, book, or word).
id'entical (41-2-1) the same; exactly alike; *Identical twins = twins* (= two babies born at the same time) formed from the same *ovum* (= egg) and looking exactly like each other;
id'entify (——41) show or prove to be the same, e.g. *To identify a thief* = recognize a certain person as the thief; *To identify oneself with* = show that one is interested in; **id'entity** (——1), e.g. *To prove one's identity* = prove who one is.
ideogram (1-167-3) **ideograph** (1-167-44) picture-sign in writing, e.g. in Chinese.
'ide'ology (41-15-9j1) e.g. *Communist ideology* = set of ideas on which Communism is built.
id est (1 + 2) that is.
idiocy (1-19s1) complete lack of understanding, great foolishness.
idiom (1-19) group of words which have a special meaning when used together, e.g. *To cut no ice* = produce no result; adj. **idiom'atic** (1-19-3-1).
idios'yncrasy (1-19-1ngk-9-1) way of feeling or behaving peculiar to one person, e.g. *It is an idiosyncrasy of mine not to eat eggs.*
idiot (1-19) person having no power of mind; a fool.
idle (41) **(1)** doing no work; *To stand idle* = do nothing; be not in use, e.g. *The machines are lying idle; I have not an idle moment* = am always busy; **(2)** lazy; **(3)** of no use or effect; *An idle attempt* = which failed; *It is idle to expect* = useless —; **(4)** empty, valueless, e.g. *Idle talk; To idle away one's time* = waste —.
idol (41) holy object made in the form of a man or animal; person or thing which is greatly admired or respected; **id'olater** (41-5-9-9) one who believes in idols; **idolize** (41-9-41) regard as holy, admire greatly; **id'olatry** (41-5-9-1).
idyl(l) (41-1) short poem describing simple country life; **id'yllic** (41-1-1) of an idyl, very delightful and charming.
i.e. (Latin), **id est** (1 + 2) that is.
igloo (1-77) hut made of ice.
igneous (1-19) having to do with fire; — **rocks** (+ 5) rocks formed by great heat.
ign'ite (1-41) set fire to, start to burn; **ign'ition** (1-1shn) setting fire to; **the ign'ition**, instruments which set fire to the gas in a motor-car to make it go.
ign'oble (1-67) of low birth, of low character.

ignominious (1-9-1-19) shameful; **'ignominy** (1-9-1-1) dishonour.

ignor'amus (1-9-21-9) one who knows nothing.

ignorant (1-9) having no knowledge; not having been told of something; n. **ignorance** (———s).

ign'ore (1-55) take no notice of; refuse to know.

igu'ana (1-1744-9) large *lizard* (= creature with skin and head like a snake, but having four legs and long tail).

ikon (41) see Icon.

ilk (1) *Of that ilk* = of that name, of that kind.

ill (1) (**1**) in bad health; (**2**) of bad character; (**3**) harmful, e.g. *An ill turn* = harmful action; *Ill blood, Ill will* = hatred; *Ill-usage* = bad treatment; *A bird of ill omen* = sign of bad fortune; *Ill-tempered* = bad-tempered, angry; *I take it ill* = I am angry at it; *Ill at ease* = uncomfortable; *I can ill afford it* = it is difficult for me to pay the money to buy it, or to suffer the loss of money which will result from this action.

'ill-adv'ised (+ 9-41z) unwise.

'ill-aff'ected (+ 9-2-1) not favouring; feeling dislike.

'ill-br'ed (+ 2) not polite.

'ill-disp'osed (+ 1-67z) wishing to do harm; not in favour of.

ill'egal (1-11) not according to law.

ill'egible (1-2j9) not clear enough to be read.

'ill-f'avoured (+ 21-9) ugly, unpleasant.

illeg'itimate (1-1j1-1-1) unlawful; (of a child) one whose parents were not married.

ill'iberal (1-1-9) narrow-minded; ungenerous.

ill'icit (1-1s1) not lawful.

ill'imitable (1-1-1-9) measureless; very large.

ill'iteracy (1-1-9-9s1) state of not being able to read or write.

'ill-n'atured (+ 21tsh9) having a bad temper.

ill'ogical (1-5j1) not according to reason.

'ill-st'arred (+ 44) fated to evil.

ill'uminate (1-177-1-21) give light to; make clear to the mind; cause the mind to have noble thoughts; make the page of a book beautiful with coloured letters and pictures.

ill'umine (1-177-1) give light to.

ill'usion (1-1773n) belief which is not according to facts; seeing what is really not there; adj. **ill'usive** (1-177-1) **ill'usory** (1-177-9-1) deceiving the senses or mind.

illustrate (1-9-21) make clear by means of an example; add pictures to a book; **ill'ustrative** (1-8-9-1) serving as an example.

ill'ustrious (1-8-19) famous.

im- (**1**) not; (**2**) in, into.

image (1-1j) likeness or copy of anything made of wood, metal, etc.; picture in the mind; *To speak in images* = use words which bring pictures into the mind; *He is the living image of his father* = is exactly like his father.

imagery (1-1j9-1) figures of men, animals, etc., made of stone or metal; (in writing or speech) use of words which cause pictures to come into the mind.

im'agine (1-3j1) form a picture of a thing in the mind; believe without proof; **im'aginary** (1-3j1-9-1) imagined, not real; adj. **im'aginative** (person) (1-3j1-9-1) one who thinks of many new ideas—or of ideas which are of no use in practice.

im'am (1-44) leader of prayer, leader among Muslims.

imbecile (1-1s11) of weak mind, foolish.

imb'ed (1-2) fix firmly in any matter, e.g. *Plants imbedded in the earth*. See Embed.

imb'ibe (1-41) drink in; take in as if drinking, e.g. ideas.

imbr'oglio (1-67-167) difficulty caused by ideas or plans being mixed.

imbr'ue (1-77) to colour, make dirty, e.g. *Imbrue the hands with blood*.

imb'ue (1-177) to wet completely; to colour; *To imbue with hate* = cause the mind to be full of —.

imitate (1-1-21) to copy; act or behave in the same way as; appear the same.

imm'aculate (1-3-17-1) pure, without fault.

immanent (1-9-1) remaining within; present everywhere.

imm'ediate (1-11-19) (**1**) close to, very near; *His immediate family* = his father, mother, brothers and sisters; (**2**) (in time) following at once; *Do it immediately* = without delay.

immem'orial (1-1-55-19) beyond the reach of memory; very old.

imm'ense (1-2) very large.

imm'erse (1-99) to put into water; *Immersed in a book* = deeply interested in reading —; *Immersed in difficulties* = having difficulties all round, deep in —.

immigrant (1-1-9) one who comes to a country to settle and live there; **immigrate** (1-1-21) come to a country as an immigrant.

imminent (1-1-9) very near; which will probably happen very soon.

immolate (1-9-21) kill as an offering to a god.

imm'oral (1-5) adj. wrong, evil, of bad character.

imm'ortal (1-55) adj. which will never die; famous for all time.

imm'une (1-177) free from; not able to be attacked by, e.g. *I have had that disease and so am immune* = and so cannot be attacked by it again.

imm'ure (1-179) to shut up within walls.

imm'utable (1-177-9) which cannot be changed.

imp (1) small devil; evil spirit; troublesome child.

impact (1-3) striking together of two objects; **to imp'act**, press tightly together.

imp'air (1-29) make weak, to harm or make less useful.

imp'ale (1-21) push a sharp-pointed instrument through.

imp'alpable (1-3-9) not able to be felt because so fine.

impanel (1-3) see Empanel.

imp'art (1-44) give, e.g. *To impart colour* = give colour to, to colour; *To impart news* = tell —.

imp'artial (1-44shl) not favouring one side; just.

impasse (3ⁿ-4) road open at one end only; place from which one cannot escape; great difficulty; point in a talk at which the two sides or persons are quite unable to agree.

imp'assioned (speech) (1-3shnd) full of strong feeling.

imp'assive (1-3-1) showing no sign of feeling.

imp'atient (1-2ɪshnt) unable to suffer delay; eager to go or act; *Impatient of blame* = angry at —.

imp'each (1-11) say that a person has been dishonest or disloyal; bring a person (e.g. a nobleman) before a court of law for this reason.

imp'eccable (1-2-9) faultless; unable to do wrong.

impec'unious (1-1-177-19) having no money.

imp'ede (1-11) to delay or prevent from moving.

imp'ediment (1-2-1-9) thing which stops or delays an action from going on; difficulty in speaking caused by the muscles of the throat and tongue.

impedim'enta (1-2-1-2-9) all the things carried with a traveller (the carrying of which causes delay in the journey).

imp'el (1-2) to push on or urge.

imp'ending (1-2-1) very near; which will happen soon, e.g. danger, storm.

imp'enetrable (1-2-1-9) not able to be passed through, e.g. *This wall is impenetrable to shots*; *Impenetrable darkness* = which cannot be seen through.

imp'erative (1-2-9-1) commanding; *It is imperative for him to go* = it is very necessary.

imp'erial (1-19-19) having to do with an empire or the ruler of an empire; **imp'erial m'easure** (+ 239) e.g. *Imperial gallon* = British—not American (Imperial gallon = 277·3 *cubic* inches of liquid; American gallon = 231 *cubic* inches; cubic inch = 1 × 1 × 1 inch); **an imp'erial** (1-19-19) small beard.

imp'eril (1-2-1) cause to be in danger.

imp'erious (1-19-19) (person) one who loves to command or use power; *An imperious manner* = rude and commanding.

imp'ersonate (1-99-9-21) pretend to be another person; act the part of a person in a play.

imp'ertinent (1-99-1-9) not polite, not showing proper respect.

impert'urbable (1-9-99-9) calm; not easily made angry or excited.

imp'ervious (1-99-19) not allowing to pass through, e.g. *Rubber is impervious to liquid*; *He is impervious to reason* = cannot be made to understand.

impet'igo (1-1-41-67) disease of the skin.

imp'etuous (1-2-179) moving with great force; (of a person) acting hastily without thinking first.

impetus (1-1-9) force which moves or drives anything.

imp'iety (1-419-1) lack of respect for God; lack of respect for one's parents.

imp'inge (1-1nj) strike against or upon, e.g. *Light impinges upon the eye*; *To impinge upon Mr. X's authority* = do what Mr. X alone has the right to do.

impious (1-19) adj. of Impiety (2nd above).

impl'acable (1-3-9) feeling anger or hate which cannot be changed or softened; unforgiving.

impl'ant (1-44) to set deeply into, e.g. *To implant ideas in the mind*.

implement (1-1-9) any instrument; **to implement** (1-1-2) (a law paper) complete or fulfil.

implicate (1-1-21) show that a person has a share in, e.g. *He was implicated in the murder*.

impl'icit (1-1sɪ) understood but not expressed; unquestioning, e.g. *Implicit faith*.

impl'ore (1-55) beg or pray a person to do something, to pray with tears.

imply (1-4ɪ) to mean without saying, e.g. *You do not say that you were present, but your words imply that you were*.

imp'olitic (1-5-1-1) unwise; done or said at the wrong time and place.

imp'onderable (1-5-9-9) unable to be weighed or measured; too small or light to be measured.

imp'ort (1-55) bring (goods) into a country; **'import** (1-55) meaning; n. **'imports**, goods brought into a country.

imp'ortant (1-55) serious; of great value; which will probably produce a great effect; (of a person) having power.

imp'ortunate (1-55-17-1) continuing always and at all times to ask or claim, so that the hearer is made angry; n. **import'unity** (1-55-177-1-1).

imp'ose (1-67z) lay a load or unpleasant duty upon a person; *You have been imposed upon* = have been tricked or deceived.

imp'osing (1-67z) fine, causing one to admire.

impos'ition (1-9zɪshn) act of putting on; laying of a load or unpleasant duty, or punishment upon; **an impos'ition**, unpleasant duty; unreasonable demand for money; school-child's punishment, e.g. to copy out a poem.

impost (1-5) *tax* or *duty* demanded by the government (*tax* = money paid to the government; *duty* = money paid to the government on goods brought into the country).

imp'ostor (1-5-9) person who pretends to be something which he is not; deceiver; **imp'osture** (1-5-tsh9) act of pretending; a trick.

impotent (1-9) having no powers; unable to act.

imp'ound (1-47) to shut in; seize by power of the law, e.g. cattle which go into another person's garden.

imp'overish (1-5-9-1) cause to become poor; take away all the goodness of the earth so that plants will not grow in it.

imprac'ticable (1-3-1-9) not able to be done or used.

imprecate (1-1-21) to curse or call down evil upon.

impreg'nable (1-2-9) able to be defended against all attacks.

impreg'nate (1-2-21) cause to bear fruit; *Impregnated with salt* = left in salt water so that there is salt in all parts.

impresa'rio (1-2-4-167) one who has charge of the business-matters of a play, of a famous singer, or other performer.

impr'ess (1-2) **(1)** to mark by pressing; **(2)** press upon the mind, to cause to remember; *He impressed on me the need of hard work* = told me that I must work hard; *I am much impressed by this book* = it moves my feelings — I admire it; *Mr. A did not impress me at all* = did not seem clever or nice; **impr'ession** (1-2shn) n. act of pressing; mark left by pressing; number of copies of a book printed at one time; effect produced in the mind; general idea; *I have an impression that* = I think but am not sure; **impr'essionable** (person) (1-2sh9-9) one whose feelings or opinions are easily changed by other persons or by experience.

impr'essionist (1-2sh9-1) painter who paints, not the real scene, but the effect produced by the scene in his mind.

impr'essive (1-2-1) grand, solemn.

imprim'atur (1-1-44-99) permission to print a book; *The work has received the — of the government* = government has shown that it is in favour of the work.

imprint (1-1) mark made by pressing; effect produced on the mind or character; printer's name in a book.

impr'ison (1-1z) to put into prison.

impr'omptu (1-5-177) without preparation, e.g. *To speak impromptu.*

impr'ove (1-77) make better or become better; *There is room for improvement* = it could be made better; *To improve the occasion* = use this chance of teaching a lesson; *Improve upon it* = make something better.

impr'ovident (1-5-1) not looking to the future, e.g. not laying aside money for future needs.

improvise (1-9-41z) do something which one has not prepared before, e.g. play music; *To improvise a bed (meal, etc.)* = make hastily and without having the proper material.

impudent (1-17) rude; not showing proper respect.

imp'ugn (1-177) to question with the idea of proving untrue.

impulse (1-8) sudden desire to act, usually without careful thought; *An* **imp'ulsive** (1-8-1) *person* = person who acts without first planning what to do.

imp'unity (1-177-1-1) *To do it with impunity* = without fear of being punished.

imp'ute (1-177) consider as belonging to; *To impute evil to* = say that a person is bad or did wrong.

in- not, e.g. **inability** (1-9-1-1-1) state of not being able.

inadv'ertence (1-9-99-s) lack of care or attention.

in'alienable (1-21-19-9) not able to be separated or taken away, e.g. *An inalienable right.*

in'ane (1-21) very foolish or silly.

in'apt (1-3) not skilful; not concerned with the matter which is being talked about.

inartic'ulate (1-44-1-17-1) unable to express one's thoughts or feelings.

inasm'uch as (1-9z-8 + 9z) because.

in'augurate (1-55-17-21) begin in a solemn way and with ceremony, e.g. open a show, open a building, start new work.

inborn (character) (1-55) that which one has at birth.

inbr'ed (1-2) that which is born in one; natural.

inbr'eeding (1-11-1) (of animals) choosing parents always from the same family.

inc'alculable (1-3-17-9) so great that it cannot be measured or counted.

incand'escent (1-3-2) able to become white with heat without burning, e.g. electric lamps.

incant'ation (1-3-21shn) something sung or spoken in order to produce a magic effect.

inc'apable (1-21-9) helpless, unable to move; unfit for one's work; *Incapable of telling the truth* = unable to —.

incap'acitate (1-9-3s1-21) make unfit or useless.

inc'arcerate (1-44s9-21) to put in prison.

inc'arnadine (1-44-9-41) make red.

inc'arnate (1-44-1) appearing in a body, in human shape; **incarn'ation** (1-44-21shn) act of taking on a body.

inc'endiary (1-s2-19-1) having to do with burning houses on purpose; person who sets fire to a building on purpose; person who excites others to fight against the government.

inc'ense (1-s2) cause to become angry.

incense (1-s2) material burned to make a sweet-smelling smoke.

inc'entive (1-s2-1) that which gives one a desire to act, to work hard, etc.

inc'eption (1-s2-shn) the beginning.

inc'essant (1-s2) continuing without stopping.

inchoate (1-k672I) in a very early state, not yet complete or arranged in order.

incidence (1-s1-s) direction of falling or way of having an effect; *The incidence of a disease* = number, or kind, of people who catch the disease.

incident (1-s1) a happening; unimportant

event; **incid'ental** (I-SI-2) small, unimportant; happening without any special purpose or meaning; *The duties incidental to an office* = which are a necessary but less important part of one's work.

inc'inerator (I-SI-9-2I-9) large enclosed fire for burning waste matter.

inc'ipient (I-SI-I9) just beginning.

inc'ise (I-S4Iz) to cut into; **an inc'ision** (I-SI3n) act of cutting in; a cut; **inc'isive** (I-S4I-I) sharp, cruel; *An incisive remark* = words which are clever and cause pain; **inc'isor** (I-S4Iz9) large teeth in front of the mouth which cut the food.

inc'ite (I-S4I) urge on.

incl'ement (weather) (I-2-9) = bad —.

incl'ine (I-4I) lean, or cause to lean towards, or away from; to turn from the straight or usual direction; to slope; cause to turn, bend towards; *I am inclined to go* = I feel a slight wish to go; **an incline**, slope; *An incline of I in 4* = hill rising one foot in every four feet of distance.

inclose (I-67z) see Enclose.

incl'ude (I-77) contain; consider as belonging to a group, e.g. *I include him among my friends*; **incl'usive** (——I) containing or counting all, e.g. *From May 10th to 18th inclusive*, i.e. counting both the 10th and 18th.

inc'ognito (I-5-I-67) using a different name in order to escape notice, e.g. *The Prince arrived incognito* = not travelling as Prince but as (Mr. John Smith).

incoh'erent (I-67-I9) (of the expression of ideas) in bad order, not well arranged; (of a person) unable to express his ideas clearly.

income (I-8) money coming in; amount of money which one receives each year.

incomm'ensurable (I-9-2-SI9-9) (of two things) not able to be *compared* with each other, not able to be measured the one with the other (*compare* = to set side by side and notice the sameness or difference); **incomm'ensurate** (I-9-2-SI9-I) not equal, not enough.

incomm'ode (I-9-67) give trouble to; make uncomfortable.

inc'omparable (I-5-9-9) which cannot be *compared* (see 2nd above); better than all others.

incomp'atible (I-9-3-9) having opposite or disagreeing natures, e.g. fire and water.

inc'ompetent (I-5-I) unskilful, unable to do one's work properly.

'incomunic'ado (I-5-I7-I-44-67) shut in prison with no way of sending messages to people outside.

inc'ongruous (I-5ngg-779) not *suitable*, not agreeing with, e.g. a lady's hat on a man.

inconsequ'ential (I-5-I-2-shl) not following the natural order, not making sense, e.g. to say "I am ill but it is raining."

incons'iderable (I-9-I-I9) small; not worth noticing.

inconv'enient (I-9-II-I9) causing trouble or difficulty, uncomfortable.

inc'orporate (I-55-9-2I) take into one's own group or body, e.g. *The English language sometimes incorporates foreign words*; *I have incorporated the idea in my speech* = used, taken into; form a business company according to law.

inc'orrigible (I-5-Ijr) not able to be set right or made to behave well; hopelessly bad.

incr'ease (I-II) become greater in size, number, value, etc.; make greater; n. **'increase**.

incr'edible (I-2-9) unbelievable; **incr'edulous** (I-2-I7-9) disbelieving, not willing to believe.

increment (I-I-9) an increase; amount of an increase; *Unearned increment* = money obtained without actually working for it, e.g. money received as rent from a house which one owns.

incr'iminate (I-I-I-2I) show that a person had something to do with a wrong act.

incrust'ation (I-8-2Ishn) hard outer shell or covering.

incubate (I-I77-2I) bring the young out of eggs by keeping them warm; form a plan in the mind.

incubus (I-I7-9) evil spirit supposed to descend and sit upon sleeping persons; any trouble which is a weight on the mind, causing one to be anxious.

inculcate (I-8-2I) fix firmly in the mind of another person.

inculpate (I-8-2I) say that another has done wrong as well as oneself.

inc'umbent (I-8-9) lying on or pressing on; *It is incumbent upon me to* = it is my duty to; **an inc'umbent**, person who holds an office, e.g. as priest.

inc'ur (I-99) run into; *To incur debt* = get into debt, to owe money; *I incurred his anger* = I caused him to be angry with me.

inc'ursion (I-99shn) sudden quick bursting in, e.g. attack by enemy soldiers, unexpected visit from a large number of unwelcome guests.

ind'ebted (I-2-I) owing money; owing thanks or *gratitude* (= gratefulness).

ind'ecent (I-IIs) not proper; (of behaviour) dirty and low.

indec'ision (I-ISI3n) state of being unable to decide.

ind'ecorous (I-2-9-9) not according to good manners.

ind'eed (I-II) in fact; in truth; *Indeed!* = expression of surprise or doubt.

indef'atigable (I-I-3-I-9) untiring; not resting until one has obtained one's purpose.

ind'elible (I-2-9) not able to be rubbed out or cleaned off, e.g. *Indelible pencil*.

ind'elicate (I-2-I-I) not such (a thing) as a nice polite person would say or do.

ind'emnify (1-2-1-41) repay for loss or damage; n. **an ind'emnity** (1-2-1-1) such payment.

ind'ent (1-2) make a small hollow in; to start the first line of a block of printing further in than the others; to give an order for goods; **an 'indent**, an order for goods; **indenture** (1-2-tsh9) agreement between a master and a learner of a trade; any agreement of which two copies are made.

indep'endent (1-1-2-9) not controlled by or depending on another; self-governing; free to live one's own life and think one's own thoughts; having enough money to live without working.

indeterm'inate (1-1-99-1-1) uncertain; not fixed in time, place or meaning.

index (1-2) that which points out or guides; list of names or subjects in a book arranged in A.B.C. order at the back; *Index finger* = finger with which one points; *Index number*, e.g. $a^3 \times b^{3-3}$ is the index number.

Indiaman (1-19-9) large old sailing-ship trading with India.

'indian f'ile (1-19 + 41) in a single row one behind the other.

'Indian s'ummer (+ 8-9) pleasant warm days late in the year.

India-rubber (1-19 + 8-9) rubber, especially in a small piece used for rubbing out pencil marks.

indicate (1-1-21) show signs of; point out; cause one to see; **ind'icative** (1-1-9-1) acting as a sign of; that part of a *verb*, (e.g., Be, Do, Write, etc., are verbs) which tells an action or a fact.

indices (1-1s11z) pl. of Index.

ind'ict (1-41) say that a person has broken the law; *Indictable offence* = serious wrong-doing for which one can be tried in a court of law.

ind'ifferent (1-1-1) not interested in or not caring for; without any very good or bad qualities, e.g. *An indifferent book.*

ind'igenous (1-1j1-9) born or produced in the country, not foreign.

indigent (1-1j) very poor.

indig'estion (1-1j2stshn) illness or pain caused by the stomach being unable to deal with the food which has been eaten.

ind'ignant (1-1-9) angry, usually with just cause.

ind'ignity (1-1-1-1) very rude treatment of a person, causing him shame and loss of self-respect.

indigo (1-1-67) plant from which a blue colouring-matter is obtained; deep-blue colour.

indiscr'etion (1-1-2shn) any act done without good judgment or thought of possible results.

indiscr'iminate (1-1-1-1-1) not choosing carefully.

indisp'ensable (thing) (1-1-2-9) thing without which a certain action or piece of work cannot be done, e.g. *Air is indispensable for* (to) *life.*

indisp'osed (1-1-67z) unwilling; ill and unfit for work; **indispos'ition** (1-1-9zIshn) illness which is not serious.

ind'ite (1-41) write, e.g. a poem, a letter.

indiv'idual (1-1-1-179) single person or thing; alone, single or being apart from everything else; having to do with a single person; *An agreeable individual* = a nice man; **indiv'idualism** (1-1-1-179-1z) teaching that the rights of each person are more important than the rights of the group; unwillingness to work with others; **individu'ality** (1-1-1-173-1-1) special character different from others.

ind'octrinate (1-5-1-21) teach; teach the particular ideas and beliefs of one group.

indolent (1-9) lazy.

ind'omitable (1-5-1-9) unyieldingly courageous.

'ind'oor(s) (1-55z) in the house, not in the open air.

ind'orse (1-55) see Endorse.

ind'ubitable (1-177-1-9) not able to be doubted; certain.

ind'uce (1-177s) to cause; lead a person to act by giving reasons or causing desire; (electricity) cause electricity to flow along an inner wire by sending electricity through a wire twisted round it, but not touching it.

ind'uct (1-8) lead into office, e.g. *A priest is inducted* = put in charge of a church; **ind'uction** (1-8-shn) way of reasoning from many known facts to one general law; (electrical) see Induce.

ind'uctive (1-8-1) adj. of Induce (2nd above), e.g. *Inductive reasoning* = using facts to prove a general rule.

ind'ulge (1-8-j) yield to and please the tastes or desires; give pleasure to; *To indulge in* = allow oneself to enjoy; *He indulges too much* = he drinks too much wine; **ind'ulgence** (1-8-j9-s) the act of satisfying one's desires; (in religion) freedom given by a priest from the punishment for wrong-doing.

indurate (1-179-21) make hard.

ind'ustrial (1-8-19) having to do with the making of goods for trade.

industry (1-9-1) (1) quality of working hard; adj. **ind'ustrious** (1-8-19); (2) making of goods in large numbers with the help of machines; adj. **ind'ustrial** (1-8-19); **an ind'ustrialist** (1-8-19-1) owner of a large mill or workshop where things are made.

'indw'elling (1-2-1) being in one's mind or spirit.

-ine, of the nature of, like a, e.g. eleph'antine (2-1-3-41).

in'ebriated (1-11-121-1) *drunk* (= having lost all reason because of taking too much wine).

in'effable (1-2-9) that which cannot be expressed or described, because it is too beautiful or too good.

ineff'ectual (1-1-2-179) unable to produce the desired result.

in'ept (1-2) silly; out of place; n. **in'eptitude** (1-2-1-177).

iner'adicable (1-1-3-1-9) deeply rooted; difficult to change.

in'ert (1-99) lifeless and soft, as when asleep; **in'ertia** (1-99shI9) state of being powerless, too lazy to move; (scientific) that force which prevents a thing from being moved when it is standing still, and keeps it moving (prevents it from being stopped) when it is moving.

in'estimable (1-2-1-9) not able to be measured or valued; of very great value.

in'evitable (1-2-1-9) which must happen, allowing no escape; *An inevitable conclusion* = judgment which must follow from the reasons given.

in'exorable (1-2-9-9) which cannot be changed or prevented, working regularly and without pity, e.g. *The inexorable laws of nature.*

inexp'erience (1-1-19-19-s) lack of experience.

in'extricable (1-2-1-9) which cannot be untied or set in order.

inf'allible (1-3-9) unable to fail or be mistaken.

infamous (1-9-9) having a very bad character; very evil; **infamy** (1-9-1) dishonour; very bad behaviour.

infant (1-9) very young child; adj. very small or young; **infancy** (1-9-sI) state or time of being very young; **infantile** (1-9-4I) as of an infant; **inf'anticide** (1-3-Is4I) killing of an infant.

infantry (1-9-1) foot-soldiers.

inf'atuate (1-3-172I) cause one to admire or love so completely as to lose judgment or reason.

inf'ect (1-2) pass on disease to another; cause to have wrong ideas; **inf'ectious** (1-2-sh9) able to be passed on from one person to another, like a disease.

inf'er (1-99) reach an idea by reasoning.

inf'erior (1-19-19) lower in value, importance, place, rank; *He has an inferiority complex* = he behaves very proudly because he believes that he is really inferior to others.

inf'ernal (1-99) having to do with *hell* (= place of punishment for evil-doers after death); *An infernal nuisance* = great trouble-maker; *An infernal machine* = one containing explosive material placed in a building to destroy it.

inf'erno (1-99-67) *hell* (see above); any very hot place, e.g. *The burning house became an inferno.*

inf'est (1-2) be in great numbers, e.g. *A bed infested with insects* = full of —.

infidel (1-1) one who does not believe in certain teachings about God.

infid'elity (1-41-2-1-1) act or state of being disloyal or unfaithful, especially to the person whom one has married.

infiltrate (1-1-2I) pass through and into, as liquids pass through sand; (of ideas) get into people's minds.

infinite (1-1-1) without *limits* (= lines marking outside edges); not able to be measured or counted; *The Infinite* = God.

infinit'esimal (1-1-1-2-1) so small that it cannot be measured.

inf'initive (1-1-1-1), e.g. *"To be"* is the infinitive of *Am.*

inf'irm (1-99) weak in body or mind; **inf'irmary** (1-99-9-1) place for sick people.

infl'ame (1-21) to set on fire; excite; make red and *swollen* (= p.p. of Swell); **inflamm'ation** (1-9-21shn) painful swollen place on the body; adj. **infl'ammatory** (1-3-9-9-1); *Inflammatory speeches* = such as excite people to fight against the government.

infl'ate (1-21) cause to swell with air or gas.

infl'ation (1-21shn) increase in the amount of money, but the money can buy less, so prices are higher.

infl'ect (1-2) raise' or lower the voice while speaking; change the form of a word to show person and number, e.g. *I do, he does*; n. **infl'exion** (1-2kshn).

infl'exible (1-2-9) that which cannot be bent; (of purpose) unchangeable.

infl'ict (1-1) cause to suffer (pain or a wrong, etc.).

inflor'escence (1-5-2s9-5) act or state of having flowers.

influence (1-79-s) have an effect on; n. an effect, cause of an effect, e.g. *He is an influence for good*; **influ'ential** (1-72-shl) having influence, important.

influ'enza (1-72-9) feverish *cold* (= liquid flowing from the nose, pain in the throat, etc., with fever).

influx (1-8) flowing in, especially in great amounts.

inf'orm (1-55) tell; *To lay information against* = tell the police about law-breakers; *Well informed* = having knowledge about many subjects.

inf'ormal (1-55); without ceremony or ceremonial dress; *An informal dinner* = not a special meal or large gathering, and the guests will not wear ceremonial dress.

infra- under, below.

infr'action (1-3-shn) act of breaking, e.g. a law or rule.

'infra d'ig (1-9 + 1) below the *dignity* (= honour, self-respect and respect of others) of; unworthy of one's high position and the respect with which others regard one.

'infra-r'ed (rays) (1-9 + 2) part of light which cannot be seen by the eye.

infr'inge (1-1nj) break a law or rule; *Infringement of copyright* = printing something written by another person without the right to do so.

inf'uriate (1-179-12I) make very angry.

inf'use (1-177z) pour into; to put into boiling water, e.g. tea leaves; **an inf'usion** (1-1773n) liquid in which a vegetable has been boiled so as to get out its special taste or medical quality.

infus'oria (1-17z55-19) very small living creatures found in water containing decayed vegetable matter.

ing'enious (1nj11-19) clever, skilful; (of a thing) cleverly planned and skilfully made.

'ingénue (3ⁿ321-177) (French) young inexperienced girl.

ingen'uity (1nj1-1771-1) cleverness and skilfulness.

ing'enuous (1nj2-179) simple and inexperienced.

'inglę-n'ook (1ngg + 7) corner near the fire in a room.

ingot (1ngg9) short thick bar of metal.

ingrained (1n·g-21) fixed deeply in the nature or character.

ingrate (1n·g-21) ungrateful person.

ingr'atiate (1n·g-21shi21) get oneself into the favour of a person.

ingred'ient (1n·g-11-19) part of a mixture.

in'gress (1n·g-2) act of entering.

inh'abit (1-3-1) live in (a country); **inh'abitant** (1-3-1) one who lives in (a city, country).

inh'ale (1-21) draw in the breath.

inh'ere (1-19) be a necessary part of; belong as a quality; adj. **inherent** (1-19).

inh'erit (1-2-1) receive money, a title, etc., as the descendant of a person at his death; receive qualities of character from the persons from whom one is descended; **an inh'eritance** (1-2-1-s) anything so received.

inh'ibit (1-1-1) prevent from doing.

inh'uman (1-177-9) not human; cruel, evil.

inim'ical (1-1-1) not friendly; unfavourable.

in'imitable (1-1-1-9) which cannot be *imitated* (= copied); very good, very unusual.

in'iquitous (1-1-1-9) very evil.

in'itial (1-1shl) first, e.g. *An initial attempt*; first letters of a person's names, e.g. the initials of *John Smith* are *J.S.*

in'itiate (1-1shl-1) begin, to set going; *Initiate a person into* = take in as a member of a group.

in'itiative (1-1shl9-1) quality or power of starting new courses of action; *He did it on his own initiative* = he did it by himself, not because he was ordered to do it; *To have the initiative* = have the power or right to make the first move; *To take the initiative* = begin, make the first move (e.g. in a battle).

inj'ect (1-2) force liquid or gas into; put medicine into the body through a hollow needle.

inj'unction (1-8ngkshn) a command; written order from a court of law saying something shall (or shall not) be done.

injure (1-9) do harm to; adj. **inj'urious** (1-79-19).

ink (1ngk) coloured liquid used for writing and printing books.

inkling (1ngk-1) slight idea or sign of.

inkwell (1ngk-2) pot for ink.

inl'aid (1-21) p.t. and p.p. of Inlay.

inl'and (1-3) adv. away from the coast; adj. **inland** (1-9).

-in-law (1-55) by marriage, e.g. *Mother-in-law* = wife's (or husband's) mother; *Brother-in-law* = wife's (or husband's) brother; *Son-in-law* = the man who has married one's daughter.

inl'ay (1-21) cut a hollow place in a surface and fill it with ornamental material such as gold, silver, bone, etc.; n. **'inlay**.

inlet (1-2) small arm of the sea; entrance.

inmate (1-21) one who lives in a place, e.g. *The inmates of a prison* = prisoners.

in mem'oriam (1 + 2-55-19) in memory of.

inn (1) house in which travellers may eat, drink and sleep.

inn'ate (1-21) born in one; natural.

inner (1-9) inside; having to do with the inside; *The inner man* = mind and soul; Sl. stomach.

innings (1-1-z) time of being in; in cricket, the time during which each player in turn has a chance of hitting the ball; one's chance of showing one's skill or power.

innocent (1-9s) knowing or doing or having done no evil.

inn'ocuous (1-5-179) causing no harm.

innovate (1-9-21) start something new.

innu'endo (1-172-67) words having a hidden bad meaning.

in'oculate (against) (1-5-17-21) put the dead or harmless *germs* (= seeds) of a disease into the body of a person so that the person may become free from the danger of the disease; **in'oculate with**, cause a person to have a disease.

in'operable (1-5-9-9) e.g. *Inoperable cancer* (*cancer* = diseased growth in the body; *inoperable* = which the doctor cannot cut away).

in'ordinate (1-55-1-1) uncontrolled, too great, e.g. *Inordinate desire*.

inorg'anic (matter) (1-55-3-1) matter which is not part of the body of any living thing.

inquest (1-2) examination to find the reason for a person's death or to decide the lawful owner of valuable things, e.g. money found hidden in the ground.

inqu'ire (1-41) ask; examine into some important matter.

inquis'ition (1-1zIshn) act of questioning, usually with the idea of punishing those who do not believe in certain teachings.

inqu'isitive (1-1zI-1) eager to know other people's business.

inroad (1-67) sudden attack made into the enemy's country; *Makes inroads on one's money* = uses large amounts of —.

ins and outs (1-z + 47) *To know all the — —* = know a matter thoroughly.

ins'ane (1-21) mad.

ins'atiable (1-21shI9) not able to be satisfied.

inscr'ibe (1-41) write in or on; **inscr'iption** (1-1-shn) that which is written in or on some-

inscrutable   171   **insuperable**

thing, e.g. the words cut on a stone in memory of a dead person.

inscr'utable (1-77-9) not able to be understood, e.g. *The — ways of Fate.*

insect (1-2) any small creature having six legs; Sl. any small creature; **ins'ecticide** (1-2-1s41) substance used for killing insects; **insect'ivora** (1-2-1-9-9) insect-eating animals.

insemin'ation (1-2-1-21) putting seeds in; *Artificial insemination* = putting male substance into (e.g.) a cow with an instrument so as to produce young.

ins'ensate (1-2-21) without common sense; without feelings of right and wrong.

ins'ensible (1-2-9) having no feelings; *Insensible to shame* = not feeling shame (when one ought); not knowing about, e.g. *Insensible of any danger*; so slight as to be unnoticed, e.g. *Moving insensibly.*

ins'ert (1-99) to put into or add to.

inset (1-2) thing set in, e.g. a small picture inside a larger one.

'insh'ore (1-55) near the shore.

ins'idious (1-1-19) doing harm secretly.

insight (1-41) power of seeing into the real meaning; knowledge gained by careful thought and study.

ins'ignia (1-1-19) signs of rank or honour.

insign'ificant (1-1-1-1) unimportant.

ins'inuate (1-1-1721) push oneself gently or secretly; say something unkind or harmful indirectly; *To make insinuations against a person* = say indirectly things which cause others to think evil of him.

ins'ipid (1-1-1) possessing no taste or interest.

ins'ist (1-1) declare with force, e.g. *He insisted on the importance of* = said that it was very important; *He insisted on having the money* = said it must be paid.

insolent (1-9-9) very rude, especially to elders or persons of higher rank.

ins'oluble (1-5-17) which cannot be melted; impossible to understand or explain.

ins'olvent (1-5) unable to pay one's debts.

ins'omnia (1-5-19) state of being unable to sleep.

ins'ouciant (3ⁿ-77s144ⁿ) careless, untroubled.

'insp'an (1-3) join the horses or cattle to a cart.

insp'ect (1-2) look carefully at, examine carefully; **insp'ectorate** (1-2-9-1) whole group or number of *inspectors* (= persons who inspect).

insp'ire (1-419) breathe in air; cause an increase of fine feelings or great thoughts in the mind; inspired, receiving thoughts from God; filled with great thoughts; *An inspired article* = something written in a newspaper containing facts or opinions obtained from a person in the government; *The poet had an* **inspir'ation** (1-9-21shn) = had a great thought for a poem.

inst. = instant; *The 2nd inst.* = 2nd of this month and year.

instab'ility (1-9-1-1-1) lacking steadiness, especially of character.

inst'all (1-55) put a person into an office; settle, e.g. in a chair, or house; to fix machines into; *To install electric light* = put — into a house.

inst'alment (1-55-9) part payment of a debt; piece of anything supplied part by part at different times, e.g. one part of a story printed part by part each week.

instance (1-9-s) example; *For instance* = as an example; *In the first instance* = at the beginning; *At the instance of Mr. X* = Mr. X asked that it should be done, or first gave the idea of doing it.

instant (1-9) very short time; adj. active, ready, not delaying, not stopping; **instant'aneous** (1-9-21-19) happening at once and without delay; **inst'anter** (1-3-9) without any delay, at once.

inst'ead (1-2) in place of.

instep (1-2) curved inner part of the middle of the foot.

instigate (1-1-21) cause an act.

inst'il (1-1) pour in slowly; *To instil knowledge* = teach.

instinct (1-1ngk) natural desire or inborn skill which causes animals to act in a certain way without teaching or experience.

institute (1-1-177) to set up, e.g. *To institute a new custom*; group of men working for some common purpose; **an institute**, group formed for some special purpose; building in which its work is carried on; **instit'ution** (1-1-177shn) something that has been set up, e.g. a custom, law; group of persons which supplies some public need, or the buildings used for this purpose, e.g. *A university is an institution of learning.*

instr'uct (1-8) teach; *I instructed him to* = ordered —.

instrument (1-7-9) thing by means of which something is done; **instrum'ental** (——2) causing something to happen; *Instrumental music* = music produced by means of instruments, not by the human voice.

insub'ordinate (1-9-55-1-1) not obeying higher officers.

insular (1-17-9) of an island; *Insular ideas* = narrow, not thinking of other nations.

insulate (1-17-21) to separate from everything around; (in electricity) cover (a wire) with material which will not allow electricity to pass away from (the wire).

insulin (1-17-1) medicine obtained from certain parts of sheep which helps the body to use the sugar which is eaten, and prevents those who have too much sugar in the blood from dying.

ins'ult (1-8) be rude to; **an 'insult.**

ins'uperable (difficulty) (1-177-9-9) difficulty with which one cannot deal, by which one is beaten.

insupp'ortable (1-9-55-9) which cannot, or should not, be suffered.

ins'urance (1-sh79-s) act or business of *insuring* (see 1st below).

ins'ure (1-sh79) pay money each year so that an agreed sum may be paid to one's family at one's death; or pay money each year so that an agreed amount may be paid if a certain accident happens.

ins'ure (1-sh79) make certain that a thing shall happen or be done.

ins'urgent (1-99j) rising up to fight against the government; n. **insurr'ection** (1-9-2-shn).

int'act (1-3) unharmed, whole and complete.

int'aglio (1-3-167) figure cut down into stone (etc.) as for pressing into soft wax, or for printing from the ink left in the cut-out pieces.

intake (1-21) a taking in, e.g. *Intake of men into the army*; *Intake pipe* = pipe through which (air, etc.) is taken.

int'angible (1-3nj9) not able to be felt by touch; so slight that it cannot be noticed.

integer (1-1j9) a whole number; **integral** (1-1) having to do with the whole; whole and complete; **integrate** (1-1-21) bring all parts together to make a whole; **int'egrity** (1-2-1-1) condition of being complete; *A man of integrity* = honest man.

intellect (1-1-2) power of mind by which we think and know; **int'elligence** (1-2-1j-s) condition of having this power; *To have intelligence of* = have news of; *Intelligence Service* = group of men whose duty is to collect news secretly about the plans of the enemy—or of law-breakers; **intellig'entsia** (1-2-1j2-19) learned people in a country.

int'end (1-2) have the purpose of.

int'ense (1-2) very great or very strong; *An intense young lady* = one who is very serious about anything; *An intense pain* = very great —; *Intensive study* = study of a subject with great care.

int'ent (1-2) *With intent to kill* = with the purpose of killing; *Intent on his work* = attending carefully to —.

int'ention (1-2-shn) purpose or plan; *He has intentions* = he desires to marry her; *The wound healed with the first intention* = did not become poisoned or have to be cut open again, but got well at once.

int'er (1-99) to put in the grave.

inter- between or among, e.g. **intern'ational** (1-9-3sh9) = between the nations.

'inter 'alia (1-9 + 21-19) among other things.

inter'act (1-9-3) have an effect upon each other.

interc'ede (1-9s11) ask for a favour for someone, e.g. that his punishment be lighter.

interc'ept (1-9s2) catch or stop on the way; prevent from going farther; stop messages passing from one place to another.

interc'ession (1-9s2shn) act of *interceding* (see 2nd above)

interch'ange (1-9-21nj) give and receive; put each in place of the other.

'interc'om (1-9-5) telephones inside an aeroplane so that officers can talk to each other.

intercourse (1-9-55) dealings with, e.g. *Social intercourse* = meeting other people at dinners, dances and other gatherings.

'interd'ict (1-9-1) prevent by order of a court, church, etc.

int'erest (1-9) **(1)** a share or right in, e.g. in a business; *To look after one's own interests* = one's own gain or chances of gain; *It is to your interest* = for your good; **(2)** eager attention, e.g. *The book aroused* (= caused) *great interest*; **(3)** thing to which one gives eager attention, e.g. *Music is one of his interests*; **(4)** money paid for the use of money, e.g. *He lent me the money at 5 per cent. interest* = and I pay £5 a year for each £100 lent; *To return a blow with interest* = give a blow harder than that which was received; **to interest**, cause a person to have interest, to gain the attention or help of.

'interf'ere (1-9-19) come between; push oneself into a matter which does not concern one; prevent a person from carrying out his plans.

'interf'use (1-9-1772) cause to flow together.

interim (1-9-1) time between two events; meant to serve for the present, e.g. *An interim report* = one given before the real long report is ready; *An interim payment* = small payment before the whole amount is settled and paid.

int'erior (1-19-19) the inside; *Minister of the Interior* = member of the government in charge of the home country.

'interj'ect (1-9-2) throw in, between; throw in a word, as when a man is speaking and someone interjects, "Good!"; **an interj'ection** (1-9-2-shn) word expressing sudden feeling, e.g. *Oh!*

'interl'ace (1-9-21s) twist together.

'interl'ard (1-9-44) mix foreign words in one's speech.

'interl'eave (1-9-11) put leaves in between, e.g. empty pages in a book on which one may write notes.

interl'inear (1-9-1-19) between the lines of print.

'interl'ock (1-9-5) lock together firmly.

interl'ocutor (1-9-5-17-9) person who takes part in the talk; *My interlocutor* = person who is talking to me and to whom I am talking.

interloper (1-9-67-9) one who forces himself in where he has no right to be.

interlude (1-9-77) a pause or rest, e.g. in a play.

interm'ediary (1-9-11-19-1) acting between two people or groups, etc.; coming or happening between.

interm'ediate (1-9-11-19) having a middle place.

int'erment (1-99-9) act of putting into the grave.

interm'ezzo (1-9-2ts67) short piece of music performed between two longer pieces.

int'erminable (1-99-1-9) unending, too long.

'interm'ingle (1-9-1ngg) mix together.

'interm'ission (1-9-1shn) *interval* (= time between acts in the theatre).

'interm'ittent (1-9-1) happening, then stopping, then beginning again . . . ; not continuous.

int'ern (1-99) keep a person as a prisoner in order to prevent him from doing harm; **an 'intern,** Am. person studying who lives in the school or place of study; a young doctor who lives in a hospital.

int'ernal (1-99) having to do with the inside of a thing; obtained from inside.

intern'ational (1-9-3shn9) having to do with different nations; **'intern'ationalism** (1-9-3shn9-1) idea that all men are brothers, that they should not be separated by differences of nation or race, and that all the nations should work together as one.

intern'ecine (war) (1-9-11s41) causing great harm to both sides.

int'erpellate (1-99-9-21) demand an *explanation* (n. of Explain) from (the government).

'interpl'ay (1-9-41) action between parts (of a machine), or between persons in a group.

int'erpolate (1-99-6-21) to put into a book parts which were not written in it at first.

'interp'ose (1-9-67z) to put between or come between.

int'erpret (1-99-1) explain the meaning of, e.g. of a foreign language; **int'erpreter** (——9) one who puts into the language of the hearer things spoken in a foreign language.

interr'egnum (1-9-2-9) time between, e.g. the death of one king and the date on which the next king begins to rule.

int'errogate (1-2-9-21) to question; **interr'ogative** (1-9-5-9-1) asking a question; **interrog'ation mark** (1-2-9-21shn + 44) = **?**; **interr'ogatory** (1-9-5-9-9-1) = questioning.

interr'upt (1-9-8) break in upon, e.g. speak to a person who is speaking; to get in the way of or cause to stop, e.g. *To interrupt the flow of electricity.*

inters'ect (1-9-2) to cut across; **inters'ection** (1-9-2-shn) act of crossing or the place of crossing.

intersp'erse (1-9-99) to set here and there among other things, e.g. *Flowers interspersed among the corn.*

'interst'ellar (1-9-2-9) between the stars.

int'erstice (1-99-1s) small space or opening between the parts of a thing.

'intertw'ine (1-9-41) twist two threads together.

'inter'urban (1-9-99) between cities.

interval (1-9) time or space between; *At intervals* = here and there, from time to time.

interv'ene (1-9-11) come in between, e.g. as a third person between two who are fighting; to come between (in time); *I will come should nothing intervene* = if nothing happens to prevent it.

interview (1-9-177) meeting for the purpose of getting a person's opinion or for doing business.

int'estate (1-2-21) dying without having made a *will* (= written paper telling what is to be done with money, lands, etc., after death).

int'estine (1-2-1) bowel.

intimate (1-1-1) inside, secret, e.g. *One's intimate thoughts*; *An intimate friend* = a very close friend; **to intimate** (1-1-21) tell in an indirect way.

int'imidate (1-1-1-21) cause to be afraid.

int'olerable (1-5-9-9) which cannot or should not be suffered.

int'olerant (1-5-9) unwilling to allow other people to think or act differently from oneself.

int'one (1-67) say in a singing voice; **inton'ation** (1-6-21shn) up and down movements of the voice in speaking.

int'oxicate (1-5-1-21) cause loss of control or great excitement, e.g. by the use of wine; **int'oxicants** (1-5-1-9) wine and other strong drinks.

intra- in, inside, within.

intr'actable (1-3-9) not easily controlled; unwilling to obey.

'intram'ural (1-9-17) within the walls; within a city, university, etc.

intr'ansigent (1-3-1j) not willing to come to an agreement.

intr'epid (1-2-1) fearless.

intricate (1-1-1) having a great many small parts, difficult to understand.

intr'igue (1-11) (1) to make a secret plan; (2) interest greatly; *An intrigue* = secret lovemaking.

intr'insic (1-1-s1) having to do with the real nature of a thing.

intro- to the inside.

introd'uce (1-9-177s) lead in, bring in, put in, e.g. *To introduce a new law*; *Introduce me to Mrs. X* = lead me up to Mrs. X and make me known to her; n. **introd'uction** (1-9-8-shn).

introsp'ect (1-67-2) look into one's own mind and feelings.

introvert (1-9-99) to turn inwards; draw into itself; *He is an introvert* = is always looking into his own mind to examine his thoughts and feelings.

intr'ude (1-77) enter without being invited or welcome; adj. **intr'usive** (1-77-1).

intu'ition (1-171shn) knowledge obtained without reasoning; the power of knowing things in this way, e.g. *A woman's intuition as to the feelings of a man.*

inundate (1-8-21) to flow over and cover with water; *Inundated with letters* = receiving a large number of ——.

in'ure, en'ure (1-179) harden and make used to, e.g. *Soldiers are inured to cold and hunger.*

invade (1-21) go into another's country as an act of war; rush into.

invalid (1-9-11) person in weak health; *An invalid chair* = special chair for the use of a sick person; *To invalid a person* = send a person away from his work because of illness.

inv'alid (1-3-1) of no force; useless, e.g. a claim, reason, agreement.

invaluable (1-3-179) of the greatest possible value.

invariable (1-29-19) not changeable.

invasion (1-213n) a rushing into and attacking.

invective (1-2-1) strongly expressed blame; cursing.

inveigh (against) (1-21) attack with words.

inveigle (1-11) use dishonest means to lead a person to do something.

invent (1-2) think out something new, e.g. a new machine or instrument, a new way of doing a task, an untrue story; **an invention** (1-2-shn) new thing or idea thought out.

inventory (1-9-9-1) list of things.

'**inverse** (1-99) opposite; **inversion** (1-99shn) state of being in the wrong or opposite order; **inv'ert,** turn *upside-down* (= bottom upwards).

invertebrate. (1-99-1-1) having no backbone; person of weak will.

invest (1-2) (1) put upon a person clothes which are a sign of rank or office; (2) *To invest a city* = set an army round it to take it; (3) lend money or put money into a business so that one may get more money by means of it; *Invest in a (car)* = buy.

investigate (1-2-1-21) inquire into and examine.

investiture (1-2-1tsh9) solemn act of giving rank or office to a person.

investment (1-2-9) act of *investing* (3rd above); money invested.

inveterate (1-2-9-1) firmly fixed by custom.

invidious (1-1-19) causing ill-feeling or dislike.

invigilate (1-1j1-21) watch over, e.g. watch persons writing an examination paper in order to prevent dishonesty.

invigorate (1-1-9-21) make a person feel strong.

invincible (1-1-s9) unconquerable.

inviolate (1-419-1) unharmed; kept holy; **inviolable** (1-419-9) that which may not or cannot be harmed.

invisible (1-1z9) which cannot be seen.

invite (1-41) (1) ask politely, e.g. *He invited her to sing*; *I invite questions* = welcome questions; *The fort is so weak that it invites attack* = seems to ask the enemy to attack it; (2) ask a guest to a meal or gathering, or to stay at one's house; n. **invitation** (1-1-21shn).

invocation (1-9-21shn) a calling upon God; prayer.

invoice (1-51s) list of goods sent and their prices.

invoke (1-67) call upon God; ask for solemnly, e.g. *He invoked the power of the law*.

involuntary (1-5-9-9-1) not under control of the will; **involuntarily** (1-5-9-9-1-1) without meaning to do it.

involve (1-5) (1) roll up in; mix up with, as a person gets *tied up* in a net, e.g. *Involved in debt*; (2) bring with it as a necessary result, e.g. *Living in a hot country always involves some loss of health*; (3) mixed up and difficult to understand, e.g. *His reasoning is very involved*.

invulnerable (1-8-9-9) not able to be wounded.

inwards (1-9-z) towards the inside; adj. **inward,** inside, e.g. *My inward thoughts; The true inwardness* = real meaning.

iodine (419-11) salt-like material from which a brown liquid is obtained, used to put on cuts and wounds.

ion (419) — An atom is a piece of matter so small that it cannot be divided except into positive (+) and negative (—) electricity. The + and — electricity in an atom is equal in strength. In an ion the + and — are not equal; so the ion is electrically + or —.

i'ota (4167-9) Greek letter ι; *Not one iota of truth* = not a bit of —.

I.O.U. (41 + 67 + 177) = I owe you—a promise to pay money.

ipecacu'anha (1-1-3-1744-9) medicine which causes one to throw up all that is in the stomach.

'**ipso f'acto** (1-67 + 3-67) by that fact itself.

irascible (1-3-1) easily made angry.

irate (41-21) angry.

ire (419) anger.

iridescence (1-1-2s-s) having a surface which breaks up light and shows many changing colours.

iridium (41-1-19) white, very hard metal.

iris (41-1) beautiful flower; coloured part of the eye; **iritis** (41-41-1) disease of the eye.

irk (99) make tired; cause trouble to; *An irksome task* = tiring and uninteresting piece of work.

iron (419) very common hard metal; *Strike while the iron is hot* = act while conditions are favourable; *To rule with a rod of iron* = control very firmly; *A man of iron* = hard unyielding man; *To have too many irons in the fire* = be trying to do too many things at once; *To put a man in irons* = fasten the arms and legs with iron bands; **an iron,** instrument, especially one for making clothes smooth and flat; **to iron,** make clothes smooth by means of a hot iron.

'**Iron C'urtain** (419 + 99-1) the closely-guarded line between the countries controlled by Russia and the others through which no news is allowed to pass.

iron lung (419 + 8) — A sick person is put inside the iron lung. Air is pushed in and out of it so that it causes him to take air in and out of his body as in breathing

ironmonger (4I9-8ngg9) one who sells metal goods.

irony (4I-9-I) use of words which are opposite to one's meaning, usually with an amusing purpose, e.g. *This is lovely weather*—when one means that it is bad weather; course of events which has the opposite result from what is expected, appearing to be directed by a spirit of evil, e.g. *The irony of fate*; adj. **ir'onical** (4I-5-I).

irr- (= in + r) not, e.g. *Ir-regular* = in-regular = not regular.

irr'adiate (I-2I-I2I) shine light on to; make bright.

irr'efragable (I-2-9-9) not able to be proved untrue.

irr'elevant (I-2-I-9) having nothing to do with the subject.

irr'eparable (I-2-9-9) not able to be repaired.

irrepr'oachable (I-I-67-9) without fault of any kind, especially in behaviour.

irr'esolute (I-2z9-77) not decided and so unable to act; weak in character.

irresp'ective (of) (I-I-2-I) in spite of, without thinking of or troubling about.

irresp'onsible (I-I-5-9) not caring about the results of one's acts; not to be trusted to do work carefully.

irr'evocable (I-2-9-9) not able to be changed, e.g. *An irrevocable decision* (= act of deciding).

irrigate (I-I-2I) bring water to dry land by canals; pour water on to.

irritate (I-I-2I) excite; cause pain or discomfort in a part of the body, e.g. by rubbing or by a strong medicine; (of the mind) make angry; **irritable** (I-I-9) easily excited or made angry.

irr'uption (I-8-shn) sudden bursting in.

isinglass (4IzIngg-44) sticky liquid used for keeping eggs from going bad and to make beer clear.

island (4I-9) piece of land with water all round it; raised place of safety in the middle of a wide street; **isle** (4I) island (in poetry); **islet** (4I-I) small island.

iso- equal in value, e.g. **isobar** (4I-67-44) line on the map showing places on the earth that have the same heaviness of the air (and so, probably the same weather) at any particular time.

isolate (4I-9-2I) to put apart or alone; separate from others of the same kind.

'isol'ationist (4I-9-2Ish9-I) a person in U.S. who believes that his country should keep out of the affairs (wars, etc.) of other countries.

is'osceles (4I-5-I-IIz) *triangle* (= 3-sided figure) having two sides equal.

isotope (4I-6-67) — All matter is made up of (about) 90 *elements* (= substances which cannot be broken up into simpler substances). Some elements have two forms, one form having *atoms* (see under Ion, above) which are heavier than the atoms of the other. These two forms are isotopes.

issue (I-I77) come out; send out; *Issue with* (boots) = supply (boots) to, e.g. a soldier in the army; *These boots are an army issue*; **an issue** (1) flowing or sending out; *The next issue of a newspaper* = next printing and selling of —; (2) a result; *To bring to a successful issue* = to a successful finish; *The matters at issue* = which are not decided yet; *To face the issue* = see clearly what the facts are and what must be done about them; *To abide the issue* = wait for the result; *He died without issue* = children; *To join issue with* = disagree, quarrel.

isthmus (I-9) narrow neck of land joining two large bodies of land.

it'alics (I-3-I) sloping kind of *printing*.

itch (I) feeling on the skin which gives one a desire to *scratch* (= rub with the fingernails).

item (4I-2) one separate thing written in a list; one part of a whole; a piece of news.

iterate (I-9-2I) say again and again.

it'inerant (4I-I-9) travelling round from place to place; **it'inerary** (4I-I-9-9-I) course followed or to be followed on a journey.

ivory (4I-9-I) valuable white bone obtained from the long teeth of an elephant.

ivy (4I-I) plant with large green leaves which grows on walls and sides of buildings; its leaves do not change in winter.

-ize (4I) bring into a certain state, e.g. *Equalize*.

J

jab (3) push roughly with the finger or *fist* (= closed hand) or a stick, etc.

jabber (3-9) talk quickly and in a way that is difficult to understand.

j'abot̯ (33-67) loose ornamental piece of material on the front of a lady's dress, or formerly on a man's shirt.

jack (3) (1) one of a set of playing-cards (for picture, see Knave); (2) machine for raising heavy weights; (3) flag; *Every man jack* = every one; *Jack Ketch* = name for the man who hangs law-breakers; *Before you could say Jack Robinson* = in a moment; *Jack-of-all-trades* = man skilled in all kinds of work; *Jack-in-office* = officer of low rank who thinks himself very important; *Jack Tar* = seaman.

jackass (3-3) (1) male ass; (2) fool; (3) Australian bird.

jackal (3-55) wild animal like a dog. It was believed that the jackal finds food for the lion, for this reason a man who acts as the servant of another and gets business for him (e.g. for a lawyer) is called a jackal.

jackanapes (3-9-21) troublesome child; rude person.

jackboot (3-77) large high boot.

jackdaw (3-55) noisy bird which steals small bright objects.

jacket (3-1) (1) short coat; *Dust a person's jacket* = give a beating to —; (2) any covering, e.g. of a hot-water pipe.

j'ack-in-office (3 + 1 + 5-1s), **j'ack-of-'all-trades** (3 + 9v + 55 + 21-2) see Jack.

j'ack-in-the-box (3 + 1 + ð9 + 5) box from which an amusing wooden figure jumps when the top is opened.

j'ack-knife (3 + 4I) large knife with a blade which folds over into the handle.

jackpot (3-5) the biggest prize in a game (e.g. card-game) played for money.

Jacob'ean (3-9-11*9) of the time of James I of England, 1566-1625; **Jacobite** (3-9-41) a person who wished to make a descendant of James II King of England.

jade (21) old, worn-out horse; **jaded** (21-1) tired and ill.

jade (21) (1) bad woman; (2) playful word used in speaking about a woman.

jade (21) precious green stone.

jagged (3-1) rough, having sharp points, e.g. *A jagged tooth.*

jaggery (3-9-1) dark brown sugar.

jaguar (3-1744) large wild cat found in South America.

JAGUAR

jail (gaol) (21) prison.

jam (3) press into a small space; become fixed, e.g. *The door is jammed and will not open*; *Radio jamming* = stopping radio from being heard by sending out other radio waves; Sl. *In a jam* = in a difficulty and not knowing how to get out of it.

jam (3) fruit boiled in sugar.

jamb (3) side post of a door or window.

j'ambor'ee (3-9-11) joyful gathering, e.g. of Boy Scouts.

jangle (3ngg) make an unpleasant sound as of many bells ringing at once.

janitor (3-1-9) door-keeper, or man who takes care of a building.

jap'an (9-3) hard paint; **to jap'an,** cover with japan.

jape (2I) amusing saying.

jar (44) bottle with a short neck and large opening.

jar (44) (1) unpleasant sound; (2) shock or shaking caused when two things run into each other or are struck together; **to jar** (1) make an unpleasant sound; (2) cause shock or shaking; (3) be very unpleasing to; *The news gave me a nasty jar* = shock; *He jars on me* = he displeases me, makes me angry.

jargon (44) language which cannot be understood.

jasmih(e) (3-1) **jessamin(e)** (2-9-1) sweet-smelling bush.

jasper (3-9) precious stone, red, yellow, or brown.

jaundice (55-1s) yellowness of the skin caused by illness; *A jaundiced* (55-1st) *outlook* = *distrustful* (= not trusting) way of looking at things.

JASMINE

jaunt (55) short journey taken for pleasure; **jaunting-car** (55-1 + 44) carriage with two wheels used in Ireland.

jaunty (55-1) feeling self-satisfied and pleased with life.

javelin (3-1) light spear for throwing.

jaw (55) one of the bones in which the teeth are set; Sl. *Hold your jaw* = be silent; Sl. **to jaw** = talk, scold; **a jaw-breaker** (55 + 21-1) word which is difficult to say.

jay (2I) noisy bright-coloured bird.

jaywalker (21-55-9) person who crosses the street in a careless and dangerous way.

jazz (3) (1) sort of music to which people dance; (2) unusual mixture of bright colours.

jealous (2-9) (1) guarding carefully, e.g. *Jealous of one's good name*; (2) wanting something which another possesses; fearing that another will take what one has, and therefore hating him.

jeep (11) a car as shown used for very rough work and across rough country.

jeer (at) (19) laugh rudely at; **jeers** (19z) rude words and laughter.

Jehu (11-177) fast, dangerous driver (named in the Bible).

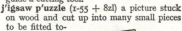
JEEP

jej'une (11-77) poor, uninteresting, unsatisfying.

jell (2) jelly. When a liquid becomes a jelly (see below), it "jells". Sl. A plan or story which cannot be made just right "will not jell".

jelly (2-1) soft clear material made by boiling bones; such material given a sweet taste (e.g. of fruit) and served for food; any material, neither liquid nor solid but between the two states.

jelly-fish (+ 1) sea-creature with a body like jelly.

jemmy (2-1) bar used by a thief for breaking open doors, etc.

jenny (2-1) machine which twists several threads of cotton or wool at one time.

jeopardy (2-9-1) danger.

jerem'iad (2-1-419) long complaint.

jerk (99) sudden movement; **to jerk**, pull suddenly.

jerkin (99-1) tight coat, usually of leather.

jerry built (2-1 + 1) badly built.

jersey (99z1) tight *knitted* (see Knit) covering for the body made of wool, often worn by seamen.

jest (2) something said to produce a laugh; *A standing jest* = thing at which people always laugh; **jester** (2-9) paid fool in a king's court.

Jesuit (zz171) member of the religious *Society* (= company) of Jesus (started in 1534). The Jesuits are a company of men working in all parts of the world who serve God and try to do good.

jet (2) hard black material used for ornament on dresses; **j'et-bl'ack** (+ 3) quite black.

jet (2) stream of liquid coming out of a small hole; small hole from which liquid comes out with force; **j'et-'engine** (+ 2-j1) **j'et prop'ulsion** (+ 9-8-shn) causing an aeroplane to go forward by drawing in air in front, mixing it with oil and sending out hot burning gases at the back.

jetsam (2) goods thrown out to make a ship lighter.

jettison (2-1) throw goods out of a ship to make it lighter.

jetty (2-1) place where one gets on to a ship, or gets down on to land from a ship.

Jew (77) member of the people whose history is told in the first part of the Bible.

jewel (779) precious stone; ornament made with precious stones; any very precious thing; **jeweller** (——9) one who sells jewels; **jewelry**, **jewellery** (——1) things made of precious metals and stones.

jib (1) (1) small sail; (2) the long bar which stands out at an angle from a *crane* (= machine used to lift heavy things, e.g. into or out of a ship); (3) to stop and refuse to go on.

jibe, gibe (j41) laugh disrespectfully at a person.

jiffy (1-1) Sl. short time.

jig (1) quick dance, music for it; **to jig**, dance up and down quickly.

jig (1) instrument used to guide a cutting tool.

JIB

j'igsaw p'uzzle (1-55 + 8zl) a picture stuck on wood and cut up into many small pieces to be fitted together as a game.

jilt (1) send away a lover after pretending to love him (her); one who does this.

jingle (1ngg). sound like that of small bells; make such a sound; words which bring in the same sound again and again, e.g. in a simple poem.

JIGSAW PUZZLE

jingo (1ngg67) person who cries out for war; *By jingo!* cry expressing surprise or pleasure, etc.; **jingoism** (1ngg67·1z) eagerness for war.

jinks (1ngk) *High jinks* = noisy merry-making.

jitterbug (1-9-8) Sl. to dance with wild rough ugly movements; a person who does this.

jitters (1-9) feeling of excitement and fear.

jiu-j'itsu (177 + 1-77) see Ju-jutsu.

jive (41) a noisy sort of music; to dance to such music.

job (5) (1) piece of work; (2) employment; (3) dishonest piece of work; *That's a good job* = is fortunate; **to job**, to work irregularly, e.g. *A jobbing gardener*; hire out horses or carriages, e.g. *A job-master* = one who lets out horses, etc., on hire; buy and sell goods; **jobbery** (5-9-1) dishonest use of one's power as an officer of government.

jockey (5-1) one who rides horses in horse races.

jockey (5-1) do something dishonestly, e.g. *To jockey a person into doing something* = force him to do it by some trick.

joc'ose (9-67) **jocular** (5-17-9) merry and trying to make people laugh.

jocund (5-9) merry.

jog (5) (1) push a person suddenly so as to get attention; *To jog a person's memory* = try to make him remember; (2) go at a slow steady run.

jog-trot (5 + ·5) slow steady run.

John Bull (5 + 7) any Englishman; the English nation; English character.

join (51) to put together, fix together; **a joiner** (——9) wood-worker; **joinery** (——1) wood-work; **a joint**, place of joining, arrangement by which things are joined; bone with the meat on it; **joint**, adj., shared by two or more people, e.g. *Our joint opinion; To take joint action*.

jointure (51-tsh9) money (etc.) given to be used by a wife during her life after her husband's death.

joists (51) beams on which the floor is fixed.

joke (67) thing said or done to make people laugh; **to joke**, say amusing things; *It's no joke* = it is a serious matter; *A practical joke* = trick played upon one person to give amusement to others; **joker** (67-9) *The joker* = a playing-card which may have any value.

jolly (5-1) happy, merry; *A jolly good fellow* = very nice —; *To jolly a person along (up)* = treat a person very nicely so as to get him to do what one wishes; n. **j'ollific'ation** (5-1-1-21shn) merry-making.

jolly-boat (5-1 + 67) small boat carried on a ship.

jolt (67) sudden movement throwing one up from one's seat in a car or carriage; unpleasant surprise.

Jonah (67-9) person supposed to bring bad fortune.

josh (5) Sl. to play tricks on a person and laugh at him.

joss (5) figure of a Chinese god; **joss-house** (+ 47) building containing such a figure.

jostle (5) to knock or push against.

jot (down) (5) write a short note.

jot (5) *Not a jot* = none at all.

journal (99) (1) report written every day; a daily newspaper; (2) that part of a turning bar in a machine which rests upon a support; **journal'ese** (99-9-11z) kind of writing found in newspapers; **journalism** (99-9-1z) writing and preparing journals, story papers, etc.; **a journalist** (99-9-1) person who works at journalism.

journey (99-1) a travelling to; distance travelled.

journeyman (99-1-9) hired worker paid by the day; a skilled worker.

joust (47) fight with spears between knights; **to joust.**

Jove (67) Roman god; *By jove!* = cry of surprise, pleasure, etc.

jovial (67-19) merry.

jowl (47) lower part of the face; *jaw* (= that part of the face which is moved when eating); *Cheek by jowl* = very close together.

joy (51) gladness.

jubilate (77-1-21) rejoice; **jubilant** (——9) rejoicing.

jubilee (77-1-11) fiftieth year after an event; rejoicing for this reason; *Silver jubilee* = 25th year; *Diamond jubilee* = 60th year.

Judas (77-9) disloyal person.

judge (8j) one who decides questions and tries prisoners in a court of law; person chosen to decide any question; **to judge**, to give an opinion on; **a judgment** (——9) *decision* (n. of *Decide*) of a court of law; power of judging; *It's a judgment on him* = God has punished him.

judicature (77-1-9tsh9) all the judges and law-officers of a country; their work.

jud'icial (77-1shl) having to do with a judge; able to decide wisely.

jud'iciary (77-1sh19-1) having to do with a court of law; **The jud'iciary**, all the judges.

jud'icious (77-1sh9) wise, having good judgment.

judo (77-67) another name for Ju-jutsu.

jug (8) pot for liquids, with a handle; **to jug**, boil meat in a closed pot.

Juggernaut (8-9-55) Indian god under the wheels of whose car people used to throw themselves; any great force which destroys all in its path.

juggle (8) do clever tricks with the hands for amusement; *To juggle out of* = take away by a trick; *To juggle with facts* = choose facts to show what is not really true.

jugular vein (7-17-9 + 21) great blood-pipe in the neck leading blood back to the heart.

juice (77s) liquid part of a plant, or of food; Sl. electricity, motor-spirit.

ju-ju (77 + 77) magic charm in West Africa.

jujube (77-77) jelly-like sweet.

ju-j'utsu (77-77-77) Japanese way of fighting with the hands and feet.

juke box (77 + 5) machine which plays music when money is put into it.

julep (77-2) sweet medicinal drink.

jumble (8) mix in disorder; disorderly mixture; *A jumble sale* = selling cheap of various used things to help some good work with the money so obtained.

jump (8) to spring up off the ground; move suddenly; *Jump at the chance* = accept gladly; *You made me jump* = gave me a shock; *Jump a claim* = seize land claimed by another; Sl. *Jump upon* = blame, scold; *A jump in prices* = sudden increase.

jumper (8-9) loose short coat put on over the head.

jumpy (8-1) in an excited and easily frightened state of mind.

junction (8ngkshn) a joining; place of joining; railway station where two or more lines join.

juncture (8ngktsh9) *At this juncture* = just at the moment when things were in this state.

jungle (8ngg) land covered with wild bushes, plants and trees; **jungly** (——1) as of the jungle, untrained.

junior (77-19) younger.

juniper (77-1-9) bush whose oil is used for its pleasant smell.

junk (8ngk) old rope; salt meat; old things of little value.

junk (8ngk) a Chinese sailing-ship.
junket (8ngkɪ) milk made solid, with sugar added; **to junket,** to feast.
jur'idical (79-1-1) having to do with the law.
jurisd'iction (79-ɪz-ɪ-shn) (1) giving of law; (2) land or country over which a law-court, judge, or officer has power.
j'urispr'udence (79-ɪ-77-s) art and science of law-giving.
jurist (79-ɪ) one skilled in the law.
juror (79-9) member of a *jury* (see below).
jury (79-ɪ) twelve persons chosen to decide questions of fact in a law-court, having solemnly promised to give an honest opinion.
jury-mast (+ 44) *mast* (= upright pole which carries sails) put up in a ship in place of a broken one.

JUNK

just (8) fair, right, true.
just (8) exactly; *Just now* = a very short time ago; *He just succeeded* = nearly failed; *Just perfect* = quite perfect.
justice (8-ɪs) (1) fairness, justness; (2) action of the law; (3) a judge, e.g. *Justice of the Peace*; *To bring a person to justice* = cause to be punished.
justify (8-1-4ɪ) show to be right, true, blameless; **justifiable** (———9) able to be proved just; **justific'ation** (8-1-1-2ɪshn) action of justifying; that which justifies.
jut (out) (8) to stand out from the main mass.
jute (77) plant whose skin is used for making rope and rough cloth.
juvenile (77-1-4ɪ) young.
juxtapose (8-9-67z) to set side by side.

K

Kaffir (3-9) member of the native Bantu race of South Africa (Bantu peoples call themselves by their own names, e.g. Xhosa, Zulu, etc., not Kaffir).

Kaiser (41z9) *emperor* (= one who rules an empire).

kale, kail (21) vegetable whose leaves are boiled and eaten for food.

kal'eidoscopic (9-41-9-5-1) quickly changing.

k'anaka (3-4-4) native of the South Sea Islands.

k'angar'oo (3ngg9-77) Australian animal which jumps along on its large back legs.

KANGAROO

kaolin (219-1) fine white earth used for making cups, plates, etc.

kapok (21-5) kind of cotton used for filling *cushions* (= bags of soft material put under the head or body when resting).

kar(r)'oo (9-77) high land in South Africa which has no water for a great part of the year.

kat'abolism (3-3-9-1z) the destroying or breaking down of matter in the body, as a result of work.

kay'ak (41-3) small boat as shown.

KAYAK

kedgeree (2j9-11) Indian dish of *rice* (= white food-grain), fish, etc.

keel (11) the long bar along the bottom of a boat or ship from which the whole frame of the ship is built up; *To keel over* = turn over on one side.

keen (11) (1) having a sharp edge; (of sound or light) strong; *A keen wind* = very cold; (of the senses) good, e.g. *Keen sight; Keen hearing; A keen sense of smell*; (2) eager, quick of understanding; *Keen on* = much interested in, in love with.

keen (11) to weep over the dead in Ireland.

keep (11) (1) hold, continue to possess; *To keep track of a person* = know what he is doing; (2) protect, e.g. *God keep you*; (3) have charge of, e.g. *To keep a shop* = own and make money by —; *To keep cows* = own and take care of —; (4) support or pay for, e.g. *To keep a family; To keep a horse; He keeps open house* = has many guests; (5) to stay; *To keep good health* = be in good health; *Keep cool* = do not get excited; *To keep at it* = go on working at it; *Keep down, Keep under* = hold under one's power; *Keep in (a boy)* = make him stay and work after school hours; *Keep him from going* = prevent; *Keep one's feet* = not fall; *Keep oneself to oneself* = not make friends; *Keep up* = support; *Keep it up* = continue; *Keep up appearances* = try not to seem poor; *Keep the law* = not break.

keep (11) great tower of a castle.

keeper (11-9) guard, person in charge of.

keepsake (11-21) thing kept as a memory of a person.

keg (2) small barrel.

kelp (2) kind of plant which grows in the sea.

ken (2) *Beyond my ken* = beyond my knowledge.

kennel (2) small wooden hut for a dog; place in which dogs are kept.

kept (2) p.t. of Keep.

kerb (99) **kerbstone** (99-67) line of raised stones separating the footpath (for walkers) from the road.

kerchief (99-1) cloth covering for the head as worn in ancient times.

kernel (99) soft centre part of a nut.

kerosene (2-9-11) lamp-oil obtained from under the earth.

kersey (99z1) rough narrow cloth made of wool.

KERCHIEF

kestrel (2) red-brown bird which feeds on mice, insects and small birds.

ketch (2) small sailing-ship.

ketchup (2-9) sour liquid used to give a pleasant taste to meat.

kettle (2) pot with a handle and a pipe from which liquid is poured, used for boiling water; *This is a pretty kettle of fish* = I am in great difficulty, things look bad.

kettledrum (2-8) drum with a round curved-up bottom.

key (11) (1) instrument used to open a lock; (2) set of notes having a certain *keynote* (= starting note); (3) **keyboard** (11-55) part of a *piano* or *organ* (= musical instruments) struck by the fingers; (4) **keynote** (11-67) chief sound of a musical key; the chief idea of a speech or book; **keystone** (11-67) middle stone in the top of an arch; **to key** (up) = raise the note of a musical instrument by tightening the strings: *Keyed up* = excited.

khaki (44-1) yellow-brown cloth worn by soldiers.

Khan (44) (1) title of ruler in Asia; (2) an inn in the East.

kick (1) strike with the foot; *The gun kicked* = came back at the moment of firing the shot; *Has no kick left in him* = is beaten and has no more power of fighting; Sl. *Kick the bucket* = die; Sl. *Kick up a dust* = make trouble; *Kick up one's heels* = have a good time, enjoy oneself; *Kicked out of a job* = sent away from employment.

kickshaws (1-55z) fancy dishes at a meal.

kid (1) young goat; leather of goat-skin; (in common speech) child; Sl. **to kid**, deceive a person in order to laugh at him afterwards; adj. **kid-glove** (manner) (+ 8) not wishing to dirty the hands with hard work; *One cannot fight a war in kid gloves* = without hard fighting.

kidnap (1-3) take away (e.g. a child) so as to ask money for returning him (her).

kidney(s) (1-1z) two *organs* (= parts) of the body which take poisons out of the blood and pass them out of the body in the water; *A man of that kidney* = of that kind.

kill (1) cause the death of; destroy; *A kill-joy* = one who ruins the pleasure of a party of friends; *Kill-time* = way of making time pass easily; **the kill**, the animal killed, e.g. in hunting; Sl. *Killing* = very amusing.

kiln (1) large closed fireplace, e.g. in which bricks are made.

kilo- one thousand, e.g. **kilometre** (1-9-11-9) 1,000 metres = about ⁸⁄₁₀ths of a mile.

kilocycle (1-9s41) 1,000 flows of electricity backwards and forwards along a wire or in radio.

KILT

kilt (1) short skirt worn by Scotsmen.

kim'ono (1-67-67) long coat as worn in Japan.

-kin (1) e.g. *Lambkin* = small lamb.

kin (1) members of one's family, relations by blood; adj. being of the same family; related; like.

kind (41) sort, class; *After their kind* = according to their character or nature; *Payment in kind* = in goods, not money; *Repay his rudeness in kind* = be as rude to him as he has been to me.

KIMONO

kind (41) gentle, good, loving.

kindergarten (1-9-44) school for very young children.

kindle (a fire) (1) to light —; **kindling** (1-1) dry wood used for lighting a fire.

kindly (41-1) pleasant, gentle.

kindred (1-1) state of being of the same family; sameness.

kinema (1-1-9) see Cinema.

king (1) male ruler of a country; *King's evil* = a disease (Scrofula) causing swellings, usually in the neck.

kingdom (1-9) country ruled by a king.

kingfisher (1-1-9) small brightly-coloured bird which catches fish.

kingpin (1-1) pin which holds the wheel of a car in place; most important person or thing on whom everything depends.

kink (1ngk) backward turn or twist in a rope or chain; peculiarity of the mind.

kinsfolk (1-z-67) members of one's family, relations; **kinship** (1-1) relationship; likeness.

kiosk (115) small open hut, e.g. one used for selling newspapers.

kipper (1-9) dried fish salted, from which the inside organs have been taken out.

kirk (99) church (Scottish word).

kismet (1-2) fate.

kiss (1) touch with the lips as a greeting or sign of love; *Kiss the dust* = yield completely.

kit (1) clothes, etc., which a soldier carries in his bag; all one's clothes, etc., as taken on a journey.

kitchen (1-1) room used for cooking; **k'itchen- g'arden** (+ 44) garden where vegetables are grown for food; **kitchener** (1-1-9) large iron fire-place used for cooking.

kite (41) bird which catches and eats other birds, etc.

kite (41) light frame covered with paper which is made to fly up in the air by children.

kith (1) *Kith and kin* = friends and members of one's family.

kitten (1) young cat.

kittle cattle (1 + 3) people who are troublesome and difficult to deal with.

kitty (1-1) childish name for a cat; all the money to be gained at one time in a game of chance.

kiwi (11-11) wingless bird.

KIWI

kl'eptom'ania (2-67-21-19) mad desire to steal things; **kl'eptom'aniac** (——13) one who has a —.

knack (3) special skill in some one kind of work.

knapsack (3-3) bag carried on the back by a traveller or soldier.

knave (21) tricky dishonest fellow; playing-card as shown; **knavery** (21-9-1) dishonesty; **knavish** (21-1) as of a knave.

knead (11) press and mix flour, water, etc., with the hands so as to make bread.

knee (11) middle joint of the leg, where the leg bends; *On the knees of the gods* = uncertain.

KNAVE

kneel (11) go down on the knees.

knell (2) sound of a bell at death.

knelt (2) p.t. of Kneel.

knickerbockers (1-9-5-9z) loose garment covering the body from the waist down to just below the knees; **knickers** (1-9z) same, especially as women's underclothing or a child's outer garment.

knick-knack (1 + 3) any small object used as an ornament for the house or dress.

knife (41) blade fixed in a handle used for cutting; *War to the knife* = without mercy; *Before you can say knife* = very suddenly; *Knife-grinder* = one who sharpens knives.

knight (41) soldier of noble rank; man of rank allowed to set "Sir" before his name.

knit (1) join together a thread of wool or cotton in a close network so as to form a garment, e.g. for the hands or feet; join closely, e.g. *He knit his fingers together*; *Knit one's brows* = draw down the *eyebrows* (= curved lines of hair above the eyes) so as to express deep thought, or anger.

knives (41-z) pl. of Knife.

knob (5) round mass used as a handle, e.g. on the end of a stick, as handle of a door, etc.

knock (5) strike with a hard blow; strike the door as a sign of desire to enter; *Knock on the head* = kill or make senseless with a blow; Sl. *Knock a. person's head off* = win easily against; *Knock a person about* = strike a person many times; *Knock about* = lead a rough and wandering life; *Knock against* = meet without expecting to do so; *Knock down* = strike and cause to fall; *Knock a thing down to* = sell for the highest offer; *Knock off work* = stop work; *Knock off a (picture)* = finish hurriedly; *Knock out* = strike so as to make senseless; *Knock together* = make quickly; *The engine is knocking* = is making a noise which shows that its work is too hard, or the petrol is not good; *Knock-kneed* = having the legs bent inwards; **knocker** (5-9) a metal instrument used by visitors for knocking at a door.

knoll (67) small round hill.

knot (5) (**1**) join two pieces of string together; a knot, joining of string or rope; (**2**) hard mass in wood where a branch has come out of the main stem of a tree; *A knotty question* = difficult question.

knot (5) measure of speed—of a ship, about 6,080 feet in one hour.

knout (47) long piece of leather tied to a stick and used for beating persons.

know (67) have facts in the mind; understand; remember; recognize; experience, e.g. *To know fear*; *He knows what's what* = understands things and is not easily deceived; *To my knowledge, been there* = so far as I know.

knowing (67-1) clever, having common sense; **knowledge** (5-1j) things known; *He had not, to my knowledge, been there* = so far as I know.

knuckle (8) bone where a finger joins on to the hand; *To knuckle down to* = yield to; **kn'uckle-duster** (+ 8-9) instrument made of metal fixed to the back of the hand so that a blow may do more damage.

kodak (67) trade name of an instrument used for taking photographs on a roll of thin glass-like material called *celluloid*.

kohl (67) powder used in the East to darken the skin above the eyes.

kohlrabi (67-44-1) vegetable used for food.

kopje (5-1) in South Africa, a small hill.

Kor'an (5-44 or 55-3) *sacred* (= holy) book of the Muslims.

kosher (5-9) food, especially meat, which it is lawful for the Jews to eat.

KOHL-RABI

kowtow, kotow (47-47) in China, touch the ground with the head as a sign of respect.

kraal (44) native village in South Africa with a fence round it.

Kremlin, the (2-1) buildings in Moscow which are the centre of the Russian government.

kris (11) Malayan knife with a *wavy* (wave + y) blade.

Kt. = **knight** (41).

kudos (177-5) praise, honour.

kukri (7-1) heavy curved knife used by the Gurkhas, a people of Nepal.

kursaal (99-44) building in which music, plays, and other amusements are provided for visitors, e.g. at a seaside place.

L

L, Roman numeral meaning 50.

£, pound (100 pence).

laager (44-9) camp, e.g. one made inside a circle of carts.

label (21) piece of paper fixed to a thing, e.g. to a book showing its number, to a box showing the address to which it is to be sent; **to label**, put things in classes, fix labels on.

labial (21-19) of the lips.

lab'oratory (9-5-9-9-1) place in which scientists work.

lab'orious (9-55-19) working hard.

labour (21-9) **(1)** work; *A labour of love* = work done because one likes doing it, not for pay; *Hard labour* = work given to prisoners as part of their punishment; **(2)** group of persons who work with their hands; the workers—not the owners of a business; party in the government which tries especially to help the common working-man; **(3)** pains of a woman in giving birth to a child; **to labour**, work; have difficulty in doing something; *A very laboured poem* = one which shows signs of hard work, which does not flow easily; *To labour under a delusion* = have a wrong idea; *To labour the point* = explain a matter with unnecessary care.

lab'urnum (9-99-9) tree with yellow flowers.

labyrinth (3-1-1) number of paths or *passages* (= path with walls on each side) through which it is difficult to find one's way.

lac (3) liquid made by very small creatures in India, used, when hard, for ornamenting wood and for making paint.

LABURNUM

lace (21s) **(1)** string used to draw the edges of a thing together, e.g. *a shoe-lace*; **to lace up**, tie together with a lace; **(2)** sort of network of cotton or silk used as an ornament for dresses; **to lace**, draw together with a string; *Red laced with blue* = having lines of blue in it; *Tea laced with brandy* = mixed with *brandy* (= a strong drink).

lacerate (3s9-21) to wound.

lachrymal (3k-1) of tears; *Lachrymal gland* = part of the eye from which tears come; **lachrymose** (3k-1-67) tearful, easily made to weep.

lack (3) want of, absence of; **to lack**, be without; *Money was lacking* = there was no —;
l'ack-l'ustre (+ 8-9) having no brightness.

lackad'aisical (3-9-21zr) behaving in a weak, lazy and unnatural way.

lackey (3-1) manservant; person who behaves like a servant.

lac'onic (9-5-1) expressed in few words.

lacquer (3k9) hard paint.

lacr'osse (9-5) game in which the ball is caught and carried in a net fixed to an L-shaped handle.

lact'ation (3-21shn) producing of milk in the breast; **lacteal** (3-19) **lactic** (3-1) having to do with milk.

lad (3) **laddie** (3-1) boy.

ladder (3-9) two long bars (or ropes) with short bars across as steps, used for climbing up; *Ladder in a stocking* = long line in a lady's *stocking* (= silk or cotton leg-covering) where the downward thread has broken and come untwisted from the cross-threads.

lade (21) (p.p. **laden**) to load; *A bill of lading* = list showing the goods put on a ship.

la-di-da (44 + 1 + 44) Sl. (person) one who behaves in a proud, foolish and unnatural way.

ladle (21) spoon with a long handle used for liquids.

lady (21-1) woman of good class; **Lady —**, title of a woman of rank, e.g. wife of a knight; **Our Lady**, the Blessed Mary (= mother of Christ).

ladybird (21-1-99) small red or yellow insect with black spots.

L'ady-d'ay (21-1 + 21) March 25th.

ladykiller (21-1-1-9) one who thinks himself very pleasing to the ladies.

ladyship (21-1-1) *Her Ladyship* = "she," in speaking of a lady of high rank.

lag (3) *An old lag* = one who has been often in prison.

lag behind (3 + 1-41) be slow and fall behind.

lager (44-9) light *beer* (= bitter strong drink made from grain).

laggard (3-9) one who is slow in action.

lag'oon (9-77) salt-water lake cut off from the sea.

laid (21) p.t. of Lay.

lain (21) p.p. of Lie.

lair (29) home of a wild animal; *Go to my lair* = to my home, to my own room.

laird (29) a Scottish land-owner.

l'aissez-f'aire (21-21 + 29) *A policy of laissez-faire* = idea of certain persons in the government that one should not make too many laws but allow things to go on in their own way.

laity (21-1-1) general public other than the members of a *profession* (e.g. doctors, lawyers, priests, etc.).

lake (21) large sheet of water with land all round it.

lake (crimson lake) (1-z + 21) red paint.

lakh (3) 100,000 *rupees* (= Indian coin value about ⅟₁₃th of £1).

lama (44-9) priest in Tibet.

lamb (3) young of a sheep; *lovable* (= such as is loved, worthy of love) and helpless creature; *As well be hanged for a sheep as a lamb* = if you do wrong, do the whole of the wrong act, for you will get no less punishment for the smaller wrong.

l'ambent fl'ame (3-9 + 21) burning gently.

lame (21) having a bad leg and not able to walk properly; *A lame duck* = person who is lame; *A lame excuse* = weak reason for not doing something.

lam'ent (9-2) show great grief; **lamentable** (3-9-9) very sad; so bad as to cause grief—and anger.

laminated (3-1-21-1) made up of very thin plates or sheets of material.

lamp (3) instrument used to give light.

l'amp-black (3 + 3) black powder used to make paint.

lamp'oon (3-77) written attack upon a person.

lamprey (3-1) fish-like creature with a long body, like a snake, about 16 inches long.

lance (44-s) spear used by horse-soldiers; **lancer** (44-s9) a horse-soldier who uses a lance: **lance** (44-s) to cut with a *lancet* (see 2nd below).

l'ance-c'orporal (44-s + 55-9) lowest rank in the British army, just above the common soldier.

lancet (44-s1) small knife used by doctors.

land (3) ground; country; **to land**, go off a ship on to the land; **landing** (3-1) flat place between two sets of stairs; *A landing-stage* = place where one gets off a ship.

landau (3-55) four-wheeled horse-carriage with a movable top.

landlady (3-21-1) woman who *lets lodgings* (= gives the use of furnished rooms for rent).

land-locked (3 + 5-t) (piece of water) shut in by land.

landlord (3-55) *My landlord* = the owner of my house or of the ground on which my house stands.

landmark (3-44) mark showing the edge of one's land; any clearly seen object used in telling or finding the way to a place.

L'and Rover (3 + 67-9) car used for hard work over very rough ground.

landscape (3-21) beautiful natural scene, stretch of country.

landslip (3-1) **landslide** (3-41) fall of earth, e.g. from the face of a cliff.

landsturm (3-779) part of the German army (till 1918) which could be called up in special danger, and in which men over sixty years of age served; not the regular army.

lane (21) narrow road; *It's a long lane that has no turning* = things will get better after some time.

language (3nggwɪ) speech, words, way of speaking or writing; *To use bad language* = curse, express anger by means of impolite words.

languid (3nggwɪ) weak, without interest; **to languish**, become weak; *To languish in prison* = live very unhappily in—; *A languishing look* = sad and loving look; **languor** (3nggg) weakness.

lank (3ngk) **lanky** (3ngkɪ) thin and tall.

lanolin (3-9-11) fat of wool made pure and used as a medicine for the skin.

lantern (3-9) glass case for a lamp or candle; top of a building or small tower with windows on all sides.

LANTERN

lanyard (3-9) string worn round the shoulder or neck with a knife or whistle, etc., on the other end.

lap (3) person's knees and upper part of legs used as a seat for a child; *Lapped in luxury* = living in great comfort; **lap-dog** (+ 5) small dog.

lap (3) turn or twist of string round (a stick, etc.); *To run one lap round the field* = run once round —.

lap (3) drink with the tongue as a cat does; *The waves lapped the shore* = touched the shore with a sound as of lapping.

lap'el (9-2) that part of the front of a coat which is turned back towards the shoulders.

lapidary (3-1-9-1) man who cuts precious stones to shape.

l'apis l'azuli (3-1 + 3-17-41) bright blue precious stone.

lapse (3) a mistake; a fall from goodness; passing of time; **to lapse**, fall away from, e.g. *He has lapsed back into his old bad ways*; (of land or goods) pass from one person to another because some rule or law has not been fulfilled; (of a claim) come to an end, be of no more use or effect.

l'apsus l'inguae (3-9 + 1nggwɪɪ) mistake in speaking.

lapwing (3-1) small bird which flies up and down and calls "*pee-wit!*"

larboard (44-9) left-hand side of a boat as one faces forward.

larceny (44s9-1) stealing.

larch (44) tall straight tree whose wood is used for making posts.

lard (44) pig's fat.

larder (44-9) store-room for food.

large (44j) taking up much space; able to contain a great amount; big; *He has a large heart* = he is kind and generous; *At large* = not in prison; *To the world at large* = all people; **largely** (44j-1) in great amount, chiefly.

larg'ess(e) (44j2) money scattered by a king or lord to the people.

largo (44g67) (music) slowly, solemnly.

lariat (3-19) rope for tying up horses.

lark (44) singing bird.

lark (44) be merry; play in a merry way; *Larks* = happy play, merry tricks; *He only said it for a lark* = to amuse, not meaning it seriously.

larva (44-9) pl. **larvae** (44-11) form in which an insect first lives after it leaves the egg.

larynx (3-ɪngks) upper part of the throat in which the voice is produced; **laryngitis** (3-ɪnj41-1) pain and redness in the larynx.

lascar (3-9) Indian seaman.

lasc′ivious (9sɪ-19) full of evil desire.

lash (3) to hit with a *whip* (= short stick with a string on the end used in driving a horse and for beating men or animals); a **lash**, stroke given with a —; string of a —; *To lash with the tongue* = scold.

lash (3) fasten with string or rope.

lashes (3-ɪz) small hairs (Eyelashes) on the edge of the covering of the eye.

lass (3) **lassie** (3-1) girl.

lassitude (3-1-177) tiredness.

lasso (3-67) rope made of leather used for catching cattle in America.

last (44) wooden or iron shape of a foot on which shoes are made; *To stick to one's last* = do one's own work, not other people's.

last (44) after all others, coming at the end.

last (44) continue, stay alive or in use.

latch (3) simple lock for a door, made of a short falling bar which is pulled up with a string from outside, or pressed up with a short handle; **latchkey** (3-11) key of the front door of a house.

latchet (3-1) shoe-*lace* (= string).

late (21) after the proper time; far on in time; not long ago, e.g. *The late headmaster* = the headmaster before the present one, the headmaster who is just dead; **lately** (——1) not long ago; *Of late years* = in the last few years.

latent (21) lying hidden.

lateral (3-9-9) at the side; of the side.

latest (21-1) most late; newest; *Have you heard the latest* = what has just happened, the newest story.

latex (21-2) white liquid which comes out of plants, e.g. out of the rubber-tree.

lath (44) long thin piece of wood.

lathe (21δ) machine which turns a piece of wood or metal round while it is cut or shaped.   LATHE

lather (3δ9) white mass made by rubbing up soap and water.

Latin (3-1) having to do with the ancient Romans; the language of ancient Rome.

latitude (3-1-177) freedom—especially of opinion; *Give him some latitude (of choice, of movement)* = some width of —.

latitude (3-1-177) imaginary lines drawn round the world or drawn on a map of the world by means of which one tells how far north or south a place is.

latr′ine (9-11) place in a camp where men go to leave the waste matter of the body.

latter (3-9) later; second of two things just spoken about.

lattice (3-ɪs) network made of wood, e.g. one on which climbing plants grow upward; **l′attice w′indow** (+ 1-67) window in which the glass is fixed in cross-pieces of metal.

laud (55) to praise; **laudable** (55-9) worthy of praise; **laudatory** (55-9-9-1) praising.

laudanum (5-9) liquid used to make people go to sleep, the liquid form of *opium* (= medicine made from the *poppy*).

laugh (44f) make sounds showing pleasure or amusement; *He laughs best who laughs last* = you may laugh at me now, but I shall win in the end and laugh at you; *To laugh in a person's face* = show great disrespect to; *To laugh up one's sleeve* = secretly; *Laugh on the wrong side of one's face (mouth)* = be sad at the *failure* (n. of Fail) of one's plans; *Laugh at* = be amused at, show disrespect to; *Have the laugh on a person* = be more successful than, and so be able to laugh at; **laughable** (44f9) causing persons to laugh; *A laughing-stock* = person (or thing) at whom all laugh, something very foolish; **laughter** (44f-9) act or sound of laughing.

l′aughing-gas (44fɪ + 3) gas used to put people to sleep, e.g. when a tooth is to be pulled out.

launch (55) small *power-driven* (= driven by motor-spirit or steam) boat, e.g. one carried on a large ship; **to launch** (a ship), send a newly built ship into the water; **to launch** (an attack) = start; *To launch out on* = begin (new work); *To launch out* = spend much money.

launder (55-9) wash clothes; **laundress** (55-1) woman who —; **laundry** (55-1) place where clothes are washed.

laureate (55-19) crowned with *laurel* (see below), e.g. a poet; *Poet Laureate* = title of honour given for life to a poet specially appointed by the king.

laurel (5) a bush with bright green leaves, also called the Bay-tree).

lava (44-9) liquid thrown out by a *volcano* (= mountain from which fire bursts out) which afterwards becomes hard rock.

lavatory (3-9-9-1) place where one washes oneself; place where one leaves the waste matter of the body.

LAUREL

lave (21) to wash.

lavender (3-1-9) plant with small blue-red flowers with a pleasant smell.

lavish (3-1) giving freely, generous; **to lavish**, spend or give freely.

law (55) (**1**) rule made by government or the king; *To lay down the law* = speak as if one was very sure of the rightness of one's opinions; *To go in for law* = become a lawyer; *To go to law against* = make a claim in a law-court against; *Take the law in one's own hands* =

defend one's rights oneself, without the use of the law-courts; (2) any set of rules, e.g. those of a game; (3) regular events of nature which happen as expected by scientists; l'aw-abiding (+ 9-41-1) keeping the laws; l'aw-c'ourt (+ 55) place where a judge settles matters of law; lawful (55) according to the law; lawless (55-1) not keeping the laws; -in-l'aw, by marriage, e.g. *Son-in-law* = the man who has married one's daughter.

lawn (55) fine white cloth; this cloth as a sign of rank as a *bishop* (= high officer of the Church).

lawn (55) piece of carefully kept grass near a house; l'awn-mower (+ 679) machine for cutting grass; l'awn-t'ennis (+ 2-1) game in which a ball is hit over a net on a piece of open ground 78 feet long, 36 feet wide.

lawsuit (55-177) making of a claim in a law-court before a judge.

lawyer (55y9) person who has studied the law and has the right to give advice on matters of law.

lax (3) loose, careless.

laxative (3-9-1) medicine which clears out waste matter from the body.

lay (21) (1) to place, to put, cause to lie; *Lay stress on it* = say it is important; *Lay one's finger on* = discover; *Don't dare to lay a finger on* —! = do not harm; *Can't lay my hands on it* = find; *Lay oneself out for* = arrange to do; *Lay it at his door* = blame him for it; *Lay by the heels* = catch and put in prison; *Lay a ghost* = cause the spirit of a dead man to cease appearing to the living; *Lay the dust* = prevent dust from rising, e.g. with water; (2) to set ready; *Lay the table, Lay the cloth* = set knives, spoons, plates, etc., on the table ready for a meal; *Lay heavy odds that* = promise to pay much money if it does not happen; *Lay his cheek open* = cut open with a knife or blow; *Lay one's heart bare* = tell all one's secrets; *Lay aside, Lay by (money)* = save up money for the future; *Lay it down* = say that it is true that; *Lay in stores* = take stores into the house; *Lay on (blows)* = hit; Sl. *Lay it on thick* = praise too much; *Lay down the law* = give opinions in a very sure and certain manner; Sl. *Lay a man out* = hit and make senseless; *Lay out one's money* = spend carefully.

lay (eggs) (21) produce (eggs).

lay (21) a song.

lay (21) of the general public, other than the members of a *profession* (e.g. doctors, lawyers, priests, etc.).

lay (21) p.t. of Lie.

lay-by (21 + 41) place at the side of a road where cars may be stopped.

LAY-BY

layer (21g) thin covering spread over, e.g. sugar on a cake.

lay'ette (212) clothes for a new-born child.

l'ay figure (21 + 1-9) wooden figure of a man with movable limbs used to help an artist in painting a picture.

layout (2147) (of a printed page, etc.) arrangement.

lazar (3-9) person having *leprosy* (= a disease which eats away the skin and other parts of the body); lazaret, lazarette (3-9-2) home for lepers or other sick persons; store-room in a ship.

lazy (21-1) not liking work; *Lazy-bones* = lazy person; to laze, be lazy.

£E, Egyptian pounds (money).

lea (11) field of grass.

lead (2) soft heavy metal; *Black-lead* = the black matter (*graphite*) in a pencil; *Leaden sky* = grey —; *Leaden limbs* = tired —; leads (——z) part of roof covered with lead; *To swing the lead* = be lazy while others work; leadsman (2-z-9) seaman who throws a line with lead on it to find how deep the water is.

lead (11) (p.t. and p.p. led (2)) (1) to guide; to direct; *Lead by the nose* = have complete control of; *Lead her to the altar* = marry; (2) get a person to follow; *I am led to believe* = I have knowledge which causes me to —; (3) act as chief; be in charge of, e.g. *To lead an army*; (4) serve as a path to, e.g. *This road leads to the church*; *This leads nowhere* = this will produce no useful results; (5) pass or spend (time), e.g. *To lead a happy life*; *To lead a dog's life* = to be very unhappy; *Lead him a dance* = give much trouble to, cause to follow one about; (6) go in front; play first in a card-game; a lead, n., act of leading, the right to play first; chief part in a play; string used for leading a dog; l'eading 'article (11-1 + 44-1) part of a newspaper in which the opinions of the chief or head of the newspaper are expressed; *Leading lady* = woman acting chief part in a play; a l'eading c'ase (+ 21) judgment in a law-court which is used as an example in later cases.

leaf, pl. leaves (11-z) green blade of a plant; two printed pages of a book; part of the top of a table which can be taken out so as to make the table smaller; *To take a leaf out of someone's book* = copy a person and make use of his ideas; *Turn over a new leaf* = decide to behave better in future.

leafage (11-1j) leaves, leafy covering of trees.

leaflet (11-1) small leaf of a plant; printed paper folded but not sewn; small book.

league (11) an agreement between persons or nations to help each other.

league (11) measure of distance, about 3 miles or 5 kilometres.

leak (11) small hole through which liquid escapes or breaks in; to leak, enter or escape through a small hole; leakage (11-1j) a leaking.

leal (11) loyal.

lean (11) thin; of bad quality; small in amount; *Lean years* = years when crops are small.

lean (11) bend towards; rest against; *He has a leaning towards* = has a liking for, will probably become interested in.

leap (11) to jump; *Leap-frog* = game in which children jump over each other's backs; *Leap year* = year in which there are 366 days; *A leap in the dark* = risky action of which the result cannot be guessed; *By leaps and bounds* = very quickly.

learn (99) gain knowledge; practise doing something; **learned** (99-1) having much knowledge.

lease (11) agreement to give the use of a house or land for a certain number of years on payment of certain money as rent; *A new lease of life* = chance of living longer or more happily owing to some trouble or disease ending; **leasehold** (11-67) land or a house rented (as above).

leash (11) string for holding a dog.

least (11) smallest, in the smallest amount.

leather (2ðg) skin of an animal prepared for use; beat fiercely; **l'eather'ette** (2ðg-2) cloth made to look like leather.

leave (11) *To ask for leave* = ask to be allowed to; *To get leave off* = be allowed to be absent from; *To go on leave* = go away for a *holiday* (= time of rest and absence from work); *3 months' home leave* = 3 months' holiday at home; *To take French leave* = go without asking to be allowed to go.

leave (11) p.t. **left** (2) (1) allow to remain; *Leave a person alone* = not trouble; *Leave a thing alone* = have nothing to do with, not touch; *Leave go* = loosen one's hold on; Sl. *To get left, be nicely left* = be tricked; (2) give money to a person at one's death; (3) trust a person to, e.g. *Leave it to me* = trust me to do it; *It leaves much to be desired* = is not good, should be better; *Leave off* = stop; *Leave out a word* = not say or not write; *You have left out the fact* = have not considered; *leavings* = things left as not needed.

leaven (2) soft grey-white material used to make bread *light* (*light bread* = bread which is full of little holes, not a solid mass).

lebensraum (2-9-47) extra space needed by a country (e.g. Germany) so that it may grow greater.

lectern (2-9) sloping table on which the Bible is put in a church.

lecture (2-tshg) speech given to teach a class; **lectureship** (——1) employment as a lecturer.

led (2) p.t. of Lead.

ledge (2j) narrow flat place in a wall or cliff, e.g. one on which one can put one's feet; flat rock under the sea.

ledger (2jg) book in which accounts of money are written.

lee (11) *In the lee of* = in the shelter of; **l'ee-sh'ore** (+ 55) shore on to which the wind blows; **leeward** (11-9) on the side away from the wind; **leeway** (11-21) movement off the right course caused by wind; loss of time in doing work, e.g. *I have a lot of leeway to make up.*

leech (11) small water creature which fixes itself on the skin and drinks blood; doctor (in ancient times).

leek (11) strong-smelling vegetable which is cooked for food.

leer (at) (19) look at in an evil and unpleasant way.

lees (11z) thick liquid at the bottom of a bottle or barrel of wine.

LEEK

leeward (11-9), **leeway** (11-21) see Lee.

left (2) p.t. of Leave.

left (2) that side of the body on which the heart is.

leg (2) (1) one of the limbs used for walking; *Have no leg to stand on* = have nothing more to say in favour of oneself (or of the idea which one is supporting); Sl. *Pull a person's leg* = laugh at, make a fool of; *On its last legs* = near death or near the end; Sl. *Give a person a leg up* = help; (2) a support, e.g. *The leg of a table*; (3) that part of a garment which covers the leg.

legacy (2-9s1) money or other things passed on to another at death.

legal (2) according to law; having to do with the law; **l'egal t'ender** (+ 2-9) money such as must be accepted according to law.

legalize (11-9-41) make lawful (according to law).

legate (2-1) officer of the *Pope* (the Pope is the head of one part of the Christian Church—the Roman Catholic Church) sent to carry messages or do work in foreign countries.

legat'ee (2-9-11) one who receives money at the death of another person.

leg'ation (1-21shn) A legate is an officer of the government sent to a foreign country to act there for his government; a legation is a legate with all the officers under him; also the house in which they live.

legend (2j9) old story passed down by word of mouth; **legendary** (2j9-1) as told of in legends.

l'egerdem'ain (2j9-9-21) quickness and skill of hand in doing tricks to deceive and amuse.

leggings (2-1-z) leather coverings for the lower part of the legs.

leggy (2-1) having long legs.

legh'orn (2-55) kind of hen; kind of hat.

legible (2j1) easily read.

legion (11jg) company of soldiers in the Roman army; *My enemies are legion* = I have many —; *The Foreign Legion* = French soldiers in Africa, etc.; **a legionary** (11jg-9-1) Roman soldier; *Member of the*

LEGHORN HAT

Legion of Honour = title given by the French Government.

legislator (2j1-21-9) maker of laws; **the legislature** (2j1-21tsh9) men who make laws.

leg'itimate (1j1-1-1) according to law; allowable; *His legitimate son* = son born in marriage; **leg'itimize** (1j1-1-41) make legitimate.

leg'uminous (plant) (2-1 77-1-9) like a bean, of the same kind as the bean-plant.

leisure (time) (239) time not given to work; *To be at leisure* = be free, not working; **leisurely** (239-1) slowly, not in a hurry; **leisured** (239) having plenty of free time.

lemming (2-1) small animal like a rat.

lemon (2-9) yellow, very sour fruit; tree bearing this fruit; the colour; **l'emon'ade** (2-9-21), LEMMING **l'emon squ'ash** (+ 5) a drink made from lemons.

lemur (11-9) kind of monkey with a hairy tail.

lend (2) give the use of a thing on the understanding that it will be given back; *It lends itself to* = it is well fitted to; *Lend me your ears* = listen; *Lend a hand* = help.

length (2) *The length is 3 feet* = it is three feet long; *At length* = after a long time; *Keep him at arm's length* = as far away as possible, do not be friendly with him; **lengthen**, make or become longer; **lengthwise** (——4lz) along the length; **lengthy** (——1) long.

lenient (11-19) gentle and forgiving.

lens (2-z) piece of glass which collects light into one beam (or scatters it).

Lent (2) time of year when some Christians eat simple food and give up things they like.

lent (2) p.t. of Lend.

lentil (2-1) yellow seed of a kind of bean-plant.

leonine (11·9-41) like a lion.

leopard (2-9) meat-eating animal, yellow with black spots, found in the forests of India and Africa.

LEOPARD

leper (2-9) one suffering from *leprosy* (=disease which eats away the skin and other parts of the body).

lepid'optera (2-1-5-9-9) insects with four wings covered with flat plates, e.g. the *moth* (= insect which flies into a lamp, also destroys clothes).

leprosy (2-9-1) see Leper (2nd above).

lesion (113n) a wound.

less (2) not so much; taken from; **lessen**, make less; **the lesser** (2-9) the smaller.

less'ee (2-11) person who rents a house; **less'or** (2-55) person who owns and lets a house for rent.

lesson (2) thing to be learnt; amount of teaching given at one time; *Teach him a lesson* = punish him so that he may not do that thing again.

lest (2) for fear that ——.

let (2) to leave, allow; *Let me be*, *Let me alone* = do not trouble me; *Let the business alone* = take no part in; *Let us have a song* = we wish to ——; *Let drive at* = aim a blow at; *Let go* = loosen one's hold; *Let oneself go* = not control oneself any more; Sl. *Let a man down* = deceive, not do what one was trusted to do; *Let him down easily* = be kind to, forgive; Sl. *I was let in over this business* = deceived; *Let off a gun* = fire; *Let him off* = forgive; *Let out* = tell a secret; Sl. *Don't let on* = do not tell; *Let out a garment* = make larger or longer.

let (a house) (2) give the use of a house for rent.

let (2) get in the way of; stop the action of.

-let, a small ——, e.g. **streamlet** (11-1) small stream.

lethal (11) causing death.

lethargy (2-9j1) sleepiness; lack of spirit or interest; adj. **leth'argic** (2-44j1).

letter (2-9) (1) A, B, C, etc., are letters; (2) written message, a note; (3) *A man of letters* = man who writes books or studies good writings.

l'etter-p'erfect (+ 99-1) knowing one's words in a play perfectly.

l'etterpress (2-9-2) printed matter.

lettuce (2-1s) vegetable with green leaves eaten uncooked, often with cold meat.

lev'ant (1-3) go away without paying one's debts.

levee (2-1) (1) meeting to which the chief men of a country go and *bow* (= bend the body as a sign of respect) to the king; (2) bank to prevent a river from flowing over the land.

level (2) flat, not hilly; *To find one's level* = find that set of people with whom one is equal, that part of the work which is not too difficult; Sl. *On the level* = honest; **to level**, make flat; **level-crossing** (+ 5-1) place where road and rail cross without a bridge; **l'evel-h'eaded** (+ 2-1) not easily excited; **a leveller** (2-9) one who would make all men equal in rank.

lever (11-9) bar with a fixed support at one point, used for lifting things; **leverage** (11-9-1j) power of a lever.

LEVER

lev'iathan (1-4I9-9) very large sea-creature; any very large thing.

levitate (2-1-21) cause a body to be lifted up from the ground as if by magic.

levity (2-1-1) state of mind in which solemn things are treated lightly and disrespectfully.

levy (2-1) collect money from the people, e.g. for government; raise an army; **a levy**, collecting of money or soldiers; soldiers so collected.

lewd (177) nasty, dirty (way of behaving, story, etc.).

lexicon (2-1-9) book giving the meanings of words, *dictionary*; **lexic'ographer** (2-1-5-9-9)

ley (21) a field which is sown with new grass (about) every four years.

liable (419) (1) bound by law; *I am liable for his debts* = I shall have to pay if he does not; (2) open to attack, e.g. *Liable to illness* = open to attacks of illness; **liab'ilities** (419-1-1-1z) debts.

li'aison 'officer (121z + 5-1s9) officer who keeps an (e.g. English) army in touch with what is being done in another (e.g. French) army.

liar (419) one who does not speak the truth.

lib'ation (41-21shn) wine poured out as an offering to a god.

libel (41) something printed or written which is damaging to a person's good name.

liberal (1-9) free in opinion, generous in giving money; *Liberal allowance of food* = plenty; *The Liberal Party* = name of one of the groups of men in England who are interested in the government of the country; *A liberal education* = such education as is fit for a gentleman.

liberate (1-9-21) to set free.

libertine (1-9-41) pleasure-seeker of loose character.

liberty (1-9-1) freedom; *To take liberties (with)* = do acts which one has no real right to do.

library (41-9-1) collection of books; place where books are kept; reading-room in a house; **a libr'arian** (41-29-19) one who is in charge of a library.

libr'etto (1-2-67) book of words of a musical play.

lice (41s) pl. of Louse.

licence (41s-s) leave, *permission* (n. of Permit); paper permitting one to (e.g. drive a car); too great freedom, lack of control; *Poetic licence* = poet's freedom from rules of language or from exactness of fact.

license (41s-s) give *permission* (n. of Permit); **a lic'entiate** (41s2-sh121) one who is permitted to (teach, act as a doctor, etc.); **licens'ee** (41s-11) holder of a licence.

lic'entious (41s2-sh9s) rough and badly behaved.

lichen (41k9) very small plant which covers rocks.

lick (1) pass the tongue over; *To lick one's lips* = show desire for food; *Lick a person's boots* = lower oneself before; Sl. to beat; **a licking** (1-1) beating; *To lick into shape* = teach an unpromising or difficult learner; finish work which is already in a rough state.

lid (1) cover, e.g. of a box; **eyelid** (41-1) cover of the eye.

lido (11-67) place in the open air where people can swim and lie out in the sunshine.

lie (41) remain flat on, be at rest on; be kept in, e.g. *Lie in prison*; *It lies with you to decide* = you have the right or power to decide; Sl. *Lie doggo* = keep quiet; *The claim does not lie* = is not according to law; *Lie in* = stay in bed at childbirth; *Lie up* = stay ill in one's room; *Let sleeping dogs lie* = not ask about a matter which is causing no trouble, but might cause trouble if —; *Take it lying down* = not fight against an evil or punishment; *See how the land lies* = see how matters are at present.

lie (41) say what is not true.

lief (11) *I'd as lief* = I would like as much to —; *I'd liefer* = I would rather —.

liege (11j) lord whom I am bound to serve.

lien (11·9) *To have a lien on* = have the right to keep something until a debt is paid.

lieu (177) *In lieu of* = instead of.

lieutenant (2ft2-9) officer of low rank in the army or on a ship; one who is acting for (doing the work of) another.

life (41) (1) power of living; (2) living creatures; (3) time between birth and death; (4) *A life of Mr. N* = story of Mr. N from birth to death; (5) spirit, quickness.

life-belt (+ 2) thing put round the waist so as to prevent one sinking in water.

lifeboat (41-67) boat used to save men from a wreck.

life-buoy (+ 5I) floating thing to which men hold when in water.

l'ife-insurance (+ 1-sh79-s)—A person pays a small amount of money (a *premium*) every year to a company which pays to his wife or family an agreed amount at his death.

lifelong (41-5) during the whole of life.

l'ife-preserver (+ 1z99-9) short heavy stick used for hitting an enemy on the head.

lift (1) raise up; **a lift**, machine which raises goods or people up in a building; *Give a lift to* = take a person in one's motor-car.

ligament (1-9-9) band joining two bones in the body, or holding some part of the body in its place.

ligature (1-9tsh9) string used for tying up the end of a blood-vessel.

light (41) (1) that which comes from the sun (etc.) by which we see; (2) lamp; lighted match; *Ancient lights* = windows which must not have their light taken away by a new building built up in front of them; *I can't see it in that light* = understand the matter that way; *That puts things in a different light* = makes them seem different; *High lights* = brightest parts of a picture; **to light**, give light to; set fire to; **lighter** (41-1-9) small instrument for lighting cigarettes.

light (41) not dark; light colour, e.g. *Light blue* = not deep or dark in colour.

light (41) not heavy; active; graceful; not serious or painful, e.g. *A light attack of illness*; *A light punishment*; *Light reading* = amusing books, etc., not difficult to understand.

light upon (+ 9-5) find when not expecting to do so.

lighter (4I-9) flat-bottomed boat used for unloading ships.

lighthouse (4It·h47) tower with a lamp in it to warn ships of rocks.

lightning (4I-I) flash of light seen in the sky during a storm.

lights (4I) (of an animal) the *lungs* (= part with which one breathes).

lignite (I-4I) sort of coal.

lignum (I-9) wood; **ligneous** (I-I9) woody.

LIGHTHOUSE

like (4I) not different from; *It was like him to do that* = he is the kind of man who would —; *That's just like your foolishness* = that is the foolish sort of thing which you often do; *Ah! that's something like!* = just what I wanted; *We shall not see his like again* = not see a man like him —.

like (4I) find pleasant; Sl. *I like that!* = I am surprised at that and it does not please me; *I do not like to trouble you* = not wish to —, am sorry to —.

likely (4I-I) probable; *A likely person for the work* = suitable, one who will probably do the work well; **likelihood** (4I-I-7) probability.

likeness (4I-I) *A good likeness* = good picture of a person.

likewise (4I-4Iz) in the same way; also.

lilac (4I-9) bush with a blue-red or white flower.

lilt (I) regular beat of music.

lily (I-I) beautiful flower.

limb (I) arm or leg or wing; branch of a tree.

limber (I-9) A gun-carriage is made in two parts, (1) the limber (the part in which the powder and shot is carried), and (2) the gun itself; **to limber up**, join a gun on to its limber ready for pulling away.

LILY

limber (I-9) easily bent; active.

limbo (I-67) place after death between *heaven* (for good people) and *hell* (for bad —).

lime (4I) (1) white powder mixed with sand to make *mortar* (used to join bricks in building); (2) sticky material used for catching birds; **l'ime-light** (+ 4I) very powerful light obtained by blowing burning gas on to a piece of special white stone; powerful light used in the theatre; *In the lime-light* = being noticed, important at the present time.

lime (4I) small sour fruit; tree.

limerick (I-9-I) amusing poem of five lines, usually beginning " There was a (young lady, etc.) of (name of place)."

limestone (4I-67) kind of rock.

limit (I-I) farthest edge; **to limit**, keep within a certain space, within certain rules; Sl. *That's the limit!* = that is very bad, too bad to be allowed; **limit'ation** (I-I-2Ishn) act of limiting, state of being limited; *To have one's limitations* = have weak points in one's character or powers; *Limited Company*, see Ltd.

limn (I) paint a picture of.

limous'ine (I-7zII) closed motor-car with a separate place for the driver.

limp (I) not stiff.

limp (I) walk as if with a wounded leg.

limpet (I-I) shell-fish which holds tightly on to rocks.

limpid (I-I) clear.

linchpin (I-I) pin which prevents a wheel falling off a cart.

linden (I-9) *lime* tree (tree with sweet-smelling flowers).

line (4I) (1) string, e.g. *A fishing line*; (2) thin mark; *To toe the line* = obey orders, stay under control; *Draw the line at* = not be willing to do (or allow) a thing so bad as that; *Know where to draw the line* = know what is too bad to be allowed; (3) *a line of* = a row of, e.g. *A line of soldiers*; *Read between the lines* = find more in a written paper than is actually expressed; *Marriage lines* = paper showing that one is married; *Come into line with* = agree to; *A ship of the line* = big warship; (4) set of ships giving regular service, e.g. *The Cunard Line*; (5) track upon which trains run; (6) *The line*, *To cross the line* = pass over the *equator* (= an imaginary line round the middle of the earth); (7) way of behaving, e.g. *To take a strong line* = show no pity, be firm; (8) descendants, e.g. *A long line of kings* = father and son, etc., becoming king one after another; (9) business, e.g. *What is his line?* = what things does he sell or make or do?; *That's not in my line* = I am not interested in it; Sl. *Hard lines!* = that is unfortunate, you deserved better fortune; *To shoot a line* = claim to have done much more than one has done; *boast* (see Boast); **to line**, set in line, stand in line; *To line (a box, coat, etc.)* = to cover the inside of — with cloth or other material.

lineage (I-I·Ij) line of persons from whom one is descended; one's father, grandfather, great-grandfather, etc.; **a lineal** (I-I9) *descendant* = in the direct line of father—son—grandson, etc.

lineament (I-I9-9) part of the face which gives it its special character, is most easily recognized.

linen (I-I) (1) cloth made of *flax* (= plant grown in Ireland and other places whose stem is used to make thread); (2) clothes and cloths used in the house; *To wash dirty linen in public* = let people know of unpleasant matters which need not concern them.

l'inen-draper (+ 2I-9) one who sells women's clothes and things made of cloth used in the house.

liner (4I-9) large ship which carries people across the ocean.

linger (Inggg9) stay a long time, stay behind.

lingerie (3ⁿ39-11) women's undergarments.

lingo (1ngg67) language (the word shows disrespect for someone else's language).

l'ingua fr'anca (1ngg79 + 3ngk9) mixed language serving as a common tongue for several peoples.

lingual (1ngg79) of the tongue, of language.

linguist (1ngg71) one who speaks many languages; **lingu'istic** (——1) having to do with languages; **lingu'istics**, scientific study of language.

liniment (1-1-9) medical oil rubbed into the skin.

lining (41-1) (of a coat) covering of the inside; *Every cloud has a silver lining* = misfortune is often followed by happiness.

link (1ngk) ring of a chain; a measure, $7\frac{9}{10}$ inches; **to link**, join with a link; *To link arms* = join arms.

link-man (1ngk + 9) man carrying a *torch* (= burning material carried in an upright holder used to give light).

links (1ngk) grassy sandhills; place where *golf* (see Golf) is played.

linnet (1-1) singing bird common in England.

linoleum (1-67-19) floor covering made of cloth covered with a mixture of *cork*-dust and hardened oil (*cork* = soft outside shell of a tree).

linotype (41-9-41) machine which makes flat plates of metal with raised letters on the edge, used for printing.

linseed (1-11) seed of *flax* (= plant whose stem is used for making strong white cloth, e.g. for tablecloths, bed-sheets, etc.) from which oil is obtained, used in making paint, etc.

lint (1) soft cotton material used for covering wounds.

lintel (1) top beam or bar of a door or window.

lion (419) large meat-eating animal found in Africa; important person; *The lion's share* = largest share; **to lionize** (419-41) treat a person as if he were important; **lioness** (419-1) female lion.

lip (1) edge of the mouth; edge of a thing; *To smack one's lips* = show pleasure in food; Sl. *None of your lip* = show me more respect; *Lip-service* = saying that one will serve a person but not meaning to do so; **lipstick** (1-1) red pencil used by women to colour the lips.

liqu'eur (1k179) sweet strong drink taken in a very small glass, usually after dinner; *Liqueur whisky* (*brandy*) = specially good quality of these strong drinks, usually taken without added water.

liquid (1-1) matter in a form which can be poured like water; *My ideas are still very liquid* = not fixed or settled; (of sound) flowing easily and pleasantly; (in money matters) easily sold or changed for money; **liquefaction** (1-1-3-shn) causing to become a liquid; **liquescent** (1-2) in course of becoming liquid.

liquidate (1-1-21) pay off debts; break up a business company; *Liquidate an enemy* = kill —.

liquor (1k9) a liquid; strong drink (e.g. *Whisky*).

liquorice (1k9-1s) black material used in medicine, also eaten as a sweet.

l'isle thr'ead (41 + 2) specially hardened cotton thread.

lisp (1) speak saying the s sound as *th*, e.g. *He lithpth in thpeaking*.

lissom (1-9) graceful and active.

list (1) *To make a list* = write down things in order one under another; **a list**, note of things so written.

list (1) edge of cloth; long narrow pieces of cloth used to make bedroom *slippers* (= soft shoes worn in the house).

list (1) to desire.

list (1) (of a ship) lean to one side.

listen (1-9) hear and attend to; *Listen in* = hear speeches, music, etc., on the *radio* (= sending of music electrically without wires).

listerine (1-9-11) liquid used to kill *germs* (= microscopic living things which cause disease) and prevent wounds from becoming poisoned.

listless (1-1) weak and uninterested.

lists (1) place where knights fought with spear and shield.

lit (1) p.t. and p.p. of Light.

litany (1-9-1) form of prayer to God to forgive our wrong-doing and bless all men.

litchi (11-1) small fruit in a rough paper-like shell found in India, China, etc.

literacy (1-9-9s1) state of being able to read and write.

literal (1-9-9) of letters; exact as to words; according to the actual meaning of the words; *It means, literally* = taking the exact meaning of the words; *Literally the nastiest fellow I've ever known* = really, truly —.

literary (1-9-9-1) having to do with writing books.

literate (1-9-1) able to read and write.

literature (1-1tsh9) books and writings of poets and good writers.

lithe (4īð) easily bent or turned, e.g. *Lithe as a snake*.

lithograph (1-67-44) something printed from a drawing made on a special kind of stone or prepared surface.

litigate (1-1-21) go to law; make a claim in a law-court; *A* **lit'igious** (1-1j9) *person* = one who is always going to law.

litmus (1-9) blue colouring matter which is turned red by an acid.

litre (11-9) French measure of liquid, equal to $1\frac{3}{4}$ *pints*.

Litt.D. Doctor of Letters.

litter (1-9) bed used for carrying people about, e.g. for carrying wounded.

litter (1-9) waste paper and useless bits of things lying about.

litter (1-9) the young of an animal at birth, e.g. *A litter of puppies* = the young of a dog.

little (1) small; not much; young; **a little,** small amount; *For a little* = for a short time; *Little by little* = slowly, a small amount at each time.

littoral (1-9-9) land lying along the sea-shore.

liturgy (1-9)1 form of public prayer to God.

live (1) (1) have life, not be dead; (2) *To live at* —, have a home at; *He lives on his father* = depends on —; *Lives by his wits* = gets money by deceiving people; *Live and let live* = forgive the weakness of others and hope that they may forgive one's own; *Live from hand to mouth* = get with difficulty enough money to live, not being able to see the future; *Live down one's past* = live so as to make people forget the wrong which one has done in the past; *Live and learn!* = I have lived long but never learnt that until now.

live (41) adj., living, not dead; *A live broadcast* = speaking over the radio by a living person; *Live load* = things moving, e.g. over a bridge; *Live wire* = wire along which electricity is passing; *A live wire* = a keen and active person.

livelihood (41-1-7) means by which one *earns* (= gets by work) the money to live.

livelong (night) (1-5) during all the night.

lively (41-1) quick, full of life and action; *A lively time* = difficult and dangerous time.

liver (1-9) large *organ* (inside part) of the body which takes poisons out of the blood and stores up sugar; *To feel liverish* = feel ill from a disordered liver; *White-livered, Lily-livered* = not brave.

livery (1-9-1) special dress worn by the servants of a nobleman or rich man, or of an ancient City Company in London; dress used as a sign, e.g. *To wear the livery of grief*.

livery-stable (+ 21) place where horses are kept for hire.

livestock (41-5) horses, cows, sheep, etc., on a farm.

livid (face) (1-1) blue-white, bloodless because of illness or fear.

living (1-1) *To make one's living* = get enough money to live; *Good living* = good food and comfort; *A living-room* = room for general use in the day; *A living wage* = enough money (as pay for work) in order to live; **a living,** employment as a priest to serve a church.

lizard (1-9) cold-blooded creature with four legs and a long tail.

llama (44-9) animal like a sheep with a long neck and long hair, found in South America.

LL.D., Doctor of Laws.

Lloyd's (51-z) *society* (group of persons) which has to do with *insurance* (= paying a certain amount of money so that, if the ship is lost, the company or society may pay the whole or part of the value of the ship) of ships.

Lo! (67) Look! See!

load (67) put on a ship (horse, cart, etc.) the goods which it is to carry; add weight to, e.g. *A loaded stick* = one with heavy metal at one end; put powder and shot in a gun; **a load,** goods carried by a ship (horse, cart, etc.); a weight; *That's a load off my mind* = now I feel less anxious; *Load-shedding* = cutting off electricity in some parts of a city when more is being used than can be supplied.

load, lode (67) see Lode.

loadstar, lodestar (67-44) Pole star, a bright star seen in the north by which ships are guided.

loadstone, lodestone (67-67) iron-stone which always turns to the north, once used for compasses.

loaf (67) mass of bread as baked; large block of sugar.

loaf (67) to waste time doing no work.

loam (67) good soil.

loan (67) thing lent; lend.

loath, loth (67) unwilling.

loathe (67ð) to hate; **loathly** (67ð-1), **loathsome** (67ð-9) hateful, very nasty.

loaves (67-z) pl. of Loaf.

lob (5) ball sent high in the air.

lobby (5-1) *passage* (= path or way leading from one part of a house to another) into which rooms open; **to lobby,** ask members of the government to *vote* (= show an opinion) in a certain way.

lobe (67) soft hanging part, e.g. of the ear.

lobster (5-9) shell-fish with a long tail. It turns red when boiled.

local (67) having to do with a place; *Local colour* = description of a certain place put in a story to make the story seem real; *The local* = the public-house (inn); **loc'ality** (67-3-1-1) a place; **localize** (67-9-41) keep to a certain place; **loc'ate** (67-21) find the place of.

loc'ation (6-21shn) place; *Working on location* = making a cinema film outside, in the country.

loch (5k) lake in Scotland; narrow arm of the sea.

lock (5) *A lock of hair* = a curl of hair; number of hairs hanging down together.

lock (5) enclosed place in a river, used for moving boats to the upper or lower part of the stream.

lock (5) instrument for fastening a door; part of a gun; *Lock, stock and barrel* = the whole of it; **to lock,** fasten a door; become fixed or united; *To lock up capital in* = put money into a business in such a way that one cannot get it back when one may need it; **l'ock-jaw** (+ 55) disease in which the body becomes stiff and the mouth cannot be opened.

locker (5-9) small box with a lock, fixed to the wall.

locket (5-1) small box made of precious metal, worn round the neck, containing a picture or the hair of a loved one.

lockout (5-47) keeping workmen out of their place of work.

locksmith (5-1) one who makes locks.

l'ock up (5 + 8) *The lock-up* = prison.

locomotive (67-9-67-1) having the power of moving from place to place; *a locomotive*, engine which moves itself about; engine of a train.

l'ocum t'enens (67-9 + 11-2-2) priest or doctor who during another's absence does his work.

l'ocus st'andi (67-9 + 3-41) the right to make a claim in a court of law; the right to take part in a matter.

locust(s) (67-9) winged insects which move together in thousands and destroy crops.

lode, load (67) line of natural metal in a rock.

LOCUST

lodestar (67-44) star by which a ship is guided;

lodestone (67-67) stone which acts like a compass needle.

lodge (5j) house for a shooting or hunting party; small house used by the gate-keeper of a great house; **to lodge**, put in a place; take a person into one's house; live in another's house on payment; become fixed after being thrown; *To lodge a complaint* = make — before a judge or officer; **lodger** (——9) paying guest;

lodgings (5j1-z) rooms for paying guests.

loft (5) room at the top of a house.

loft (5) send a ball high in the air.

lofty (5-1) very high; showing a very high opinion of oneself.

log (5) rough unprepared piece of a tree.

log (5) instrument for measuring the speed of a boat.

l'og-book (+ 7) book in which the events of a sea journey are written down each day by the captain.

logarithm (5-9-1) figure showing the number of times a number called " the base " must be *multiplied* (= 3 × 3 = 9, 3 multiplied by 3 makes 9) by itself in order to yield a certain other number; e.g. number 1000, " base " 10, logarithm 3—for 10^3 = 10 × 10 × 10 = 1000.

loggerheads, at — (5-9-2-z) quarrelling.

logic (5j1) art of reasoning; **logical** (5j1) having to do with logic; according to reason; able to reason well; **log'ician** (5j1shn) one who teaches logic.

-logist, one who studies the science of—e.g. **ge'ologist** (j115-9j1) = one who studies the surface of the earth, rocks, etc.

log'istics (5j1-1) art of moving armies in war.

loin (5i) part of the body on either side just above the top of the legs; *To gird up one's loins* = get ready to act; *Sprung from the loins of* = descended from.

loiter (51-9) to waste time in going to a place; stand about.

loll (5) sit or lie lazily.

lone (67) alone, by oneself; **lonely** (67-1), **lonesome** (67-9) feeling sad because alone.

long (5) having length; *A long arm* = power of reaching far; *Make a long arm* = stretch out as far as you can, e.g. in taking a thing without moving from one's seat; *A long face* = sad look; *Make a long nose* = put the hand to the nose as a sign of disrespect; *Have a long tongue* = talk too much; *In the long run* = as the *final* (= last) result.

long (5) feel great desire for.

l'ong-b'ow (5 + 67) *To draw the* — = to tell stories which are difficult to believe.

l'ong-cloth (5 + 5) strong cotton cloth.

long'evity (5nj2-1-1) length of life.

longhand (5-3) usual kind of writing, not *shorthand* (= special writing which can be done very quickly).

longitude (5nj1-177) imaginary lines drawn on the world (or lines drawn on a map) by means of which one can tell how far east or west a place is.

longit'udinal (5nj1-177-1) of length or *longitude* (above).

longshoreman (5-55-9) man who works on the shore.

l'ong-s'uffering (5 + 8-9-1) suffering without complaining.

l'ong-w'inded (5 + 1-1) talking much, without expressing many ideas.

loofah (77-9) framework of a certain plant from which all the soft fruity part has been taken away, used for washing oneself.

look (7) (1) turn the eyes towards; *Look before you leap* = do not act without first planning your action; *Look daggers at* = angrily —; *Look a gift horse in the mouth* = find fault with*!* a gift; (2) seem; *Look blue* = seem unhappy; *It looks as if* = seems probable that; *Look after* = take care of; *Wouldn't look at it* = will certainly not accept or agree to it; *Look down on* = have a low opinion of; *Look forward to* = expect with pleasure; *Look in on* = visit; *Look into* = examine; *Look on him as* = think him to be —; *Look out!* = be careful; *Look up* = be careful of; *Business is looking up* = is becoming better; *Look up a fact* = find it in a book; **a look,** act of looking; appearance of the face; *Good looks* = beauty (especially of a man).

l'ooking-glass (7-1 + 44) glass in which one can see one's face.

l'ook-'out (7 + 47) place from which one watches; a watchman; *Keep a good look-out* = watch carefully.

loom (77) machine for making cloth.

loom (77) *Loom through the mist* = be seen *dimly* (= not clearly) and larger than the real thing.

loon (77) fool; water-bird found in North America.

loop (77) line curved back upon itself; string so curved.

loophole (77p·h67) narrow hole in a wall through which men shoot; way of escape.

loose (77) (1) free, uncontrolled; *To break loose* = escape, become free; *Loose cash* = money not locked up; (2) not tight; (3) not controlled by rule or law; *A loose life* = bad way of living; *He has a screw loose* = is mad; *Play fast and loose* = behave dishonestly or foolishly; *At a loose end* = having nothing to do; **loosen**, make loose.

loot (77) goods taken from the enemy in time of war.

lop (5) cut away the branches.

lop (-eared) (5) hanging down loosely.

lope (67) move easily in long steps.

l'ops'ided (5-41-1) with one side lower than the other.

loqu'acious (9-21sh9) talking a lot; **loqu'acity** (9-3s1-1).

loquat (67-5) small red or yellow sour fruit found in Japan and other countries.

lord (55) one ruling others; owner; God; title of a nobleman; *To lord it over* =. behave proudly to —; *Our Lord* = Jesus Christ.

lordling (55-1) unimportant lord.

lordly (55-1) proud, behaving like a lord.

lordship (55-1) power or rule of a lord; state of being a lord; *Your Lordship* —one addresses a lord in this way.

lore (55) learning; set of facts, e.g. facts handed down by word of mouth.   LORGNETTE

lorgn'ette (55ny2) eye-glasses with a handle.

lorn (55) deserted; alone—and sad.

lorry (5-1) long, low cart (horse or motor) used for moving heavy goods.

lose (77z) fail to keep; be unable to find; not to win; be too late for, e.g. *Lose one's train*; *Lose one's way* = be unable to find the right path; *Lose one's head* = become too excited to act wisely; *I shall lose no time in doing it* = do it at once.

loss (5) act of losing; thing lost; *I am at a loss* = do not know what to do.

lost (5) p.t. and p.p. of Lose.

lot (5) collection of things; large amount of.

lot (5) one of a set of objects used to decide something by chance; *To cast lots* = to decide by chance; *My lot* = my fate.

lottery (5-9-1) game of chance in which part of the money paid for *tickets* (= pieces of paper showing that money has been paid) is given to the owner of one ticket chosen by chance.

loth (67) see Loath.

lotion (67shn) liquid for putting on the skin, on wounds, etc.

lotus (67-9) plant (told of in LOTUS stories) supposed, when eaten, to cause one to forget everything; a water-lily.

loud (47) making much noise, easily heard; (of colours) bright; (of behaviour) noisy and rude; **l'oud-sp'eaker** (radio) electrical instrument used to make sounds louder.

lounge (47nj) sitting-room with large comfortable chairs in it; **l'ounge s'uit** (+ 177) suit of clothes as usually worn by Europeans in the day.

lour, lower (479) look at a person as if one hated him.

louse (47) pl. **lice** (41s) small insect which lives on the body or in the hair; **lousy** (——z1) having lice; Sl. bad, worthless.

lout (47) ungraceful fellow with bad manners.

louver (77-9) sloping boards fixed in a window frame to let in air without rain or too much sunlight.

love (8) feeling of great friendliness for; feeling of desire for; *There's no love lost between them* = they hate each other; *Give my love to Jack* = give him greetings from me; *Fall in love* = begin to love; *Make love to* = behave in a loving way towards; *A labour of love* = work done not for pay but because one likes doing it; **to love**, have great friendliness or desire for.

love (8) (in a game) = none, nothing, e.g. *The score is 2-love* = A has two points, B has none.

l'ove-bird (+ 99) small green bird.

l'ovelock (8 + 5) curl of hair hanging down over the face.

l'ove-lorn (+ 55) sad because left by one's lover.

lovely (8-1) beautiful, very nice, very good.

l'ove-philtre (+ 1-9) a medicine supposed to cause love.

l'oving-cup (8-1 +.8) large drinking-cup with three handles for passing round at a feast.

low (67) not high; *In a low voice* = speaking quietly; (in music) deep; *Of low rank* = not noble; *A low fellow* = bad; *Low-down* = dishonest; *To lie low* = keep quiet, not be active; *To be laid low* = be killed; *Low-brow* = a person not interested in good music or books; Sl. *Give him the low-down* = tell him the secret facts.

low (67) make the noise of a cow.

lower (679) make less high; cause to descend; *To lower oneself* = behave in an unworthy way or without pride; adj. less high, less important, of less high rank.

lower (479) see Lour.

lowly (47-1) not proud, not of high birth.

loyal (519) faithful (e.g. to one's king).

lozenge (5-1nj) (1) four-sided figure; (2) medicine for the throat made in the form of a sweet.

L. s. d. (2l + 2s + ·d11) .pounds, shillings, pence—Obs. now L. p.

Lt. *lieut'enant* (2ĭt2-9) rank in the army.

Ltd. *Limited* (1-1-1) — A *limited* company is one whose shareholders cannot lose more than the amount of money which they put into the company.

lubber (8-9) untrained seaman; rough and careless worker.
lubber's line (8-9 + 4I) line on a compass showing the direction of the front of the ship.
lubricate (77-1-21) to oil a machine; **lubricant** (77-1) oil.
luc'erne (7s99) plant with three leaves on each stem, much used as food for cattle.
lucid (77s1) clear, easily understood.
Lucifer (77s1-9) Satan, the Spirit of Evil.
luck (8) fortune, good or bad; **lucky** (——1) having good luck; **luckless** (——1) having bad luck.
lucrative (77-9-1) bringing in money or gain.
lucre (77-9) gain; Sl. *Filthy lucre* = money thought of as an evil.
lucubr'ations (77-17-21shnz) hard study, e.g. done sitting up late at night.
ludicrous (77-1-9) silly, making people laugh.
luff (8) part of a sail; **to luff,** turn a sailing-ship so that it points in towards the wind (so that the wind is blowing more from the front, less from the side).
Luftwaffe (7-v4-9) German air force.
lug (8) to pull along with difficulty.
luge (77j) carriage which slides over snow—high kind of *sleigh* (see Sleigh).
luggage (8-1j) boxes and bags of a traveller.
lugger (8-9) small sailing-boat.
lug'ubrious (7-77-19) sad.
lukewarm (77-55) slightly warm; not eager.
lull (8) to calm with sounds; sing to sleep; make quiet; be quiet; **a lull,** short time of quiet in a storm or in pain.
lullaby (8-9-4I) song for sending a child to sleep.
lumb'ago (8-21-67) illness causing pain in the *loins* (see Lumbar).
lumbar (8-9) having to do with the *loins* (= part of the body just above the top of the legs).
lumber (8-9) move heavily; useless things; *To lumber up* = fill with useless things.
lumber (8-9) to cut down trees and prepare them for selling; wood and trees so cut and prepared; **lumberjack** (8-9-3) **l'umber-man** (+ 9) man employed in this work.
luminary (77-1-9-1) star; person well-known for learning.
luminous (77-1-9) bright, giving light.
lump (8) shapeless mass; swelling; *A lump sum* = one amount of money to pay for various small things; **to lump,** put things together in one mass or in one class; *If you don't like it, you can lump it* = you must suffer it without complaining.
lunar (77-9) having to do with the moon.
lunatic (77-9-1) a madman; **lunacy** (77-9s1) madness.
lunch (8) **luncheon** (8-9) meal taken in the middle of the day.

lunge (at) (8nj) move forward as if pushing the point of a sword into.
lungs (8-z) the (two) part(s) of the body with which we breathe.
lurch (99) *To leave in the lurch* = leave in difficulties.
lurch (99) sudden roll to one side; **to lurch,** roll suddenly.
lurcher (99-9) dog used by a *poacher* (= man who kills birds or animals on another's land).
lure (1779) instrument for calling back a *hawk* (= bird used for catching other birds); **to lure,** draw a person on by promising gain or pleasure
lurid (177-1) looking like flames seen through smoke, white-yellow; *A lurid story* = very exciting and unpleasant story.
lurk (99) lie in wait, lie hidden.
luscious (8sh9) very sweet and pleasant to the taste; too sweet.
lush (grass) (8) growing freely and very green.
lust (8) strong desire for; evil desire.
lustre (8-9) brightness; glory; cloth which has a very shining, polished appearance.
lusty (8-1) young and strong.
lute (77) musical instrument.
luxury (8ksh9-1) possession and enjoyment of beautiful and costly things; enjoyable but not necessary thing; **lux'urious** (8gz179-19) very comfortable; **lux'uriant** (vegetation) (8gz179-19) plants growing very freely.

LUTE

lycée (11s21) school in France for children aged about 14-18.
lye (4I) water passed through wood *ashes* (= that soft material which is left after burning) used for washing.
l'ying-'in (4I·1 + 1) time spent in bed at childbirth.
lymph (1) colourless liquid in the body, a sort of blood without any red material in it.
lymph'atics (1-3-1) vessels (pipes) which carry the *lymph* (see above).
lynch (1) *The crowd lynched him* = the crowd killed him without giving him a proper hearing according to the law; **l'ynch l'aw** (+ 55) punishment by a crowd or group not according to the law.
lynx (1ngks) very fierce, wild cat-like animal which has keen sight.
lyre (4I9) musical instrument with strings held in a D-shaped frame.
LYNX
lyrics, lyrical poems (1-1 + 671-z) poems meant to be sung; short poems telling the poet's own thoughts and feelings.
lysol (4I-5) a dark oily acid used to kill *germs* (= microscopic living things which cause disease).

M

M, Roman figure, one thousand.

M.A. (2m + 21) Master of Arts, title given by a university to one who completes a certain course of study.

ma (44) child's cry for its mother.

ma'am (3 or 9) *madam* — title used by servants and shopkeepers in speaking to a lady.

mac'adam (9-3-9) road made of broken stones which are rolled very flat; **macadamized** (road) (9-3-9-41) road so made.

macaro'ni (3-9-67-1) dried flour and water formed into small pipes, made in Italy and other countries, boiled for food.

macar'oon (3-9-77) small sweet cake made of eggs, sugar, and powdered nuts.

mac'aw (9-55) large brightly coloured bird.

mace (21s) stick with a metal head, formerly used as a weapon, now carried by an officer as a sign of his office.

mace (21s) dried outer covering of a seed (*nutmeg*), used for giving a pleasant taste to food.

macerate (3s9-21) make soft by keeping in water; cause to become thin and weak.

Mach number (m4h + 8-9) A Mach number higher than 1 shows a speed of an aeroplane greater than the speed of sound.

mach'an (3-44) wooden tower, or floor in a tree, from which to shoot wild animals, e.g. tigers in India.

Machiav'ellian (3k19-2-19) very clever and dishonest, especially in dealings between one government and another.

machin'ation (3k1-21shn) making of plans to do evil; **to m'achinate** (3k1-21).

mach'ine (9sh11) instrument made up of several parts used to do work or to move itself or other things about; **to mach'ine**, prepare with the help of a machine; **sew** (= join together cloth with needle and thread) with a sewing-machine; **mach'inery** (——9-1) parts of a machine; a set of machines; **mach'inist** (——1) one who makes or works machines; **mach'ine-gun** (+ 8) gun which shoots one shot after another without being loaded each time.

mackerel (3-9) sea fish with a blue and silver skin.

mackintosh (3-1-5) coat which keeps out the rain.

macro- large, long, e.g. **macrocosm** (3-9-5z) = the great world — all the stars and heavenly bodies in the sky.

mad (3) having a disordered mind; very unwise; *To run like mad* = very fast.

madam(e) (3-9) = Mrs., title of a French lady; used also by servants and shopkeepers in speaking to an English lady.

madcap (3-3) very daring girl.

madden (3) make mad.

madder (3-9) plant from which a red colouring matter is obtained.

made (21) p.t. of Make.

Madeira (9-19-9) rich sweet wine; kind of cake.

m'ademoiselle (4-9-74z2) French title for an unmarried woman = Miss.

Madonna (9-5-9) Mary, the Mother of Christ; picture or figure of —.

madrigal (3-1) short love-poem or song; song for three or more voices.

maelstrom (21-67) part of the sea near Norway where the water turns round and round very quickly and draws ships down into it; any great disorder, e.g. of the mind.

magazine (3-9-11) storehouse for gunpowder and things used by soldiers; box-like part of a gun in which *cartridges* (= small round box containing powder and shot) are kept ready for firing.

magazine (3-9-11) book of stories, etc., by different writers sold usually every month.

magenta (9j2-9) blue-red colouring matter obtained from coal.

maggot (3-9) small creature without legs, e.g. found in bad meat or food.

magic (3j1) art of causing things to happen with the help of spirits and strange powers; adj. **magic, magical**, of magic, wonderful, done as if by magic; **magician** (9j1shn) one who works with magic.

m'agic-l'antern (3j1 + 3-9) instrument by which pictures are thrown in a beam of light on to a white sheet in a dark room.

magistrate (3j1-1) a judge; officer of government; **magistracy** (3j1-9s1) office of magistrate; all the magistrates, adj. **magisterial** (3j1-19-19).

magn'animous (3-3-1-9) having a great soul, generous and high-thinking; n. **magnanimity** (3-9-1-1-1).

magnate (3-21) person who has much money and power.

magnesium (3-11z19) white metal which burns with a bright light; **magnesia** (3-11z19) white powder made from magnesium, used as a medicine for the stomach.

magnet (3-1) piece of iron which draws to it other pieces of iron and, if hung up, always points north and south; **magnetism** (3-1-1-z) power of a magnet; study of magnets; (in a person) charm and power of making others do what one wishes.

magneto (3-11-67) electric machine which sets fire to the gas in making a motor-car go.

magnificent (3-1-1-1s) very fine, very good.

magnify (3-1-41) make a thing seem larger, e.g. by looking at it through a curved glass.

magn'iloquent (3-1-9-9) speaking in a foolishly solemn way.

magnitude (3-1-177) size, importance.

magn'olia (3-67-19) tree with large sweet-smelling flowers.

magnum (3-9) large bottle of wine.

magpie (3-41) black and white bird which makes a lot of noise and steals small objects; outer ring of a *target* (= board at which men shoot for practice).

Magy'ar (3-144) a people and the language spoken by them in Hungary.

Mahar'aja (44-9-44-9) great prince or king in India; **Mahar'ani** (44-9-44-11) Indian princess or queen.

mahatma (4-4-4) Indian title of respect for one who is very holy.

mah'ogany (9-5-9-1) red-brown wood.

mahout (4-77) driver of an elephant.

maid (21) young unmarried woman; woman servant; **m'aid-of-h'onour** (+ 9v + 5-9) noble lady who waits upon and serves a queen; **'old m'aid**, old unmarried woman; very careful and particular person.

maidan (41-44) open grassy space or public playing-fields in an Indian town.

maiden (21) young unmarried woman; **m'aiden n'ame** (+ 21) woman's name before she was married; **m'aiden v'oyage** (+ 51j) first journey made by a new ship.

mail (21) armour.

mail (21) letters, the general post; **to mail**, to post letters.

maim (21) cause a person to lose the use of a limb; make an animal unfit for use.

main (21) (in poetry) the ocean.

main (21) chief, most important; **a w'atermain** (55-9 + 21) water pipe under the street; **m'ainland** (21-3) large piece of land, not small islands near it; **mainly** (——1) chiefly; **m'ain-spring** (+ 1) chief spring, e.g. of a clock; most important cause of an event or reason for action.

mainstay (21-21) rope holding up the *mainmast* (= middle upright pole carrying sails) of a ship; the chief support, e.g. of a family.

maint'ain (2-21) to support; pay the costs of; *To maintain an opinion* = to speak in favour of —; n. **m'aintenance** (21-9-9-s) payment of the costs of.

m'aison'ette (21-5-2) small house or part of a house used as a home for one family.

maize (21) Indian corn.

majesty (3-1-1) honour and glory; **Your Majesty** (one speaks to a king in this way); adj. **maj'estic** (9-2-1).

major (21-9) greater; *Smith major* = elder of the two Smith brothers in a school.

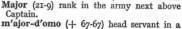
MAIZE

Major (21-9) rank in the army next above Captain.

m'ajor-d'omo (+ 67-67) head servant in a large house.

maj'ority (9-5-1-1) the greater number; *To reach one's majority* = become 21 years old.

make (21) put together things so as to produce a new object; cause to do; *To make a bed* = set the sheets, etc., in order again, ready for use; *I'll make him do it* = force him to —; *What time do you make it?* = what do you think is the time?; *Make away with* = destroy; *Make for* = go towards; *Make off* = run away; *Make out* = see or read with difficulty; *Make over* = give; *Make it up* = end a quarrel; *Make up to* = make oneself pleasant to; *Make it up to you* = pay for damage done; *Make tea (or coffee)* = prepare for drinking; n. **make**, *Of good make* = well made; *On the make* = trying to get money or success; *The Maker* or *Our Maker* = God; **m'ake-bel'ieve** (21 + 1-11) pretended; act of pretending; **makeshift** (21-1) means or instrument used because the right one is not obtainable; **m'ake-up** (21 + 8) powder and paint put on a woman's or actor's face; **m'akeweight** (21-21) a little added to make something seem stronger or better.

mal- bad, badly, e.g. **malformed** (3-55) = badly formed; **malcontent** (3-9-2) = not contented, discontented.

malachite (3-9k41) green stone used for ornament.

m'aladj'usted (3-9-8-1) fitting badly.

malady (3-9-1) illness.

mal'aise (3-21z) slight discomfort of the body, e.g. caused by illness.

mal'aria (9-29-19) illness caused by the bite of a *mosquito*.

m'al de m'er (3 + 9 + 29) sea-sickness.

male (21) animal which can become a father; having that power which makes seeds able to grow.

maled'iction (3-1-1-shn) speaking evil against a person.

malefactor (3-1-3-9) wrong-doer.

mal'evolence (9-2-9-9-s) desire to do harm to others; adj. **mal'evolent** (9-2-9-9).

m'alform'ation (3-55-21shn) bad shape of a part of the body.

malice (3-1s) desire to do harm to others; **mal'icious** (9-1shə) desiring to —.

mal'ign (9-41) speak evil of; adj. evil.

mal'ignant (9-1-9) feeling great hatred against; *Malignant disease* = a disease which will probably cause death.

mal'inger (9-1ŋg9) pretend to be ill.

mallard (3-9) kind of wild duck.

malleable (3-19) able to be shaped or beaten into a thin sheet with a hammer, e.g. gold.

mallet (3-1) small hammer usually made of wood.

mallow (3-67) plant with blue-red flowers.

m'alnutr'ition (3-177-1shn) not getting enough food—or getting wrong food.
mal'odorous (3-67-9-9) having a nasty smell.
malt (55) grain which has begun to grow in water and is then dried and used for making strong drink.
m'altr'eat (3-11) treat badly.
mamm'a (9-44) **mammy** (3-1) childish name, or cry, for its mother.
mammal (3) animal of the kind which feeds its young with its milk.
mammon (3-9) wealth—especially as an evil.
mammoth (3-9) animal like an elephant, but hairy, which lived many thousands of years ago; adj. very large.
man (3) (1) a human; *To a man* = all; *The inner man* = stomach; (2) grown man, not a boy; *Man of the world* = experienced person; *Man in the street* = any man who has no special knowledge of the subject spoken of; *Be a man! Play the man!* = be brave; (3) small piece of bone or wood used in a game; **to man,** supply with men, e.g. put seamen on a ship, soldiers in a place to be defended.
manacle (3-9) iron bands and a chain for the hands of a prisoner.
manage (3-1j) (1) to control, to direct, e.g. *Manage a horse* = ride and control; *Manage a business* = have charge of; (2) do successfully; *I can't manage it alone* = I need help to do it; *I'll manage somehow* = I will do it, though it is difficult; the **management** (3-1j-9) group of persons controlling a business; *a very* **managing** (3-1j1) *woman* = one who likes to control others.
Manchester goods (3-1-9 + 7-z) cotton goods, as for shirts, etc.
mandarin (3-9-1) officer of the government in ancient China; small orange.
mandate (3-21) command of; power to act for another.
mandible (3-1) lower *jaw*-bone (*jaw* = the bone in which the teeth are set).
m'andol'in (3-9-1) musical instrument with strings.
mandrake (3-21) plant which helps to bring sleep.
mandrill (3-1) large creature like a monkey.
mane (21) long hair at the back of the neck of a horse or lion, etc.   MANDOLIN
manful (3) brave.
m'angan'ese (3ngg9-11z) grey metal.
mange (21nj) skin disease, especially of dogs and cats.
mangel wurzel, mangold wurzel (3ngg+99) large root, used as food for cattle.
manger (21nj9) container, fixed to the wall, in which a horse's food is put.
mangle (3ngg) machine used for pressing washed clothes to dry them; to mangle clothes.
mangle (3ngg) to cut and make useless.

mango (3ngg67) Indian fruit, green outside, yellow inside, with a large stone.
mangrove (3ngg-67) tree or bush found on very wet land.
mangy (21nj1) suffering from *mange* (see 7th above); Sl. bad, weak, nasty.
man-handle (3 + 3) treat roughly.
manhole (3-67) hole (e.g. in the street) through which a man may pass to repair underground pipes, etc.
mania (21-19) madness; great interest in, e.g. *She has a mania for the theatre*; **maniac** (21-13) madman.
-mania (21-19) (1) madness, e.g. **klepto-m'ania** (2-9-21-19) mad desire to steal; (2) great interest in, e.g. **bibliom'ania** (1-1-67-21-19) great interest in books.
manicure (3-1-179) treatment of the finger-nails and hands to make them beautiful.
manifest (3-1-2) to show or express clearly; adj. **manifest**, clearly shown; *A ship's manifest* = list of goods carried on a ship; **manifest'ation** (3-1-2-21shn) showing, e.g. *A manifestation of feeling*.
manif'esto (3-1-2-67) declaration of future plans made by a group of men, a ruler, etc.
manifold (3-1-67) (1) many and various; (2) make many copies of —.
manikin (3-1-1) small man; small copy of the human figure made of wood.
man'ila (9-1-9) (hemp) material of which rope is made; (paper) strong brown paper.
manioc (3-15) plant from which *tapioca* (= white grains, glass-like when boiled, used as food) is obtained.
man'ipulate (9-1-17-21) to handle; deal with cleverly or dishonestly.
m'ank'ind (3-41) race of man.
manly (3-1) brave and noble.
manna (3-9) food given by God to the people of Israel in the desert.
mannequin (3-1k1) figure made of wax used to show clothes in a shop; a woman in a shop who puts on dresses to show a possible buyer what they look like when being worn.
manner (3-9) (1) way in which a thing happens or is done; *After this manner* = in this way; *To the manner born* = as if having done something in a special way ever since birth; (2) way of speaking and behaving in public; *Good manners* = polite behaviour; *To have no manners* = be impolite; *By no manner of means* = certainly not.
mannerism (3-9-1z) action used too often by a person in his behaviour, speech, writing, etc.
mannish (3-1) like a man, e.g. *A very mannish woman*.
man'oeuvre (9-77-9) (1) move armies or ships of war; (2) arrange matters to suit one's own purposes; n. **manoeuvres** (———z) movements of warships or armies for practice; tricks to obtain one's aims.
man-of-war (3 + 9v + 55) warship.

manor (3-9) certain amount of land held by a Lord of the Manor in England.

manse (3) house of a Scottish priest.

mansion (3nshn) large house, e.g. of a rich man.

manslaughter (3-55-9) unlawful killing of a person without meaning to kill him (or her).

mantelpiece (3-11s) ornamental square built round and above the fire-place in a room; **mantelshelf** (3-2) flat place on top of the mantelpiece on which a clock and ornaments may be put.

MANTELSHELF

mant'illa (3-1-9) piece of cloth worn as a *head-dress* (= covering for the head) especially in Spain.

mantle (3) loose outer garment; cap of specially treated cotton which forms part of a gas lamp; **to mantle**, to cover, to spread over.

manual (3-179) (1) done with the hands; (2) short book on a special subject; (3) that part of an *organ* (= large musical instrument with many pipes often found in churches) which is played by the hands.

manuf'actory (3-17-3-9-1) place where things are made in large numbers, usually by machines; **manuf'acture** (3-17-3-tshg) make things in a manufactory.

m'anum'it (3-17-1) to set free; **manum'ission** (3-17-1shn) setting free.

man'ure (9-179) spread matter on the soil so as to give food to plants; matter so used, e.g. the *droppings* (= waste of food passed out of the body) of cattle.

manuscript (3-17-1) adj. written by hand; n. book written by hand and ready for printing.

many (2-1) large number of.

map (3) flat plan of a country or of the world; **to map**, to make a map; *To map out* = to plan.

maple (21) tree (from some maples sugar is made).

maqu'is (4k11) (1) thick forest of small trees; (2) secret French fighters against the Germans; (3) such fighters elsewhere.

mar (44) make useless; to ruin.

marabou (3-9-77) African bird; its feathers are very soft and are used for women's dress.

Marathon (race) (3-9-9) a very long race (for men, not horses), e.g. 26 miles.

mar'aud (9-55) make an attack so as to carry away money and goods.

marble (44) (1) hard stone which is polished and used for buildings, graves, etc.; (2) to colour in wavy lines so as to look like marble; (3) small stone or glass ball used by children in playing.

march (44) to walk like a soldier; cause to walk —; distance walked; music to help soldiers to march well; *A march past* = show of soldiers marching past the king or some important officer; *A forced march* = unusually long march; *To steal a march on* = do secretly something which another person was meaning to do and so be better placed than he.

marches (44-1z) borders of a country.

marchioness (44shg-1) wife of a *marquess* (= title of nobleman in England, second below a prince).

mare (29) female horse; *To go on Shanks's Mare* = walk; **m'are's nest** (29z + 2) wonderful discovery imagined, not real.

m'argar'ine (44jg-11) fat obtained from plants or animals and made to look and taste like butter.

marge (44j) Sl. margarine.

margin (44j1) border; white part round a printed page; further amount allowed beyond what is necessary, e.g. *A margin of time* = more time than is needed for doing a certain piece of work; *To deal in margins* = buy and sell shares in business companies, not paying for them, but paying only the difference between the buying- and the selling-price.

marginal (land) (44j1) land too poor to be used by farmers unless helped by the government.

marguerite (44-9-11) flower, as shown.

mariage de convenance (3-1443 + 9 + k5ⁿ-9-44ⁿs) marriage made not for love but for reasons of money.

marigold (3-1-67) yellow flower.

MARGUERITE

m'ariju'ana, m'arihu'ana (3-1h74-4) (= hashish, Indian hemp) plant sometimes put in cigarettes, which causes excitement and dreams.

mar'ine (9-11) (1) of the sea; (2) all the ships of a country; (3) soldier serving on a ship; **mariner** (3-1-9) seaman.

m'arion'ette (3-19-2) wooden figure moved by strings in a theatre.

MARIGOLD

marital (3-1-9) having to do with a husband or marriage.

maritime (3-1-41) bordering on the sea.

mark (44) any sign or line made on a clean surface; *To make one's mark* = get fame; *A trade mark* = sign on a thing showing who made it; *Beside the mark* = having nothing to do with the question being talked about; *To miss the mark* = fail in one's purpose; *Grey hairs are a mark of age* = sign of —; *Below the mark* = not good enough, ill; *Up to the mark* = good enough, well; *School marks* = numbers showing the quality of children's work in school; **to mark**, make a mark on; give school-marks to; *Mark my words* = remember what I say; *To mark time* = move the feet as if marching, without moving forward; stand waiting for orders or for a chance to act.

mark (44) piece of German money.

market (44-1) (**1**) public meeting of people to buy and sell; (**2**) open space for this purpose; *To come into the market* = be offered for *sale* (= selling); (**3**) trade in a certain kind of goods; (**4**) *demand* (= need) for certain goods, e.g. *There is no market for these goods in Canada* = no one wants to buy them; *The market rose* = prices became higher; **marketable** (44-1-9) such as can be sold; **m'marketg'arden** (+ 44) garden in which vegetables are grown for *sale* (= selling).

marksman (44-9) man who shoots well.

marlinespike (44-1-4I) instrument used for separating the threads of a rope.

marmalade (44-9-2I) oranges cut up and boiled in sugar (also other fruit so cooked).

m'armos'et (44-9zz) small monkey with a hairy tail.

marmot (44-9) small animal with a big tail which makes holes in the ground.

mar'oon (9-77) brown-red colour.

MARMOSET

mar'oon (9-77) round box of gunpowder which makes a loud noise when set fire to.

mar'oon (9-77) leave a person on a desert island.

marque (44k) *Letters of marque* = letter written by the king allowing the owner of a private ship to attack the enemy's ships.

marqu'ee (44kII) large tent, e.g. one in which tea is served at a public gathering in the open air.

MARMOT

marquis (44-1) title of a nobleman, second below a prince.

marriage (3-Iij) n. of Marry.

marrow (3-67) (**1**) fat inside a bone; (**2**) large fruit which grows on the ground and is cooked for food.

marry (3-1) join as husband and wife; take as husband or wife; n. **marriage** (3-Iij); **marriage settlement** (+ 2-9) arrangement made about money at the time of marriage.

marsh (44) a low-lying wet land.

marshal (44) high officer in the court of a king; **Field-Marshal** (II +) highest rank in the army; **to marshal**, arrange in order, to lead solemnly.

marshalling-yard (44-9-1 + 44) place where goods carried by rail are regrouped according to where they are sent.

mars'upial (44sI77-19) animal which carries its young in a pocket, e.g. the *kangaroo* (see Kangaroo).

mart (44) market-place.

marten (44-1) small animal valued for its fur.

martial (44shl) having to do with war, warlike.

martin (44-1) small bird.

m'artin'et (44-1-2) person who demands very exact *obedience* (n. of Obey).

mart'ini (44-II-1) small strong drink taken before a meal (gin and French vermouth).

martyr (44-9) one who is put to death for refusing to give up his faith; one who is in continuous suffering; *To make a martyr of oneself* = suffer *needlessly* (= unnecessarily) in order to be thought well of.

marvel (44) wonderful thing; adj. **marvellous** (44-9-9).

m'arzip'an (44-1-3) mixture of powdered nut, sugar and egg, often put on the top of a cake.

masc'ara (3-44-9) dark paint used round the eyes to make them beautiful.

mascot (3-9) thing, person, or animal supposed to bring good fortune.

masculine (3-17-1) having to do with men, not women; strong; in language the opposite of feminine, e.g. "he" is a masculine word, "she" is the feminine.

mash (3) warm food for horses; any soft food; **to mash**, make into a soft wet mass.

mask (44) small piece of cloth, usually silk, used to cover the upper half of the face; painted shape of an animal's face or strange human face used to hide one's real face; any covering or protection for the face; *A death mask* = shape of the face taken by pressing *clay* (= soft sticky earth) on it after death; **to mask**, cover with a mask, hide.

masochism (3-6kI) taking pleasure in suffering pain, as seen in some mad people.

mason (21) man who works with stone; **masonry** (——-1) stonework; **fr'eem'asonry**, secret brotherhood.

masque (44-k) short play with a grand show— and sometimes no speaking.

m'asquer'ade (3-k9-2I) dance at which *masks* (see 4th above) are worn; **to m'asquer'ade**, pretend to be some other person; make a false appearance.

Mass (3) religious ceremony in the Church of Rome in which Christ's Last Supper is remembered.

mass (3) quantity of matter; number of separate things pressed together to make one solid body; large quantity; **the masses** (——-Iz) the people.

massacre (3-9k9) a general killing of men, women and children.

massage (3-443) rubbing of the body as a means of lessening pain or bringing back health to a certain part; **a mass'eur** (3-9) man skilled in that art; **mass'euse** (3-99z) woman —.

massive (3-1) having great size and weight.

m'ass-observ'ation (3 + 5-z9-2Ishn) study of the customs and ways of living of ordinary people.

m'ass prod'uction (3 + 9-8) making very

large numbers of things so that they may be produced cheaply.

mast (44) upright pole in a ship to which the sails are fixed.

master (44-9) one who employs another; head of a house; owner; chief or leader; teacher; writer or painter of great fame; **to master**, conquer; learn thoroughly; **masterful** (44-9) having a strong will; not listening to others.

master-key (+ 11) key which opens several locks.

masterly (44-9-1) very cleverly done.

masterpiece (44-9-11s) best piece of work done by a writer, painter, etc.

mastery (44-9-1) thorough learning of a subject.

masticate (3-1-21) bite thoroughly.

mastiff (3-1) large dog.

mastodon (3-9-5) very large animal which lived in the world many thousands of years ago.

mastoid (3-5I) part of the bone behind the ear.

mat (3) small floor covering; small piece of cloth or other material put under a flower-pot or plate.

mat (3) having a rough surface.

matador (3-9-55) man who kills the *bull* in a bull-fight in Spain.

match (3) small stick with a head used for making fire; **m'atchwood** (3-7) small sticks.

match (3) (1) person or thing exactly like another; one's equal in a game; a game played between two persons or groups; (2) marriage; *He is a good match* = good person to marry, e.g. because rich; **to match**, get something which is like something else in colour or in shape; be like something else; **matchless** (——1) very good, without an equal.

matchboard (3-55) thin board with the edge so cut as to fit into the edge of another board.

matchmaker (3-21-9) woman who interests herself in arranging marriages.

mate (21) fellow-worker; husband or wife; officer in rank next below the captain on a ship; **to mate**, marry.

mat'erial (9-19-19) of matter, not of the spirit; very important; n. matter from which anything is made; cloth; **mat'erialist** (9-19-19-1) one who believes that there is nothing except matter, no soul or spirit; **mat'erialize** (9-19-19-41) make material become real; **mat'erially** (9-19-19-1) actually, very much.

mat'ernal (9-99) like a mother, gentle and loving; *Maternal uncle* = uncle on my mother's side—mother's brother; **mat'ernity** (9-99-1-1) motherhood.

mathem'atics (3-1-3-1) science of space and numbers; adj. **mathem'atical** (3-1-3-1).

matinée (3-1-21) morning or afternoon show in a theatre.

matricide (21-1s41) one who kills his mother; act of —.

matr'iculate (9-1-17-21) enter into a university; pass an examination.

matrimony (3-1-9-1) marriage.

matrix (21-1) pl. **matrices** (21-1s11z) shape into which hot metal is poured.

matron (21) married woman; woman in charge of the food and housework in a school; woman in charge of the nurses and nursing in a hospital.

matted (3-1) twisted together, e.g. *Matted hair* = disordered hair twisted together into a mass.

matter (3-9) (1) that of which all things are made; (2) poisonous liquid which comes out of a wound; (3) subject being talked about; (4) ideas of a book or speech; *As a matter of fact* = this is the truth; *A matter of course* = something expected, a natural result; *No laughing matter* = a serious business; *No matter* = it is not important; *What's the matter?* = what is troubling you?; *For the matter of that* = so far as that is concerned; *A matter of £10* = about £10; *Printed matter* = printed books and papers; **to matter**, be important; **m'atter-of-f'act**, keeping to real things, not imagining things.

matting (3-1) floor-covering made of dried stems of plants or other rough vegetable material.

mattock (3-9) instrument, as shown, used for breaking up ground.

mattress (3-1) large flat bag of hair or other soft material laid on a bed; **w'ire m'attress** (419 +) arrangement of wire in the frame of the bed supporting the (hair-) mattress.

MATTOCK

mat'ure (9-179) fully grown; made perfect; ready for use; carefully thought out; **to mat'ure**, become fully grown, etc.

maudlin (55-1) full of weak and silly feeling.

maul (55) beat, treat roughly.

maulstick (55-f) stick used by painters to steady the hand.

maunder (55-9) move, act or talk in a dreamy way.

m'ausol'eum (55-9-11·9) beautiful building used as a grave.

mauve (67) light red-blue colour.

maw (55) stomach.

mawkish (55-1) having a nasty rather sweet taste; (of a book, play, etc.) full of weak and silly feeling.

maxim (3-1) short saying expressing a general truth; rule of behaviour.

m'axim g'un (3-1 + 8) gun which shoots one shot after another without being loaded each time, the *cartridges* (= boxes of shot) being carried in a long cloth band.

maximum (3-1-9) greatest possible size, number, quality, etc.

maybe (21-11) possibly, perhaps.

m'ayonn'aise (219-21z) thick yellow cream (oil, eggs, *vinegar* (= a very sour liquid)) put on fish and uncooked green vegetables.

mayor (29) chief officer of a town or city.

maypole (21-67) high post ornamented with flowers round which people dance.

mayst (21) *Thou mayst* = you may.

maze (21) many paths turning this way and that way, so that it is difficult to find one's way through them; any very difficult matter.

maz'urka (9-99-9) a dance for 8 or 16 people.

mead (11) strong drink made from *honey* (= sweet liquid made by bees).

mead (11) **meadow** (2-67) grassy field.

meagre (11-9) thin, not enough.

meal (11) *coarsely* (= not fine) powdered grain.

meal (11) time when food is taken; food taken.

mealy-mouthed (11-1 + 47δ) unwilling to use plain words.

mean (11) low, bad, unkind, or dishonest in small ways; too careful of money.

mean (11) amount or state just half-way between two quantities or qualities, neither very great nor small, good nor bad; 4 is the mean of 2, 3 and 7 (2 + 3 + 7 = 12, 12 ÷ 3 = 4); *The golden mean, The happy mean* = that action which is just right, neither too much nor too little.

mean (11) (1) have an aim or purpose in mind; *He means business* = he will really do something—not just talk; *What do you mean by saying that!* = how dare you — !; (2) (of a word or group of words) express a certain idea, e.g. *The Latin word "homo" means "a man"*; (3) be important, e.g. *This work means a lot to me*.

me'ander (11-3-9) (of a river) flow along a very wandering course.

means (11-z) (1) that by which something is done, e.g. *I cut it by means of a knife; To do it by fair means or foul* = get work done in a dishonest way if the honest way is impossible; *By all means* = certainly, of course; *By no means a nice person* = not at all nice—very nasty; (2) money; being able to pay; *To live within one's means* = not spend more money than one has; *A man of means* = a rich man; *Means test* = asking how much money a person is getting before giving help (money, a cheap house, etc.) from the government.

m'eant'ime (11-41) **meanwh'ile** (11-41) in the time between two events; at the same time.

measles (11z-z) disease which spreads from one person to another, causing red spots on the skin and liquid running from the eyes and nose.

measly (11z-1) poor and of no value.

measure (239) (1) size, weight, or amount expressed as feet, pounds, etc.; *To give short measure* = give less than the right amount; *Clothes made to measure* = made specially for the buyer; *I've taken his measure* = I know what he can do, how clever (or foolish) he is; (2) instrument used for measuring; way of measuring, e.g. *An inch is a measure of length; Beyond measure* = very much; (3) regular beat of poetry or music; *To tread a measure* = to dance; (4) the plan of a law being considered by the government; (5) action, e.g. *To take measures against wrongdoers* = do something to stop wrong-doing, punish wrongdoers; **measured** (239) slow and steady; **measureless** (239-1) so large or great that it cannot be measured.

meat (11) part of the body of an animal used as food; (in old books) any food; *This book is full of meat* = has many ideas in it; **meaty** (11-1) full of meat.

mech'anic (1k3-1) having to do with a machine; one employed in working machines; **mech'anical**, having to do with machines, done by machines; behaving like a machine, acting in the same way again and again without thought; **mechanism** (2k9-1z) piece of machinery; **mechanize** (2k9-41) make mechanical, e.g. *The mechanized part of the army* = that part of the army in which all is done by machines, no horses being used.

medal (2) piece of metal with a picture and writing cut or pressed upon it, given as an honour, e.g. to a soldier; **med'allion** (1-3-19) round piece of stone or metal with a picture on it.

meddle (2) to busy oneself with the concerns of other people; *He is a* **meddlesome** (2-9) *fellow* = he is always concerning himself with other people's business.

media (11-19) pl. of Medium.

medi'aeval (2-1-11) having to do with the Middle Ages, about A.D. 500 to A.D. 1500.

mediate (11-121) make peace between two people; settle a quarrel.

medicate (2-1-21) give medicine to; put medicine into, e.g. *Medicated wool*; a **med'icament** (2-1-9-9) form of medicine.

medicine (2-sn) science and art of bringing sick persons back to health; powders, liquids, etc., used for this purpose; charms thought by simple people to have magic power; *A medicine man* = one who does magic.

mediocre (11-167-9) not very good; **medi'ocrity** (11-15-1-1) state of being not very good; person who is not very clever—nor foolish.

meditate (2-1-21) think deeply.

medium (11-19) (1) middle; (2) means by which a thing is done; *a medium*, person supposed to be able to receive messages from the spirits of the dead; (3) that place in which a creature can live, e.g. *Fish live in a watery medium*; (4) material used in painting or drawing; adj. having a place half-way between two things; not having one quality nor the other, but between the two; not good, nor bad.

medlar (2-9) small brown fruit eaten when it begins to decay.

medley (2-1) mixture; mixed piece of music.

meed (11) that praise or payment given one who has done well.

meek (11) gentle, not proud.

meerschaum (19sh9) white soft stone-like material of which pipes are made for smoking.

meet (11) come together from opposite directions; *To meet a person's wishes* = do what he wants; *Meet a person half way* = yield some of one's opinions in order to agree; *Meet a bill* = pay a debt; *Make both ends meet* = make one's cost of living no greater than the money one has; *To meet with trouble* = suffer; *It is meet that I should* = it is right and proper; **a meet** (11) gathering of dogs and men for a hunt; **meeting** (11-1) coming together of persons for some special purpose.

mega- great.

megalith (2-9-1) very large stone used in building by ancient people; ancient building made of very large stones.

m'egalom'ania (2-9-67-21-19) mad desire for greatness, or mad idea that one is great.

m'egalos'aurus (2-9-67-55-9) very large animal which lived on the earth thousands of years ago.

megaphone (2-9-67) metal horn used to make the voice louder.

MEGALOSAURUS

megrim (11-1) pain in the head; *To have the megrims* = feel sad and without hope.

melanch'olia (2-9-k67-19) feeling of great sadness; loss of all hope.

mélange (21-44ⁿ3) mixture.

mêlée (2-21) mixed-up fight, in which all seem to be fighting against each other.

mell'ifluous (voice) (2-1-79) smooth and sweet.

mellow (2-67) made soft, sweet or gentle by time.

mel'odious (1-67-19) sweet sounding.

melodrama (2-9-44-9) play, full of exciting events, which ends happily.

melody (2-9-1) set of notes, one after another, which make a pleasing piece of music, e.g. *The melody of a song*; any pleasing music.

melon (2-9) large sweet fruit which grows on the ground and has a very watery inside.

melt (2) become liquid by heat; cause to become liquid; soften, e.g. *Her tears melted my heart* = made me feel pity; *To melt away* = disappear.

member (2-9) limb; one of a group.

membrane (2-21) thin covering of skin inside the body.

mem'ento (1-2-67) thing which helps one to remember a person.

memo (2-67) a note to help the memory.

memoir (2-744) written account of events; **memoirs** (———z), story of interesting events and experiences remembered in one's life.

memorable (2-9-9) worth remembering; easily remembered.

memor'andum (2-9-3-9) note to help the memory; a report.

mem'orial (1-55-19) thing used to cause persons to remember, e.g. stone put up in honour of the dead; paper written on a subject in order to make certain opinions known to the government; **to mem'orialize** (———4Iz) send a *memorial* (= written paper) to a government.

memorize (2-9-41) fix in the memory.

memory (2-9-1) (1) power of remembering; *In living memory* = remembered by those alive now; (2) something remembered; *A stone in memory of* = intended to cause people to remember.

mem-sahib (2 + 4-1) title used in speaking to a European woman in India.

menace (2-9s) probable danger; **to menace**, say that one will do harm to a person.

mén'age (2-44з) general arrangement, work, and servants of a house.

men'agerie (1-3j9-1) collection of wild animals kept for show.

mend (2) to repair, to put right; become better in health.

mend'acious (2-21sh9) untruthful.

mendicant (2-1-9) person who begs for money.

menial (11-19) having to do with a servant in a house; (work) such as a servant does; a house servant.

m'ening'itis (2-inj41-1) disease of the *membrane* (= thin skin) covering the brain.

men'iscus (2-1-8) curved top of liquid in a tube; piece of glass curved out on one side, in on the other; a soft plate so shaped between two bones in the body.

menopause (2-6-55) "change of life" in a woman at about the age of 50.

mensur'ation (2-179-21shn) science and art of measuring or of calculating length and size.

mental (2) having to do with the mind; *A mental case* = mad person; *Mental arithmetic* = adding, dividing, etc., done without the help of pen and paper; n. **ment'ality** (2-3-1-1).

menthol (2-5) white material which, when rubbed on the skin, makes it feel first hot, then very cold—used as a medicine for the nose, also to lessen pain.

mention (2-shn) speak of; *Not to mention others* = and other things (or people) of which (whom) it is not necessary to speak; *He was given an honourable mention* = his work was praised though he did not get the *prize* (= money or things given to one who has done the best work).

mentor (2-55) trusted adviser.

menu (2-17) list of foods which will be served at a meal.

mercantile (99-41) having to do with trade; employed in trade; *The mercantile marine* = ships which carry goods or travellers—not warships.

mercenary (99sI-1) eager for money; working only for money, not for honour, or loyalty; hired soldier.

mercer (99s9) seller of cloth and silk.

mercerize (99s9-41) treat cotton cloth in such a way as to make it strong and silk-like.

merchandise (99-41z) goods bought and sold.

merchant (99) one who carries on trade in a large way; *The merchant service* = ships which carry travellers and goods; **merchantman (99-9)** ship which carries goods and sometimes travellers.

merciful (99sI-9) merciless (99sI-1) see Mercy.

merc'urial (99-179-19) like *mercury* (see below); quickly changing in mind and feelings.

mercury (99-17-1) liquid white metal.

mercy (99sI) gentleness; pity; forgiveness; *To show mercy to* = not to harm one whom one has the power to harm; *At the mercy of* = in the power of; *Left to the tender mercy of* = in the power of one who will probably do one harm; *That's a mercy!* = a thing for which one should be thankful (to God).

mere (19) a lake.

mere (19) only, not more than; **merely (19-1)** only.

meretr'icious (2-1-1sh9s) making an outward (but unreal) show of beauty or goodness.

merge (99j) join one thing completely with another; **a merger (99j9)** uniting of several business companies.

mer'idian (9-1-19) (1) imaginary line drawn on the earth from north to south; such a line on a map; (2) twelve o'clock, or the middle of the day; (3) highest point reached by a star; time of greatest power or success.

mer'ingue (9-3) mixture of egg and sugar baked into a light cake.

mer'ino (9-11-67) kind of sheep; soft cloth made from its wool.

merit (2-1) (1) be worthy of; n. that of which one is worthy; *To reward a person according to his merits* = give a person that praise or punishment (etc.) of which he is worthy; (2) goodness; **merit'orious (2-1-55-19)** good; worthy.

mermaid (99-21) imaginary sea creature, half woman and half fish; **merman (99-3)** half man and half fish.

merry (2-1) full of happiness; gay; *To make merry* = have a happy time, to feast and drink; n. **merriment (2-1-9)**.

m'erry-go-round (2-1 + 67 + 47) machine having seats made in the shape of animals, on which people are carried round in a circle as an amusement.

MERRY-GO-ROUND

merry-thought (2-1 + 55) V-shaped bone of a hen (pulled by two people while wishing for good fortune).

més'alliance (2z3-19-s) marriage between a person of high and one of low rank.

mes'eems (1-11-z) it seems to me.

mesh (2) one of the open spaces of a net; **meshes (——Iz)** threads of a net; (of wheels) **to mesh**, fit one wheel on to another so that the one wheel causes the other to turn.

mess (2) (1) state of dirt and disorder; (2) make dirty; (3) mixture; (4) (in old books) dish of food; Sl. *To mess about* = move about in a lazy way, not doing any real work.

mess (officers', sergeants') (2) meals served to a group of —; *To mess together* = eat at a common table.

message (2-1j) news or orders sent by letter or word of mouth; **messenger (2-1nj9)** one who carries a message.

Mess'iah (1-4I9) expected deliverer of the Jews; Jesus Christ; any hoped-for deliverer.

messmate (2-21) fellow soldier or seaman whom one meets at meals; friend.

Messrs. (2-9z) e.g. *Messrs. Smith and Jones* = Mr. Smith and Mr. Jones.

met (2) p.t. of Meet.

met'abolism (2-3-9-1z) complete change, e.g. building up of food into the body.

metal (2) certain kind of substance, such as gold, iron, etc.; *Road-metal* = broken stones; *The metals* = railway lines; adj. **met'allic (1-3-1)**.

met'allurgy (2-3-9jr) art of making metals pure.

metam'orphosis (2-9-55-9-1) change of shape or character.

metaphor (2-9-9) way of stretching the meaning of a word and using it to express an idea different from its own usual meaning, e.g. The sea—A sea of troubles.

metaph'ysics (2-9-1zI) study of the beginning of everything, of the character and cause of life, the nature of God, etc.

mete (II) to measure out, e.g. *To mete out punishment*.

meteor (11-19) shining mass which appears for a short time in the sky; a falling star.

m'eteor'ology (11-19-5-9j1) scientific study of the weather, and telling what future weather will be.

meter (11-9) instrument for measuring, e.g. **ped'ometer (2-5-1-9)** = instrument for measuring the distance walked.

meth'inks (1-1ngks) it seems to me; I think.

method (2-9) way of doing something; regular arrangement.

Methodist (2-9-1) member of a group of Christian people following the teaching and practice of John Wesley.

meth'ought (1-55) it seemed to me.

m'ethylated sp'irits (2-1-1zI-1 + 1-1) *alcohol* (= that clear liquid which gives wine and strong drink its effect on the mind and body) made unfit for drinking, used for burning in lamps to produce heat.

met′iculous (1-1-17-9) too careful about small things.

métier (2-121) that work for which one is specially fitted.

metre (11-9) regular arrangement of sounds in poetry; adj. **metrical** (2-1).

metre (11-9) French measure = 39·37 inches; **m′etric s′ystem** (2-1 + 1-1) the weights and measures used in France.

Metro, The (2-67) underground railway in Paris.

metr′opolis (1-5-9-1) chief city of a country; adj. **metrop′olitan** (2-9-5-1); *Bishop Metropolitan* = *bishop* (= high officer of the Church) who has control over other bishops.

mettle (2) courage; high spirits; *Put him on his mettle* = make a person try to do his best.

mew (177) to put in a cage.

mew (177) to cry like a cat.

mews (177z) line of small houses for horses and carriages.

mezzanine floor (2z9-11) low floor between two other floors of a house—usually between the first (ground) floor and the floor above it.

M.I.5 (2m + 4I + f4Iv) secret service of the War Office in Britain.

mi′aow (147) cry of a cat.

mi′asma (13z-9) harmful mist.

mica (4I-9) material found in the ground which looks like glass, easily broken into very thin leaves or sheets.

mice (4Is) pl. of Mouse.

Michaelmas (1k9-9) feast of St. Michael, September 29th, the end of the third quarter of the year.

micro- small.

microbe (4I-67) very small living thing, seen only with the help of a *microscope* (see 5th below) e.g. one causing disease.

microcosm (4I-9-5z) a small world which shows the arrangement and nature of a large world, e.g. an ant-hill—of a city.

micr′ometer (4I-5-1-9) instrument used for measuring very small distances.

micron (4I-5)—A millimetre is $\frac{1}{1000}$th of a metre; a micron is $\frac{1}{1000}$th of a millimetre; 0·00004 inch.

microphone (4I-9-67) instrument used for changing sound-waves into electric waves.

microscope (4I-9-67) instrument by which very small things can be seen; **m′icrosc′opic** (4I-9-5-1) very small.

microtome (4I-9-67) instrument for cutting very thin pieces of material so that they may be seen under the microscope.

MICROSCOPE

mid- the middle of, e.g. **mid-day** (1 + 21).

middle (1) centre; equal distance between two points; *Middle-age* = middle part of life, age 40 to 60; *The Middle Ages* = A.D. 500 to A.D. 1500; *Middle class* = not noblemen, not common working men, but those in between, e.g. shopkeepers, doctors, teachers, etc.

middleman (1-9) trader who buys goods in large quantities from the maker, and sells in smaller quantities to shops.

middling (1-1) of middle-size; not good, nor bad; *To feel middling* = not ill, not very well.

middy (1-1) see Midshipman (4th below).

midge (1j) very small winged insect which bites.

midget (1j1) very small person.

midriff (1-1) wall of muscle separating the stomach from the *lungs* (= that part of the body with which we breathe).

midshipman (1-1-9) young man learning to be a ship's officer in the *Navy* (= king's ships).

midst (1) middle.

midwife (1-4I) woman who helps women in childbirth.

mien (11) person's appearance and behaviour.

might (4I) p.t. of May.

might (4I) power, strength.

m′ignon′ette (1-19-2) plant with sweet-smelling green-white flowers.

migraine (11-21) very bad pain in the head.

migr′ate (4I-21) move from one place to another, e.g. to leave one's own country and go to live in another—as birds do in winter.

Mik′ado (1-44-67) title of the ruler of Japan (as said by Europeans; the word really means the great gate of the palace in Tokyo).

mike (4I) Sl. microphone.

milage (4I-1j) see Mileage.

m′ilch cow (1-tsh + 47) cow kept for giving milk.

mild (4I) gentle; calm; not strong.

mildew (1-177) sort of plant which grows on wet things, e.g. on leather, books, clothes.

mile (4I) measure of length, 1760 yards or 1·609 kilometres.

mileage (4I-1j) number of miles travelled.

militant (1-1) fighting; **militarist** (1-1-9-1) one who believes in war; **military** (1-1-9-1) having to do with soldiers and war; **militate** (1-1-21) act against; be a reason against; **mil′itia** (1-1sh9) members of a nation who are trained as soldiers to be called on when needed to defend their country.

milk (1) white liquid on which animals feed their young; *A land of milk and honey* = country where there is great plenty and comfort; **to milk**, get milk from; *Milk-and-water* = having no strength, e.g. of character.

milksop (1-5) weak and womanlike man.

milktooth (1-77) one of the first set of teeth of a child.

Milky Way (1-1 + 21) broad band of light across the sky made up of countless stars.

mill (1) machinery for making grain into flour; building containing this; machines used in making goods; building in which goods are made; Sl. a fight.

mill (1) to cut lines, e.g. on the edge of a coin.

millboard (1-55) thick card.

mill'ennium (1-2-19) one thousand years; the thousand years during which Christians thought that Christ would rule on earth; a time of great happiness.

millepede, millipede (1-1-11) small creature with many legs.

miller (1-9) one who owns or works in a flour mill.

millet (1-1) grain-bearing grass.

milli- one-thousandth part of, e.g. **milligramme** (1-1-3) = $\frac{1}{1000}$ th part of a gramme.

milliner (1-1-9) one who makes or sells women's hats and other small articles of women's dress; **millinery** (1-1-1) things sold by a milliner.

milling (1-1) lines cut on the edge of a *coin* (= piece of money made of metal), e.g. of a shilling.

million (1-19) 1,000,000; **m'illion'aire** (1-19-29) one who has a million pounds or dollars; a very rich man.

millstone (1-67) round stone used for pressing grain into flour.

mime (41) kind of play, acted by dancing, with little or no speaking.

mimeograph (1-19-44) machine for printing letters by pressing ink through a waxed sheet.

mimic (1-1) copy another person's behaviour or voice in order that he may be laughed at; **a mimic**.

mim'osa (1-67z9) tree with sweet-smelling flowers which grows in warm countries.

minaret (1-9-2) tower of a *mosque* (= building in which Muslims pray).

mince (1-s) to cut meat into very small pieces; speak in a silly unnatural way; to walk with short steps in a foolish manner; *Do not mince matters* = speak the plain truth; **mincemeat** (1-s-11) mixture of dried fruits, fat, sugar, flour, etc.; *Mince-pie* = pastry container with mincemeat in it.

MIMOSA

mind (41) (1) memory; *To call to mind* = remember; *Put in mind of* = cause one to think of; (2) thought, not matter; power of thinking; *Out of his mind* = mad; *Have something on his mind* = be anxious; *Absence of mind* = not thinking of the work one is doing, but of something else; *Presence of mind* = power of deciding quickly when one is in danger; *To speak one's mind* = say plainly what one thinks; *Make up one's mind* = decide.

mind (41) (1) remember; (2) attend to; *Mind your own business* = do not try to take part in matters which do not concern you; *Mind the step* = be careful not to fall over the step; *Mind one's ps and qs* = be careful of what one says; (3) to dislike; *Do you mind my smoking?* = will it displease you if I —?; (4) take care of, be in charge of, e.g. *Mind the children*; Sl. *Mind out!* = be careful; *Never mind* = it does not matter; **mindful**, careful; **mindless** (——1) foolish.

mine (41) belonging to me.

mine (41) deep hole from which coal, metals, etc., are obtained; **to mine**, make a hole underground; **miner** (41-9) one who works in a mine.

mine (41) box of explosive material placed in the sea or under the ground in order to destroy an enemy.

mineral (1-9) any material not animal or plant; *Mineral waters* = water with gas in it used as a pleasant drink.

mingle (1ngg) mix.

mingy (1-j1) Sl. small, ungenerous.

miniature (1-19tsh9) very small picture of a person; any very small thing.

minim (1-1) (1) formerly a very short note of music, now a long note; (2) measure of liquid (16,894 minims = 1 *litre*).

minimize (1-1-41z) make a thing unimportant; make seem small.

minimum (1-1-9) smallest possible size or quantity.

minion (1-19) one who serves another like a slave and is treated with great favour.

minister (1-1-9) (1) person in charge of one part of the government; (2) officer who acts for his government in a foreign country; priest in charge of a church; **to minister to**, serve, be helpful to; **ministry** (1-1-1) (1) act of serving; (2) building in which the work of a minister (government) is done; (3) number of priests; (4) work of a priest.

mink (1ngk) animal valued for its fur.

minnow (1-67) very small freshwater fish.

minor (41-9) smaller; under the age of 21; **min'ority** (41-5-1-1) smaller number in a group or meeting, holding opinions different from those of the rest; state of being under the age of 21.

MINK

minster (1-9) large and important church used, or formerly used, by religious men living apart, giving their lives to God.

minstrel (1) wandering singer in ancient days.

mint (1) place where money is made from metal; *A mint of money* = lot of —; **to mint** = make money out of metal.

mint (1) plant whose leaves are used to give a pleasant taste to sweets and food.

m'inu'et (1-172) slow, graceful dance; music for this.

minus (41-9) less, e.g. *3 minus 1 = 2*; *Minus an eye* = without, lacking —.

minute (1-1) $\frac{1}{60}$th of an hour.

minute (1-1) short note, e.g. one written in a government office on a matter which has to be decided; **minutes** (of a meeting) written account of opinions expressed and things decided in a meeting.

min'ute (41-177) very small.

min'utiae (4I-177shI·II) very small, less important matters.

minx (Ingks) rather rude and daring girl.

miracle (I-9) wonderful event not according to the laws of nature; adj. **mir'aculous** (I-3-17-9); **m'iracle-play** (+ 21) play showing some part of the Bible story.

mirage (I-443) trees, lakes, etc., seen in the sky over a hot desert.

mire (4I9) wet ground; mud.

mirror (I-9) glass in which one can see one's face.

mirth (99) joy and laughing.

mis- wrongly, badly, unfortunately.

m'isadv'enture (I-9-2-tsh9) unfortunate event.

m'isall'iance (I-9-4I9-s) marriage to one of lower birth.

misanthrope (Iz9-67) one who hates all men.

misbeh'ave (I-I-2I) behave badly.

misc'arriage (I-3-Ij) failure to complete successfully; *Miscarriage of justice* = wrong judgment.

miscell'aneous (I-9-2I-I9) of various kinds mixed together.

mischief (I-I) (1) damage; *To do him a mischief* = do harm to; *To make mischief between* = to cause people to quarrel; (2) harm done on purpose, not by accident; *The children are up to mischief* = are planning some wrongdoing; **mischievous** (I-I-9) causing trouble; trying to cause trouble.

m'isconc'eive (I-9-sII) judge wrongly.

m'isconstr'ue (I-9-77) understand wrongly.

miscreant (I-I9) evil-doer.

m'isd'eal (I-II) give out playing-cards wrongly so that one player gets less or more than the proper number; **misdealings** (I-II-I-z) wrong and dishonest acts.

m'isdem'eanour (I-I-II-9) unlawful act of a not very serious nature.

misd'oubt (I-47) not to trust; feel uncertain.

miser (4Iz9) one who saves and loves money.

miserable (Iz-9) very unhappy; bad; **misery** (Iz9-I) state of great unhappiness.

misg'ivings (I-I-I-z) feelings of doubt and fear.

misgu'ided (I-4I-I) led by others into wrong.

mish'ap (Is·h3) unfortunate event.

misl'ay (I-2I) to put in a wrong place and be unable to find.

misn'omer (I-67-9) wrong name.

mis'ogyny (4I-5jI-I) hatred of woman.

m'ispr'int (I-I) mistake in printing.

miss (I) fail to hit; fail to catch a ball; fail to get what one wants; *It just missed being a great success* = was nearly but not quite; *I was sorry to miss you* = sorry that I did not meet you; *Miss out a word* = not say, not write; *We shall miss you very much* = feel sad at your absence; Sl. *To give a person a miss* = try not to meet, escape from.

Miss (I) title of an unmarried woman or girl.

missile (I-4I) thing which is thrown in order to wound or do damage.

mission (Ishn) sending or being sent on some service; group of persons so sent; man's duty in life; group of persons teaching about God in a foreign land; **missionary** (Ish9-9-I) person sent to teach about God in a foreign land.

missive (I-I) letter or message.

m'is-st'ate (I + 2I) say incorrectly.

mist (I) cloud close to the ground; rain in very small drops.

mist'ake (I-2I) not to understand; form a wrong opinion; to take one person or thing for another; incorrect thought or action; — *and no mistake* = without doubt.

mistletoe (I-67) plant with a small white fruit which grows on various trees and is used to ornament houses at Christmas-time.

mistress (I-I) woman who employs other persons; woman teacher.

mite (4I) very small insect; very small child; very small piece of money.

mitigate (I-I-2I) make less serious.

mitre (4I-9) (1) kind of crown worn by high officers of the Church; (2) way of fitting two pieces of wood to each other; instrument for doing this.

mitten, mitt (I) covering for the hand which leaves the ends of fingers free and uncovered.

mix (I) put things together to form one mass; join in, e.g. *To mix in society* = go to see people, go out as a guest; *He is all mixed up* = not clear in his ideas; *A good mixer* = a friendly man who gets on well with people; **mixture** (I-tsh9) mass or liquid formed by putting two or more things together.

mizzen (I) third *mast* (= upright pole which carries sails) of a ship.

mnem'onic (I-5-I) helping the memory.

moan (67) make a low sound in pain or grief.

moat (67) deep hole with water in it round the walls of a town or castle.

mob (5) disorderly crowd of people; **to mob**, to attack in a crowd.

mobile (67-4I) easily moved; **mobilize** (67-I-4I) call up soldiers for war.

moccasin (5-9-I) soft shoe, made of deerskin, used in North America.

mock (5) (1) cause people to laugh disrespectfully at; (2) act like another person in a way that makes people laugh at him; (3) deceive; *To make a mock of* = to make people laugh at; **mock —**, e.g. *Mock solemnity* = pretending to be solemn, but not really being so; *A mock-orange* = bush with flowers like orange-flowers; **mockery** (5-9-I) act of mocking; thing mocked at; *A mere mockery of* = a very bad copy of.

m'ock-up (+ 8) a roughly made thing of the same size as a (future, planned) aeroplane or fighting machine (etc.), so as to show what it will look like.

mode (67) custom; manner; *The mode* = the kind of dresses worn by women at any particular time.

model (5) (1) small copy of some larger thing, e.g. *A model railway*; (2) small thing made to be copied larger, e.g. *A model for a ship*; *A working model of a machine* = small machine which really moves, and is to be copied; (3) thing to be copied, e.g. *He is a model father* = all other fathers should try to be like him; (4) woman who shows off dresses in a shop by wearing them; dress shown as an example; (5) person employed by painters as an example to paint from; **to model**, make a model of; copy; do modelling; **modelling** (5-1) making objects of art in *clay* (= soft sticky earth).

moderate (5-9-1) not too great, not too small, not too strong, etc.; **to moderate** (5-9-21) make less strong, great, etc.

modern (5-9) having to do with the present time; new.

modest (5-1) not thinking too much of one's own powers; quiet, not proud, not making oneself noticed.

modicum (5-1-9) small amount.

modify (5-1-41) make small changes.

mod'iste (67-11) maker of women's dresses.

modulate (5-17-21) change the sound of.

m'odus oper'andi (67-8 + 5-9-3-41) way in which a thing works.

mohair (67-29) cloth made from the hair of the Angora goat; cloth like the above, but made of a mixture of wool and cotton.

Moh'ammedan (9-3-1-9) Muslim; follower of Mohammed (Muhammad).

moiety (519-1) half.

moil and toil (51 + 9n + 51) work hard.

moist (51) not dry; **moisture** (51-tsh9) wetness.

molar (tooth) (67-9) large double tooth at the back of the mouth.

mol'asses (9-3-1z) dark sugary liquid.

mole (67) small dark growth on the skin.

mole (67) small animal which makes holes in the ground.

mole (67) strong sea-wall at the mouth of a harbour.

molecule (5-1-177) smallest amount of any material which can be taken separately and still keep its character.

molehill (67-1) earth thrown up by a *mole* (= animal, 3rd above); *To make mountains out of molehills* = be anxious and troubled by small difficulties.

mol'est (9-2) give trouble to a person; touch in order to harm.

mollify (5-1-41) to calm.

mollusc (5-9) shell-fish.

mollycoddle (5-1-5) one who is too careful of himself; take too great care of (e.g. a child).

molten (67) p.p. of Melt, now used only as adj.

moment (67-9) (1) a very short time; *In a moment* = very soon; *This very moment* = at once; *Man of the moment* = very important person at the present time; (2) importance; *Of little moment* = unimportant; adj. **momentary** (67-9-9-1) lasting only for a short time; **mom'entous** (67-2-9) very important.

mom'entum (67-2-9) force of a moving body.

monarch (5-9k) king, chief, ruler.

monastery (5-9-1) house in which a group of men live, apart from the world, lives given to God.

monetary (8-1-1) having to do with money.

money (8-1) gold, silver, printed paper, etc., used in buying and selling; *To make money* = gain money; **moneyed** (8-1) having much money; *A money-grubber* = one who desires to get much money; *Money-order* = order for payment of money obtained at a post-office and used for sending money by post.

-monger (8ngg9), e.g. **fishmonger**, trader in fish.

mongoose (5ng-g77) a small Indian animal which kills snakes.

mongrel (8ngg) dog of mixed birth (of a mixed kind).

MONGOOSE

monitor (5-1-9) one who gives a warning or advice; boy who is given charge of younger boys in a school; a small warship with heavy guns; *Monitor* (radio) = person who is paid to listen to foreign radio; *To monitor* = listen thus.

monk (8ngk) one of a group of men living, apart from the world, lives given to God.

monkey (8ngk1) animal, rather like man in shape; child who plays amusing or troublesome tricks; **m'onkey-jacket** (+ 3-1) short coat worn by sailors; **m'onkey-puzzle** (+ 8) tree with many prickles on it; **m'onkey-wrench** (+ 2) instrument with a movable part so that it can hold things of different sizes, used for holding things very firmly.

mono- one, e.g. **monochrome** (5-9k-67) picture in one colour; **monorail** (5-67-21) railway with only one rail.

monocle (5-9) eye-glass (glass held in one eye to help the sight).

mon'ogamy (9-5-9-1) marriage with only one wife or husband at a time.

monogram (5-9-3) two or more letters written on top of each other so as to make a single sign.

monograph (5-9-44) short book on one subject.

monolith (5-9-1) *pillar* (= things which support an arch) made of one large stone.

monologue (5-9-5) long speech, as in a play, said by one person.

m'onom'ania (5-67-21-19) madness in which the mind is filled with one idea.

monoplane (5-9-21) machine for flying in the air having only one supporting wing on each side.

mon'opolize (9-5-9-41) possess the whole of; *To monopolize the conversation* = talk so much that no one else has a chance to talk; **mon'opolist** (9-5-9-1) person or company which alone is able to do trade in a certain article.

mon'otonous (9-5-9-9) continuing without change and therefore uninteresting; **mon'otony** (9-5-9-1) unchanging, sameness; *He spoke in a* **m'onotone** (5-9-67) = without changing the note of his voice, all on the same note.

monotype (5-9-41) machine which makes printers' type letter by letter as needed according to the writing. (Linotype makes it line by line.)

monsi'eur (9-199) French for Mr.

mons'oon (5-77) wind which blows in the Indian Ocean, from the south-west in summer, north-east in winter.

monster (5-9) large unnatural animal or plant; ugly and bad person; anything of unusual size; **a monstr'osity** (5-5-1-1) monster; **monstrous** (5-9) like a monster; very bad; *It's perfectly monstrous to* = very wrong, very impolite.

mont'age (5-443) joining together bits of different photographs to make a picture, or bits of different cinema films to give (e.g.) the idea of a journey.

month (8) $\frac{1}{12}$th of a year; *Not in a month of Sundays* = never; **monthly** (——1) happening once a month; paper which is printed and sold each month.

monument (5-17-9) thing built to keep alive the memory of a person or event; a very learned book which will always be of value. **m'onum'ental** (5-17-2) very large; (especially of a book) such as will always be of value.

moo (77) sound made by a cow.

mooch, mouch (77) wait about in the street doing nothing.

mood (77) state of the mind and feelings.

moody (77-1) sad and ill-tempered.

moon (77) small world which goes round our Earth; any small world going round a greater; *The man in the moon* = marks on the surface of the moon supposed to look like a man's face; *Once in a blue moon* = almost never; *To moon about* = walk about in a dreamy way; **moonshine** (77-41) foolish ideas; wine or strong drink made secretly and unlawfully; **moonstone** (77-67) blue-green jewel; **moonstruck** (77-8) mad; **moony** (——1) dreamy, not thinking of present things.

moor (79) large space of waste hilly land.

moor (79) fasten a ship with chains or ropes; **moorings** (79-1-z) place where a ship is so fastened.

moose (77) large North American deer.

moot (77) *A moot point* = doubtful question not yet decided.

mop (5) lot of strings or narrow pieces of cloth fixed on the end of a stick, used for cleaning floors, etc.

mope (67) be silent and sad.

moral (5-9) having to do with right or wrong actions; *A moral man* = man who does right; *To give moral support* = help by one's favourable opinion; *He gained a moral victory* = he actually lost the battle yet really was the winner—in the effect on people's opinion; *A moral certainty* = thing which is very probable; *The moral of a story* = lesson taught by a story; **morals** (——z) science of right and wrong; one's own ideas as to right and wrong; one's behaviour in matters of love and control of the desires of the body.

mor'ale (5-44) state of mind which makes men able to do great deeds.

mor'ality (9-3-1-1) set of ideas as to duty and good behaviour; goodness; control of the desires of the body in matters of love; *A morality play* = play teaching men to be good; **moralize** (5-9-41) to talk about *morality*.

mor'ass (9-3) piece of wet ground.

morat'orium (5-9-55-19) order of government permitting delay in the payment of debts.

morbid (55-1) having to do with disease; unhealthy; sad and unpleasant (thoughts).

mordant (55) (words) cruel; (disease) eating away the flesh; (liquid) destroying material like an acid; liquid which enables a *dye* (= colour) to be fixed firmly into a cloth so that it will not be washed out.

more (55) greater in quantity or quality; *Never more* = not ever again.

more'over (55-67-9) and also; and I must also say this.

m'organ'atic m'arriage (55-9-3-1 + 3-1j) marriage of a prince or princess or member of a king's family to one of far lower rank. The children do not become royal.

morgue (55) place where the bodies of persons found dead are kept in order to discover who they are; (in a newspaper office) collection of old papers, photographs, etc., kept for future use if needed.

moribund (5-1-8) dying.

Mormon (55-9) member of a group of persons in America who hold certain special beliefs in God and who were (at one time) allowed to marry more than one wife.

morn (55) morning.

morning (55-1) early part of the day.

mor'occo (9-5-67) leather with a shiny (polished) rough surface often used for book covers.

moron (55-9) person who lacks the usual power of mind.

mor'ose (9-67) very sad and ill-tempered.

morphia (55-19) **morphine** (55-11) white powder which causes sleep and lessens pain.

m'orris d'ance (5-1 + 44-s) old English way of dancing.

morrow (5-67) next day.

morse (signalling) (55) way of sending messages by long and short sounds or flashes of light.

morsel (55) a bite, small bit.

mortal (55) who (which) will die; causing death; n. man, not a god or fairy.

mortar (55-9) mixture of sand and lime to which water is added, used to join together bricks in building; **m'ortar-board** (+ 55) flat black hat worn with university dress.

mortar (55-9) stone or metal bowl in which things are beaten into powder.

mortar (55-9) large short gun which shoots high up in the air.

mortgage (55-1j) giving a house or land to a person who has lent money so as to make sure that the money will be paid back. The person to whom the money is lent is allowed to go on using the house or land so long as he continues to pay back the money part by part, or to pay for the use of the money.

mortify (55-1-41) *To mortify the flesh* = gain control over the desires of the body by living a hard life; *The wound mortified* = the skin round it died and decayed; n. **m'ortific'ation** (55-1-1-21shn) as above; also feeling of anger and shame.

mortise (55-1) hole cut in a piece of wood into which another piece fits, in order to join the two.

mortuary (55-179-1) building where dead bodies are kept before they are put in the grave.

mos'aic (9z2ĭ·1) picture made up of small pieces of coloured glass or stone.

Moslem (5z-9) Muslim = follower of Muhammad.

mosque (5-k) place where Muslims pray to God.

mosqu'ito (9-k11-67) flying insect which bites and drinks blood, and sometimes causes fever.

moss (5) small *non-* (= not) flowering plant which spreads over stones, trees, or wet ground; *A rolling stone gathers no moss* = a restless person who often changes his employment will not get wealth.

most (67) greatest number or amount, etc.; *-most* e.g. **topmost** (5-67) = highest.

mostly (67-1) generally, usually.

mote (67) very small bit, e.g. of dust.

motel (67-2) (= motor-hotel) place where motor-car drivers can spend the night.

moth (5) winged insect, which eats cloth, flies into the flame of lamps, has powdery wings; *Moth-balls* = balls of strong-smelling substance (naphthalene) which keeps moths out of clothes.

mother (8ŏ9) woman who has given birth to a child; *Mother country* = country in which one was born; *One's mother tongue* = one's own native language; **m'other-in-law** (+ 1 + 55) mother of one's wife or husband.

m'other-of-p'earl (+ 9v + 99) hard shining material found in the inside of certain shells.

mot'if (67-11) chief idea in a work of art.

motion (67shn) act of moving; *To set in motion* = cause to move; *To move a motion* = ask a meeting of people to say that they are in favour of a certain rule; *To have a motion* = pass waste matter out of the body; *He motioned me away* = made a sign to send me away.

motivate (67-1-21) cause a person to wish to work or act in a certain way.

motive (67-1) feeling or desire which causes an action; *Motive power* = power which causes a thing to move.

motley (5-1) made up of different colours; dress of a *Fool* (= man employed in the court of an ancient lord or king to do and say amusing things).

motor (67-9) machine which changes power into movement; **a m'otor-car** (+ 44) carriage moved along by an engine, e.g. a Ford car; **motorist** (67-9-1) one who drives a motor-car.

mottle (5) to mark with spots.

motto (5-67) saying or word used as a rule of life; saying or word painted below a shield.

mould (67) rich soil.

mould (67) hollow form into which liquid (e.g. hot metal) is poured; sweet jelly-like food made in an ornamental shape; **to mould**, give a desired shape to; to form (character); *Mould oneself on* = copy, try to be like.

mould (67) *non-* (= not) flowering plant which grows on wet cloth, old bread, etc.

moulder (67-9) fall to pieces through age or decay.

moulding (67-1) ornament on a wall, etc., made of soft material pressed into the shape of flowers, etc., and then allowed to become hard.

mouldy (67-1) made useless by *mould* (3rd above); Sl. valueless, uninteresting.

moult (67) lose the feathers.

mound (47) small hill.

mount (47) mountain, e.g. *Mount Everest*.

mount (47) (1) to climb; get on to, e.g. a horse; (2) to set in place, e.g. fix a picture on a stiff card; fix a jewel in an ornament; prepare the skin of an animal for use as an ornament; *To mount a friend* = lend a horse to; *To mount guard* = set men on guard; *To mount up* = increase; n. **mount**, card upon which a picture is fixed; frame in which a jewel is held in a ring or other ornament.

mountain (47-1) very high hill; **m'ountain'eer** (47-1-19) mountain-climber; one who lives in the mountains.

mountebank (47-1-3ngk) person who sells useless things in public and makes much talk and noise in doing so.

mounted (men) (47-1) men on horses.

mourn (55) be sad, show grief, e.g. for a dead person.

mourning (55-1) black clothes worn as a sign of grief.

mouse (47) small animal with a long tail found in houses, caught by cats.

mousse (77) cream and (chocolate, etc.) beaten to make a *sponge* (= with air in it) and eaten very cold.

moust'ache (9-44sh) hair growing on the upper lip.

mouth (47) (1) opening in the face which contains the teeth; *Down in the mouth* = sad; (2) opening of anything; **to mouth** (47ð) make peculiar movements of the mouth in speaking.

m'outh-organ (+ 55) small musical instrument held in the hand and played by passing it across the lips while blowing.

mouthpiece (47-11s) (1) that part of a pipe or musical instrument to which the mouth is put; (2) person who expresses the opinions of others.

move (77) go from one place to another; cause a thing to go from one place to another; *To move house* = take one's goods from one house to another; *I move that* — = I want the members of this meeting to agree to this rule; *The story moved me greatly* = made me feel pity.

movies (77-1z) Sl. *cinema* (= moving pictures).

mow (67) to cut grass.

M.P. (2 + 11) Member of *Parliament* (= the group of elected persons who govern Great Britain).

Mr. (1st9) mister, title of a gentleman; **Mrs.** (1s1z) title of a married woman.

much (8) great in amount; *To make much of* = treat a person as if very important; *I don't think much of* = think to be of little value.

mucilage (177s1-1j) liquid of a plant used for sticking.

muck (8) dirt; Sl. *To muck about* = wander aimlessly; *To make a muck of* = ruin.

m'ucous m'embrane (177-9 + 2-21) soft wet skin inside the mouth, nose, throat, etc.; **mucus** (177-9) liquid given out by the *mucous membrane*.

mud (8) soft wet soil; *Throw mud at* = speak evil of.

muddle (8) disorderly heap; **to muddle**, make disorder, cause a plan to fail; **muddled**, not clear; not well arranged; *To muddle along* = be busy without a clear plan.

mu'ezzin (72-1) man who calls out the hour of prayer for Muslims.

muff (8) piece of fur or cloth inside which the hands are put to keep them warm out of doors.

muff (8) bad player at outdoor games; **to muff**, do a thing badly; fail to catch a ball.

muffin (8-1) light flat cake eaten hot with butter.

muffle (8) put cloth round a thing to keep it warm; make sound less loud.

muffle (8) box inside a fire used for baking pots.

muffler (8-9) warm cloth worn round the neck.

mufti (8-1) plain clothes worn by soldiers, etc., when off duty.

mug (8) drinking-cup with a handle; Sl. (1) face; (2) person who is easily deceived, a fool.

muggy (8-1) hot and airless.

mugwump (8-8) Am. one who keeps himself free and separate from both parties (groups) in the government.

mul'atto (17-3-67) person of mixed birth, black and white.

mulberry (8-9-1) tree bearing a dark red fruit; its leaves are used to feed *silk-worms* (= the small creatures which produce silk).

MULBERRY

mulct (8) punish by taking money from; take money from.

mule (177) animal produced from a male ass and a female horse; person who is difficult to control, who will not listen to reason; **mulet'eer** (177-1-19) mule-driver.

mull (8) heat wine (or other strong drink).

mullah (7-4 or 8-9) Muslim learned man and priest.

mullet (8-1) a fish.

m'ulligat'awny (8-1-9-55-1) hot-tasting yellow *soup* (= liquid food).

mullion (8-19) upright bar between two parts of a window.

multi- many, e.g. **m'ulti-c'oloured** (8-1 + 8-9) having many colours.

m'ultif'arious (8-1-29-19) various.

m'ultil'ateral (8-1-3-9-9) many sided.

multiple (8-1) having a large number of parts; number which contains another number an exact number of times.

multiplex (8-1-2) made up of many parts; **m'ultipl'icity** (8-1-1s1-1) *of duties* = great number of different pieces of work which one must do.

multiply (8-1-41) make many; find the amount produced if a number is added to itself a certain number of times.

multitude (8-1-177) large number; great crowd.

m'ultum in p'arvo (8-9 + 1 + 44-67) much in little; much knowledge written in a small book.

mum (8) *To keep mum* = be silent, not tell a secret.

mumble (8) speak through closed lips; (of one who has no teeth) to bite.

mummer (8-9) one who acts a silent play; an actor.

mummy (8-1) dead body kept from decay by cleaning, drying and tying up in cloth—as in ancient Egypt.

mummy (8-1) child's name for its mother.

mumps (8) disease which causes swelling at the sides of the neck.

munch (8) eat with much movement of the mouth and some noise—as when eating hard food; *Cows munch grass.*

mundane (8-21) of this world.

mun'icipal (177-1s1) having to do with the business of the city; owned by the city-government.

mun'ificent (177-1-1s) generous.

mun'itions (177-1shnz) things used in making war, especially explosives and shot for guns.

mural (paintings) (179) (paintings) on a wall.

murder (99-9) kill a person meaning to do so, not by accident.

murky (99-1) very dark.

murmur (99-9) make a low sound as of running water, or low quiet talk, or bees.

murrain (8-1) disease of cattle; *A murrain on you!* = curse you.

muscle (8) that part of the body which causes movement, e.g. of the limbs; adj. **muscular** (8skɪ7-9) strong, having powerful muscles.

Muse (177z) goddess (= female god) of learning or the arts of music, painting, etc.

muse (177z) think deeply, taking no notice of things around.

mus'eum (17zɪ9) building containing a collection of interesting or beautiful things as examples of history, or of some special part of man's life or work.

mush (8) soft paste; **mushy** (8-1) like soft paste.

mushroom (8-7) white plant used for food—shaped like a T with a round top, and having no flowers or leaves; *A mushroom growth* (e.g. of a town) = sudden very rapid growth. MUSHROOM

music (177zɪ) art of producing sweet sounds; sound so produced; paper showing sounds to be produced; Sl. *To face the music* = meet expected trouble or punishment with courage; **mus'ician** (177zɪshn) one who produces music.

musk (8) brown sweet-smelling matter obtained from a certain kind of deer; smell like the above.

musket (8-1) light gun carried by a soldier in ancient times; **m'usket'eer** (——19) soldier who carried a musket; **musketry** (——1) art of shooting as taught to soldiers.

Muslim (7-1) follower of the religion taught by Muhammad.

muslin (8z-1) fine cloth made of cotton.

musquash (8-5) rat with a smell like *musk* (see 4th above).

muss (8) Sl. make disordered, e.g. clothes, hair, papers.

mussel (8) small shellfish.

Mussulman (8-9) *Muslim* (see 5th above).

must (8) liquid of which wine is made.

must'ache (9-44sh) see Moustache.

mustang (8-3) half-wild horse in America.

mustard (8-9) yellow powder made from the seeds of a plant, mixed with water and eaten with meat.

muster (8-9) gather together; soldiers gathered together; *To muster one's courage* = make oneself feel brave; *To pass muster* = be just good enough.

musty (8-1) made useless or unpleasant by age and *damp* (= wetness).

mutable (177-9) changeable; **mut'ation** (177-21shn) change.

mut'atis mut'andis (17-21-1 + 17-3-1) with necessary changes.

mute (177) silent, unable to speak; (of a letter) not sounded in saying the word; **a mute**, person who cannot speak; thing used to lessen the sound of stringed instrument of music.

mutilate (177-1-21) to cut off a limb; to damage.

m'utin'eer (177-1-19) seaman or soldier who will not obey orders and fights against his officers; **mutiny** (177-1-1) rising of men against their officers.

mutt (8) Sl. a very foolish person.

mutter (8-9) speak in a low voice without moving the lips.

mutton (8) meat of a sheep; *To return to our muttons* = come back to the subject of which we were speaking.

mutual (177-179) (help) help given to each other; (friend) friend of both persons.

muzzle (8) mouth and nose of an animal; thing put over the mouth of an animal to prevent biting; mouth or opening of a gun; *Muzzle-loader* = gun loaded by pushing powder and shot in at the end from which it will come out again when the gun is fired; **to muzzle**, fix a wire or leather cage over the mouth of an animal; force a person to be silent.

myopia (4167-19) state of being unable to see distant things clearly.

myriad (1-19) 10,000; very large number.

myrmidon (99-1) servant or slave who carries out orders without pity.

myrrh (99) matter obtained from a tree which has a sweet smell.

myrtle (99) bush with sweet-smelling white flowers.

mystery (1-9-1) a secret, a thing beyond man's understanding; secret knowledge or magic made known only to chosen persons; **m'ystery-play** (+ 21) play showing a Bible story; adj. **myst'erious** (1-19-19).

mystic (1-1) having to do with secret teachings and magic; **a mystic**, one who believes that he can enter into direct touch (understanding) with God; **to mystify** (1-1-41) make *mysterious* (see above).

myth (1) story of gods, fairies, etc., often showing through these persons some fact of nature.

m'yxomat'osis (1-6-9-67-1) disease which kills rabbits.

N

N.A.A.F.I. (n3fr) Navy, Army, Air-Force Institute. The NAAFI (NAFI) sells food, cigarettes, etc., cheaply to men serving in the Navy (etc.) and has rooms where they can meet, write, read, etc.

nab (3) Sl. seize.

nabob (21-5) rich person.

nadir (21-19) lowest point, e.g. of hope.

naevus (11-9) red mark on the skin caused by swelling of a blood-vessel.

nag (3) small horse.

nag (3) scold continually.

naiad (413) water-fairy.

nail (21) (**1**) piece of metal with a point and head, used for joining pieces of wood; (**2**) horny growth on the ends of the fingers; *Fight tooth and nail* = very fiercely; *Pay on the nail* = at once; *A nail in one's coffin* = something that shortens one's life; *Hit the right nail on the head* = express the really important idea in a matter; *As hard as nails* = very strong and healthy; **to nail**, fix with a nail; *Nail one's colours to the mast* = say that one will not yield; *Nail a lie down to the counter* = prove that a thing is untrue; *Nail a man down to his promise* = force him to do as he promised.

nainsook (21-7) fine cloth made of cotton.

na'ive (4411) simple and natural in speech and manner; n. **na'iveté, na'ivety** (4411-1-1).

naked (21-1) without clothes; not kept secret; open, uncovered; *To see with the naked eye* = without the help of a glass.

name (21) word by which a person or thing is known; *Not a penny to his name* = having no money; *Take his name in vain* = speak disrespectfully of; *My good name* = people's opinion of my character as good; *Give a dog a bad name and hang him* = decide that a man is bad only because people say bad things about him; **to name**, give a name to; *Named after his father* = given the same name as —; *Name the day* = fix a day for the marriage; **nameless** (——1) not named, too bad to be spoken of; **namely** (——1) that is to say, I mean; **namesake** (21-21) person having the same name as another.

nanny (3-1) a nurse; **n'anny-goat** (+ 67) female *goat* (= sheep-like animal).

nap (3) short sleep; *Caught napping* = surprised when not keeping watch.

nap (3) card game; Sl. *To go nap on* = be quite sure that a thing will happen, or is true.

nap (3) hairs on the surface of cloth.

nape (21) back of the neck.

napery (21-9-1) fine cloths used at the dinner-table and in the house.

naphtha (3-9) light oil obtained from coal;

naphthalene (——11) white glassy material with a strong smell, obtained from coal, used to keep insects out of clothes.

napkin (3-1) (**1**) small cloth used when eating to keep the clothing clean, also to clean the hands and mouth; (**2**) cloth tied round a young baby.

narc'issus (44s1s9) flower, usually white or yellow.

narc'otic (44-5-1) medicine which produces sleep; adj. producing sleep.

narr'ate (9-21) tell a story; **n'arrative** (3-9-1) story; adj. of stories.

narrow (3-67) not broad or wide; *I had a narrow squeak* = I only just escaped great danger; *Narrow-minded* = not able to take in great ideas or to understand other people's opinions.

NARCISSUS

nasal (21z) having to do with the nose; *He spoke in a nasal voice* (*accent*) = spoke through the nose.

nasc̨ent (3) just coming into being; beginning to grow.

nast'urtium (9-99sh9) plant with red-yellow flowers and hot-tasting seeds.

nasty (44-1) unpleasant; dirty; *To turn nasty* = to become bad-tempered.

natal (day) (21) birth-(day).

nation (21shn) race of people under one government; **nationalism** (3sh9-9-1z) strong feeling for one's nation; demand for the freedom of one's nation; **nation'ality** (3sh9-3-1-1) fact of belonging to a nation; state of being a nation (also, wrongly, a nation); **nationalize** (3sh9-9-41) cause to belong to the nation.

native (21-1) born in a certain place; *A native of* = belonging by birth to a country; *My native land* = land of my birth; *Native powers* = born in one, not learnt.

nat'ivity (9-1-1-1) birth; *The Nativity* = Birth of Jesus Christ.

natter (3-9) Sl. talk a lot; complain.

natty (3-1) neat and of nice appearance.

natural (3tshr9) according to the usual laws which govern events in the world; *inborn* (= born in one); usual and to be expected; produced by the forces of the earth and weather, not by man; *Natural son* = actual but not in lawful marriage; **naturally** (3tshr9-9-1) according to nature; of course; as expected; **nat̨uralist** (3tshr9-9-1) one who studies plants, animals, insects, etc.; **naturalized** (3tshr9-9-41) e.g. *Naturalized Frenchman* = French by law but not by birth; **n'atural sel'ection** (3tshr9+ 1-2-shn) that killing off of the weak and unfit and *reproduction* (= having young ones) of the fit which causes change and improvement in all

naught 214 **neighbour**

living *species* (= kinds of living things); **nature** (21tshǝ) inborn character of a thing; class; sort; life force; the power which causes changes in the world; world of plants, animals and matter as a whole; *One's nature* = one's character; *Something in the nature of a* = something rather like a.

naught (55) nothing.

naughty (55-1) bad, giving trouble, e.g. *A naughty child*.

nausea (55-19) feeling sick in the stomach; **nauseate** (55-121) cause a feeling of sickness; **nauseating** (55-121-1), very nasty.

nautch (55) show given by paid dancers in India.

nautical (55-1) having to do with ships and seamen; **n'autical m'ile** (+ 41) about 6080 feet or 1·85 kilometres.

nautilus (55-1-9) fish with a shell curved round and round like a screw.

naval (21) having to do with war-ships.

nave (21) main part of a church.

navel (21) the little hollow in the middle of the front of the body.

navigate (3-1-21) to sail a ship; **navigable** (river) (3-1-21-9) river up which a ship can pass.

navvy (3-1) unskilled workman employed for digging, for making roads, railways, etc.

navy (21-1) warships of a country; officers and men of these ships; *Navy blue* = very dark blue.

naw'ab (9-44) title of Muslim noblemen in India; Muslim ruler.

nay (21) no.

naze (21) piece of land standing out into the sea like a nose.

N.B. (2n + b11) (Latin, *nota bene*) (67-9 + 11-1) note well.

neap (tide) (11) smaller (than usual) rise and fall of the sea in the first and third quarter of the moon.

near (19) close; not far away; very careful of one's money.

nearly (19-1) almost; *Nearly related* = closely —.

neat (11) cattle; *Neat's foot oil* = oil made from the feet of cattle.

neat (11) clean and in good order; careful, e.g. *Neat writing*; skilful, e.g. *A neat piece of work*; *He drank it neat* = without adding any water.

nebula (2-17-9) cloud of brightly burning gas or small stars seen in the sky; **nebulous** (2-17-9) cloudy, not clearly seen or understood.

necessary (2s1-9-1) needed; which must be; must be done or obtained; **nec'essity** (1s2-1-1-1) something which makes one act in a certain way; need; a thing needed; **nec'essitate** (1s2-1-21) make necessary.

neck (2) part of the body between the head and the shoulders; Sl. *Get it in the neck* = suffer some very unpleasant experience, be punished; *Neck and crop* = completely; *Neck and neck* = side by side; *Neck or nothing!* = I will succeed in spite of the risks; *Stiff necked* = not yielding to control or reason; *Neck of a bottle* = narrow upper part.

necklace (2-1s) string of jewels (or other small ornamental objects) worn round the neck.

necklet (2-1) a *necklace* (see above); covering for the neck, e.g. a piece of fur.

necktie (2-41) band of coloured silk worn by a man round the neck.

necro- having to do with death.

necromancer (2-9-3-s9) one who claims that he can speak to the spirits of the dead; **necr'opolis** (2-5-9-1) large piece of ground used for graves; **n'ecr'opsy** (2-5-1) examination of a dead body to discover the cause of death; **necr'osis** (2-67-1) decay of part of the living body.

nectar (2-9) wine of the Greek gods; sweet liquid found in plants.

nectarine (2-9-1) fruit with a rough stone and very soft outside.

née (21) born, e.g. *Jane Smith, née Jones* = her name before marriage was Jones.

need (11) (1) lack; *necessity* (n. of Necessary); (2) state of being poor; **to need,** be in want of; *He need not do it* = is not forced to; *He needs must* = is forced to; **needful,** needed; *Do the needful* = do what is necessary.

needle (11) instrument used for joining cloth together with thread; any sharp pointed instrument; the iron bar in the middle of a compass.

needless (11-1) not necessary.

needy (11-1) poor.

ne'er (29) never; *Ne'er do well (weel)* = worthless fellow.

nef'arious (1-29-19) unlawful, very bad.

neg'ation (1-21shn) act of saying No; n. of Negative; **negative** (2-9-1) *A negative answer* = No; *A negative order* = order not to do a thing; *Of negative value as proof* = not proving or disproving; *A negative* = photograph in which all the light parts are dark and dark parts light—used for printing copies of the picture.

negl'ect (1-2) take no care of; fail to do; **n'egligible** (2-1j1) not worth troubling about; **n'egligent** (2-1j9) not taking care; **négligé** (2-1j21) long loose dress.

neg'otiate (1-67shı21) try to reach an agreement with; give or get money for; **neg'otiable** (1-67shı9) which may be bought or sold.

negro (11-67) man of the black race of Africa; **negress** (11-1) woman of —; **negroid** (11-51) having some of the character or appearance of a negro.

negus (11-9) hot drink of wine, mixed with water, sugar, *lemon* (= a sour yellow fruit).

neigh (21) cry of a horse.

neighbour (21-9) person who lives near; **neighbourhood** (21-9-7) country or streets near any particular place; people in that part;

neighbouring (——1) near; **neighbourly** (——1) friendly.
neither—nor (41ō9) (55) not this, not that.
Nemesis (2-1-1) fate which brings punishment.
neo- new, e.g. **Neolithic** (1167-1-1) = new stone; the Neolithic Age was the later Stone Age when some 10,000 years ago the new and better stone instruments were made.
ne'ologism (15-9j1z) making of a new word; using words in a new way; new word or new use of words.
neon (11.5) gas used in making those electric signs in the streets in which words are formed by a glass pipe filled with light.
neophyte (119-41) beginner; one lately brought over to a new faith.
nephew (2f17) son of one's brother or sister.
nephr'itis (2-41-1) disease of the *kidneys* (= part of the body which takes waste matter from the blood and passes it out in the water).
nepotism (2-9-1z) showing special favour and giving offices to members of one's own family.
nerve (99) thread-like parts of the body which carry feelings to the brain, or carry messages which produce action in the limbs, etc.; *To have the nerve to* = be brave enough to; *Suffer from nerves* = be in an unhealthy state of mind, easily excited or frightened; *It gets on my nerves* = it makes me troubled or angry whenever I see (hear) it; **nerveless** (——1) without strength or courage; **nervous** (——9) having to do with the nerves; in an unhealthy state of mind, easily excited or frightened; *A nervous breakdown* = illness of the mind caused by *anxiety* (n. of Anxious) or overwork; **nervousness** (——1) a state of fear and excitement.
nest (2) place built by a bird in which it lays its eggs; *To feather one's nest* = make oneself rich, sometimes dishonestly; *Foul one's nest* = behave badly in one's own home or home-town; say bad things about one's home; *A nest of crime* = place full of law-breakers; *A nest of tables* (*boxes, etc.*) = set of — fitting one inside the other; *Nest-egg* = stone egg left in a nest to make birds lay there; store of money laid up for the future.
nestle (2) lie closely and comfortably against.
nestling (2-1) young bird not yet able to leave the nest.
net (2) knotting of string into squares, used, e.g., to catch fish; **to net**, catch with a net; cover with a net; make nets.
net (2) e.g. *Net gain* = that amount left when all costs, etc., have been taken off; *Net weight* = weight without the box, paper or packing.
nether (2ŏ9) lower; **nethermost** (2ŏ9-67) lowest.
netting (2-1) net; cloth made like net.
nettle (2) plant which, when touched, causes pain and redness of the skin.
nettled (2) made angry.

n'ettle-rash (2 + 3) redness of the skin often caused by eating certain food, e.g. shell-fish.
network (2-99) a net; many lines crossing each other, e.g. *A network of railways*.
neur'algia (17-3-j9) pain in the *nerves* (= parts of the body which carry messages to or from the brain).
neurasth'enia (17-9-11-19) general weakness resulting not from any actual disease of the body but from some *mental* (= of the mind) cause.
neur'itis (17-41-1) pain and swelling in a *nerve* (see Neuralgia, above).
neur'otic (17-5-1) excitable and uncontrolled.
neuter (177-9) neither male nor female; (of a word) of that form which means neither a male nor female thing.
neutral (177) taking neither side in a war; belonging to neither of two classes; *Neutral shade* = not any one clear colour; *Electrically neutral* = not +, not —; *In neutral* = with the engine of the car not in any *gear* (Gears make the engine drive the car faster or slower).
never (2-9) not at any time; *Well I never!* = I am surprised; Sl. *On the never-never plan* = paying for something a little each week for a long time.
nevermore (2-9-55) never again.
n'everthel'ess (2-9ŏ9-2) although that is true, yet —.
new (177) not old; fresh; not seen before; lacking experience.
n'ew-f'angled (177 + 3ngg) of a new kind (which the speaker does not like).
news (177z) report of events which have happened lately; *To break the news to* = tell something unpleasant in a gentle way; **newspaper** (177s-21-9) a paper giving the news; **newsreel** (177z-11) cinema film showing the news of the day or week.

NEWT

newt (177) small water creature with four legs and a long tail.
next (2) nearest, coming after this one.
nib (1) metal point of a pen.
nibble (1) take little bites of.
nice (41s) (1) pleasing; (2) hard to please; (3) difficult to judge, e.g. *A nice point of law*.
nicety (41s1-1) very small difference; *He judges it to a nicety* = exactly right.
niche (17) hollow place in a wall, usually meant to contain a stone figure.
nick (1) small V-shaped cut in (a stick) made by cutting out a piece; *In the nick of time* = just in time.
nickel (1) hard white metal used as a covering for spoons, boxes, etc.; Am. piece of money, 5 cents.
nicknack (1-3) see Knick-knack.

nickname (1-21) name used by friends instead of one's real name.

nicotine (1-9-11) poison found in *tobacco* (= plant which one smokes in a pipe or cigarettes).

niece (11s) daughter of one's brother or sister.

niggardly (1-9-1) ungenerous, careful of money.

nigger (1-9) impolite word for a member of a black race.

nigh (41) near.

night (41) time of darkness; *Make a night of it* = spend the night in enjoyment; **nightcap** (41-3) drink taken just before going to bed; **nightfall** (41-55) end of the day.

nightingale (41-1ngg21) small bird which sings beautifully at night.

nightmare (41-29) terrible dream.

nightshade (41-21) very poisonous plant.

nihilist (41-1-1) one who is against all forms of government.

nil (1) nothing.

nimble (1) quick in movement, active.

nincompoop (1-9-77) fool.

ninepins (41-1-2) game in which a ball is thrown at nine wooden "pins" (shaped like bottles) the purpose being to knock them down.

ninon (11-5^n) very thin light silk material for ladies' dresses.

nip (1) press a small piece of skin between the fingers, causing pain; stop the growth of plants, e.g. *Nipped by the frost*; *Nipped in the bud* = killed before the flower opened; *There's a nip in the air* = it is cold; *To take a nip* = take a small drink; Sl. *Nip off* = run away; **nipper** (1-9) thing used for nipping, e.g. *The nippers of a shell-fish*; small boy; **nipping** (1-1) very cold.

nipple (1) point of the breast; anything so shaped.

nippy (1-1) quick in movement.

nirv'ana (19-44-9) state after death in which the spirit of a man becomes united with God.

nitrogen (41-9j9) colourless gas found in the air and very necessary to the life of plants.

nitwit (1-1) Sl. foolish person.

nobble (5) damage a horse in order to prevent it winning a race; deceive or trick.

noble (67) of very fine character; high in rank; **a noble**, person of high rank, a lord; **nob'ility** (67-1-1-1) goodness of character; *The nobility* = all the persons of high rank and birth.

n'oblesse obl'ige (67-2 + 67-113) one who is of high rank must behave in a noble way.

noct'urnal (5-99) happening at night; *A nocturnal animal* = which seeks food at night.

nod (5) bend the head down as a sign of agreement or greeting, or because one is feeling sleepy; *A nodding acquaintance* = person whom one knows only very distantly; *The land of Nod* = sleep.

noddle (5) Sl. head.

node (67) place on a stem at which a leaf is joined on; hard swelling on a muscle or bone; point at which a curve crosses another curve, or where a curve turns and crosses itself.

Noel (672) Christmas.

noise (51z) loud sounds; Sl. *A big noise* = important person or event.

noisome (51s9) very harmful and unpleasant.

nomad (67-3) one of a wandering people; adj. wandering.

n'om de pl'ume (5 + 9 + 77) name (other than his real name) used by a writer.

nom'enclature (67-2-9tsh9) way of naming.

nominal (5-1) having to do with names; *Nominal price* = very low —.

nominate (5-1-21) put forward (say or write down) a person's name so that he may be chosen for an office; **nomin'ee** (5-1-11) person nominated.

non- not.

nonagen'arian (67-9j1-29-19) person who is 90 years old.

nonce, for the (5-s) for the present.

nonchalant (5-sh9-9) not eager.

n'oncomm'ittal (5-9-1) not telling what one intends to do.

n'onconf'ormist (5-9-55-1) one who refuses to act or believe as others do, especially in matters of belief in God.

n'on-co'operator (5 + 675-9-21-9) one who refuses to work with or help others.

n'ondescript (5-1-1) not easily described; peculiar.

non'entity (5-2-1-1) thing which does not *exist* (= be, live); person of no importance.

n'onpl'us (5-8) surprise a person so much that he does not know what to say or do.

nonsense (5) not sense; silly talk.

n'on s'equitur (5 + 2-1-9) (Latin = it does not follow) bad piece of reasoning which does not lead up to the judgment intended.

noodle (77) Sl. fool; *Noodles* = little flat sticks made from egg and flour cooked in soup.

nook (7) sheltered corner.

noon (77) midday.

noose (77) circle of rope which becomes tight when one end is pulled—used for hanging people.

norm (55) (1) middle or commonest (most frequent) measure in a set of measures, e.g. 3, 3, 4, 6, 7, 7, 7, 7, 8, 8, 9; 7 is the norm; (2) such a number as an aim in factory work, e.g. *Our norm is 100 cars a day but we have not reached it yet*.

normal (55) regular; natural; usual; **a Normal School** (+ sk77) Am. place where teachers are trained.

normalcy (55-s1) wrongly formed word meaning normal state, normality.

N'orth P'ole (55 + 67) north end of the earth; **northern** (55ŏ9) adj.; **northerly** (55ŏ9-1) in or from the north.

nose (67z) that part of the face with which we smell; anything of that shape; *Cut off one's* *nose to spite one's face* = do harm to oneself when angry with others; *Follow one's nose* = = go straight on; *Keep one's nose to the grindstone* = work hard; *Lead by the nose* = have complete control over; *Pay through the nose* = pay far too much; *Poke one's nose into another's business* = push into another's business; *Put her nose out of joint* = take her place, e.g. in the love of a man; *Turn up one's nose at* = show no liking or respect for, think nothing of; **to nose** *out*, find out; (of a ship) *To nose her way* = go carefully; **nosey, nosy** (67z1) interested in other people's business; *A Nosey Parker* = one who is —.

nosegay (67z-21) handful of sweet-smelling flowers tied together.

nost'algia (5-3-j19) sadness at being away from home.

nostril (5-1) one of the two openings in the nose.

nostrum (5-9) medicine not given by a doctor but sold by an untrustworthy fellow.

notable (67-9) worthy of notice; worth remembering; likely to be remembered; **notably** (——1) specially.

notary (67-9-1) man who does certain kinds of law business.

not'ation (67-21shn) writing of signs to stand for numbers, e.g. *The Roman system of notation, V, X, L, C,* etc.

notch (5) V-shaped cut.

note (67) **(1)** sign standing for a certain musical sound; the musical sound; a *key* (= piece of bone or wood) struck to produce a musical sound; **(2)** any sign or mark, e.g. ! = *A note of exclamation;* **(3)** fame, good name, e.g. *A man of note* = a famous man; **(4)** to notice; *To take note of* = to notice; **(5)** something written to help the memory, e.g. *To take notes of a speech;* **(6)** short letter or written message; **(7)** piece of paper money; written promise to pay money.

notice (67-1s) **(1)** attend to; attention; *Take notice of* = show interest in; *To give a servant notice* = say that she (he) will not be employed after a certain date; *I give you notice that* = I warn you; **(2)** short printed piece in a newspaper telling some special fact, e.g. notice of things to be sold, or a report of a birth, death, etc.; paper fixed up in public giving news or orders.

notify (67-1-41) make known; make public; warn.

notion (67shn) idea.

not'orious (67-55-19) well known for something bad; **notor'iety** (67-9-419-1).

notwithst'anding (5-1-3-1) in spite of; although.

nougat (77-44) soft white sweet with dried fruit in it.

nought (55) nothing; o.

noun (47) word used as the name of a thing.

nourish (8-1) give food to; *To nourish ill-feeling* = keep — in the mind.

nous (47) common sense.

n'ouveau r'iche (77-67 + 11sh) (French) new rich; person who has lately become rich and does not behave well.

novel (5-9) new, strange; **a novel,** long imaginary story written in a book; **n'ovel'ette** (5-9-2) short novel; **novelist** (5-9-1) one who writes novels; **novelty** (5-9-1) some new thing, e.g. in a shop.

novice (5-1s) beginner, one new to the work.

now (47) at this time; *Now and again, Now and then* = sometimes, from time to time; *Now, now!* = warning, e.g. to stop children making too much noise; *Now* = listen, as when beginning to tell a story; **nowadays** (479-21z) in these times.

noxious (5ksh9) harmful.

nozzle (5) pointed end of a pipe used to direct a stream of liquid.

nuance (1744^{n}s) very slight difference in the meaning of a word; slight difference in colour, in the quality of a feeling.

nub (8) small piece or point; point of a story or chief point in a difficulty.

nubile (17-41) old enough for marriage.

nuci– nut, e.g. **nuciform** (17s1-55) shaped like a nut.

n'uclear f'issi̧on (177-19 + 1shn) first see Atom, Atom bomb. The *nucleus* (see below) of an atom is the centre part; electrons go round the outside. Fission means breaking in two. In Nuclear Fission the nucleus of an atom breaks up and sets free *energy* (= power) which breaks up another nucleus, so causing the explosion of an atom bomb.

nucleus (177-19) centre part about which matter collects or grows; adj. **nuclear** (177-19).

nude (177) uncovered, having no clothes.

nudge (8j) to touch with the *elbow* (= middle joint of the arm).

nudist (177-1) person who believes in the value of *nakedness* (= wearing no clothes) for health.

nugatory (17-9-9-1) of no importance, useless, having no effect.

nugget (8-1) rough piece of gold as found in the ground.

nuisance (177-9-s) harmful or troublesome thing or person.

null (8) of no effect; *Null and void* = having no force according to the law.

nullify (8-1-41) make of no effect, of no force.

numb (8) having no feeling, e.g. because of cold.

number (8-9) **(1)** quantity or amount; **(2)** sign, e.g. 1, 2, 3, etc.; *Look after number one* = take care of oneself; **(3)** copy of a newspaper; *A back number* = person who has *lost touch with* (= does not know or try to know) present ideas; **to number,** count; write numbers on; say numbers (as soldiers do); *His days are numbered* = he will soon die; **numberless** (——1) very many.

numeral (177-9) word or figure showing how many; adj. expressing a number.
num'erical (17-2-1) having to do with numbers.
numerous (177-9-9) many in number.
num'ismatist (17-1z-9-1) one who collects and studies *coins* (= metal pieces of money).
numskull (8-8) fool.
nun (8) woman living with a group of other women a life given to God; **nunnery** (8-9-1) house for nuns.
nuptial (8-shl) having to do with marriage.
nurse (99) person trained to take care of the young, or sick persons; **to nurse**, take care of a child or sick person; *To nurse a hatred* = keep in the mind; *To nurse a business* = take great care of; *a wet nurse*, woman who gives milk to another's child.
nursery (99-1) room for the use of children.
nursery-garden (99-1 + 44) garden where young plants are grown for *sale* (= selling); **nurseryman** (99-1-9) one who owns such a garden.
nursling (99-1) young child.
nurture (99tsh9) training and care of the young.
nut (8) seed of a tree, contained in a hard shell; Sl. rich and foolish young man; Sl. one's head; Sl. *I can't play for nuts* = not at all; Sl. *Dead nuts on* = very interested in; Sl. *A tough nut* = strong, determined and unpleasant person; Sl. *He's nuts* = mad.
nut (8) small block of metal with a hole in it which may be screwed on to a bar.
nutmeg (8-2) hard seed of a Malayan tree used, when powdered, to give a pleasant taste to food, especially to foods made from milk.
nutriment (177-1-9) food; **nutr'ition** (177-1shn) giving or receiving of food; food; adj. **nutr'itious** (177-1sh9), **n'utritive** (177-1-1), **nutrient** (177-19) useful as food, supplying power of growth to the body.
nutshell (8-2) *In a nutshell* = in as few words as possible.
nutting (8-1) gathering nuts.
nutty (8-1) having a taste like nuts; having a good taste; Sl. mad.
nuzzle (8) push with the nose, as a dog does.
nylon (41-5) very strong silk-like thread used for ladies' stockings and dresses; *My nylons* = my stockings made of nylon.
nymph (1) a *goddess* (= female god) living in rivers, forests, etc.
n'ymphom'aniac (1-6-21-13) woman who has madly strong desires for men.

O

o', of, e.g. **o'clock** (9-5).
oaf (67) ungraceful foolish fellow.
oak (67) tree which grows to a great age and has very hard wood; **'oak-apple** (+ 3) diseased growth on an oak.
oakum (67-9) loose material got by opening up old rope, used for filling cracks between the boards on a ship.
oars (55z) (a pair of —) two long bars of wood with flat ends used for rowing a boat; *Put (stick) one's oar in* = try to take part in another person's business.
o'asis (672I-I) pl. **o'ases** (——IIz) place in a desert where there are trees and water.
oat (67) grain used for food; *To sow one's wild oats* = enjoy life and behave foolishly while young (so as to be wiser and quieter when old).
oath (67) (1) *To take an oath* = to promise in the name of God that one will speak the truth; *an oath*, such a promise; (2) disrespectful use of the name of God or any holy name.
'obblig'ato (5-1-44-67) part of a piece of music which is different from the rest but must not be missed out.
obdurate (5-17-1) not easily moved from an opinion.
ob'edient (9-11-19) willing to do as ordered.
ob'eisance (9-21-s) *To make an* —— = bend oneself down as a sign of respect.
obelisk (5-1-1) tall pointed stone with flat sides.
ob'ese (67-11) very fat.
ob'ey (9-21) do as ordered; to act according to a rule or law.
ob'ituary (notice) (9-1-179-1) notice of death.
object (5-1) (1) thing; (2) word telling the person or thing to whom an action was done; (3) purpose.
obj'ect to (9-2) to dislike; not agree to; **obj'ection** (9-2-shn) disagreement; **obj'ectionable** (9-2-shg-9) nasty, unpleasant.
obj'ective (9-2-1) (1) which is real, outside the mind; (2) purpose, aim, e.g. aim of an attack by soldiers.
obl'ation (67-21shn) offering to God.
obl'igatory (9-1-9-9-1) which must be done.
oblig'ation (5-1-21shn) (1) duty; (2) state of *indebtedness* (= being in debt) or thankfulness to another person who has helped one.
obl'ige (9-41j) (1) force a person to act; (2) do a kindness to; **obl'iging** (9-41j1) kind and eager to help.
obl'ique (9-11k) indirect; in a sideways direction.
obl'iquity (9-1-1-1) moral ——, turning aside from good behaviour.
obl'iterate (9-1-9-21) rub out (e.g. a word); destroy.

obl'ivion (9-1-19) act of forgetting; state of being forgotten.
oblong (5-5) shape like a square but with two sides longer than the ends.
obloquy (5-9-9-1) words spoken against a person; loss of respect and honour.
obn'oxious (9-5ksh9) unpleasant, nasty.
oboe (67-67) wooden musical instrument played with the breath. OBOE
obsc'ene (5-11) nasty and dirty (in idea).
obsc'ure (9-179) dark, not easily understood; not well known; **to obsc'ure**, make dark, or difficult to understand.
obsequies (5-1-1z) ceremonies performed at a funeral.
obs'equious (9-11-19) too eager to obey and serve.
'observ'ation (5-z9-21shn) act of watching; power of noticing; things noticed; sayings or writings about things noticed.
obs'ervatory (9-z99-9-9-1) place from which scientists watch the stars.
obs'erve (9-z99) (1) keep or act according to, e.g. *Observe the laws*; (2) to watch, to notice; (3) say.
obs'ession (9-2shn) fixed idea from which the mind cannot be freed; **to obs'ess**, fill the mind with a ——.
obs'idian (5-1-19) dark glass-like rock.
obsolete (5-9-11) not now in use; of an old kind not such as is now used.
obstacle (5-9) something which stands in the way and prevents action or movement.
obstinate (5-1-9) not giving up an opinion; not moved by reasoning; unwilling to obey.
obstr'eperous (9-2-9-9) noisy and uncontrollable, e.g. children.
obstr'uct (9-8) get in the way of; to stop up a pipe or block a path.
obt'ain (9-21) get; *The custom has obtained for many years* = has been in use.
obtr'usive (9-77-1) pushing forward and causing oneself, or some object, to be noticed; **to obtr'ude**.
obt'use (9-177) (1) not sharp; an angle greater than a *right angle* (the corners of a square are right angles); (2) slow of understanding.
obviate (5-121) clear away a difficulty from the path.
obvious (5-19) clearly seen; which must be noticed.
occ'asion (9k2I3n) event; a chance to; *On the occasion of* = at the time of; *Having occasion to* = having need to; *No occasion for* = no reason or need for; *Occasioned by* = caused by; **occ'asional** (9k2139) happening from time to time.

occiden'tal (5ksɪ-2) of the West.

occlude (5-77) stop up a hole so that liquid or air cannot pass; *Occluded air* (in melted metal) = air shut in so making a *bubble* (= a small empty space) inside the metal when it is cold.

occult (9k8) hidden, secret; *Occult science* = study of magic and strange, not natural, powers.

occupant (5kɪ7-9) person holding land or living in a house.

occupation (5kɪ7-2ɪshn) (1) act of holding in one's possession; (2) holding by armed force of an enemy's country; (3) time during which a thing is held in possession; (4) employment; *Occupational disease* = illness caused by one's work, e.g. poisoning in a painter; *Occupational risk* = special danger caused by one's work, e.g. falling from a wall to a builder; *Occupational therapy* = curing illness of the body or mind by making the sick person do certain work.

occupy (5kɪ7-4ɪ) (1) take and hold possession of; (2) hold an enemy's country; (3) live in a house; (4) fill a certain space, e.g. *Occupy a house*; (5) employ, e.g. *Occupy oneself in* = work at.

occur' (9k99) happen; be found; *It occurs to me* = the thought comes to me; **occur'rence** (9k8-s) happening.

ocean (67shn) great sea.

ochre (67k9) yellow earth used as a colouring matter, e.g. in paints.

octa- eight, e.g. **oct'agonal** (5-3-9) eight-sided; **octave** (5-ɪ) eight equal musical notes above or below a certain note.

octane (number) (5-2ɪ) number which shows the power and goodness of petrol (gasoline): 100 octane petrol is very good.

oct'avo (5-2ɪ-67) piece of paper folded three times so as to give eight pages.

octopus (5-9-9) deep-sea creature with eight arms.

OCTOPUS

octroi (5-trw4) money paid to the government on all goods coming into a town; place where this money is paid.

ocular (5-ɪ7-9) of the eye or eyesight; **oculist** (5-ɪ7-ɪ) eye-doctor.

odd (5) not one of a set, e.g. *An odd shoe* = only one shoe; peculiar; *Odd numbers* = 1, 3, 5, etc.; *Odd jobs* = not regular employment; *One hundred odd* = a few more than one hundred; **oddity** (5-ɪ-ɪ) peculiarity; an unusual person; **odds** (5-z) *The odds are 2 to 1 on* = there are two *chances* (= probabilities) to one in favour of; *odds and ends* (5-z + 2-z) = loose bits of things left over.

ode (67) song or poem of a solemn kind.

odious (67-ɪ9) hateful.

odium (67-ɪ9) wide-spread hatred; *I shall get the odium of it* = I shall be blamed and disliked because of it.

odorif'erous (67-9-ɪ-9-9) carrying smell.

odour (67-9) smell; *He is in bad odour* = people do not think well of him.

o'er (679) over.

oesophagus (ɪɪ-5-9-9) food-pipe leading from the mouth to the stomach.

oestrum (ɪɪ-9) time of sex-excitement in an animal.

offal (5) waste matter; waste part of animal killed for food.

off (5) (1) at a distance; *Be off!* = go away; *Five miles off* = distant; (2) adj. not on; more distant, e.g. *The off side* = far —; *Put off* = to delay to a later date; *An off-day* = day of no work; Sl. *The fish is a bit off* = not fresh; *Off and on* = sometimes, not always; *Off colour* = (of a jewel) of bad colour; (of a person) not in good health; *Off the record* = not to be written down in the notes of this meeting; *Voices off* = sounds made off the stage in the theatre, not made by those at whom we are looking.

off'ence (9-2-s) a wrong; *To commit an offence* = do a wrong or unlawful act; *To take offence* = be displeased; *To give offence* = displease.

off'end (9-2) do wrong; displease.

offensive (9-2-ɪ) (1) unpleasant, e.g. *An offensive smell*; (2) causing anger, e.g. *Offensive remarks* = sayings which displease; (3) having to do with attack, e.g. *Offensive weapons* = weapons used in attack; *To take the offensive* = to attack.

offer (5-9) (1) give to a god; (2) hold out to a person as a gift; give a chance of accepting, e.g. *I offer £100 for your car* = I will buy it at —; *As occasion offers* = when there is a chance; **an offer**, thing offered; **an offering** (———ɪ) gift, e.g. to a god; **an offertory** (5-9-9-ɪ) money given by the people at a church *service* (= religious ceremony).

'off-h'and (5 + 3) at once, without preparation; *An off-hand manner* = a careless disrespectful manner.

office (5-ɪs) (1) work done, e.g. *Your good offices* = your help; (2) employment and special duties, e.g. *The office of headmaster*; (3) house or room used as a place of business, for writing letters, etc.; **offices** (5-ɪsɪz) parts of a house where house-work and cooking are done; *The last offices* = prayers for a dead person; **an officer** (5-ɪs9) one who holds an office or is employed by government, e.g. *An officer in the army*; **official** (9-ɪshl) having to do with an office; having to do with the government; *Official news* = news made public by the government; **An official**, person employed by the government; **to officiate** (9-ɪshɪ2ɪ) do the work of an officer who is away or ill; carry out a ceremony in a church.

offing (5-ɪ), **in the** — (used of a ship) at a

offset (5-2) *This will offset my other losses* = make a gain equal to —, so that there will be no loss in the end.

offspring (5-1) children.

oft (5) **often** (5-9 or 55-9) many times.

ogle (67) look at in a loving way.

ogre (67-9) imaginary man-eating *giant* (= man-like creature of more than human size).

ohm (67) measure of *electrical resistance* (= the difficulty with which electricity passes along a certain wire).

-oid, in the form of, e.g. **metalloid** (2-9-51) like a metal.

oil (51) fatty liquid, used for burning, for making machines run easily, also for cooking; *Pour oil on troubled waters* = bring peace when people are quarrelling; *To strike oil* = make a valuable discovery; *To burn the midnight oil* = read or work until very late at night.

oilcake (51-21) mass of seeds from which the oil has been pressed, used to feed cattle.

oilcloth (51-5) cloth covered with a special thick paint, used as a floor-covering.

oilskin (51-1) cloth specially treated with oil to keep out rain.

ointment (51-19) medicine made up with fat to be rubbed on the skin.

O.K. (67k21) Sl. I agree; correct.

old (67) having lived (or been used) for a long time; belonging to an earlier time; *Old maid* = old unmarried woman; person who is very careful and difficult to please; *An old hand at the game* = experienced person; *Men of old* = who lived long ago; **olden** (67) old; *In olden times* = long ago.

ole'aginous (67-13j1-9) oily.

olf'actory (5-3-9-1) of smell.

oligarchy (5-1-44k1) government by a few.

olive (51-1) tree grown especially in Italy which has a small egg-shaped fruit, used for food, also for its oil; any small *oval* (= egg-shaped) thing; *The olive branch* = sign of peace; (adj. of colour) light green.

omelet (51-1) eggs beaten together with salt and pieces of pleasant-tasting leaves, etc., and cooked with butter.

omen (67-2) sign showing that something (good or bad) is going to happen; **ominous** (51-1-9) showing future evil.

om'it (6-1) miss out, e.g. not write or say a certain word or not read a certain part of a book; *To omit to* = fail to, not do; n. **om'ission** (6-1shn).

omni- all, for all.

omnibus (51-1-9) car travelling along a fixed course to various places and carrying people for a small payment; *Omnibus book* = one big book containing several long stories which were first printed each as one book.

omn'ipotent (5-1-1-9) all-powerful.

omn'iscient (5-1-1-19) all-knowing.

omn'ivorous (5-1-9-9) eating all kinds of food—meat, plants, etc.

on (5) *The play is on* = is being shown; *Breakfast is on now* = can be had now; *On and on* = continuing without stopping; *Off and on* = from time to time; *And so on* = etc.; *The on side* = near side.

once (w8-s) at one time; some time ago; *All at once* = all together; *At once* = now without waiting; Sl. *Give the car a once-over* = look quickly at all the parts, or clean (mend) all the parts quickly.

one (w8) *It is all one to me* = it makes no difference; it does not matter; *One must do it* = I must—any person must.

onerous (duty) (5-9-9) heavy, troublesome.

onion (8-19) round white vegetable made up of one skin within another, strong smelling, much used in cooking.

onset (5-2) attack.

onslaught (5-55) fierce attack.

onus (67-9) weight; duty; *The onus of proof lies with you* = you must prove it.

onward (5-9) forward, towards the front.

onyx (5-1) precious stone having lines of various colours in it.

oodles (of money) (77dlz) Sl. a great deal of —.

ooze (77) thick liquid, e.g. at the bottom of a river; **to ooze**, (of liquid) pass slowly through.

opal (67) precious stone of the colour of milk-and-water; **'opal'escent** (67-9-2) like an opal.

op'aque (67-21k) not allowing light to pass through; n. **op'acity** (67-3s1-1).

open (67) not shut; free; generous; *Keep open house* = have many guests; *An open question, Leave the matter open* = undecided; *To be open with a person* = keep nothing secret; **to open**, cause to be open; *Open the dance* = start —; **'open-h'anded** (+ 3-1) generous; **openly** (——1) not secretly.

open-cast mining (67 + 44 + 41-1) getting coal out of the earth by taking off the upper part of the ground—not as usual by making holes under the ground.

opera (5-9-9) musical play of a serious kind; **oper'atic** (5-9-3-1) of the opera; **oper'etta** (5-9-2-9) light (not serious) musical play.

'opera-glasses (+ 44-1z) glasses used in a theatre to see the actors as if nearer.

operate (5-9-21) to work, cause to work; have an effect; cut the body in order to set right a diseased part; **oper'ation** (5-9-21shn) working; the way a thing works; cutting of the body by a doctor; *Operations of an army* = movements; *Not in operation* = not in use;

operative (5-9-9-1) having power to work; *An operative* = workman; *The operative word* = most important word in the sentence.

ophth'almia (5-3-19) disease of the eyes.

opiate (67-19) sleep-producing medicine.

op'inion (9-1-19) what one thinks about a

subject; *To have no opinion of* = think badly of; **op'inionated** (9-1-19-21-1) very sure of the rightness of his opinions.

opium (67-19) sleep-producing material made from the seed of the white *poppy*.

op'ossum (9-5-9) small American tree-climbing animal which pretends to be dead when it is caught. OPOSSUM

opp'onent (9-67-9) person who takes the other side in a game, talk or fight.

opportune (5-9-177) coming just at the right time.

opport'unity (5-9-177-1-1) chance to do something.

opp'ose (9-67z) to stand or fight against a person or idea.

opposite (5-9z1) facing one, in the front of; quite different from, e.g. *Black is the opposite of white.*

oppos'ition (5-9z1shn) act or state of being opposite to; act of fighting or struggling against.

oppress' (9-2) rule in a hard and cruel way; cause to feel ill or sad.

oppr'obrious (9-67-19) rude (word), showing disrespect.

oppr'obrium (9-67-19) shame; thing or words which cause a feeling of shame.

optic (5-1) having to do with the eyes; **optical**, having to do with light and eyesight; **opt'ician** (5-1shn) one who makes or sells glasses for the eyes.

optimism (5-1-1z) belief that everything will come right, will end happily; hopefulness; **an optimist** (5-1-1) one who believes that all will be well.

optimum (5-1-9) best; *Optimum temperature* = heat best for the work.

option (5-shn) a choice; *To have an option on it* = first right to buy it; **optional** (5-sh9), which may or may not be done, at choice.

opulent (5-17-9) rich.

oracle (5-9) place where a god was believed to speak to people; person through whom the god was believed to speak; answers given by the god; any wise and wonderful adviser; **or'acular** (5-3-17-9) as of an oracle.

oral (55) by mouth; of the mouth; *Oral examination* = examining a person's knowledge by spoken questions and answers.

orange (5-1nj) very common sweet golden-coloured fruit; colour; **orange'ade** (5-1nj21) drink made from oranges.

'orang-'outang (5-3 + 77-3) large monkey-like creature with no tail. ORANG-OUTANG

or'ation (9-21shn) solemn speech; **orator** (5-9-9) good speaker; **orat'orical** (5-9-5-1) as of an orator.

orat'orio (5-9-55-167) long piece of music and singing, telling a Bible story.

oratory (5-9-9-1) art of speaking; small house of prayer.

orb (55) round thing, ball; star or world.

orbit (55-1) hollow in which the eye is set; path of a star or other world in the sky which moves round another star.

orchard (55-9) field of fruit trees.

orchestra (55k1-9) group of persons who play music together; *Orchestra stalls* = front seats in a theatre.

orchid (55k1) plant with three brightly coloured *petals* (= coloured leaves), often curiously shaped, found usually in hot countries (most orchids grow on the branches of trees).

ord'ain (55-21) to order; *God has ordained that* —; to make a man a priest.

ord'eal (5-19) difficult or painful experience; *Trial by ordeal* = judging a person by giving him a painful or frightening experience.

order (55-9) (1) arrangement, e.g. *In alphabetical order* = in A.B.C. arrangement; (2) neat arrangement; (3) state of law and good control; *To rise to a point of order* = get up and say that the rules of a meeting are not being obeyed; (4) healthy state, e.g. *My stomach is out of order*; (5) class; *The lower orders* = common people; (6) group of persons holding a certain rank, e.g. *The Order of the Bath* (title given to famous men in England); (7) *To take orders* = become a priest; *He is in holy orders* = is a priest; (8) a command; *Made to order* = made specially for the buyer; **to order**, command; tell a shop to supply goods; **orderly** (55-9-1) well arranged; loving good arrangement; peace-loving and well behaved.

orderly (55-9-1) soldier who carries orders from one officer to another.

ordinal (numbers) (55-1) e.g. first, second, third ...

ordinance (55-1-9-s) a rule or law.

ordinary (55-1-1) usual; meal served at a fixed price; an eating-house.

ordin'ation (55-1-21shn) act and ceremony of making a man a priest.

ordnance (55-9-s) guns and army stores.

ordure (55-179) waste matter of animal bodies; dirt.

ore (55) rock from which metal is obtained.

organ (55-9) part of a plant or animal which serves some special purpose (does some special duty); instrument; newspaper used as a means of having an effect on public thought; musical instrument made of many pipes blown by air —much used in churches.

organdie (5-9-1) very fine rather stiff cotton material used for ladies' dresses.

org'anic (55-3-1) having to do with some *organ* (2nd above) of the body; **org'anic ch'emis-**

try (+ k2-1-1) study of the nature of materials found in living things.

organism (55-9-1z) living thing; group of parts each performing its special duty.

organize (55-9-41) arrange parts so that they may work together to make an active whole.

orgy (55j1) wild gathering of wine-drinkers.

oriel (55-19) large upper window built out from the wall.

Orient (55-19) The East; **ori'ental** (55-12) of the east, a native of an Eastern country, e.g. China.

orientate (55-12-21) plan a church so that one end may be towards the east; *To orientate oneself* = find where one is, e.g. in order to know the right path.

orifice (5-1-1s) opening; the small mouth of a large hole.

origin (5-1j1) place from which a thing began; first beginning of a thing; first cause; *One's origin* = one's birth and family, e.g. *A man of humble origin* = man of low birth.

or'iginal (9-1j1) earliest; new, not like any other; thinking and acting for oneself; peculiar in behaviour; **or'iginally** (——1) in the beginning; in a way not copied from other people; **origin'ality** (9-1j1-3-1-1) power of thinking out new ideas; **or'iginate** (9-1j1-21) cause to begin; to start.

orison (5-1z) prayer.

ornament (55-9-9) thing used to add beauty to something else.

orn'ate (55-21) having many ornaments; ornamented too much.

'ornith'ology (55-1-5-9j1) scientific study of birds.

orphan (55) child whose father and mother are dead; **orphanage** (55-9-1j) home for orphans.

ortho- right, e.g. **orthodox** (55-9-5) holding accepted opinions.

orth'ography (55-5-9-1) correct *spelling* (= choice of letters in writing a word).

Oscar (5-9) prize given for the best cinema actor, cinema writer, etc., in a certain year.

oscillate (5-1-21) to swing from side to side.

oscular (5-17-9) of the mouth.

osier (6739) tree whose smaller branches are used to make baskets.

osprey (5-1) fish-eating bird.

osprey (5-1) group of fine white silky feathers found on the back of an *egret* (= bird, not the osprey above), and formerly used for ornamenting hats.

osseous (5-19) made of bone; **ossify** (5-1-41) to change into bone.

ost'ensible (reason) (5-2-1) seeming or pretended.

ostent'ation (5-2-21shn) unnecessary show; **ostent'atious** (5-2-21shgs) making much show.

'oste'opathy (5-15-9-1) curing diseases by pressing, pulling (etc.) the bones with the hands, e.g. pressing up the bones in the arch of the foot to cure pain in walking.

ostler (5-9) man who takes care of horses.

ostracize (5-9s41) to drive out from a group of people.

ostrich (5-1) very large bird with long legs and a long neck, which runs very quickly, found in Africa, Arabia and Syria.

otherwise (8ŏ9-41z) in a different way; if this is not so.

otter (5-9) fish-eating animal with beautiful brown fur.

OSTRICH

ottoman (5-9-9) long soft seat without back or arms.

ought, aught (55) anything (cf. nought); Sl. nothing, o.

ought (55) *I ought to* = I must.

ounce (47-s) 1/16th of a pound *Avoirdupois* (= 28·35 grammes); 1/12th of a pound *Troy* (= 31 grammes) (N.B. 1 pound Troy = ·82286 pound Avoirdupois).

oust (47) push a person out of—e.g. out of employment, favour, etc.

out (47) *The secret is out* = is known; *My daughter is not out yet* = not old enough to go to dances, etc.; *Out in one's guess* = incorrect; *Acted out of kindness to* = because of; *Out and away the finest* = by far; *Out and out* (bad) = very, in every way —.

out- more than, better than, freely.

'out-b'id (47 + 1) offer more than.

'outboard m'otor (47-55 + 67-9) machine as shown fixed on to a boat to drive it.

'outcast (47-44) homeless, friendless person.

'outcl'ass (47-44) be in a higher class; be better than.

OUTBOARD MOTOR

outcome (47-8) the result.

outcrop (of rock) (47-5) rock which stands up out of the ground.

outcry (47-41) show of anger by the people.

outd'istance (47-1-9-s) go farther or faster than.

outd'o (47-77) do better than.

'outd'oors (47-55z) not in the house; adj. **'outdoor.**

outermost (47-9-67) farthest outside.

outfit (47-1) all the things necessary for a certain piece of work.

'out-gr'ow (47 + 67) grow too large for.

outing (47-1) *To go for an outing* = go on a short pleasure-journey.

outl'andish (47-3-1) strange.

outlaw (47-55) one who is put outside the protection of the law.

outlay (47-21) money spent, e.g. in doing a certain piece of work.

outlet (47-2) way through which a thing may go out; good chance for using one's powers.

outline (47-41) line showing the shape of a thing; **to outline**, draw the shape of; give a general idea of.

outl'ive (47-1) live longer than.

outlook (47-7) (1) view seen from a window; (2) general appearance of future events; *His general outlook* = his way of considering things; *An outlook tower* = a high tower from which watch is kept.

outn'umber (47-8-9) be more in number than.

outpost (47-67) guard at some distance from the main army keeping watch while the army is at rest, e.g. during the night.

outrage (47-21j) very wrong or cruel act which causes great anger; **to outrage**, attack; *To outrage public opinion* = do something which everyone thinks very wrong; **outr'ageous** (47-21j9) very bad, causing great anger.

outré (77-21) very peculiar or unusual.

outrider (47-41-9) servant on a horse riding at the side of, or in front of, a carriage.

'outr'ight (47-41) at once; freely and truthfully.

outset (47-2) the beginning.

outs'ider (47-41-9) person who is not a member of a certain group; horse not expected to win a race; person who has very bad manners.

outsizes (47-41-1z) coats, dresses, shoes, hats, etc., for very big men or women.

outskirt(s) (47-99) outer edge of a town.

'outstr'ip (47-1) to pass in running.

'outw'it (47-1) deceive; win by greater cleverness.

oval (67) egg-shaped.

ovary (67-9-1) egg-producing organ; seed-producing organ in a plant.

ov'ation (67-21shn) joyful welcome given by the people to some person greatly admired.

oven (8) box used for baking.

over (67-9) above; across; on the other side of; more than; finished, e.g. *The day is over*; *All over* = quite finished; *It's all over with him* = he is ruined, must die; Sl. *She was all over him* = tried hard to please him; *To go over* = examine carefully.

over- too much, e.g. **to over'eat** (67-9-11) eat too much; **'over-'anxious** (67-9 + 3ngsh9) too —.

overall (67-9-55) loose dress covering the usual clothes and protecting them during work.

over-all length (67-9 + 55 + 2) length from one end to the other, e.g. of a ship.

'over'awe (67-9-55) fill a person with fear so that he obeys.

'overb'alance (67-9-3-s) fall over; cause to fall over; be greater in weight or value than.

'overb'earing (67-9-29-1) taking no notice of other people's ideas or feelings.

'overb'oard (67-9-55) *To fall overboard* = fall from a ship.

'overc'ast (sky) (67-9-44) cloudy.

overcoat (67-9-67) warm coat used to wear in the street.

'overc'ome (67-9-8) conquer.

'overd'o (67-9-77) do too much, e.g. to be foolishly eager in an attempt; work too hard; cook (meat) too much.

'overdr'aw (67-9-55) take more money from a bank than one put in; **n. overdraft** (67-9-44).

overh'aul (67-9-55) examine and repair thoroughly.

overh'ear (67-9-19) hear by accident.

'overj'oyed (67-9-51) very pleased.

'overl'ap (67-9-3) to lie partly covering something else.

'overl'ook (67-9-7) (1) look over; *The windows overlooked the street* = one could look out over the street from those windows; (2) look at and fail to see; (3) pretend not to see; forgive.

overn'ight (67-9-41) on the night before; during the night.

'overp'ower (67-9-479) conquer by greater power; **overp'owering** (——1) more than one can bear.

'overr'each (oneself) (67-9-11) fail by trying to do too much or to be too clever.

'overr'ide (67-9-41) take no notice of (another person's orders, claims, etc.), give opposite orders from those of another person.

overseer (67-9-11·9) one who watches to see that work is properly done.

oversight (67-9-41) a mistake.

'oversl'eep (67-9-11) to sleep on past the proper time for waking.

ov'ert (67-99) public, not secret.

'overt'ake (67-9-21) come up level with a person from behind.

overtime (67-9-41) time worked beyond the regular working-hours.

overture (67-9-179) piece of music played at the beginning of a musical play; *To make overtures to* = make an offer to a person; begin to deal with a person in the hope of reaching an agreement.

'overt'urn (67-9-99) cause to fall over.

'overw'eening (67-9-11-1) proud and too sure of himself.

'overwh'elm (67-9-2) cover or swallow up completely.

'overwr'ought (67-9-55) tired and too excited.

owe (67) be in debt; feel that one should be grateful to; *Owing to (the rain)* = because of.

owl (47) night-bird with large eyes, supposed to be very wise.

own (67) possessed by oneself; *To come into one's own* = get that which belongs to one, get the fame of which one is worthy; *Hold one's own* = be able to stand against attack; (in illness) not lose strength; *On one's own* = alone; *Do it on*

OWL

one's own = without help; **to own,** possess; agree that an opinion is right; **own to, own up, own up to,** say that one did a wrong act.

ox (5) male form of cattle which cannot cause the production of young; pl. **oxen.**

oxidize (5-1-41) cause to unite with *oxygen* (2nd below).

'oxy-ac'etylene welding (5-1 + 9s2-1-11 + 2-1) cutting or joining metal by using the very hot flame of the two gases *oxygen* and *acetylene*.

oxygen (5-1j) gas necessary for all animal life.

oyez (6712s) listen!

oyster (51-9) flat shell-fish in which *pearls* (= beautiful round white-grey jewels) are sometimes found.

ozone (67-67) form of *oxygen* (3rd above); very pleasant air, e.g. at the sea-side.

P

Pa (44) child's word for Father.
pace (21s) a step; speed; **to pace, to walk,** e.g. *He paced up and down the room;* to ride along beside a runner so as to help him.
pacha (44sh9) see Pasha.
pachyderm (3k1-99) thick-skinned animal.
pacify (3sI-41) make peaceable; **pac'ific** (9sI-1) peaceful, peace-loving; **pacifist** (3sI-1) **pac'ificist** (9sI-1-1) one who desires to put an end to all war.
pack (3) (1) set of things tied or fastened together; load carried on the back or on an animal; (2) group of animals, e.g. *A pack of hounds* (= dogs used for hunting); (3) set of playing-cards; **to pack,** fit closely into a box; to cover with material so as to protect from damage; to load an animal; *To pack a committee* = choose the members of a group so that the group may decide as one wishes; *To send a person packing* = send away quickly; Am. *To pack meat* = put meat into tins.
packet (3-1) **package** (3-1j) small collection or amount tied up together usually in paper; **packing** (3-1) soft material used for putting round things which are sent in boxes; material used to make a joint tight in an engine.
p'acket-boat (3-1 + 67) ship which carries letters and people and goods regularly on fixed days.
pact (3) agreement.
pad (3) piece of soft material, e.g. one used to protect the body from blows; number of sheets of writing-paper fixed together on a piece of card; **padding,** matter used to fill a pad or make chairs, etc., soft; useless words in a book; soft round part on the bottom of some animals' feet, e.g. cats.
paddle (3) wooden blade used to move a boat along in the water; **to paddle,** move a boat with a paddle; row slowly; *Paddle one's own canoe* = work unhelped.
paddle (3) walk in water with *bare feet* (= having no shoes on the feet).
p'addle-wheels (+ 11-z) large wheels fixed to the sides of a ship, turned by a steam-engine to make the ship move forward through the water; **a p'addle-steamer** (+ 11-9).

PADDLE-STEAMER

paddock (3-9) small field.
padlock (3-5) lock, not fixed to the door, but passed through rings.
padre (44-1) (= father) priest.
paean (11·9) song of praise or victory.
p'aedi'atrics (11-13-1) treatment of the diseases of children.

pagan (21-9) person who is not a Christian; a person who believes in false gods.
page (21j) one side of a piece of paper in a book.
page (21j) boy servant.
pageant (3j9) fine show or public performance; acting in the open air of scenes from the history of a town; **pageantry** (3j9-1) fine or useless shows and ceremonies.
pag'oda (9-67-9) *temple* (= house of prayer) of Buddha.
paid (21) p.t. of Pay.
pail (21) open vessel with handle used for carrying liquids.
paillasse (3-13) see Palliasse, Pallet.
pain (21) suffering of body or mind; *On pain of death* = with death as the punishment; *He took great pains* = he was very careful; **painstaking** (21-z-21-1) careful.

PAGODA

paint (21) liquid colouring matter laid on with a brush; to put on paint; **a painting** (21-1) picture; *Paint the town red* = have a very merry evening.
painter (21-9) one who paints; rope at the front of a boat with which it is tied to the shore.
pair (29) two; **to pair,** put in groups of two.
pajamas (9-44-9z) see Pyjamas.
pal (3) Sl. friend.
palace (3-1s) house of a king or other ruler; any large fine house.
paladin (3-9-1) very brave and perfect knight.
palaeo- old, e.g. **palaeolithic** (3-16-1-1) old Stone Age, time of earliest man.
palatable (3-9-9) pleasing to the taste.
palate (3-1) roof (inside, bony arch) of the mouth.
pal'atial (9-21shI) of or like a palace.
pal'aver (9-44-9) a talk, at which many people sit round in a circle; unimportant talk.
pale (21) having little colour, white, bloodless, e.g. *A pale face; Pale-face* = name used by American Indians for the Europeans.
pale (21) **paling** (21-1) fence; *He is beyond the pale* = not a gentleman, very badly behaved.
palette (3-1) board with a hole for the thumb, on which a painter of pictures mixes his paints.
palis'ade (3-1-21) fence used in defending against attack.
pall (55) ornamental covering of cloth or silk thrown over a box in which a dead body is carried.
pall (55) become uninteresting.
pallet (3-1) *mattress* (= flat bag of soft material used for sleeping on) filled with *straw* (= dry stems of grain-bearing plants). •

palliasse (3-13) *pallet* (above).

palliate (3-121) make a thing seem less wrong; lessen pain without setting right the cause.

pallid (3-1) (of the skin) white, bloodless; n. **pallor** (3-9).

palm (44) flat inside of the hand; *To grease his palm* = pay him money to do wrong.

palm (44) tree with broad leaves growing out of the top; *Bear away the palm* = win a victory; *Yield the palm to.*= be beaten by.

palmist (44-1). one who tells character and the future, from lines on the hand.

palmy days (44-1 + 21z) happy care-free times.

PALM

palpable (3-9) which can be felt or observed.

palpitate (3-1-21) move quickly, e.g. the heart.

palsy (55-zI) disease which causes shaking of the hands and limbs.

paltry (55-1) worthless; **to palter with**, refuse to deal seriously or boldly with; *Palter with the facts, truth* = speak about — in such a way as to deceive the listener.

pamper (3-9) treat too kindly, e.g. a child.

pamphlet (3-1) small book.

pan (3) flat open pot.

pan- all, for all, e.g. **p'anac'ea** (3-9s19) medicine for all diseases.

pancake (3-21) thin, flat cake.

p'anchrom'atic film (3-kr6-3-1 + 1) On ordinary photographic film red comes out too black, blue comes out too white. In panchromatic film this is not so.

pancreas (3-1-3) part of the body which produces a liquid that helps the bowel in dealing with sugar.

p'andem'onium (3-1-67-19) scene of great noise and disorder.

pander to (3-9) help a person to satisfy bad desires.

pane (21) *A window-pane* = sheet of glass.

p'aneg'yric (3-1j1-1) speech in praise of.

panel (3) (1) large board set in a door, or fixed to the wall; **panelling** (——) wooden covering of a wall; (2) list of names; (3) list of people chosen to deal with a certain sort of question, e.g. *A panel of doctors*; *Panel-game* = radio game in which three or four people (the panel) try to guess the right answer.

pang (3) sudden great pain.

panic (3-1) sudden fear spreading through a crowd.

panniers (3-19z) baskets carried on each side of a donkey (ass) or horse.

pannikin (3-1-1) small tin cup.

panoply (3-9-1) complete set of armour.

panor'ama (3-9-44-9) view all round; a picture painted on a long *strip* (= narrow piece of material) which is unrolled from one end and rolled up on the other.

pansy (3-zI) small plant with broad flat flowers.

pant (3) breathe quickly.

pantal'oons (3-9-77-z) wide garments covering the legs; **pantal'oon**, man paid to amuse others by his foolishness.

pant'echnicon (3-2k-1-9) large covered cart used for moving furniture.

pantheism (3-11-1z) belief that the whole world is God.

panth'eon (3-19) (1) large hall, e.g. one built in honour of many gods or of famous men; (2) all the gods of a certain nation.

PANSY

panther (3-9) large wild cat.

pantograph (3-9-44) instrument for copying pictures by moving a point along the lines while a pencil is moved by bars so that it draws larger or smaller on another sheet of paper.

pantomime (3-9-41) fairy-play acted at Christmas in the theatre.

pantry (3-1) store-room for cups, plates, knives, spoons, etc., in a house; a serving-room for meals.

pants (3) garments worn on the legs.

pap (3) soft food for babies.

pap'a (9-44) child's name for father.

papacy (21-9s1) office of *Pope* (= head of part of the Christian Church—the Roman Catholics); **papal** (21) of the *Pope*.

pap'aya (9-419) **pap'aw**, **pawp'aw** (9-55) fruit of tree which grows in hot countries, green outside, yellow inside with black seeds and a sweet-salt taste.

paper (21-9) material on which a book is printed; *On paper* = as judged by printed figures; *A paper* = newspaper; written or printed paper; written examination; *Send in one's papers* = give up an office; **to paper**, stick paper on to, e.g., a wall.

p'aper-chase (21-9 + 21) game in which one set of runners throws down bits of paper to mark the track, and others follow.

p'apier m'âché (3-121 + 3sh21) paper boiled into a soft mass and used for making boxes, ornamental figures, etc.

papist (21-1) Roman Catholic (used as a word of disrespect).

pap'oose (9-77) American-Indian baby.

papr'ika (9-11-9) red, hot-tasting powder.

pap'yrus (9-419-9) leaf of a plant used by ancient Egyptians for paper.

par (44) state of being equal; *At par* = equal to its usual or correct value; *On a par with* = equal to, level with.

parable (3-9) short story teaching some lesson about God or goodness.

par'abola (3-9-9) curve made by the flight of a ball when thrown.

parachute (3-9sh77) large circle of thin cloth which opens to let a man fall slowly through the air. (See next page for picture.)

parade (9-21) (**1**) show, march-past or drilling of soldiers; (**2**) raised road along the sea-front; *To parade one's knowledge* = show proudly —.

paradise (3-9-41) place to which the souls of good people go after death; any very happy place.

paradox (3-9-5) saying that seems foolish yet may be true.

paraffin (3-9-11) oil used in lamps; fat from this oil used in making candles.

paragon (3-9-9) example of goodness which all should copy.

PARACHUTE

paragraph (3-9-44) block of writing or printing of which the first word is set a little inwards to the right.

parak'eet (3-9-11) small bright-coloured bird.

parallel (lines) (3-9-2) straight lines running side by side yet never meeting.

parall'elogram (3-9-2-9-3) four-sided figure whose opposite sides are equal and *parallel* (see above).

par'alysis (9-3-1-1) disease causing loss of power and feeling in part of the body; **to p'aralyse** (3-9-41z) make unable to move; adj. **paral'ytic** (3-9-1-1).

paramount (3-9-47) highest (importance).

paramour (3-9-79) lover.

p'aran'oia (3-9-51g) form of madness in which the mad person thinks that he is very great, e.g. a king, Napoleon, etc.

parapet (3-9-1) wall at the edge of a roof or at the side of a bridge.

paraphern'alia (3-9-9-21-19) many and various things belonging to a person, or used in some work.

paraphrase (3-9-21z) say or write the meaning of a *passage* (= piece of writing), using other words.

parasite (3-9-41) plant or animal which joins on to another and lives on its food or blood; person who lives at another's cost.

p'aras'ol (3-9-5) cloth stretched on a frame of metal, which can be opened and shut, carried by a lady to give shade from the sun.

paratrooper (3-9-77-9) soldier who is dropped by *parachute* (see Parachute.)

parboil (44-51) boil for a short time.

parcel (44s) something *wrapped up in* (= covered with) paper as for the post or for carrying; *A parcel of land* = piece of land; *To parcel out* = divide into shares; *Part and parcel of (the plan)* = very important part of, a part which cannot be left out.

PARATROOPER

parch (44) burn slightly, to dry up.

parchment (44-9) animal skin used for writing on.

pardon (44) forgive; forgiveness; *I beg your pardon* = I am sorry, allow me to trouble you, forgive me for troubling you.

pare (29) cut away the outside or edge of.

parent (29-9) father or mother.

par'enthesis (9-2-1-1) words put inside *brackets* (= ( )) to keep them separate from the words round them.

par 'excellence (44 + 2ks2-44ⁿs) far the best.

pariah (3-19) Indian of the lowest rank or class in the order of *Hinduism* (= religion of the Hindus in India); wild dog in India.

parish (3-1) piece of country served by one church; **par'ishioner** (9-1-9-9) one who lives in a parish.

parity (3-1-1) state of being equal.

park (44) large piece of enclosed ground used by the public, or lying round a great man's house; **to park** = put a motor-car in an open place where it may be left safely, e.g. in a quiet street.

parlance (44-9-s) way of speaking.

parley (44-1) talk with an enemy so as to make peace.

parliament (44-9-9) group of persons elected by the people to make laws.

parlour (44-9) sitting-room.

parlous (state) (44-9) dangerous, very bad.

par'ochial (9-67k19) having to do with a *parish* (= piece of country served by a church); narrow in opinion.

parody (3-9-1) write or speak in the manner of another person so as to make others laugh at him; **a parody**, thing said or written with this purpose; a laughable copy of a thing.

par'ole (9-67) promise given by a prisoner not to try to escape.

paroxysm (3-9-1z) sudden fierce attack, e.g. of pain.

parquet (flooring) (44k21) floor made of blocks of wood fitted together like bricks.

parricide (3-1s41) killer of, killing of, one's father or near relative.

parrot (3-9) bird which is able to speak; **to parrot**, say words learnt without thought of their meaning.

parry (3-1) to turn aside, e.g. a blow, the blade of an enemy's sword.

PARROT

parse (44z) describe a word showing its relation to other words in a *sentence* (= group of words expressing a complete meaning).

parsim'onious (44-1-67-19) too careful of money; n. **parsimony** (44-1-9-1).

parsley (44-1) vegetable whose leaves are put on food to make it look nice, used also in cooking.

parsnip (44-1) sweet yellow root, boiled for food.

parson (44-9) priest; **parsonage** (44-9-1j) house in which the priest of a church lives,

part (44) one of the pieces into which a thing is divided; *True in part* = part of it is true; *Take it in good part* = do not be angry at it; *Spare parts of a motor* = new pieces of a machine used when part is broken or worn out; *I live in these parts* = near here; *I for my part* = speaking for myself only; *Foolish behaviour on the part of Mr. X* = Mr. X behaved foolishly; *To take a part in a play* = act one character in; *To take part in* = help in; *Take the part of* = speak in support of; **to part**, divide; separate; *To part with* = give up, sell.

part'ake (44-21) take a part of.

partial (44shl) (1) in part, e.g. *A partial success* = not completely successful; (2) in favour of; *She is partial to sweets* = she likes —; *Partial in his judgments* = not fair to both sides.

partic'ipate (44-Isi-21) to share in.

participle (44-Isi) part of a *verb* (= word expressing being or doing), e.g. Doing, Done, are participles of Do.

particle (44-I) (1) very small piece; (2) word such as *And, To,* or *Oh!*

p'arti-coloured (44-I + 8-9) having different colours in different parts.

partic'ular (9-I-I7-9) (1) special or separate and different from others, e.g. *Each works in his own particular way*; *In a particular case* = in one special example; *He is particularly careful of* = specially; (2) difficult to please, e.g. *Very particular about one's food*; **a partic'ular**, single point or part, e.g. *Correct in every particular*; **to part'icularize** (9-I-I7-9-41) give a list of all the special parts of.

parting (44-I) (1) act of separating; *A parting of the ways* = time when we must choose one of two lines of action; (2) line from which one's hair is brushed to right and left.

partis'an (44-Iz3) eager supporter of a group or of a set of ideas.

part'ition (44-Ishn) thin dividing wall; a cutting up into parts.

partner (44-9) one who works or plays with another.

partridge (44-Ij) bird, shot and used for food.

parturi'tion (44-I7-Ishn) act of giving birth to a child.

party (44-I) group of persons who share the same opinion; small group; gathering of friends for food and amusement; *To be a party to a plan* = know of, to help in; Sl. *An ugly old party* = person.

PARTRIDGE

part'ook (44-7) p.t. of Partake.

parvenu (44-9-17) person who has suddenly become rich or powerful.

pasha (44shg) an officer of the army or government in Turkey or Egypt.

pass (44) (1) go as far as and beyond a thing; to change from one state into another; *To pass the ball* = hit, kick or throw it to another player; *All things must pass* = end; *To pass away* = die; *To pass out* = die, faint; (2) accept, allow, e.g. *A law was passed*; *It will pass* = it is good enough; *To pass an examination* = satisfy the examiners; (3) cause to pass, e.g. *To pass a string through a hole*; *Pass water* = cause waste liquid to flow out of the body; *Please pass the butter* = give me; *Pass the time of day with* = greet; (4) be better than, be too great for; *The peace of God that passes all understanding* = cannot be understood by men; *To pass for* = be accepted as, be thought to be; *Pass oneself off as* = pretend to be; **a pass**, act of passing; paper which allows one to pass through a door or gate; road through mountains; *Things have come to a bad pass* = are in a bad state; **passable** (44-9) just good enough.

passage (3-Ij) act of passing; journey by sea; way by which one passes; narrow way joining the rooms of a house; part of a book; *A passage of arms* = a fight.

passbook (44-7) book showing money paid into and taken out of one's bank.

passé(e) (3-21) old and no longer beautiful.

passenger (3-Inj9) traveller by train, ship, or car.

p'asse-part'out (3 + 44-77) key which opens all the doors in a hotel, office, etc.

passion (3shn) strong feeling; eager desire; *The Passion* = the sufferings of Christ on the cross.

passive (3-I) suffering, without taking action.

Passover (44-67-9) feast of the Jews in memory of their escape from Egypt.

passport (44-55) paper allowing one to visit a foreign country.

password (44-99) word which, when spoken to the guard, allows one to pass.

past (44) adj. gone by; **to go past**, go as far as and beyond a thing.

paste (21) soft matter, such as a mixture of flour and water; such matter used for sticking papers together; **to paste**, to stick.

pasteboard (21-55) stiff thick paper.

past'el (3-2) sticks of dry colour used for drawing.

pasteurize (3-9-41) to heat (milk) so as to kill all seeds of disease in it.

past'ille (3-11) small sweet containing medicine for the throat.

pastime (44-41) amusement.

p'ast-m'aster (44 + 44-9) one who is very skilled in some art.

pastor (44-9) priest in charge of a church; **pastoral** (44-9-9) of country life; of church duties.

pastry (21-I) flour, water, butter, etc., mixed and baked.

pasture (44-tsh9) grass-land for cattle.

pasty (21-I) (of a face) white, unhealthy-looking.

pasty (3-I) pastry cooked with meat in it.

pat (3) touch lightly with the flat hand; *To*

pat oneself on the back = be pleased at one's own cleverness; *A pat of butter* = small round piece of —; *To answer pat* = answer cleverly and at once.

patch (3) piece of material fixed on to or into another material to repair it; *It's not a patch on* = not nearly so good as —; *A patch of ground* = small piece of; *To patch up a quarrel* = settle for a time; **patchy** (——1) irregular in colour, not all of one quality.

p'atchouli (3-7-1) sweet-smelling plant; liquid obtained from it.

pate (21) head.

patent (21) open; clear to see.

patent (21) government order giving to one person or one group of people only, the right to make a certain article for sale; *To patent a thing* = get such an order; **patent'ee** (21-11) person who owns a patent.

p'atent-l'eather (+ 289) leather with a covering of hard polished matter.

p'aterfam'ilias (21-9-9-1-13) father of a family.

pat'ernal (9-99) of a father, like a father; n. **pat'ernity** (9-99-1-1) fatherhood.

p'atern'oster (3-9-5-9) the prayer "Our Father which art in Heaven . . ."

path (44) narrow road for walking on; line of action; track followed by a moving object.

path'etic (9-2-1) causing a feeling of pity.

path'ology (9-5-9jI) study of the signs, causes and treatment of disease.

pathos (21-5) power of causing pity.

patience (21sh9-s) (1) power of suffering without complaining; *To be out of patience with* = be angry with; (2) card game for one person; **patient** (21shnt) bearing trouble without complaining; sick person being treated by a doctor.

patois (3-w44) special form of a language spoken in one particular place.

patriarch (21-144k) father and ruler of a family.

patr'ician (9-rshn) nobleman of ancient Rome; adj. of noble birth.

patrimony (3-1-9-1) land, money, etc., handed down to descendants.

patriot (21-19) one who loves and defends his country.

patr'ol (9-67) small group of men who march about and guard a place; **to patr'ol**, go round and guard.

patron (21-9) helper and protector; rich man who helps a writer, painter, etc.; one who buys regularly at a certain shop; **patronize** (3-9-41) act as protector and helper; show that one thinks a person lower and less important than oneself.

patter (3-9) sound of a number of quick light blows or short steps; special talk of a certain class, e.g. thieves; **to patter**, make a pattering sound; talk quickly.

pattern (3-9) thing made so that other things may be made like it; ornamental drawing made or printed on cloth, paper, etc., e.g. *The pattern on a cup*.

patty (3-1) flour, water and butter mixed, and baked with meat or fish in it.

paucity (55s1-1) small number or amount.

paunch (55) stomach, especially a big one.

pauper (55-9) poor person, especially one helped with public money.

pause (55z) to stop or rest; a time during which work or speaking ceases.

pave (21) to cover with stone; *Pave the way for* = prepare for, help to arrive or happen; **pav'ement** (——9) paved floor, the path at the side of a street used by people walking.

pav'ilion (9-1-19) big tent; tent-shaped building.

paw (55) soft foot of an animal; **to paw**, touch with the paw or hand.

pawn (55) get money by leaving an article of value which will be given back when the money is repaid; **p'awn-broker** (55 + 67-9) one who lends money on things so offered.

pawn (55) smallest piece in the game of *Chess* (see —); unimportant person used by another.

pawpaw see Papaya.

pay (21) (1) give money for; *To pay through the nose* = pay too high a price; *Pay one's way* = pay one's own costs as they come; *My pay* = money which I am paid for my work; (2) produce gain, e.g. *The shop is not paying* = not bringing in enough money; (3) give or offer; *Pay one's respects* = go and greet a person with respect; *Pay a call* = go to a person's house and visit him; Sl. *I'll pay him out!* = punish him for the wrong which he has done to me.

PEA(-POD)

p'ay-roll (21 + 67) list of workers with the amount paid to each.

pea (11) small round green seed which grows in a green *pod* (= seed case) eaten as a vegetable; the kind of plant which produces this food.

peace (11s) calm; quietness; freedom from war.

PEACOCK

peach (11) soft fruit with a rough stone; Sl. beautiful girl; Sl. **to peach**, tell of the wrongdoings of others.

peacock (11-5) bird with a big brightly coloured tail.

peak (55) pointed top, e.g. of a rock or hill; front part of a cap which stands out over the eyes.

peal (11) loud and continuous ringing of bells.

PEANUT

peanut (11-8) hard-shelled seed, white outside, yellow inside, grown under the ground.

pear (29) a fruit.
pearl (99) jewel, white and round, found in shell-fish; **m'other-of-p'earl** (8ö9r + 9v + 99) white inside of the shell of certain shell-fish.
peasant (2z) small farmer or worker on a farm; **peasantry** (——1) people who work on farms.
peat (11) mass of decayed plants, leaves, etc., cut from the ground and used for burning.
pebble (2) small stone.
peccad'illo (2-9-1-67) small unimportant fault.
peck (2) a measure of grain, 7½ litres.
peck (2) strike at with a pointed thing, as a bird in eating; Sl. **pecker** (2-9) nose; Sl. *Keep one's pecker up* = be cheerful; Sl. **peckish** (2-1) hungry.
pectoral (2-9) of the chest, e.g. *Pectoral muscles*.
peculate (2-17-21) steal.
pec'uliar (1-177-19) one's own; not like any other; strange.
pec'uniary (1-177-19-1) of money.
pedagogue (2-9-5) teacher.
pedal (2) part of a machine pressed by the foot; **to pedal**, move pedals with the feet.
pedant (2) one who is interested in words and rules rather than in making wise use of knowledge; n. **pedantry** (2-1) this character; adj. **ped'antic** (1-3-1).
peddle (2) sell from door to door.
pedestal (2-1) square or round block upon which a stone figure or pillar stands.
ped'estrian (1-2-19) going on foot.
pediatrics see Pae/-.
pedicure (2-1-179) treatment of the feet to make them comfortable or beautiful; cf. Manicure = such treatment of the hands.
pedigree (2-1-11) line of persons (e.g. father, grandfather, etc.) from whom one is descended.
pedlar (2-9) one who sells from door to door.
peek (11) look at secretly.
peel (11) take off the outer skin, e.g. of a fruit; skin so taken off.
peep (11) cry of a young bird.
peep (11) look at secretly and for a moment.
peer (19) look at with half-closed eyes.
peer (19) one of equal rank; nobleman; **peerless** (19-1) without equal; **a peerage** (19-1j) rank of nobleman; all the noblemen; list of noblemen.
peevish (11-1) easily angered like a child.
peg (2) wooden nail; *To peg away at* = work patiently; Sl. glass of strong drink; Sl. *Peg out* = die.
P'ekin'ese (dog) (11-1-11z) small dog as shown; **Peke** (11) short for——.
pelf (2) money, wealth.
pelican (2-1-9) bird with a very large beak.
pellet (2-1) little ball, e.g. of bread pressed together in the fingers.
p'ell-m'ell (2 + 2) in a disorderly rush.
pell'ucid (2-177s1) very clear, like water.
pelmet (2-1) narrow band of curtain across the top of a window.
pelt (2) skin of an animal.
pelt (2) throw many things at; *Pelting rain* = heavy ——.
pelvis (2-1) great bone at the bottom of the body on to which the legs join.
pemmican (2-1) dried meat.
pen (2) enclosed place for sheep.
pen (2) instrument for writing; **to pen**, write carefully.
penalty (2-1) punishment; **penal** (11) having to do with punishment; **penance** (2-9-s) suffering given to oneself as a sign of sorrow for wrong-doing.
pence (2-s) pl. of Penny.
penchant (44ⁿsh44ⁿ) liking for.
pendant, pendent (2-9) hanging ornament, e.g. jewelled ornament hanging round the neck.
pending (2-1) during; waiting for; not yet settled.
pendulous (2-17-9) hanging down.
pendulum (2-17-9) weight swinging from side to side, e.g. on a large clock.
penetrate (2-1-21) enter into; make a hole in.
penguin (2nggw1) bird with short legs, not able to fly, found in very cold countries.
p'enic'illin (2-1s1-1) substance made from a *mould* which kills *bacteria*.
pen'insula (9-1-17-9) piece of land with water nearly all round it, joined to the shore by a narrow neck of land; adj. **pen'insular**.
penitent (2-1) sorry for wrong done.
penit'entiary (2-1-2-sh9-1) prison.
penknife (2-41) small knife kept in the pocket.
pennon, pennant (2-9) long, narrow, three-cornered flag.
penny (2-1) 1/160th of a pound; *A pretty penny* = large amount of money.
pension (2-shn) money paid to an officer, worker, etc., from the time he gives up work until his death.
pensive (2-1) thoughtful.
penta- five, e.g. **pentagon** (2-9-9) five-sided figure; *The Pentagon* = war office of U.S.A. in Washington.
p'ent-house (2 + 47) sloping roof over a window; hut built against a wall or on the top of a flat roof.
p'ent 'up in (2 + 8 + 1) enclosed tightly in.

PELICAN

pen'ultimate (2-8-1-1) last except one, e.g. P is the penultimate letter of EXCEPT.

penury (2-17-1) state of being very poor.

peon (11·9) (in S. America) a farm-labourer; (in India) a letter-carrier.

people (11) persons; *A people* = nation; *Peoples* = nations.

pep (2) Sl. quickness, activity, interest.

pepper (2-9) hot-tasting powder, white, black or red, made from a seed and used with food; *To pepper with* = hit with many small shots; *Pepper-and-salt* (colour of cloth) = small black and white spots.

peppermint (2-9-1) oil used for giving a taste to sweets—tasting hot at first, cold afterwards.

peppery (2-9-1) hot-tasting; easily angered.

pepsin (2-1) one of the liquids formed in the stomach which helps to change food into body material.

per- through, completely, thoroughly, over the whole.

per, by, for each, e.g. **per h'ead** (9 + 2) for each person.

peradv'enture (9-9-2-tsh9) perhaps; by chance.

per'ambulate (9-3-17-21) to walk through; to walk about; **per'ambulator** (9-3-17-21-9) carriage for a baby, *pushed* by hand.

perc'eive (9s11) see, feel, hear, taste, or smell; understand.

per c'ent (9 + s2) %, in each hundred.

perc'eptible (9s2-9) which can be *perceived* (see 2nd above); **perc'eption** (——shn) power of perceiving; **p'ercept** (99s2) thing perceived.

perch (99) fresh-water fish.

perch (99) bar on which a bird stands in a cage; stand on a branch or bar like a bird.

percolate (99k9-21) (of liquid) to pass through —as through sand; **percolator** (——9) instrument used for making coffee.

perc'ussion (99k8shn) act of striking one thing against another; (medical) striking the chest and listening to discover what part (if any) is diseased; *Percussion instruments of music* = such as are struck, e.g. a drum; *Percussion cap* = small container full of matter which explodes when hit, used in firing a gun.

perd'ition (99-1shn) ruin; loss of hopes of heaven.

peregrin'ation (2-1-1-21shn) wandering.

per'emptory (order) (9-2-9-1) sharp and allowing no answer.

per'ennial (9-2-19) lasting from year to year; lasting all through the year.

perfect (99-1) finished, which cannot be better; **to perf'ect** (9-2).

perfidy (99-1-1) disloyalty, unfaithfulness.

perforate (99-9-21) make a hole through.

perf'orce (9-55s) (done) because necessary.

perf'orm (9-55) carry out (e.g. a ceremony); do in a solemn ceremonial way or in public; to show in a theatre.

perfume (99-177) pleasant smell; pleasant smelling liquid; **to perf'ume** (9-177).

perf'unctory (9-8ngk-9-1) done quickly and badly as an unpleasant duty.

pergola (99-9-9) wooden arches along a path over which plants grow.

perh'aps (9-3) it is possible that —; possibly.

peri- around, or near (9-1-1-9) measure round the outside of —.

peril (2-1) great danger.

period (19-19) certain length of time; a *sentence* (= set of words expressing a complete thought); little mark (.) at the end of a sentence; adj. **peri'odic** (19-15-1); **a peri'odical** (19-15-1) newspaper or book of stories, etc., printed from time to time, e.g. every month.

peripat'etic (teacher) (2-1-9-2-1) going round from place to place.

per'iphrasis (9-1-9-1) roundabout way of saying a thing.

periscope (2-1-67) instrument used by *submarines* (= under-sea boats) for seeing above the water.

perish (2-1) die; to decay; *Perishable goods* = goods which *spoil* (= become useless) if left too long, e.g. eggs; *Perished with cold* = feeling very cold.

periwinkle (2-1-1ngk) small shell-fish; small low-growing plant with light-blue flowers.

perjury (99-9-1) act of breaking a promise; act of saying, in the name of God, things which are not true.

perky (99-1) full of life, active in an amusing way, e.g. a bird.

permanent (99-9-9) continuing unchanged; *Permanent way* = railway line; *Permanent wave* = way of making curls which last a long time in women's hair (about 6 months).

permeate (99-121) to spread through, as a smell through the air of a room.

perm'it (99-1) allow; **a p'ermit** (99-1) written paper allowing a certain act; **perm'ission** (9-1shn) act of allowing.

pern'icious (99-1sh9) harmful.

pern'ickety (9-1-1-1) difficult to please.

peror'ation (2-9-21shn) end of a long speech.

perpend'icular (9-9-1-17-9) standing (line) at right angles (90°) to (another line).

perpetrate (a crime) (99-1-21) do (a thing which is against the law).

perp'etual (9-2-179) continuing for ever; **perp'etuate** (9-2-1721) cause to continue for ever; **in p'erpet'uity** (99-1-1771-1) for ever.

perpl'ex (9-2) cause difficulty in understanding.

perquisite (99-121) extra payment or gain beyond one's regular pay.

per se (99 + 11) in itself, of its own nature.

persecute (99-1-177) continue to treat cruelly, e.g. because of some belief.

persev'ere (99-1-19) go on trying; continue to try.

persifl'age (99-1-443) unimportant amusing talk.

pers'ist (9-1) continue steadily in a course of action in spite of difficulty.

person (99) man, woman or child; *To come in person* = oneself; **personable** (99-99) good-looking; **personage** (———1j) person of importance; **personal** (99-9) of one's own; **personality** (99-9-3-1-1) character; **p'ersonalty** (99-9-1) things owned other than houses and land; **personn'el** (99-9-2) persons employed in a business, on a ship, etc.; **pers'onify** (99-5-1-41) speak of a quality as if it were a person, e.g. Come, Mercy, and speak to the hearts of men.

pers'ona gr'ata (9-67-9 + 21-9) favoured or welcome person.

persp'ective (9-2-1) art of drawing in such a way as to show depth and distance; *To see things in perspective* = have a true judgment of the relative importance of events; **perspic'acious** (99-1-21shg) having good understanding and judgment.

Perspex (99-2) clear glass-like plastic (see Plastics) (Trade name).

persp'ire (9-41g) pass liquid out through the skin when hot; **perspir'ation** (99-9-21shn) this natural act; liquid so passed.

persu'ade (9-72I) bring a person round to one's opinion, or get him to do as one wishes; **persu'asive** (9-72I-1) able to persuade; **persu'asion** (———213n) act of persuading; belief.

pert (child) (99) child who tries to amuse but forgets to show respect to his elders.

pert'ain to (9-21) belong to; be a natural character of —.

p'ertin'acious (99-1-21shg) holding firmly to an opinion; not giving up work begun.

pertinent (99-1-9) well fitted to the subject.

pert'urb (9-99) make anxious or afraid.

per'uke (9-77) ornamental covering for the head, made of hair, used formerly.

per'use (9-77z) to read carefully; n. **per'usal.**

perv'ade (9-21) to spread through.

perv'ert (9-99) turn to a wrong use; **a p'ervert** (99-99) person turned away from right and natural behaviour; **perv'ersity** (9-99-1-1) stiff refusal to do right.

pessimist (2-1-1) one who always expects the worst to happen.

pest (2) thing which causes trouble or harm; spreading disease.

pester (2-9) continue to trouble.

pest'iferous (2-1-9-9) carrying disease; harmful.

pestilence (2-1-9-5) dangerous disease which spreads widely.

pestle (2) striker used for breaking things to powder in a strong stone or metal bowl called a *mortar*.

pet (2) animal kept in the house as a plaything;

PESTLE AND MORTAR

Pet aversion = most disliked thing; **to pet**, play lovingly with.

petal (2) coloured leaf of a flower.

pet'ard (2-44) box of explosive material, e.g. one used to blow open a door; *Hoist with his own petard* = caught and hurt by his own evil plans.

peter out (11-9 + 47) slowly end or disappear.

pet'ite (9-11) neat and small (woman).

pet'ition (1-1shn) prayer; letter from a lower to a higher officer asking for some favour; letter signed by many making some demand of the government.

petrel (2-9) black and white sea bird.

petrify (2-1-41) change into stone; n. **petrif'action** (2-1-3-shn).

petrol (2) light oil used in motor-cars; in U.S.A. called *gasoline*.

petr'oleum (1-67-19) heavy oil obtained from the earth.

petr'ology (2-5-9jI) study of rocks.

petticoat (2-1-67) woman's underskirt.

pettish (2-1) ill-tempered and complaining.

petty (2-1) unimportant; *Petty cash* = small amounts of money spent on various small matters.

petulant (2-17-9) impatient and ill-tempered.

pews (177z) fixed seats in a church.

pewter (177-9) mixture of *tin* (= valuable white metal used to cover the surface of iron boxes which contain food) and *lead* (= very heavy metal used to make pipes), used for making drinking pots.

phaeton (21-9) light horse carriage.

phalanx (3-3ngks) company of heavily armed Greek soldiers in ancient times; a tightly packed body of men or animals; bone of the fingers or *toes* (= finger-like things on the feet).

phantasm (3-3z) supposed appearance of the spirit of an absent person.

phantasy (3-9zI) see Fantasy.

phantom (3-9) appearance of a dead person seen by a living person.

pharmacy (44-9sI) shop which sells medicines; **pharmac'eutical** (44-9sI77-1) of or for medicines; **pharmacop'oeia** (44-9-9-11-9) list of medicines.

phase (21z) appearance of a thing as seen in one state of growth, e.g. *The first phase of the moon, of the war.*

pheasant (2z) bird with a very long tail, shot for food.

phen'omenon (1-5-1-9) natural event as seen or felt by the senses (not the hidden force by which the event is caused); uncommon event; **phen'omenal**, strange and unusual.

phial (41g) small glass bottle.

phil'ander (1-3-9) make love often and not with serious intentions.

phil'anthropist (1-3-9-1) one who loves his fellow-men; one who uses his money for the good of his fellow-men.

phil'ately (1-3-9-1) collecting postage-stamps.

philo- love, loving, a lover of —.

phil'ologist (1-5-9j1) one who studies the history of language; n. **phil'ology** (1-5-9j1).

phil'osopher (1-5-9-9) (1) one who tries to find the first causes of events, of the world, etc.; (2) one who always takes things calmly as they come.

phlegm (2) thick liquid which comes from the nose and throat; heavy slowness of character; adj. **phlegm'atic** (2-3-1) slow.

-phobia (67-19) fear and dislike of.

phone (67) = *Telephone* (see —).

phoneme (67-11) sound in a language.

phoney (67-1) Sl. imitation, not real.

phon'etics (67-2-1) study of the sounds of speech; *Phonetic spelling* = writing words exactly as they are said, e.g. Fonetik.

phono- of sound.

phonograph (67-9-44) instrument for *reproducing* (= producing again) sounds which have been written down on wax material.

ph'osphor'esce (5-9-2) shine in the dark as does *phosphorus* (= material used in making matches).

photo (67-67) see Photograph; *Photo-finish* = end of a race in which horses are so close that only a photograph can decide the winner.

ph'otog'enic (person) (67-9j2-1) one who looks well when photographed, e.g. for the cinema.

photograph (67-9-44) picture made by light passing through a *lens* (= glass curved on both sides) on to a glass plate covered with a special preparation of silver; **to photograph**, make such a picture; **phot'ography** (9-5-9-1) this art or science.

phrase (21z) small group of words; **phrase'ology** (21z15-9j1) manner of expression.

phren'etic (2-2-1) wild, mad.

phut, go phut (8) Sl. explode, become useless.

physic (1z1) medicine.

physical (1z1) having to do with the body; having to do with the natural world.

phys'ician (1z1shn) doctor.

physics (1z1) study of matter and the forces of the natural world; **physicist** (1z1s1) one who studies —.

physi'ognomy (1z15-9-1) judging character by the face; the face.

physi'ology (1z15-9j1) study of the way in which a living body (e.g. of a man) works.

ph'ysiothe'rapy (1z16-2-9-1) treatment of a sick person by rubbing, exercises, and movements of the legs, arms, etc.

phys'ique (1z1k) the form and character of the body; *A man of strong physique* = one who does not easily become ill; *Of powerful physique* = strong in the arms, legs, etc.

PIANO

pi'ano (13-67) **pi'anof'orte** (13-67-55-1) musical instrument with strings which are hit by little hammers when the *keys* (= pieces of wood and bone struck by the fingers in playing music) are pressed; **p'ianist** (19-1) one who plays the —.

pi'ano (144-67) (Music) quietly.

pi'azza (13ts9) open place with houses round it; path under a roof along the front of the house.

piccan'inny (1k9-1-1) small black child.

piccolo (1k9-67) musical instrument making a very high whistling sound.

PICCOLO

pick (1) **pick-axe** (1 + 3) pointed iron cross-bar with a wooden handle, used for breaking the earth; **to pick**, break up earth.

pick (1) choose one thing out of many; *To pick holes in* = find fault with; *To pick fruit* = gather fruit; *To pick a lock* = open — without a key; *To have a bone to pick* = have a quarrel; *To pick a quarrel* = make a quarrel on purpose; *To pick up* = take up, make friends with; *The pick of the bunch* = the best of all.

pick-a-back (1 + 9 + 3) to carry a child on the back with its arms round one's neck.

picket (1-1) (1) wooden post fixed in the ground; (2) small group of soldiers acting as a guard; (3) any group of persons acting as a guard.

pickle (1) put food in salt water to keep it for eating; *In a sad pickle* = bad state; **pickles** (—z) food, e.g. vegetables boiled in *vinegar* (= very sour liquid).

pickpocket (1-5-1) one who secretly steals things from people's pockets.

picnic (1-1) short journey taken for pleasure, with a meal eaten out of doors.

picture (1-tsh9) a drawing or painting; *The pictures* = moving pictures (cinema); **to picture** = imagine; **pictur'esque** (scene) (1-tsh9-2sk) such as would make a good picture; **pict'orial** (1-55-19) of a picture.

pie (41) dish of fruit or meat with pastry above or below it.

piebald (41-55) having irregular markings in two colours.

piece (11s) bit of; *A piece in the theatre* = a play; *To piece together* = put pieces together; **piecemeal** (11s-11) bit by bit; **piecework** (11s-99) work paid for according to the amount done (not by time).

pied (41) spotted.

pier (19) (1) strong post, e.g. of iron; (2) road, built out into the sea on iron posts, on which one comes to land from a ship; used also as a place of amusement.

p'ier-glass (19 + 44) large looking-glass.

pierce (19s) make a hole through; see through or understand.

pierrot (19-67) one man of a group of public

piety (4ɪ9-ɪ) goodness—in doing one's duty towards God and the Church.

piffle (ɪ) foolish talk or writing.

pig (ɪ) fat animal used for food; *To buy a pig in a poke* = buy something which one has not properly seen; *He's a pig* = he eats too much, takes too much interest in food; *Make a pig of oneself* = eat too much; a pig (of metal) large rough mass of; *Pig iron* = iron in rough masses as shaped after it is first made from the ore (= rock).

PIERROT AND PIERRETTE

pigeon (ɪjɪ) bird which has a wonderful power of finding its way home; also used for food; *Pigeon-chested* = with the chest (breast) pushed forward; *Pigeon-toed* = with the feet pointing inwards.

pigeon-holes (ɪjɪ + 67-z) set of small open boxes in which papers are put; *To pigeon-hole a thing* = lay aside for later attention.

p'ig-h'eaded (ɪ + 2-ɪ) unwilling to listen to reason.

p'ig-iron (ɪ + 4ɪ9) iron in rough square masses.

pigment (ɪ-9) colouring matter.

pigmy (ɪ-ɪ) see Pygmy.

pike (4ɪ) long spear; *Plain as a pike-staff* = very easily seen or understood.

pike (4ɪ) large fresh-water fish.

pilchard (ɪ-9) sea-fish; small pilchards are sometimes preserved in oil and sold as *sardines*.

pile (4ɪ) a heap; *To make one's pile* = get all the money one wants.

pile (4ɪ) soft hair, e.g. on cloth.

pile (4ɪ) large post driven into the ground on which a building is built.

piles (4ɪ-z) soft swellings in the bowel.

pilfer (ɪ-9) steal small things.

pilgrim (ɪ-ɪ) one who goes to a holy place; a wanderer; **pilgrimage** (ɪ-ɪ-ɪj) journey to a holy place.

pill (ɪ) small ball of medicine.

pillage (ɪ-ɪj) take away things from a house or town seized in war.

pillar (ɪ-9) strong post made of stone, brick, or iron.

pillion (ɪ-ɪ9) seat to carry a second person behind the rider of a motor-bicycle or horse.

pillory (ɪ-9-ɪ) bar with holes in it in which the head and hands were fixed as a punishment.

pillow (ɪ-67) case full of feathers or other soft material for putting under the head; *To take counsel of one's pillow* = think about during the night; **pillow-case** (+ 2ɪ) **pillow-slip** (+ ɪ) covering for a pillow.

pilot (4ɪ-9) man who guides a ship into a harbour; man who has charge of and guides an aeroplane.

pilot plant (4ɪ-9 + 44) Before making a new factory with big machines to produce a large amount of some new thing, a pilot plant is used to produce a small amount so as to be sure of success.

pim'ento (ɪ-2-67) the dried sweet-smelling fruit of a West Indian tree.

pimpernel (ɪ-9-2) small flower.

pimple (ɪ) small poisoned spot on the skin.

pin (ɪ) very small metal bar with a point and head used for fastening cloth, papers, etc.; *Don't care a pin* = don't care at all; *Pins and needles* = feeling in the arms or legs as if needles were being pushed into the skin; Sl. *Quick on his pins* = legs; *To pin a person down* = demand an answer, promise, etc.; *Safety pin* = curved pin with a cover for the point.

pinafore (ɪ-9-55) loose outer covering worn by children to protect their clothes in play.

p'ince-nez (3ⁿˢ + 2ɪ) eye-glasses held on the nose by means of a metal spring.

pincers (ɪ-s9z) instrument used for holding things tightly; *Pincer-movement* = movement of two armies curving in to meet behind an enemy.

pinch (ɪ) press a small amount between the finger and thumb (or between any two small surfaces); *A pinch of* = small amount; Sl. steal.

pine (4ɪ) tree with needle-like leaves and white soft wood.

pine (4ɪ) to waste away with grief.

pineapple (4ɪ-3) large yellow fruit with pointed leaves growing out of the top, found in hot countries.

p'in-feather (ɪ + 2θ9) young feather still inside its case before it opens out.

PINE-TREE

pinion (ɪ-ɪ9) wing of a bird; to pinion, hold or tie up the arms of a person.

pinion (ɪ-ɪ9) small toothed wheel which joins with another wheel and turns it (or is turned by it).

pink (ɪngk) colour made by mixing red and white; a flower; *To pink with a sword* = make a small wound —.

PINEAPPLE

p'in-money (ɪ + 8-ɪ) amount of money given to a woman for small unexpected costs.

pinnace (ɪ-ɪs) boat for eight rowers (or with an engine) carried on a ship.

pinnacle (ɪ-9) pointed piece of stonework on a building; pointed piece of rock.

p'in-point (1 + 41) hit exactly the place aimed at.

pion'eer (419-19) one who goes in front, e.g. of an army, and prepares the way; one who goes first into a new country or into a new subject or branch of study.

pious (419) loving to serve God and the Church.

pip (1) small seed in a fruit; Sl. *It gives me the pip* = makes me sad and angry.

pipe (41) (1) round bar with a hole through it, used to carry liquid or gas from one place to another; (2) musical instrument; (3) wine barrel; *To smoke a pipe* = draw in *tobacco* (= plant whose leaves are dried and used for smoking) smoke through an L-shaped pipe; **pipeclay** (41-21) white earth used for making shoes white; **piping** (41-1) (1) set of pipes; (2) round fold used to make an edge or ornament on cloth; (3) *A piping voice* = thin and high like a young bird's; (4) *Piping hot* = very hot; Sl. *Pipe down!* = Do not talk so much—not make so much noise!

pipe-line (41 + 41) long pipe carrying oil, e.g. from the oil-well to the sea and ships.

piper (41-9) Scotsman playing the *bag-pipe* (= musical instrument with a wind-bag held under the arm).

PIPER

pipkin (1-1) small pot made of baked earth.

piquant (11k44ⁿ) having a pleasant sharp taste; clever and amusing.

pique (11k) to hurt the *pride* (n. of Proud) of a person; to interest.

pirate (419-1) one who attacks and steals from ships; print a book or story, etc., without the right to do so and without paying the writer.

pirou'ette (1-72) turn round on the point of the foot.

pistil (1-1) that part of a flower where the seeds come to growth.

PISTIL

pistol (1) short gun fired with one hand.

piston (1-9) round block inside a pipe (the *cylinder*) which is pushed forward and backward by a gas or steam in an engine.

pit (1) (1) deep hole in the ground; (2) **the pit**, back seats on the lowest floor of a theatre; *To pit against* = set to fight against.

pitch (1) black sticky material used to stop cracks between the boards of ships; *Pitch dark* = very dark, black.

pitch (1) (a tent) set up a tent; (a ball) throw; **cr'icket p'itch** (1-1 +) narrow length of grass in a *cricket-* (see —) field between the *wickets* (= 3 upright sticks); *To pitch forward* = fall —; *The ship is pitching* = going up and down from end to end; *Pitch into* = scold; *Pitch of the voice* = highness; *Pitch of a roof* = slope; *Pitched* (1-t) *battle* = large battle carefully arranged and prepared for.

pitcher (1-9) large pot with handle.

pitchfork (1-55) instrument with two metal fingers used for moving *hay* (= dried grass), etc.; *Pitchforked into* = pushed suddenly into (an employment or duty).

piteous (1-19) worthy of pity.

pitfall (1-55) covered hole for catching animals; a trap.

pith (1) soft centre of a stick; most important part of a speech or book.

pitiful (1-1) worthy of pity; *A pitiful attempt* = attempt so bad as to make one feel angry.

pittance (1-s) small amount of food or money; *A mere pittance* = very little, just enough to keep one alive.

pitted (1-1) having many small hollows in it, e.g. the skin after an illness; set to fight against.

pity (1-1) sorrow for the pain of others; *It's a pity that* = I am sorry because.

pivot (1-9) point upon which anything turns; centre bar upon which a wheel turns; to turn on a pivot.

p'izzic'ato (1ts1-44-67) (Music) picking at the strings, not rubbing them.

placard (3-44) public notice stuck on a wall; stick up notices.

plac'ate (9-21) make peaceful; take away the anger of.

place (21s) *St. James's Place* = St. J.'s *Square* (= an open space in a town with buildings round it); *Have got a place as a* — = employment —; *My place in the country* = house —; *He knows his place* = rank and duty; *It's not my place to* = I have no right to; **to place**, put; find a place for, e.g. get employment for; *I cannot place him* = cannot remember who he is or where I met him.

placid (3s1) calm, peaceful.

plagiarize (21j19-41) use another's writings as if they were one's own.

plague (21) easily spread dangerous disease; to trouble.

plaice (21s) a flat sea-fish much used as food.

plaid (3) cloth of various bright colours, the colours showing to what family group a Scotsman belongs.

plain (21) flat; easily understood; without ornament; not beautiful; *Plain-clothes man* = officer of the law dressed so as not to be known as such; *Plain dealing* = honesty; *The Plains* = lower flatter part of the country, not the mountains.

plaint (21) complaint; writing given to a court of law to ask for justice.

plaintiff (21-1) one who makes or begins a claim in a law court.

plaintive (voice) (21-1) sad, asking for pity.

plait (3) join three or more strings together by turning each one over the other in turn; *She had two long plaits down her back* = her hair was plaited into two ropes.

plan (3) map of anything, e.g. machine, house; way of acting thought out for the future.

plane (21) tree with large leaves.

plane (21) instrument for making wood smooth; **to plane**, make wood smooth; *A plane surface* = flat level space.

plane (21) aeroplane; **to plane,** move in an aeroplane without using the engine.

planet (3-1) world going round the sun.

plank (3ngk) board; *To walk the plank* = be forced to walk along a board and fall off the end into the sea; Sl. *To plank down (money)* = pay quickly and willingly.

plankton (3ngkt5) very small animals and plants in the sea on which fishes feed.

plant (44) flower, tree, etc.; **to plant**, to set in the ground; cause to grow in the ground.

plant (44) buildings, machines, etc., used for any special purpose.

plantain (3-1) common wild plant with broad leaves.

plantain (3-1) tree which produces *bananas* (= long yellow fruit); fruit of this tree.

plant'ation (44-21shn) wood planted by man; large amount of land on which tea, sugar, etc., is grown; **planter** (44-9) man in charge of a plantation.

plaque (44) flat piece of metal or other material used as an ornament.

plaster (44-9) (1) material spread over the walls of buildings to make them smooth; **to plaster**, cover walls with plaster; (2) material of this kind used for shaping into figures as ornaments; (3) sticky mixture put on the skin as a medicine; cloth covered with sticky matter used to protect a wound.

plastic (3-1) soft and able to be shaped; substance which, heated and pressed into shape, becomes hard.

plastics (3-1) substances made chemically from coal or oil which, when soft, can be pressed into a shape and then become hard.

plate (21) flat thin sheet of metal; flat open dish from which food is eaten; **to plate**, cover a common metal with a more valuable one, e.g. *Silver plated*; **pl'ate-glass** (+ 44) large thick sheets of glass, like those in large shop windows.

plateau (3-67) level high land.

platform (3-55) raised part of the floor on which a speaker or teacher stands; plans of a group in the government about which they will speak to the people when asking to be elected.

platinum (3-1-9) white, soft, heavy, very valuable metal.

platitude (3-1-177) uninteresting fact or opinion so well known that it is not worth saying again.

plat'oon (9-77) group of about 35 soldiers.

platter (3-9) large flat dish, especially a wooden one.

plaudit (55-1) expression of praise or agreement, e.g. by *clapping*.

plausible (55z9) seeming to be just or true, but perhaps not so.

play (21) (1) move freely; (2) amuse oneself; join in a game; *Play the game* = be honest and fair; (3) act a part in a theatre; (4) use an instrument of music; n. **play** (21) (1) free movement; *There is too much play in this joint* = it is loose, it shakes; (2) amusement; *High play* = playing a card game for large amounts of money; (3) piece in a theatre.

plea (11) prayer; what the prisoner in a law-court says in defending himself.

plead (11) make a *plea* (see above).

pleasant (2z) enjoyable, comforting.

pleasantry (2z-1) speech or talk which causes laughter.

please (11z) give enjoyment to; *Please do it* = I ask you to —.

pleasure (239) enjoyment; *To be put in prison during the king's pleasure* = for so long as the king orders.

pleat (11) part of the cloth in a garment which is folded down flat; **pleated** (———1) having many flat folds.

pleb'eian (1-11·9) belonging to the common people.

plebiscite (2-1-1) giving of an opinion by all the people in a country to decide a question of government.

pledge (2j) thing given by A to B to be held by B so as to make sure that A carries out a promise; a promise; **to pledge**, give a pledge, e.g. for payment of money; to drink to the health of.

plenary (11-9-1) full (powers); **a plenary session** (+ 2shn) meeting of all the members.

plenipot'entiary (2-1-9-2-sh9-1) having full powers.

plenitude (2-1-177) fullness, large amount.

plenty (2-1) amount which is more than enough; adj. **plenteous** (2-19), plentiful.

plethora (2-9-9) too large an amount; overfullness; diseased state of the body caused by too much blood.

pleurisy (77-1-1) disease of the outer covering of the *lungs* (= part of the body with which we breathe).

pliable, pliant (419) easily bent; (of a person) easily controlled, readily changing his opinion to suit the wishes of others.

pliers (419z) instrument used for holding things tightly, also for bending and cutting wire.

plight (41) (bad) state.

plight (41) to promise; to promise to marry.

plinth (1) raised floor of stone or brick on which a house or tall stone figure stands.

plod (5) to walk or work steadily on.

plot (5) small piece of land.

plot (5) plan of a story; secret plan against a person; *To plot a curve* = draw a line showing the relation between two changing quantities.

plough (47) instrument used for turning up the

plover (8-9) bird with long pointed wings and short tail.

pluck (8) pull off feathers, or flowers; give a sudden pull at; n. a sudden pull; *He has plenty of pluck* = he is brave; **plucky** (8-1) brave; *Pluck up your courage* = be brave; *To be plucked* = fail in an examination.

plug (8) something which fits into a hole to prevent liquid flowing out; to stop or block up a hole; *Plugging away* = working hard.

plum (8) red or blue-red fruit with a stone in it; dried fruit; Sl. greatly desired object.

plumage (77-1j) feathers.

plumb (8) ball of *lead* (= heavy white metal) on a string used to find whether a wall is upright, or to find how deep water is; **to plumb**, get to the bottom of; study thoroughly.

plumber (8-9) man who fits pipes or repairs pipes used for the water-supply, gas-supply, etc., in a house; **plumbing** (8-1) all the pipes which have to do with the water and gas supply in a house.

plume (77) feather; ornament made of feathers.

plump (8) nicely fat.

plump (8) sit or fall suddenly; *To plump for* = give all one's *votes* (see Vote) to one person in an election instead of giving to two (or more).

plunder (8-9) steal openly or by force.

plunge (8nj) jump into, e.g. into water.

pl'up'erfect tense (77-99-1 + 2) e.g. *I had gone*.

plural (77) form of a word expressing more than one.

plus (8) +, added to.

pl'us-f'ours (8 + 55z) loose lower garment for men covering the legs and knees, but not the lower part of the legs.

plush (8) soft cloth made of wool with short hairs standing up on one side.

plutocrat (77-9-3) man who has power because of his wealth; **plut'ocracy** (77-5-9si) rule by such persons.

ply (41) to work at (a trade); go regularly, e.g. *Ships plying between England and India*.

ply wood (41 + 7) *Three-ply wood* = three thin pieces of wood stuck together to make one strong board (five-ply, seven-ply, etc., are also made).

pneum'atic (177-31-1) containing air; (of a machine) worked by air.

pneum'onia (177-67-19) serious illness of the *lungs* (= part of the body with which we breathe).

P.O. (11 + 67) Post Office.

poach (67) steal birds or animals from someone's land.

poached (egg) (67ct) cooked without the shell in water.

pock (5) hollow mark on the skin, caused by certain diseases.

pocket (5-1) small bag fixed in a garment; any small bag; **pocket-book** (+ 7) small notebook; small case for money and papers; **pocket-knife** (+ 41) small folding knife; *To pocket a thing* = take for one's own.

pod (5) long seed-vessel of a plant.

podgy (5j1) fat, thick.

poetry (671-1) beautiful language arranged in lines of regular length and form; **a poem** (671) one example of such writing; **a poet** (671) one who writes poetry; adj. **po'etical** (672-1).

poignant (51-19) moving the feelings; sharp.

point (51) sharp end of; exact place or time; *To see the point* = understand the main idea; *Get to the point* = get to the main idea; **to point**, show with the finger or a stick; *A pointed remark* = saying aimed at some one person; **pointless** (——1) foolish and meaningless; **p'oint-bl'ank** (+ 3ngk) *To fire —* = shoot straight at a thing when close to it; **points** (51) movable *rails* (= iron bars on which trains run) used for sending trains in different directions; **pointer** (51-9) (1) thing used for pointing, e.g. a long stick; (2) dog used to show where birds or animals are when one is out shooting.

poise (51z) place a thing so that it stays steady; way of holding the head and body; calmness and good judgment.

poison (51z) matter which causes harm if allowed to enter the body.

poke (67) push with the finger or with a stick; *Poke the fire* = break up coals in a fire with an iron bar called a *poker*; *To poke one's nose into* = try to take part in another's business; *To poke fun at* = try to make people laugh at.

poker (67-9) (1) iron bar used to break up coals in a fire; (2) card game played for money; Sl. *Poker-face* = having the face of a poker player, showing no feeling.

poky (67-1) small, e.g. *A poky little house*.

polar (67-9) see 2nd below.

pole (67) long strong stick.

pole (67) farthest north (or south) point of the earth; end of a *magnet* (= piece of iron such as moves in a compass); adj. **polar** (——9).

polecat (67-3) small animal which has a very bad smell.

pol'emic (5-2-1) attack in speech or writing.

pol'ice (9-11s) set of men who keep order in a country.

policy (5-1si) plan of government; *It is not good policy to —* = not wise to; *An Insurance Policy* = agreement to pay a certain amount of money in a certain event, e.g. accident or death.

p'oliomyel'itis (67-16-412-41-1) polio (67-167) disease of the nerves inside the *spine* (= backbone) which can cause loss of power to move the muscles.

polish (5-1) rub smooth and shining; *A polished*

POLECAT

polite — 239 — **porpoise**

man = having fine manners; *Polish off work* = finish quickly; *To polish (up) a poem* = make it better in small ways.

pol'ite (9-41) pleasing in manner; acting like a gentleman.

politic (5-1-1) having to do with government; wise, carefully thought out; **pol'itical** (9-1-1) having to do with the art of government or with public business; **polit'ician** (5-1-1shn) (1) one who takes part in the government of a country; (2) one who is more interested in the success of his party in the government than in the well-being of the people governed; **politics** (5-1-1) art of government; one's opinion about matters of government.

polka (5-9) quick jumping dance.

poll (67) to *vote* (= to mark on a paper the names of those one wishes to elect to the government) and put the paper into a box; **the poll**, act or place of voting.

poll (67) head; **p'oll-t'ax** (67 + 3) *tax* (= money paid to the government) on every head—i.e. paid by every person.

pollen (5-1) yellow dust in a flower which makes the seed begin to grow.

poll'ute (9-77) make dirty.

Polly (5-1) name for a *parrot* (= brightly coloured bird which talks).

polo (67-67) game played with a ball and sticks by men on horses; **w'ater-p'olo** (55-9 +) hand-ball played in the water.

poltr'oon (5-77) man who is not brave.

poly- many; **pol'ygamy** (5-1-9-1) act or custom of having more than one wife; **polyglot** (5-1-5) having many languages; **polygon** (5-1-9) many-sided figure; **polyt'echnic** (5-1-2k-1) school teaching many arts and sciences.

pom'ade (9-44) thick oily material rubbed on the hair.

p'omegranate (5-3-1) large fruit containing many red seeds.

pommel (8) (1) round end of the handle of a sword; (2) front of a *saddle* (= leather seat on horse); **to pommel**, continue to hit with the *fists* (= tightly closed hands).

pomp (5) solemn ceremonial show; **pompous** (5-9) behaving in a foolishly solemn way.

pond (5) hole in the ground with water in it, e.g. where cattle drink and ducks live.

ponder (5-9) think carefully and for a long time about a question.

ponderous (5-9-9) heavy; (of a person or manner) slow and too solemn and serious.

poniard (5-19) small knife with sharp point used for killing people.

pontiff (5-1) high-priest.

pont'oon (5-77) flat boat used to support a bridge.

pony (67-1) small kind of horse.

poodle (77) dog which usually has its hair cut in a peculiar way.

pooh! (77) sound showing *scorn* (= feeling that a thing is of no value or importance).

pool (77) small hole in the ground with water in it.

pool, the (77) amount of money made up of payments from each person taking part in a game or business; *Football pool* = a lot of people pay money into a *pool* (= one large amount); this money is divided up among those who say correctly the results of games of football next week.

poop (77) raised part at the back of a ship.

poor (79) (1) having little money; (2) unhappy; unfortunate; (3) bad, e.g. *A poor speaker*, *Poor soil*; *Feeling poorly* (——1) = not feeling well.

pop! (5) sound of opening a bottle; *To pop up* = come up or appear suddenly; *Pop in* = come in suddenly; Sl. *Pop off* = die; Sl. *To pop the question* = ask a lady to marry one; Sl. *To pop one's gold ring* = have money lent upon —.

Pope (67) head of the Roman Catholic Church (one part of the Christian Church).

popinjay (5-1-21) well-dressed foolish fellow.

poplar (5-9) very tall tree often grown along the sides of rivers or roads.

poplin (5-1) cloth made of silk and wool, not smooth, but with raised lines on it.

poppy (5-1) red (or white) flower. From the seeds of the white poppy *opium* (= a medicine causing sleep) is made.

populace (5-17-1s) the common people.

popular (5-17-9) liked by all people; n. **popul'arity** (5-17-3-1-1).

POPPY

popul'ation (5-17-21shn) all the people in a country; number of people in a country; **populous** (——9) thickly populated, having many people in it.

porcelain (55s-1) fine *china* (= baked white earth used to make cups, plates, etc.).

porch (55) raised floor covered with a roof built outside the front door of a house, church, etc.

porcupine (55-17-41) animal like a rat covered with long prickles.

PORCUPINE

pore (over) (55) fix the eyes and mind upon.

pore(s) (55z) small opening(s) in the skin from which liquid comes when the body is hot.

pork (55) meat obtained from a pig.

porker (55-9) pig.

porous (55-9) allowing liquid to pass through, e.g. *A porous pot* = one used to keep water cool.

PORPOISE

porpoise (55-9) large sea animal which swims about in groups, going over and under the water in curves.

porridge (5-1j) grain boiled in water to a thick mass, eaten by Scottish people and others; **porringer** (5-1njg) bowl from which porridge or liquid food is eaten.

port (55) harbour; town with a harbour; left-hand side of a ship as one faces forward.

p'ort w'ine (55 + 41) sweet thick wine.

portable (55-9) which can be carried easily.

portage (55-1j) place where boats or goods have to be carried from one stream to another.

portal (55) grand gate or door.

portc'ullis (55-8-1) network of iron bars hung above the gate of a castle and lowered during attack.

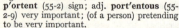
PORTCULLIS

port'end (55-2) be a sign of a future event; a **p'ortent** (55-2) sign; adj. **port'entous** (55-2-9) very important; (of a person) pretending to be very important.

porter (55-9) (1) door-keeper; (2) man who carries goods; (3) dark-coloured *beer* (= bitter strong drink).

portf'olio (55-67-167) (1) case for papers; (2) office of a member of the government.

p'ort-hole (55 + 67) round window in the side of a ship.

portico (55-1-67) roof supported by pillars covering a path, or built outside the entrance to a building.

portière (55-129) curtain over a door.

portion (55shn) part or share; money given to a girl at her marriage.

portly (55-1) solemn and important-looking; fat.

portm'anteau (55-3-67) large bag for carrying clothes when travelling.

portrait (55-1) picture of a person; **to portr'ay** (55-21) make a picture of; describe.

pose (67z) put (a question); stand still holding the body in a certain way while a picture is made; *To pose as* = pretend to be; *That's a poser!* = difficult question; **pos'eur** (67zg9) one who behaves in an unnatural way so as to appear clever or important.

posh (5) Sl. e.g. *Posh clothes* = very fine, very expensive, very smart —; so also *A posh car, house*, etc.

pos'ition (9z1shn) way in which a thing is placed; state; employment; place to be defended; *I am not in a position to do it* = not able to.

positive (5z1-1) sure; +, greater than 0.

posse (5-1) group of officers of the law.

poss'ess (9zz) to own; *Possessed* = under the control of evil spirits; *Self-possessed* = calm and sure of oneself; **poss'essive** (———1) as if owning; eager to own or show that one owns; *The possessive case* = that form of a word which shows possession, e.g. *Man's*.

posset (5-1) drink of hot milk and wine.

possible (5-1) which can be done; which can or may happen.

post (67) (1) bar of wood, metal or stone fixed upright in the ground; *To be driven from pillar to post* = be made to move about continually; (2) *The General Post* = government office in charge of the carrying of letters; *Have a general post* = all go to someone else's place; (3) place to which an officer is sent for his work; (4) group of houses where trade is done; **to post,** (1) fix up a notice in public; *Keep me well posted* = tell me all the news; (2) send a man to work in a certain place; (3) travel quickly; (4) to put a letter in the letter-box; (5) *To post a cash-book, etc.* = copy amounts of money from the cash-book, etc., into another book called the ledger; *The Last Post* = music played to call soldiers back to camp, also over the grave of a soldier.

postage (67-1j) cost of sending a letter by post.

p'ost-d'ate (67 + 21) write a date later than the real one.

poster (67-9) public notice, e.g. for selling goods.

post'erior (5-19-19) later; farther back; back part of the body on which one sits.

post'erity (5-2-1-1) descendants.

p'ostern (gate) (5-99) small back gate.

p'ost-fr'ee (67 + 11) without having to pay for the postage.

p'ost-h'aste (67 + 21) as quickly as possible.

posthumous (5-17-9) (child born) after the death of (the father); (book) printed after the death of (the writer).

post'il(l)ion (9-1-19) rider of one of the horses pulling a carriage.

p'ost-m'ortem (67 + 55-2) examination of a body after death to find the cause of death.

postp'one (9-67) to *put off* (= delay) till a later date.

p'ostpr'andial (67-3-19) adj. after dinner.

postscript (67skr1) writing added afterwards to a letter or book.

postulate (5-17-21) take a fact as known or as true, in order to reason from it.

posture (5-tsh9) way of standing or of holding the body.

posy (67z1) a few flowers tied together.

pot (5) vessel, usually of baked earth, used for holding liquid; *Take pot luck* = as a guest to eat the usual food of the family; Sl. *To go to pot* = be ruined; Sl. *To take a pot at* = shoot at; Sl. *Potty* = mad; **to pot,** put in a pot, e.g. plants.

potash (5-3) white powder used in making glass and soap.

pot'ation (67-21shn) drinking; **potable** (67-9) drinkable.

pot'ato (9-21-67) root very commonly used as a vegetable.

potency (67-s1) power; **potent,** powerful; **potentate** (———21) powerful king.

pot'ential (9-2-shl) possible, which might be if —; *Electric potential* = possible amount of work a certain electric flow can do.

pot-hole (5 + 67) hole in the road which will shake a car going over it; a deep underground cave; *Go pot-holing* = go into such caves.

potion (67shn) liquid medicine—or poison.

pottage (5-1j) food boiled in water.

potter (5-9) work in a lazy careless way.

potter (5-9) man who makes pots, cups, etc., out of baked earth; **pottery** (5-9-1) such cups, plates, etc.; the place where they are made; the art of making —.

pouch (47) small bag.

poultice (67-1s) mass of hot material put on the skin as a medicine.

poultry (67-1) hens and other birds kept for eggs and food; **poulterer** (67-9-9) one who sells birds for food.

pounce (on) (47-s) jump suddenly upon.

pound (47) break up into powder; to hit heavily and often.

pound (47) place in which wandering cattle, horses, etc., are imprisoned.

pound (47) measure of weight; 100 pence of English money; *An 18-pounder* = gun which fires a shot weighing 18 pounds.

pour (55) cause liquid to flow; come out freely and in a mass, e.g. *The people poured out of the building*; fall or flow rapidly, e.g. *Pouring rain* = very heavy —.

pout (47) push out the lips as a sign of being displeased.

poverty (5-9-1) state of having little money.

powder (47-9) any dry material broken into very small pieces; **g'unpowder** (8-47-9) powder which explodes with force when touched with fire; **to powder**, make into a powder; put powder on, e.g., the face.

power (479) force; *He has the power to* = he is able to; *The Great Powers* = *powerful* (= strong) countries in the world.

p'ow-w'ow (47 + 47) meeting, e.g. of army officers or Boy Scouts, to talk over various questions.

practicable (3-1-9) which can be done or used.

practical (3-1) concerned with doing real things, rather than thinking and ideas.

practically (3-1-1) usefully; really; *Practically dead* = almost dead.

practice (3-1s) doing (rather than thinking); *Practice in —* = doing a thing often so as to become skilful; *It is my practice to* = custom to —; *A doctor's practice* = people whom he serves; *Knows the theory but not the practice* = the ideas but not how to put them into action; **pract'itioner** (3-1sh9-9) one who has a practice, e.g. *A doctor is a medical practitioner*.

practise (3-1s) do often so as to learn and become skilful; to put into action; *Practise what you preach* = do yourself what you advise others to do.

prairie (29-1) grass-land without trees.

praise (21z) say that one admires; speak in honour of.

pram (3) (1) perambulator (see —); (2) small flat-bottomed boat.

prance (44-s) to jump along.

prank (3ngk) childish trick.

prate (21) talk meaninglessly and too much.

prattle (3) talk a lot, like a child.

prawn (55) small water-creature with a soft shell which becomes red when boiled.

pray (21) ask eagerly or solemnly; ask God for; *Pray, what is that?* = I ask you to tell me what —; **prayer** (29) an act of praying; words said in praying, e.g. to God.

pre- before, e.g. **pr'e-w'ar** (11 + 55) before the war.

preach (11) talk solemnly—as a priest in a church; *To preach war* = speak, urging people to go to war; *Practise what you preach* = do yourself what you advise others to do.

pre'amble (11·3) first part, e.g. of a law, giving reasons for making it.

prec'arious (1-29-19) uncertain, dangerous.

prec'aution (1-55shn) care taken before an event in order to prevent it happening or in order to cause it to happen without doing harm.

prec'ede (1s11) go in front of; *To give precedence to* (2s1-s) = give a higher place to.

precedent (2s1) something done or settled before, which is now used as an example or rule.

precept (11s2) rule of behaviour; **prec'eptor** (1-2-9) teacher.

precinct (11s1ngk) land round a church, school, government office, etc.

precious (2sh9) of great value; (in art or writing) too careful about little things, not natural.

precipice (2s1-1s) very steep cliff.

prec'ipitance (1s1-1-s) a rushing into action without thinking first.

prec'ipitate (1s1-1-21) (1) throw down; (2) cause a thing to happen at once; (3) cause the solid part of a liquid to separate out and fall to the bottom.

prec'ipitous (1-1-1-9) very steep.

précis (21s11) ideas of a long speech or book written down in as few words as possible.

prec'ise (1s41) exact; n. **prec'ision** (1s13n).

preclude (1-77) prevent; to shut off from.

prec'ocious (1-67sh9) growing up too soon; (child) unusually clever for one so young.

prec'ursor (11-99-9) fore- (= before, in front) runner, something which comes or happens before, e.g. *A red sky is the precursor of a storm*.

predatory (2-9-9-1) (animal) animal which lives by killing others; (tribe) group of persons who live by stealing.

predecessor (11-1s2-9) one who came before, e.g. in office or employment.

pred'estined (11-2-1) already settled by fate.

pred'icament (1-1-9-9) dangerous or unpleasant difficulty.

predicate (2-1-21) say something about a subject; *Subject and* **predicate** (2-1-1), e.g. He is ill = "he" is the subject, "is ill" is the predicate.

pred'ict (1-1) say that an event will happen.

predil'ection (11-1-2-shn) greater liking for.

pr'edisp'ose (11-1-67z) have such an effect on the body or mind as to make a certain event probable, e.g. *To predispose the body to disease, — the mind to certain ideas*; n. a **pr'edispos'ition** (11-1-9-zIshn).

pred'ominate (1-5-1-21) be greater in number, strength, etc.

pre-'emption (11 + 2-shn) *The right of—* = right to buy things first before they are offered to others.

preen (11) (of a bird) set the feathers in order.

pref'abricate (11-3-1-21) make it ready before it is put in place, e.g. the walls, floor, roof, etc., of a prefabricated house (= a **pr'efab**) are made in a factory and then put together on the land.

preface (2-1s) note written at the beginning of a book.

prefect (11-2) officer of government in ancient Rome; school-boy set to keep other boys in order.

pref'er (1-99) to like better; **pref'erment** (1-99-9) rising to a higher office in the Church; *Preferred shares* = shares in a business on which money is paid first, before the common shares; n. **pr'eference** (2-9-9-s).

pref'ix (11-1) fix in front of; a **pr'efix** (11-1) group of letters fixed in front of the root of a word, e.g. *Pre-* is the prefix in *Prefix*, and *Fix* is the root.

pregnant (2-9) full of meaning; in the state before childbirth.

preh'ensile (foot) (1-2-41) able to seize and hold.

prejudice (2-7-1s) opinion formed before examining the facts; *To the prejudice of* = so as to cause harm to; **to prejudice**, make a person form such an opinion.

prelate (2-1) high officer of the Church.

prel'iminary (1-1-1-9-1) preparing for —.

prelude (2-177) piece of music which leads up to another; any act or performance which is meant to lead on to something else.

prematu're (2-9-179) happening or done before the proper time.

prem'editate (11-2-1-21) think over a thing before doing it; *A premeditated act* = done on purpose, after careful thought.

premier (2-19) first, of highest rank; **the Premier**, the chief of the government in Britain.

premise (2-1) (in reasoning) thing taken as true and used as a starting point; **to prem'ise** (1-41) say the facts on which a piece of reasoning is built.

premises (2-1-1z) house or building with all that belongs to it.

premium (11-19) special payment; money paid to a teacher by a learner; money paid for an *insurance* (see —); special amount added to the value of an insurance; *Sold at a premium* = sold for more than the usual price.

premon'ition (11-9-1shn) a feeling that a certain event is going to happen.

pre'occupied (11.5-17-41) thinking of other things.

prepare (1-29) get ready before; **prep'aratory** (1-3-9-9-1) getting ready.

prep'onderate (1-5-9-21) be in greater weight or power.

preposi'tion (2-9zIshn) word such as To, By, With, etc.

preposs'essing (appearance) (11-9z2-1) such an appearance as produces a good opinion at first sight.

prep'osterous (1-5-9-9) very foolish or unbelievable.

prer'ogative (1-5-9-1) special power or right, e.g. of a king.

presage (2-1j) to be a sign of a future event.

Presbyt'erian (2z-1-19-19) Church (e.g. that of Scotland) ruled by Elders who are all of the same rank.

prescience (2-19-s) knowledge of what will happen in the future.

prescr'ibe (1-41) order the use of—e.g. a book or medicine; **prescr'iption** (1-1-shn) list of things to be mixed to make up a medicine.

present (2z) here; now; n. **presence** (2z-s); *In the presence of* = being with a person; standing in front of; *Presence of mind* = quickness in thinking and acting when in danger.

pres'ent (1zz) bring a person before another and make him known; give; *To present arms* (of soldiers) = hold the guns upright in honour of a high officer.

pr'esent (2z) gift; n. **present'ation** (2z-zIshn).

pres'entiment (1zz-1-9) feeling that something bad is going to happen.

presently (2z-1) soon, after a little time.

pres'erve (1z99) keep from harm or decay; fruit preserved from decay by cooking it in sugar.

pres'ide (1z41) act as head of and control (a meeting); **pr'esident** (2z1) head and controller of a business company, government; etc.

press (2) to push together; *To press clothes* = make flat and neat; *Hard pressed* = in difficulty; *To press a person to act* = urge; *To press money on* = try to make a person accept —; *Pressing business* = which must be done at once; *Press on* = hurry forward; *Press for* = continue to ask for; **a press**, instrument used for pressing; piece of furniture used for storing clothes; printing machine; *The Press* = newspapers.

pressure (2sh9) act of pressing; force with which one thing presses against another, e.g. *The pressure of gas in a container*; state of difficulty; *To bring pressure to bear on* = urge or force a person to act; *To work at high pressure* = very hard.

pressure-cooker (+ 7-9) closed metal container in which food is cooked by steam pressure instead of simple boiling.

pressurized (aeroplane) (2sh-4I) with the air inside the aeroplane kept at about the same pressure as the pressure of air on the ground.

prest'ige (2-113) *To have —* = have power because of one's fame.

pres'ume (1z17) take as being known to be true, or as allowed to be done; to guess; be too bold in behaviour; **pres'umption** (1z8-shn) act of presuming; a thing taken as known; boldness of behaviour; *The heir* **pres'umptive** (1z8-1) = son who, it is imagined, will get the father's money, etc. (or become king), after the father's death; **pres'umptuous** (1z8-179) bold and bad-mannered.

pret'end (1-2) act in such a way as to make people believe that —; to claim; **pret'entious** (1-2-sh9) pretending to be very important.

preter- past, beyond, outside, e.g. **pretern'atural** (powers) (11-9-3tsh9) outside nature.

pretext (11-2) pretended but not real reason for an action.

pretty (1-1) beautiful in a simple way; charming; quite, e.g. *Pretty far* = quite a long way; Sl. *Pretty good* = very good; *A pretty penny* = large amount of money.

prev'ail (1-21) win; gain power over; become generally accepted as a custom; *The prevailing wind* = most usual at some time of year; adj. **prevalent** (2-9-9).

prev'aricate (1-3-1-21) try to hide the truth by refusing to give straight or clear answers to questions.

prev'ent (1-2) to stop from happening.

preview (11-177) seeing (a cinema film or other show) before it is shown to the public (to anyone who pays to see it).

previous (11-19) happening before.

prey (21) animal (or bird) which is hunted by other animals (birds); *A beast of prey* = animal which eats other animals; *To prey on his mind* = continue to make him sad and anxious.

price (4Is) money for which a thing is sold; *Put a price on the head of —* = offer money to whoever makes a prisoner of —; **priceless** (4Is-1) of great value; Sl. very good, very amusing.

prick (1) make a small hole, e.g. with a needle; *To prick up the ears* (of an animal) = make the ears stand up straight as when listening.

prickle (1) sharp needle-like part of a plant or animal.

pride (4I) feeling of being proud.

priest (11) one who has the right to lead prayers and perform ceremonies in a church (or other religious building).

prig (1) person who makes a show of goodness or wisdom.

prim (1) stiff in manner and behaviour; like an old lady.

pr'ima d'onna (11-9 + 5-9) chief woman singer.

pr'ima f'acie (4I-9 + 21s1-11) at first sight, as first seen.

primal (4I) earliest, of the earliest times.

primary (4I-9-1) first in order; simplest; *Of primary importance* = more important than anything else.

Primate (4I-1) head of the Church of England.

primate (4I-21) one of that class of animals which includes men and monkeys.

prime (4I) (1) first in order, chief, e.g. *Of prime importance*; *The Prime Minister* = highest officer of government; (2) very good, e.g. *In prime condition*; (3) *A prime number* = one which cannot be divided except by itself and the number 1, e.g. 2, 3, 5, etc.; (4) *The prime of the year* = best time; *Cut off in his prime* = killed just when he was at his best; **to prime**, prepare for use or action, e.g. put gunpowder ready for firing a gun; tell a person facts so as to prepare him to make a speech.

primer (1-9 or 4I-9) child's first book.

primitive (1-1-1) of the earliest times; simple.

primog'eniture (4I-67j2-1tsh9) right of the eldest son to receive the whole of the land, etc., at the father's death.

primrose (1-67z) yellow wild flower.

primus stove (4I-9 + 67) burner which blows out oil mixed with air (Trade name).

prince (1-s) son of a king; ruler; **princ'ess** (1-s2) daughter of a king; wife of a prince.

principal (1-s1) chief; head of a school; *My principal* = person for whom I am acting in this business; an amount of money put into business for gain.

princip'ality (1-s1-3-1-1) country ruled by a prince.

principle (1-s1) general truth or law at the bottom of other laws; general reason for action; ideas according to which one guides one's life; *A man of no principles* = of no fixed beliefs, not to be trusted.

print (1) mark made by pressing; press marks upon paper, as in a printed book; *Large print* = large printed letters; *A print dress* = one made of cotton with ornament printed on it.

prior (4I9) earliest; head of a *priory* (= house in which men lead lives given to God); **prioress** (——1) head of a priory for women.

pri'ority (4I5-1-1) the right to get something or have something done before other people can get or have it done.

prise (open) (4Iz) to open by force.

prism (Iz) block of regular shape with three or

prison

more flat sides; piece of glass with three sides used for breaking up light into its colours.

prison (1z) building in which law-breakers are shut up; **prisoner** (1z-9) person put into prison.

pristine (1-41) belonging to the earliest times; in its first simple and pure state.

privacy (1-9s1 or 41-9s1) state of being alone, of being secret.

private (41-1) belonging to one person; not public; **a private**, common soldier.

privat'eer (41-9-19) ship which does not belong to the government but is allowed to attack enemy ships.

priv'ation (41-21shn) lack of food and comforts.

privilege (1-1-1j) special favour or right.

privy (1-1) having special knowledge of (a secret); *Privy Council* = the king's own special advisers; *A privy* = place where one leaves the waste matter of the body.

prize (41) something given as a return for, or as a sign of, very good work—e.g. given to one who is first in a race, or who is head of his class in school; enemy ship seized in war; **to prize**, value greatly.

pro- in front of, forwards, e.g. **proc'eed** (9s11) = go forward; for, e.g. **proc'ure** (9-179) = get a thing for a person; in favour of, e.g. **pr'o-G'erman** (67 + j99-9).

pro. (67) a *professional* (= one who plays a game for money).

pro(s) and con(s) (67z + 5-z) reasons for and against.

probable (5-9) which is thought to be true, though it cannot be proved; which is expected to happen; n. **probab'ility** (5-9-1-1-1).

probate (67-1) examining of a *will* (= paper showing to whom a man's possessions are to be given after his death) and saying that it is in order and according to law.

prob'ation (9-21shn) *On probation* = not fixed in an office, but allowed to hold it for a time so as to show one's fitness or unfitness; (of a prisoner) allowed to remain out of prison if he behaves well.

probe (67) thin bar of metal used by a doctor to feel for a shot (etc.) in a wound; **to probe**, examine into.

probity (67-1-1) honesty.

problem (5-9) difficult question; **problem'atic** (5-1-3-1) doubtful.

prob'oscis (9-5-1) long nose of an animal, e.g. an elephant; (insects) lengthening of parts about mouth.

proce'dure (9s11j9) way of going forward; way of carrying out a business.

proc'eed (9s11) go forward; carry on work; come out from; *To proceed against* = go to law against.

proc'eeding (9s11-1) course of action; *Legal proceedings* = action in a court of law; *The proceedings of the meeting* = things said and settled in —.

process (67s2) number of actions all leading to one aim; way of acting or doing something; *In process of completion* = now being finished.

proc'ession (9s2shn) number of persons going along in line, in a fixed order, e.g. at a marriage or funeral.

procl'aim (9-21) make public; **a proclam'ation** (5-9-21shn) thing made known to the public; act of proclaiming.

procl'ivity (9-1-1-1) leaning towards (a certain sort of behaviour).

procr'astinate (67-3-1-21) to delay.

pr'ocre'ate (67-121) produce children.

proctor (5-9) one who acts for another; an officer who keeps good order, e.g. in a university.

proc'ure (9-179) obtain; buy; cause a result to happen.

prod (5) to push with a pointed object; to urge to action.

prodigal (5-1) wasteful, careless in spending.

prodigy (5-1j1) a wonder; person who has some wonderful power; adj. **prod'igious** (9-1j9) unusual; very big; wonderful.

prod'uce (9-177s) (1) bring forward; *To produce a play* = get a play ready for performance in a theatre; (2) to bear, to yield, e.g. *The soil produces corn*; be the cause of, e.g. *My work has produced no result*; (3) make, e.g. *To produce motor-cars*; (4) make a line longer; n. **pr'oduce** (5-177s) things produced, e.g. crops; **pr'oduct** (5-9) thing produced, a result; $2 \times 2 = 4$; 4 is the product.

prof'ane (9-21) not holy; having to do with this life (not the life after death); disrespectful to God; *Profane language* = bad language, cursing.

prof'ess (9-2) say openly; make a claim to; claim to be able to do; pretend; be a teacher of; **prof'ession** (9-2shn) declaration; pretending; learned employment, e.g. doctor, teacher, lawyer; **prof'essional**, having to do with a profession; **a professional**, one who plays games for money; **prof'essor** (9-2-9) teacher in a university.

proffer (5-9) to offer.

prof'icient (9-1shnt) well practised, clever.

profile (67-11) *outline* (= line round the edge) of a thing, e.g. of a face seen from the side.

profit (5-1) gain, e.g. of money; **to profit**, be of use to; **profit'eer** (——19) one who gains much money in time of war or difficulty.

profligate (5-1-1) given up to bad ways; evil-liver.

prof'ound (9-47) deep; very learned; **prof'undity** (9-8-1-1) depth.

prof'use (9-177) poured out freely; **prof'usion** (9-1773n) plenty.

prog'enitor (67j2-1-9) person from whom one is descended; earlier member of the family; **progeny** (5j1-1) descendants.

progn'osticate (5-5-1-21) tell the future; **progn'osis** (5-67-1) probable result of a disease.

programme (67-3) list of things which will be done in public, e.g. of songs, etc., in a public show.

progress (67-2) onward movement; improvement; **to progr'ess** (9-2) go forward, improve.

proh'ibit (9-1-1) forbid; **prohib'ition** (671-1shn) act of forbidding; forbidding of all strong drink in a country; *A proh'ibitive* (9-1-1-1) *price* = price which forbids buying, is so high that one cannot buy.

project (5-2) a plan.

proj'ect (9-2) throw forward; stand out; **proj'ectile** (9-2-41) thing shot forward, e.g. from a gun; **proj'ector** (9-2-9) (1) person who makes *projects* (= plans), usually of a foolish kind, or intended to deceive; (2) instrument for throwing pictures on a sheet by means of a bright light, or for throwing light forward, as in the lamps of a motor-car.

prolet'ariat (67-1-29-19) all the common people; all the workers.

prol'ific (9-1-1) fruitful, producing much.

prolix (67-1) using many words to express little meaning.

prologue (67-5) speech made before a play begins.

prol'ong (9-5) make longer.

promen'ade (5-1-44) quiet walk; wide road; road along the sea-front.

prominent (5-1-9) standing out; easily seen; well known to all.

prom'iscuous (9-1-179) mixed; of all classes.

promise (5-1) say that one will do something; cause a person to hope; **a promise**, act of promising; thing promised; *His work shows promise* = causes one to hope that he will do well; **promising** (——1) causing one to hope.

promissory note (5-1-9-1 + 67) paper saying that money will be paid on a certain date.

promontory (5-9-9-1) point of high land standing out into the sea.

prom'ote (9-67) to move up to a higher rank or place; to help forward; to help to start (e.g. a business).

prompt (5) ready; done at once.

prompt (5) (1) move or urge a person to action; to cause action; (2) help an actor who has forgotten his words.

promulgate (5-21) make known to the public, e.g. a law, news.

prone (67) lying face downward; sloping towards; *Prone to anger* = becoming angry very easily.

prong (5) sharp point of an instrument.

pronoun (67-47) (for noun) word such as I, You, He, etc.

pron'ounce (9-47-s) say solemnly; form the sounds of a language; **pron'unci'ation** (9-8-s121shn) way of saying words or of forming the sounds of a language; **pron'ounced** (9-47-st) strongly marked, clear, e.g. *His fear was very pronounced*.

proof (77) that which shows a thing to be true (or untrue); first printing which the writer will correct; *Spirits 10 per cent. under proof* = strong drink which is 10 per cent. less strong than the greatest strength allowed by law.

prop (5) a support; to support.

propag'anda (5-9-3-9) arrangements for spreading a certain belief; beliefs so spread.

propagate (5-9-21) cause to increase, e.g. plants; spread an idea among people.

prop'el (9-2) push forward; **prop'eller** (9-2-9) set of sloping blades which drive a ship or aeroplane forward.

prop'ensity (9-2-1-1) a leaning towards a certain kind of behaviour.

proper (5-9) right and fitting; peculiar to one's self; one's own; polite; *A proper noun* = name of a person or place.

PROPELLER

property (5-9-1) that which is owned; special and peculiar character of a thing; things used in a play in a theatre.

prophecy (5-1s1) telling of a future event; **prophesy** (5-1-41) tell the future; **prophet** (5-1) one who declares the will of God to men, who tells the future.

pr'ophyl'actic (5-1-3-1) used to guard against disease.

prop'inquity (9-1ngkw1-1) nearness.

prop'itiate (9-1sh121) gain the favour of; lessen the anger of.

prop'itious (9-1sh9) favourable; fortunate.

prop'ortion (9-55shn) size of a thing when considered as a part of a whole; *Equal in proportion to* = equal when considered as part of a whole, e.g. 2 is to 5 as 4 is to 10, $\frac{5}{2} = \frac{10}{4}$; *Of large proportions* = of large size; *A proportion of the gains* = a share of —.

prop'ose (9-67z) *put forward* (= say, offer) an idea for consideration; offer marriage; in **pro-p'osal**; **propos'ition** (5-9z1shn) an offer; in *geometry* (= science of measuring) a thing to be proved.

prop'ound (9-47) put forward an idea for consideration.

propr'ietor (9-419-9) owner; *A* **propr'ietary** (9-419-9-1) *medicine* = medicine made by a business company, not one specially ordered by a doctor.

propr'iety (9-41-1-1) state of being proper, or according to the rules of good behaviour.

prop'ulsion (9-8-shn) n. of Propel (= to drive forward).

pror'ogue (9-67) to close down for an unknown time, e.g. *parliament* (= meeting in which laws are made).

pros′aic (67z21·1) containing no new or interesting ideas.

proscr′ibe (67-41) declare to be outside the law; forbid the use of.

prose (67z) not poetry; adj. **prōsy** (67z1) saying much and causing little interest.

prosecute (5-1-177) follow (a plan); take action against or make a claim against in a court of law.

proselyte (5-1-41) person won over to a belief.

prosody (5-9-1) laws which govern the regular arrangement of sounds in poetry.

prospect (5-2) scene; looking forward or expecting; **to prosp′ect** (9-2) look for, e.g. gold; **prosp′ective** (9-2-1) expected.

prosp′ectus (9-2-9) plan or short description.

prosper (5-9) be successful, do well in business; **pros′perity** (5-2-1-1).

prostitute (5-1-177) use for a bad purpose.

prostrate (5-21) lying stretched out; **to prostr′ate** (oneself) (5-21) throw oneself down on the ground as a sign of great respect.

prot′agonist (67-3-9-1) chief actor; leader.

prot′ect (9-2) to guard, to shelter from evil; **prot′ector** (———9) one who protects; ruler of a kingdom while the king is too young; **prot′ectorate** (9-2-9-1) such rule; weaker country placed in charge of a stronger one.

protégé (67-2321) one who is under (my) protection.

protein (67-11) kind of body-building food, contained in, e.g. meat, egg—not in bread or fat or sugar.

prot′est (9-2) say that one is not in favour of; say that a thing should not be done; n. a **pr′otest** (67-2).

Protestant (5-1-9) one of a group of Christians who separated themselves from the Church of Rome.

protocol (67-9-5) rules of behaviour for officers of a government in dealing with officers of a foreign government; also of persons in any gathering where a king or queen, etc., is present.

protoplasm (67-9-3z) living material from which the bodies of plants and animals grow.

prototype (67-9-41) first example according to which other later things are made.

protozo′a (67-9-679) very small and simple living things found in water.

protr′act (9-3) make long; **protr′actor** (9-3-9) instrument used for measuring angles.

protr′ude (9-77) stand out from.

prot′uberance (9-177-9-9-s) a swelling out.

proud (47) holding a high opinion of oneself or one's possessions.

prove (77) show that a thing is true; try whether a thing is true, e.g. *Prove me and examine my thoughts* = examine, try me.

provender (5-1-9) food for cattle.

proverb (5-99) short wise saying.

prov′ide (9-41) supply; prepare for; *Provided that* = if —; **providence** (5-1-9-s) care and preparation for the future; the care of God for man; **provident** (5-1) caring for the future; **provid′ential** (5-1-2-shl) very fortunate.

province (5-1-s) part of a country; space within which a certain person or thing has power; adj. **prov′incial** (9-1-shl).

prov′ision (9-13n) preparation; **prov′isions** (9-13nz) food; **prov′isional** (9-139) serving for the present time only, but able to be changed later.

prov′iso (9-41z67) *On the proviso that* = if —.

prov′oke (9-67) make angry; adj. **prov′ocative** (9-5-9-1); *How provoking!* = that is very unfortunate and makes me feel angry.

provost (5-9) head of a *college* (= school for youths); holder of an office in the Church; chief officer of Scottish cities.

prow (47) front of a ship.

prowess (47¹) courage.

prowl (47) wander about like an animal seeking to kill.

prox′imity (5-1-1-1) nearness.

proxy (5-1) the right to act for another person, e.g. *To vote by proxy* = show the opinion of a person absent from a meeting.

prude (77) woman who is over-correct and careful in her behaviour.

prudent (77) wise and careful.

prune (77) dried *plum* (= kind of fruit).

prune (77) to cut off parts of a tree to make it grow better.

prurient (77-19) interested in unpleasant things.

pry (41) look into, inquire into secretly—especially into a thing which is not one's concern.

psalm (44) song in honour of God, e.g. those songs found in the Bible.

pseudo (177-67) not real, pretending to be; **pseudonym** (177-9-1) name other than the real name.

pshaw (55) sound made with the lips to show disbelief.

psych′iatry (s41k419-1) science and art of curing disorders of the mind.

psychic (41k1) of the soul; having to do with the spirits of the dead.

psych′ology (41k5-9j1) scientific study of the mind; adj. **psychol′ogical** (41k9-5j1).

psychopath (s41k6-3) person of rather disordered mind, but not mad.

psych′osis (s41k67-1) disorder of the mind.

pt′omaine p′oisoning (67-21 + 51z9-1) poisoning by bad food.

pub (8) inn, public house (see 2nd below).

puberty (177-9-1) earliest age at which it is possible to become a parent.

public (8-1) general; open to all people; *A public house* = house where strong drink is sold; Am. *A public school* = school in which teaching is provided by the government for all; *The English Public Schools* = number of schools in England which are used mainly by the wealthier classes and are *not* provided by the government.

publican (8-1-9) owner of a *public house* (see above); collector of money owed to the government.

public'ation (8-1-21shn) printed thing, e.g. a book; act of printing and selling books.

publ'icity (8-1s1-1) making something widely known.

publish (8-1) (1) make known; (2) print and sell a book or paper.

puce (171s) colour made by mixing red, blue and brown.

puck (8) small round, flat piece of rubber used instead of a ball in playing *hockey* (= a game played with J-shaped sticks) on the ice.

pucker (8-9) gather into small folds.

pudding (7-1) (1) sweet dish served at the end of a meal; (2) meat boiled inside a thin pipe-like skin; meat cooked inside pastry.

puddle (8) small quantity of water lying in a hollow, e.g. in the road; **to puddle**, cover the inside of a water-way with a kind of earth through which water does not pass.

pudgy (8j1) short, thick and fat.

puerile (179-41) childish, silly.

puff (8) (1) short sharp breath of wind; (2) small cloud of smoke; (3) any soft round object, e.g. one made of feathers used to put powder on the face; (4) piece of writing praising a book in order to sell it; **puffy** (——1) soft and swollen.

pug (nose) (8) a short broad nose; **pug-dog** (+ 5) small fat dog with a tightly curled tail.

puggaree (8-9-1) **pugree** (8-1) long piece of cloth bound round the head of an Indian or round a hat.

PUG-DOG

pugilist (171-1) person who fights with his *fists* (= tightly closed hands).

pugn'acious (8-21-sh9) loving to fight.

puissant (171) powerful.

pull (7) *Pull one's weight* = do a fair share of the work; *Pull a horse* = prevent it winning; *Pull a ball* = strike it round towards the left; *Pull a face* = make the face look ugly as a sign of disrespect; Sl. *Pull a person's leg* = deceive in order to laugh at; *Pull down a building* = destroy; *Pull him round from an illness* = bring back to health; *Pull oneself together* = gather all one's strength, give up bad ways; *Pull up* = stop; **a pull**, act of pulling; *Take a pull at the bottle* = take a drink from —; *He has a pull with the government* = has power to make it do what he wants.

pullet (7-1) young hen.

pulley (7-1) wheel over which a rope passes, used to raise weights.

pullover (7-67-9) woollen garment pulled on to the body by passing it over the head.

pulmonary (8-9-0-1) having to do with the *lungs* (= part of the body with which we breathe).

pulp (8) soft inside material of a plant or fruit.

pulpit (7-1) raised place in a church from which a priest speaks to his people.

puls'ate (8-21) to beat, like the heart.

pulse (8) heart-beat.

pulse (8) plants such as beans; their seeds used as food.

pulverize (8-9-41) make into powder.

puma (177-9) fierce animal like a large cat.

pumice (8-1s) light stone with little holes in it (like bread) used for cleaning the hands.

PUMA

pummel (8) strike many times with the hands.

pump (8) machine for raising liquid, or pressing air into things; also for taking liquid or air out.

pumpkin (8-1) very large round yellow fruit which grows on the ground and is used for food.

pumps (8) shoes used for dancing.

pun (8) play on words, e.g. Those who make *puns* should be *punished*.

punch (8) strike with the closed hand.

punch (8) make a small hole in; instrument for this purpose..

punch (8) strong drink made of spirits (e.g. *whisky*), hot water, sugar, etc.

punct'ilious (8ngk-1-19) very careful over small matters of politeness.

punctual (8ngkt179) coming at the exact time.

punctuate (8ngkt1721) put the *stops* (, ; : . etc.) into writing.

puncture (8ngktsh9) make a hole in; make a hole and let out the air, e.g. from the wheel of a motor-car.

pundit (8-1) (Indian word) learned man.

pungent (8nj9) strong-smelling; sharp and painful, e.g. speech.

punish (8-1) cause pain or discomfort to a person as a return for wrong-doing; treat roughly.

punitive (177-1-1) punishing.

punkah (8ngk9) instrument used in hot countries for keeping the air in a room moving.

punt (8) flat boat pushed along with a pole.

punter (8-9) one who risks money on horse-races.

puny (177-1) small and weak.

PUNT

pup (8) see Puppy.

pupil (177) (1) person being taught; (2) black opening in the centre of the eye.

puppet (8-1) small wooden figure moved by strings to make it dance; person who is completely under the control of another.

puppy (8-1) **pup** (8) young dog; foolish young man.

purchase (99-1) buy; *To get a purchase on* = get in a good place for pulling or raising a heavy thing.

purdah (99-9) (Indian word) curtain; custom of keeping women separate and in hiding.

pure (179) unmixed with anything else; simple; clean; *A pure accident* = event caused wholly by chance.

purée (179-21) thick *soup* (= liquid food made of meat and vegetables).

purgative (99-9-9-1) medicine used to drive waste matter downwards from the body.

purgatory (99-9-9-1) place in which souls after death are made pure and fit to enter heaven.

purge (99j) make pure and clean; to clear waste matter out of the body.

purify (179-1-41) make pure; **purist** (179-1) one who demands great correctness in language; n. **purity** (179-1-1).

puritan (179-1) one who leads a very plain simple life and believes that church *services* (= prayer and singing in a church) should be performed in a very plain way.

purlieus (99-177z) neighbouring lands.

purl'oin (99-51) steal.

purple (99) colour obtained by mixing red and blue.

purport (99-9) the meaning.

purpose (99-9) aim, desire, plan.

purr (99) low sound made by a cat when pleased.

purse (99) bag for money; amount of money given or collected for some purpose.

purse (99) one's lips; draw the mouth together into a small round o.

purser (99-9) officer in charge of the money and stores on a ship.

purs'uant (99-1779) *Pursuant to, In* **purs'uance** (9-1779-s) *of* = according to; *In the pursuance of my duties* = while performing my —.

purs'ue (9-177) run after and try to catch; n. **purs'uit** (9-177).

purv'ey (9-21) provide, to supply.

pus (8) liquid which comes out of a poisoned wound.

push (7) press forward; *A pushing person* = person who tries to make himself important; *Pushed for time* = not having enough time; *I can do it at a push* = if I try hard, if it is very necessary; Sl. *Get the push* = be sent away from one's employment; so also *Give him the push* = send him away.

pusill'animous (177-1-3-1-9) not brave or generous.

puss (7) **pussy** (7-1) name used in calling a cat.

pustule (8-177) small poisoned spot in the skin.

put (7) (**1**) move into a certain place or cause to remain in a certain place; *To put a book on the table* = set down; (**2**) bring into a certain state; to cause; Sl. *Put it across* = cause it to succeed; Sl. *To put it across him* = beat him, win against; *Put a stop to* = cause to end; *Put things right* = cause things to be right; Sl. *Put him wise* = tell him the truth; *Put to death* = cause to die, kill; *Put a person in the wrong* = make him feel or appear wrong; (**3**) change the direction of movement or cause movement in a certain direction; *Put a horse at a fence* = cause to jump; *Put a ship about* = cause to go in the opposite direction; *The ship put out to sea* = went away from the land; **put about,** *Put about a story* = cause to be known; *Much put about* = anxious and troubled; **put across,** Sl. *Put the idea across* = cause people to understand —; **put aside,** *Put aside work* = stop doing it meaning to do it at some other time; *Put aside money* = keep for use at a later date; **put away,** *Put away one's books* = put back into their proper place; *Put away money* = save; Sl. *Put away food* = eat a lot of; **put back,** *Put back* = put it in its proper place; **put by,** *Put money by* = save; **put down,** *Put down a rising against the government* = cause to cease; *Put one's foot down* = show that one is firmly decided; *Put down on paper* = write; *Put it down on my account* = write it down as owed by me; *I put him down as a fool* = think that he is a fool; **put forth,** *Put forth all one's powers* = use; **put forward,** *Put forward an idea* = explain and ask people to accept; **put in,** *Put in an appearance* = go to a meeting and cause oneself to be seen; *Put a law in force* = cause it to be obeyed; *Put in hand* = begin; Sl. *Put in a hole* = cause a person to have difficulties; *Put one in mind* = cause to remember; *Put in possession* = cause to possess; *Put in work* = do; **put in for,** *Put in for employment* = ask to be appointed; **put off,** *Put off* = delay to a later time or date; *Put a person off his game* = cause to play badly; *A bad smell put me off my food* = caused me to dislike; **put on,** *Put on airs and graces* = behave in a proud and silly way; *Put on a play* = cause to be shown in a theatre; *Put on weight* = become fatter; *Put money on a horse* = pay money which will be lost if the horse loses, but will gain more if the horse wins the race; **put out,** *Put out* = cause to be outside; *Put out one's knee* = put the bone out of the joint; *Put out a light* = cause to cease burning; *He is put out with me* = angry; **put over,** Sl. *Put it over* (e.g. a play, the sale of some new thing) = make it successful; **put through,** *Put work through* = cause to be finished; *Put a horse through his paces* = examine, watch it walk and run; **put together,** *Put two and two together* = examine the facts and understand what they mean; **put up,** Sl. *Put his back up* = make angry; *Put up a prayer* = pray; *Put a person up for* = ask that he be elected; *Put up for sale* (= selling) = try to sell; *Put up goods in boxes* = pack; *Put up your sword* = put back in its place, not fight; *Put up at a hotel* = go and stay at; *Put a person up* = take in as a visitor; *A put-up* (*bed*) =

(bed) which you can put together yourself; *A put-up job* = dishonestly arranged trick or plan; **put upon**, *I will not be put upon* = treated unfairly, made to do more than my fair share of work; **put up with**, *Put up with the Smiths* = stay in the house of —; *Put up with (evil)* = suffer without complaining.

putrefy (177-1-41) to decay; n. **putref'action** (177-1-3-shn); **putr'escent** (177-2) decaying; **putrid** (177-1) decayed.

puttees (8-1z) long pieces of cloth bound round the lower part of the legs by soldiers.

putty (8-1) white powder and oil mixed to make a soft material used for fixing glass in windows.

puzzle (8) difficult question; plaything which provides some difficult task to pass the time; **to puzzle**, set a difficult question; cause difficulty of thought; *To puzzle it out* = think hard and find the correct answer.

pygmy, pigmy (1-1) very small man or woman, e.g. member of a race of very small people found in Africa.

pyj'amas (9-44-9z) loose trousers as worn by Indians; coat and trousers of cotton or silk or wool, worn in bed.

pylon (41-9) tall upright stone or post; steel tower to carry electric wires across country.

pyramid (1-9-1) thing square at the bottom and pointed at the top (or of this shape but having three or more sides); **The Pyramids** (——z) great buildings in Egypt in which the dead bodies of kings were put in ancient times.

pyre (419) heap of wood on which a dead body is burned.

pyr'exia (41-2-19) fever.

p'yrot'echnics (41-6-2k-1) *fireworks* (= coloured lights and explosions).

python (41-9) large snake which kills by twisting itself tightly round the body of an animal.

Q

quack (3) cry of a duck.

quack (3) a person who pretends to have knowledge of (e.g. of medicine) which he does not possess.

quad- four.

quadrangle (5-3ngg) figure with four sides, e.g. a square; square courtyard in a *college* (= building in a university).

quadrant (5-9) one quarter of a circle; instrument used for measuring *angles* (= corner formed by the meeting of two straight lines).

quadr'ennial (5-2-19) happening once in four years.

quadr'ille (9-1) dance performed by eight or more people standing in a square.

quadr'illion (9-1-19) **1** followed by twenty-four 0s; (France and America) **1** followed by fifteen 0s.

quadruped (5-7-2) animal with four legs.

quadr'uple (5-77) four times.

quads (5-z) quadruplets (5-7-1) four children born of the same mother at the same time.

quaff (5) to drink.

quagmire (3-419) very soft piece of ground.

quail (21) small bird.

quail (21) draw back from fear.

quaint (21) pleasing because old or unusual.

quake (21) to shake.

Quaker (21-9) member of a group, called *The Society of Friends*; they hold certain special beliefs in God and are very much against war; they do many good works.

qu'alific'ation (5-1-1-21shn) act of *qualifying* (see below); *He has many qualifications for the work* = qualities of character and experience which make him fit for —.

qualify (5-1-41) **(1)** get or give the qualities necessary for, e.g. *To become qualified as a doctor* = pass the necessary examinations; **(2)** make less or weaker, e.g. *To qualify what one has said* = add something which makes one's words less strong or less general.

qualitative (5-1-9-1) having to do with quality, e.g. *Qualitative analysis* = scientific examination of a material to find what things are in it, rather than how much of each thing is found.

quality (5-1-1) that which makes a person or thing different from others; real nature; goodness or badness; *A lady of quality* = of rank; *The quality* = persons of high rank.

qualm (55) sudden feeling, e.g. of sickness or faintness.

quandary (5-9-1) state of doubt or difficulty.

quantity (5-1-1) amount; *He's an unknown quantity* = we know nothing of his powers or character.

quantum (5-9-1) certain amount; *Quantum mechanics* = way of making calculations about atoms and very small things.

quarantine (5-9-11) separation from other people for fear of spreading disease.

quarrel (5) disagreement.

quarry (5-1) place from which stone is got.

quarry (5-1) hunted animal; anything which is eagerly searched for or followed.

quart (55) measure of liquid = 1·136 litres in England, but ·96 litres in America.

quarter (55-9) **(1)** one fourth part of; **(2)** one of the four limbs of an animal, e.g. *The hind quarters* = back legs; **(3)** one of the four points of the compass, e.g. *From every quarter* = from all sides; **(4)** part of a town, e.g. *The Chinese quarter* = that part where the Chinese live; **(5) quarters** (——z) place given to soldiers to live in; *Living in close quarters* = in a crowded room or house; *At close quarters* = near; **(6)** mercy, e.g. *To give quarter to* = to show mercy to, not kill; **to quarter,** cut into four parts; *To quarter oneself on* = go and live with.

qu'arter-day (+ 21) the day on which debts must be paid, March 25th, June 24th, Sept. 29th, Dec. 25th (the days are different in Scotland).

qu'arter-deck (+ 2) back part of the top of a ship below where the officers live.

quarterly (55-9-1) happening four times a year; **a quarterly,** a paper printed and sold four times a year.

quartermaster (55-9-44-9) army officer who supplies food, clothes, etc.; ship's officer who is in charge of keeping watch by night and is on duty at the wheel by day.

qu'arter-staff (+ 44) long stick which was used for fighting as a game in ancient times.

quart'et(te) (55-2) set of four.

quarto (55-67) full-size sheet of paper folded twice, making four pages.

quartz (55ts) hard rock in which gold is sometimes found.

quasi- (44zI) almost, seeming as if.

quassia (5sh9) medicine with a very bitter taste.

quatrain (5-21) four lines of poetry.

quaver (21-9) to shake; **a quaver,** short note of music.

quay (kII) place where ships are loaded or unloaded.

queasy (11zI) feeling sick; difficult to please.

queen (11) wife of a king; female ruler of a country.

queer (19) unusual; *To feel queer* = feel sick; *He's a bit queer* = rather mad; *In Queer Street* = (of a business man) in money difficulties; **to queer,** cause things to go wrong.

quell (2) to put down, cause to cease (e.g. a rising against the government); *To quell fears* = calm —.

quench (2) (thirst, fire) to put an end to by means of water.

quern (99) hand-mill for making grain into flour.

querulous (2-17-9) full of complaints; eager to quarrel.

query (19-1) to question; a question.

quest (2) a search.

question (2-tshn) (1) an asking for knowledge; *Out of the question* = impossible, not to be considered; (2) difficult matter; **to question, to ask questions of**, to doubt; **questionable** (———9) doubtful; **qu'estionn'aire** (2stI9-29) set of printed questions sent out to many persons in order to get facts on a certain subject.

queue (kI77) line of people waiting, e.g. to get into a theatre.

quibble (1) answer intended to deceive—or to escape from telling the truth.

quick (1) (1) swift, keen, active, clever; (2) living, e.g. *The quick and the dead*; *Cut to the quick* = cut down to the living and painful part of the skin, very much hurt (in the mind or feelings); (3) (of things) active, e.g. **quicklime** (1-41) with water boils and becomes building lime; **quicksand** (1-3) soft sand which swallows up ships; **quicksilver** (1-1-9) = *mercury*; **quicken**, make or become alive; cause to move faster; move faster.

qu'ickset h'edge (1-2 + 2j) line of growing bushes as a fence for a field or garden.

quid (1) (1) piece of *tobacco* (= plant used for smoking) kept in the mouth; (2) Sl. £1; (3) *A quid pro quo* (Latin = something for something) = payment of some kind for help or for something given.

qui'escent (412-9) resting.

quiet (419) free from noise or movement; calm; (of colours) not bright; **qui'etus** (41-11-9) (payment of debt); death.

quill (1) central stem of a feather; feather used as a pen; any sharp pointed object, e.g. prickles growing on the backs of certain animals.

quilt (1) bed-covering filled with wool or feathers *sewn* (*to sew* = use a needle and thread) across many times so as to keep the inside material in place; **quilted** (———1) made like a quilt.

quince (1-s) hard fruit like an apple.

quin'ine (1-11) bitter medicine got from the *cinchona* tree used for fever.

quinque- five, e.g. **quinqu'ennial** (1-2-19) happening every five years.

quins (1-z) **quintuplets** (1-17-1) five children born of the same mother at the same time.

quinsy (1-zI) poisoned swelling in the throat.

quintal (1) a measure, 101 pounds.

quint'essence (1-2-s) real nature of a thing; perfect example of something, e.g. *The — of politeness*.

quip (1) clever saying.

quire (419) twenty-four sheets of paper.

quisling (IzlI) person of the country who is set up by an enemy to rule that country.

quit (1) go away from; *He quitted (acquitted) himself well* = behaved —; Sl. **a quitter** (1-9) one who gives up a piece of work before it is finished; one who is afraid.

quite (41) (1) completely, in all ways, e.g. *To feel quite well*; (2) almost, rather, e.g. *Your boy is quite a man now*; *She's quite pretty*; *Oh quite!* = I agree.

quit(s) (1) free; *We're quits* = neither owes the other anything.

quiver (1-9) case in which arrows are carried.

quiver (1-9) to shake.

qu'i v'ive (kiI + II) *To be on the qui vive* = awake and on the watch.

quix'otic (1-5-1) generous; full of imagination, and taking no care of one's own business interests.

quiz (1) to question; *A quiz* = game in which groups of persons try to answer more questions than the other group.

quoit (k5I) ring for throwing over a small post as part of a game.

quondam (5-3) at one time, but not now, e.g. *Quondam friends*.

quorum (55-9) number of persons who must be present at a meeting according to the rules.

quota (67-9) share which one must receive (or pay); amount of goods which any one nation may send into a certain foreign country.

quote (67) repeat the words of another person, saying whose words they are; speak of some person as a supporter of one's opinion or tell some fact or event which serves as an example; tell what the price of a thing will be; **quot'ation** (67-2Ishn) *marks* = " ".

quoth he (67 + II) said he.

quotient (67shn) number of times one number can be divided into another.

R

rabbi (3-41) Jewish teacher or priest.
rabbit (3-1) small common animal with long ears, which lives in a hole in the ground.
rabble (3) crowd of low noisy people.
rabid (3-1) mad, e.g. mad with anger; **rabies** (21-11z) serious illness caused by the bite of a mad dog.

RABBIT

race (21s) an attempt to move faster than another, e.g. *Horse-races*; strong stream of water; **to race**, try to win by running faster; move very quickly.
race (21s) group of people or animals of the same blood; class of persons or living things; adj. **racial** (21sh9).
rack (3) to stretch; cause great pain to; *a rack*, frame fixed to the wall on which things are kept, e.g. for drying; frame of wood and string on which light bags, etc., are put in a railway carriage; *Rack and pinion* = toothed bar moved along by a toothed wheel (= *pinion*).
racket (3-1) noisy talk and play; Am. dishonest trick done by a group of bad men to get money; Am. **r′acket′eer** (3-1-19) one who arranges such dishonest tricks.
racquet, racket (3-1) instrument used for hitting the ball in *tennis*.
racy (21s1) full of life.
radar (21-44) way of seeing aeroplanes, etc., by means of electric waves *reflected* from the thing and seen on a bright glass plate.
radiate (21-121) send out light or heat; *A radiant* (21-19) *smile* = showing great happiness.
radiator (21-121-9) instrument for sending out heat in a house; instrument for cooling the engine of a motor-car.
radical (3-1) from or of the root; *Radical changes* = thorough, complete —; *A radical* (in government) = person who wishes to make great changes in the government of the country.
radio (21-167) sending out of music, speech or messages through the air by means of electrical waves; **r′adio′active,** behaving like *radium* (see 2nd below); **radi′ography,** taking *X-ray* photographs.
radish (3-1) red root with a hot taste.
radium (21-19) very costly metal which changes very slowly, giving off light and electricity as it does so.
radius (21-19) straight line from the centre of a circle to the *circumference* (= line round the edge of a circle).
raffia (3-19) long pieces of soft paper-like substance from a plant, used to make baskets, mats, etc.
raffle (3) sale in which each person pays a small part of the value of a thing and a name is drawn by chance to decide who shall become the owner.
raft (44) large pieces of wood joined together to make a rough flat boat.
rafter (44-9) one of the main beams of a roof.
rag (3) bit of cloth; **ragged** (3-1) torn; dressed in bad torn clothes; **ragamuffin** (3-9-8-1) boy dressed in ragged clothes; Sl. *To rag a person* = make a person angry for one's own amusement.
rage (21j) wild uncontrolled anger; *Large hats are all the rage* = everyone is wearing or buying —.
r′agtag and b′obtail (3-3 + 5-21) all sorts of people of the worst kind.
raid (21) sudden attack.
rail (21) cross-bar of a fence; **the rails** (———z) iron bars on which a train runs; *To go by rail* = go by train; *To go off the rails* = go wrong, do wrong; **railing,** bars put up to stop people from falling off stairs, off a cliff, etc.; *Railhead* = end of the railway, where it stops or begins.
rail (against) (21) speak angrily to or about a person.
raillery (21-9-1) laughing at a person in a good-tempered way.
railway (21-21) Am. **railroad** (21-67) lines and track on which a train runs; lines, trains, stations and all things used in carrying people and goods by train.
raiment (21-9) clothing.
rain (21) water falling from the clouds.
rainbow (21-67) many-coloured arch of light in the sky.
raise (21z) lift up; produce or cause to grow, e.g. *To raise sheep*; *To raise an army* = collect and prepare an army; Sl. *To raise a dust, the roof, etc.* = make trouble; *To raise Cain* = make great trouble; *To raise the money* = get the money; *To raise the offer* = increase —; *To raise the question* = bring up and talk about —; Am. *A raise* = increase of one's pay.
raisin (21z) dried *grape* (= fruit from which wine is made).
r′aison d′′être (21z5ⁿ + 21-9) reason which explains why a thing was made or continues to remain.
raja(h) (44-9) Indian ruler.
rake (21) instrument with teeth fixed to a cross-bar, used for drawing together leaves, dry grass, etc.; **to rake,** use a rake; *Rake out* = discover by searching; *Rake up* = cause people to remember things better forgotten; *Rake a ship with fire* = shoot at from end to end.

rake (21) slope of a floor or *mast* (= upright pole carrying sails).

rake (21) man of bad character.

rake-off (21 + 5) Sl. dishonest gain by a person who is selling or buying something for another person.

rally (3-1) bring together the scattered soldiers of an army; **a rally**, meeting, e.g. of Boy Scouts.

rally (3-1) talk to and laugh at a person; get back one's strength after an illness.

ram (3) male sheep.

ram (3) any heavy instrument used for pushing or striking with great force, e.g. in order to break open a door or break down the wall of a castle; pointed front of a warship with which it strikes another ship; **to ram**, strike with a ram; run a ship into another; push into, e.g. *He rammed his clothes into a bag.*

ramble (3) walk about in the country; talk in a foolish wandering way; **rambler** (3-9) climbing rose-tree with groups of small flowers.

ramify (3-1-41) spread out in branches.

ramp (3) sloping place, e.g. in a fort.

ramp (3) stand up on the back legs like a horse; *Ramping and raging* = angry and making much noise and movement; **rampant**, standing upon the back feet; not controlled, e.g. *Disease is rampant in that part of the town.*

ramp (3) Sl. dishonest attempt to get money out of a person.

ramp'age (3-21j) *Be on the rampage* = run about wildly in great excitement.

rampart (3-44) bank made to defend a fort or castle against attack.

ramrod (3-5) stick used for pushing gunpowder and shot into an old kind of gun.

ramshackle (3-3) (house) nearly falling down.

ran (3) p.t. of Run.

ranch (44) large cattle farm.

rancid (3-s1) (fat or oil) bad, decayed.

rancour (3ngk9) deep-rooted, unforgiving hatred.

random (3-9) without order or plan, by chance.

rani (44-11) Indian queen.

rang (3) p.t. of Ring.

range (21nj) (1) set things in line, e.g. *He ranged his soldiers in order of size*; (2) put oneself in a certain class, e.g. *Range oneself on the side of law and order*; (3) be stretched out, e.g. *The forest ranges from A to B*; to wander about, e.g. *Beasts ranging in the forest*; (4) to change between certain fixed points, e.g. *The prices range from 5p to 50p*; n. **range** (1) line, e.g. *A range of mountains*; (2) distance, e.g. *Beyond the range of my voice* = too far for —; (3) *A wide range of prices* = many different prices; (4) large iron fireplace used for cooking.

range-finder (21nj + 41-9) instrument used by soldiers to find how far away the enemy is and so aim guns correctly.

ranger (21nj9) wanderer; **bush-ranger** (7+) one who protects a forest from fire.

rank (3ngk) single line of soldiers; certain class or level; *Rank and file* = common soldiers, people, etc.; *He rose from the ranks* = he was of common birth but became great; **to rank**, put in a rank; have an opinion as to the value of; *To rank with* = take place among, be considered equal to.

rank (3ngk) growing roughly and in plenty, e.g. grass in a wet place; bad-smelling; *Rank dishonesty* = complete, very bad —.

rankle (3ngk) continue to cause anger or pain.

ransack (3-3) search thoroughly.

ransom (3-9) pay money so as to set a prisoner free.

rant (3) noisy meaningless speech.

rap (3) strike with a sharp quick blow; Sl. *I don't care a rap* = not at all.

rap'acious (9-21shg) seizing by force; seizing everything possible.

rape (21) seed from which oil is made.

rapid (3-1) moving quickly; **a rapid**, place in a stream where the water is swift and rough.

rapier (21-19) long thin sword.

rapine (3-41) carrying off goods by force, as by soldiers attacking a city.

rapport (3-55) close relationship with, and understanding of each other.

rapt (3) lost in thought.

rapture (3-tshg) delight; great joy.

rare (29) thin, e.g. air; not often found and therefore valuable; *To have a rare time* = enjoy oneself greatly; Am. lightly cooked (meat); **rarely** (——1) not often.

rascal (44) bad man; (used 1 layfully) fellow.

rash (3) foolishly daring.

rash (3) redness of the skin caused by illness.

rasher (3-9) thin piece of bacon (= salted pig-meat).

rasp (44) instrument used for rubbing away or smoothing wood, metal, etc.; *A rasping voice* = rough sounding.

RASPBERRY

raspberry (44z-9-1) small red fruit containing many seeds; Sl. *Give the* —, *Give him a* —, *Blow a* — — = put one's tongue out and make a rude noise as a sign of disrespect.

rat (3) animal like a mouse, but larger; *To smell a rat* = think that some secret plan is being made, feel doubtful; **to rat**, to desert one's party; Sl. *Rats!* = I do not believe it.

ratchet (3-1) toothed wheel with a bar resting on it allowing it to go round only in one direction.

RATCHET

rate (21) amount of one thing measured in relation to another, e.g. *The birth rate* = number of births considered in relation to the number of the people; *Rate of travel* = distance travelled in a certain time; *The rates* = money paid by householders to the government of the town in which the house is; -rate, e.g. *First-rate* = very good; *Second-rate* = not very good; **to rate**, consider; fix a relationship; decide the quality of.

rate (21) speak angrily to.

rather (44ð9) (1) not very, e.g. *Rather good* = good, but not very good; *Rather better* = slightly —; *Rather!* = certainly; (2) *I would rather have this than that* = I like this better, I want this more than that.

ratify (3-1-4I) to settle, to fix, e.g. a written agreement.

rating (21-I) class to which a thing (e.g. ship) belongs; *Naval ratings* = men other than officers on a warship.

ratio (21sh167) number of times one quantity contains another, e.g. *The ratio of 2 and 8 is one to four, or a quarter.*

ration (3sh9) fixed amount of (food) given each (day); **to ration**, give a fixed quantity each day.

rational (3sh9-9) reasonable, having common sense.

rattle (3) make a noise as of shaking stones in a tin; *To rattle along* = go fast; *Rattle off (one's lessons)* = do quickly, say quickly; **a rattle**, instrument for making a rattling noise; **rattlesnake** (3-21) American snake which makes a noise with its tail; **a r'attle trap** (+ 3) old noisy carriage or motor-car.

raucous (voice) (55-9) unpleasant sounding like the tired voice of one who has been shouting.

ravage (3-1j) destroy everything in (a country).

rave (21) talk and behave in a mad way; *To rave about* = say that a person or thing is wonderful.

ravel (3) twist together (threads); **unravel**, **ravel out**, untwist, become untwisted (threads), make (become) clear (difficulties).

raven (21) large very black bird.

ravenous (3-1-9) very hungry.

rav'ine (9-11) long deep narrow valley.

ravish (3-1) carry away by force; **ravishing** (——1) very charming.

raw (55) uncooked, unprepared; (of a part of the body) having no skin on it, painful; (of weather, wind) cold and wet.

ray (21) beam of light; large flat sea-fish.

rayon (215) silk-like material, obtained by special treatment of wood made into a liquid by acid, and pressed through very small holes.

raze (21) to level to the ground.

razor (21-9) knife used for cutting hair off the face.

re, in re (11) concerning, on the subject of.

re- again, e.g. **r'et'ell** (11-2) to tell again.

reach (11) (1) to stretch out; (2) obtain by stretching out the hand; (3) arrive at a place; get what one wishes; (4) be stretched out as far as, e.g. *The garden reaches down to the river; Beyond my reach* = too far, not obtainable; *The reach of a river* = straight piece of river; *A reach-me-down* = piece of *ready-made* clothing (see 4th below).

reach (11) **retch** (2) make the sound or movement of being sick (throwing up food from the stomach).

re'act (11·3) to act in return; to act as the result of an act; **re'action** (11·3-shn) movement coming as a result of, or answer to, some exciting cause; returning to the condition of things before a change was made; *What was his reaction to it?* = what did he seem to feel or think when he saw (or heard) it?; **re'actionary** (11·3-sh9-9-I) one who wishes to return to things as they were.

read (11) p.t. **read** (2) get ideas from print or writing; to study; *My reading of the law is* = I understand the law to mean.

ready (2-1) prepared; near at hand, easily obtained; *I am ready to go anywhere* = willing —; *Ready-made clothes* = not made specially for the buyer; *To pay ready money* = pay at once, not owe; *Ready-reckoner* = book of tables of figures which saves the trouble of *reckoning* (= calculating).

real (19) actual; true; *Real-estate* = houses, land, etc.; **realist** (19-1) one who believes in painting or describing things exactly as they really are; **re'ality** (11·3-1-1) state of being real; real, not imaginary, thing; **realize** (19-41) make real; understand as being real; get money for things owned; **really** (19-1) truly, in fact; *Really!*—expresses surprise, doubt or anger according to the way in which the word is said.

realm (2) kingdom.

ream (11) 480 sheets of paper; **to ream**, make a hole in metal larger.

reap (11) cut and gather in a crop.

rear (19) back part; back part of an army.

rear (19) to set up on end; rise up on the back legs, as a horse does; to nurse and bring up young.

reason (11z) cause for belief; power of thinking; **to reason**, consider facts and get from them some meaning, idea or result; **to reason with**, talk to a person in order to make him accept one's ideas; **reasonable** (11z-9) having common sense, willing to listen to reasoning.

rebate (11-21) small lessening of the price.

rebel (2) one who fights, e.g. against the government; **to reb'el** (1-2) fight against (the government).

reb'ound (1-47) to jump back from, e.g. a ball from a wall.

reb'uff (1-8) *To get a* —— = be treated rudely when one is trying to be friendly.

reb'uke (1-177) find fault with; to blame.

reb'ut (1-8) push back; prove what has been said to be wrong.

rec'alcitrant (1-3-sI-9) refusing to obey.

rec'ant (1-3) say that one no longer believes in a former opinion.

recap'itulate (11-9-1-17-21) repeat the chief ideas of a speech in a few words.

recede (1s11) go back; slope back.

rec'eipt (1s11) a receiving; paper showing that money has been paid.

rec'eive (1s11) take, get, accept; *To receive a person* = allow a person to visit and talk to one.

recent (11s) happening not long ago.

rec'eptacle (1s2-9) any vessel or container.

rec'eption (1s2-shn) act of receiving; meeting at which many guests are received.

rec'eptionist (1s2-shg-1) man or woman who receives people in a hotel; woman who receives those visiting a doctor, etc.

rec'ess (1s2) space hollowed out; break in school work when the children go out to play.

rec'ession (1s2shn) weakening of trade and so less buying and selling.

recipe (2s1-1) paper telling how to mix and make a cake or other form of food.

rec'ipient (1s1-19) one who receives.

rec'iprocal (1s1-9) done or given to each other.

rec'iprocate (1s1-9-21) have an effect upon each other; give and take; *A reciprocating engine* = engine in which steam or gas causes a part to move backwards and forwards (see Piston).

r'ecipr'ocity (2s1-5s1-1) arrangement to give and take, or to buy and sell, from each other.

rec'ite (1s41) say from memory; tell; a **rec'ital**, *performance* of music by one person, or of the music of one writer; a saying of poetry in public.

reck (2) *Reck nothing of* = not care about, not be afraid of; **reckless** (2-1) careless about the results; not caring about danger.

reckon (2-9) to count; consider; make accounts; calculate; Am. think.

recl'aim (1-21) bring back, e.g. a person from wrong, land from the sea.

recl'ine (1-41) lie down.

recl'use (1-77) person who lives alone and does not like meeting people.

recognize (2-9-41) know again; accept as true or real, or as belonging to oneself; n. **recogn'ition** (2-9-1shn).

rec'oil (1-51) (of a gun) to spring backwards after firing; draw back from.

r'ecoll'ect (2-9-2) remember.

r'ecomm'end (2-9-2) speak in favour of; advise.

recompense (2-9-2) something given as a return for good (or evil) done to the giver.

reconcile (2-9-s41) make friends again; *He is reconciled to living here* = he did not like — at first but is getting used to it.

rec'ondite (1-5-41) very learned and difficult to understand.

r'econn'oitre (2-9-51-9) find out where the enemy is, his numbers, the general nature of the land, etc.; n. **a rec'onnaissance** (1-5-1-9-s).

rec'ord (1-55) to set down in writing; to set down sounds on a flat plate (a *gramophone* (= talking machine) record); **a r'ecord** (2-55) writing so done; plate used in playing on a gramophone; *To break (make) a record* = do something better, quicker, etc., than anyone else has done it.

r'ec'ount (11-47) count again; **to rec'ount** (1-47) tell (a story).

rec'oup (1-77) get back money lost; make a gain which pays back a former loss.

rec'ourse (1-55) *To have recourse to* = turn to — for help.

rec'over (1-8-9) get back again; become well again after illness.

recreant (2-19) person who is afraid and does not keep his promises.

recre'ation (2-12Ishn) rest or amusement after work.

recr'iminate (1-1-1-21) blame each other.

r'ecrud'escence (11-77-2-s) breaking out again, e.g. of war, illness, trouble.

recr'uit (1-77) person who has just joined, e.g. the army; **to recr'uit**, get soldiers for the army; collect helpers; get new strength, e.g. by rest and good food.

rectangle (2-3ngg) four-sided figure, having opposite sides equal, and four equal angles.

rectify (2-1-41) to set right, e.g. a mistake.

rectitude (2-1-177) honesty.

rector (2-9) man in charge of a church; head of a large school.

rec'umbent (1-8-9) lying down.

rec'uperate (1-177-9-21) get well after an illness.

rec'ur (1-99) come back again; happen again; adj. **rec'urrent** (1-8).

recusant (2-17z9) refusing to obey.

red (2) colour of blood; *Red Cross* = sign used by those who care for the wounded in war; *Draw a red herring across the trail* = bring some new subject into a talk so that people may not speak about a certain other subject; *Red-hot*, metal (etc.) so hot that it shines red; *Red-letter day* = feast day; *Redskin* = American Indian; *Red tape* = mass of silly rules delaying business; *Caught red-handed* = caught while actually doing some deed; *In the red* = owing money to the bank.

Red (2) of Russia, of Communism; *A Red* = communist; *The Red Army* = Russian army.

Red-cap (+ 3) army policeman; railway *porter* (= man who carries boxes and bags) in U.S.A.

red'eem (1-11) bring back; pay off a debt; buy the freedom of a person; save from the punishment of evil-doing; *A redeeming feature* = something good in a thing which is bad in all other ways; n. **red'emption** (1-2-shn).

redolent (2-9-9) smelling of.

red'oubt (1-47) small fort.

red'ound (1-47) be a result; *It redounds to his credit* = it adds to his good name.

redr'ess (1-2) setting right of a wrong, or repayment for loss caused by it.

red'uce (1-177s) make less; break up into parts. e.g. *To reduce pounds to pence*; to conquer; n. **red'uction** (1-8-shn).

red'undant (1-8-9) more than is necessary.

reed (11) tall grass-like plant found in wet places; (of musical instrument) that part which shakes and makes the sound when the breath passes over it; *A broken reed* = helper who cannot be trusted.

reef (11) part of a sail which can be rolled up; line of rocks in the sea; **reefer** (——9) short coat; Sl. cigarette which contains *marijuana* (= hashish).

reek (11) smell strongly of.

reel (11) (1) frame or roller on which string (or any long band) is kept; (2) a dance; **to reel off**, pull quickly off a reel; tell something quickly and easily; **to reel along**, walk as if drunk with wine.

ref'ectory (1-2-9-1) large room in which meals are served to many people.

ref'er (1-99) (1) point to as a cause; (2) pass on a matter to some other person; *Let us refer the matter to Mr. X* = ask Mr. X to settle it; *He referred me to X* = told me to ask —; *To refer to a book* = look in a book for a certain fact; *This rule does not refer to girls* = girls need not keep this rule; *He referred to me in his speech* = spoke of —; **refer'ee** (2-9-11) judge, e.g. in a game; **reference** (2-9-s) act of referring; thing referred to (see above); *A book of reference* = book to which one turns to find facts, e.g. dictionary, book of maps, etc; **refer'endum** (2-9-2-9) asking all the people of a country to give an opinion on a law or question of government.

refine (1-41) make pure; **refined** (of a person) very polite, having a nice mind.

refl'ect (1-2) throw back light as from a looking-glass; think; *To cast reflections on* = say bad things about.

reflex (11-2) bent back; *A reflex action* = action done without meaning to do it and without power to prevent it, e.g. shutting the eyes at a flash of light.

ref'orm (1-55) to change and make better; **reformatory** (1-55-9-9-1) school for young wrong-doers; n. **reform'ation** (2-9-21shn).

refr'act (1-3) to bend a beam of light, e.g. by passing it through a three-sided glass.

refr'actory (1-3-9-1) troublesome and unwilling to obey; **a refr'actory**, **refr'actory (material)** (1-3-9-1) substance which stands well against great heat, e.g. in a *furnace* (= fire) for melting iron.

refr'ain (1-21) part of a song which is repeated.

refr'ain (1-21) *To refrain from doing* = not to do, prevent oneself doing.

refr'esh (1-2) make fresh; get new strength; **refr'eshments** (——9) food and drink.

refr'igerator (1-1j9-21-9) machine which keeps food cold.

refuge (2-17jj) a shelter; **refug'ee** (2-17j11) one who seeks shelter from danger, e.g. in a foreign land.

ref'und (11-8) pay back.

ref'use (1-177z) be unwilling to do or give what is asked.

refuse (2-177) waste matter.

ref'ute (1-177) *disprove* (= prove not to be true); n. **refut'ation** (2-17-21shn).

regal (11) as of a king; **reg'alia** (1-21-19) signs of kingship used when a king is crowned, e.g. the crown, jewelled sword, etc., etc.

reg'ale (1-21) supply with and cause to enjoy (e.g. food, music).

reg'ard (1-44) look at; consider; to respect; *In regard to* = in respect of, concerning; *My regards* = my good wishes; **reg'ardless** (——1) without thinking of; careless of, e.g. of the cost.

reg'atta (1-3-9) meeting of many people for boat races.

regent (11j9) one who rules a country until a child-king is old enough to rule it himself or if the real king is mad.

reg'enerate (1j2-9-21) make better after decay; cause to grow again and better.

reg'ime (21311) way of governing; the government.

regimen (21311) **reg'ime** (21311) fixed plan of food, sleep, etc., in order to bring a person back to health.

regiment (2j1-9) group of four companies of soldiers—about 1,000 men; **to regiment** (2j1-2) arrange people in groups, make them obey many rules, treat them as if they were soldiers.

region (11j9) part of the country; space round a certain place.

register (2j1-9) written list, e.g. *A register of births* = book in which — are written, list of —; instrument for showing an amount, e.g. of heat, light, etc.; *The register of the voice* = range; **to register**, write down in a register; *To register surprise* = show on the face (as in moving-pictures); *To register a letter* = pay an amount of money so that a valuable letter may be taken through the post with special care; **registr'ar** (2j1-44) officer who registers; **r'egistry** (2j1-1) office for registering; *Registry office* = place where people may be married—it also keeps a list of births and deaths; office which keeps a list of servants needing employment; **registr'ation** (2j1-21shn) act of causing a thing to be written in a register.

regr'et (1-2) grief for a mistake or wrong done.

regular (2-17-9) according to rule; not changing; *The regular army* = that part of the army which is kept always ready for war (not those

regurgitate   257   **reminiscence**

men called up from time to time); *A regular slave* = complete —; **to regulate** (2-17-21) to make according to rule; *To regulate a clock* = make it keep good time.

reg'urgitate (1-99j1-21) pour out again, e.g. from the stomach.

rehab'ilitate (11-9-1-1-21) to put back in his former office, to clear from blame; make strong enough (after illness) to do his usual work again.

rehearse (1-99) repeat aloud; practise a play; n. **rehearsal**.

reign (21) rule as a king; n. rule; time of rule.

reimburse (11-1-99) pay back.

reins (21-z) leather bands used in driving a horse.

r'einc'arnate (11·1-44-21) be born again.

reindeer (21-19) kind of deer with large horns, found in cold parts of northern Asia and northern Europe.

r'einf'orce (11·1-55s) bring up new forces, e.g. move soldiers up to help the front line in a battle; make stronger; *Reinforced concrete* = stone-like material with iron bars in it.

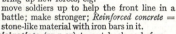

REINDEER

r'einst'ate (11·1-21) to put back as before.

re'iterate (11·1-9-21) repeat.

rej'ect (1-2) throw back; to refuse.

rej'oice (1-51s) feel or show gladness.

rej'oin (1-51) return to a person or persons after being separated; to answer; **rej'oinder** (——9) an answer.

rej'uvenate (1-77-1-21) make young again.

rel'apse (1-3) fall back into evil or illness.

rel'ate (1-21) tell (a story); show the relation between; **rel'ation** (1-21shn) (1) joining of two things, e.g. *The relation between cause and effect; The relation of the weather to the quality of crops*; (2) way in which persons are united, or the effect which they have on each other, e.g. *My relations with him are quite friendly*; (3) member of one's family; (4) a telling or account, e.g. *The relation of a story*; **r'elative** (2-9-1) being in some way joined to; having an effect on or resulting from; having to do with; *Relatively (large)* = (large) when considered with other things; *The relative duties of master and servant* = their duties to each other; **a relative**, a family relation; **relat'ivity** (2-9-1-1-1) state of being relative.

rel'ax (1-3) loosen; become loose; **relax'ation** (11-3-21shn) rest, amusement.

rel'ay (1-21) supply of fresh men or horses to take over work from tired ones; *To rel'ay* (11-21) *a message* = receive and send on again.

rel'ease (1-11) to set free; give up; allow a thing to be made public.

relegate (2-1-21) send away; to put in a lower place.

rel'ent (1-2) become less hard or cruel; **rel'entless** (——1) without pity.

relevant (2-9-9) concerned with the matter being considered.

rel'iable (1-41-9) able to be trusted; **rel'iance** (1-41-9-s) act or state of trusting.

relic (2-1) thing left, e.g. *This custom is a relic of a by-gone age* = is an old custom which still remains; *Sacred relics* = parts of some holy thing, e.g. the bone of some very good man.

rel'ief (1-11) *Figures cut in relief* = shapes of men, etc., made to stand out from the surface of stone by cutting away the rest of the surface; *A relief map* = map in which the mountains stand out, and seas, lakes, etc., are shown as below the surface.

rel'ief (1-11) (1) lessening of pain or trouble; (2) help given to the poor, e.g. *Outdoor relief* = help given to poor persons in their own homes; (3) driving away of an enemy which is attacking a town; (4) being set free from a duty; person who takes over one's work to set one free.

rel'ieve (1-11) (1) make pain or trouble less; *To relieve one's feelings* = express one's feelings in some way, e.g. by weeping, and so make them easier to bear; (2) drive away an enemy attacking a town; (3) set a person free from duty; (4) *To relieve a person of his money* = take away, steal; (5) make less uninteresting, less same, e.g. *To relieve the dullness of the evening with a few songs* = break the sameness and uninterestingness of —.

rel'igion (1-1j9) all those acts, feelings and beliefs which are concerned with doing one's duty to God; adj. **rel'igious** (1-1j9).

rel'inquish (1-1ng-1) to yield, give up.

relish (2-1) taste; thing used to give taste to food; have a taste or liking for.

rel'uctant (1-8-9) unwilling.

rel'y (on) (1-41) depend on; to trust.

rem'ain (1-21) be left after part has been taken or destroyed; continue to be; **rem'ains** (——z) parts left; **rem'ainder** (1-21-9) rest; what is left.

rem'and (1-44) send back to prison until the *trial* (= examining of a prisoner in a court of law) is carried on again.

rem'ark (1-44) (1) to notice; (2) speak about; **a rem'ark**, saying drawing attention to something; **rem'arkable** (——9) worthy of notice.

remedy (2-1-1) anything used to cause a person to get well (get health again) from illness; setting right of a wrong; **to remedy**, set right.

rem'ember (1-2-9) to have in mind; not to forget; *He wishes to be remembered to you* = he sends his greetings; **rem'embrance** (——9-s) act of remembering, thing which causes one to remember.

rem'ind (1-41) cause to remember.

remin'iscence (2-1-1-s) remembering; *My*

reminiscences = my memories, the written story of the interesting things which I remember in my life.

rem'iss (1-1) careless, not attending to duty.

rem'ission (1-1shn) freeing from debt; forgiveness; **to rem'it** (1-1) forgive; *To remit money* = send.

rem'ittance (1-1-s) sending of money; money sent; *A remittance man* = man living in a distant country on money sent to him from home.

rem'ittent (fever) (1-1) sometimes becoming better or less, sometimes worse.

remnant (2-9) small piece left over.

rem'onstrate (1-5-21) complain against; show reasons against.

rem'orse (1-55) grief for one's wrong-doing.

rem'ote (1-67) distant.

rem'ove (1-77) move to another place; take away, e.g. a cause of pain; *My first cousin once removed* = child of my first *cousin* (= child of my father's or mother's brother or sister).

rem'unerate (1-177-9-21) to pay for work or loss.

Ren'aissance, The (9-21-9-s) that time when a new interest in learning arose in Europe, about 1300 to 1500.

renal (11) having to do with the *kidneys* (= parts of the body which separate waste matter from the blood and pass it out of the body in the water).

rend (2) to tear.

render (2-9) give, e.g. *Render good for evil*; *Render an account of* = tell about; *Account rendered* = bill sent asking for payment of money; *Render useless* = make useless; *To render the meaning of* = explain; *Render from English into Latin* = write the meaning of the English in Latin; *Render help* = give help to; *Rendering of a part in a play* = way of acting —.

rendezvous (5-1-77) agreed place of meeting.

rend'ition (2-1shn) act of giving back to the lawful owner; a *rendering* (see 2nd above).

renegade (2-1-21) one who changes his religion; one who deserts the group or army to which he belonged.

ren'ew (1-177) make fresh and new again.

ren'ounce (1-47-s) say that one does not own; give up all claim to.

renovate (2-6-21) make like new.

ren'own (1-47) fame.

rent (2) a tear, e.g. in cloth.

rent (2) money paid for the use of (a house); **rental**, the amount demanded as rent.

renunciation (1-8-s1z1shn) giving up (n. of Renounce, 5th above).

rep'air (1-29) to put into good condition again after being damaged; *He repaired to Paris* = went to —; **r'eparable** (2-9-9) which can be repaired; **repar'ations** (2-9-21shnz) payment to set right damage done.

repart'ee (2-44-11) quick, clever answer.

rep'ast (1-44) meal.

rep'atriate (11-3-121) send back to his own country.

rep'eal (a law) (1-11) make (a law) of no further force, end it.

rep'eat (1-11) say or do again; **rep'eatedly** (1-11-1-1) again and again; often.

rep'el (1-2) drive back (an enemy); push back; **rep'ellent** (1-2-9) causing dislike.

rep'ent (1-2) feel sorry for having done (wrong).

reperc'ussion (11-9-8shn) beating back; act of coming back after going out, e.g. when a ball strikes a wall; far-reaching effect.

repertoire (2-9tw44) **repertory** (2-9-9-1) set of plays which a company of actors has ready for acting (so also songs or other things which may be performed in public).

repet'ition (2-1-1shn) saying or doing again.

rep'iné (1-41) feel sad.

repl'ace (1-21s) to put back in its former place; give in the place of a thing lost or damaged.

repl'enish (1-2-1) fill up again; **repl'ete** (1-11) full.

replica (2-1-9) exact copy of a work of art.

repl'y (1-41) to answer; an answer.

rep'ort (1-55) tell about; account of; *There is a report that* — = people are saying that; *I shall report you* = tell (the teacher) about you; *A loud report* = noise, e.g. of a gun; **rep'orter** (1-55-9) one who gathers news for a newspaper.

rep'ose (1-67z) to rest, lie on.

rep'ository (1-5z1-9-1) shop; storehouse.

repreh'ensible (2-1-2-9) worthy of blame.

repres'ent (1zz) cause to be present in the mind, cause one to think of, or be a sign of, e.g. *A picture representing a ship*; *This mark on the map represents a city*; to act for, e.g. *Mr. X will represent me at the meeting*; *To represent one's grievances* = complain; a **repres'entative** (2-1zz-9-1) one who acts for another; *Representative government* = government by elected persons.

repr'ess (1-2) to beat down; to put under control.

repr'ieve (1-11) to free from punishment for a short time, or for all time.

reprimand (2-1-44) scold; to blame for a fault.

repr'isal(s) (1-41z-z) wrong done as repayment or punishment for wrong.

repr'oach (1-67) blame sadly or angrily; a **repr'oach**, thing which brings shame upon one.

reprobate (2-6-21) *disapprove* (= think a thing is bad) of; **a reprobate**, very bad person.

reprod'uce (11-9-177s) cause to be seen or heard again, e.g. a *gramophone* (= talking machine) reproduces sound; (2) make a perfect copy of a thing; (3) bring children (or young) into the world; n. **reprod'uction** (11-9-8shn).

repr'ove (1-77) speak to a person blaming him; scold; n. **repr'oof** (1-77).
reptile (2-41) cold-blooded egg-laying creature, e.g. a snake; low and evil person.
rep'ublic (1-8-1) country governed not by a king but by persons elected by the people.
repudiate (1-177-121) to say that a thing is not one's own; be unwilling to accept a gift; be unwilling to claim; say that one does not owe a debt.
rep'ugnant (1-8-9) greatly disliked; hateful.
rep'ulse (1-8) to drive back; treat with coldness a person who tries to be friendly; **rep'ulsive** (1-8-1) very ugly or unpleasant.
reput'ation (2-17-21shn) fame, good or bad; **reputable** (2-17-9) having a good name; worthy of trust; **rep'ute** (1-177) fame; *Reputed to be* = thought to be.
requ'est (1-2) ask; **a requ'est**, thing asked for; act of asking; *Much in request* = being asked for by many people.
requiem (2-12) *service* (= religious ceremony) of prayer for a dead person.
requ'ire (1-419) to need; **requisite** (2-121) necessary; **to requis'ition** (2-1zIshn) demand supplies for the use of, e.g. an army.
requ'ite (1-41) pay back good with good or evil with evil.
resc'ind (a law) (1-1) put an end to, cause (a law) to have no more force.
rescue (2-177) save from danger.
res'earch (1-99) scientific study in order to discover new facts.
res'emble (1zz) look like.
res'ent (1zz) show anger about.
res'erve (1z99) (1) keep back for future use, e.g. *Reserve one's strength*; (2) keep for the use of a particular person, e.g. *To reserve a seat in a theatre*; (3) *He is very reserved* = he does not show his feelings; n. **res'erve**, *His Company was in reserve* = was kept at the back of the army for use later in the battle; **a res'erve**, piece of country kept for a special purpose, e.g. for wild animals, e.g. in Africa; *To be sold without reserve* = at any price offered; *The well-known reserve of the English* = self-control, hiding their feelings; **r'eserv'ation** (2z9-21shn) part of the country set aside for a special people, e.g. Red Indians in America; *My reservation* = seat which I have ordered to be kept for me on an aeroplane or in a train; *I agree, with the reservation that* — = I agree, but only on the understanding that —; **reservoir** (2z9-744) large container built to hold water, e.g. all the water for a city.
res'ide (1z41) live in —; **residence** (2z1-s) house; **residency** (2z1-s1) house of a *Resident* (= officer of the British Government at the court of a Native Ruler in India or elsewhere);
resid'ential (2z1-2-shl)—*part of the town*, that part where there are houses, not shops.
residue (2z1-177) what is left; adj. **res'iduary** (1z1-179-1).

res'ign (1z41) give up an office; *To resign oneself to* = accept and suffer calmly; **resign'ation** (2z1-21shn) calm suffering without complaint.
res'ilient (1z1-19) springing back to its former place, like a stick bent and let go.
resin (2z1) sticky material which comes out of trees and later becomes hard, like yellow glass.
res'ist (1z1) stand against; try to prevent.
resolute (2z9-77) firmly decided.
res'olve (1z5) decide; *Resolve a doubt* = drive away — by making certain; *Resolve into* = change into a simpler form; **res'olved**, firmly decided; n. **resol'ution** (2z9-77shn).
resonant (2z9-9) deep sounding; sending sounds back as in a large empty hall.
res'ort (1z55) go to; turn to for help; *A seaside resort* = place near the sea to which people go for health and enjoyment.
res'ound (1z47) to ring with; send sounds back as in a large empty hall.
res'ource (1-55s) cleverness in finding a way of doing a thing; *My resources* = my money and all the things which may help me in doing what I want; **resourcefulness** (——1) cleverness in finding a way of carrying out one's plans.
resp'ect (1-2) (1) attention to, care of, e.g. *We should have respect for his wishes* = do as he wishes; *He is no respecter of persons* = he does what is right and is not moved by what (important) people say; (2) honour; *To pay respects to* = to visit and greet a person of higher rank; *In respect of* = concerning; *In all respects* = in all ways; *Self-respect* = proper regard for one's character and position; **to resp'ect**, show honour to; **resp'ectable** (——9) worthy of honour; of such size or importance as to be worth notice; of good character; **resp'ectful**, showing honour to; **resp'ecting**, concerning.
resp'ective (1-2-1) of each; *Let each go to his respective place* = to the place which belongs to him.
resp'ire (1-419) breathe; n. **respir'ation** (2-9-21shn).
respite (2-41) short pause in, e.g. work, pain, etc.
respl'endent (1-2-9) shining, very fine, splendid.
resp'onse (1-5) answer.
resp'onsible (1-5-9) trusted to do, in charge of, e.g. *He is responsible for it* = he will be blamed if things go wrong, he is trusted to make things go right; *A responsible person* = trustworthy person; *A responsible post* = important work needing a man who can be trusted.
resp'onsive (1-5-1) answering; showing results, e.g. showing feeling when spoken to with deep feeling.
rest (2) (1) a pause in work so as to get new strength; (2) place of rest; *Be laid to rest* = put

in a grave; *A rest* = instrument used to support or steady the hand; **to rest,** stop work; *Rest on* = be supported by; *Rest on one's oars* = stay quiet after heavy work, be satisfied with what one has done and do no more; *Everything rests on his answer* = depends on —; *It rests with you* = you must decide.

rest (2) *The rest* = that which still remains.

restaurant (2-9-5) eating-house.

restitu'tion (2-1-177shn) payment for damage done.

restive (2-1) **restless** (2-1) not willing or not able to stay still.

rest'ore (1-55) to put back as it was; build up again.

restr'ain (1-21) hold back; to control; n. **restr'aint.**

restr'ict (1-1) keep within a certain space or amount.

res'ult (1z8) that which is produced by a cause.

res'ume (1z177) begin again; continue after a pause; n. **res'umption** (1z8-shn).

résumé (2z17-21) short account of a speech, book, etc.

resurr'ection (2z9-2-shn) rising again from the dead.

res'uscitate (1-8-1-21) bring to life one who is almost dead.

ret'ail (11-21) sell goods in small quantities, as in a shop; adj. **retail,** selling only in small quantities.

ret'ain (1-21) to keep for or within oneself; **ret'ainer** (——9) (1) servant, (2) money paid to a lawyer so that one may be sure that he will work for one when necessary.

retal'iate (1-3-121) do evil to others as they have done to you.

ret'ard (1-44) cause a delay.

ret'ention (1-2-shn) a *retaining* (see 3rd above); **ret'entive** (——1) able to retain or keep; *A retentive memory* = good power of remembering.

reticent (2-1s) not telling; keeping things secret.

retina (2-1-9) back of the eye where light falls on the nerve-endings.

retinue (2-1-177) followers and servants of a prince or nobleman.

ret'ire (1-419) go back; go to bed; go away; give up one's work when one is old; *A retired spot* = quiet place far from noise or crowds; *He has a retiring nature* = is quiet, not eager to show himself or meet others.

ret'ort (1-55) quick or angry answer; bottle with a bent neck.

r'et'ouch (11-8) improve or repair a picture by small touches.

retr'ace (1-21s) go back over; *Retrace one's footsteps* = go back along the path by which one came.

retr'act (1-3) take back something said, say that it was not meant, or was not true.

r'etr'ead (a tyre) (11-2) put a new surface on the outside edge of a worn motor tyre.

retr'eat (1-11) go back from a battle; **a retr'eat** (1) act of going back, e.g. from an enemy; (2) place to which one goes for peace and quiet.

retr'ench (1-2) arrange to spend less money.

retribu'tion (2-1-177shn) punishment.

retr'ieve (1-11) get back something lost; **retr'iever** (1-11-9) dog which brings back shot birds to its master.

retro- backwards, e.g. **retrograde** (2-6-21) moving backwards; n. **retrogr'ession** (2-6-2shn) a moving backwards; n. **retrospect** (2-6-2) looking backwards; a considering of the past.

ret'urn (1-99) go back; give back; send back; elect a person to the government; *In return for* = as thanks for, as a payment of; *Small profits, quick returns* = if one asks a small price, the gain is small, but is quick; *Answer by return* = by the next post; *The return fare* = cost of travelling there and back again; *Many happy returns* (said on a birthday) = may you live long; *To make a return of (money spent, etc.)* = give a written account of.

rev'eal (1-11) make known what was hidden.

rev'eille (1-2-1) music which wakens soldiers in the morning.

revel (2) feast merrily; **revels** (——z), **revelry** (——1) merrymaking and feasting.

revela'tion (2-1-21shn) a *revealing* (see 3rd above); *It was quite a revelation to me* = I was surprised to hear, see —.

rev'enge (1-2nj) doing wrong to another as a punishment for wrong done by him to oneself.

revenue (2-1-177) money coming in, e.g. to the government.

rev'erberate (1-99-9-21) (of sound) be thrown back; continue to sound as in a large empty hall.

rev'ere (1-19) feel great respect for; **rev'erence** (2-9-s) feeling of great respect.

reverend (Rev.) (2-9) title of a priest, e.g. *Rev. George Smith*; worthy of great respect.

reverent (2-9) feeling or showing great respect.

reverie (2-9-1) day-dream.

rev'erse (1-99) turn the wrong way up; turn the other way round; *The reverse side* = the back; *To suffer a reverse* = be beaten in battle; *The reverse of* = opposite of.

rev'ert (1-99) go back to a former condition or subject; **rev'ersion** (1-99shn) giving back to the first owner; becoming as before.

rev'iew (1-177) look over a thing again; write an opinion on a book; weekly, monthly or three-monthly paper which gives opinions on new books, public events, etc.; *A review of the army* = grand show of the army which is seen by the king or officer of high rank.

rev'ile (1-41) use unkind language to; call cruel names.

rev'ise (1-41z) look over and correct a thing written.

rev'ive (1-41) come fully back to life; cause to —.

rev'oke (1-67) *To revoke an order* = say that it need not be fulfilled; (in playing cards) play a card of the wrong kind even though one has one of the kind needed.

rev'olt (1-67) rising of the people against the government; **rev'olting** (1-67-1) very nasty.

revol'ution (2-9-77shn) turning, e.g. of a wheel; sudden change of government.

revolve' (1-5) turn round and round.

revol'ver (1-5-9) pistol which holds six or more shots in a barrel which turns round after each shot is fired.

REVOLVER

rev'ue (1-177) amusing musical play with no story in it.

revul'sion (1-8-shn) sudden change of feeling, e.g. from love to hate.

rew'ard (1-55) something given in return for service, or as a sign that one is grateful.

rhapsody (3-9-1) poem or piece of music written when very excited.

rhetoric (2-9-1) art of good writing or speaking.

rheumatism (77-9-1z) disease causing painful swelling of the joints.

rhin'oceros (41-5s9-9) large animal.

rhubarb (77-44) garden plant, boiled and eaten; also used as a medicine for the stomach.

RHINOCEROS

rhyme (41) get the same sound at the ends of lines of poetry; *a rhyme*, two words ending with the same sound, e.g. *school, fool*.

rhythm (1ŏ) regular beat of poetry, music, or dancing.

rib (1) one of the curved bones of the breast; any narrow curved piece of material, e.g. as part of a boat or building; any narrow raised part of a surface, e.g. *Ribbed silk*.

ribald (1) low, unpleasant, e.g. song.

ribbon (1-9) narrow band, e.g. of silk; *Ribbon development* = building a lot of houses along the sides of a main road.

rice (41s) white grain boiled for food, very common in India and China; the plant.

rich (1) (1) having much money; (2) producing much, e.g. *Rich soil*; (3) of great cost or value, e.g. *Rich silks*; (4) (of food) fat, oily; (5) *Rich in* = containing much —; (6) (of colour) deep; Sl. *That's rich!* = is amusing; **riches** (——1z) wealth; **richly** (——1) *He richly deserves punishment* = he very much deserves —.

rick (1) heap of hay shaped like a small house.

rickets (1-1) disease in which the bones of children become soft.

rickety (1-1-1) not steady.

ricochet (1-9sh21) jumping of a *bullet* (= shot from a gun) when it hits the ground.

rid (1) *To get rid of* = get free of; *Good riddance* (——s) = I am glad to be free of it.

ridden (1) p.p. of Ride (3rd below); (*priest*)-*ridden* = too much under the control of —.

riddle (1) difficult or amusing question, e.g. " I always follow you, yet I am nothing: what am I? "—*Answer*, my shadow.

riddle (1) vessel with many holes in the bottom for shaking small things through and keeping back the larger; make many holes in.

ride (41) be carried on a horse or in a car or carriage; *Ship riding at anchor* = moving only up and down while held to the bottom by a weight and chain; *To ride rough-shod over* = treat a person roughly and with disrespect.

rider (41-9) something added to a written paper; extra piece of advice added to the judgment of a *jury* (= group of persons in a court of law who decide questions of fact).

ridge (1j) long narrow hill; any long narrow raised object.

ridicule (1-1-177) laugh at; **rid'iculous** (1-1-17-9) silly, laughable.

rife (41) found everywhere.

riff-raff (1 + 3) low common people.

rifle (41) gun such as a soldier uses.

rifle (41) to search through things in order to steal.

rift (1) a crack; narrow piece of clear sky.

rig (1) arrangement of sails on a ship; Sl. *My rig-out* = my clothes, etc.

rigging (1-1) ropes which hold up the sails and *masts* (= upright pole carrying the sails) on a ship.

right (41) (1) straight, e.g. *Go right on* = go straight on; *A right angle* = 90°; (2) correct, proper, e.g. *The right way to the town*; *To guess right*; *To put a machine right* = make it work well; (3) very completely; *Right sad we were* = we were very sad; *Turn right over* = completely —; *Right here, Right now* = just here, just now; (4) *Right hand* = that hand on the opposite side from the heart; (5) just, fair, according to law and good behaviour; **a right**, just claim, e.g. *I have a right to speak*; *By right of my office* = because of the power of —; **to right**, make right; to set up in the correct way, e.g. *To right a boat*; **r'ight-about** (turn) (+ 9-47) turn round and face the opposite way; **righteous** (41-19) just and good.

rigid (1j1) stiff.

rigmarole (1-9-67) long meaningless talk.

rigor (41-55) stiffening of the muscles; *rigor mortis* = such stiffening in a dead body.

rigour (1-9) hardness; unmercifulness; adj. **rigorous** (1-9-9).

rile (41) make angry.

rill (1) little stream.

rim (1) edge, e.g. of a cup.

rime (41) frozen drops of water seen on leaves or on the grass (etc.) in winter.

rind (41) outer covering of a fruit, of meat, or cheese.

ring (1) circular band, e.g. of gold, worn on the finger; circle of any metal or material; *The Ring* = place closed in with ropes in which two men *box* (= fight with their hands).

ring (1) cause a bell to sound; (of a bell) to sound; to sound out clearly like a bell; *To ring true* = show by sign or sound that it is true; *Ring the changes on* = give the same thing in different forms or different things in regular order; *To ring up* = call on a *telephone* (see —).

ringleader (1-11-9) leader of a group joined together for wrong-doing.

ringlet (1-1) small curl of hair.

ringworm (1-99) disease usually on the skin of the head causing circular hairless rings.

rink (1ngk) sheet of ice for *skating* (= moving on ice with iron blades fixed to the boots).

rinse (1) wash soap off; wash lightly.

riot (419) noise, disorder, and unlawful acts done by a crowd; disorderly behaviour.

rip (1) to tear; Sl. *Let things rip* = be careless of results; *A rip* = worthless fellow.

ripe (41) (of a fruit) ready to be eaten; **ripen**, make or become ripe.

ripping (1-1) Sl. very nice.

ripple (1) small wave.

rise (41z) (1) go up; stand up; get out of bed; *To rise again* = come back from being dead; (2) to increase, e.g. *The river is rising*; *To rise to an occasion* = show oneself able to deal with a specially difficult matter; *To rise up against the government* = begin to fight against —; (3) begin, e.g. *The river rises in those mountains*; a rise, *A rise of prices* = an increase; *A gentle rise* = small hill; *To give rise to* = to cause; Sl. *Take a rise out of* = deceive and laugh at a person; p.p. **risen** (1z).

risible (1z1) able to laugh; making people laugh.

risk (1) danger; *To run a risk* = put oneself in danger, be in danger of failing; **to risk**, take a chance; endanger a thing; adj. **risky** (1-1).

rissole (1-67) meat cut small and made into a roll.

rite (41) fixed form of prayer and song as in a church; any set of actions fixed by custom; **ritual** (1-179) set of rites or fixed forms; adj. having to do with rites.

rival (41) one who tries to do better than another, or to win something desired also by another.

river (1-9) wide stream.

rivet (1-1) thing like a nail with an end that is not very hard; **to rivet**, put a rivet through two pieces of metal and beat the soft end flat to hold them together.

rivulet (1-17-1) little river.

roach (67) fresh-water fish; Am. = *cockroach* (see —).

road (67) hard prepared way for carriages, etc.; *On the road* = travelling; *Get in one's road* = get in the way; prevent one doing what one wishes to do; **r'oad-hog** (+ 5) driver of a motor-car who goes too fast; **r'oad-metal** (+ 2) stones used in road-making.

roadstead (67-2) place near the shore where ships *anchor* (= stop and let down a hooked weight and chain to the bottom).

roadster (67-9) open motor-car for two persons.

roam (67) wander.

roan (67) (colour of a horse) dark brown.

roar (55) loud deep cry, as of a lion.

roast (67) to cook in front of an open fire or in a hot iron box; piece of meat cooked in this way.

rob (5) steal; steal by force; a **robber** (5-9) thief.

robe (67) long indoor garment.

robin (5-1) very common small bird with a red breast.

robot (67-5) machine made in the form of a man which works as a slave; any machine-like worker.

rob'ust (9-8) strong and healthy.

rock (5) large mass of stone; *On the rocks* = being in money-difficulties.

rock (5) move from side to side or backwards and forwards; **rockers** (5-9z) curved pieces of wood fixed to a chair, etc., which enable it to move in this way; **rockery** (——1) heap of stones or small rocks with flowers among them, as part of a garden.

rocket (5-1) stick shot into the air which lets out stars of coloured flame when it gets high up; object driven by burning gases, used as a weapon or to carry things into space, a rope to a wrecked ship, etc.; Sl. *I got a rocket* = was blamed and spoken to angrily.

rococo (9-67-67) much ornamented.

rod (5) straight bar or stick.

rode (67) p.t. of Ride.

rodent (67) animal like a mouse or rat.

rod'eo (67-21-67) gathering together of *cattle*; show of riding by *cowboys* (= cattle-drivers).

roe (67) small deer; female red deer; **roebuck** (67-8) male deer.

roe (67) eggs of a fish.

rogue (67) dishonest fellow; troublesome but playful child.

role (67) part taken by an actor.

roll (67) (1) move along by turning over and over; *Rolling in money* = very rich; (2) cause to roll; *To roll one's eyes* = move the eyes round; (3) flatten with a roller, e.g. *To roll the grass*; (4) make a deep sound, e.g. *The music rolled; He rolled out his speech*; *To roll a drum* = beat a drum with many quick blows; *To roll in* = come in large numbers; *To roll up* = form paper, etc., into a shape like a pipe; Sl. arrive unexpectedly; **a roll**, pipe of paper; very small loaf of bread; list; *Call the roll* = read out names to see if all are present; *To strike a lawyer off the rolls* = not allow him to work as a lawyer any more; **rolled gold** (+ 67) metal with a thin covering of gold on it.

roller (67-9) solid, pipe-shaped piece of iron or metal used for flattening grass or a path, or as a part of a machine.

rollicking (5-1-1) noisy and merry.

rolling-pin (67-1 + 1) round piece of wood used for rolling out paste for cooking.

roly-poly (67-1 + 67-1) pastry rolled up with *jam* (= fruit boiled in sugar) in it.

rom'ance (9-3-s) fanciful story, e.g. of knights; a love story; **a Rom'ance l'anguage** (+ 3ŋggwɪj) language which comes from Latin; **rom'antic** (——1) fanciful; dealing with love; *poetical* (adj. of poetry).

romp (5) (of children) play noisily; **rompers** (5-9z) clothes of a small child, made in one piece.

roof (77) outside upper covering of a house.

rook (7) large black bird; **rookery** (7-9-1) collection of the nests of such birds.

ROMPERS

rook (7) Sl. take away a person's money by a trick.

room (7 or 77) space; part of a house; **roomy** (——1) having plenty of space.

roost (77) bar on which hens sit at night; **to roost**, sit and sleep thus; **a rooster** (77-9) male form of hen; *To rule the roost* = be a leader and force others to obey.

root (77) underground part of a plant; that from which something grows; first cause or beginning; *The root of a word* = that part of a word to which endings are added to make other words; **square root** (29 +) e.g. $\sqrt{4} = 2$.

rope (67) very strong string-like thing, as used in ships; *The rope* = hanging as a punishment; *Know the ropes* = know the customs and arrangements; *Give him rope* = let a foolish person do what he wishes; **to rope**, tie with a rope; *To rope a person in* = make him join in one's plans.

rosary (67z9-1) string of *beads* (= small ornamental balls) used for counting the number of prayers said.

rosary (67z9-1) *rose*-garden (see 2nd below).

rose (67z) p.t. of Rise.

rose (67z) beautiful sweet-smelling flower; *It's not all roses* = having some unpleasant sides to it; *Under the rose* = secretly.

rosemary (67z-9-1) sweet-smelling bush.

ros'ette (67z2) piece of silk material in the shape of a rose to be fixed to the coat as an ornament, or sign of office; piece of stone so cut and shaped.

rosewood (67z-7) hard dark wood (not the wood of the rose-tree).

rosin (5zɪ) **resin** (2zɪ) sticky liquid from a tree which hardens into a yellow glass-like mass.

roster (67-9) list of persons showing the order in which they will do work.

rostrum (5-9) raised place for a speaker.

rosy (67zɪ) of light red colour; *The future is rosy* = seems hopeful.

rot (5) to decay; Sl. *Don't talk rot* = do not talk foolishly.

rotary (67-9-1) turning round; **to rot'ate** (67-21) turn round; cause to turn round; **rot'ation of cr'ops**, planting different things in a field each year, so as not to use up the food in the soil.

Rotary Club (+ 8) group of men, each having a different sort of work, who meet to exchange ideas.

rote (67) *To say by rote* = say from memory without thought of the meaning.

Rotodyne (67-9-4ɪ) flying machine which can leave and return to the ground without running along it. Trade name.

rotor (67-9) part inside a machine which turns round and round.

rotten (5) decayed; Sl. very bad; Sl. **a rotter** (5-9) useless bad person.

rot'und (67-8) round and fat.

rot'unda (67-8-9) round building.

rouge (773) red matter put on their faces by women.

rough (8f) (1) not smooth; (2) not level, e.g. *Rough country*; (3) full of uncontrolled force, e.g. *A rough sea*; *A rough game* = noisy fighting sort of game; Sl. *Rough house* = disorder and fighting; (4) not polite; *A rough diamond* = impolite person who is really kind; *A rough customer* = rude fellow who uses force; (5) unfinished, unpolished; *A rough draft of a letter* = first writing which will be made better later; *Rough and ready* = made in a hurry to serve for a short time only.

rough-cast (8f + 44) covered with very rough *plaster* (= liquid, containing little stones, which becomes hard).

roul'ette (77-2) game played with a wheel and a small ball falling into holes opposite numbers; the person who guesses the number wins money.

ROULETTE

round (47) *circular* (adj. of circle); *A round number* = number ending in 0; *A round game* = game in which all take part in turn; *The round trip* = journey there and back; *Rounded off* = nicely finished; *A postman's (doctor's) round* = course from house to house done each day; *The (second) round of a fight* = (second) meeting of fighters after a short rest; *To go round to* = go to see a friend; (trade) call for orders; *Not enough to go round* = not enough for all; *All round the house* = in a circle about the house; *He shot 20 rounds* = 20 shots; *In round terms* = in plain speech; **roundabout** (way) (47-9-47) not the straight and shortest way; **roundly** (47-1) with great force, e.g. *To scold a person roundly*; **r'ound'up** (47 + 8) drive together, e.g. cattle, lawbreakers, etc.; **r'ound upon** (47 + 9-5) turn round and attack or blame.

rouse (47z) wake up; excite; drive to action.

rout (47) disorderly crowd; army driven back in disorder; **to rout,** to drive back in disorder.
route (77) track; road; *A route march* = a march done by soldiers for exercise.
rout′ine (77-11) regular order of work.
rove (67) wander about.
row (67) move a boat forward by means of *oars* (= long sticks with flat ends).
row (47) noise; a quarrel; **rowdy** (——1) noisy.
row (67) line of things.
rowel (479) small wheel at the end of a *spur* (= instrument fastened to the foot used for pricking a horse to make it go faster).
rowlock (5-9) pin or U-shaped piece in which an *oar* (see Row, 4th above) rests.
royal (519) of a king; splendid; **royalty** (519-1) state of being a king; ROWLOCK persons of the king's family; part of the price of a book paid to the writer on every book sold; royalties are also paid on plays, music, and to men who plan or think out some clever machine.
R.S.V.P. (French, *répondez s'il vous plaît*) please answer (this letter).
rub (8) press down and move something over a surface, e.g. in order to clean or polish; *To rub out pencil marks* = cause — to disappear by rubbing; *To rub up a subject* = learn again, make one's memory fresh; *To rub along* = continue to do a thing, but with difficulty; Sl. *Don't rub it in* = do not continue to speak about a subject which is unpleasant to me; **a rub,** some small thing on the ground which prevents a ball from rolling straight; *Aye, there's the rub* = yes, that is the difficulty; *To rub a person the wrong way* = make angry.
rubber (8-9) material obtained from a tree grown in hot countries, used to rub out pencil marks, used for the wheels of motor-cars, overshoes, rain-coats, etc.; *My rubbers* = shoes made of rubber put on over the other shoes on a wet day.
rubbish (8-1) unwanted useless things or matter; silly talk or writing.
rubicund (77-1-9) red in the face.
ruby (77-1) red precious stone.
ructions (8-shnz) Sl. noisy quarrelling or scolding.
rudder (8-9) movable blade at the back of a boat or ship used to guide it.
ruddy (8-1) red and healthy-looking.
rude (77) untaught, rough; not gentle, not polite; *In rude health* = very healthy.
rudiment(s) (77-1-9) earliest things taught; simplest and most important part of a study.
rue (77) be sorry.
ruff (8) circle of stiff material standing out round the neck as part of a dress.
ruffian (8-19) rough lawless fellow.

ruffle (8) (of a bird) make the feathers stand up; *To ruffle the feelings* = make angry; *The wind ruffled the water* = made little waves on —; **a ruffle,** cloth gathered together to make a loose edge to a garment, e.g. round the neck or at the end of the arm.
rug (8) thick floor-covering made usually of wool; large piece of thick woollen material used to cover the legs when travelling.
Rugby (8-1) form of football in which the ball is touched with the hands as well as the feet.
rugged (8-1) rough, unpolished; *Rugged character* = rough but strong.
ruin (77ı) condition of complete loss or destruction; old building in bad repair; **to ruin,** destroy completely.
rule (77) law or custom followed by all; *A foot-rule* = piece of straight wood used for measuring; **to rule,** govern; control; *To rule lines* = make straight lines with the help of a straight edge; *To rule out* = say that a matter may not be considered; **ruler** (77-9) person who rules; straight edge used in ruling lines; **a ruling** (77-1) judgment given by a judge or by the chief man in a meeting.
rum (8) strong drink made from sugar.
rum (8) **rummy** (8-1) strange, unusual; **rummy,** card game in which one tries to collect sets of cards of a special kind.
rumble (8) make a noise like distant thunder; *The rumble seat* = seat at the back of a carriage or motor-car.
ruminate (77-1-21) bite food over and over again, like a cow; think.
rummage (8-1j) search thoroughly; *A rummage sale* = selling of various used articles so as to get money for a good cause, e.g. to help the poor.
rumour (77-9) common talk, probably untrue.
rump (8) tail end of an animal.
rumple (8) gather up a smooth thing in a careless way, causing marks of bending or folding.
rumpus (8-9) noisy quarrelling or scolding.
run (8) (**1**) move quickly on the legs; (**2**) move or travel, e.g. *A train runs*; (**3**) change and become mixed, as the colours in some kinds of cloth when washed; *The machine is in running order* = is working properly; *The road runs over the hill* = lies over —; *Run dry* = become empty; *The story runs* = is told; *To run it fine* = allow oneself just enough time; *To run a knife into* = put — in quickly; *To run a business* = be in charge of —; *To run the risk* = do a thing when there is a chance of danger or failing; *His temper ran away with him* = he lost control of his feelings; *To run down (or run over) a person* = hit with a motor-car; *He is run down* = is weak and tired; *To run a person down* = say bad things about; *We have run out of food* = the food is finished; *To run up a flag* = put up a flag quickly; *To run a car in* = drive a new motor-car slowly at first, e.g. for the first thousand miles; n. **run,**

(1) act of moving quickly, e.g. *Go for a run*; (2) distance moved, e.g. *London is an hour's run from here*; (3) time during which a thing lasts, e.g. *The play had a run of 100 days*; (4) eager rush, e.g. *A run on the bank* (when people are afraid and go to get their money from a bank); (5) enclosed place for animals, e.g. *A sheep run*; *In the long run* = in the end, at last; *Give him a run for his money* = let him have a chance of winning; *The ordinary run of mankind* = the common people.

rung (8) p.p. of Ring.

rung (8) cross-bar, e.g. between long bars of a *ladder* (= long bars with short bars (rungs) across as steps).

runner (8-9) (1) person who runs; (2) long cloth for a table; (3) kind of plant which climbs up walls, trees, etc.; (4) one of the two iron bars on which a wheel-less carriage slides over snow; **r'unner-'up** (+ 8) person next after the winner in a race.

r'unning-board (8-1 + 55) board on each side of a railway carriage or car.

runway, hard surface in an air-field from which aeroplanes go up or on which they come down.

rup'ee (77-11) a silver coin in India (etc.) about $\frac{1}{18}$ of a £.

rupture (8-tsh9) (1) bursting or breaking; a quarrel; (2) the pushing out of a part of the bowel through a weak place in the muscles of the front of the body.

rural (77) of the country.

ruse (77z) a trick.

rush (8) tall grass-like plant which grows in wet places.

rush (8) press rapidly forward; seize by a sudden attack; *To rush a person* = hurry a person into deciding.

rusk (8) piece of bread baked hard; *biscuit* (=. flat dry hard cake) of this sort.

russet (8-1) red-brown.

rust (1) red coating formed on iron left in a wet place; disease of plants; *I am rusty on that subject* = I have forgotten —.

rustic (8-1) of the country people; man from the country; **rusticate** (8-1-21) live in the country; send away from a school or the university as punishment for bad behaviour.

rustle (8) make a noise as of dead leaves.

rut (8) deep track of a wheel; *To be in a rut* = be unable to do anything or think anything new.

ruthless (77-1) merciless.

rye (41) grain-bearing plant.

S

Sabbath (3-9) holy day for the Jews, Saturday; for Christians, Sunday.

sable (21) small meat-eating animal; valuable brown fur; adj. dark coloured.

sabot (3-67) wooden shoe.

sabotage (3-9-443) damage done by workmen to their machines or materials so as to prevent work going on.

sabre (21-9) curved sword.

sac (3) small bag of liquid inside the body of an animal, or in a plant.

saccharin(e) (3k9-1) very sweet white powder.

sacerd'otal (3s9-67) having to do with priests and the work of priests.

sachet (3sh21) small bag holding sweet-smelling material.

sack (3) large cloth bag; **sacking** (3-1) rough cloth of which such bags are made; *Sackcloth and ashes* = signs of great grief.

sack (3) attack a town and carry off everything of value.

sack (3) Sl. send away a workman or servant because he (she) is no longer wanted.

sacrament (3-9-9) outward sign with an inward *spiritual* (= of the soul) power; church *service* (= religious ceremony), such as that in which Christ's Last Supper is solemnly remembered; adj. **sacram'ental** (3-9-2).

sacred (21-1) holy.

sacrifice (3-1-41s) make an offering to God; give up a thing for some noble reason; sell goods at a loss; n., an act of sacrificing; a thing sacrificed; adj. **sacrif'icial** (3-1-1shl).

sacrilege (3-1-1j) doing a disrespectful act to a holy thing.

sacrosanct (3-67-3ngk) very holy, and therefore protected from harm.

sacrum (21-9) large bone on to which the legs and backbone join.

sad (3) feeling sorrow; causing sorrow; (colour) dark.

saddle (3) leather seat fixed on a horse for riding; back of an animal used as meat; top of a hill; **to saddle**, fix a saddle on; *To saddle with* (a duty) = lay as a load upon; **saddler** (3-9) one who makes all those things (chiefly of leather) necessary..for riding or driving horses.

sadism (3-1z) mad desire to be cruel.

saf'ari (9-44-1) a journey hunting wild animals, e.g. in Africa.

safe (21) out of danger; not dangerous; trustworthy; a **safe**, strong box for valuables; **safeguard** (21-44) protection; SAFETY-PIN

safety-pin (21-1 + 1) pin of which the point is bent over into a hook which prevents it from opening.

saffron (3) yellow colour.

sag (3) hang down in the middle.

saga (44-9) story of the brave deeds of great men of old in Norway, Denmark, Sweden, and Iceland; set of books telling the story of the same family or group over many years.

sag'acious (9-21shg) wise, clever, e.g. *A sagacious animal*; n. **sag'acity** (9-3s1-1).

sage (21j) sweet-smelling plant, used in cooking.

sage (21j) wise.

sago (21-67) white material obtained from the inside of certain trees and boiled with milk for food.

sahib (44-1) title of respect used in India; a European in India.

said (2) p.t. of Say.

sail (21) stretched cloth used to catch wind and so drive a ship forward; **a sailor** (——9) seaman; **to sail**, travel on the water; *To sail close to the wind* = come very near to breaking a law; *To set sail* = (of any ship) leave the harbour to begin a journey.

saint (21) title of a holy man or woman.

sake (21) *For the sake of* = in order to help or please.

sal'aam (9-44) greeting used in the East.

salad (3-9) uncooked leaves and vegetables used as food.

s'alamander (3-9-3-9) small cold-blooded four-legged creature (people used to believe that it was able to live in fire).

salary (3-9-1) regular fixed payment made to workers of higher rank.

sale (21) the act of selling; **a sale**, special selling at low prices; **salesmanship** (21-z-9-1) art of selling.

salient (21-19) standing out; clearly seen; **a salient**, part that stands out in front, e.g. in a line of battle.

saline (21-41) containing salt.

sal'iva (9-41-9) liquid of the mouth.

sallow (3-67) (of the face) of a yellow-white colour.

sally (3-1) sudden attack made from inside a town; short clever speech or answer; *To sally forth* = to go out, e.g. for a walk.

salmon (3-9) large fish with red meat used for food, often preserved in a tin.

salon (3-5ⁿ) room in which guests are received; meeting of persons for talking about books, art, etc.; show of paintings.

sal'oon (9-77) large room; sitting-room in a ship or train; closed motor-car; place for buying and drinking strong drink.

salt (5) white powder commonly eaten with food; **salt-cellar** (+ s2-9) pot made of glass, silver, etc., for salt; *An old salt* = old seaman;

Take it with a grain of salt = not believe it all; *The salt of the earth* = really good people.

saltpetre (5-11-9) white powder, often used in making gunpowder.

sal'ubrious (9-77-19) resulting in good health.

salutary (3-17-9-1) health-giving; having a good effect.

sal'ute (9-77) greet; raise the hand in greeting like a soldier.

salvage (3-1j) payment for saving a ship; goods so saved; act of saving.

salv'ation (3-21shn) saving of the soul; that which saves.

salve (44) medicine mixed with fat and used to rub on painful places on the skin.

salver (3-9) silver or metal plate used by servants for carrying small things, e.g. glasses.

salvo (3-67) firing of many guns at once.

Sam Browne (belt) (3 + 47) leather *straps* (= bands) worn across the shoulder and round the waist by an officer in the army.

SAM BROWNE

samov'ar (3-67-44) large container for tea-making, used in Russia.

sampan (3-3) flat-bottomed boat used in China.

sample (44) example—of goods for sale.

sanat'orium (3-9-55-19) place to which sick persons go in order to get back their health.

sanctify (3ngk-1-4I) make holy.

sanctim'onious (3ngk - 1 - 67 - 19) pretending to be very holy.

sanction (3ngkshn) *To give sanction to* = allow, give a person the right to —; *Sanctions* = *penalties* (= punishments) for breaking an agreement or a *treaty* (= agreement between nations).

SAMOVAR

sanctity (3ngk-1-1) holiness.

sanctuary (3ngk-179-1) holy place; place in which a wrong-doer might (in ancient times) claim protection from the officers of the law; east end of a church where the priest stands.

SAMPAN

sanctum (3ngk-9) holy place; room in which a writer writes his books; headmaster's room in a school.

sand (3) dust made of broken stone and shells, as on the sea-shore; *The sands* = sandy shore; *Make ropes of sand* = try to do something useless or impossible.

sandal (3) kind of shoe of wood or leather tied to the foot with strings or leather bands leaving most of the upper part uncovered.

s'andal-wood (+ 7) sweet-smelling red wood.

sandbag (3-3) bag filled with sand used as a protection in war; to hit with a —.

sandwich (3-1j) meat (etc.) between two pieces of bread; **s'andwich-man** (+ 3) man walking with two boards hung, front and back, over his shoulders covered with notices of goods to be sold, of a play in the theatre, etc.

sane (21) not mad; having good sense; according to common sense.

sang (3) p.t. of Sing.

sang-froid (44ª + frw4) calmness.

sanguinary (3nggy71-9-1) bloody.

sanguine (3nggy71) hopeful; red-faced.

sanit'arium (3-1-29-19) American way of writing Sanatorium.

sanitary (3-1-1) according to the laws of health.

sanity (3-1-1) state of being healthy in mind— opposite of madness.

sank (3ngk) p.t. of Sink.

Sanskrit (3-1) ancient language of India.

S'anta Cl'aus (3-9 + 55z) old man with a white beard supposed to come down the chimney at Christmas, bringing gifts to children.

sap (3) liquid in a plant.

sap (3) dig a hole in the ground, e.g. under the wall of a town; *To sap the strength* = weaken slowly; Sl. *A sap* = hard-working schoolchild; Am. Sl. fool.

sapling (3-1) young tree.

SANTA CLAUS

sapper (3-9) soldier who has to do with digging, making roads and bridges, building forts, etc.

sapphire (3f4I9) blue jewel.

Saracen (3-9s9) old name for an Arab.

sarcasm (44-3z) bitter wounding words; adj. **sarc'astic** (44-3-1).

sarc'oma (44k67-9) dangerous growth in the body usually starting in a bone or muscle.

sarc'ophagus (44-5-9-9) stone box for a dead body.

sard'ine (44-1I) small fish usually preserved for food in oil in a tin.

sard'onic (smile) (44-5-1) bitter, cruel.

sari (44-1) dress of an Indian woman.

sar'ong (4-5) dress of people in Malaya.

SARI

sart'orial (44-55-19) having to do with making men's clothes.

sash (3) broad band of silk worn round the waist or over the shoulder.

sash (3) window frame.

sat (3) p.t. of Sit.

Satan (21) the Prince of Evil; adj. **sat'anic** (9-3-1).

satchel (3) small bag, e.g. for a schoolboy's books.

SARONG

sate (21) give all and more than is wanted.

sat'een (3-1I) woollen or cotton cloth with a very silky appearance.

satellite (3-9-41) small world moving round a larger one, e.g. the moon; a follower of a great man; *Satellite state* = country which is controlled by some stronger country, e.g. by Russia.

satiate (21shi-21) give more (food, etc.) than is desired; n. **sat'iety** (9-419-1).

satin (3-1) silk material of a very *shiny* (= shining) appearance.

satire (3-419) poem or other form of writing meant to make something seem foolish and laughable; adj. **sat'irical** (9-1-1).

satisfy (3-1-41) supply a need; fulfil a wish; give what is claimed; *Satisfy yourself* = see for yourself, make sure; n. **satisf'action** (3-1-3-shn); *Demand satisfaction* = tell a person to pay for damage done, call a person out to fight; adj. **satisf'actory** (——9-1).

saturate (3tsh9-21) make as wet or full of liquid as possible; *A saturated solution of salt* = water with as much salt in it as possible.

saturnine (3-9-41) heavy, solemn-looking.

satyr (3-9) god of the forest, half man half beast.

sauce (55s) pleasant-tasting liquid added to food; Sl. rudeness, disrespect; **sauceboat** (55s-67) curved pot used to contain sauce.

saucepan (55s-9) cooking pot with a handle.

saucer (55s9) small curved plate put under a cup.

saucy (55s1) disrespectful to elders; rude.

sauerkraut (479-47) *cabbage* (= a vegetable with thick leaves) leaves, cut and preserved in salt water.

saunter (55-9) walk slowly.

sausage (5-1j) meat cut small and put into a pipe-like skin.

savage (3-1j) wild; fierce.

savant (3-9) wise man.

save (21) take out of danger; keep for future use; *To save time* = prevent waste of —; *A saving grace* = some good quality which saves a person from being completely bad; **savings** (21-1-z) money put by for future use.

save (21) except.

saveloy (3-1-51) kind of *sausage* (see 5th above) made from brains, or young pig's meat.

saviour (21-19) one who saves; *Our Saviour* = Jesus Christ.

s'avoir-f'aire (3-744 + 29) knowledge of how to behave; common sense.

savour (21-9) taste or smell; to taste; **savoury** (——1) nice tasting.

saw (55) toothed blade used for cutting; to cut with a saw; p.p. **sawn.**

saw (55) p.t. of See.

saxophone (3-9-67) metal wind instrument of music (like a horn with many finger-pieces). SAXOPHONE

scab (3) hard mass of dried blood formed on a wound; Sl. man who works when other men are *on strike* (= refusing to work).

scabbard (3-9) case of a sword-blade.

scabies (21-11) disease causing rough places on the skin especially between the fingers.

scaffold (3) raised floor of wood upon which evil-doers were killed in public; **scaffolding** (——1) frame put up round a building which is being built or repaired.

scald (55) damage the skin with boiling water; to clean or cook with boiling water; to heat but not boil (e.g. milk).

scale (21) climb.

scale (21) set of musical notes of any particular key; set of marks for measuring; *The scale of a map* = figure showing how many miles of country are shown in one inch of map.

scales (21-z) thin flat plates, e.g. on the skin of a fish.

scales (21-z) *A pair of scales* = instrument used for weighing.

scallop (5-9) shell-fish.

scallywag (3-1-3) lazy useless fellow.

scalp (3) skin of the head; to scalp, cut off the scalp as a sign of victory. SCALLOP

scalpel (3) small knife used by a doctor.

scamp (3) do work carelessly and in a hurry; a scamp, lazy worthless fellow.

scamper (3-9) run about quickly, e.g. as children playing.

scan (3) (1) turn the eyes to look carefully at one part, then another; (2) divide up poetry according to its regular beat.

scandal (3) spreading of evil reports about a person; action such as might cause such reports; adj. **scandalous** (3-9-9) very bad, such as will cause scandal.

scansion (3-shn) act of scanning poetry (see 2nd above).

scant (3) **scanty** (3-1) not enough.

scantling (3-1) size to which stone or wood is to be cut; small beam, less than 5 inches square.

sc'ape-goat (21 + 67) one who is made to bear the blame for the wrong-doing of others.

sc'ape-grace (21 + 21s) worthless person.

scapula (3-17-9) flat bone of the shoulder.

scar (44) mark left on the skin by an old wound.

scar (44) cliff.

scarab (3-9) insect with a hard skin, once considered very holy in Egypt.

scarce (29s) few and hard to find; **scarcely** (29s-1) *any* = very little, hardly any.

scare (29) frighten.

scarecrow (29-67) wooden figure dressed in old clothes used to frighten birds; very badly-dressed person. SCARAB

scarf (44) long piece of cloth worn round the neck.

scarify (3-1-41) make many small cuts in the skin.

scarlet (44-1) blood-colour.

sc'arlet f'ever (+ 11-9) disease which causes redness of the skin, pain in the throat, swellings in the neck.

sc'arlet-r'unner (+ 8-9) kind of bean.

scathing (attack) (21ŏ1) very fierce and wounding speech or writing.

scatter (3-9) throw loosely about; drive in different directions; go in different directions; *A scatter-brain* = foolish person who cannot think of one thing for very long.

scavenger (3-1ŋ9) one who gathers up waste matter; street-cleaner.

scen'ario (1-44-167) written plan of a story to be shown in the *cinema* (= moving pictures), theatre, etc.

scene (11) that which is seen by the eye, e.g. trees, fields, mountains, etc.; place where an event happened; part of a play; one set of painted pictures used in a theatre; *To have a scene* = a noisy quarrel.

scenery (11-9-1) (1) general appearance of the country; (2) painted pictures used in showing a play in a theatre.

scent (2) pleasant smell; that smell left by an animal on the ground which enables other animals to follow it; *On the scent* = on the track of, following successfully; **to scent**, cause to smell; to smell; *To scent out* = try to find, e.g. wrong-doers.

sceptic (sk2-1) one who doubts; **sceptical**, doubtful.

sceptre (s2-9) ornamental bar of gold held in the hand by a king.

schedule (shə2-177) (in America sk2-177) list.

scheme (sk11) plan of future work; **to scheme**, to plan, especially so as to do unfair or wrong things.

schism (1z) *division* (= dividing) of opinion in the Church.

Schnorkel (shn55-9) tube carrying air down to a submarine when it is under the water; also called a *snort*.

SCHNORKEL

scholar (5-9) one who goes to school; one who studies; learnèd person; **a scholarship** (——1) money given to a promising learner to enable him to go on learning; adj. **schol'astic** (9-3-1).

school (77) place in which the young are taught; any place of teaching; *A school of painting* = particular kind of painting, as done in a particular place or country or by the followers of one man; *A school of fish* = large group of —; **to school**, teach; bring under control.

SCHOONER

schooner (77-9) sailing ship, as shown; the back *mast* (= pole for the sails) is higher than the front one.

sci'atica (413-1-9) disease causing pain in the upper part of the leg and the back.

science (419-s) (1) careful study, e.g. of the nature of matter, of natural forces; (2) set of facts about these; **sc'ientist** (419-1) one who studies science; **scient'ific** (419-1-1) having to do with science.

scimitar (1-1-9) curved sword with a broad blade.

scintillate (1-1-21) give off small bits of shining or burning matter; shine like a star; *Scintillating talk* = very clever and amusing —.

scion (419) descendant.

scissors (1z9z) instrument with two blades which open and shut, used for cutting cloth, etc.

schizophr'enic (skɪts67-2-1) person whose mind is divided so that he behaves at different times like two different persons.

scler'osis (19-67-1) hardening of the blood-vessels, usually caused by old age.

scoff (5) use bitter words to and laugh at a person.

scold (67) to blame, find fault with; **a scold**, noisy ill-tempered woman.

scone (5) flat rather sweet cake, often eaten hot with butter.

scoop (77) make a hole in; get out matter from a hole; **a scoop**, instrument used for these purposes; (in a newspaper) important piece of news printed by only one newspaper.

scoot (77) Sl. move away quickly; **scooter** (77-9) toy with two wheels as shown; *Motor-scooter* = motor-cycle with very small wheels. See Corgi.

SCOOTER

scope (67) range of view; field of action.

scorch (55) burn the outside of.

score (55) make marks on a surface with a sharp point, e.g. *He scored the table with a nail*; win points in a game; n. **score**, points won in a game; *Musical score* = printed music in which the parts for the different instruments and kinds of voice are shown on sets of lines one above another; *Pay the score* = the bill; *To pay off old scores* = do evil to those who have harmed one; Sl. *Score off a person* = get the better of a person.

score (55) twenty; (as weight of a pig) 20 or 21 pounds.

scorn (55) feel no respect for a thing; *I would scorn to do it* = I should be ashamed to —; **scorn**, n. lack of respect for; feeling that a thing is bad and worthless.

SCORPION

scorpion (55-19) small creature with eight legs having poison in its tail, found only in hot countries.

scotch (5) kill or make harmless, e.g. a snake. **Scotch** (5) of Scotland; e.g. *Scotch tweed* (= woollen cloth); **Scottish** (5-1) of Scotland, Scottish people, the *Scots* (Scotch is used of things; Scottish, of people).

sc'ot-f'ree (5 + 11) *To get off —* = escape punishment.

Scots, see Scotch (2nd above).

scoundrel (47) very bad man.

scour (479) to clean; to polish; rub away; *To scour the country* = go quickly over — searching everywhere.

scourge (99j) number of strings tied together used for beating as a punishment; anything which causes great suffering, e.g. a widespread disease; **to scourge,** beat with a —.

scout (47) person sent in front of an army to get news of the enemy; member of *The Boy Scouts* (*Boy Scouting* = way of training boys in character, helpfulness to others, and self-help by means of camp-life); **to scout,** act as a scout; *To scout round* = search; *To scout an idea* = refuse to consider.

scow (47) flat-bottomed boat.

scowl (47) pull down the muscles above the eyes as a sign of anger.

scrabble (3) make meaningless marks; gather things together hastily; make quick searching movements of the hands.

SCOW

scraggy (3-1) thin and bony.

scram (3) Sl. Go away!

scramble (3) to climb using the hands and knees; to struggle against others for something; *Scrambled eggs* = eggs broken up and cooked in butter; **a scramble,** short climb; disorderly struggle.

scrap (3) small piece; *Scrap-iron* = pieces of waste iron; Sl. *To have a scrap* = fight; *A scrap-book* = book in which one sticks pictures, pieces cut from newspapers, etc.; *To throw on the scrap-heap* = throw away as useless.

scrape (21) rub with a knife or sharp edge; sound so caused; *To scrape through an examination* = pass — with difficulty; *To get into scrapes* = into trouble; *To scrape up* = gather together, e.g. money, with difficulty.

scratch (3) make marks on a surface with a pointed object, e.g. with the nails; **a scratch,** mark so caused; *A scratch player* = one who counts his strokes or points from 0, not from any + or — amount; *A scratch collection* = group hastily collected, not the best to be had; *To scratch* (in a game) cut out one's name from a list of players; *Not up to scratch* = not as good as usual.

scrawl (55) write in a bad, careless way; make meaningless marks.

scream (11) give a loud long cry, e.g. of pain.

screech (11) high loud cry.

screed (11) long and uninteresting piece of writing.

screen (11) protect; hide; *To screen (people)* = test and examine so as to send away those who are not to be trusted; **a screen,** frame covered with cloth, paper or other material used to hide or protect the user; stretched sheet on which light-pictures are thrown, e.g. in the *cinema* (= moving-picture house).

screen (11) net-like instrument used to separate larger pieces from smaller pieces (e.g. of coal or earth); also used in making pictures for printing in books, so as to divide up the black parts of a photograph into a number of smaller squares or circles which will hold the ink.

screw (77) thing like a nail which is driven into wood by being turned round and round; a three-bladed object at the back of a ship which is turned round and round to drive the ship forward; **to screw,** fix with a screw; turn round; **a scr'ew-driver** (+ 41-9) instrument with a flat end used to drive in screws; *He's a screw* = hard in money matters; *To screw up one's courage* = force oneself to be brave; Sl. *He has a screw loose* = is mad.

scribble (1) write quickly and carelessly.

scribe (41) writer.

scrimmage (1-1j) disorderly struggle.

scrip (1) paper showing that one owns shares in a business company.

script (1) writing done by hand; *The script* = written words from which a *cinema* (= moving pictures) film is made or which are to be spoken on radio.

Scripture(s) (1-tshgz) the Bible; holy book or writing.

scrofula (5-17-9) disease causing swelling of the neck.

scroll (67) old book written on a long piece of paper or skin rolled up on two rollers.

scrub (8) land covered with bushes; **to scrub** (a floor) wash with a brush; **scrubby** (8-1) small and not pleasant.

scruff (8) back of the neck.

scrumptious (8-shg) Sl. very nice to eat.

scruple (77) small weight = 1·3 grammes; very small amount; feeling of doubt, e.g. as to the rightness of what one is asked to do;

scrupulous (77-17-9) very careful and afraid of doing wrong.

scrutinize (77-1-41) look at carefully; n. **scrutiny** (77-1-1).

scud (8) (of a ship) run before the wind; wind-driven mist.

scuff (8) to walk rubbing the feet on the ground.

scuffle (8) disorderly fight.

scullery (8-9-1) room in which plates, etc., are washed; **scullion** (8-19) man employed in the scullery.

sculls (8-z) two *oars* (= poles flattened at the end) held one in each hand to row a light boat.

sculptor (8-9) one who cuts figures of men, etc., in stone, wood or other materials; **sculpture** (8-tsh9) beautiful figures cut in stone, etc.; this art.

scum (8) mass of dirt which collects on the top of boiling liquid; *The scum of the earth* = bad, worthless people.

scupper (8-9) hole in a ship's side which allows the water from waves falling on the ship to flow back into the sea.

scurf (99) small pieces of dry skin found among the hairs on the head.

scurrilous (8-1-9) using low and rude language in speaking against a person.

scurry (8-1) move hastily.

scurvy (99-1) disease caused by lack of fresh fruit; *A scurvy knave* = low bad fellow; *A scurvy trick* = low dishonest trick.

scutcheon (8-9) a shield; *A blot on the —* = dishonour to the family.

scuttle (8) coal box; **to scuttle**, run hastily away; **scuttle** (8) window in the side of a ship; *To scuttle a ship* = let water in so as to sink it on purpose.

scythe (41ŏ) long curved blade set at an angle to a long bent handle, used for cutting grass.

sea (11) mass of water, not land; *We are all at sea on this subject* = we do not understand —; **seasickness** (11-1-1) illness caused by the movement of a ship; **seaman** (11-9) man who works on a ship; **seamanship** (——1) art of guiding and controlling a ship.

seal (11) large sea animal hunted for its skin.

seal (11) close a letter with hot wax; print a mark upon hot wax; close up tightly so as to keep out air, e.g. *To seal up a pot of food*; instrument used for this; decide and make firm, e.g. *Seal a promise*.

SEAL

seam (11) joining-line of two pieces of cloth; part of a rock containing coal or metal; **seamstress** (2-1) needlewoman; **seamy** (11-1) *The seamy side of life* = low unpleasant side —.

séance (2144ⁿs) meeting in which attempts are made to call up the spirits of the dead.

sear (19) dried up, e.g. leaf; **to sear**, burn with a hot iron.

search (99) look in a place in order to find; examine in order to find; **a search-light** (+ 41) electric lamp throwing a very powerful beam of white light.

season (11z) (1) one of the four parts of the year, summer, winter, etc., (2) right time for doing a thing; short time; **to season**, make (wood) fit for use; give a good taste to food; **seasonable** (——9) well fitted for the time of the year; done at the right time; **seasonal** (11zg) lasting only during a certain season; **seasoning** (——1) material used to give a good taste; *Season-ticket* = pass on the railway paid for several journeys, days or months at one time, instead of paying for each journey separately.

seat (11) piece of furniture on which one sits; part (of a chair or of one's garment) on which one sits; place where a thing happens or is done, e.g. *The seat of government*; place where the cause is, e.g. *The seat of the trouble*; place paid for in a theatre or train; *A seat in the country* = country house; **to seat**, give a chair to; have enough room for, e.g. *This hall seats 500 people*; *Be seated* = please sit down.

sea-urchin (11 + 99-1) small sea animal covered with sharp prickles.

sebaceous (1-21sh9) containing or producing oil, e.g. *A sebaceous gland at the root of a hair* = one producing natural oil for the hair.

secede (1s11) to leave, cease to be a member of; **secession** (1s2shn) giving up membership of.

seclude (1-77) to shut away from; *A secluded spot* = quiet distant place; **seclusion** (1-773n) being alone and shut off from others.

second (2-9) next after the first; *My second* = my helper in a fight; *To second a motion* = say that one agrees with an opinion already expressed by another person in a meeting; **to second** (1-5) take an officer from his usual work and send him to some special duty; **secondary** (2-9-9-1) coming later, of less importance; *Secondary school* = school for children aged about 14 to 18; **second-hand** (2 + 3) not new, bought from another; **second-rate** (+ 21) not the best; second-best; **second sight** (2-9 + 41) power of seeing things happening far away or in the future.

secret (11-1) not to be made known to others; *The Secret Service* = persons paid by a government to find out the plans of an enemy; n. **secrecy** (11-1s1).

secretariat (2-9-29-19) building containing the offices of the government; the people working in it.

secretary (2-9-1) helper who writes letters and does duties for the employer.

secretion (1-11shn) a liquid formed within the body, e.g. *Saliva is a secretion (liquid) formed in the mouth*; **to secrete**, make a secretion.

secretive (1-11-1) keeping *secret* (see 4th above).

secretory (1-11-9-1) forming *secretions* (see 2nd above).

sect (2) group of persons following one leader or holding a particular set of opinions in religion, etc.; **sectarian** (2-29-19) belonging to a certain small party; narrow-minded.

section (2-shn) part cut off; part of.

secular (2-17-9) concerned with this world (not the world of after-life); concerned with every-day matters rather than those of the Church.

sec'ure (1-179) protect from danger; fasten well; adj. safe, in good keeping; trustworthy; n. **sec'urity** (1-179-1-1) safeness; *To give security for a loan* (= money lent) = give something valuable to the lender which will be kept by him if the money is not paid back; *My securities* = papers which prove that I own shares in a business, a house, land, etc.

sed'an (1-3) covered chair carried by two men; closed motor-car.

sed'ate (1-21) calm and solemn.

sedative (2-9-1) calming medicine.

sedentary (work) (2-9-1) which one does sitting down.

SEDAN CHAIR

sedge (2j) grasses growing in wet places.

sediment (2-1-9) matter which settles at the bottom of a liquid.

sed'ition (1-1shn) words or acts intended to make people disobey the government.

sed'uce (1-177s) lead a person (e.g. young woman) into wrong-doing; n. **sed'uction** (1-8-shn).

sedulous (2-17-9) working steadily and carefully.

see (11) (1) use the eyes; to notice with the eyes; *See the last of* = be free of and not wish to see again; *I'll see you home* = go with you to your —; *See a person off* = go with him to the (train) and say good-bye; *See a thing through* = help to finish a piece of work; *See you through your troubles* = help —; (2) understand, e.g. *I see why you did that*; *Don't you see?* = I hope you understand; *Well, I'll see* = I will consider the matter; *I see through your plan* = understand the real aim or meaning of it; (3) to experience; *To see life* = have many experiences; (4) to meet; to visit; go and get advice from, e.g. *To see a doctor*; *I'll see about it, see to it* = attend to; *See after* = take charge of; *See into* = examine; *See something out* = wait till the end of.

See (11) place where a higher officer of the Church, e.g. the *Pope* (= head of the Church of Rome) lives; country or countries over which he has control.

seed (11) that small object (put in the ground) from which a plant grows; *To go (run) to seed* = become careless or useless; *Seeded players* = strong players who do not play against each other in the first games of a *tournament* (= number of games played to see who is best of all).

seedy (11-1) ill.

seek (11) look for; try to get; *Seek to* = try to.

seemly (behaviour) (11-1) proper; correct.

seen (11) p.p. of See.

seep (11) (of liquid) pass slowly through; n. **seepage** (11-1j).

seer (19) one who sees and tells the future.

see-saw (11 + 55) board laid over a barrel or other object (a child sits on each end and they move up and down).

seethe (11ð) to boil; be in a state of very strong feeling.

segment (2-9) one of the natural parts into which a fruit or jointed stick is divided; *A segment of a circle* = part cut off a circle by a straight line.

segregate (2-1-21) keep separate.

seine (21) large fishing-net.

seize (11) take hold of by force; *Seized with* = suddenly attacked by (illness or strong feeling, e.g. pity); become fixed (e.g. a machine when overheated); **seizure** (11ჳ9) sudden illness.

seldom (2-9) not often.

sel'ect (1-2) choose; *A very select school* = one which takes only carefully chosen boys or girls.

s'elf-c'oloured (2 + 8-9) all of one colour; of the natural colour of the wool (silk, leather, etc.); **self-c'onscious** (+ 5-sh9) unable to forget oneself when in the company of others, feeling one is being looked at and talked about all the time; **s'elf-cont'ained** (+ 9-21) (house) complete in itself; (person) self-controlled; **selfish** (2-1) thinking only of one's own interests; **s'elf-poss'essed** (+ 9zzst) calmly sure of one's own behaviour; **s'elf-w'illed** (+ 1) determined to have things done according to one's own wishes; not guided by others.

sell (2) give in return for money; *To sell up a person* = sell his goods so as to get back money lent to him; Sl. *To be sold* = be deceived; Sl. *What a sell!* = we cannot have what we expected or hoped for.

selvedge, selvage (2-1rj) edge of cloth made specially strong to prevent threads coming out.

sem'antics (1-3-1) scientific study of the meaning of words.

semaphore (2-9-55) way of sending messages by holding the arms up in various ways, each way meaning a letter.

semblance (2-9-s) outside appearance, e.g. *To have a semblance of honesty* = pretend to be honest.

sem'ester (1-2-9) half-year in a school.

semi- (2-1) half-.

s'emic'olon (2-1-67-9) a mark (;).

seminar (2-1-44) small group of learners studying the more difficult parts of a subject under a teacher.

seminary (2-1-9-1) school.

sem'itic (1-1-1) having to do with the Jews.

s'emiv'owel (2-1-479) e.g. the sounds W and Y.

sempstress (2-1) see Seamstress; needle-woman, e.g. one who makes clothes.

senate (2-1) meeting of law-givers in ancient Rome; meeting of persons for the government of a country; meeting which controls a university; **senator** (2-9-9) member of a senate.

send (2) cause to go; *To send word* = a message; *Send him victorious* = make him win the battle; *Send for him* = send a person to call him; *They gave him a good send-off* = said good-bye to him in a very kind way.

sen'escent (1-2) growing old.

senile (11-4I) old and weak.

senior (11-19) older; higher in rank; longer in service.

señ'or (2ny55) Mr., Sir (in Spain); **señora** (2ny55-9) Mrs., Madam; **señor'ita** (2ny5-11-9) Miss.

sens'ation (2-2Ishn) a feeling; great excitement; **sensational,** causing great excitement.

sense (2) power to feel, see, hear, etc.; power to understand; *Common sense* = good judgment; *Good sense* = good understanding; *I cannot see the sense of it* = the meaning of —; **to sense,** to feel; **senseless** (——1) foolish, meaningless; *To fall senseless* = faint; **sensib'ility** (2-1-1-1-1) power of feeling; power of understanding beauty; *My sensibilities* = feelings of what is right and proper; **sensible** (2-9) able to feel; having good judgment; **sensitive** (2-1-1) having keen powers of feeling; *A sensitive instrument* = one which shows the effect of, or answers to, only slight causes, e.g. to a very small amount of light, sound, heat, etc.; **sensory** (2-9-1) having to do with the carrying of feelings, e.g. *A sensory nerve* = nerve carrying feelings of heat, pain, etc., to the brain.

sensual (2-179) having to do with the pleasures of the body; too much interested in the —.

sentence (2-9-s) group of words expressing a complete meaning; punishment given by a judge to a wrong-doer.

sent'entious (2-2-sh9) expressing much meaning cleverly in few words; *Sententious person* = one who tries to appear wise.

sentiment (2-1-9) a feeling, e.g. love; expression of feeling; opinion.

sentim'ental (2-1-2) expressing too much feeling; feeling too much; feeling rather than thinking; loving in a weak and silly way.

sentinel (2-1), **sentry** (2-1) soldier on guard.

separate (2-1) apart; **to separate** (2-9-21) keep apart; go away from.

sepia (11-19) brown paint.

sepoy (11-51) Indian soldier.

sepsis (2-1) poisoning of any part of the body caused by *germs* (= microscopic living things); adj. **septic** (2-1) so poisoned.

sept- seven.

septuagen'arian (2-179j1-29-19) one who is 70 years old.

sepulchre (2-9-k9) grave cut in the rock or built of stone; *A* **sep'ulchral** (1-8lkrgl) *voice* = solemn voice as from the grave.

sequel (11-9) that which follows or is the result of; *The sequel of a book* = second book going on with the story of the first.

sequence (11-9-s) chain of events following each other; *In sequence* = one after another.

sequ'ester (1-2-9) keep apart from; take away goods from the supposed owner until the true ownership is decided; *A sequestered spot* = quiet distant place.

sequin(s) (11-1-z) little plates of bright metal fixed on a dress as an ornament.

ser'aglio (2-44-1·67) part of a house (in an Eastern country) in which the women are kept.

ser'ai (2-41) building for travellers in the East.

seraph (2-9) *angel* (=heavenly spirit, messenger of God) of the highest rank; pl. **seraphim** (2-9-1); adj. **ser'aphic** (2-3-1).

sere (19) dry, e.g. leaf.

seren'ade (2-1-21) playing or singing by a lover outside a lady's window in the evening; quiet piece of music.

ser'ene (1-11) calm and peaceful; n. **ser'enity** (1-2-1-1).

serf (99) slave; in ancient times a land-worker who was not allowed to leave his land.

serge (99j) strong rough woollen cloth.

sergeant (44j9) rank in the army, third from the bottom.

serial (19-19) happening in, or as part of, a *series* (see below); *A serial story* = story which appears in parts daily, weekly or monthly.

series (19-11z) number of things coming one after another.

serious (19-19) solemn; thoughtful; important; *A serious illness* = dangerous —.

sermon (99-9) speech given by a priest in a church.

serpent (99-9) snake.

serr'ated (2-21-1) having a toothed edge (like a saw).

serried (ranks) (2-1) closely packed.

serum (19-9) white liquid of the blood; liquid taken from the blood of an animal which has had a disease and put into men's bodies to protect them from that disease.

servant (99) one who works for another for pay, especially one who works at housework.

serve (99) (1) to work for another; help another; *That will serve, will serve my purpose* = will do what is needed; *That serves him right* = that is what he deserves; (2) bring or supply food to; (3) strike the ball to another person in a game, e.g. in *tennis*; (4) *To serve a notice* = give a person a printed paper according to law, e.g. one telling him to appear at a court of law on a certain day.

service (99-1s) act of serving (see above); work done for another; *The service in the hotel is bad* = servants do not work well; *A church service* = form of prayer and praise to God; *A dinner service* = set of plates, etc., for use in eating; *The train service is good* = there are plenty of fast trains; *At your service* = ready to do what you want; *The Civil Service* = officers of government other than those in the fighting forces; *The Services* = Army, Navy (= king's

serviette   274   shammy

warships) and Air Force; **serviceable** (99-1s9) useful.

servi'ette (99-12) cloth spread over the knees while eating.

servile (99-4I) behaving like a slave; **servitude** (99-1-17) condition of being a slave; *Penal servitude* = forced work in a prison.

servo- helped by machine, e.g. **servo-steering** (99-67 + 11-1) having a machine to help to *steer* (= guide by changing the direction) a big car, etc.

sesame (2-9-1) plant whose seeds are used for oil.

session (2shn) a sitting, e.g. of a law-court; work-time in a school.

set (2) become hard and solid, e.g. certain liquid mixtures used in building.

set (2) to put in a place; to put in the proper place or condition, e.g. *Set a clock* = put the hands at the right hour; *To set a broken bone* = put the broken ends firmly together; *To set a hen* = put it on eggs; *To set eyes on* = see; *To set an example* = be good so that others can copy one; *To set the table* = put everything ready for the dishes for a meal; *To set to work* = begin work; *To set a jewel* = fix it in a (ring, etc.); *To set sail* = start out on a sea journey; *To set out* = start on a journey; *To set the teeth* = press them together, as in pain; *The sun set* = went down at evening; *To set up for oneself* = start one's own business; *A set time* = time fixed for (a meeting, etc.); *Set phrases* = words which everybody uses at certain times; **a set**, group or collection, e.g. *A tea-set* = plates, cups, etc., used in taking tea; *A set of Shakespeare* = complete collection of books written by —; *A set of tennis* = certain number of games of —; *A set-back* = some accident which causes loss; *A set-to* = a fight; *A cinema set* = built-up scene in which part of the story will be acted to make a moving picture.

sett'ee (2-11) long seat.

setter (2-9) dog used when shooting birds.

settle (2) **(1)** fix in one place; **(2)** decide; *To settle a quarrel* = end —; *To settle a debt* =

SETTER

pay off —; **(3)** come to rest, e.g. *A bird settled on the branch*; *They have settled in England* = made a home in; **(4)** sink down, e.g. *The tea-leaves settled at the bottom of the pot*; *The earth has settled and become firm*; **a settle**, long seat with a high back; **a settler** (2-9) one who makes a home in a distant country; **settlement** (2-9) way in which a quarrel has been ended; place where people are starting to live; money given to a woman at her marriage.

set-up (2 + 8) an *organization* (= arrangement of parts to work together), e.g. *A new set-up in the office*.

sever (2-9) to cut off; keep apart.

several (2) more than two but not many; *Each in their several places* = own separate —.

severe (1-19) plain, without ornament; hard and merciless; n. **sev'erity** (1-2-1-1).

sew (67) join with a needle and thread.

sewage (171j) waste matter of a house or city.

sewer (179) pipe carrying away waste matter from a house or city.

sex-, sexi- six, e.g. **s'exp'artite** (2-44-41) having six parts.

sex (2) condition of being male or female.

sexton (2) one who has charge of a church-building and graveyard.

sexual (2-179) having to do with *sex* (see 2nd above).

shabby (3-1) badly dressed; (of a garment) much worn and bad; (of behaviour) ungenerous.

shack (3) hut.

shackle (3) fasten with a chain.

shade (21) protect from light; *In the shade* = in a place protected from the full light; *An eye-shade* = thing used to protect the eyes from light; *A shade of colour* = richness of colour, e.g. *That's the wrong shade of red*; *it's too dark*; *The shades of the dead* = spirits of —.

shadow (3-67) dark form of a thing thrown by light on the ground; *To shadow a person* = follow secretly.

shady (21-1) (place) protected from the heat of the sun; (person) dishonest.

shaft (44) stick of an arrow; any long handle of an instrument; bar turning round and round to carry power; main part of a *pillar* (= support of an arch); poles of a carriage between which the horse runs; deep hole in the ground leading to a *mine* (= underground place from which coal, etc., is obtained); *A shaft of light* = beam of —.

shag (3) finely cut strong tobacco.

shaggy (3-1) having rough hair.

shagr'een (3-11) leather with a rough surface usually made green in colour.

shake (21) cause to move quickly from side to side or up and down; make less firm, e.g. *To shake one's belief*; Sl. *In two shakes* = very soon; *A shake-down* = hastily prepared bed; **shaky** (——1) unsteady; p.p. **shaken**.

shako (3-67) high hat worn by soldiers.

shale (21) soft rock which breaks easily into thin sheets of material.

shall'ot (9-5) small strong-tasting vegetable.

shallow (3-67) not deep (water or container).

sham (3) pretend; adj. not real.

shamble (3) to walk in an ungraceful way.

shambles (3-z) place in which animals are killed for food; any place of great killing.

shame (21) painful feeling of having done wrong; **to shame**, cause this feeling in another; *It's a shame* = is very unjust.

shammy (3-1) (chamois) soft leather used for polishing.

shampoo   275   **shingle**

shamp'oo (3-77) wash the hair.
shamrock (3-5) plant with leaves in sets of three, the national sign of Ireland.
shangh'ai (3-4I) make a man senseless and carry him off to be a seaman.
shank (3ngk) leg; part of an instrument between the working part and the handle.
shanty (3-1) hut; seaman's song.

SHAMROCK

shape (2I) form of a thing; hollow form into which liquid is poured and taken out when it has become solid; **to shape**, cut or press into a certain form; *My son is shaping well at school* = is getting on in a promising way; **shapeless** (——I) not having a regular shape; **shapely** (——I) of good shape.
shard (44) broken piece of a pot; hard wing-cover of an insect.
share (29) *My share* = that part of the whole which belongs to me; *A share in a company* = ownership of part of the business, part of the gain being paid to the part-owner; **to share**, divide up among; take a part of.
shark (44) large fish which eats men; person who tricks people out of money.
sharp (44) having a keen edge; acid; clever; a sharp, small needle; a sharper (44-9) dishonest man; *A sharp pain* = quick, strong pain; *2 o'clock sharp* = exactly at 2 o'clock.

SHARK

shatter (3-9) break into small pieces.
shave (2I) cut the hair from the skin with a *razor* (= very sharp knife); Sl. *Young shaver* = boy.
shaving(s) (2I-I-z) very thin bands of wood cut off by a *plane* (= flat instrument with a knife in it, used for smoothing wood).
shawl (55) loose square cloth worn over the shoulders by women.
sheaf (II) number of objects, e.g. arrows, pieces of paper, etc., gathered and tied together.
shear (I9) to cut with *scissors* (= instrument with two blades used for cutting cloth); **shears** (——z) large pair of scissors as for cutting branches, the wool of sheep, etc.
sheath (II) case or covering, e.g. one to hold a blade; **sheathe** (IIð) to put into a sheath.
sheaves (II-z) pl. of Sheaf.
shed (2) hut.
shed (2) cause to fall, e.g. tears, leaves.
sheen (II) brightness, polish.
sheep (II) animal useful for its wool, also for food; *A black sheep* = bad member of a family; *To make sheep's eyes* = look at lovingly; **sheepish** (II-I) foolish, ungraceful and afraid in the company of others.
sheer (I9) steep; (cloth) very fine; *Sheer nonsense* = quite foolish, very foolish talk.

sheer (I9) *To sheer off* = turn suddenly away from.
sheet (II) flat piece of paper or metal, glass, etc.; rope tied to the corner of a sail; *A pair of sheets* = two squares of cotton (or other thin material) on a bed, between which one sleeps.
sheik (2) or (2I) head of an Arab family or group.
shekel (2) piece of money spoken of in the Bible; *The shekels* = money.
shelf (2) board (fixed to the wall) on which things are put, e.g. *A bookshelf*; flat rock or sand-bank in the sea.
shell (2) hard outside covering of an egg, fish or fruit, etc.; frame; metal case full of explosive material fired from a big gun; **to shell**, take off the shell from an egg, a fruit, etc.; in war, to fire shells at; Sl. *To shell out* = pay out.
shell'ac (9-3) glass-like material formed by insects, used to make colourless paint and *sealing-wax* (= wax for closing letters).
sh'ell-sh'ock (+ 5) disorder of the mind, or madness, caused by terrible experiences in war.
shelter (2-9) protect; take protection from; thing which protects, e.g. hut with an open front and its back turned against the direction of cold winds.
shelve (2) slope slowly down; lay aside (a question) without deciding it.
shelves (2-z) pl. of Shelf.
shepherd (2-9) one who takes care of sheep.
sherbet (99-9) cool drink made from fruit.
sheriff (2-I) chief officer of the law in a particular part of the country.
sherry (2-I) strong yellow wine.
shibboleth (I-9-2) word showing that one belongs to a certain party; password.
shied (4I) p.t. of Shy.
shield (II) piece of armour carried on the arm or in the hand; any plate which protects, e.g. wind-shield, dress-shield, etc.; **to shield**, protect.
shift (I) to move; cause to move; a shift, trick; shirt; *The night shift* = group of workmen who work at night; **shiftless** (——I) careless and foolish in business matters; **shifty** (——I) tricky and deceiving.
shilling (I-I) Obs. worth 5 pence; *I'll cut him off without a shilling* = I shall leave no money to him after my death.
shimmer (I-9) to shine in movement, e.g. *A lake shimmering in the moonlight.*
shin (I) front bone of the lower part of the leg; *To shin up* = climb.
shindy (I-I) noise; Sl. *Kick up a shindy* = make a noise, complain.
shine (4I) give out light; be bright and polished.
shingle (Ingg) small stones at the border of the sea.
shingle (Ingg) flat bits of wood used in making a roof; *To shingle hair* = cut a woman's hair

shingles

short at the back, leaving the front and sides long.

shingles (1ngg-z) disease causing painful spots on the skin following the path of a nerve, often half-way round the waist.

shiny (41-1) shining.

ship (1) large sea-going boat; **to'ship**, send (goods) by ship; *Ship oars* = pull in the *oars* (= flat blades with which a boat is rowed).

-ship (1) e.g. *Friendship* = state of being a friend.

shipshape (1-21) in good order.

shire (419) one of the parts into which England is divided, Hampshire, Yorkshire, etc.

-shire (9) e.g. Berkshire.

shirk (99) to escape from doing a duty; not to do one's work.

shirt (99) loose garment worn over the upper part of the body; **shirting** (——1) material for making shirts.

shiver (1-9) shake with cold or fear.

shiver (1-9) break into small pieces.

shoal (67) *shallow* (= not deep) place in the sea.

shoal (of fish) (67) large group of.

shock (5) sudden blow and shaking; sudden great pain or great sorrow; loss of strength or disorder of mind caused by a great pain or sorrow; *An electric shock* = feeling produced by passing electricity through the body; **to shock**, cause sudden pain or sorrow; to surprise by talking or acting in an improper way; **shocking** (——1) surprisingly bad; shameful.

shock (5) lot of cut corn stood up on end in a field; *A shock of hair* = mass of thick hair.

shod (5) wearing shoes; *Shod with iron* = having the lower part protected with —.

shoddy (5-1) cloth made by tearing up old cloth and using it again; (of any object) made of bad materials.

shoe (77) covering for the foot; *Horse-shoes* = curved bands of iron put on horses' feet; **sh'oe-lace** (+ 21S) **sh'oe-string** (+ 1) string used to tie up a shoe; Sl. *On a shoe-string* = with very little money.

shone (5) p.t. of Shine.

shook (7) p.t. of Shake.

shoot (77) fire a gun, let fly an arrow; put or send out quickly, e.g. *He shot out his arm*; move quickly, e.g. *A shooting star*; *Shooting pains* = sudden sharp pains; *A shoot of a tree* = young branch; *A (coal) shoot* = sloping way down which (coal) is poured.

shooting-stick (77-1 + 1) walking-stick on which one can sit.

shop (5) room or building in which one buys things; room in which there are machines; **to shop**, go to the shops and buy; *To talk shop* = talk about one's own business interests; **sh'op-lifter** (+ 1-9) one who steals things from a shop while pretending to buy; **sh'op-walker** (+55-9) man

SHOOTING STICK

shrapnel

who walks about in a shop to see that all the people are being served properly.

shore (55) land on the edge of the sea.

shore (55) *To shore up* = support with wooden posts or beams.

shorn (55) (p.p. of Shear); cut short.

short (55) not long; not tall; not enough; *Selling short* = selling more than one actually has; **a shortage** (——1j) lack of, not enough of; **sh'ort c'ircuit** (+ s99-1) touching of two electric wires so that the electricity finds a short way round instead of passing through the lamp or machine; **shortc'omings** (55-8-1-z) faults, weaknesses; **shortening** (55-1) fat put into cakes, etc.; **shorthand** (55t·h3) very quick way of writing down spoken words; **shortly** (55-1) soon; **shorts** (55) short garment worn by a man covering the body from the waist to above the knees; **sh'ort-s'ighted** (+ 41-1) not able to see distant objects clearly; **sh'ort-t'empered** (+ 2-9) easily made angry.

shot (5) p.t. of Shoot; **a shot**, metal ball shot from a gun; sound of a gun; firing of a gun; *A good shot* = one who shoots well, well-aimed shot or stroke in any game; *Within ear-shot* = near enough to be heard; Sl. *To have a shot at it* = make an attempt; **shot**, e.g. *Shot silk* = silk having threads of other colours running through it; **sh'ot-gun** (+ 8) gun with barrel (or two barrels) smooth inside for firing many small *shots* (= metal balls) at once.

shoulder (67-9) part of the body between the neck and the top of the arm; **to shoulder**, put on the shoulder; push with the shoulder.

shout (47) loud cry; give a loud cry.

shove (8) to push.

shovel (8) broad blade fixed in the end of a handle used for moving coal, snow, etc.; **to shovel**, move loose material with a shovel.

SHOVEL

show (67) cause to see; *Show a person round the house* = lead round; *Show him the door* = send or lead him out of the house; *Show up a person* = let people know that he is dishonest; *To show up at* = be present at; **a show**, thing shown; showing, e.g. of horses, flowers; public performance; **showy** (——1) bright, such as will be noticed—but probably not good.

shower (479) slight fall of rain; number of things falling or arriving at once, e.g. *A shower of letters*; **a sh'ower-bath** (+ 44) bath in which water falls on one like rain.

showmanship (67-9-1) art of showing things so that they look very good; art of arranging shows (e.g. of dancing, singing, animals, etc.) for people to see.

shown (67) p.p. of Show.

shrank (3ngk) p.t. of Shrink.

shrapnel (3) metal case full of iron balls and

shred explosive matter which is fired from a gun and explodes in the air.

shred (2) to tear or cut into long narrow pieces; piece so torn or cut off.

shrew (77) bad-tempered, scolding woman; kind of field-mouse.

shrewd (77) of keen mind, sharp in business matters.

shriek (11) give a high loud cry.

shrift (1) *To give short shrift to* = give little time to a man to say his prayers before one kills him; punish without delay.

shrill (1) high and loud (sound), e.g. *A shrill whistle.*

shrimp (1) small white salt-water creature with ten legs and a long tail, which turns red when boiled.

shrine (41) case containing holy things; the grave of a holy man; *altar* (= holy table) in a church; any small building considered holy.

shrink (1ngk) become smaller, e.g. woollen cloth when boiled; draw back from a dangerous or unpleasant thing; **shrinkage** (——1j) amount by which a thing becomes smaller.

shrivel (1) become curled and bent by the action of heat or dryness, e.g. *Shrivelled leaves.*

shroud (47) garment put on a dead body; **to shroud**, cover with a sheet, or as with a sheet, e.g. *Shrouded in mist.*

shrouds (47-z) main ropes holding up the *mast* (= upright pole carrying sails) of a ship.

shrub (8) low bush; **shrubbery** (——9-1) low bushes, e.g. planted round a house.

shrug (8) draw up the shoulders, meaning " I don't care."

shrunk (8ngk) p.p. of Shrink; as adj. **shrunken.**

shudder (8-9) shake with fear or cold.

shuffle (8) walk rubbing the feet along the ground; say sometimes one thing, sometimes another; mix up playing-cards before a new game.

shun (8) keep away from, try not to meet.

shunt (8) move a train from one line (track) to another; send electricity down a different wire.

shut (8) to close; be closed; closed; Sl. *Shut up!* = stop talking.

shutter (8-9) wooden covering for a window used to keep out light.

shuttle (8) instrument which carries the thread from side to side in making cloth; *Shuttle-train* = train which moves backwards and forwards along a short line.

shy (41) easily frightened; careful; not sure of oneself in the company of others; Sl. *I am shy of £5* = I have £5 less than I need; Sl. *-shy*, e.g. *Work-shy* = afraid of work, not willing to work; (of a horse) **to shy**, turn aside suddenly.

shy (41) to throw; Sl. *Have a shy at* = make an attempt.

shyster (41-9) Sl. dishonest lawyer.

sibilant (1-1-9) making a sound like a snake, or like the letter S.

sibs (1-z) **siblings** (1-1-z) children of the same father and mother.

sic (1) (Latin) thus.

sick (1) ill; *To be sick* = throw up food from the stomach; *I was sick* (English) = threw up food, (American) = was ill; *Sick of* = tired of; *Sick for* = desiring; *Homesick* = greatly desiring to go home; **sicken**, become sick, make sick, make tired of; Sl. **sickening** (——1) such as makes one feel very sad and angry; **sickly** (——1) not having strong health; (colour) unpleasant weak colour.

sickle (1) curved knife used for cutting corn, grass, etc.

SICKLE

side (41) (1) edge, e.g. *The side of a square*; (2) surface, e.g. *One side of a sheet of paper*; (3) not the end, e.g. *The side of a box*; (4) direction, e.g. *Look on the right-hand side*; (5) group; e.g. *On the side of the government, To take sides, To side with* = agree with and help; (6) adj. not in the main road, e.g. *A side road*; Sl. *To put on side* = behave in a proud way.

sideboard (41-55) closed-in table in a dining-room in which food, drink, plates, knives, etc. are kept; dishes of fruit, etc., are put on the top.

SIDEBOARD

sidelong (41-5) to the side, e.g. *A sidelong movement; A sidelong glance* = a look to the side.

sid'ereal (41-19-19) having to do with the stars.

sidewalk (41-55) Am. *footpath* (= path for people walking) at the side of a road.

siding (41-1) short side-line of a railway, e.g. one where carriages are kept when not in use.

sidle (up to) (41) go sideways to a person as if afraid.

siege (11j) *To lay siege to a town* = keep an army round a town and attack it in order to take it.

si'enna (12-9) brown colouring matter.

si'esta (12-9) short midday sleep.

sieve (1) round frame with a wire net at the bottom used for separating small things from large.

sift (1) pass through a *sieve* (see above); examine, separating the truth from that which is untrue.

sigh (41) draw in the breath as when sad, tired, or suddenly ceasing to be anxious.

sight (41) (1) power of seeing; something seen, e.g. *A beautiful sight*; (2) instrument for guiding the eye, e.g. *The sights of a gun; At sight, On sight* = as soon as seen; **to sight**, to notice; look carefully at as when aiming.

sightly (41-1) good-looking; *unsightly* = ugly.

sign (41) mark or letter or movement which stands for an idea; something which shows the future, e.g. *Clouds are a sign of rain;* **to sign,** send an idea without writing or speaking, e.g. *I signed to Mr. — to come; To sign one's name* = write one's name; *To sign on* = write one's name accepting employment; *To sign off* (in radio) = to say good-bye to the listeners; **a signboard** (41-55) notice-board telling the way, or telling about goods to be sold; **s'ignpost** (41-67) post at a crossing of roads showing the places to which the roads go.

signal (1-9) sound, movement or flag (etc.) which carries an order or idea to another person; *A railway signal* = board moved up or down to stop trains or let them pass; **to signal,** make signs.

signalize (1-9-41) add importance, e.g. *The victory was signalized with rejoicing.*

signatory (1-9-1) one who writes his name under an agreement.

signature (1-9tsh9) name of a person written by himself or herself; *Signature tune* = music played every time just before a certain person sings or plays on radio.

signet (1-1) piece of stone or metal cut as a *seal* (= thing used for pressing figures upon melted wax); **a s'ignet-ring** (+ 1) finger-ring used for this purpose.

sign'ificant (1-1-1-9) having special meaning; important.

signify (1-1-41) show by a *sign* (see 7th above); to mean; be important.

signor (11ny55) (in Italy) Mr., Sir; **sign'ora** (11ny55-9) Mrs., Madam; **signor'ina** (11ny9-11-9) Miss.

silent (41-9) not speaking or making a noise; quiet; n. **silence** (41-9-s).

silhou'ette (1-72) picture made by cutting round the edge of a shadow thrown on paper; black, shadow-like picture; picture-like shadow of a person.

silica (1-1-9) material such as sand and many glass-like kinds of stone.

silk (1) thread made by an insect, and used for making the best kinds of dress-materials.

sill (1) flat shelf at the bottom of a window.

silly (1-1) foolish.

silo (41-67) tower in which grass, etc., is put in order that it may change into a dark, strong-smelling mass eaten by cattle; **silage** (41-1j) food so made.

silt (1) fine earth and sand left on the land by a river.

silvan (1-9) of the forest.

silver (1-9) white metal used for money; colour of this metal; **silverware** (1-9-29) silver instruments and vessels, e.g. knives, spoons, plates, etc.

simian (1-19) of or like a monkey.

similar (1-1-9) like; n. **simil'arity** (1-1-3-1-1).

simile (1-1-1) saying that a thing is like something else, e.g. *Her teeth are like pearls.*

simmer (1-9) boil gently.

sim'oom, -n (1-77) very hot wind in Arabia.

simper (1-9) silly smile; to smile in a silly way.

simple (1) plain, unmixed; not clever; medicine made from one plant; **simpleton** (1-9) fool; **simpl'icity** (1-1s1-1) condition of being simple; **simply** (1-1) in a plain way; *Simply terrible* = very bad, as bad as possible.

simulate (1-17-21) pretend.

simult'aneous (1-9-21-19) happening at the same time.

sin (1) break the laws of God; act which breaks.—.

since (1-s) (1) after; from the time that —; (2) because.

sinc'ere (1-s19) (of feeling) not pretended, real.

sinecure (41-1-179) paid office in which the duties are very light.

s'ine d'ie (41-1 + 41·1) (Latin, without a day) *To postpone a meeting sine die* = put off a meeting to a later date without fixing the future date.

s'ine qu'a n'on (41-1 + 21 + 5) (Latin, without which, not) necessary part of an agreement.

sinew(s) (1-177z) strong threads fixing a muscle on to a bone; *Of mighty sinews* = strong; *The sinews of war* = money necessary for war.

sing (1) make musical sounds with the voice.

singe (1nj) burn slightly, e.g. the ends of hairs.

single (1ngg) one only; not married; *In single file* = line of men one behind the other; *To single out* = choose one special person (thing); **s'ingle-h'anded** (+ 3-1) without help.

singlet (1ngg-1) light, tight-fitting garment worn under the shirt.

singly (1ngg-1) one at a time.

singular (1ngg17-9) (1) meaning one person, e.g. "Man" is a singular noun, "men" is plural; (2) unusual.

Sinhal'ese (1-9-11z) native of Ceylon, not of (e.g.) Indian descent.

sinister (1-1-9) of the left hand; being a sign of future evil; *Having a sinister look* = looking as if intending to do evil; *Bar sinister, Bend sinister* = mark on a shield showing that the person is not a lawful descendant of the family.

sink (1ngk) go slowly down; go down to the bottom of water; become worse or weaker; *To sink a well* = make a deep hole to get water; **a sink,** square container with a waste pipe at the bottom, fixed to the wall (plates and dishes are washed in it); **a sinker** (1ngko) weight on a string used in fishing; **s'inking-fund** (1ngk1 + 8) money set aside year by year so as to pay off a debt.

sino- of China, e.g. **Sinophil** (41-67-1) a lover of China and the Chinese.

sinuous (1-179) not straight, but bending from side to side.

sinus (41-9) small hollow or pocket, e.g. inside a bone, in the brain, etc.

sip (1) to drink, taking a small quantity each time.

siphon (41-9) pipe of this shape ͡ with a longer downward arm used to draw liquid up over the edge and down out of a vessel; bottle filled with water into which gas has been pressed.

sir (99) title used in addressing a knight, or an older man than oneself.

SIPHON

sire (419) father; old form of *Sir* (see above); (of a horse or other animal) father.

siren (419-1) sea-fairy which sings and draws ships on to rocks; instrument which makes a loud noise, used on ships, also to call workers to work and warn of air-attack.

sirloin (99-51) meat from part of the back of cattle.

sir'occo (1-5-67) hot dry wind.

sissy (1-1) Sl. a boy who behaves like a girl.

sister (1-9) girl born from the same father and mother as oneself; nurse in charge of a room in a hospital; **a sisterhood** (——7) number of women joined together in a group for good works.

sit (1) *Sit on the fence* = not join one or other group; Sl. *Sit tight* = hold firmly to one's purpose; *The hen is sitting* = is covering eggs to make the young birds come out; *The judge (law-court) is sitting* = is working; *To sit in Parliament* = be a member of *Parliament* (= group of elected law-makers); *The coat sits well* = fits nicely; *Sit down under* = suffer without making any answer; *Sit for a portrait* = have a picture made of oneself; *To sit on a person* = be rude to him so as to make him less proud and more polite; *Sit out a play* = stay to the end; *Make a person sit up* = surprise, excite; *Sit up (late)* = not go to bed.

site (41) piece of ground on which a building might be built or is built.

situated (1-1721-1) placed; **situ'ation** (1-1721shn) a place; employment.

sizable (41-9) rather large.

size (41) big-ness; *Size in hats* = number showing how large a hat is; **to size**, arrange in order of size; *To size up a situation* = understand — thoroughly.

size (41) sticky liquid used to make cloth stiff, also mixed with colours for painting scenes in theatres, on walls, etc.

sizzle (1) make a sound as fat does in a hot cooking-pot.

skate (21) large flat fish.

skate (21) move over ice on iron blades fixed to the boots.

skein (21) quantity of wool or thread tied up loosely together.

skeleton (2-1) bony frame of the body; general plan of action; *A skeleton in the cupboard* = family secret.

skep (2) light basket; *hive* (= house) for bees.

sketch (1) rough unfinished drawing or painting; short account of anything; short play; **sketchy** (——1) incomplete; Sl. *She looks a sketch* = is dressed in an ugly and foolish way.

skew (177) turned to the side, not straight.

skewer (179) pin of iron or wood put through meat to hold it together.

ski(s) (sk11z or sh11z) shoes about 7½ feet long used for going over snow.

skid (1) to slip, e.g: a motor-car on a wet road; **a skid**, piece of wood or iron put under a cartwheel to prevent it turning.

skiff (1) small boat.

skill (1) that power of doing which is the result of practice.

skim (1) to clear thick matter from the top of liquid; run along over the surface of; to read hastily; **sk'im-m'ilk** (+ 1) milk from which the *cream* (= fatty part) has been taken.

skimp (1) not to supply enough of; not to use enough material or labour in a piece of work; adj. **skimpy** (1-1) not large enough, narrow.

skin (1) outer covering, e.g. of the body, of a fruit; container for liquid, made of the whole skin of an animal; **to skin**, to take the skin off; Sl. take all the money from.

skinflint (1-1) one who is very careful of money.

skinny (1-1) (of a person) very thin.

skip (1) jump a short distance; swing a rope under the feet and jump over it; pass quickly from one thing to another; miss out parts in reading.

skipper (1-9) master or captain of a ship.

skirmish (99-1) small irregular fight.

skirt (99) woman's dress from the waist downward; the edge; **to skirt**, go along the edge of.

skit (on) (1) piece of writing *imitating* (= copying) some book or play in such a way as to make people laugh at the thing copied.

skittish (1-1) playful, easily excited, e.g. horse, or an old woman behaving as if very young.

skittles (1-z) game in which one throws a ball to knock down bottle-shaped pieces of wood.

sk'uld'uggery (8-8-9-1) Sl. dishonest tricks.

skulk (8) hide so as to escape danger or work.

skull (8) bones of the head.

skunk (8ngk) small American animal with a very nasty smell; nasty person.

sky (41) space above us where clouds and stars are; **to sky**, hit a ball high in the air.

skylark (41-44) small bird which sings as it flies upward.

skylark (41-44) play noisily.

skylight (41-41) window in the roof.

skyscraper (41-21-9) very high building, as in New York.

slab (3) large flat block, e.g. of stone.

slack (3) not tight; lazy and careless; *Slack water* = time when the sea is neither coming in nor going out; *Slacks* = loose trousers; **a**

slacker (3-9) lazy person who does not do his duty.
slack (3) coal dust.
slag (3) waste matter left from melted metal.
slain (2I) p.p. of Slay.
slake (thirst) (2I) satisfy; *Slaked lime = lime* mixed with water, as used with sand for joining bricks.
slalom (2I-9) race on *skis* (= boards fixed to the feet for going over snow) downhill, turning from side to side to avoid posts.
slam (3) shut (a door) with noise; throw down with force.
slander (44-9) untrue report spoken to damage a person's character.
slang (3) words commonly used in speech but not always considered suitable or correct; **to slang**, scold.
slant (44) to slope.
slap (3) strike with the flat of the hand.
slapdash (3-3) bold and careless.
slash (3) to cut boldly and carelessly; hit with a thin stick or *whip* (= string tied to a stick).
slat (3) narrow board.
slate (2I) blue-grey rock which breaks easily into sheets, used for roofs; piece of this material used in schools for writing on; *To have a clean slate* = have no wrong acts remembered against one; Sl. **to slate**, scold.
slattern (3-9) woman who is careless and dirty in her dress, or in the house.
slaughter (55-9) act of killing; kill in large numbers.
slave (2I) unpaid servant owned by a master;
slavery (2I-9-I) state of being a slave.
slay (2I) kill.
sled (2) **sledge** (2j) **sleigh** (2I) carriage which slides over the snow on metal or wooden blades.
sl'edge-hammer (2j + 3-9) heavy hammer.
sleek (II) (of hair) smooth, oily; (of a person) too neat.
sleep (II) be in a state of complete rest—as in bed at night; **sleeper** (——-9) railway carriage with beds in it; **sleepers** (——-9z) wooden crosspieces under railway lines; **sl'eeping p'artner** (II-I + 44-9) part owner of a business who does not do any work in the business.
sleet (II) snow and rain mixed.
sleeve (II) that part of a garment which covers the arm; *To laugh in (up) one's sleeve* = to be secretly amused.
sleigh (2I) carriage which slides over snow on metal or wooden blades.
sleight-of-hand (4I + 9v + 3) cleverness of the hand; magic tricks which deceive the eye.
slender (2-9) long and thin; *Slender means* = little money.
slept (2) p.t. of Sleep.
sl'euth-hound (77 + 47) dog which follows the track of a man or beast by the smell;
sleuth, a *detective* (= one who tries to discover who has done a bad deed and to catch the wrong-doer).
slew (77) p.t. of Slay.
slew (77) see Slue.
slice (4Is) thin broad piece, e.g. of bread or cake; **to slice**, cut in this way.
slick (I) quick, clever; *I ran slick into* = ran straight against, came head to head against.
slid (I) p.t. of Slide.
slide (4I) move smoothly over; move quietly; to cause to slide; **a slide**, ice on which children slide; picture on glass to be shown by light on a sheet; *A slide rule* = instrument used for calculating; *A sliding scale of payments* = payments which are made greater or less according to changes in the amount of something, e.g. the needs of the person paid.
slight (4I) thin; weak; small in amount; unimportant; **to slight**, treat rudely, as if of no importance.
slim (I) thin.
slime (4I) soft sticky matter almost liquid.
sling (I) throw with a free movement of the arm; hang from a band, e.g. *A sword slung at his side*; *To sling up a box to put it on a ship*; **a sling**, piece of cloth or leather used for throwing a stone; band passed round a thing so as to lift or hang it up, e.g. *His arm was in a sling* = in a cloth tied round the neck to support it; *To sling mud at* = say bad things about.
slink (Ingk) move quietly and secretly.
slip (I) (1) move smoothly over, e.g. over ice; (2) slide by accident, e.g. *He slipped and fell on the ice*; Sl. *To slip up* = make a mistake; (3) to escape secretly, e.g. *He slipped away from the meeting*; *The name has slipped my memory*; *To slip on a dress* = put on quickly; **a slip**, mistake; garment worn by women under their outer clothes; loose covering; long thin piece, e.g. of wood, of paper; *A slip of a girl* = young girl; *A slip-carriage* = carriage which is let loose from the end of a train, while the rest of the train goes on; **slips**, rails down which a newly built ship moves into the sea.
slipper (I-9) loose shoe.
slippery (I-9-I) very smooth so as to cause slipping, e.g. *Ice is* —.
sl'ipshod (I-5) careless.
slit (I) long cut; narrow hole; to cut a narrow hole in.
slither (Iŏ9) to slip.
sliver (I-9) narrow piece, e.g. torn from a piece of wood.
slobber (5-9) allow liquid to run from the mouth.
sloe (67) small blue-black fruit with a bitter taste.
slog (5) to hit (a ball) hard; Sl. to work hard.

SLIP

slogan (67-9) war-cry in Scotland; easily remembered saying used in trading or in getting laws (or plans) made.

sloop (77) small sailing-ship with one *mast* (= upright pole carrying sails).

slop (5) let water fall carelessly, e.g. over the edge of a pot; **slops**, simple food for sick persons; waste water; **a sl'op-pail** (+ 21) container for waste water, e.g. from bedrooms; **a sl'op-basin** (+ 21) bowl into which the tea left in cups is poured.

slope (67) to lean, be not upright; **a slope**, leaning side, neither flat nor upright.

sloping (67-1) not flat nor upright, like the side of a hill.

sloppy (5-1) wet and dirty; careless; *Sloppy sentiment* = weak and silly feelings of love, etc., foolish talk about such feelings.

slops (5) loose-fitting clothes bought ready to wear.

slot (5) long narrow hole; track of a deer;

sl'ot-machine (+ 9sh11) a machine which pushes out a small box of sweets (etc.) when a piece of money is put into the slot.

sloth (67) laziness; **a sloth**, large South American animal, like a bear; it lives in trees.

slouch (47) lazy ungraceful way of walking or standing; *A slouch hat* = soft hat with the sides turned down.

SLOTH

slough (47) very wet muddy land.

slough (8f) (of a snake) throw off the old dead skin; piece of dead skin which comes off, e.g. from a burn.

sloven (8) lazy, dirty, careless person; **slovenly** (——-1) careless and lazy.

slow (67) not fast; not clever; uninteresting; *The clock is slow* = behind the right time; *A slowcoach* = person who is slow in thought and action.

sl'ow-worm (+ 99) small harmless black-brown snakelike creature.

sludge (8j) thick oily mixture of earth and water; thick waste liquid from houses in a city.

slue (77) to turn round on a centre.

slug (8) creature like a *snail* (= creature with a shell on its back, slow-moving and leaving a silvery track behind) but without a shell.

slug (8) small piece of metal used as a shot; Sl. **to slug**, hit hard.

sluggard (8-9) lazy person; **sluggish** (8-1) slow-moving, lazy.

sluice (77s) water-way with a door which can be opened or shut; **to sluice**, pour water over.

slum(s) (8) dirty back streets of a city; **to slum**, visit the poor.

slumber (8-9) sleep; to sleep.

slump (8) fall suddenly; sudden fall in the prices of goods.

slung (8) p.t. of Sling.

slunk (8ngk) p.t. of Slink.

slur (99) say in a careless not-clear way; *A slur on his character* = something said against —, a cause of blame.

slush (8) half-melted snow; watery dirt; bad poetry (etc.) in which there is unreal feeling and too much of it.

slut (8) dirty careless woman.

sly (41) deceiving cleverly and secretly.

smack (3) slight taste; to taste of; give a faint idea of.

smack (3) give a blow with the open hand; such a blow.

smack (3) small sailing-boat used for fishing.

small (55) not large, little, unimportant; *To look (feel) small* = foolish, ashamed; **sm'all arms** (+ 44-z) weapons (especially guns) which can be carried by soldiers.

sm'allpox (55-5) dangerous easily spread disease causing spots on the skin.

smarm (44) Sl. be too polite in an unpleasant way; adj. **smarmy** (44-1).

smart (44) feel a sharp pain in the surface of the skin.

smart (44) (1) done quickly and with force, e.g. *A smart blow*; *A smart pain* = sharp pain; (2) quick, skilful, clever; (3) clever but dishonest; (4) neat in appearance, e.g. *Smart clothes*; (5) according to the custom of the rich and well-born; *The smart set* = group of people who consider themselves to be the leaders in matters of dress and amusement.

smash (3) break to pieces; (of a business) to be ruined; **a smash**, serious accident; very hard blow, e.g. in the game of *tennis* (see —); Sl. **smashing** = very good.

smattering (3-9-1) *To have a — of a subject* = know a little of something and that not well, e.g. a foreign language.

smear (19) rubbed mark made with a thick oily liquid; **to smear**, mark in such a way.

smell (2) e.g. *I smell with my nose*; *My nose smells*; *Roses smell nice*; **a smell**.

sm'elling-salts (2-1 + 5) medicine used for smelling when one feels weak or ill.

smelt (2) small sea-fish; silver grey with a green back.

smelt (2) melt the metal out of rock.

smelt (2) p.t. of Smell.

smile (41) turn up the corners of the mouth showing pleasure or amusement.

smirch (99) make dirty; do harm to (one's good name).

smirk (99) to smile in a forced, unnatural way.

smite (41) to hit.

smith (1) worker in metal; **a blacksmith** (3-1) worker in iron, maker of horse-shoes; **a smithy** (101) place in which a blacksmith works.

smither'eens (109-11-z) small bits.

smitten (1) p.p. of Smite; *Smitten with* = admiring greatly.

smock (5) *sew* (= join with a needle and thread) regular folds in cloth as an ornament; **a smock**, loose outer garment so ornamented.
smog (5) smoke mixed with *fog* (= mist) in a large city so that one cannot see or breathe easily.
smoke (67) cloud given off by fire; **to smoke**, give off smoke; draw in smoke, e.g. from a cigarette; *To smoke meat or fish* = dry in a smoky place so as to keep it from decay and give it a pleasing taste.

SMOCK

smolder (67-9) see Smoulder.
smooth (77ō) polished; not rough; (of movement) easy and without shaking.
smote (67) p.t. of Smite.
smother (8ŏ9) keep air from; *To smother in (liquid)* = cover thickly with.
smoulder (67-9) burn slowly without flame.
smudge (8j) mark made by rubbing writing while it is still wet; rub wet writing or painting; rubbed mark of ink or dirt, e.g. on the face.
smug (8) very self-satisfied.
smuggle (8) take in or out secretly; take goods secretly into a country without paying money to the government.
smut (8) black bits that fall down out of smoke; disease of grain-growing plants.
snack (3) small hasty meal.
snaffle (3) two curved bars in a horse's mouth used to control the animal in riding; Sl. steal.
snag (3) log hidden in water, dangerous to boats; unexpected difficulty.
snail (21) small creature with a shell on its back, slow-moving and leaving a silvery track behind.
snake (21) long creature with no legs; some snakes have very poisonous bites.

SNAKE

snap (3) (1) break suddenly, like a dry stick; (2) make a sudden bite at; (3) to close with a sharp sound; *To take a snap (snapshot) of* = take a photograph of; *A cold snap* = sudden cold weather; **snappy** (——1) ill-tempered; (of a play or of writing) short and amusing.
snapshot (3-5) see Snap above.
snare (29) trap for birds or animals.
snarl (44) sound of an angry dog.
snatch (3) seize suddenly and without asking; get quickly or hurriedly, e.g. *To snatch a meal.*
sneak (11) move quietly and secretly; tell the teacher of another child's fault; *A sneaking regard for him* = feeling of friendship for him although he is unworthy.
sneer (19) to smile in such a way as to show disrespect.
sneeze (11) sudden outburst of breath through the nose and mouth; *Not to be sneezed at* = not to be treated as if worth nothing.

snicker, snigger (1-9) to laugh quietly and foolishly.
sniff (1) draw air up the nose; to smell; *To sniff at* = show that one thinks a thing of no importance.
snip (1) one cut (act of cutting) with *scissors*; Sl. *It's a snip* = it is certain; this horse is certain to win; **snippet** (1-1) very small piece cut off; *A snippet of poetry* = a few lines of —.
snipe (41) small bird with a very long beak which lives in wet or muddy ground.

SNIPE

sniper (41-9) single soldier who shoots from a hiding-place.
snivel (1) to cry with liquid running from the nose.
snob (5) one who has too great respect for persons of wealth and rank.
snoop (77) Sl. go about *spying* (= secretly watching people).
snooty (77-1) Sl. proud and unfriendly.
snooze (77) take a short sleep.
snore (55) make a loud unpleasant noise while sleeping.
snort (55) blow out or draw in air through the nose with a loud noise.
snout (47) nose of an animal, e.g. of a pig.
snow (67) water frozen in a white form like wool.
snowdrop (67-5) small white flower.
snub (8) behave rudely and coldly to a person whose behaviour does not please one; *A snub nose* = short thick nose.
snuff (8) (1) draw in through the nose; powder drawn up the nose; (2) to cut off the black burnt top of a candle.
snuffle (8) breathe noisily.
snuffy (8-1) Sl. ill-tempered.
snug (8) warm and comfortable.
snuggle (8) move and lie close to, e.g. as a child to its mother; *Snuggle down in bed* = get warm and comfortable in —.
s'o-and-so (67 + 67) some person whose name is not given.
soak (67) become wet through; make very wet; continue to drink too much wine.
soap (67) matter used with water to clean the hands, etc.; *A soapy fellow* = one who tries too hard to please; **s'oap-suds** (+ 8-z) soap mixed with water.
soar (55) to fly up in the air; increase very quickly, e.g. prices.
sob (5) draw in the breath while weeping.
sober (67-9) self-controlled and careful in the use of wine; living a quiet life; serious; *A sober judgment* = calm and wise; *Sober colours* = not bright; n. **sobr'iety** (6-419-1).
sobriquet (67-1k21) special name given to a

soccer | 283 | **songster**

person, e.g. Nosey as a name for a person who has a long nose.

soccer (5-9) Association Football, a form of the game in which the ball may not be touched with the hands, except by the *goal-keeper* (= player who stands between the posts at the end of the field).

sociable (67sh9) interested in meeting others; friendly.

social (67sh) living in a group, e.g. *Man is a social animal*; *Social life* = going to other people's houses and inviting guests to one's own house.

socialist (67sh9-1) one who believes that all means of producing wealth (all land, mills, works, etc.) should be owned by the government.

society (9s419-1) (1) way in which men live together ordering their lives according to law and custom, helping each other, and working together for common aims; (2) any group of men so living together; (3) particular group joined together for some special purpose, e.g. *A scientific society*; (4) persons of wealth and high rank; (5) company of others, e.g. *To enjoy the society of one's friends*; **soci'ology** (67s15-9j1) study of the nature and growth of human society.

sock(s) (5) short cotton, silk, or woollen coverings for the feet and part of the leg; Sl. to hit.

socket (5-1) hollow in which something turns, e.g. *The eye-socket*; hole into which something fits, e.g. *A socket for an upright pole*.

sod (5) mass of growing grass cut from the earth with its roots.

soda (67-9) white powdery material used to make washing easier; **s'oda-water** (+ 55-9) **soda**, water filled with gas, used as a pleasant drink; **soda fountain** (+ 47-1) machine for selling sweet drinks.

sodden (5) very wet.

sodium (67-19) white metal which burns in water.

-so'ever (672-9), e.g. *Whatsoever* = whatever.

sofa (67-9) long seat with a back and end, on which one can lie in the day-time.

soft (5) not hard; (of colour) not bright; (of sound) not loud; (of lines in a picture) not sharp, not clear; (of speech) gentle; (of persons) kind, weak; Sl: *He's a bit soft (in the head)* = mad; *Soft water* = not chalky; *Soft drinks* = not wine or strong drink; *Soft currency* = money which can be changed into dollars only according to certain rules.

soggy (5-1) heavy with water, e.g. wet earth.

soi-disant (sw4 + 1z4$4^n$) *A soi-disant soldier* = he calls himself a soldier (but really is not one).

soil (5I) that part of the earth in which plants grow.

soil (5I) make dirty.

soir'ée (sw44-2I) evening gathering of people.

sojourn (5-99) to stay for a time in a place.

solace (5-9s) comfort in trouble.

solar (67-9) of the sun.

s'olar pl'exus (67-9 + 2-9) mass of nerves behind the stomach.

sold (67) p.t. of Sell.

solder (5-9) easily melted metal used for joining other metals.

soldier (67-j9) fighting man in the army.

sole (67) under part of the foot or shoe.

sole (67) flat sea-fish, good to eat.

sole (67) only, e.g. *The sole support*.

solecism (5-1s1z) a mistake, especially in speaking or writing.

solemn (5-9) slow, serious.

solemnize (5-9-4I) make solemn; carry out a ceremony, e.g. *The marriage was solemnized in the church*.

sol'icit (9-1s1) invite; ask for.

sol'icitor (9-1s1-9) one who advises on law and prepares law cases for a *barrister* (see Barrister).

sol'icitous (9-1s1-9) eager to do; anxious about; n. **sol'icitude** (9-1-1-1-177).

solid (5-1) not liquid; firm, hard, strong.

sol'iloquize (9-1-9-4I) to speak one's thoughts aloud; n. **sol'iloquy** (9-1-9-1).

solit'aire (5-1-29) single jewel in a ring; a card game for one person.

solitary (5-1-9-I) living or being alone; n. **solitude** (5-1-177).

solo (67-67) piece of music played or sung by one person.

soluble (5-17) which can be melted in liquid, e.g. *Salt is soluble in water*; **sol'ution** (9-77shn) the act of mixing with a liquid; liquid in which something is mixed, e.g. salt water; *The solution of the difficulty* = finding an answer to a question or a way out of a difficulty.

solve (5) find the *solution* (see above) of a question or difficulty; **solvent** (5) (1) liquid, in which certain matter is *soluble* (see above), e.g. *Water is a solvent of salt*; (2) able to pay one's debts.

sombre (5-9) dark; sad.

sombr'ero (5-29-67) hat with a broad edge as worn in Mexico.

-some, causing, e.g. **quarrelsome** (5-9) = producing quarrels, eager to quarrel; **tiresome** (4I9-9) = causing one to feel tired; **troublesome** (8-9) = causing much trouble.

SOMBRERO

somersault (8-9-55) jumping, and turning the body completely over.

somn'ambulism (5-3-17-1z) sleep-walking.

somnolent (5-9-9) sleepy.

son (8) male child.

son'ata (9-44-9) piece of music divided into three or four parts, and played by one or two instruments.

song (5) music produced by the voice; words and music written for the voice.

songster (5-9) singer; singing bird.

sonic (5-1) having to do with sound.

sonnet (5-1) poem of 14 lines arranged in a special way.

son'orous (9-55-9) producing a deep and beautiful sound.

soon (77) in a short time.

soot (7) black powder which is left by smoke.

soothe (77ŏ) to calm an excited person.

soothsayer (77-219) one who tells the future.

sop (5) (1) bread which has been put in water, milk or other liquid; (2) something given to a person to please him or to keep him quiet for a time.

sophist (5-1) one whose reasoning is clever but not true.

soph'isticated (9-1-1-21-1) not natural; too wise in the ways of the world.

sophomore (5-9-55) Am. youth in his second year at a university.

sopor'ific (67-9-1-1-1) causing sleep.

sopr'ano (9-44-67) highest kind of singing voice in boys or women.

sorcerer (55s9-9) one who can do things by magic; **sorcery** (——-1) art of magic.

sordid (55-1) poor; dirty; ungenerous.

sore (55) painful; painful place on the body; *A sore grief* = great ——; *He's very sore about it* = angry.

sor'ority (9-5-1-1) group of women students in a university in U.S. Compare a *fraternity* (= group of men students).

sorrel (5) (1) sour-tasting plant eaten uncooked or boiled; (2) colour of a horse (red-brown).

sorrow (5-67) sadness.

sorry (5-1) sad, because of loss or wrongdoing; poor, worthless, e.g. *A sorry fellow*; *I feel sorry for him* = I pity him.

sort (55) kind, class; **to sort**, arrange each according to its kind; *He is out of sorts* = ill.

sortie (55-1) attack made by the soldiers in a town on those outside it.

S.O.S. (2s + 67 + 2s) message sent (by a ship) calling for help.

s'o so (67 + 67) not good, not bad.

sot (5) one who always drinks too much strong drink.

s'otto v'oce (5-67 + 67tshɪ) in a low voice.

sough (47) make a low sound like the wind.

sought (55) p.t. of Seek.

soul (67) man's spirit; a man's real nature or character; *I did not meet a soul* = did not meet anyone; *He was the life and soul of the gathering* = he kept everyone amused; *Poor soul!* = poor fellow; **soulful**, seeming to be full of fine feelings; **soulless** (67l·lɪ) not having any fine feelings.

sound (47) unbroken; healthy; strong; *Sound sleep* = deep ——; *A sound reason* = good ——; *Of sound mind* = not mad.

sound (47) waves in the air which cause hearing in the ear; **to sound**, cause to make a noise, e.g. *To sound a bell*; examine a thing (e.g. man's chest) by hitting it and listening to the sound.

sound (47) to measure the depth of water.

sound (47) long narrow piece of water, e.g. between an island and the mainland.

soup (77) liquid food made by boiling meat and vegetables in water.

sour (479) acid-tasting; ill-tempered.

source (55s) spring from which a river comes; first cause of anything.

souse (47) throw into water; preserve food in salt water.

south (47); adj. **southern** (8ŏ9); **southerly** (8ŏ9-1) in or from the south.

souvenir (77-9-19) thing kept in memory of a place or person.

sovereign (5-1) chief ruler; adj. *A sovereign state* = country which has full power to rule itself; piece of gold once used in English money; *A sovereign remedy* = medicine which is sure to drive away an illness.

Soviet (67-12) group of persons governing a town or piece of country in Russia who choose one of themselves to be member of the group which governs the whole country; the Russian government.

sow (47) female pig.

sow (67) scatter seeds.

spa (44) spring whose water is used as medicine; place where there is such a spring.

space (21s) any emptiness in which things are put, or might be put, or through which a thing might move, e.g. *There are many stars in space*; *There is space on this page for more words*; *There is a space between these two words*; *For a space of time* = for a length of time; **to space**, set out with regular spaces between; adj. **spacious** (21sh9).

spade (21) instrument used for digging; *To call a spade a spade* = be plain and truthful in speech; one sort of playing-card.

SPADE

spagh'etti (9-2-1) long thin sticks made from flour, cooked and eaten, especially in Italy.

spake (21) formerly p.t. of Speak.

span (3) to stretch from side to side; distance between the little finger and thumb when stretched out; distance from end to end of a bridge; pair of horses or cattle used to pull a cart; *For a span* = for a short time.

spangle (3ngg) any small bright object used as an ornament; *To spangle* = ornament with spangles.

SPADE (CARD)

spaniel (3-19) dog with long hair and long ears.

spank (3ngk) strike with the open hand.

spanner (3-9) instrument used for tightening or loosening *nuts* (*a nut* = small block of metal with a hole in it into which a screw fits); Sl.

Throw a spanner in the works = do something which causes work to stop.

spar (44) pole used on a ship for holding up and stretching out the sails.

spar (44) practise *boxing* (= fighting in a ring).

SPÁNIEL

spare (29) (1) not in plenty; (2) thin; (3) more than is necessary, kept for future use; *The spare wheel* =5th wheel carried on a motor-car; *Spare parts* = parts of a machine kept to be used when repairing; *The spare room* = guest-room in a house; **to spare** (1) keep from using something which one has; *To spare oneself* = not to work too hard; *To spare the rod* = not punish a child enough; (2) give away, do without; *He cannot be spared* = we need him, we cannot do without him; (3) show pity, e.g. *Spare my life* = do not kill me; (4) protect or save from; *I will spare you the painful story* = not pain you by telling you.

spark (44) very small piece of burning matter; flash made by electricity jumping from one wire to another; *A gay spark* = merry gentleman; **to spark**, give off sparks.

sparkle (44) give off *sparks* (see above); to flash light like a jewel.

sparrow (3-67) small common grey-brown bird.

sparse (44) thinly scattered.

spasm (3z) sudden tightening of the muscles of the face or body; any sudden great feeling, e.g. *A spasm of fear*; **spasm'odic** (3z-5-1) happening with great force but not lasting long.

spastics (3-1) people who cannot use their limbs because of damage to the brain before birth.

spat (3) p.t. of Spit.

spats (3) cloth coverings worn on the feet over the shoes or boots.

spatter (3-9) scatter liquid over.

spatula (3-17-9) flat instrument used to mix paint or powders; an instrument used by doctors to hold down the tongue when looking down the throat.

spawn (55) (of fish) produce eggs; the eggs produced; thread-like things from which a *fungus* (= plant containing no green material, found growing usually on wet decayed vegetable matter) grows.

speak (11) to talk; to talk to a meeting; *Speak up* = talk louder; *A speaking likeness* = picture which is very like the person; *Nothing to speak of* = very little; *He is, so to speak, head of the business* = is actually in charge of —; *Not on speaking terms* = having quarrelled.

spear (19) metal point fixed to a long stick used as a weapon; to strike with a spear.

special (2shl) not general; not for general use; not the usual; **a specialist** (2shg-1) one who has made particular study of one subject; **a sp'ecialty** (2shl-1), **speci'ality** (2sh13-1-1) thing which one does particularly well; one kind of goods for which a shop is well-known.

specie (11sh11z) money made of metal.

species (11sh11z) kind, sort.

spec'ific (1s1-1) having to do with one particular subject; medicine for one particular disease; **spec'ific gr'avity** (+ 3-1-1) relation of the weight of any matter to the weight of an equal amount of water.

specify (2s1-41) to name a particular thing, or write it in a list of things to be supplied; **sp'ecific'ation** (2s1-1-21shn) careful description of a thing to be made and the materials to be used.

specimen (2s1-1) thing, or part of a thing, used as an example.

specious (11sh9) seeming to be good but not really good.

speck (2) very small spot or mark; **speckled** (2) covered with small spots of colour, e.g. *A speckled hen*.

spectacle (2-9) a show, a grand sight; *A pair of spectacles* = glasses worn in front of the eyes to correct the eyesight.

spect'acular (2-3-17-9) very grand, providing a fine show.

spect'ator (2-21-9) one who looks on at a public show.

spectre (2-9) spirit of a dead person appearing to a living person.

spectrum (2-9) light broken up by a three-sided glass into bands of colour.

speculate (2-17-21) think; to guess; buy shares in business companies in the hope of gaining money by selling them again later.

sped (2) p.f. of Speed.

speech (11) power of *speaking* (= talking); long talk given in public.

speed (11) swiftness; move quickly; *At full speed* = as fast as possible; *Bid him Godspeed* = wish him a safe journey; **to speed**, to go quickly; *To speed up* = cause to go more quickly.

speed'ometer (1-5-1-9) instrument which shows how fast a motor-car is going.

spell (2) magic charm; *Spell-bound* = held as if by magic.

spell (2) time during which one works turn by turn with another; short time, e.g. *A spell of bad weather*.

spell (2) *To spell correctly* = write a word using the correct letters; p.t. **spelt**.

spend (2) pay out money; use up; p.t. **spent**; adj. **spent**, tired out, with no force left.

spendthrift (2-1) one who wastes money.

sperm (99) **sp'ermac'eti** (99-9s2-1) oil or fat obtained from a *whale* (= large sea creature)

spew (177) throw out of the mouth or up from the stomach.

sphere (19) ball; the earth; *One's proper sphere* = duty, kind of work which one can do best, sort of people with whom one should mix.

sphinx (1ŋgks) creature with the head of a woman, body of a lion, and wings; great stone image of this in Egypt; strange person about whom little is known.

spice(s) (4ɪsɪz) materials used to give a pleasant taste to food; **to spice**, to add spices to; *Spicy* = tasting of spice.

spick and span (1 + 3) clean and neat.

spider (4ɪ-9) 8-legged creature which lives in a fine net and eats flies.

spied (4ɪ) p.t. and p.p. of Spy.

spigot (1-9) wooden pin used to control the flow of liquid.

spike (4ɪ) pointed thing; *To spike his guns* = spoil his plans.

spill (1) (1) cause liquid to flow over; (2) to waste liquid; *To spill blood* = cause death or wounds; *To have a spill* = a fall, e.g. from a horse; p.t. spilt.

spill (1) thin piece of wood or paper used for lighting a candle, etc.

spin (1) pull and twist wool or cotton so as to make it into a thread; *To spin out a story* = tell at great length; *To go for a spin* = go for a drive or ride; *To spin round* = turn round and round; *To spin a coin* = cause a *coin* (= piece of money made of metal) to turn round and round by itself so as to decide a matter by chance.

spinach (1-1j) plant whose leaves are boiled into a soft mass for food.

spindle (1) bar on to which the thread is rolled or twisted in a machine used for *spinning* (= making thread from wool); thin bar or pin upon which anything turns; *Spindle-shanks* = a person with long thin legs.

spine (4ɪ) backbone; any needle-like thing, e.g. part of a plant or animal which pricks; *A spineless person* = weak-willed useless person.

spin'et (1-2) ancient stringed instrument played by striking *keys* (= blocks of wood) with the fingers.

spinster (1-9) unmarried woman.

spiral (4ɪ9-9) (1) going round and round and up and up, like a screw; (2) figure, as shown, like a watch-spring.

spire (4ɪ9) tall pointed roof on a tower.

SPIRAL

spirit (1-1) strong drink, e.g. *Whisky, Eau de vie, Brandy*; adj. **spirituous** (——179);

sp'irit-level (+ 2) glass tube containing liquid with a ball of air in it used in getting a flat level surface.

SPIRIT-LEVEL

spirit (1-1) soul; shadow-like form of a person supposed to be seen sometimes after death; fairy; *A generous spirit* = character; *In high spirits* = full of life and happiness; *He has no spirit* = no life, no eagerness; *To spirit away* = take away secretly as if by magic; *A spirited speech* = full of force and feeling; **spiritual** (1-1-179) having to do with the soul; **spiritualist** (——1) one who believes that the souls of the dead can be made to appear to and send messages to the living.

spirt (99) see Spurt.

spit (1) large pin or bar on which meat is cooked before a fire; narrow piece of land standing out into the sea; **to spit**, to push a spit through.

spit (1) throw out (liquid) from the mouth; make a noise as of spitting; Sl. *He's the dead spit of his father* = exactly like —— in appearance.

spitfire (1-4ɪ9) hot-tempered person.

spite (4ɪ) hatred and anger; **to spite**, do a thing in order to make a person angry; **in spite of**, not caring about, e.g. *I shall go in spite of the weather*.

spittle (1) liquid of the mouth.

spitt'oon (1-77) pot into which one *spits*.

spiv (1) over-dressed, dishonest young man.

splash (3) noise made by something falling into water; water thrown out by an object falling in; Sl. *To make a splash* = make a show, cause oneself to be noticed, e.g. by spending much money; **to splash**, throw drops of liquid over.

splay (21) to slope outwards; *Splay feet* = feet turned outwards.

spleen (11) part of the body found just behind the stomach which helps to make the blood pure (it was once thought to be the seat of ill-temper and grief).

splendid (2-1) fine; beautiful; bright; n. **splendour** (2-9).

splice (4ɪs) join two ropes by working the threads of one into the threads of the other; join wood by putting a tongue of one piece into the other; Sl. *Spliced* = married.

splint (1) thin piece of wood; boards used to hold a broken bone in place.

splinter (1-9) thin long piece of wood torn off (or standing out from) a larger piece.

split (1) divide into parts; break a piece of wood from end to end; Sl. *To split (one's) sides) with laughing* = laugh uncontrollably; *To split hairs* (in reasoning) = make much of very small and unimportant differences.

splutter (8-9) talk so quickly that the lips get in the way of the words and liquid is thrown from the mouth.

spoil (5ɪ) steal all that is valuable from a place; to damage and make useless; *A spoilt child* = child treated too kindly and not taught to obey; **the spoil(s)**, things stolen, e.g. by soldiers from a town.

spoke, spoken (67) p.t. and p.p. of Speak.

spoke(s) (67) bars joining the outer part of a

spokesman (67-9) one who speaks for others.

spoli'ation (67-12Ishn) stealing; act of *spoiling* (see 4th above).

sponge (8nj) soft yellow thing (used in one's bath) which takes in water and lets it out when pressed; real sponges are made by small creatures in the sea; *Throw up the sponge* = yield in a fight; **to sponge**, to clean with a sponge; *To sponge upon a person* = live at his cost.

sponsor (5-9) person who promises that another person will do certain things; business man who pays for music, etc., on radio to advertise his goods.

spont'aneous (5-21-19) happening without any outside cause, e.g. *Spontaneous combustion* = a fire which begins of itself; *To act spontaneously* = act without being asked or ordered to do so.

spook (77) spirit of a dead person.

spool (77) H-shaped wheel on which thread or any long band is kept; the thread is turned round and round the middle and the sides keep it from slipping off.

spoon (77) flat bowl on the end of a handle used in eating liquids, etc.

spoon (77) Sl. (of two people) make loving speeches, and kiss.

spoor (79) track of a wild animal.

spor'adic (9-3-1) happening in scattered places or from time to time.

spore (55) kind of seed.

sport (55) amusement; outdoor exercise; hunting, shooting and fishing; *He said it in sport* = to amuse, not meaning it; *To make sport of* = cause people to laugh at; *It is a sporting chance* = not probable but just possible; a **sportsman** (——9) one who loves sport; a **sport**, one who plays honestly; one who is not angry when he loses; **sporting** (——1) having to do with sport; not angry at losing a game; **sportive** (——1) playful.

spot (5) particular place; a mark; **to spot**, make a mark on; see or recognize; **spotted** (——1), **spotty** (——1) covered with spots.

spouse (47z) husband or wife.

spout (47) water coming out with force; pipe which stands out from any container (e.g. a tea-pot) from which liquid is poured; **to spout**, pour out with force, e.g. water from a pipe; Sl. speak quickly and continuously.

sprain (21) pull or turn a limb with such force as to cause damage; damage so caused.

sprang (3) p.t. of Spring.

sprat (3) small sea-fish; *Set a sprat to catch a mackerel* = offer something small so as to get something big.

sprawl (55) spread out the limbs ungracefully.

spray (21) (1) fine drops of water flying through the air; liquid forced out of a pipe into a fine mist; (2) small branch of a tree with its leaves; **to spray**, direct a stream of fine drops of liquid upon, e.g. to spray one's throat.

spread (2) to cover with, e.g. *Spread butter on bread* = cover bread with ——; send or go in all directions, e.g. *To spread a story*; *The disease spread*.

spree (11) *To have a spree* = have an amusing time; Sl. *To go out on the spree* = go out for drinking and wild amusement.

sprig (1) part of a branch of a tree bearing a few leaves or flowers; **sprigged**, ornamented with pictures of sprigs.

sprightly (41-1) gay and amusing.

spring (1) to jump; *A breeze springs up* = small wind starts to blow; *To spring a surprise* = do something which surprises people; (of a ship) *To spring a leak* = let in water through the side or bottom.

spring (1) water coming out of the earth, e.g. as the beginning of a river; *This springs from* = is caused by.

spring (1) piece of metal which, when bent, unbends itself (or, if a curled spring, when curled up, uncurls again).

spring (1) the next season after winter; *To spring-clean a house* = clean everything very thoroughly (usually in the spring).

spr'ing-t'ide (1 + 41) specially large *tide* (= inflowing of the sea on to the land caused by the moon) at the new or full moon.

sprinkle (1ngk) scatter liquid over.

sprint (1) run as fast as possible.

sprite (41) fairy.

sprocket (5-1) tooth on a *chain-wheel* (= wheel with teeth fitting into a chain, as on a bicycle).

sprout (47) begin to grow; very young plant; small group of young leaves on a plant.

spruce (77s) well and carefully dressed; *To spruce oneself up* = set one's hair, clothes, etc., in order.

spruce (77s) kind of tree; the white wood of this tree.

sprung (8) (1) p.p. of Spring; (2) bent out of shape, cracked by bending.

spry (41) quick in action and full of life.

spud (8) (1) instrument with a narrow blade used for getting *weeds* (= unwanted wild plants in a garden) out of the soil; (2) Sl. *potato* (= round root, floury when boiled, used for food).

spun (8) p.p. of Spin.

spunk (8ngk) dry wood which burns easily; courage; spirit.

spur(s) (99z) instruments worn on the back of the foot, used for pricking a horse to make it go fast; sharp point on the back of a bird's leg; anything standing up in this way, e.g. a hill from a range of hills; **to spur**, drive on faster; **to spur on**, urge a person to do something; *To win one's spurs* = prove one's courage or worth.

spurious (179-19) not real, but made to look like the real, e.g. paper money printed by thieves.

spurn (99) kick away; treat as worthless or bad.

spurt (99) (of liquid) rush out suddenly and with force; sudden stream of liquid, e.g. from a pipe; *To make a spurt* = try hard for a short time, e.g. to run very fast when nearing the winning-post.

sputnik (7-1) case containing scientific instruments sent up so high that it goes round the earth like a moon.

sputter (8-9) throw out small pieces, e.g. *A wet candle sputters*; speak so quickly that drops of liquid are thrown out.

sputum (177-9) sticky liquid thrown out from the throat.

spy (41) one who goes secretly to find out about the enemy; to watch secretly; see at a distance; **spy-glass** (+ 44) glass used for seeing distant objects.

squabble (5) to quarrel about an unimportant matter.

squad (5) small party, e.g. of soldiers.

squadron (5-9) group of 120-200 horse-soldiers; number of warships acting together; group of 12 aeroplanes.

squalid (5-1) dirty; poor.

squall (55) (of a baby) cry loudly.

squall (55) sudden storm.

squalor (5-9) dirtiness and *poverty* (= state of being poor).

squander (5-9) to waste money.

square (29) figure shaped as diagram; open space in a city with houses on four sides of it; *A square inch* = 1 inch each way; **squared**, e.g. $3^2 = 9$; **squ'are r'oot** (+ 77) e.g. $\sqrt{9} = 3$; *To square up with* = pay off debts; *All square* = owing nothing to each other; *I've squared him* = paid all I owe, or paid money so that he will do as I wish; *A square deal* = piece of business fair to both buyer and seller; *A square meal* = a good satisfying meal.

SQUARE

squash (5) flatten by pressing; silence a person by an unkind speech; game played by hitting a ball against a wall; Am. very large vegetable-fruit, green outside, yellow inside, boiled for food.

squat (5) sit down on the *heels* (= back of the foot); *A squat person* = short thick-bodied person.

squatter (5-9) person who settles on public land without having the right to do so; in Australia, a wealthy farmer.

squaw (55) American-Indian woman.

squawk (55) short cry of pain or fear, e.g. of a hen when hurt.

squeak (11) short high cry, e.g. of a mouse; *I had a narrow squeak* = only just escaped something (great danger).

squeal (11) long high cry, e.g. of a pig in pain; **to squeal**, give such a cry; Sl. tell of the wrong-doing of a friend.

squeamish (11-1) feeling sick, e.g. on a ship; easily made to feel sick; very careful about matters of honesty.

squ'eeg'ee (11j11) thing like a brush, but with a rubber edge, used to drive the water off a wet floor, street, etc.

squeeze (11) press into a smaller space, e.g. in order to get out the liquid; get money with difficulty out of a person.

squelch (2) (1) flatten by pressing—especially something with liquid in it, e.g. a fat insect; (2) noise of walking in a wet field.

squib (1) small paper case of gunpowder which bursts with a loud noise; short written attack upon a person.

squint (1) look cross-eyed (the two eyes not pointing in the same direction); Sl. *Have a squint at* = look at.

squire (419) country gentleman; servant of a knight in old days; man attending lovingly on a lady.

squirm (99) turn the body about like a snake, e.g. when feeling great pain or shame.

squirrel (1-9) pretty tree-animal with four legs and a very large bushy tail.

squirt (99) send out a small stream of water; instrument used for this, e.g. for watering flowers.

SQUIRREL

St., street; *saint* (s9nt), e.g. *St. John*.

stab (3) to wound with a pointed weapon.

stable (21) steady, not easily changed; **stab-ilize** (21-1-41) make steady; **stab'ility** (9-1-1-1) steadiness.

stable (21) house in which horses or cattle are kept.

stacc'ato (9-44-67) (of sounds) short, sharp and not joined to other sounds (notes).

stack (3) neat heap of wood, bricks, etc.; **ch'imney-stack** (1-1 + 3) one tall chimney, or several chimneys together; **to stack**, form into a stack.

stadium (21-19) open space for games with seats all round it.

staff (44) stick used in walking, or as a sign of office; **a flagstaff** (3-44) pole for a flag.

staff (44) group of persons who help a leader, e.g. *The staff of a school* = all the teachers; *The staff of the leader of an army* = officers who help to draw up plans; **to staff**, supply with helpers or workers.

stag (3) male deer.

stage (21j) (1) raised part of a hall or theatre on which the performers stand; *To go on the stage* = become an actor; (2) resting-place on a journey; distance between two resting-places; certain point in growth or change, e.g. *At this stage of life*; *At an early stage in the history of India*; **to stage**, put a play on the stage; *Stage directions* = orders to an actor written in a play showing what things he

stagger (3-9) walk unsteadily; surprise greatly; *Staggered office hours* = times arranged so that all the workers do not come (go) at the same time, thus causing less crowding in buses and trains.

stagnant (water) (3-9) not flowing, dirty and bad-smelling from standing long in one place; **to stagn'ate** (3-21) (of liquid) cease to flow; (of a person) remain *inactive* (= not in action) in an uninteresting place, or (of the mind) lose interest.

staid (21) steady and serious (person).

stain (21) change the colour of; make a coloured mark on; *Stainless steel* = steel (= strong form of iron) which cannot be stained.

stair(s) (29z) steps, e.g. for going up and down; **staircase** (29-21) **stairway** (29-21) steps inside a house.

stake (21) (1) post driven into the ground; (2) money risked on an event, e.g. the *stakes* (= money) of Mr. A, Mr. B and Mr. C will be given to Mr. C if his horse wins; *At stake* = in danger of being lost.

stale (21) not fresh; heard before.

st'alem'ate (21-21) condition in which neither person can win.

stalk (55) stem of a plant on which the leaves and flowers grow; stick of a leaf or fruit which joins it on to the plant.

stalk (55) move slowly and carefully towards an animal so as to kill it; walk proudly.

stall (55) that part of a cow-house in which one cow is kept; place for one horse in a *stable* (= house for horses); small lightly built shop, e.g. *The bookstall in a railway station*; seat in a theatre or church; *To stall one's engine* = stop the engine of a motor-car by careless driving; *To stall* = to delay, cause delay so as to gain time.

stallion (3-19) male horse.

stalwart (55-9) strong and brave.

stamen (21-2) *pollen-bearing* (= having dust which starts growth in the seed) part of a flower.

stamina (3-1-9) strength.

stammer (3-9) speak with difficulty, e.g. "I m-m-must g-go."

stamp (3) press a mark upon; bring the foot down heavily; **a stamp**, instrument used for printing marks on; a small piece of paper stuck to a letter to pay for sending it; *Men of that stamp* = of that kind; *To stamp out a fire, a disease, an evil* = put out, put an end to.

stamp'ede (3-11) sudden rush of frightened animals.

stanch (44) see Staunch.

stanchion (44-sh9) iron post used as a support.

stand (3) be upright on; to set upright on; *£ stands for "pounds"* = means —; *Stand for an office* = try to be elected to —; *I can't stand it!* = bear, suffer; *It stands to reason* = it is not necessary to explain that —; *To stand drinks* = give drinks to; *To stand by a person* = help and support; **a stand,** ornamental *base* (= bottom) on which things are set, e.g. *A flower-stand*; rows of seats rising behind each other on which people sit to watch a game; *A stand-in* = man or woman who takes the place of an actor (actress) when unimportant or dangerous work is being done in making a cinema film; *A man of good standing* = of good rank, of good name; **st'and-'offish** (5-1) proud and unwilling to be friendly.

standard (3-9) flag; fixed weight, length, strength, etc., to which things must be made equal; *Not up to standard* = not as good as is demanded by law or by agreement; class or level of study in a school; *A standard author* = writer accepted by all as good; **standardize** (3-9-41) fix according to a standard so as to prevent change and *variety* (= various-ness).

standpoint (3-51) *point of view* (= way of considering things).

stank (3ngk) p.t. of Stink.

stanza (3-9) group of lines in a poem.

staple (21) U-shaped nail pointed at both ends, ∩.

staple (21) most produced, most used; e.g. *Rice is the staple crop of Bengal—it is also the staple food*.

star (44) other worlds and suns seen in the sky at night; figure of this shape ★; very well-known actor or singer.

starboard (44-9) right side of a ship when one faces forward.

starch (44) white powder mixed with water and used to make clothes stiff.

stare (29) look steadily at with wide-open eyes.

stark (44) quite; *Stark naked* = having no clothes on at all; *Stark staring mad* = quite mad.

starling (44-1) small noisy bird.

starry-eyed (44-1 + 41) looking at the stars not at the earth; thinking of beautiful but impossible plans.

start (44) (1) begin; set out on a journey; cause others to begin; (2) to jump with sudden fear; *His eyes starting out of his head* = wide-open with fear; *By fits and starts* = not regularly, from time to time.

startle (44) to surprise and frighten.

starve (44) be without food; keep a person without food.

state (21) condition; nation; *He lives in great state* = in a very fine and rich way; **stately** (——1) solemn, fine.

state (21) say as a fact; *At stated times* = at times fixed and made known; **a statement** (——9) fact said or written; written paper telling certain facts.

statesman (21-9) one skilled and learned in the art of government.

static (3-1) standing still; electricity in the air which causes difficulty when sounds are sent through the air by electricity (in radio).

station (21shn) place where people stand; stopping-place for railway-trains; one's place in life; place to which a person goes to serve as an officer of government; *A fire station* = place where *fire-engines* (= engines for putting out fires) are kept.

stationary (21sh9-9-1) not meant to be moved about, e.g. *A stationary engine*; *To remain stationary* = to stay still.

stationery (21sh9-9-1) writing materials, e.g. paper, pens, etc.; **stationer**, one who sells —.

stat'istics (9-1-1) facts shown by numbers; **statist'ician** (3-1-1shn) one who deals with statistics.

statuary (3-179-1) art of making *statues* (see below); collection of —.

statue (3-177) figure of a man, animal, etc., cut out of stone or made in metal, wood; **statu-'esque** (3-172-k) beautiful and calm like a statue; **statu'ette** (3-172) small statue.

stature (3tsh9) natural height of the body.

status (21-9) rank or place in relation to others; **st'atus qu'o** (21-9 + kw67) same state as before a certain date.

statute (3-177) law.

staunch (55) stop the flow of blood; adj. firm, loyal.

stave (21) curved piece of wood forming part of a barrel; short pole; wooden cross-bar; few lines of poetry; five lines on which music is written; *To stave in* = break inwards, e.g. a boat or barrel; *To stave off* = keep off, prevent.

stay (21) (1) stop or delay action; *Stay one's hand* = delay taking action; *Stay judgment* = delay carrying out the orders of a court of law; *Stay the course* = have strength to finish a race; *Staying power* = strength to continue; (2) remain in a place for a short time, e.g. on a visit.

stay (21) a support; a post; strong rope or wire holding up a post; *To stay one's appetite* = satisfy hunger; **stays** (——z) = stiff body support worn by women.

stead (2) *Instead of* = in place of; *Will stand you in good stead* = will help you.

steadfast (2-9) not changing; determined; loyal.

steady (2-1) firmly fixed, regular, unchanging.

steak (21) thick piece of meat or fish.

steal (11) take away secretly a thing which belongs to another; move quietly.

stealthy (2-1) acting in such a way as not to be noticed, secret; n. **stealth**.

steam (11) gaseous form of water; **steamer** (11-9) ship which goes by steam; instrument used for cooking food by steam.

steed (11) horse.

steel (11) iron mixed with *carbon* (e.g. black burnt wood or coal is carbon) to make it stronger; *To steel one's heart* = to harden —, show no pity.

steep (11) sloping up quickly; Sl. *That's rather steep* = more than I will allow, more money than I will pay.

steep (11) make things wet through, e.g. *To steep vegetables in water* = leave in water for a long time.

steeple (11) church tower, usually with a tall pointed roof.

steeplechase (11-21) horse-race across the country, over walls, streams, etc.

steer (19) guide (a ship); *Steer clear of* = keep away from.

steer (19) young *ox* (= male of cattle).

steerage (19-1j) act of *steering* (2nd above); that part of a ship in which one may travel at least cost.

stellar (2-9) having to do with the stars.

stem (2) main or central stick of a plant; front part of a ship; main part of a word to which different beginnings and endings are added.

stem (2) stop the flow of (water).

stench (2) bad smell.

stencil (2-81) piece of paper or metal with holes in it through which colour is pressed as a way of printing.

sten'ographer (2-5-9-9) one who writes down speeches in a special kind of writing.

stent'orian (voice) (2-55-19) very loud.

step (2) move the foot in walking; a step, one movement of the foot; distance so moved; sound of a foot walking; one part of a stair; *Our next step is to* = the next thing we must do is —; *A pair of steps, a step ladder* = wooden steps which can be opened into a Λ shape for climbing up; *Stepping-stones* = stones in a stream used for crossing it.

step- (-brother, -sister, etc.) child of an earlier or later marriage of one's mother or father; *My stepfather* (2-44ð9) = my mother's husband after the death of my father.

-ster, one who does, e.g. a **gamester** (21-9) one who plays games for money.

stereoscope (19-19-67) instrument through which one looks at two pictures at once, so that the figures stand out and appear to be solid.

stereotype (19-19-41) printing-plate made by pressing wet paper on to *type* (= metal letters from which printing is done) and pouring melted metal into the pressed paper; **to stereotype**, make such a plate; make fixed and unchangeable.

sterile (2-41) (soil) unable to produce crops, etc.; (book) having no ideas in it; **to sterilize** (2-1-41) make sterile; to free from seeds of disease.

sterling (99-1) of fixed value; pure; trustworthy; English money.

stern (99) very serious in manner and without mercy.

stern (99) back of a ship—or other thing.

sternum (99-9) breast-bone.

stertorous (breathing) (99-9-9) noisy.

stethoscope (2-9-67) instrument for listening to sounds in the body, especially the breathing or the heart.

stevedore (11-1-55) man in charge of loading or unloading a ship.

stew (177) cook meat and vegetables in water; dish so made; Sl. *In a great stew* = very excited.

STETHOSCOPE

steward (179) man-servant on a ship; man in charge of the food and living arrangements in a large house; person giving help at a public gathering; **stewardess** (——1) woman-servant on a ship.

stick (1) long thin piece of wood broken from a plant or tree; long thin piece of anything, e.g. *A sugar stick*; *He's a stick* = is ungraceful and uninteresting.

stick (1) (1) push a pointed thing into; put, e.g. *Don't stick your head out of the window*; *To stick out one's tongue*; *His nose sticks out from his face* = stands out; (2) fix on to, e.g. *To stick a stamp on*; *Stick close to me* = keep close; (3) become fixed, e.g. *This door sticks*; *A stick-in-the-mud* (*mud* = wet earth) = person without imagination or interest in new ideas; *He sticks at nothing* = is afraid of nothing, will use any trick however dishonest.

stickler (1-9) one who is stiff in his opinions about unimportant matters.

sticky (1-1) sticking, e.g. *Melted sugar is sticky*; *A sticky person* = uninteresting, difficult to amuse, solemn.

stiff (1) unbending; not easily moved; difficult; *The wind stiffened* = became stronger.

stifle (41) prevent from breathing; *This room is stifling* = the air is too hot or too bad to breathe; *To stifle one's tears* = try to stop or at least hide —.

stigma (1-9) burnt sign on a slave; mark of shame; any small mark on the body; part of flower into which male cells are put (see Pistil); **to stigmatize** (——41z) mark as shameful; say that a thing is bad.

stile (41) step or steps for getting over a fence.

stil'etto (1-2-67) small pointed weapon; point for making holes in cloth.

still (1) not moving, peaceful; *A picture of still life* = of things that do not move, e.g. fruit; **to still**, make calm; e.g. *Christ stilled the storm*.

still (1) up till now; up till then; always; *Still more* = yet more.

still (1) but.

still (1) pipes, etc., used for making strong drink.

st'ill-born (+ 55) born dead.

stilts (1) long poles with supports for the feet so made that one is able to walk at a height above the ground; **stilted** (——1) stiff and solemn (way of speaking or writing).

stimulate (1-17-21) excite; drive on; *a stimu-*lant (1-17-9) any liquid which increases one's powers for the time, e.g. tea; **stimulus** (——9) something which excites and drives one on.

sting (1) prick the skin and drive in poison; **the sting**, e.g. of a bee, part which stings; swelling caused; *This liquid stings* = causes pain on the skin; Sl. *He stung me* = he cheated me.

stingy (1njı) too careful of money.

stink (ıngk) bad smell.

stint (1) not to give enough of; fixed amount of work, e.g. for one day.

stipend (41-2) fixed payment for work; adj. **stip'endiary** (——19-1) serving for pay.

stipple (1) draw or paint with very small spots instead of lines.

stipulate (1-17-21) arrange specially as part of an agreement.

stir (99) move; cause to move; excite; move liquid round with a spoon.

stirrup (1-9) D-shaped piece of iron in which one puts one's foot when riding a horse, ⌂.

stitch (1) join with a needle and thread; single in-and-out action of a needle; *Without a stitch on* = wearing no clothes at all; *To get a stitch* = get a sharp pain in the side as a result of running fast; *A stitch in time saves nine* = action now may save much trouble later.

stock (5) (1) main stem of a tree; (2) family or birth, e.g. *He is of good stock*; (3) handle of a gun; (4) store of goods for selling in a shop; *To take stock* = to count and make a list of such goods; (5) liquid of boiled bones and meat kept for use in cooking; (6) money lent to the government; or shares in a business company; (7) band of cloth worn round the neck; **to stock**, supply with goods; keep a store of goods in a shop; **livestock** (41-5) cattle; *A laughing-stock* = person or thing at which all laugh.

stock'ade (5-21) place encircled by a wall made of upright posts.

stockbroker (5-67-9) one who sells shares in business companies.

St'ock Exchange (+ 1-21nj) place where shares in business companies are bought and sold.

st'ock-farmer (+ 44-9) one who keeps cattle or sheep.

stocking (5-1) tight-fitting garment of wool, silk, or cotton pulled over the foot and leg.

st'ock-in-tr'ade (5 + 1 + 21) goods used in carrying on a business.

st'ock-market (+ 44-1) = *Stock Exchange* (see 4th above).

stockpile (5-41) big store of some important substance (e.g. cotton, wheat, oil) kept in case of special need, e.g. in a future war; **to stockpile**, to store up.

stocks (5) frame in which men were fixed as a punishment; frame in which a ship is built or repaired.

st'ock-st'ill (+ 1) quite still, not moving.

st'ock-whip (+ 1) *whip* (= string fixed to a stick used for beating) for cattle.

stocky (man) (5-1) short and strong.

st'ock-yard (+ 44) place where animals are killed for meat.

stodgy (5j1) heavy; stiff; uninteresting.

stoep, stoop (77) unroofed steps and raised flat-roofed space in front of houses in South Africa, etc.

stoic (67i) person who accepts pleasure and pain equally calmly.

stoke (67) put coal into a *furnace* (= large closed fire); eat a lot hastily; **st'okehold, stokehole** (67-67) part of a ship where the coal is put on the fires to make steam.

stole (67) **stolen** (67-9) p.t. and p.p. of Steal.

stole (67) long band of silk worn by a priest; long band of fur or feathers worn by a woman.

stolid (5-1) not easily excited.

stoma (67-9) scientific word for mouth; **stomata** (67-9-9) mouths.

stomach (8-9k) bag-like part of the body into which food goes; *I cannot stomach it* = allow such a thing to be said (or done) without complaining.

stone (67) small piece of rock; hard centre in a fruit; hard mass formed inside the body in certain diseases; measure of 14 pounds; jewel; **to stone**, throw stones at; to cover with stone; take fruit-stones out; *Stone blind* = completely —

stood (7) p.t. of Stand.

stooge (77j) Sl. foolish person who does whatever he is told, e.g. helping an actor to make his jokes.

stool (77) small seat with no back; *To pass a stool* = drive waste matter downwards out of the body.

st'ool-pigeon (+ 1j1) person employed to go with wrong-doers in order to find out their plans.

stoop (77) bend the body forward and down; *To stoop to do* = not to be too proud to —.

stoop (77) (of a house) see Stoep.

stop (5) to close; to block up; cease; to stay (at); **stop** (of an *organ*) set of pipes producing a certain set of sounds; **stop** (of *camera* = an instrument for taking photographs), means of making the hole for letting in the light smaller; **stopper** (5-9) round block of glass used to close the mouth of a bottle.

storage (55-1j) act of or price for storing (see below); **st'orage battery** (+ 3-9-1) **st'orage cell** (+ s2) box with metal plates and acid in it, which stores up electricity.

store (55) keep a supply ready for use; the supply so kept; large shop which sells all kinds of things; Am. any shop; *To set great store on* = value greatly.

storey, story (55-1) first, second, etc., floor of a house.

stork (55) large bird with very long legs.

storm (55) wind, rain and thunder; any great show of force or excitement; *To storm a fort* = attack and seize; *A storm in a teacup* = great excitement over nothing.

story (55-1) account of events, real or imagined; *To tell stories* = tell untruths.

stout (47) strong; fat; dark brown bitter strong drink, made from grain.

stove (67) enclosed fire used for cooking or heating.

stove (in) (67) broken inwards, e.g. a boat.

stow (67) pack tightly into; to load on to a ship.

stowaway (67-9-21) one who hides on a ship so as to travel without paying.

straddle (3) stand or sit with one's legs far apart over something.

straggle (3) move about (or lie about) loosely and irregularly; (of tired soldiers) to spread out behind the army.

straight (21) direct; not bent; honest; *Straight away* = at once; **straightf'orward** (21-55-9) adj. honest.

strain (21) (1) pull as much as possible; (2) to damage by pulling too much; (3) try hard; (4) pass liquid through a cloth or wire net in order to get out solid matter; *Strained him to his breast* = pressed —; *It was a great strain* = the work was very hard; **a strainer** (——9) instrument used for straining liquid.

strait (21) narrow, e.g. *Enter in at the strait gate*; *A strait jacket, A strait waistcoat* = special coat for tying up mad persons; **a strait**, narrow piece of water joining two larger pieces; **straiten**, make narrow; *In straitened circumstances* = having very little money; **str'aitlaced** (21 + 21st) stiff and hard in character and behaviour.

strand (3) one of the threads that make up a string or rope.

strand (3) shore; **to strand**, run a ship on the shore; *Left stranded* = deserted by one's friends when in difficulty.

strange (21nj) not one's own; not well known; foreign; peculiar; **a stranger** (——9) foreigner; person from another place.

strangle (3ngg) kill by holding the throat tightly.

strap (3) leather band; any narrow band; **to strap**, beat with a strap; **to strap up**, put leather bands round a box or bag in order to close it.

strapping (boy) (3-1) big and strong.

strata (44-9) pl. of Stratum (see 3rd below).

stratagem (3-1j9) a trick to deceive.

strategy (3-1j1) art of moving armies before a battle (*Tactics* is the art of war during a battle).

stratum (44-9) *layer* (= a thickness of material spread over a surface) of rock or other material forming part of the earth's surface.

straw (55) stem of a grain-bearing plant; *A man of straw* = unimportant person treated as if important—usually for dishonest purposes.

strawberry (55-9-1) small red fruit with little seeds on its surface (it grows on the ground).
strawboard (55-55) very thick yellow card as used inside the covers of books and for boxes.
stray (21) wander from the path; go wrong; *A stray cat* = lost or homeless cat, wandering about.
streak (11) line of colour.

STRAWBERRY

stream (11) small river; flowing of any liquid or gas; crowd of people or things all moving in one direction; **streamlet** (——1) small stream.
streamer (11-9) long narrow flag.
streamlined (11-41) e.g. motor-car—shaped so that the air may flow easily over its surface.
street (11) public way in a city; *Not in the same street with* = not nearly as good as.
strength (2) quality of being strong, strongness.

STREAMLINED MOTOR-CAR

strenuous (2-179) needing great strength, using much strength, e.g. *A strenuous game; A strenuous worker.*
stress (2) lay special weight on; say with special force, e.g. *He stressed the word "If"*; difficulty, trouble, e.g. *Under stress of bad weather the ship had to return; Times of stress* = of difficulty and danger.
stretch (2) make larger or longer by pulling; pull tight; to spread out, e.g. *He stretched himself out on the bed; Three hours at a stretch* = without stopping to rest; *A stretch of country* = wide piece of.
stretcher (2-9) frame used for carrying sick persons.
strew (77) to scatter.
stricken (1) old p.p. of Strike; *Stricken with age* = very old; *The stricken* = the wounded.
strict (1) unyielding; exact; demanding exact *obedience* (n. of Obey).
stricture (1-tsh9) blame; narrowing of a pipe so that liquid cannot pass.
stride (41) take long steps; *He will take it in his stride* = do it without pausing or without special work.
strident (voice) (41) high and unpleasant.
strife (41) quarrelling, fighting.
strike (41) (1) to hit; (2) to sound, e.g. *The clock strikes one*; (3) to print, e.g. *To strike off 20 copies* = print 20 of a paper; (4) make, e.g. *To strike a bargain* = make an agreement; *To strike a light* = light a match; (5) find; *To strike oil* = find oil on one's land, get sudden wealth by good fortune; *How does this strike you?* = what do you think of it?; **striking** (41-1) surprising; fine; unusual; (6) *To strike up* (e.g. *music*) = begin; (7) *To strike a flag* = take down, show that one is beaten; (8) *Workers go on strike* = stop work to force better conditions or pay from employers; (9) *To strike out (a word)* = cut out a word by drawing a line through it; *Strike out for oneself* = begin to work unhelped, set up one's own business.

string (1) strong thread; any long and narrow thing used for tying; part of a musical instrument; line of things, e.g. *A string of cars*; *Give a promise with no strings to it* = without making the other person promise to do something in return; **to string**, fix a string on to; put on a string, e.g. jewels as an ornament for the neck.
stringent (1nj9) tight; demanding exact *obedience* (n. of Obey); *Financial* **stringency** (——s1) = lack of money.
strip (1) pull off the outer covering, e.g. from a tree; to take everything off, e.g. clothes; *Stripped of all his wealth* = having lost —; a **strip**, narrow piece.
stripe (41) long narrow mark, e.g. on cloth; *Forty stripes* = blows as punishment.
stripling (1-1) boy, about 16 years old.
strive (41) try hard.
strode (67) p.t. of Stride.
stroke (67) a blow, e.g. from a stick; sudden bursting of a blood vessel in the brain; *A stroke of business* = successful piece of —; line drawn with a pen; one sound of a bell, e.g. *On the stroke of nine o'clock*; **to stroke**, rub gently; *To stroke a boat* = set the time when rowing.
stroll (67) walk in an unhurried way.
strong (5) powerful; firm; forceful; *Strong drink* = powerful wine or *spirits* (e.g. *whisky, brandy*); **stronghold** (5-67) fort.
strop (5) piece of leather used for sharpening a *razor* (= knife used to cut hair from the face).
strove (67) p.t. of Strive.
struck (8) p.t. and p.p. of Strike; Sl. *Struck all of a heap* = very surprised.
structure (8-tsh9) thing built or fitted together; way in which a thing is built up, its inner form.
struggle (8) try hard; to fight.
strum (8) play music in a noisy careless way.
strung (8) p.t. of String; (of a person) *Highly strung* = easily excited.
strut (8) walk proudly throwing out the feet.
strut (8) piece of wood or metal used as a support.
strychnine (1k-11) medicine which causes excitement and quickness of movement; in large amounts it causes death.
stub (8) short thick piece, e.g. of pencil; **to stub**, strike the foot against a stone by accident.
stubble (8) (1) the cut ends of corn remaining in the field after the corn has been cut; (2) hair on the face looking like this.
stubborn (8-9) fixed in purpose or opinion.
stubby (8-1) short and thick.
stucco (8-67) fine white paste (which later becomes hard like stone) used to cover the

stuck (8) p.t. of Stick; *I'm stuck* = am in difficulties and cannot go on; Sl. **st'uck-up** (8 + 8) proud.

stud (8) thick nail with a large head; a thing used for joining pieces of cloth or leather by passing the small head through both pieces, the large bottom remaining on the other side.

stud (8) collection of horses kept for racing or producing young; *A stud mare* = female horse kept for producing young.

student (177) one who studies.

studio (177-167) room in which a painter or other *artist* (= worker in art) works.

study (8-1) to work at a subject in order to learn it; subject to be learnt; rough drawing or painting, or unfinished piece of music; reading- and writing-room of one person; *In a brown study* = deep in thought and not noticing those around.

stuff (8) any material, liquid or solid; (of writing or speaking) foolishness; **to stuff**, pack tightly; put a nice-tasting mixture into the inside of a bird before cooking it; fill the skin of a dead animal with wool, etc., so as to make it look as in life; Sl. *Stuffed shirt* = solemn self-important person.

stuffy (8-1) hot and airless.

stultify (8-1-41) make a thing useless; make it seem foolish.

stumble (8) make a wrong step and fall forward; make a mistake; *To stumble on* = find by accident.

stump (8) part of a tree which remains in the ground after the tree has been cut down; broken or useless end of anything; *Stump speaker* = common out-of-doors speaker; Sl. *Completely stumped* = not knowing what to do or say; *To stump about* = walk heavily; Sl. *Stump up* = pay; **the stumps**, sticks which are put upright in the ground in the game of *Cricket*.

stun (8) make senseless by a blow on the head; *She looked stunning* = very beautiful.

stung (8) p.t. and p.p. of Sting.

stunk (8ngk) p.p. of Stink.

stunt (8) stop the growth of; **a stunt**, some act done to show how clever one is.

stupefy (177-1-41) make dull and *stupid* (see 2nd below).

stup'endous (177-2-9) very large; very surprising.

stupid (177-1) slow of understanding; foolish; n. **stup'idity** (17-1-1-1).

stupor (177-9) slowness of mind; deep sleep-like condition caused by poison or serious illness or shock.

sturdy (99-1) strong and well-grown.

sturgeon (99j9) large fish; its eggs are eaten as *caviare* (see —).

stutter (8-9) talk with difficulty, e.g. "I c-c-can't t-t-talk."

sty (41) hut in which a pig is kept.

sty(e) (41) poisoned swelling near the eye.

style (41) pointed instrument used for writing, e.g. on wax in old days; a manner of speaking or writing, e.g. *A simple style, A forceful style*, etc.; manner of doing anything, e.g. drawing, dancing, etc.; part of flower (see Pistil); **stylish** (clothes) (41-1) nice and of the newest kind.

su'ave (744) specially polite, with smooth easy manners.

sub- under; less than.

subaltern (8-9) army officer of low rank.

s'ubc'onscious (8-5-sh9) e.g. *To know subconsciously* = to know a thing without actually thinking or attending (it is the subconscious mind that makes you wake up at the right time when you have to catch an early morning train).

subcut'aneous (8-17-21-19) under the skin.

s'ubdiv'ide (8-1-41) divide the parts of a thing.

subd'ue (9-177) conquer; **subd'ued** (sound, voice) quiet; (colour) not bright.

subject (8-1) adj. under the control of; n. one of the persons ruled by a king; a thing studied; word in a *sentence* (= group of words expressing a complete idea) about which the sentence tells more; *Subject to your approval* = if you agree or think it good; **to subj'ect** (9-2) bring under control.

subj'ective (9-2-1) thinking of one's own feelings or thoughts, rather than of things or persons with which (whom) one is dealing (objective, which is real, outside the mind).

subjugate (8-7-21) bring under control.

s'ubl'et (8-2) *To let a house* = rent a house to a *tenant* (= person to whom a house is rented); the tenant sublets when he rents the house to someone else.

sublimate (8-1-21) make pure; **sublimate** (8-1-1) very pure form of a material.

subl'ime (9-41) very grand and very noble.

submarine (8-9-11) under-sea; a **submarine**, under-sea ship.

subm'erge (9-99j) to put under water.

subm'it (9-1) to put under the control of; ask a person to consider; to yield; n. **subm'ission** (——shn).

s'ubn'ormal (8-55) less or worse than the usual.

sub'ordinate (9-55-1-1) lower in rank; person who is lower in rank; **to sub'ordinate** (9-55-1-21) bring under control.

sub'orn (8-55) get a person to do an unlawful act, e.g. by giving him money.

subp'oena (8-11-9) paper ordering a person to appear in (a court of law, and saying that he will be punished if he does not do so.

subscr'ibe (9-41) write one's name at the bottom of a paper; write one's name on a list of persons who will pay money; pay money

subsequent	**295** **sullen**

with others for some good purpose, e.g. a hospital; n. **subscr'iption** (9-1-shn).

subsequent (8-1-9) later; next.

subs'erve (9-99) to help; adj. **subs'ervient** (9-99-19) helping towards a certain aim.

subs'ide (9-41) sink down to a lower level; become quiet.

subs'idiary (9-1-19-1) helping, e.g. a company which makes motor-cars has subsidiary companies which supply materials, electrical parts, etc.

subsidy (8-1-1) money given by government, e.g. to an owner of ships to help him to keep them running without loss; **to subsidize** (8-1-41).

subs'ist (9-1) continue to live; **subs'istence all'owance** (——9-s + 9-479-s) money given to pay the cost of living.

substance (8-9-s) material of which a thing is made; real nature of a thing; chief ideas of a speech or book; firmness; *solidity* (= solidness); **subst'antial** (9-3-shl) solid; real; wealthy; **to subst'antiate** (9-3-shi21) prove that a thing is real; prove that a saying is true.

substantive (8-9-1) noun.

substitute (8-1-177) thing used in place of something else; person who works in place of someone else; to put a person or thing in place of another.

s'ubstr'atum (8-44-9) thickness of material spread under another, e.g. the soil has a substratum of rock; *A substratum of truth* = some truth at the bottom, though the rest of the reasoning is untrue.

subterfuge (8-9-177j) something done to escape blame or difficulty.

subterr'anean (8-9-21-19) under the earth.

subtle (8) fine, not solid; difficult to feel or to understand; clever.

subtr'act (9-3) take away from, e.g. *2 subtracted from 3 = 1*.

s'ubtr'opical (8-5-1) near the hottest part of the earth.

suburb (8-99) outlying part of a city; adj. **sub'urban** (9-99-9) living in or having to do with a suburb; having the good qualities neither of the town nor of the country.

subv'ention (9-2-shn) money given as a help.

subv'ert (8-99) overturn or destroy, e.g. beliefs, a government; adj. **subv'ersive** (8-99-1).

subway (8-21) underground way; Am. underground railway.

succ'eed (9ksI1) come after; do what one has planned and wished to do; win; n. **succ'ess** (9ks2) things happening as planned or hoped; **a succ'ession** (9ks2shn) (of persons or things) one coming after another.

succ'inct (9ksIngt) clearly expressed in few words.

succour (8k9) help.

succulent (8kI7-9) (of fruit or food) full of liquid, pleasing to the taste.

succ'umb (9k8) to yield to, be conquered by.

such (8) of that kind; *At such-and-such a time* = at some time, I do not know (or need not tell) just when; *Such-like things* = things of that sort.

suck (8) draw liquid in with the mouth; Am. **a sucker** (8-9) person who is very easily deceived; **suckle**, give milk to the young from the breast; **suction** (8-shn) the act of sucking.

sudden (8) happening quickly and unexpectedly.

sudor'ific (177-9-1-1) causing one to *sweat*.

suds (8-z) white mixture of soap, air and water which floats on top of a wash-bowl.

sue (177) make a claim against a person in a court of law.

suede (721) kind of soft leather.

suet (1771) hard fat of animals, used in cooking.

suffer (8-9) to bear (pain); *To suffer damage* = be damaged; *He is here on* **sufferance** (8-9-s) = he has no right to be here but is allowed to remain.

suff'ice (9-41s) be enough; *Suffice it to say* = it is enough if we say.

suff'icient (9-1shnt) enough.

suffix (8-1) ending of a word, e.g. /-ing, /-ity, /-ly.

suffocate (8-9-21) cause difficulty in breathing; kill by so doing.

suffrage (8-1j) right to take part in electing a person to the government; the act of so doing.

suff'use (9-177z) to spread over, e.g. *Eyes suffused with tears* = filled with —; *Sky — with light*.

sugar (sh7-9) white powder commonly used to give a sweet taste; **s'ugar-cane** (+ 21) **s'ugar-beet** (+ 11) plants from which sugar is obtained.

sugg'est (9j2) cause an idea to arise in the mind; *put forward* (= offer) an idea for consideration; **sugg'estive** (——1) suggesting.

suicide (171s41) act of killing oneself; one who kills himself.

suit (177) be well fitted to; complete set of outer garments for a man; all the playing cards of one of the four kinds; *To bring a suit against* = make a claim in a law-court; *To press one's suit* = make love to a lady so as to get her in marriage; *To follow suit* = act in the same way; **suitable** (177-9) well fitted for.

suit-case (177 + 21) light travelling-box for clothes, carried in the hand.

suite (711) group of servants; set of rooms; set of tables, chairs, etc., all of the same kind.

suitor (177-9) one who is making love to a lady so as to get her in marriage; person who makes a claim in a law-court.

sulk (8) be silently ill-tempered (see Sullen below).

sullen (8-9) silently ill-tempered (*Sulky* is a state of mind which soon passes; *Sullen* is a matter of character and lasts longer); *A sullen sky* = covered with dark grey clouds.

sully (8-1) make dirty.

sulphur (8-9) yellow material which burns with a blue flame and a very bad smell.

Sultan (8-9) king, e.g. *The Sultan of Turkey in 1914*; **Sult'ana** (8-44-9) wife of a sultan; **sult'ana** (9-44-9) small yellow dried fruit used in cakes.

sultry (day) (8-1) hot and airless.

sum (8) whole amount resulting from adding; amount of money; calculation; e.g. *To do sums* = work with figures, to add, divide, etc.; **to sum up**, collect all the important ideas in a few words; **a summary** (8-9-1) short account of the ideas of a book, etc.; *A summary act* = done quickly and without order of a court of law.

summer (8-9) hottest season of the year; *Summer-time*—in many countries the clocks are put forward one hour in summer (see Daylight-saving under Day).

summer-house (8-9 + 47) hut in the garden in which one sits in hot weather.

summit (8-1) the top.

summon (8-9) order a person to come (e.g. to a court of law) at a certain time; **a summons** (——z) such an order.

sump (8) bottom part of an engine where the dirty, used oil collects.

sumptuous (8-179) comfortable, fine and costing much money, e.g. *A sumptuous meal*.

sun (8) large ball in the sky which gives the earth heat and light; any large central star; adj. **sunny** (8-1) having sunlight; *A sunny person* = bright and happy person.

sundae (8-21) frozen *cream* (= fat part of milk) with fruit, nuts and other things served in a tall glass.

sunder (8-9) to separate.

sundial (8-419) flat plate with marks on it and a sloping metal bar fixed to the middle; the shadow of the bar thrown by the sun shows the time.

sundry (8-1) various.

sunflower (8-479) large yellow flower with a mass of black seeds in the middle.

sung (8) p.p. of Sing.

sunk, sunken (8ngk) p.p. of Sink.

SUNFLOWER

sunstroke (8-67) pain in the head or senselessness (fainting) caused by the heat of the sun on the head.

sup (8) eat supper; to drink, taking a little at a time; *Take just one sup of* = one small drink of.

super- (177-9) above; more than.

super'annuate (177-9-3-1721) cause a person to leave employment (or a school) because he is too old.

sup'erb (177-99) very grand and beautiful.

s'uperc'argo (177-9-44-67) officer on a ship who has charge of the *cargo* (= goods carried on the ship).

superc'ilious (177-9s1-19) proud, treating other people as if they were not so good as oneself.

superf'icial (177-9-1shl) on the surface only, not deep.

superfine (177-9-41) very fine.

sup'erfluous (177-99-79) more than is necessary; n. **superfl'uity** (177-9-771-1).

superimp'ose (177-9-1-67z) to put on the top of.

sup¸erint'end (177-1-2) watch people working to see that they do things well and correctly; have charge of.

sup'erior (177-19-19) higher or better.

sup'erlative (177-99-9-1) better than all others; Loud*est* is the superlative of Loud.

supers'ede (177-9-11) to put in the place of; be used instead of; n. **supers'ession** (——z shn).

s'upers'onic (177-9-5-1) faster than the speed of sound.

superst'ition (177-9-1shn) unreasonable belief in *supernatural* (= more than natural) powers, such as fairies and magic, and in things supposed to bring good or bad fortune, e.g. black cats, number 13.

superv'ene (177-9-11) happen while something else is happening, or soon after.

supervise (177-9-41z) to watch over persons working to see that they work well and honestly.

supine (177-41) lying on the back, face upwards; lazy.

supper (8-9) last meal of the day.

suppl'ant (9-44) take the place of.

supple (8) easily bent; easily led by others; changing one's opinions cleverly so as to suit those of other people.

supplement (8-1-2) to complete by adding something; n. **supplement** (8-1-9).

suppliant (8-19) one who prays for a favour.

supplicate (8-1-21) pray.

suppl'y (9-41) bring or give what is wanted; store of things needed.

supp'ort (9-55) bear the weight of; hold up; to help.

supp'ose (9-67z) imagine to be true; *Suppose that I were king* = if —; n. **suppos'ition** (8-9z1shn).

suppr'ess (9-2) to put down (e.g. a rising of the people); prevent from being known; put an end to an evil.

supp'urate (8-17-21) produce *pus* (= white liquid formed in a poisoned wound).

supra- (177-9) higher than; beyond.

supr'emacy (17-2-9s1) state of being *supreme* (see below).

supr'eme (177-11) highest in power or rank; greatest or best possible.

sur- above, over, too much; e.g. **surcharge** (99-44j) = money to be paid beyond what has been paid already.

sure (sh79) certain; trustworthy.

surety (sh79-1) one who promises to make sure that another pays his debt or does as ordered.

surf (99) broken water where the sea runs up on the land.

surface (99-1s) outside part of; that which has length and *breadth* (= broadness) but no depth.

surfeit (99-1) too much, e.g. eating or drinking; the results of —.

surge (99j) move up and down like the sea.

surgeon (99j9) one who cuts away diseased parts of the body, sets right broken bones, etc.; **a surgery** (99j9-1) room in which a doctor gives advice.

surly (99-1) bad-tempered.

surm'ise (99-41z) suppose; to guess; n. **s'urmise.**

surm'ount (99-47) climb over, get over (overcome) a difficulty; be above.

surname (99-21) family name, e.g. John *Smith*.

surp'ass (99-44) be better or bigger than.

surplice (99-1s) loose white garment worn in church by a priest.

surplus (99-9) amount above what is needed.

surprise (9-41z) feeling caused by something sudden and unexpected; cause this feeling; attack suddenly.

surr'ender (9-2-9) to yield, say that one is beaten.

surrept'itious (8-9-1sh9) done secretly.

surr'ound (9-47) be on all sides of.

surtax (99-3) extra tax paid to the government on very large incomes (money received each year).

surv'eillance (99-21-9-s) careful watch.

surv'ey (99-21) (**1**) look at carefully; (**2**) measure land and make a plan of it; **a s'urvey** (99-21).

surv'ive (99-41) live longer than; continue to live; *Survival of the fittest*, see Fit.

susc'eptible (9-2-9) easily *affected* (*affect* = to have an effect on) by.

susp'ect (9-2) to have a general idea that —; to doubt; *I suspect him* = I believe that he is not honest, but have no proofs; **a s'uspect** (8-2) person suspected; adj. **s'uspect.**

susp'end (9-2) hang up; *I suspend judgment* = delay —; *Matter in suspension in liquid* = floating in —.

susp'ender(s) (9-2-9z) Am. bands worn by men to keep up the trousers; (England) bands worn to keep up the *socks or stockings* (= foot and leg coverings made of wool, silk, or cotton).

susp'ense (9-2) feeling of fear and uncertainty whether a thing will happen or not.

susp'icion (9-1sh9) act of *suspecting* (see 4th above); *A suspicion of salt* = slight taste of —.

sust'ain (9-21) hold up; support or keep alive; to bear; prove; **sustenance** (8-1-9-s) act of sustaining; food.

suzerain (77-9-21) king, ruler.

svelte (woman) (2) thin and graceful.

swab (5) piece of cloth tied to a handle for cleaning a *deck* (= floor of a ship); a piece of cotton-wool on a stick used for putting medicine on the inside of the throat; Sl. unskilful and useless seaman, or person.

swaddle (5) tie up in cloth, e.g. *To swaddle a baby.*

swag (3) Sl. stolen goods.

swagger (3-9) walk in a proud self-satisfied way; behave or talk in such a way; Sl. *Swagger clothes* = splendid, very nice-looking —; *A swagger-stick (cane)* = light short stick carried by soldiers when not on duty.

swain (21) young countryman; lover.

swallow (5-67) small bird with long wings and a V-shaped tail, ∧.

swallow (5-67) take food down the throat into the stomach; *All my money was swallowed up* = was used up; *Swallowed up in the clouds* = lost in, hidden in —; *He swallowed his anger* —; tried to control and hide —; Sl. *I can't swallow that!* = can't believe —.

swam (3) p.t. of Swim.

swamp (5) soft, very wet land; *To swamp a boat* = fill with water and sink.

swan (5) large beautiful bird with a long neck which lives on the water; *Swan-song* = last and most beautiful song, last work, speech just before death.

swank (3ngk) Sl. proud outward show; proud behaviour.

swap, swop (5) Sl. to *exchange* (= take one thing in return for another).

sward (55) grassy land.

swarm (55) large crowd of bees or other flying creatures; any large crowd; **to swarm**, move in crowds; be crowded; be found in large numbers; *The place is swarming with people* = there are large crowds in the place.

swarm (up) (55) climb up as one climbs a rope.

swarthy (skin) (55ŏr) dark.

swashbuckler (5-8-9) noisy rough fellow.

swastika (5-1-9) sign as shown in the picture.

swat (a fly) (5) kill.

swath (55) line of cut grass in a field.

swathe (21ŏ) bind with cloth.   SWASTIKA

sway (21) move unsteadily in different directions; cause to move in a certain direction, e.g. *Sway his judgment*; n. **sway,** power, e.g. *Hold sway over*.

swear (29) say solemnly in the name of God; use bad language.

sweat (2) liquid which comes out of the skin when one is hot; **to sweat,** produce such liquid; work hard; *Sweated labour* = hard work done for very low pay.

sweater (2-9) woollen covering for the upper part of the body, usually worn before and after games.

sweep (11) (p.t. and p.p. Swept) (**1**) to brush;

(2) move quickly, driving all before one (it), e.g. *The river sweeps by; The storm swept all before it;* **(3)** search quickly and thoroughly, e.g. *Sweep the seas;* **a sweep,** quick circular movement, e.g. of the arm; curve, e.g. *The sweep of the drive* = curved part of a road up to a house; **a sweep, a chimney-sweep** (1-1 +) man who cleans chimneys; *He made a sweeping statement* = he said something which was too general and not wholly true, e.g. "All unemployed men are lazy."

sweepstakes (11-21) *Example:* Mr. A, Mr. B, C; D (etc.) pay five pence each; the names of horses are divided among them: Mr. B's horse wins; Mr. B gets all the money (or holders of 2nd and 3rd may also get a share).

sweet (11) tasting of sugar; nice; gentle; *The sweet* = sweet-tasting dish in a meal; **a sweet, sweets,** small pieces of boiled sugar, *chocolate,* etc., enjoyed by children.

sweetbread (11-2) part of the body which produces a liquid that helps the stomach in dealing with sugar; also called the *Pancreas.*

sweetheart (11t·h44) dearly loved person.

sweetmeat (11-11) a *sweet* (see 3rd above).

sw'eet-p'ea (11 + 11) sweet-smelling flower.

sw'eet-t'ooth (11 + 77) a person who loves eating sugar is said to have a —.

swell (2) become larger; be blown out with air, gas or liquid; *The river is swelling* = has more water in it; (in music) become louder; **a swell** (of the sea) large unbroken waves; Sl. rich well-dressed person.

swelter (2-9) feel very hot.

swept (2) p.t. and p.p. of Sweep.

swerve (99) to curve aside from the straight path, e.g. motor-car, runner, ball.

swift (1) rapid; **a swift,** small bird.

swig (1) Sl. to drink; **a swig,** one mouthful of drink.

swill (1) wash out (a pot); drink large quantities; n. **swill,** pigs' food.

swim (1) move in the water (like a fish); be full of, e.g. *Eyes swimming with tears; My head swims* = feels as if it were going round and round—as in illness; *To be in the swim* = have a part in all the important events in one's own group.

swindle (1) get money by deceiving.

swine (41) pigs.

swing (1) move from side to side like a thing hanging from a string, door opening and shutting, etc.; cause to swing; *To swing the lead* = escape work by pretending to be ill; **a swing,** seat hanging by ropes as a child's plaything; *The play went with a swing* = went off nicely; *The party was in full swing* = going on well, at its height; **swing music** (+ 1772i) dance-music in which the beat keeps changing.

swipe (41) to hit with a strong circular movement; Sl. steal.

swirl (99) move quickly like liquid turning in circles as it flows on.

swish (1) sound of a woman's skirt as she walks; also of a stick moved quickly; Sl. **swish,** adj. very fine; Sl. *A swish (car)* = very smart and showy (car, etc.); **to swish,** to beat with a stick.

sw'iss r'oll (1 + 67) cake covered with *jam* (= fruit boiled in sugar) when flat and then rolled up.

switch (1) very thin stick; **to switch,** to hit with a thin stick; move (a tail) quickly.

switch (1) send a train on to another line; send electricity along another wire; **a switch,** instrument for doing this; *A switchboard* = a collection of electrical switches on a board.

sw'itch-back (+ 3) railway which runs up and down steep slopes, used for pleasure.

swivel (1) ring turning on a pin, e.g. at the end of a chain.

swollen (67-9) p.p. of Swell.

swoon (77) to faint, fall senseless, e.g. from sudden fright or illness; **a swoon,** sudden fainting.

swoop (77) to fly down upon, e.g. *A bird swoops down upon an animal to kill it.*

swop (5) see Swap.

sword (55) cutting weapon used by soldiers.

swore, sworn (55) p.t. and p.p. of Swear.

swum (8) p.p. of Swim.

swung (8) p.t. and p.p. of Swing.

sybarite (1-9-41) person who loves comfort and rich-living.

sycamore (1-9-55) a kind of tree.

sycophant (1-9-9) one who tries to win favour by behaving in a slave-like way.

syllables (1-9-z) separate sound groups (or letter groups) into which a word can be divided.

syllabus (1-9-9) course of study in a school or university; written list of subjects to be studied.

syllogism (1-9j1z) piece of reasoning, set out in three parts, e.g. **1** *all insects have 6 legs,* **2** *this creature has 8 legs,* **3** *therefore it is not an insect.*

sylph (1) fairy; *Sylph-like* = thin and graceful.

sylvan (1-9) see Silvan.

symbol (1) sign, e.g. £, √ ; adj., **symb'olic** (1-5-1).

symmetry (1-1-1) sameness of parts, e.g. any object (picture, etc.) which if divided in half by an imaginary line, shows either side in pleasing relation or as a pleasing opposite to the other side; adj. **symm'etrical** (1-2-1).

sympathize (1-9-41) share the feelings of another, e.g. be glad when he is glad, sad when sad, etc.; n. **sympathy** (1-9-1); adj. **sympath'etic** (1-9-2-1).

symphony (1-9-1) pleasant mixing of sounds; piece of music (e.g. by Beethoven, Brahms, etc.) for many persons playing many instruments together.

symp'osium (1-67zı9) collection of writings by different writers all treating the same subject.
symptom (1-9) sign of (especially of disease).
Synagogue (1-9-5) house of prayer of the Jews.
synchronize (ııgkr9-4ı) cause to agree as to time; cause things to happen at the same time.
syncopate (ıngk9-2ı) (a word) shorten; (music) change the regular and usual beat, beginning a note after one beat and carrying it on into the next.
syncope (ıngk9-ı) sudden senselessness or fainting, e.g. caused by failing of the heart.
syndicate (1-ı-ı) company of persons united in carrying out some plan, usually one needing a large amount of money; **to syndicate** (1-1-2ı) join together into a syndicate; print a story in many (syndicated) newspapers at the same time.
synod (1-9) meeting of officers of the Church.
synonym (1-9-ı) word which has almost the same meaning as another word, e.g. *Start—begin*; adj. **syn'onymous** (1-5-1-9).
syn'opsis (1-5-1) short account of a book, etc.
syntax (1-3) science or art of joining words together correctly to express thought; adj. **synt'actic** (1-3-1).
synthesis (1-1-1) a putting together; things put together; **synth'etic** (1-2-1) e.g. *Synthetic wine* = wine made by putting together various materials in a scientific way—not made from real fruit.
syringe (1-ınj) instrument for pushing liquid out through a small pipe, e.g. for putting medicine under the skin.
syrup (1-9) very sweet, pleasant-tasting liquid.
system (1-1) (1) a grouping of things or ideas so as to make one well-ordered whole, e.g. *A system of thought;* (2) plan for arranging things so that they may work well together; things so arranged, e.g. *The school system of Egypt; Too much smoking is bad for the system* = for the body; adj. **system'atic** (1-1-3-1).

T

T (11) *It suits me to a T* = it is just right, just what I need.

ta (44) Sl. (or child's word) thank you.

tab (3) small piece of cloth or paper fixed on to the edge of a larger piece, e.g. the tab on a coat, used for hanging it up, or for showing the maker's name; Sl. *To keep tabs on* = keep an account of, to watch.

tabard (3-9) coat worn in ancient times.

tabby (cat) (3-1) cat of mixed brown-grey colour, generally female.

tabernacle (1-9-3) place used for religious ceremonies; small lightly built church.

TABARD

table (21) piece of furniture; *He keeps a good table* = he provides good food; flat piece of stone or metal with writing on it; list of figures or facts arranged one below another.

tableau (3-67) scene in a theatre in which people stay still, as if it were a painted picture.

t'able d'h'ôte (44 + 67) meal supplied at a fixed price, giving a choice of only a certain number of dishes.

tablet (3-1) small flat surface with writing on it; number of sheets of paper fixed together for writing on; small amount of powdered medicine pressed together.

tabloid (3-51) small amount of medicine pressed together into a round or egg-shaped ball; small form of anything, e.g. *A tabloid newspaper*.

tab'oo (9-77) set a thing apart ordering that it is not to be touched nor spoken of; forbid.

tabor (21-9) small drum.

tabulate (3-17-21) arrange facts one below another; adj. **tabular** (———9) arranged in the form of a table, one below another.

tacit (consent) (3s1) silent (agreement); understood without being spoken.

taciturn (person) (3s1-99) one who speaks little.

tack (3) small nail with a big head; fasten with small nails; fix loosely with needle and thread; Sl. *Come down to brass tacks* = get to the real facts.

tack (3) make a ship sail from side to side so as to move against the wind; *On the right (wrong) tack* = doing the —— thing.

tackle (3) ropes, etc., used on a ship; all the instruments needed for a certain game or piece of work, e.g. *Fishing tackle*; **to tackle**, put questions to; begin a difficult piece of work; (in football) to seize a person.

tacky (3-1) feeling sticky when touched.

tact (3) power of understanding other people's feelings and of doing or saying just the right thing at the right moment.

tactics (3-1) art of moving troops on the field of battle; any clever plans.

tactile (3-41) **tactual** (3-179) having to do with touch.

tadpole (3-67) first form of a *frog* when it comes out of the egg.

taffeta (3-1-9) a kind of silk.

taffrail (3-21) *rail* (=bar with upright supports) round the back part of a ship to prevent people falling off.

tag (3) bit of cloth fixed to the back of a boot for pulling it on; card fixed on to a box to show where it is to be sent; running game played by children; *The tag end* = loose end.

tail (21) that movable part of an animal's body formed by the lower backbone continuing some distance beyond its body; anything hanging down at the back, e.g. *The tail of a coat*; back part of anything; *I can't make head or tail of it* = can't understand it; *To turn tail* = turn and run away.

tailor (21-9) person who cuts out, makes and sells outer garments.

tainted (21-1) having a bad smell or taste; beginning to decay.

take (21) *The work will take 3 hours* = will be finished in ——; *Do you take me?* = understand; *You may take it from me* = believe; *Did not take* = had no effect (e.g. medical treatment to prevent illness); *Take aback* = surprise; *Take after* = look like; *Take down (notes)* = write ——; *Take for* = treat as, believe to be; *Take in* = deceive; *Take in for the night* = receive as a guest; *Take off* = copy the behaviour of a person so as to make others laugh; *Take off* from an airfield = go up in an aeroplane; *The take-off* = the start; *Take him on at a game* = agree to play against; *The play did not take on* = failed; *Didn't take to him* = did not like; *A taking manner* = pleasing; *Take to gardening* = become interested in; *To take it upon oneself* = put oneself in charge of, do a thing without being asked; *To take up music* = begin to study music.

talc (3) natural glass-like material found in thin sheets; used also as a powder for the skin; **talcum** (3-9) fine powder made from talc.

tale (21) story; *To tell tales* = tell of another's wrong-doing; *A tale-teller, tale-bearer* = one who tells of another's wrong-doing.

talent (3-9) piece of money used in and before the time of Christ; natural power of the mind, e.g. *A talent for music*.

talisman (3-1z-9) thing supposed to possess magic power.

talk   301   tariff

talk (55) speak; Sl. *Talk the hind leg off a donkey* = talk too much; talkative (person) (55-9-1) one who talks much.

talkie (55-1) moving (*cinema*) picture which also speaks.

tall (55) high; *A tall order* = piece of work difficult to fulfil; *A tall story* = unbelievable story.

tallow (3-67) hard fat, usually of animals, e.g. that used in making some kinds of candles.

tally (3-1) two pieces of wood tied together, from the edge of which small pieces are cut as a way of keeping accounts (one stick being for the buyer, the other for the seller); to tally, agree exactly.

tally-h'o! (3-1 + 67) cry for urging on dogs at a hunt.

talon (3-9) *claw* (= nail) of a bird; long sharp finger-nail.

tamarind (3-9-1) Indian tree whose fruit is used in cooking.

tamarisk (3-9-1) bush which grows in sand, has feathery branches, and white or light-red flowers.

t'ambour'ine (3-9-11) light drum with pieces of metal at the sides, shaken or beaten with the hand.

TAMARISK

tame (21) not wild, not fierce; spiritless and uninteresting.

t'am-o'-sh'anter (3 + 9 + 3-9) round cap worn by the people of Scotland.

tamp (3) press down matter into a hole, e.g. into a hole containing an explosive so that it may not explode outwards.

TAMBOURINE

tamper (with) (3-9) change dishonestly or in such a way as to damage, e.g. *Tamper with a written paper* = change words dishonestly; *Tamper with a machine* = put out of working order, cause not to run properly.

tan (3) turn the skin of an animal into leather; *His skin is tanned* = made brown by the sun; yellow-brown colour; Sl. punish with a stick.

TAM-O'-SHANTER

tandem (3-9) two horses pulling a carriage one behind the other; bicycle for two riders.

tang (3) strong taste, e.g. *The air has a tang of the sea*.

tangent (3nj9) straight line touching a curve at one point; *To fly off at a tangent* = suddenly talk of something else.

t'anger'ine (3nj9-11) small orange.

tangible (3nj9) which can be touched; real.

tangle (3ngg) disorderly mass of threads, string, etc.; to tangle, mix up threads in a disorderly way.

tango (3ngg67) slow dance for two persons.

tank (3ngk) metal container for gas or liquid; heavy motor-car with guns in it, used in battle.

tankard (3ngk9) large drinking-pot.

tanker (3ngk9) ship used for carrying oil.

tantalize (3-9-41) keep a person always hoping for something which he will never obtain.

TANK

tantamount (3-9-47) equal to.

tantrum (3-9) sudden burst of ill-temper.

tap (3) instrument fitted on the end of a pipe with which one turns the (water) on or off; *Wine on tap* = ready for sale in small quantities from the barrel; to tap, draw out liquid, e.g. from a swelling in the body; *To tap an electric wire* = draw off electricity from —.

tap (3) strike lightly; a tap, light blow.

tap-dancing (+ 44-sI) way of dancing in which the dancer makes a tapping sound with his feet.

tape (21) strong narrow piece of cloth used for tying up things; *Red tape* = mass of silly rules, making it difficult to do business quickly; t'ape-m'easure (+ 239) long narrow band of cloth used for measuring.

taper (21-9) thin candle.

taper (21-9) become narrower and come towards a point.

tapestry (3-1-1) large piece of cloth whose threads make a picture; cloth picture.

t'api'oca (3-167-9) white grains obtained from a root, boiled for food.

tapir (21-9) pig-like South American animal.

tapis (3-11) *Question on the —* = being talked about but not yet settled.

tappet (3-1) bar standing out from a wheel which strikes up another part of a machine every time the wheel turns, thus changing a round-and-round movement into an up-and-down movement.

t'ap-room (3 + 7) room in an inn in which drinks are served.

t'ap-root (3 + 77) chief root of a plant.

tar (44) black oily liquid obtained from wood and coal; *A tar, A jack-tar* = sailor; *Tarred with the same brush* = having the same faults.

taradiddle, tarradiddle (3-9-1) untruth.

tar'antula (9-3-17-9) large poisonous *spider* (= creature with 8 legs that makes a net and eats flies).

tarb'oosh (44-77) see Fez.

tardy (44-1) late, slow.

tare (29) *weed* (= wild plant not wanted in a garden or field).

tare (29) weight of a cart or box without the goods in it.

target (44-1) a shield; object to be aimed at with a gun, etc.

tariff (3-1) list of goods on which money must

tarmac   302   **teem**

be paid when brought into a country; list of prices, e.g. of food in a hotel.

tarmac (44-3) (= tar-macadam) road made with small stones held together with *tar* (= black oily matter obtained from coal).

tarn (44) small lake.

tarnished (44-1-t) having lost its brightness or polish.

tarp'aulin (44-55-1) cloth covered with *tar* (= black oily matter obtained from coal) to keep out wet.

tarpon (44-9) large fish.

t'arrad'iddle (3-9-1) see Taradiddle.

tarry (3-1) to delay; to wait.

tarry (44-1) like *tar* (= black oily matter obtained from coal); covered with tar.

tart (44) acid; *A tart reply* = sharp answer.

tart (44) fruit, etc., cooked in a dish with pastry above or below it.

tartan (44) woollen cloth with coloured squares, worn in Scotland.

tartar (44-9) (1) hard covering formed on dirty teeth; (2) *To catch a Tartar* = have to deal with a very difficult or hot-tempered person.

Tartarus (44-9-9) place of punishment for souls after death.

task (44) piece of work which must be done; *To take to task* = find fault, to blame; *It tasks my powers* = is very difficult.

task-force (+ 55s) small army or a few warships sent to do some special piece of work, and then come back.

tassel (3) number of threads tied together at the upper end, hanging down from a cap, flag, etc.

taste (21) that feeling which we get only by the tongue; good judgment in matters of art, poetry, etc.; *He has a taste for* = he likes; *To my taste* = as I like it; **tasty** (——1) having a pleasant taste.

tat (3) make **tatting** (3-1) (= ornament for clothes made of open-work threads).

tat'a (3-44) childish way of saying good-bye.

tatters (3-9z) torn pieces of cloth; *His coat was in tatters* = torn in many places; **t'atterdem'alion** (3-9-9-21-19) person dressed in very dirty and torn clothes.

tattle (3) unimportant talk.

tatt'oo (3-77) coloured picture drawn on the skin by pricking it and rubbing colouring matter into the holes.

tatt'oo (9-77) beating of the drum calling soldiers back for the night; public show given by a large number of soldiers, usually at night.

taught (55) p.p. and p.t. of Teach.

taunt (55) say cruel things so as to make a person feel shame.

taut (55) tight.

taut'ology (55-5-9jI) waste of words.

tavern (3-9) drinking place, inn.

tawdry (things) (55-1) which look nice but are of bad quality.

tawny (55-1) light brown.

tax (3) money which has to be paid to the government; **to tax**, demand money from the people; *This work taxes my powers* = is almost too hard for me; *To tax with* = say that a person has done some wrong.

taxi (3-1) motor-car for hire with a machine showing the amount to be paid; **taximeter** (——11-9) this machine; **to taxi** (of an aeroplane), run along the ground.

taxidermist (3-1-99-1) one who fills the skins of dead birds or animals and sets them up to look like live ones.

T.B. (t11 + b11) *tuberculosis* (see ——).

tea (11) (1) drink made by pouring hot water on tea-leaves; (2) light meal eaten in the afternoon.

teach (11) try to make a person learn and help him in so doing; *I'll teach him (not) to* = will punish him so that he will not do that again.

teak (11) large Indian tree whose hard redbrown wood is used especially in shipbuilding.

teal (11) kind of wild duck.

team (11) (of horses or dogs) two or more, pulling a cart; (of players) group, e.g. of 11 football players; **teamster** (11-9) one who works with a team of horses.

tear (29) break by pulling apart (e.g. cloth); **tear up**, destroy; *To tear one's hair* = show signs of great grief or trouble; *To tear along* = go very quickly.

tear (19) drop of water from the eyes, e.g. as a sign of grief.

tease (11z) (1) pull threads apart; (2) make a hairy surface on cloth; (3) trouble a person; Sl. **a teaser** (11z9) difficult question.

teasle, teazle (11z) plant with hooked needles used for raising and smoothing out the surface of cloth.

teat (11) part of the breast from which a child draws out milk; anything so shaped.

technical (2k-1) having to do with some special art; having to do with machines and making things by machines; n. **technic'ality** (2k-1-3-1-1).

techn'ician (2k-1shn) person trained in the making of certain things in factories.

technicolor (2k-1-8-9) trade name for a certain kind of coloured cinema film.

techn'ique (2k-11k) art of doing some special thing; one person's (e.g. a painter's) special way of doing his art.

techn'ology (2k-5-9j1) scientific study of the making of things in factories.

T'e D'eum (11 + 11-9) Christian song of thanks to God (Latin *Te* = You, *Deum* = God).

tedious (11-19) long and uninteresting; **tedium** (11-19) tiredness caused by lack of interest.

tee (11) place from which a ball is struck in certain games, e.g. in *Golf* (see ——).

teem (11) produce a large number or amount

teens (11-z) *In her teens* = aged 13 to 19.

teeth (11) pl. of Tooth; **teethe** (11ð) produce the first teeth in childhood.

teet'otal (11-67) using no wine or strong drink.

t'eetot'um (11-67-8) small *top* (= wheel with a bar through the centre, made to turn round by itself by giving it a sharp twist between the finger and thumb, or with the help of a string) with numbers on its sides.

tele- far, e.g. **t'elecommunic'ation** (2-1-9-17-1-21shn) sending messages far away by electricity; **teleprinter** (2-1-1-9) The sender typewrites his message on a machine which causes it to be written on many other machines far away.

telegram (2-1-3) message sent in signs (not by voice) on an electric wire or wave; **telegraph** (2-1-44) instrument for doing this; send messages thus; **tel'egraphy** (1-2-9-1).

tele'ology (2-1-15-9j1) idea that everything was made by God in order to carry out some special purpose.

tel'epathy (1-2-9-1) strange power of passing thought direct from one mind to another without speaking or making signs.

telephone (2-1-67) instrument for sending the sound of the voice on an electric wire or wave or receiving sounds so sent; to send such messages; **tel'ephony** (1-2-9-1).

telescope (2-1-67) instrument used for seeing distant objects; adj. **telesc'opic** (2-1-5-1) (1) having to do with telescopes; (2) made with parts that can be closed by pushing one into another.

television (2-1-13n) sending and receiving of pictures by electric waves.

tell (2) (1) to count; (2) say a story; (3) express or show, e.g. *A clock tells the time*; (4) discover, e.g. *I can't tell which is which*; (5) to order, e.g. *Tell him to go*; (6) have an effect, e.g. *Good work tells in the end*; *The hard work is beginning to tell on him* = to have an effect.

teller (2-9) one who pays out money in a bank.

telltale (2-21) one who tells of others' wrongdoing; *Telltale signs* = signs which show what is secret or hidden.

tem'erity (1-2-1-1) daring, boldness.

temper (2-9) treat metal or other material so as to make it of just the right hardness; hardness so obtained.

temper (2-9) general condition of the feelings, e.g. *Bad-tempered*, *Hot-tempered* = easily angered; *Good-tempered* = calm and pleasant; *To get into a temper* = become angry.

temperament (2-9-9) general character, especially in regard to the feelings; **temperam'ental** (2-9-9-2) easily excited.

temperance (2-9-s) state of self-control, e.g. not eating too much; *A temperance meeting* = meeting to urge people to stop drinking wine.

temperate (2-9-1) self-controlled; not eating or drinking too much; (of parts of the earth) not very hot or cold.

temperature (2mpr1ch9) heat or cold; *To take one's* — = discover the heat of the body by means of a special instrument put in the mouth.

tempest (2-1) storm; adj. **temp'estuous** (2-2-179).

template (2-1) see Templet.

temple (2) building in which prayers are said to a god.

temple (2) part of the head just above and in front of the ear.

templet, template (2-1) shaped plate used as a guide in cutting wood (or other material).

tempo (2-67) speed at which music is played.

temporal (2-9) lasting only for a certain time; having to do with this earth (not heaven).

temporal (2-9) having to do with the *temple* (= part of head in front of ear).

temporary (2-9-9-1) lasting for a short time.

temporize (2-9-41) behave in such a way as to gain time; delay doing an important action.

tempt (2) try to make a person do something (e.g. something wrong) by promises; excite desire in.

tenable (opinion) (2-9) which can be held with reason.

ten'acious (1-21shn) holding on tightly; n. **ten'acity** (1-3s1-1).

tenant (2-9) person who holds and pays rent for a house or land; **tenancy** (2-9-s1) state or time of being a tenant; **tenantry** (——1) group of tenants.

tench (2) fresh-water fish.

tend (2) to watch over, e.g. the sick.

tend (2). lean towards; *He tends to cruelty*, *He tends to be cruel* = he is by character bent towards —; *Wars tend to settle nothing* = usually settle nothing; n. **tendency** (2-9-s1).

tender (2-9) small ship which carries things to a larger one; wheeled container for coal and water pulled by a railway engine.

tender (2-9) to offer; *Legal tender* = that which must (according to law) be accepted as money.

tender (2-9) soft; easily damaged; easily hurt; kind and loving.

tenderfoot (2-9-7) inexperienced newcomer, e.g. in the Boy Scouts.

tendon (2-9) strong string-like part of the body which joins a muscle on to a bone.

tendril (2-1) thin outgrowth of a climbing plant which holds the plant to the wall, or stick, up which it grows.

tenement (2-1-9) that which is held by a *tenant* (= person who pays rent for a house or land); **a t'enement-h'ouse** (+ 47) house containing many sets of rooms for different (poor) families.

tenet (11-2) belief.

tennis (2-1) game played by two or four players hitting a ball over a net.

tenon (2-9) finger of wood standing out from

one board which fits into a hole in another board so as to hold the two together.

tenor (2-9) (1) general direction; general meaning; (2) high male voice; man who has —.

tense (2) form of a *verb* (= such a word as Be, Do, Write) which tells the time (past, present, or future) at which the act took place.

tense (2) tightly stretched; adj. **tensile** (2-41); n. **tension** (2-shn) stretching; excitement.

tent (2) cloth shelter as used by soldiers.

tentacle (2-9) long easily bent limb with no bone in it.

tentative (2-9-1) not fixed, but said or done as a trial to see the result; *A tentative opinion* = one given in order to hear what people say in answer.

tenterhooks (2-9-7) *On* —— = very anxious or excited.

tenuous (2-179) very fine and thin.

tenure (2-179) act of holding, or right to hold, land or a house; time during which a house, land, or an office (employment) is held.

tepee (11-11) tent of North American Indians.

tepid (2-1) slightly warm; n. **tep′idity** (2-1-1-1).

t′ercent′enary (99s2-11-9-1) 300th year after an event.

tergiversate (99j1-99-21) keep changing one's opinions or plans.

term (99) (1) part of the school year; time during which a law-court sits; any fixed length of time, e.g. time to be spent in prison; *During one's term of office* = time —; (2) special word used by lawyers, doctors, scientists, etc., e.g. *A medical term; The terms of an agreement* = arrangements agreed upon; *To come to terms* = agree; *I term this a* —— = I name or call this ——.

termagant (99-9-9) noisy scolding woman.

terminate (99-1-21) to end.

termin′ology (99-1ʳ5-9jⁱ1) special words used in a science or art.

terminus (99-1-9) railway station at the end of a line.

termite (99-41) white insect that lives in the ground and makes hills above it; it destroys wood. Also called " white ant ".

terrace (2-9s) flat raised place outside a house, or cut in the side of a hill; set of houses standing back from the road.

terraced (roof) (2-9st) flat roof as in the East.

t′erra-c′otta (2-9 + 5-9) baked red earth used especially for making ornamental figures, e.g. of men and animals.

t′erra f′irma (2-9 + 99-9) dry land.

terrain (2-21) piece of land, considered especially as a place for a battle.

TERRAPIN

terrapin (2-9-1) *turtle* (= cold-blooded animal with a hard shell from which only the head, legs and tail come out).

terr′estrial (1-2-19) having to do with this earth.

terrible (2-9) causing great fear; Sl. very bad; **terribly** (——1) Sl. very.

terrier (2-19) active strong dog which likes digging holes in the ground.

terrify (2-1-41) frighten greatly; adj. **terr′ific** (9-1-1) Sl. very great.

territory (2-1-9-1) land ruled by a government; *The Territorials* = men in England who learn to be soldiers of their own *free will* (= willingly) and in their free time; *Territorial waters* = sea which is under control of a country—3 (or 12) miles from the coast.

terror (2-9) great fear; Sl. *A holy terror* = very unpleasant person; **terrorist** (2-9-1) one who tries to bring about a change in the government by acts intended to cause terror, e.g. murder of government officers.

terse (99) short (way of speaking), using few words.

tertian (99sh19) happening every second day, e.g. a fever.

tertiary (99sh19-1) third in rank or order; *Tertiary rocks* = rocks formed about 40 million years ago.

tesselated (floor) (2-1-21-1) made up of many small blocks of stone.

test (2) trial; **to test**, try and examine a thing to see if it is pure, strong, etc.

testament (2-9-9) *The Old* —, *The New* —, parts of the Bible; *Last will and testament* = paper showing what is to be done with goods, land and other possessions after the owner is dead; **test′ator** (2-21-9) person who writes a will and testament.

testify (2-1-41) say solemnly the truth—as in a law-court; n. **testimony** (2-1-9-1).

testim′onial (2-1-67-19) letter giving an opinion as to a person's character and powers; gift intended to show **gratitude** (n. of Grateful), e.g. to a Headmaster who is leaving the school.

t′est-tube (2 + 177) small glass pipe closed at one end used in scientific work.

testy (2-1) ill-tempered.

tetanus (2-9-9) disease which causes tightening of the muscles.

tetchy (2-1) ill-tempered.

t′ête-à-t′ête (21 + 44 + 21) *private* (= not public) talk between two people.

tether (2ðɡ) tie an animal (e.g. to a small post in the ground) so that it cannot run away; *I'm at the end of my tether* = have no more money, strength, power to act.

tetra- four, e.g. **tetragon** (2-9-9) = four-sided figure.

text (2) words actually used by a writer; small piece cut of the Bible; main part of a book; adj. **textual** (2-179); **a textbook** (2-7) book about one special subject, book set for study.

textile (2-41) having to do with making cloth; **textiles** (——z) all sorts of cloth.

texture (2-tshg) way in which threads are put together to make cloth; smoothness or roughness of cloth.

thane (21) nobleman in England before A.D. 1066.

thanks (3ngk) expression used to show that one is grateful to a person who has given one something or done one a kindness; **to thank** (3ngk) say that one is grateful to a person; *Thanks to* = because of.

Thanksgiving Day (3ngk-1-1 + 21) last Thursday in November is (usually) fixed as a day when Americans give thanks to God for all His mercies, and hold big feasts.

thatch (3) roof made of dry grass or leaves.

thaw (55) (of ice and snow) melt.

theatre (19-9) public hall in which plays are acted; scene of important events; *The operating theatre* = special room in which doctors cut away diseased parts from living people; adj. **theatrical** (11·3-1).

thé dansant (t21 + 44ⁿ-44ⁿ) afternoon tea with dancing.

thee (ð11) you.

theft (2) act of stealing.

theme (11) subject of thought, speech or writing; certain set of notes coming again and again in a piece of music.

theocracy (11·5krgsı) government by priests.

theodolite (11·5-9-4ı) instrument used in measuring angles when making a map.

theology (11·5-9jı) study of the nature of God and of man's beliefs in God; adj. **theological** (11·9-5jı).

theorem (19-9) idea which has to be proved by reasoning.

theory (19-1) general idea put forward to explain a certain set of facts; the general laws of an art; *All very well in theory* = good as an idea but not possible in fact; adj. **theoretical** (19-2-1).

theosophy (11·5-9-1) belief that men can get into direct touch with God by making themselves very pure in body and mind; adj. **theosophical** (11·9-5-1).

therapy (2-9-1) medical help, e.g. *Light therapy* = treatment of diseases by light; adj. **therapeutic** (2-9-177-1) having to do with medical treatment of diseases.

there- (ð29) **thereby** (ð29-41) by means of that; **thereon** (ð29-5) on that, at that time; **therewith** (ð29-1ð) with that, then.

therefore (ð29-55) for that reason.

therm (99) measure of amount of heat, e.g. given by a gas fire.

thermal (99) having to do with heat.

thermo- heat, e.g. **thermometer** (9-5-1-9) instrument for measuring heat; **thermosetting** (99-6-2-1) becoming solid when heated.

thermos (bottle) (99-5) which keeps cold liquids cold (or hot — hot).

thesaurus (1-55-9) collection of words or of bits of poetry or other writings.

thesis (11-1) idea to be defended by a person being examined for a *degree* (= title such as M.A., Doctor of Science, etc.); book written in order to get a degree.

thews (177z) muscles; strength.

thick (1) not thin; wide, broad; *A thick wood* = trees close together; *A thick liquid* = which does not flow easily; *Thick voice* = not clear; *Thick-headed* = not able to understand; Sl. *That's a bit thick* = that is too bad, more than I can allow; *Through thick and thin* = through all difficulties; *As thick as thieves* = very friendly.

thicket (1-1) place where there are many trees and bushes.

thick-skinned (1 + 1) one who does not notice (or does not care about) other people's bad opinion of him.

thief (11) one who steals; pl. **thieves** (11-z); **to thieve**.

thigh (41) thick upper part of the leg.

thimble (1) metal cap worn on the finger to protect it when using a needle.

thin (1) not thick, not deep, not broad, e.g. *A thin sheet of paper*; having little fat, e.g. *Thin and hungry-looking*; *A thin liquid* = one which pours easily; *A thin-skinned person* = one whose feelings are easily hurt (= who is easily made angry).

thine (ð41) yours.

thing (1); *My things* = my boxes, my clothes; *It's not at all the thing to —* = not proper; *The very thing* = just what I want; *Not to feel (look) quite the thing* = not well, in bad health; *Poor thing!* = I am sorry for him (her);

thingamy, thingummy (1-9-1), word used for a thing (or person) of which one cannot remember the name.

think (1ngk) use the mind; be of opinion; get an idea.

third degree (99 + 1-11) long fierce questioning by the police.

third party risk (99 + 44-1 + 1) Mr. A insures his car with Mr. B's insurance company. If the car hurts Mr. C, Mr. C must be paid. Mr. C is the third party; his danger is the " third party risk ".

thirst (99) feeling caused by lack of drink.

thistle (1) wild plant with a red-blue flower and leaves which prick the skin, eaten by donkeys (asses).

thither (ð109) to that place.

tho' (ð67) though.

thong (5) leather band.

thorax (55-3) that part of the body between the neck and the stomach.

thorn (55) sharp part of a plant, growing out of the stem, which pricks the skin.

thorough (8-9) all through, completely; **a thoroughbred** (8-9-2) special kind of horse used for racing; (of a man) person of very good birth and character; *Thorough-going, A thorough-paced villain* = very bad man; *A thoroughfare* = street open at both ends; *No thoroughfare* = this street is not open at the far end.

thou (ŏ47) you.

though (ŏ67) *Though it is raining, I shall go* = it is —, but (in spite of this) I shall —.

thought (55) p.t. and p.p. of Think; act of thinking; *A thought less* = slightly less; **thoughtless** (55-1) careless, not considering others.

thrall (55) slave; state of being a slave.

thrash (3) (1) beat; (2) win against; (3) get out the grain from corn; *To thrash out a question* = talk over thoroughly.

thread (2) very fine single long piece of silk, cotton, etc.; *Hangs by a thread* = is in a dangerous state; *The thread of his thoughts* = the general direction; *Threadbare (cloth)* = worn down so that the threads are seen; **to thread**, put a thread through (e.g. through a needle); *To thread one's way* = go carefully, finding one's path with difficulty.

threaten (2) say that one will do harm if a person does not act as desired; *Threatening* = seeming as if it will do harm; **a threat**, saying that one will — (as above).

thr′ee-pl′y (11 + 41) three pieces of thin wood stuck together in such a way that the board will not crack whichever way it is bent; string of wool or silk made of three threads twisted together.

threnody (2-9-1) sad song, sung over a dead person.

fhresh (2) see Thrash—third meaning.

threshold (2-67) stone or board just below a door; entrance to a house.

threw (77) p.t. of Throw.

thrice (41s) three times.

thrift (1) carefulness, not wasting money.

thrill (1) excite.

thrive (41) be successful; grow strong and fat; p.p. **thriven** (1).

thro′ (77) through.

throat (67) front part of the neck; any narrow pipe-like opening leading from or into something larger.

throb (5) beat—like the heart; *Throbbing pain* = pain which comes and goes in a regular way, e.g. at each beat of the heart.

throe (67) pain; *In the throes of* = struggling with.

thromb′osis (5-67-1) forming of a solid piece in a blood-vessel (vein or artery) which stops the flow of blood.

throne (67) seat of a king; *Come to the throne* = become king.

throng (5) a crowd; to crowd.

throstle (5) (= thrush) singing bird.

throttle (5) prevent breathing by pressing the throat; **the throttle** (of an engine), small bar moved by the hand or pressed by the foot which controls the flow of steam or gas to an engine.

through′out (77-47) in every part of; during the whole time.

throve (67) p.t. of Thrive.

throw (67) cause to move through the air, e.g. by a strong movement of the arm; *Throw dust in the eyes of* = deceive; *Throw a pot* = form a pot on a potter's wheel; *Throw cold water on a plan* = say that it will fail; *Throw away* = put aside as useless; *Throw in one's hand* = cease playing (e.g. a card game), give up hope; *Throw off an illness* = become well; *Throw over a friend* = desert; *Throw up the sponge* = give up a fight, yield, say that one is beaten; *To throw up* = be sick; p.p. **thrown**.

thrush (8) singing bird.

thrush (8) redness and swelling of the tongue and mouth usually in babies.

THRUSH

thrust (8) push suddenly and with force.

thud (8) sound made by a soft thing falling.

thug (8) thief and murderer.

thumb (8) short inside "finger" of the hand; *Under the thumb of* = in the power of; *Rule of thumb* = rough way of doing things found out by experience.

thump (8) heavy blow, e.g. given with the closed hand.

thunder (8-9) loud sound heard in the sky in a storm; n. **thunderbolt** (8-9-67) mass of metal said to fall from the sky during a storm; great surprise; **thunderclap** (8-9-3) noise of thunder; **thunderstruck** (8-9-8) struck by *lightning*; very surprised.

thwack (3) a blow; to beat.

thwart (55) prevent a person from doing what he wishes; n. **thwart**, board across a boat, used as a seat; **athwart** (9-55) across.

thy (ŏ41) your.

thyme (41) sweet-smelling plant, used in cooking.

th′yroid gl′and (41-51 + 3) small part of the body, found just below that part of the throat which moves when you talk; when the thyroid gland does not do its work, you become heavy and slow, and the hair and skin are dry; when it works too much, you become easily excited, and the eyes stand out.

ti′ara (144-9) jewelled crown worn by ladies.

tibia (1-19) large bone between the foot and the knee.

tic (1) sudden uncontrolled movement of the muscles of the face.

tick (1) (1) very small creature which fixes itself on to the skin and drinks the blood; (2) sound of a clock; (3) mark showing correctness √; Sl. *To tick off* = scold; Sl. *To buy on tick* = without paying at the time.

ticket (1-1) small card showing that the owner has paid for a seat in a train, theatre, etc.;

ticking   307   **tire**

card showing the price of a thing in a shop; **Ticket-of-leave man** = prisoner allowed out of prison but still watched by the police.

ticking (1-1) strong cloth.

tickle (1) cause a person to laugh by light touches, e.g. under the arms; Sl. *That tickles me* = amuses —; **ticklish** (1-1) one who laughs easily when tickled; difficult, needing careful treatment.

t'idb'it (1-1) see Titbit.

tiddler (1-9) very small fish; Sl. small child.

tide (41) rise and fall of the sea caused by the moon; time or season; *To tide over a difficulty* = pass over successfully; adj. **tidal**.

tidings (41-1-z) news.

tidy (41-1) in good order; *A tidy sum* = rather large amount; **to tidy**, set in order.

tie (41) bind with a rope or string; **ties** (——z) fastenings; feelings which hold people together, e.g. *Ties of friendship*; *The game was a tie* = each side won the same number of points.

tie (41) band of cloth, usually brightly coloured, worn round the neck.

tier(s) (19z) rows of things one above another, e.g. of seats.

tiff (1) a slight quarrel.

tiffin (1-1) midday meal (East).

tiger (41-9) large, wild, fierce cat-like animal found in India.   TIGER

tight (41) firmly held; not easily loosened; fitting closely; *Money is tight* = scarce; *A tight corner* = difficult and dangerous set of conditions; Sl. *Tight* = drunk; **tights**, close-fitting clothes worn by persons giving a public show of dancing, rope-walking, etc.

tike, tyke (41) dog of no particular kind or value.

tile (41) flat piece of baked earth used on a floor or roof; Sl. hat.

till (1) up to the time when.

till (1) small *drawer* (= box pulled out from a table and pushed in to shut) in a shop where money is kept.

till (1) prepare land for growing seeds; **tillage** (1-1j) tilling of land, land so tilled.

tiller (1-9) bar fixed to the top of a *rudder* (= blade at the back of a ship or boat with which one guides it).

tilt (1) (1) cause to slope; (2) ride at a person with a spear (e.g. the knights of old days).

timber (1-9) wood ready for building; trees to be used for building.

timbre (3ⁿ-9) special quality of the sound of a voice or musical instrument.

timbrel (1) small drum played with the hand.

time (41) (1) e.g. past, present, future; (2) *A long time* = (idea of lasting, continuing); (3) particular moment or date; (4) e.g. *Three times two make six* = 3 × 2 = 6; *To have a good time*, *To have the time of one's life* = enjoy oneself; *At my time of life* = age; *All in good time* = at the proper time, no need for haste; *To time one's blows* = hit at just the right moment; *To time the work* = see exactly how long it takes; **timely** (41-1) coming just at the right time; **timepiece** (41-11s) clock; **t'ime-server** (+ 99-9) one who always tries to please the people who have power at the moment; **timetable** (41-21) list of days and times when certain things will be done; list of trains with time of starting and arriving; list of the times of lessons in a school.

timid (1-1) **timorous** (1-9-9) easily frightened, not daring.

tin (1) white metal; thin iron plate covered with tin; box made of iron covered with tin; **to tin**, shut up food in a metal box in order to keep it from decay.

tincture (1ngktsh9) medicine prepared in the form of a liquid.

tinder (1-9) dry material used for starting a fire; **t'inder box** (+ 5) old instrument for making fire.

tinea (1-19) disease of the skin.

tinge (1nj) to colour slightly.

tingle (1ngg) have the feeling of blood coming back into the surface of the skin, e.g. just after a blow, or when getting warm after being cold.

tinker (1ngk9) person who repairs things made of metal, e.g. kitchen pots, etc.; repair hastily or unskilfully.

tinkle (1ngk) make a sound like a small bell.

tin-pan alley (1 + 3 + 3-1) Sl. part of New York where music is bought and sold.

tinsel (1) very thin pieces of metal used to ornament dresses; anything bright and fine-looking, but of no value.

tint (1) colour, especially faint colour; to colour faintly.

t'intinnabul'ation (1-1-3-17-21shn) sound of bells.

tiny (41-1) very small.

tip (1) point or end.

tip (1) cause to slope so that what is inside falls out; *The car tipped up* = nearly fell over; *— tipped over* = actually fell over; **a tip**, place where waste matter is thrown from carts.

tip (1) small gift of money made to a servant.

tip (1) piece of advice, e.g. about which horse is going to win a race; **tipster** (1-9) one who sells such advice.

tippet (1-1) woman's garment put round the neck, covering the shoulders and breast.

tipple (1) drink too much wine, etc.

tipsy (1-1) having had too much strong drink.

t'ipt'op (1-5) the top; very good.

tir'ade (41-21) long angry speech.

tire (419) (old word for —) to dress.

tire (419) see Tyre.

tire (419) to cause to be tired; **tiredness** (419-1) that feeling which comes as a result of too much work; *Tired of* = having already had too much of, and so not wanting any more, e.g. *I'm tired of boiled eggs* = I have eaten so many

tiro boiled eggs lately that I do not want to eat any more; **tire̜some** (4I9-9) causing one to be tired or angry.

tiro, tyro (4I9-67) inexperienced person.

tissue (1-177) any very fine light material; **t'issue-paper** (+ 21-9) very thin soft paper.

tit (1) (1) small bird; (2) *teat* (= that part of the breast from which milk comes); (3) *Tit for tat* = return blow for blow, do to others as they have done to you.

tit'anic (4I-3-1) very large.

t'itb'it (1-1) specially nice piece of food.

tithe (4Ið) one-tenth of a crop, given to the Church; a small part of.

titillate (1-1-21) excite in a pleasant way.

titivate (1-1-21) make oneself clean and neat.

title (4I) name of a book or writing, picture, etc.; special word instead of Mr. showing rank, e.g. *Sir, Lord*, etc.; *He has a title to* = has a right to; **t'itle-deed** (+ 11) paper showing one's right to hold land; **t'itle role** (+ 67) that character in a play from which the play gets its name, e.g. Hamlet in *Hamlet, Prince of Denmark*.

titmouse (1-47) small bird.

titter (1-9) laugh quietly—as girls do when behaving foolishly.

t'ittle̜-t'attle (1 + 3) foolish and careless talk about other people.

titular (1-17-9) having to do with a title; having the name but not the power of an office.

toad (67) small ugly jumping creature with four legs and a large mouth, which lives in wet cool places and eats insects; *Toad-in-the-hole* = meat cooked in a mixture of flour, eggs and milk.

toadstool (67-77) T-shaped white or yellow *fungus* (= plant containing no green matter, usually found growing on wet decaying vegetable matter) with a round top, found usually in wet ground or on decayed wood.

toady (67-1) one who tries to please the great or rich, and forgets his own self-respect in so doing.

toast (67) pieces of bread made brown and hard on the surface by being held in front of a fire; *To drink a toast* = drink in honour of a person.

tob'acco (9-3-67) plant used for smoking, e.g. in a cigarette; **tob'acconist** (9-3-9-1) one who sells tobacco.

tob'oggan (9-5-9) flat wooden frame, curved up at the front, on which one slides down a snow-covered hill. TOBOGGAN

tocsin (5-1) bell used to give warning.

today (9-21) on this day.

toddle (5) walk like a baby learning to walk.

toddy (5-1) hot drink, made with *whisky* (= strong drink), sugar, fruit-*juice* (= liquid) and hot water.

to-d'o (9 + 77) *To make a great to-do* = get excited and talk a lot.

toe (67) one of the "fingers" of the feet; pointed end of a shoe or other foot-covering; *To toe the line* = do exactly as ordered.

toff (5) Sl. gentleman; finely dressed person.

toffee, toffy (5-1) boiled mixture of sugar and butter.

toga (67-9) outer garment of a Roman in ancient times.

tog'ether (9-2ð9) in company; towards each other.

togs (5-z) Sl. clothes.

toil (5I) work hard; n. hard work.

toilet (5I-1) act of washing oneself and dressing; room for washing; **t'oilet, toil'ette** (74-2) way of dressing; a lady's dress.

toils (5I-z) *In the toils* = caught in a net.

Tok'ay (67-21) very good wine made in Hungary.

token (67-9) a sign; thing used instead of money; *Token payment* = payment of a very small part of what is owed so as to show that the whole amount is really owed.

told (67) p.t. of Tell.

tolerate (5-9-21) suffer a thing which one does not like; allow such a thing to continue though one does not like it; **tolerable** (5-9-9) which can be suffered; **tolerant** (5-9-9) allowing others to think or act as they please even when they seem to be wrong; n. **toler'ation** (5-9-21shn).

toll (67) to sound a bell, e.g. as a sign that someone has died.

toll (67) money paid for going along a road or over a bridge; *A toll-bridge* = bridge at which one has to pay.

tom- male, e.g. **tomboy** (5-5I) girl who behaves like a boy; **t'om-c'at** (5 + 3) male cat; **t'omf'ool** (5-77) fool.

tomahawk (5-9-55) axe used by American Indians.

tom'ato (9-44-67) red fruit with a salt-sweet taste. TOMAHAWK

tomb (77) place in which the dead are put, a grave.

tome (67) large book.

Tommy (5-1) short for *Tommy Atkins* = an English soldier; Sl. *Tommy rot* = foolishness.

t'ommy-gun (+ 8) small machine-gun carried by one man.

tom'orrow (9-5-67) day after this one.

T'om Th'umb (5 + 8) person of very small size in an English fairy-story.

Tom Tiddler's ground (5 + 1-9z + 47) (1) children's game; (2) place where money is picked up; (3) land of doubtful ownership.

t'omt'it (5-1) a small bird.

t'omtom (5-5) Indian drum.

-tomy, cutting, e.g. **an'atomy** (9-3-9-1) cutting up and study of the body.

ton (8) 2,240 pounds weight (America, 2,000 pounds); *Tons of love* (*time*, etc.) = plenty of —.

tone (67) certain musical *interval* (= space) between two notes; musical sound; *In a loving tone* = in a tender voice; *The tone of the muscles is good* = muscles are in a good state; *The tone of a school* = general spirit of obedience (n. of Obey) and good behaviour among the boys or girls; *To tone down* = make softer, kinder, etc.

tongs (5-z) two arms of metal joined at one end or in the middle and used for seizing or holding.

tongue (8) that moving thing inside the mouth with which we talk and taste; language; anything shaped like a tongue; *To give tongue* = (of dogs) make excited noises when hunting.

tonic (5-1) keynote or first note of a musical scale; having to do with musical *tones* (3rd above); medicine used to excite or give strength to the body.

tonight (9-41) this night.

tonnage (8-1j) weight of goods which a ship can carry; all the ships of a country.

tonsil (5) two small masses at the back of the throat—sometimes cut out by doctors; **tonsill'itis** (5-1-41-1) disease in these parts.

tons'orial (5-55-19) having to do with hair-cutting.

tonsure (5-sh9) top of a priest's head from which all the hair has been cut as a mark of his office.

too (77) (1) also; (2) more than enough, e.g. *Too much, Too big.*

took (7) p.t. of Take.

tool (77) any instrument used in doing work, e.g. *A gardener's tools* = things needed for moving earth, cutting plants, etc.; *He used him as a tool* = made him do work which he did not wish to do himself.

toot (77) sound of a horn.

tooth (77) (pl. **teeth**) hard white objects in the mouth with which we bite; anything so shaped, e.g. teeth on a wheel by which it turns another wheel; *Armed to the teeth* = thoroughly well protected or completely armed; *To fight tooth and nail* = very fiercely; *To cast it in his teeth* = cause a person to remember some wrong act done by him; *To escape by the skin of one's teeth* = with great difficulty, narrowly; *To have a sweet tooth* = to like eating sweet things; **toothsome** (77-9) pleasant to taste.

top (5) highest part; adj. highest; be as high as; hit the top of (a ball); Sl. **t'op-h'ole** (5 + 67) very good.

top (5) child's plaything; wheel with a bar through the middle, made to turn by itself by twisting it sharply between the fingers, or with the help of a string.

topaz (67-3) jewel, usually yellow.

t'op-b'oots (5 + 77) boots reaching up to the knee.

toper (67-9) one who drinks too much wine.

topi (67-1) hat worn to protect the head from the sun.

topic (5-1) subject of talk; **topical**, concerned with matters of present-day interest.

t'op-n'otch (5 + 5) Sl. very good, best.

top'ography (9-5-9-1) careful description of a place; special character of a place.

topper (5-9) high silk-hat worn by men.

topping (5-1) Sl. very good.

topple (over) (5) fall slowly over.

t'opsyt'urvy (5-1-99-1) wrong side up; all mixed up and out of order.

toque (67k) lady's small close-fitting hat; small woollen cap worn by men, especially in Canada.

torch (55) piece of wood with oil on the end, burnt to give light; *Electric torch* = small electric hand light.

tore (55) p.t. of Tear.

toreador (5-19-55) a *bull-* (= male form of cow) fighter, e.g. in Spain.

torm'ent (55-2) cause great pain, n. **t'orment.**

torn (55) p.p. of Tear.

torn'ado (55-21-67) storm in which the wind blows round and round.

torp'edo (55-11-67) long round metal shell pointed at each end, filled with explosive material, sent through the water to destroy a ship.

torpid (55-1) heavy and slow; uninterested; n. **torpor** (55-9).

torque (55k) chain worn round the neck in ancient times; the turning power or movement of an engine.

torrent (5) great rush of water down a steep place; adj. **torr'ential** (5-2-shl).

torrid (5-1) hot and dried up by the sun.

torsion (55shn) state of being twisted; force with which a twisted thing tries to untwist itself.

torso (55-67) body without the limbs or head.

tortoise (55-9) land and fresh-water animal with a hard shell from which only the head, legs and tail come out.

TORTOISE

tortuous (55-179) twisting, e.g. a road; (of a piece of reasoning) difficult to understand; (of character or action) dishonest, full of tricks.

torture (55tsh9) cause great pain to; n. such pain.

Tory (55-1) party in the government of England which wishes to keep things as they are, or change only slowly.

toss (5) to throw; (of the sea) move up and down; *To toss the head* = move the head sharply up showing disagreement; *Toss off* = drink quickly; *Toss up* = throw a penny to settle a question Yes or No, according to which side of the penny falls upwards.

tot (5) (1) very young child; (2) little drink; **tot up**, add up.

total (67) whole amount; complete.

totalit'arian (government) (67-3-1-29-19) government by one party, no other party being allowed.
totalizator (67-9-41-21-9) machine used in *betting* on horses.
tote (67) *The Tote* = totalizator (2nd above).
totem (67-9) animal or plant taken as the sign of a *tribe* (= group of families) of American Indians, and considered as being a member of the tribe; tall pole cut with signs and so used.
totter (5-9) walk as if about to fall.
toucan (77-9) bird with a very large *beak* (= horny mouth) and very bright feathers.

TOUCAN

touch (8) *I have not touched food for a week* = not eaten; *The law can't touch me* = can have no effect on; *Touched my heart* = made me feel deeply; *Nothing can touch it* = it is best of all; Sl. *He touched me for £1* = made me give him £1; *The ship touched at Madras* = stopped for a short time at —; *To touch up a picture* = make better by small touches of colour; *To touch upon a subject* = speak for a short time about; *Touch down* (of an aeroplane) = come down for a very short time; *Touch off* (an explosion, a quarrel) = start by some very small act something which is very ready to explode; *A touch of the sun* = slight illness caused by the sun; *In touch* (football) = outside the playing-field; *He is slightly touched* = his mind is out of order; **touchy** (——1) = easily angered; *Touching the subject of which we spoke* = in regard to; *A touching* (*speech, book, etc.*) = one which causes deep feeling, especially pity.
touchstone (8-67) piece of stone on which gold is rubbed to see if it is pure; that which proves if a thing is true.
tough (8f) not easily torn, e.g. leather; (of a man) strong and daring; *A tough* = dangerous bad man; Sl. *Tough luck* = bad fortune.
toupée (77-21) mass of hair or feathers growing on the front of the head of a bird or animal; hair worn to hide a place on the head on which there is no hair growing.
tour (79) round journey, stopping at various places.
t'our de f'orce (+ 9 + 55s) act needing special cleverness to do it.
tourist (79-1) one who travels for pleasure.
tournament (79-9-9) number of games played between different players to see who is best of all (also = Tourney).
tourney (79-1) meeting of knights to fight each other as a game, not as in battle.
tourniquet (79-1k21) band fixed tightly round a limb to stop the flow of blood.
tousle (47z) put hair in disorder, e.g. by rubbing.
tout (47) person who goes about asking people to buy.

t'out ens'emble (77 + 44ⁿ-44ⁿ) general effect.
tow (67) pull a ship along; pull along a broken motor-car; Sl. *I took him in tow* = took charge of —.
tow (67) hair-like material got by pulling old rope to pieces.
tow'ard(s) (9-55-z) in the direction of.
towel (479) cloth used for drying the hands or body.
tower (479) tall building; **to tower**, rise high; *A towering rage* = state of great anger.
town (47) group of houses larger than a village but usually smaller than a city; *Up to town* = to London; **township** (47-1) part of the country which has certain powers of government.
tox- poison, e.g. **tox'aemia** (5-11-19) blood-poisoning; **toxic** (5-1) poisonous; a **toxin** (5-1) poison produced in an animal or plant; **toxic'ology** (5-1-5-9J1) study of poisons.
toy (51) child's plaything.
trace (21s) track or mark left by something which has passed; *A trace of* = very small amount of; follow the tracks of; copy a picture by drawing on a thin piece of paper laid over it; draw lines.
trace(s) (21s1z) leather bands joining a horse on to a carriage; *To kick over the traces* = get out of control.
tracery (21s9-1) ornamental lines; finely cut stone pillars and arches as an ornament in the upper part of a window.
trach'ea (9k11g) pipe in the throat through which we breathe.
track (3) mark left on the ground by something which has passed; path; Am. railway line; *The beaten track* TRACK = usual line of action; band on which a tank runs instead of on wheels: see picture; *A half-track car* has a track at the back but wheels in front; **to track**, follow the tracks of.
tract (3) (**1**) large piece of country; (**2**) little book usually about belief in God or about the government.
traction (3-shn) pulling; **tr'action-engine** (+ 2nJ1) large steam-engine used for pulling heavy carts along roads.
tractor (3-9) machine used for pulling farm-tools and carts.

TRACTOR

trade (21) buying and selling; employment of any kind; persons employed in a certain business; *To trade on one's name* = make dishonest use of the good opinion held of one by others; **tradesman** (21-z-9) shop-keeper; **tr'ade 'union** (+ 177-19) joining together of the men in one employment so as to get better pay, etc.; **tr'ade-wind** (+ 1) wind which always blows from the north-east and south-

tradition   311   **trap**

east towards the *equator* (= imaginary line round middle of the earth).

trad'ition (9-1shn) passing on of history or customs from father to son; old custom; story so passed on.

trad'uce (9-177s) speak against the character of a person.

traffic (3-1) buying and selling of goods; coming and going of cars and people in the street— also of ships on the sea.

tragedy (3j1-1) solemn play with a sad ending; any sad event; **trag'edian** (9j11-19) actor in tragedies; **tragic** (3j1) sad, ruinous.

trail (21) mark left by something which has passed; path.

trailer (21-9) (1) two-wheeled cart pulled behind a car or *tractor* (see 7th above); (2) short piece of cinema-film used to show what film is coming next week or soon.

TRAILER

train (21) teach; form the character; make the body strong; *In training for* = practising and getting ready for.

train (21) (1) group of followers; (2) number of railway carriages pulled along a railway line; (3) part of a lady's dress which lies on the floor behind her; (4) number of things joined together and following one after another, e.g. *A train of events, of thought*; thin line of gunpowder used to set fire to a mass of powder at a distance; *All is now in train for —* = ready —.

tr'aining college (21-1 + 5-1ij) place in which men and women learn the art of teaching.

trait (21) special and peculiar point of character.

traitor (21-9) one who does harm to his own king or country, by helping an enemy.

trajectory (3j1-9-1) curved path of a shot from a gun.

tram (3) car on an electric railway running in the streets of a town.

trammel (3) make movement difficult; n. anything which makes —.

tramp (3) walk heavily; walk far; **a tramp**, homeless poor man who walks from place to place; ship carrying goods from place to place.

trample (3) walk over and press down with the feet, e.g. flowers in a garden.

tramway (3-21) electric railway running in the streets of a town.

trance (44-s) unnatural sleep in which people sometimes see wonderful things.

tranquil (3ng-1) calm.

trans- across.

transact (business) (3-z3) do, settle.

transc'end (3-2) go beyond; be better than.

transcr'ibe (3-21) copy written or printed matter on to another paper; n. **transcr'iption** (3-1-shn).

transept (3-2) that part of a church which is built north and south across the main hall, which usually runs east and west.

transf'er (3-99) move from one place to another; n. **tr'ansfer**, act of transferring; picture printed on thin paper, which, when wetted, may be passed from the thin paper on to any other surface.

transf'igure (3-1-9) change the appearance of.

transf'ix (3-1) go through as a knife goes through a body.

transf'orm (3-55) change the shape; change from one form into another; n. **transform'ation** (3-9-21shn).

transf'use (blood) (3-177z) pass blood from one living body into another.

transgr'ess (3-2) go beyond the law, do wrong.

transient (3-z19) soon passing away, not lasting long.

transit (3-1) a moving through or across, e.g. of some other world across the face of the sun; *Goods in transit* = being carried from one place to another.

trans'ition (3-13n) a change from one condition into another.

transitive (verb) (3-1-1) verb which takes an *object* (e.g. I hit *it*—*it* is the object).

transitory (3-1-9-1) not lasting long, soon changing or disappearing.

translate (3-21) change spoken or written matter from one language into another; *Translated into heaven* = taken up into —.

transl'iterate (3-z-1-9-21) write one language using the letters of another language.

transl'ucent (3-z-77s) which allows light to pass through, although one may not be able to see through it.

transmigr'ation (3-z-41-21shn) passing of the soul at death into another body.

transm'it (3-z-1) send across, e.g. a letter; allow to pass, e.g. *Wires transmit electricity*; n. **transm'ission** (3-z-1shn).

transm'ute (3-z-177) to change into another form or substance, e.g. *Transmute lead into gold*.

transom (3-9) beam across the top of a door or window.

transp'arent (3-29) which can be seen through, e.g. glass; easily understood.

transp'ire (3-419) become known.

transpl'ant (3-44) take growing plants from one place and make them grow in another place.

transp'ort (3-55) carry from one place to another; send a prisoner to another country as a punishment; n. **tr'ansport**; *Transports of delight* = feelings of great joy; *A transport* = ship carrying soldiers.

transp'ose (3-67z) put thing A where B was and B where A was; change the order of words or letters; change music so as to make it higher or lower; n. **transpos'ition** (3-9z1shn).

transv'erse (3-z-99) lying across.

trap (3) (1) instrument for catching animals,

e.g. mice; a trick; bend in a pipe in which solid matter is caught; (2) horse-carriage with two wheels; **to trap**, catch in a trap; fix traps in a pipe; **tr'ap-d'oor** (+ 55) a door in a floor or roof.

trap'eze (9-11) short bar hanging by two ropes on which people perform clever tricks.

trap'ezium (9-11-19) irregular four-sided figure.

trapper (3-9) one who catches animals to get their skins.

trappings (3-1-2) ornaments on a horse, etc.

trash (3) worthless material; worthless writings.

travail (3-21) labour; pain in giving birth.

travel (3) to move; make a journey.

traverse (3-9) to pass across; **a traverse**, way across; movement across.

travesty (3-1-1) copy the behaviour of a person so as to make him seem foolish.

trawl (55) large fishing net; **a trawler** (55-9) ship which pulls such a net.

tray (21) flat piece of wood or metal on which cups or other light things are carried.

treacherous (2-9-9) disloyal; deceiving; not to be trusted; n. **treachery** (——-1) disloyal act.

treacle (11) thick sugary liquid.

tread (2) to press with the foot; to walk; **the tread**, (of a wheel) that part which touches the road; (of a stair) that part on which one sets one's foot.

treadle (2) part of a machine on which the foot rests in order to turn it.

treadmill (2-1) mill worked by slaves or prisoners walking inside or outside a big wheel.

treason (11z) disloyalty; helping persons to attack the king or government; *High treason* = an attempt to do harm to the king or his eldest son.

treasure (239) store of precious things; thing of great value; dearly loved person; very useful servant; **to treasure**, value greatly; **treasurer** (——-9) officer in charge of money; **treasury** (——-1) place where treasures are kept; the government office which deals with money.

treat (11) behave towards, e.g. *Treat him kindly* = be kind to him; *To treat it as serious* = behave as if it was ——; *To treat with the enemy* = talk about an agreement for peace; *To treat the illness with* —— = to use —— as a medicine for ——; to write or talk about, e.g. *He treated the subject in his book*; *He treated me to a dinner* = paid for a dinner for me; *A great treat* = unusual pleasure.

treatise (11-1z) book or writing about a subject.

treaty (11-1) agreement between nations, e.g. to end a war.

treble (2) (1) three times; make three times larger; (2) boy's voice.

tree (11) large plant from which we get wood; Sl. *Up a tree* = in a difficulty; *Family tree* = list of one's father, father's father, mother's father, and other relations from whom one is descended.

trek (2) to travel in a cart pulled by cattle.

trellis (2-1) pieces of wood crossing each other and nailed together—for plants to grow up.

tremble (2) shake—especially with fear; be afraid; *His fate is trembling in the balance* = is just about to be settled.

tremendous (1-2-9) very large.

tremolo (2-9-67) shaking notes of music.

tremor (2-9) shaking, e.g. of the limbs, or the ground in an *earthquake* (see ——).

tremulous (2-17-9) shaking; afraid.

trench (2) long deep hole dug in the ground; *To trench upon (my time)* = take some of (my time).

trenchant (speech) (2-9) keen, clever and often unkind.

trencher (2-9) wooden plate; *A good trencherman* = one who eats a lot.

trend (2) to bend or slope in a certain direction.

trep'an (1-3) **treph'ine** (1-11) cut away part of the bone of the head.

trepid'ation (2-1-21shn) fear and excitement.

trespass (2-9) go unlawfully on to another's land; do wrong.

tress (2) number of long hairs taken together, e.g. one long curl.

trestle (2) wooden support shaped like an **A.**

tri- three.

trial (419) act of trying (examining) whether a thing is good (true, etc.) or not; an examining of a prisoner in a court of law to see if he has done wrong; trouble or difficulty.

triangle (413ngg) figure with three angles; adj. **tri'angular** (413ngg17-9).

tribe (41) group of families; class or kind.

tribul'ation (1-17-21shn) grief; trouble.

trib'unal (41-177) seat of a judge; court of law.

tribune (1-177) officer of government elected by the people.

tributary (1-17-9-1) (of a river) side stream flowing into the main river; (of a king) paying money to some more powerful king.

tribute (1-177) forced payment to a conqueror; *To pay tribute to a person* = tell of the good he has done.

tricar (41-44) motor-car with three wheels.

trice (41s) *In a trice* = in a moment, quickly.

trick (1) act done to deceive; *He has a trick of* = has a *habit* (= an action done so often that it has become part of the character) of; *That will do the trick* = do what is needed; *To take a trick* (in playing cards) = win one set of cards.

trickle (1) thin stream of liquid; **to trickle**, flow in a ——.

trickster (1-9) one who tricks.

tricolo(u)r (1-9-9) three-coloured flag, e.g. that of France.

tricycle (41Is1) machine with three wheels, moved by the feet.

trident (41) spear with three points.

tried (41) p.t. and p.p. of Try; proved true or good.

tri'ennial (412-19) happening every three years.

trifle (41) thing of no importance; sweet dish of *cream* (= fat of milk), cake and fruit; **to trifle,** speak or act lightly, not seriously.

trigger (1-9) part of a gun pulled with the finger in order to fire it.

trigon'ometry (1-9-5-1-1) science which deals with *triangles* (= three-sided figures).

trill (1) sing or play so as to make a shaking note.

trillion (1-19) (English) one million million million; (Am.) one million million.

trilogy (1-9j1) three plays or stories about the same subject.

trim (1) make neat; cut the edges of; ornament the edges; make a boat float level; change one's ideas to suit other people; adj. neat.

trinity (1-1-1) three persons considered as one; **the Trinity,** Christian teaching that God the Father, Jesus Christ the Son, and the Holy Spirit are three Persons, but one God.

trinket (ıngkı) small jewelled ornament of little value.

trio (11·67) piece of music for three voices or instruments; group of three persons.

trip (1) to run with short steps; to dance; catch one's foot and fall; make a mistake; cause another to fall by catching his foot.

trip (1) short journey.

tripe (41) part of the stomach of an animal used as food; Sl. foolish talk or writing.

triple (1) make three times greater; three times; adj. made up of three persons or parts.

triplet (1-1) set of three; one of three children born at one birth.

triplex (1-2) in threes; made of three thicknesses of material.

triplicate (1-1-21) make three things exactly the same, e.g. one writing and two copies.

tripod (41-5) support with three legs.

tripper (1-9) one who goes out on a short journey for pleasure.

tris'ect (41-2) divide into three parts.

trite (41) not fresh or new, e.g. *A trite saying.*

triturate (1-17-21) rub to powder.

triumph (419) victory; a feeling of great success; **to triumph,** win; feel joy at winning, show joy at —; adj. **tri'umphant** (418-9),-**al.**

trivet (1-1) stand for a pot fixed on to the front of a fire-place; *Right as a trivet* = quite well.

trivial (1-19) unimportant.

-trix, sign that one is speaking of a woman, e.g. *Executor* = man who carries out the wishes of a dead person as to his money: **ex'ecutrix** (ıgzz-17-1) a woman who —.

trod (5) p.t. of Tread.

trog'lodyte (5-9-41) ancient cave-dweller.

troll (67) bad fairy or evil spirit.

troll (67) (1) sing in a careless way; (2) catch fish by pulling a line behind a moving boat.

trolley (5-1) light cart on two wheels pushed by hand; low four-wheeled car running on lines; **trolley-bus** (+ 8) Am. **tr'olley-car** (+ 44) electric street-car.

trollop (5-9) careless dirty woman.

tromb'one (5-67) brass instrument of TROMBONE music, played with the mouth.

troop (77) crowd of people; group of horse-soldiers; **to troop,** move forward in a crowd; *Trooping the colours* = ceremony in which respect is shown by soldiers to their own special flag; **trooper** (——9) horse soldier; **the troops,** soldiers; army; **a tr'oop-ship** (+ 1) ship which carries soldiers.

trophy (67-1) sign of victory.

tropics (5-1) hot part of the earth; adj. **tropical.**

trot (5) movement of a horse just quicker than walking; quick walk or slow run of a man; Sl. *To trot out* = bring out things for others to see, or to talk about one's ideas.

troth (67) *To plight one's troth* = promise to marry.

trotters (5-9z) (pigs') feet.

troubadour (77-9-79) singer and storyteller in France and other countries in ancient times.

trouble (8) difficulty; grief; pain; *anxiety* (= state of being anxious); **to trouble,** cause difficulty to.

trough (5f) wooden container for the food or water of animals; hollow between two waves.

trounce (47-s) beat very hard.

troupe (77) group of actors or show-people.

trouper (77-9) actor.

trousers (47z9z) man's garment covering the legs.

trousseau (77-67) clothes, etc., provided for a woman when she gets married.

trout (47) small fresh-water fish.

trove (67) *Treasure-trove* = money, gold or jewels found hidden in the earth.

trow (67) *I trow* = I believe.

trowel (479) flat blade fixed in a handle used in laying bricks for building; curved blade in a handle used for lifting small plants out of the ground.

truant (779) child who stays away from school; *To play truant* = stay away from (school).

truce (77s) arrangement to stop a battle for a time.

truck (8) low cart used on the road or on a railway line for heavy goods.

truck (8) changing goods for goods (not for money); paying for labour with goods not money; *To have no truck with* = have nothing to do with.

tr'uckle-b'ed (8 + 2) small bed which can be shut up or pushed under another bed; **to truckle to,** behave like a slave towards.

truculent (8-17-9) fierce and eager to fight.

trudge (8j) walk as when one is very tired; a **trudge**, long and tiring walk.

true (77) correct; honest; loyal.

truffle (8) black *fungus* (= plant containing no green matter which gets all its food from decaying vegetable matter) which grows below ground and is used to give a nice taste to meat.

truism (77iz) a saying which is very clearly true.

trump (8) sound of a *trumpet* (= brass instrument of music); *The Last Trump* = last day of the world, the Day of Judgment.

trump(s) (8) set of playing-cards given (by agreement) higher value than the rest; *To trump up a charge against* = tell untruths against a person, saying that he has done wrong or broken the law.

trumpery (8-9-1) looking nice but of no value.

trumpet (8-1) brass instrument of music played with the mouth; *To blow one's own trumpet* = say good things about oneself.

truncate (8ngk21) to cut off short.

truncheon (8nch9) short stick used by policemen.

trundle (8) roll a thing along.

trunk (8ngk) main stem of a tree between the root and branches; the main part of the body; long nose of an elephant; box used when travelling; *A trunk road (railway, etc.)* = chief, most important (road) into which other side-(roads) run.

truss (8) tie *hay* (= dried grass) together into a mass; mass so tied up; certain weight of hay; tie up a bird for cooking; metal support for the muscles in front of the body.

trust (8) have faith in another's honesty; believe; **a trust**, duty; union of several business houses so as to have complete control of the buying or selling of certain goods.

trust'ee (8-11) person who has charge of a dead man's money and goods so that the dead man's wishes may be carried out.

truth (77) quality of being true and according to fact; something which is true; honesty.

try (41) begin a piece of work in order to discover if it is possible to do it; use a thing to see if it is good; examine and judge a mixture; to work as hard as one can; *Try and do it* = try to; *This tries my eyes* = is tiring to —; *To try on clothes* = put on new clothes to see if they fit; *To try it on* = do something against the rules and see if punishment results; *This is very trying* = causes pain or anger.

tryst (41) a promise to meet.

Tsar (z44) ruler of Russia before 1917.

tsetse fly (2-1 + 41) fly which carries *sleeping-sickness* (= illness causing sleep usually followed by death).

T-square (t11 + 29) piece of wood shaped like a T used in drawing.

T.T. milk (t11 + t11 + 1) tuberculin-tested milk = milk from a cow which has been tested so as to be sure that it has not got *tuberculosis* (see 4th below).

tub (8) wooden container for liquids; bath;

tubby (———1) short and fat.

tube (177) pipe; adj. **tubular** (177-17-9).

tuber (177-9) swelling on the root of a plant.

tub'ercul'osis (17-99-17-67-1) disease, usually of the *lungs* (= part of body with which we breathe); adj. **tub'ercular** (17-99-17-9).

tuck (8) push a piece of cloth into a narrow crack, e.g. *To tuck up the bed-clothes*; *To tuck away* = put in a safe hiding-place; **a tuck**, cloth folded over and fixed down, for ornament or so as to make a dress shorter; Sl. food; *To tuck in* = to eat.

tuft (8) number of hairs or plants growing close together; *Tuft-hunter* = one who tries to make friends with rich or noble persons.

tug (8) to pull; small ship used to pull larger ones; *Tug-of-war* = two groups pulling a rope to see which can pull harder.

tu'ition (171shn) act of teaching; taking charge of a child for teaching.

tulip (177-1) plant with a large bell-shaped flower held upright on a long stem.

tulle (177) soft silk material for women's clothes.

tumble (8) to fall; Sl. *To tumble to* = understand suddenly.

tumbler (8-9) (1) person who does clever tricks of jumping and falling; (2) drinking glass with no foot.

tumbrel, tumbril (8-1) cart.

tumid (177-1) swollen.

tumour (177-9) diseased growth in the body.

tumult (177-8) excitement and noise.

tun (8) barrel.

tuna (177-9) very big fish, also called *tunny*.

tundra (8-9) cold desert part of Russia.

tune (177) make one musical instrument sound well with another; **a tune**, voice-music of a song; easily remembered part of a piece of music.

tungsten (8-9) grey metal, very valuable, used to make iron very strong and hard.

tunic (177-1) coat, e.g. of a soldier.

tunnel (8) long arched hole under the ground, e.g. one cut through a hill for a railway line to pass through.

tunny (8-1) large sea-fish.

turban (99-9) long piece of cloth bound round the head as a *head-dress* (= covering for the head).

turbid (water) (99-1) made cloudy by causing the mud to rise from the bottom.

turbine (99-41) machine used for making power by blowing steam or burning gas through or over wheels.

TURBAN

turbot (99-9) large flat fish.

turbulent (99-17-9) noisy and uncontrolled.

tur'een (9-11) large bowl for *soup* (= liquid

food made of meat and vegetables boiled in water).

turf (99) earth covered thickly with short grass; *On the turf* = having to do with horse-racing.

turgid (99j1) swollen up; *Turgid way of writing* = solemn in a foolish way.

turkey (99-1) large bird used for food.

turmeric (99-9-1) Indian plant used for its yellow colour, also to give a taste to food.

turmoil (99-5I) noise and disorder.

TURKEY

turn (99) (1) cause to go round and round; go round; (2) shape a piece of material by cutting it while turning it round and round; (3) change the direction of movement, e.g. *Turn to the right*; (4) change the *position* (= place) of, e.g. *Turn the stone over*; *To turn over a new leaf* = begin again and try to behave better; (5) change the state of, e.g. *To turn milk sour*; *To turn in* = go to bed; *To turn on the water* = allow water to flow through a pipe; *To turn off* = stop the flow; *To turn up* = arrive unexpectedly; *To turn down an offer* = refuse; *Turn upon* = attack; **a turn**, change; chance; *It is my turn* = my chance, or my time for work; *In turn* = one after another; *To do a good turn* = do a kindness; *Done to a turn* = perfectly cooked; *It gave me a turn* = frightened me for a moment.

turncoat (99-67) one who changes his opinions for his own gain.

turning (99-1) place where the road turns; **t'urning-point** (+ 5I) time when a great change begins, for better or worse.

turnip (99-1) large root used for food.

turnkey (99-11) man in charge of keys in a prison.

turnout (99-47) number of people at a meeting.

turnover (99-67-9) amount of money received and paid out by a business in one year; three-cornered pastry with fruit in it.

turnpike (99-41) bar across the road at which passers must pay.

turnstile (99-41) gate turned so that only one can pass at a time.

turpentine (99-41) oil obtained from certain trees, used for mixing paint.

turpitude (99-1-177) badness (of character).

turquoise (99-44z) green-blue precious stone.

turret (8-1) little tower; armoured house on a ship with guns in it.

turtle (99) creature with hard shell from which only the head, legs and tail come out; *To turn turtle* (of a ship) = turn upside-down.

turtle (99), **t'urtle-dove** (+ 8) *dove* (= a grey bird with a soft voice); *A pair of —s* = lovers.

tusk (8) long tooth, e.g. of an elephant; **tusker** (——9) elephant.

tussle (8) disorderly fight.

tut, t'ut-t'ut (8) sound made to express anger or strong disagreement.

tutelage (177-1-1j) state of being in charge of another person.

tutor (177-9) teacher; person in charge of a child or young person.

tux'edo (8-11-67) Am. short black coat, etc., as worn by men for evening dinner.

twaddle (5) foolish talk.

twain (2I) two.

twang (3) sound of a musical string being picked with the finger; sound of talking "through the nose" (with the air passage through the nose open).

tweak (II) give a sharp pull to.

tweed (I) soft woollen cloth of mixed colours.

tweezers (II-9z) two narrow pieces of metal joined at one end, used for picking up small objects.

twerp, twirp (99) Sl. low, badly-behaved young man.

twice (4Is) two times.

twiddle (I) to twist round in the fingers; *To twiddle one's thumbs* = sit with nothing to do.

twig (I) thin branch or end of a branch of a tree; Sl. to understand.

twilight (4I-4I) half-light just before and after sunset and sunrise.

twill (I) strong cotton cloth.

twin (I) one of two children born at one birth; one of two things very like each other.

twine (4I) string; *To twine round* = twist round.

twinge (Inj) sudden sharp pain.

twinkle (Ingk) to flash from time to time—as the stars do; *In a twinkling* = at once, without delay.

twirl (99) to turn or twist round quickly.

twist (I) turn one end of thread while holding the other still; change one's direction suddenly; sudden turn or curl in a rope or a road; *To twist the meaning of words* = force a wrong meaning into words; Sl. **a twister** (——9) dishonest person.

twit (I) cause a person to remember some wrong done by him and to find fault or laugh at him for it.

twitch (I) pull or move suddenly.

twitter (I-9) make a sound like a bird singing; *In a twitter* = very excited.

'twixt (I) between.

tycoon (4I-77) very important business-man.

tympanum (I-9-9) tightly stretched skin inside the ear, with which we hear = ear-drum.

type (4I) one person or thing considered as an example of a class or group; special class or kind; first form used in making other things like it; piece of metal with a letter cut on it, used in printing; write on a *typewriter* (= writing-machine).

typewriter (4I-4I-9) writing-machine.

typhoid (4I-5I) illness (also called *Enteric*) common in hot countries, carried by water or milk; *Typhoid state* = last state of a serious illness when the person is in a dream-like state.

typh'oon (41-77) great storm, especially in the China seas.
typhus (41-9) serious disease causing red spots on the body (the disease is carried by insects).
typical (1-1) being a good example of the *type* (= class or kind); **typify** (1-1-41) be an example of.
typist (41-1) one who works with a *typewriter* (= writing-machine).

typ'ography (41-5-9-1) art of printing; adj. **typogr'aphic** (41-9-3-1).
tyrant (419) ruler who has complete power; cruel and unjust ruler; **tyranny** (1-9-1) state of being under such a ruler.
tyre (419) outer ring of a wheel, made of iron on a cart, of rubber on a cycle or car.
tyro (419-67) see Tiro.
Tzar (44) ruler of Russia before 1917.

U

ub'iquitous (17-1-1-9) found everywhere.

U-boat (177 + 67) German *submarine* (= under-sea boat).

udder (8-9) that part of a cow (or other animal) from which milk comes.

ugly (8-1) not beautiful, unpleasant to look at; *It looks ugly* = dangerous; *An ugly customer* = dangerous person.

uhlan (77-44) German or Austrian horse soldier (formerly).

ukul'ele (177-9-21-1) stringed instrument of music.

ulcer (8-s9) poisoned place on the skin (or in the body) from which poisonous liquid comes out; **to ulcerate** (8-s9-21) form ulcers.

ulna (8-9) inner, larger bone of the lower part of the arm.

ulster (8-9) long loose coat with a *belt* (= band) round the middle.

ult (Latin, *ultimo*) (8-1-67) *Yours of the 5th ult.* = your letter of the 5th of last month.

ult'erior (8-19-19) further; *An ulterior motive* = some reason for behaviour other than that shown or expressed.

ultimate (8-1-1) farthest, last.

ultim'atum (8-1-21-9) last demand or warning sent by a government—if this demand is refused, war follows.

ultra- (8-9) very; more than; farther than; e.g. *Ultra-careful* = very careful, too careful; *Ultra-microscopic* = beyond the microscope, too small to be seen by a microscope.

'ultramar'ine (8-9-9-11) very bright blue colour.

'ultras'onic (waves) (8-9-5-1) waves of sound of a higher note than can be heard.

'ultrav'iolet (light) (8-9-419-1) shorter lightwaves than can be seen.

'ultra v'ires (8-9 + 419-11z) beyond one's powers; *To act ultra vires* = do what one has not the powers or right to do.

umber (8-9) yellow-brown colour; *Burnt umber* = red-brown.

umb'ilicus (8-1-1-9) little hollow in the centre of the front of the body.

umbra (8-9) shadow, e.g. of the earth on the moon.

umbrage (8-1j) *To take umbrage at* = show anger at (something said).

umbr'ella (8-2-9) instrument made of cloth or silk on a metal frame which can be shut up or opened out, used to keep off the rain.

umpire (8-419) judge in a game.

umpt'een (8-11) Sl. large number.

un- not, e.g. **'unj'ust** (8-8) not just.

un- put something back in the state in which it was before, e.g. **'unt'ie** (8-41) loosen something tied.

un'animous (17-3-1-9) being all of one opinion.

'unass'uming (8-9-177-1) not proud; not drawing attention to oneself; quiet in behaviour.

'unaw'are (8-9-29) not knowing; *Taken unawares* = surprised by some action for which one was not prepared.

unb'alanced (8-3-9-st) *Of unbalanced mind* = mad.

'unbec'oming (8-1-8-1) not according to good manners; not well-suited, e.g. *She has an unbecoming hat.*

unb'osom (oneself) (8-7z) tell one's secret thoughts and feelings.

unbr'idled (rage) (8-41) uncontrolled anger.

unc'anny (8-3-1) strange, unnatural.

unc'onscionable (8-5nsh9-9) unreasonable; without sense of fairness; *An unconscionable time* = very long —.

uncle (8ngk) brother of one's father or mother; *Uncle Sam* = America.

'unconv'ertible currency (8-9-99-9 + 8-9-s1) money which cannot be changed into dollars.

unc'outh (8-77) peculiar and lacking good manners.

unction (8ngkshn) putting on of holy oil.

unctuous (8ngk-179) too polite.

under (8-9) (1) below; (2) less than; *Under age* = less than 21 years old; (3) while; during; in the state of; *Under sail* = while sailing; *Under repair* = while being repaired; *Under the circumstances* = while (or since) things are in this condition; *Under orders* = in the state of having received orders.

undercover (men) (8-9-8-9) working as secret enemies in a country.

'underd'one (meat) (8-9-8) lightly cooked.

underg'o (8-9-67) suffer; pass through.

undergr'aduate (8-9-3-171) young student in a university studying for the *degree* (= title given by a university) of B.A., B.Sc., etc.

undergrowth (8-9-67) low bushes in a forest.

underhand (8-9-3) secret, intended to deceive.

underling (8-9-1) person holding a low office.

underm'ine (8-9-41) make a hole in the ground below a wall so as to weaken it; weaken, e.g. *Undermined health* = health weakened, e.g. by too much work.

undern'eath (8-9-11) below, under.

underp'in (8-9-1) put stones under a wall so as to strengthen it.

underr'ate (8-9-21) think that a thing is of less value than it really is.

undersc'ore (8-9-55) draw lines under words.

underst'and (8-9-3) know the meaning of; *To have an understanding with* = have an agreement with.

UKULELE

'underst'ate (8-9-21) not say fully; say less than the truth.

underst'ood (8-9-7) p.t. and p.p. of Understand.

understrapper (8-9-3-9) officer of lower rank and less importance.

understudy (8-9-8-1) one who learns the part of an actor so as to act if he is ill.

undert'ake (8-9-21) take a duty upon oneself; to promise to do a piece of work; **an undertaker** (——9) one who arranges funerals.

undertone (8-9-67) a sound lower or quieter than another; quiet (not bright) colour.

undert'ook (8-9-7) p.t. of Undertake.

undertow (8-9-67) backward flow of a wave from the shore.

underwear (8-9-29) clothes worn under one's outer garments.

underworld (8-9-99) **(1)** place of judgment and punishment after death; **(2)** group of wrong-doers and dishonest persons in any great city.

underwrite (8-9-41) to promise to bear part of the possible loss of any business, e.g. the underwriters of a ship have to pay the value of the ship if it is wrecked.

undies (8-1z) Sl. women's underclothes.

'und'o (8-77) untie (a knot); do away with (destroy) a result and put things back in their former state, e.g. *Mr. A. has undone all Mr. B.'s good work.*

'undr'ess (8-2) take off one's clothes.

'undress (uniform) (8-2) clothes worn by an officer when off duty or at times other than ceremonial gatherings.

'und'ue (8-177) more than is right or proper.

undulate (8-17-21) to move like a wave; be shaped like a sea covered with waves.

'un'earth (8-99) discover something hidden.

un'earthly (8-99-1) very strange, not of this earth; *At an unearthly hour* = very early.

un'easy (8-11z1) uncomfortable; anxious.

'unf'aithful (8-21-7) not being honest or true to one's master or friend, or to one's husband or wife.

unf'eeling (8-11-1) hard-hearted, unkind.

unf'eigned (8-21) real, not pretended.

'unf'ounded (8-47-1) having no facts to prove it true.

'unfr'ock (8-5) cause a man to cease from acting as a priest.

ung'ainly (8-21-1) ungraceful.

unguent (8nggw9) oil or fat to be rubbed on the skin as a medicine.

unh'inged (8-1nj) *His mind is unhinged* = he is mad.

uni- one, e.g. **unicorn** (177-1-55) animal (told of in stories) having only one horn.

uniform (177-1-55) having the same form, being the same as others, e.g. *A uniform heat throughout the house*; *Things of uniform weight*; **a uniform**, special dress which all members of a group wear, e.g. *Soldiers' uniforms.*

unify (177-1-41) make many things into one, e.g. *Unify our aims.*

unimp'eachable (8-1-11-9) undoubted.

union (177-19) act of making one; state of being one; group treated as one; *The Union Jack* = the flag of Great Britain and Northern Ireland; *Trade Union* = union of working men to get higher pay and better treatment; **Unionist** (177-19-1) member of the party in the British Government which desired closer union between Great Britain and Ireland.

un'ique (177-11k) quite different from all others.

unison (177-1z) *To sing in unison* = all to sing the same note at the same time (*To sing in harmony* = sing different notes which mix together to make a pleasing whole).

unit (177-1) one thing; group considered as one, e.g. *A company is one unit in an army*; one thing by which measurements are made, e.g. *A yard is a unit in measuring length.*

un'ite (177-41) make one; to join; **'unity** (177-1-1) state or feeling of being one, of being joined in one group.

univ'ersal (177-1-99) having to do with the *universe* (see below); having to do with everyone; found everywhere; *A universal rule* = rule which is always true, or must be kept by all.

universe (177-1-99) all the suns, stars, etc.— everything that there is; the world.

univ'ersity (177-1-99-1-1) place of higher learning which gives *degrees* (e.g. B.A., M.A., Dr.).

'unk'empt (8-2) badly dressed; *Unkempt hair* = unbrushed —.

unl'ess (9-2) if not; except when.

'unl'ooked-for (8-7-t + 55) unexpected.

'unm'an (8-3) take away the courage and strength from.

unm'itigated (8-1-1-21-1) not softened or lessened in any way; *An — liar* = completely untruthful person.

'unn'erved (8-99) having lost one's courage.

'unprem'editated (8-1-2-1-21-1) not thought out before, done without planning.

'unqu'ote (8-67) Write " to show the end of a *quotation* (= report of another person's words).

unr'avel (8-3) untie and straighten out a string which is knotted in a disorderly mass; make clear some difficult or hidden matter.

unrem'itting (8-1-1-1) unceasing.

unr'uffled (8-8) calm.

unr'uly (8-77-1) unwilling to be controlled or to obey laws.

uns'avoury (8-21-9-1) unpleasant, nasty.

'unstr'ung (8-8) *His nerves are all — —* = his mind and feelings are not under full control.

unt'il (9-1) up to the time that.

unt'ouchables (8-8-9-z) lowest *caste* (= class or rank) among the *Hindus* (= members of the Hindu religion in India); members of this caste are considered to be so low that to touch them makes one of a higher caste " unclean "; now called Scheduled Castes.

unt'oward (8-679) unfortunate and unexpected.

unv'arnished (truth) (8-44-1-t) plain truth without any attempt at hiding or making it look less bad.

unw'ary (8-29-1) careless, not looking out for danger.

unw'ieldy (8-11-1) too large to be moved or used easily.

unw'itting (8-1-1) not knowing; not intending.

unw'onted (8-67-1) unusual.

'unwritten l'aw (8-1 + 55) public feeling which considers certain acts allowable even though there is a law against them.

up (8) into a higher place; completely, e.g. *To eat up* = eat all; *It's up to you* = it is your duty; it is for you to decide; *What's he up to?* = what is he doing?; *Up to no good* = not doing any good; *To be up all night* = not to go to bed; *What's up?* = what is the matter?; *Come up with* = come level with; *It's all up* = all is ended, I am ruined; *The game is up* = is ended, our plans are discovered; *The up-train* = to London; *Ups and downs* = good fortune and bad; Sl. *On the up and up* = (1) becoming better; (2) honest, truthful.

upas (177-9) very poisonous tree found in Java.

upbr'aid (8-21) to scold.

uph'eaval (8p·h11) raising up of the surface of the earth by forces within; any great and sudden change, e.g. in the government.

uph'old (8p·h67) to support.

uph'olster (8p·h67-9) fix springs and soft material into chairs and cover them with coloured cloth or leather; fix *carpets* (see —) and curtains.

upkeep (8-11) cost of keeping anything (e.g. a house) in *good repair* (= in a good state, not needing repair).

uplift (8-1) Am. improvement of the mind or spirit.

up'on (9-5) on; *To put-upon a person* = get him to do more than his fair share of work.

upper (8-9) higher; **uppers** (8-9z) upper part of a shoe which covers the top of the foot; *Down on one's uppers* = poor and without hope.

uppish (8-1) pushing oneself forward; not showing respect for older and wiser people.

upright (8-41) standing straight up on end; honest.

uproar (8-55) excitement and noise.

ups'et (8-2) to turn over, e.g. a boat or carriage; to ruin, e.g. *Upset my plans*; *To upset the government* = send out of power and office; *I'm very upset about* — = troubled and anxious; *The food upset me* = caused sickness; **an 'upset**, accident; illness.

upshot (8-5) result.

'upside-d'own (8-41 + 47) with the bottom at the top.

'upst'airs (8-29z) on the upper floor of the house.

upstart (8-44) person who has suddenly risen from low rank to wealth and importance.

'up-to-d'ate (8 + 9 + 21) of the latest and newest kind.

ur'anium (17-21-19) heavy *radio-active* (see —) metal.

urban (99-9) of the town.

urb'ane (99-21) very polite; n. **urb'anity** (99-3-1-1).

urchin (99-1) street-boy; bad boy.

Urdu (99-77) a language spoken in Pakistan.

urge (99j) push a person on to action; drive an animal faster.

urgent (99j9) important; which must be done at once.

urn (99) container used for the ashes of a dead person; large metal container in which tea is made.

usage (177z1j) custom; treatment, e.g. *Rough usage* = bad treatment.

use (177z) employ for a purpose; *All the coal is used up* = has been burnt; *I used* (177st) *to go* = I went often in the past, was accustomed to go; n. **use** (177s) Sl. *I have no use for him* = I do not like him; **useful**, such as can be used, helpful; **useless** (——1) which cannot be used, not helpful.

usher (8-9) officer in charge of the door, e.g. in a law-court; schoolmaster; **to usher in**, lead into a room.

usual (177379) according to custom.

usurer (17739-9) money-lender.

us'urious (17z179-19) *A — rate of interest* = too high a payment for the use of money.

us'urp (177z99) seize by force and without right, e.g. *To usurp the throne* = make oneself king by force.

usury (17737-1) lending of money; money paid for the use of money; demanding too much from one to whom money is lent.

ut'ensil (17-2) instrument; any container used in the home and kitchen.

ut'ility (17-1-1-1) usefulness; **utilit'arian** (177-1-1-29-19) one who considers usefulness to be the real and true measure of value (e.g. of the value of a school subject); **utilize** (177-1-41) to use.

utmost (8-67) farthest; greatest.

Ut'opia (177-67-19) imaginary perfect form of government; **Ut'opian**, perfect but imaginary and impossible.

utter (8-9) complete; *An utter rascal* = very bad man.

utter (8-9). say or make a sound with the mouth; *To utter false coin* = pay out money which is not real money.

uttermost (8-9-67) farthest; greatest.

uvula (177-17-9) small hanging finger-like object at the back of the throat.

ux'orious (man) (8-55-19) one who loves his wife very much.

V

vacancy (21-9-s1) emptiness; space for; office for which a person is to be chosen; **vacant** (21-9) empty; **vac'ate** (9-21) leave empty, e.g. *To vacate a house* = go out of — taking all one's things.

vac'ation (9-21shn) time when schools, law-courts, etc. are closed; *holiday* (= time free from work).

vaccinate (3ks1-21) protect against *small-pox* (= a dangerous disease causing spots on the skin) by putting into the arm a liquid obtained from animals which have had this disease; **vaccine** (3ks11) poison obtained from an animal which has had a disease, used to protect men against that disease by giving them the disease in a slight, not dangerous, form.

vacillate (3s1-21) be uncertain in opinion.

vacuous (3-179) empty; *A vacuous look* = with no meaning or sense in it.

vacuum (3-179) space with no air in it; *A vacuum cleaner* = machine which cleans floors, etc., by drawing in air and dust together.

v'ade-m'ecum (21-1 + 11-9) small book of facts carried about for use when needed.

vagabond (3-9-5) homeless wanderer.

vagary (21-9-1) strange idea; wandering of the mind.

vagrant (21-9) homeless wanderer—usually poor and sometimes dishonest.

vague (21) not properly understood; not clearly expressed.

vain (21) valueless; useless; too proud of one's face and appearance; *In vain* = without result.

v'aingl'orious (21-55-19) very proud; talking about one's own great deeds.

valance (3-9-s) short curtain hanging above a window or round the edge of a bed.

vale (21) low land between mountains.

vale (21-1) good-bye; **valed'iction** (3-1-1-shn) saying good-bye; adj. **valed'ictory** (——9-1).

valentine (3-9-41) love message sent on February 14th; person to whom it is sent.

val'erian (9-19-19) plant with a very strong smell.

valet (3-1) man-servant, with the special duty of looking after a gentleman's clothes.

v'aletudin'arian (3-1-177-1-29-19) one who is too anxious about his own health.

valiant (3-19) brave.

valid (3-1) correct according to law; *A valid argument* = strong reason which cannot be shaken (disproved); **validate** (3-1-21) make valid; consider as correct according to law.

val'ise (9-11z) bag used when travelling.

valley (3-1) low land between mountains.

valour (3-9) great courage.

valse (44) a dance; see Waltz.

value (3-177) what a thing is worth; *Face value* = amount printed on a piece of paper-money; **to value**, say what a thing is worth; think a thing is of great worth; adj. **valuable**(3-179).

valve (3) part of a machine which allows gas or liquid to flow through it when opened; (in radio) glass ball emptied of air containing instruments which increase the power of the electric waves received from the sending station (a radio valve in the U.S.A. is called a *tube*).

vamp (3) repair a shoe; (in music) play a musical instrument (without preparation or written music) so as to join with a singer; Sl. *To vamp up* = make look like new, to prepare hastily.

vamp (3) Sl. the part (character) of the beautiful bad woman in a play or story.

vampire (3-419) evil spirit supposed to draw out the blood from people in their sleep; one who lives at the cost of another; *bat* (= flying rat-like creature) which sucks blood from people and animals at night.

VAMPIRE BAT

van (3) front of an army; *In the van of* = leading the way.

van (3) large covered cart; (England only) light covered cart; carriage on a train in which boxes and bags are put.

vandal (3) one who destroys works of art.

Vandyke (beard) (3-41) small, pointed beard; *Vandyke brown* = red-brown.

vane (21) instrument fixed to the top of a tower to show which way the wind is blowing; one blade of a wheel turned by air-power or water-power.

vanguard (3-44) that part of an army which marches in front and protects the rest.

van'illa (9-1-9) plant whose seeds are used to give a pleasant taste to sweet foods.

vanish (3-1) disappear.

vanity (3-1-1) quality of being *vain* (= too proud of one's face and appearance); emptiness, worthlessness, e.g. *The vanity of earthly greatness*; **v'anity-bag** (+ 3) small bag containing powder and paint for a woman's face; **V'anity F'air** (+ 29) world of the rich and of those who are busy amusing themselves.

vanquish (3ng-1) beat completely, usually in battle.

vantage (44-1j) *Point of vantage* = good place from which to attack.

vapid (talk) (3-1) spiritless and uninteresting.

vapour (21-9) gaseous form of anything, e.g.

Water-vapour = mist; **to vapour,** talk foolishly.

variable (29-19) able to change, changing easily or often.

variance (29-19-s) *At variance with* = disagreeing, quarrelling with.

variant (29-19) something different in form though really the same, e.g. two different ways of writing the same word.

varicoloured (29-1-8-9) marked with many different colours.

v'aricose v'eins (3-1-67 + 21-z) swollen *veins* (= blood-vessels carrying blood back to the heart).

variegated (29-1-21-1) marked with different colours.

var'iety (9-419-1) state of being different; lack of sameness; a collection of different things; one sort or kind, e.g. *This is one variety of roses*; *A variety show* = evening's amusement made up of many different shows, e.g. dancing, singing, magic tricks, etc.; **various** (29-19) of many kinds; *Various people* = many different people.

varlet (44-1) servant; low fellow.

varnish (44-1) to cover with glass-like paint.

vary (29-1) to change; make one thing unlike another.

vascular (3-17-9) having to do with the blood-vessels.

vase (44z) pot of beautiful shape used to contain flowers.

vassal (3) one who in ancient times held land, and promised (in return for the use of land) to serve his master as a soldier.

vast (44) very large.

vat (3) large barrel.

Vatican (3-1-9) palace in which the *Pope* (= head of the Roman Catholic Church) lives in Rome.

vat'icinate (3-1s1-21) tell the future.

vaudeville (67-9-1) evening's amusement made up of many different shows, e.g. dancing, singing, etc.

vault (55) to jump.

vault (55) arched roof; underground room, e.g. one used as a grave; **vaulted** (——1) having an arched roof.

vaunt (55) make a proud show of; talk proudly.

V.C. (11-s11) Victoria Cross, the highest honour which can be given to a British soldier, seaman or airman for courage in battle.

veal (11) meat of a *calf* (= young of cattle).

Veda (21-9) one of the holy writings of *Hinduism* (= a religion of India).

veer (19) change direction.

vegetable (2j1-9) adj. having to do with plants; n. a plant; a plant used for food; **veget'arian** (2j1-29-19) one who eats only vegetable food; **to vegetate** (2j1-21) live a very uninteresting and quiet life; **veget'ation** (2j1-21shn) plant life; many plants growing in one place.

vehement (11·1-9) speaking with very great force; fierce and eager.

vehicle (11·1) anything which can be used for carrying, e.g. cart, carriage, motor-car; *Milk is the vehicle by which this disease is carried* = means by which —; adj. **veh'icular** (1h1-17-9).

veil (21) covering for the face or head; curtain; *To take the veil* = become a *nun* (= woman who gives herself to the service of God and good works); **to veil,** hide, e.g. *To veil one's meaning in strange language*; **veiling** (——1) thin material used for veils.

vein (21) one of the blood-*vessels* (= pipes) which carry blood back to the heart; any fine lines which look like veins of the body, e.g. *The veins on a leaf, veins of metal in a rock*; *There is a vein of cruelty in his character* = there are signs of cruelty in him.

veldt (2) open grass country in South Africa.

vellum (2-9) fine white skin of an animal prepared for writing on.

vel'ocity (1-5s1-1) speed.

vel'ours (2-79) cloth like *velvet* (see below).

velvet (2-1) silk material with short threads standing upright on the surface; *Velvet glove* = strength hidden by a show of friendliness; Sl. *On velvet* = in a happy position with no fear of losing; **v'elvet'een** (2-1-11) material like velvet but made of mixed silk and cotton.

venal (person) (11) one who can be made to do wrong by being paid money; *A venal action* = wrong act done for money.

vend'etta (2-2-9) quarrel between families (e.g. in Corsica) in which each kills members of the other family.

vendor (2-9) person who sells.

ven'eer (9-19) cover less good material (e.g. common wood) with thin sheets of better matter (e.g. more costly wood); thin sheets so used; surface-appearance, e.g. of politeness hiding a very different real character.

venerate (2-9-21) to honour; to respect; **venerable** (2-9) worthy of respect; old and respected.

ven'ereal (disease) (1-19-19) disease passed from woman to man or man to woman.

vengeance (2-j9-s) doing of wrong to another as a punishment for wrong done to oneself; *With a vengeance* = with great power and force, very thoroughly, without doubt.

venial (offence) (11-19) mistake or wrong which may easily be forgiven.

venison (2nzn) meat of deer.

venom (2-9) poison; **venomous** (2-9-9) poisonous; full of hatred and anger.

venous (11-9) having to do with blood in the *veins* (= blood-vessels which carry blood back to the heart).

vent (2) hole; outlet-pipe; *He found vent for his anger in strong language* = he allowed the force of his feelings to escape by using strong words to express it; *To vent one's anger on* = let out the force of one's anger upon.

ventilate (2-1-21) cause fresh air to flow through a room; cause a fact to become known.

ventral (2) having to do with the stomach.

ventricle (2-1) small pocket-like space in the body, e.g. one of the two parts of the heart into which the blood flows.

ventr'iloquist (2-1-9-1) one who is able to speak in such a way that the voice seems to come not from the speaker but from some distant place or from a wooden figure held by him; adj. **ventril'oquial** (2-1-67-19).

venture (2-tsh9) risky course of action; *At a venture* = without any clear aim, trusting to chance; **to venture**, be brave, go into danger; **venturesome** (——9) daring.

venue (2-177) meeting-place; place at which a case will be tried in a court of law.

ver'acious (2-21sh9) true, truthful; **ver'acity** (2-3s1-1) truth.

ver'anda(h) (9-3-9) covered open place outside the windows of a house.

verb (99) kind of word, e.g. "be", "do", "come" are verbs.

verbal (99) (1) having to do with words; *A verbal message* = said, not written; (2) having to do with a *verb* (see above).

verb'atim (99-21-1) in exactly the same words.

verbiage (99-1·1j) use of too many words; **verb'ose** (99-67) using too many words.

verdant (99) fresh green.

verdict (99-1) opinion given by the *jury* (= persons, e.g. 12, chosen to hear the trial of a prisoner and say whether they think he has done wrong or not) in a court of law; any judgment given after careful thought.

verdigris (99-1-1) green decay of brass or *copper* (= red metal).

verdure (99j9) fresh green grass.

verge (99j) edge; **to verge**, bend towards; come near the edge of.

verger (99j9) man in a church who leads people to their seats.

veri- true; **verify** (2-1-41) make sure whether a thing is true or not; **verily** (2-1-1) truly; **verisim'ilitude** (2-1-1-1-1-177) appearance of truth; **veritable** (2-1-9) true, real.

ver'idical (2-1-1kl) true, real.

vermi- (99-1) shaped like a *worm* (= small snake-like creature which lives in the ground); **vermic'elli** (99-1s2-1) preparation of flour in the form of long round sticks.

verm'ilion (9-1-1j) bright red.

vermin (99-1) (1) animals which do harm, e.g. rats, also harmful birds; (2) nasty insects.

vermouth (99-9) bitter wine.

vern'acular (9-3-17-9) native language.

vernal (99) of the spring (time of year).

versatile (99-9-41) able to change easily; able to do many things well.

verse (99) group of lines in a poem; poetry.

versed (99st) *Well versed in* = clever at, knowing much of.

version (99sh9) *translation* (*translate* = change from one language into another) of a book; one person's account of certain events.

versus (99-9) against.

vertebra (99-1-9) one of the bones which make up the backbone; *A* **vertebrate** (99-1-21) *animal* = one which has a backbone.

vertex (99-2) the top.

vertical (99-1) standing upright.

vertigo (99-1-67) unpleasant feeling in the head caused, e.g., by turning round and round quickly.

verve (99) spirit and force in the work of a writer, painter or player of music.

vesicle (2-1) small pocket or swelling on the skin filled with liquid.

vespers (2-9z) evening prayers.

vessel (2) pot or container of any kind; a ship; *A blood-vessel* = pipe which carries the blood.

vest (2) (1) under-garment worn on the upper part of the body next to the skin; (2) *waistcoat* (= garment worn by men under the coat).

vest (2) *To vest power in* = give right or power to.

vesta (2-9) wax match which can be lit by rubbing it anywhere.

vestal virgin (2 + 99j1) pure unmarried Roman woman who spent her life in the service of a goddess (Vesta).

vestibule (2-1-177) covered entrance to a house; entrance hall.

vestige (2-1j) mark left behind by something which has now passed on or been destroyed.

vestments (2-9) special clothes worn by a priest when performing a ceremony.

vestry (2-1) room in a church where the priest puts on his *vestments* (see above).

vesture (2-tsh9) clothing.

vet (2) see Veterinary; Sl. *To vet a person* = examine him and see if he is in good health.

veteran (2-9-9) old and experienced person, e.g. soldier.

veterinary (2-9-1-9-1) having to do with the diseases of animals.

veto (11-67) right of a person (e.g. king) to forbid a law being made.

vex (2) to trouble; wave angry.

V.H.F. (v11-21tsh-2f) Very High Frequency = radio using very short waves which give better sounds than others and are not spoiled by other waves, e.g. from electric machines, etc.

via (419) by way of; passing through on the way.

viable (419) (baby) which, even if born too soon, could have lived; (of a very small country) able to go on without being part of a bigger country.

viaduct (419-8) long bridge carrying a road or railway line.

vial (419) small glass bottle.

viands (419-z) food.

vibr'ate (41-21) shake like the string of a musical instrument.

vicar (1-9) priest in charge of a church; **vicarage** (——1ij) house in which a vicar lives.

vic′arious (41-29-19) doing work for another person.

vice- acting for; working instead of, e.g. the **Viceroy** (41s-51) acted in place of the king in India (*-roy* = king); **vice** (41si) in place of, e.g. *Mr. Jones will act as headmaster vice Mr. Smith.*

vice (41s) serious fault of character; low and bad behaviour; (in an animal) fierceness.

vice (41s) instrument (fixed to a table) used for holding a piece of metal or wood very tightly while one cuts or shapes it.

v′ice-r′egal (41s·+ 11) adj. of *Viceroy* (3rd above).

v′ice v′ersa (41si + 99-9) and with the relations considered in the opposite way, e.g. *I hate him, and vice versa* = and he hates me.

vic′inity (41si-1-1) nearness; country near.

vicious (1shg) of bad character; bad; (of an animal) fierce; *A vicious circle* = set of bad conditions which act on each other so that the one produces the other, e.g. fear causes illness and illness causes more fear.

vic′issitudes (1si-1-177-z) changes of fortune.

victim (1-1) animal killed as an offering to a god; person who suffers, e.g. *The victim of my hatred*; *The victim of his own foolishness.*

victor (1-9) winner.

Vict′oria Cr′oss (1-55-19 + 5) see V.C.

victual (1) food; *To victual a ship* = supply with food; *Licensed victualler* = person allowed by the law to keep an inn.

victory (1-9-1) success in battle or in a game.

vide (41-1) see, e.g. *Vide page 51* = see page 51.

vid′elicet (1-11-1s2) see Viz.

vie (with) (41) to struggle with so as to be first or stronger.

view (177) (1) sight; looking at, e.g. *In full view of* = seen by all; *A beautiful view* = sight of beautiful country; (2) opinion; *A point of view* = way of looking at a question; *In my view* = in my opinion; *In view of* = because of; *To air one's views* = say one's opinions; (3) purpose, desire, e.g. *He has other views for his son's future*; *I will try to meet your views* = to do what you want; **to view**, look at; form an opinion of.

viewer (1779) person who looks at *television*.

vigil (1j1) act of being awake or watching; staying awake all night to pray, e.g. before a feast-day; **vigilant** (——9) watchful.

vign′ette (1ny2) small printed ornament in a book; picture of a person with the space around fading away to whiteness.

vigour (1-9) strength; power of mind or body; **vigorous** (1-9-9) full of power; strong.

Viking(s) (41-1-z) seamen from the north who attacked the coast of England, France, etc., in ancient times.

vile (41) of very bad character; (in old writings) common and of no value; **vilify** (1-1-41) speak evil of.

villa (1-9) small house standing in its own garden.

village (1-1ij) small collection of houses—not so large as a town.

villain (1-9) wrong-doer.

vim (1) strength; spirit; force.

vindicate (1-1-21) prove a claim to be just; (of a person's character) prove it to be good in spite of evil said against it.

vind′ictive (1-1-1) desiring to do harm to another as a punishment for harm done to oneself.

vine (41) (1) tree which bears *grapes* (= fruit of which wine is made); (2) any plant which grows upward by twisting its branches round a support of some kind.

vinegar (1-1-9) very sour liquid, sometimes made from wine, much used in cooking.

vineyard (1-9) place in which *vines* (2nd above) are grown.

vinous (41-9) having to do with wine.

vintage (1-1ij) act of gathering *grapes* (see Vine, 4th above); time of gathering grapes; amount of grapes gathered; wine produced in a certain year.

vintner (1-9) wine merchant.

vi′ola (167-9) (1) instrument of music slightly larger than a *violin* (4th below); (2) **v′iola** (419-9) plant of the same class as violets (3rd below).

violate (419-21) treat a holy thing with disrespect, e.g. *To violate a person's grave*; *To violate a promise* = not to fulfil =.

violent (419-9) showing great or uncontrolled force, e.g. *A violent storm,* — *struggle,* — *attack of illness.*

violet (419-1) small flower; blue-red colour.

viol′in (419-1) instrument of music played by drawing a *bow* (= stick with hair stretched from end to end) across the strings.

violonc′ello (419-9-tsh2-67) large violin giving a deep note.

VIOLIN

V.I.P. (vii-41-p11) Very Important Person.

viper (41-9) a poisonous snake.

vir′ago (1-44-67) fierce bad-tempered woman.

virgin (99j1) unmarried woman; adj. pure, untouched.

virile (1-41) having the powers and character of a full-grown man; powerful, active, strong; n. **vir′ility** (1-1-1-1).

virtu (99-77) *Object of virtu* = precious and beautiful object.

virtual (99-179) actually, though not in name, e.g. *The virtual head of the business.*

virtue (1-19) (**1**) strength; *In virtue of my office* = using the powers which my office gives me; (**2**) goodness of character; (**3**) *purity* (n. of Pure).

virtu'oso (99-176z67) person who has great skill in an art, e.g. music.

virulent (1-17-9) very poisonous; very harmful; full of hatred.

virus (41-9) that poison formed by *germs* (= very small living things seen only under the microscope) which causes disease.

visa (11z9) mark put on a *passport* (= paper allowing one to enter a foreign country) showing that it has been examined and found correct for a particular foreign country.

visage (1z1j) face.

v'is-à-vis (11z + 44 + 11) face to face with.

viscera (1-9-9) inside parts of the body, especially the bowel.

viscid (1-1) sticky.

viscount (41-47) nobleman of rank fourth below a prince.

viscous (1-9) sticky, like glue or gum; **vis- c'osity** (1-5-1-1) stickiness.

visible (1z9) able to be seen.

vision (139) power of seeing; power of imagination; thing believed to be seen, e.g. *A vision of the future*; adj. **visionary** (139-9-1) seen in a vision, unreal; (of a person) having ideas which cannot be carried out.

visit (1z1) go to see a person or place; **a visit**, short stay in a place; **visitor** (——9) one who makes a visit; **visitant**, visitor, especially a spirit of the dead coming to visit the living; **visit'ation** (1z1-z1shn) a visiting; some terrible event considered as a punishment sent by God.

visor (41z9) iron covering for the face, as shown.

vista (1-9) view seen through a long narrow space, e.g. through two lines of trees; such a view (seen in the mind) of many events one after another. VISOR

visual (1z179) having to do with sight; **visualize** (——41) call up a picture of a thing in the mind.

vital (41) having to do with life; very much alive; very important; **vitals** (——z) those parts of the body which are necessary for life, the most important parts; n. **vit'ality** (41-3-1-1).

vitamin(s) (1-9-1-z) certain materials (of unknown nature) found in fresh fruit, fresh milk, green leaves, etc. (These materials are necessary for health, and their absence from food causes various illnesses.)

vitiate (1sh1z1) destroy the force or value of, e.g. *His book is vitiated by mistakes*; to make impure and unfit for use, e.g. *To vitiate the air of a room.*

vitreous (1-19) like glass.

vitriol (1-19) powerful acid (also called *Sulphuric acid*); adj. **vitri'olic** (1-15-1) *She has a vitriolic tongue* = speaks very cruelly.

vit'uperate (41-177-9-z1) to scold, speak angrily about.

viva! (11-9) Long live —!

viv'acious (1-z1sh9) full of life and spirit.

v'iva v'oce (41-9 + 67s1) examination in which the questions and answers are spoken, not written.

vive (11) (French) Long live —!

vivid (1-1) full of life; *A vivid imagination* = great power of imagining; *Vivid colours* = bright —; *A vivid description* = clear word-picture.

vivis'ect (1-1-2) cut the body of an animal while still alive—for the purpose of making scientific discoveries.

vixen (1) female form of *fox* (see FOX); *A vixenish person* = bad-tempered —.

viz. (short for, Latin, *videlicet* = you may see) that is, these are, e.g. *Great Britain is divided into four parts, viz. England, Scotland, Wales, Northern Ireland.*

viz'ier (1-19) high officer of government in Muslim countries.

vizor (41-9) see Visor.

voc'abulary (9-3-17-9-1) whole set of words used by a writer or speaker; list of the words used in a certain book arranged in A.B.C. order.

vocal (67) having to do with the voice; spoken aloud; noisy; **vocalist** (67-9-1) singer.

voc'ation (67-z1shn) special fitness for certain work; one's usual employment.

vocative (case) (5-9-1) form of a noun used in calling or addressing a person, e.g. Latin, *Serve* (from *Servus*) = O slave.

voc'iferate (67s1-9-z1) to shout.

vodka (5-9) strong drink used in Russia.

vogue (67) state of being admired or liked by many people; *Long skirts are in vogue*, *There is a great vogue for long skirts* = all the women like wearing long skirts just at present.

voice (51s) sound produced in speaking and singing; *To have a voice in* — — have a right to help in deciding —; **to voice**, express.

void (51) empty; of no effect; *The agreement was void* = of no value according to law, useless.

voile (744) thin cotton material used for ladies' dresses.

volatile (5-9-41) (liquid) one which easily becomes a gas; (person) quickly changing one's purpose or ideas.

volc'ano (5-21-67) VOLE
mountain with a deep hole in the top from which fire and smoke come out.

vole (67) small creature like a rat.

vol'ition (67-1shn) act of choosing or using the will; power of —.

volley (5-1) number of shots fired at the same moment; *A volley of oaths* = flow of bad language; **to volley**, (in games) hit a ball before it touches the ground.

volt (67) measure of electrical force; **voltage** (67-1j) number of volts.

v'olte-f'ace (5 + 44s) complete change (e.g. in opinion or feeling).

voluble (5-17) talking with a great flow of words.

volume (5-17) (1) book; (2) large mass, e.g. *A great volume of water*; (3) space filled by a liquid or gas or by solid matter; (4) *Volume (of sound)* = power of filling a large space; **vol'uminous** (9-177-1-9) filling much space.

voluntary (5-9-9-1) acting of one's own free will, not forced; done willingly; **a voluntary** = music played on the *organ* (= instrument of music with many pipes) in a church.

volunt'eer (5-9-19) (1) person who offers to do a difficult or dangerous piece of work; (2) person who serves as a soldier of his own choice; (3) one who works without pay; **to volunt'eer**, offer to do some special piece of work; offer to serve as a soldier.

vol'uptuary (9-8-179-1) one who gives himself up to the enjoyment of pleasures of the body.

vomit (5-1) throw up food from the stomach.

voodoo (77-77) magic practised by certain people in the West Indies.

vor'acious (9-21shg) quality of eating too much.

vortex (55-2) liquid (e.g. a part of the sea) turning round very quickly.

votary (67-9-1) person who is bound by some *vow* (= promise made to God); one who gives himself up completely to some work of a public or religious kind.

vote (67) show one's choice (e.g. in electing a person to government), show one's opinion in a meeting; **a vote**, choice or opinion so shown.

votive (offering) (67-1) given in fulfilment of a solemn promise to God.

vouch (47) *Vouch for a person's honesty* = say that a person is honest.

voucher (47-9) piece of paper showing that money has been paid, or that the holder has a right to goods or service.

vouchs'afe (47-21) give as an act of special kindness or mercy.

vow (47) to promise solemnly to God, or in the name of God; **a vow**.

vowel (479) speech sound, e.g. a, e, i, o, u.

v'ox p'opuli (5 + 5-17-41) (Latin) public opinion.

voyage (51j) sea journey.

vulcanite (8-9-41) hard (usually black) material made from rubber; **vulcanize** (8-9-41) (1) make rubber harder by mixing it with *sulphur* (= yellow material which burns with a blue flame and a bad smell) and heating it; (2) mend a cut in an article made of rubber by filling the hole with rubber paste and heating it to make the filling-material hard.

vulgar (8-9) of the common people; rough, not polite; n. **vulg'arity** (8-3-1-1).

vulnerable (8-9-9) unprotected against attack; easily wounded.

vulpine (8-41) of a *fox* (see Fox); like a fox.

vulture (8-tsh9) large bird with a red or grey head with no feathers on it, which feeds on dead bodies.

vying (41·1) see **Vie**.

W

Waaf (3) member of the Women's *Auxiliary* (= helping) Air Force (now W.R.A.F.).

wabble (5) see Wobble.

wad (5) small mass of material packed round a thing to prevent it from moving, or used to fill a hole; Am. Sl. roll of *notes* (= printed money); **wadding** (5-1) soft material used for packing.

waddle (5) to walk with short steps, like a duck.

wade (21) to walk through water; *To wade through a book* = read a long book with difficulty; **waders** (21-9z) high *boots* (= high shoes covering the feet and legs) used for walking in water.

wadi (5-1) water-course in North Africa, etc., which is dry in summer.

wafer (21-9) flour, sugar, etc., cooked in the form of a very thin cake; a small round piece of paper or other material *stuck* (p.p. of Stick) on the back of a letter to close it.

waffle (5) large thin cake, usually marked with squares, eaten by Americans.

waft (44) carry lightly through the air, as wind carries a leaf.

wag (3) move from side to side or up and down, e.g. *A dog wags its tail*; *To set tongues (chins) wagging* = cause much talk by some surprising or improper action.

wag (3) clever and amusing talker.

wager (21j9) promise made between two persons that Mr. A is to pay Mr. B if a certain event happens, B is to pay A if it does not happen; amount of money so promised; **to wager**, make such a promise.

wage(s) (21j1z) money paid for work; *A living wage* = just enough money to live on.

w'age w'ar (21j + 55) carry on a war.

waggle (3) move slightly backwards and forwards.

wagon (waggon) (3-9) strong cart; container on wheels used on the railway; Sl. *On the water-wagon* = not taking any strong drink.

waif (21) homeless person or animal.

wail (21) cry out with grief.

wainscot (21-9) wooden boards fixed to the bottom of a wall touching the floor.

waist (21) narrow part of the human body just above the legs; Am. part of a dress from the neck or shoulders to the waist; **waistcoat** (21-67) close-fitting garment reaching to the waist, worn under a coat.

wait (21) (1) to stay or stop until something happens, until someone comes; (2) bring food to the table; *To lie in wait for* = hide, waiting to attack; **a waiter** (21-9) manservant who brings food to the table; **waitress** (——1) woman who—; *Lady-in-waiting* = lady of high rank attending on the queen.

waits (21) band of people who go from house to house singing Christmas songs.

waive (21) give up, for a time or for ever, e.g. *To waive a claim*.

wake (21) watching all night by the dead; a feast.

wake (21) track behind a ship moving through water; *In the wake of* = following.

wake (21) cease sleeping; not to go to sleep; **to wake, wake up, waken**, cause a person to cease sleeping; excite; **wakeful**, not sleeping; not feeling desire for sleep.

wale (21) see Weal.

walk (55) move with the help of the feet; *A walker-on* = actor who has no words to say; *Walk away with* = win easily; *Walk off with* = steal; *A walk-over* = easy victory; Sl. *Walking out with* = going out walking with and making love to; **a walk**, action of walking; way of walking; distance walked; path; *Walk of life* = rank or employment.

w'alkie-t'alkie (55-1 + 55-1) radio carried by a soldier on his back so as to talk to another (also carrying one) as he walks along.

wall (55) thing built of bricks or stone, e.g. as the side of a house; any flat upright dividing surface; *Walls have ears* = others may hear us; *Run one's head against a wall* = try to do an impossible thing; *With one's back to the wall* = fighting with no way of escape; *Go to the wall* = be pushed away as useless, be the loser.

wallaby (5-9-1) small *kangaroo* (= Australian animal with large back legs, small front legs and a pocket in which it carries its young).

wallah (5-9) person, e.g. *A box-wallah* = business man in India.

wallet (5-1) bag; pocket-case, e.g. for money.

wallflower (55-479) (1) flower; (2) woman at a party without a man to dance with her.

wallop (5-9) to beat; heavy blow; Sl. *To wallop along* = move quickly and heavily; Sl. *A big walloping fellow* = big heavy fellow.

wallow (5-67) roll about in liquid or dirt—as a pig does.

W'all Street (55 + 11) money-market in New York.

walnut (55-8) (1) eatable nut —the shell of a walnut is rough and easily divided into two parts; (2) wood of the walnut tree.

WALNUT TREE AND NUT

WALRUS

walrus (55-9) large sea creature with two large teeth standing out from the face with the ends pointing downwards.

waltz (55-s) dance made up of six steps, for two persons dancing together.

wan (5) without colour in the face, looking ill and tired.

wand (5) thin stick carried in the hand, e.g. by one who does magic tricks.

wander (5-9) move aimlessly from place to place; leave the right path; *He is wandering, His mind is wandering* = his thoughts are mixed up as in a dream, e.g. because of serious illness.

wanderlust (5-9-8) restless desire to travel.

wane (21) become less, e.g. *The moon is waning*.

wangle (3ngg) Sl. obtain by cleverness or by a trick.

want (5) to lack, to need; to wish; *To be in want* = be poor; **wanting** (5-1) incomplete, lacking something in order to be perfect; foolish or slightly mad.

wanton (5-9) wild and uncontrolled in behaviour.

war (55) fighting between nations; *War to the knife* = till one or the other is completely beaten; *Carry the war into the enemy's camp* = attack someone who has been expecting to attack you; *He seems to have been in the wars* = shows signs of having been hurt or damaged.

warble (55) sing like a bird with *trembling* (= shaking) of the voice.

ward (55) part of a city divided off for purposes of government; room in a hospital; part of a key which makes it fit only one lock; young person under the protection of a court of law.

ward (55) *To ward off a blow* = turn — aside, e.g. with the arm.

-ward(s), in the direction of, e.g. **westward** (2-9) towards the west.

warden (55) head or person in control of, e.g. a school or *college* (= school for older persons).

warder (55-9) prison guard.

wardrobe (55-67) large upright box, with a door, in which one hangs up clothes.

wardroom (55-7) officers' room on a warship.

ware (29) be careful of; look out for.

wares (29z) goods for *sale* (= selling); **warehouse** (29-47) a storehouse; **to warehouse** (——z) store.

warfare (55-29) war, fighting.

warm (55) pleasantly hot; *Warm work* = which makes one hot; *To make things warm for* = attack, cause great discomfort to; Sl. *A warm corner* = dangerous place; *A warm-hearted person* = loving, generous; *You're getting warm* = you are going in the right direction to find what you are looking for.

warmonger (55-8ngg9) person who wants war.

warn (55) tell a person about probable danger; n. **warning** (55-1).

warp (55) to bend, e.g. *Wood warped by the heat*; *Warped mind* = made unreasonable by some special like or dislike.

warp (55) pull a ship into place with ropes.

warp (55) threads running along the length of cloth (*weft, woof* = the cross threads).

warrant (5) paper giving the right to, e.g. put a person in prison; paper giving the right to pay or receive money; *You have no warrant for saying that* = no right to —, no reason for —; *I'll warrant you that* = I am quite sure that.

warren (5-1) piece of land in which there are many rabbits.

warrior (5-19) soldier; experienced fighting-man.

wart (55) small hard growth on the surface of the skin.

WART-HOG

wart-hog (55 + 5) African wild pig.

wary (29-1) careful, looking out for danger.

wash (5) to clean with water (or other liquid); *The sea washes the rocks* = flows over; *Will this wash well?* = will this cloth be undamaged by washing?; Sl. *That story won't wash* = is clearly untrue; *Look washed out* = tired; *I wash my hands of it* = I shall have nothing more to do with it and am not to be blamed; *Hair-wash* = liquid for the hair; Sl. *Eye-wash* = things done to deceive a person into thinking that the work done (e.g. in a school, company of soldiers, etc.) is good.

washer (5-9) round piece of metal or leather with a hole through which a screw passes; machine for washing clothes.

washout (5-47) Sl. *It was a* —— = it failed completely.

w'ash-stand (5 + 3) table on which all things necessary for washing the hands and face are put.

wasp (5) *stinging* (*sting* = prick the skin and drive in poison) insect, like a bee, but with black and yellow lines on its body.

wassail (5-21) drinking-party; drink.

wast (5) *Thou wast* = you were.

wastage (21-1j) wasting; matter wasted.

waste (21) use up without getting any good; cause to lose strength; lose strength; n. **waste**, act of wasting; a thing wasted; unused land; adj. **waste**, unused, unwanted, useless; **waster** (——9) **wastrel**, lazy useless person.

watch (5) stay awake; keep the eyes on; be on guard; **a watch**, person who watches; the act of watching; time spent in keeping guard (e.g. on a ship); pocket clock.

watchword (5-99) word spoken to a guard in time of war to prove that one is not an enemy.

water (55-9) commonest liquid; Sl. *To get into hot water* = trouble; *The story won't hold water* = can be proved to be untrue; *Throw cold water on a plan* = speak against, pointing out difficulties; *High water (low water)* = when the sea comes up high (goes down) on the land because of the pull of the moon; *I'm in low water* = have no money; *Jewel of the first water*

watt — of very good quality; **to water**, pour water on; give water to; *Make one's mouth water* = fill one with desire; *Watered silk* = having *wavy* (= shaped like waves, 〜〜〜〜) lines; *Watered stock* = shares in a business which are much greater in number than the value of the business; **w'ater-closet** (+ 5zI) *A closet* = place in which one leaves the waste matter of the body; *A water-closet* = such a place fitted with an instrument which gives a flow of water when needed; **w'ater-colour** (+ 8-9) colours to be mixed with water (not oil) used for painting pictures; **watercress** (55-9-2) hot-tasting plant grown in water and used as food; **w'ater-diviner** (+ 1-41-9) person who finds where water is under the ground, by the use of a Y-shaped stick; **waterfall** (55-9-55) water falling straight down over a rock; **w'ater-gas** (+ 3) gas produced by passing steam through red-hot coals; **w'ater-glass** (+ 44) liquid used to keep eggs from going bad; **w'atering-place** (55-9I1 + 2Is) place to which people go to drink medical waters; sea-side place; **w'ater-logged** (+ 5) filled with water so that it cannot become wetter, e.g. wood, earth; filled with water so that it cannot float, e.g. a ship; **waterman** (55-9-9) boatman; **watermark** (55-9-44) mark of the maker seen on paper when it is held up to the light; **waterproof** (cloth) (55-9-77) cloth which keeps out water; **watershed** (55-9-2) line of hills between two river valleys; **watertight** (55-9-4I) able to keep water out (or in); *A watertight argument* = piece of reasoning which cannot be proved to be wrong; *A watertight agreement* = written agreement in which no weakness can be found, from which neither person can escape; **waterworks** (55-9-99) place from which water is sent out through pipes to a town or city.

watt (5) measure of electrical power.

wattle (5) **(1)** sticks bent in and out between thicker upright sticks so as to form a kind of wall; *Wattle and daub* = a wall so made and covered with *clay* (= sticky earth); **(2)** red skin hanging down from the neck of a bird.

wave (2I) up and down and rolling movement on the surface of water, e.g. *A wave of the sea*; any movement of the same kind, e.g. *Sound waves, Light waves*; steady forward movement, rapidly spreading change, e.g. *A wave of feeling*; *A cold wave* = short time of cold weather; **to wave**, move from side to side, e.g. a flag, a branch; move up and down; lie in a hill-and-valley form, e.g. *Hair waves*.

waver (2I-9) move unsteadily; change often and be in doubt between two opinions.

wavy (2I-I) covered with waves; bending from side to side, e.g. *A wavy line* = 〜〜〜〜.

wax (3) become larger; *They waxed merry* = became more and more merry; *The moon waxes and wanes* = becomes bigger and smaller.

wax (3) easily melted material made and used by bees in building; also used in making candles; **waxworks** (3-99) wax figures of well-known persons used as a show.

way (2I) **(1)** road; direction; *Which way did he go?* = in which direction?; **(2)** distance travelled or to be travelled, e.g. *It is a long way from here to London*; **(3)** space, e.g. *Make way for the King*; **(4)** manner, e.g. *The right and the wrong way of doing the work*; *To pave the way for* = to prepare for, make it easy for it to come; *By the way*—(this shows a sudden change of subject in speaking); *Out-of-the-way* = distant, unusual; *The ship is under way* = moving forward; *To give way* = yield, bend, break; *To have one's way* = get what one wants; *Anything else in a small way?* = (in a shop) can I sell you anything else?; *She's in a bad way* = bad state, very ill; *Ways and means* = all the things necessary for doing the work, e.g. plans, money, etc.

w'ay-bill (+ I) list of things (or people) carried in a ship or on a train.

wayfarer (2I-29-9) traveller.

w'ayl'ay (2I-2I) wait for a person in order to attack them or to speak to him.

-ways, e.g. **sideways** (4I-2Iz) to the side, from side to side.

wayward (2I-9) uncontrolled; not obeying orders.

W.C. (d8blI7 + sII) see Water-closet under Water.

weak (II) not strong; not able to stand up against attack; not able to do a thing well; **weaken**, make weaker; become weaker; **a weakling** (——I) weak person.

weal (II) success; good, e.g. *For the public weal* = for the good of the people.

weal (II) **wale** (2I) mark of the blow of a stick, etc.

wealth (2) riches; plenty.

wean (II) accustom a child to food other than milk; draw a person slowly away from, e.g. make a person slowly begin to be able to do without a former friend, custom, etc.

weapon (2-9) instrument used for fighting.

wear (29) to put on clothes; carry on the body; *To wear whiskers* = have hair growing at the sides of the face; *To wear a troubled look* = look anxious; *To wear away* = be rubbed away, rub away, e.g. *Water wears away a stone*; *To wear out* = make useless by much wearing (e.g. clothes); *These clothes will wear well* = are strong and will last long; *The day is wearing on* = passing slowly on; *Wear and tear* = damage caused by use or accident; clothes, e.g. *Men's evening wear*; *Underwear* = clothes worn under the outer garments.

weary (I9-I) make tired by work; cause loss of interest; adj. tired, in need of rest; having lost interest in —; **wearisome** (I9-I-9) uninteresting.

weasel (IIz) small fierce red-brown animal.

weather (2ŏ9) state of the sky and air, e.g. *Bad weather* = rain, storm, etc.; Sl. *Under the weather* = sad or ill; *To weather a storm* = come through safely; **weathercock** (2ŏ9-5) instrument sometimes made in the shape of a bird, fixed to the top of a tower, where it can turn so as to show which way the wind is blowing.

weave (11) form threads into cloth; twist flowers together to make a crown; fly an aeroplane to and fro or round an enemy.

web (2) threads laid across each other to form cloth or net; *Web-footed, With webbed feet* = having feet like those of a duck with skin between the *toes* (= finger-like things on the feet); **webbing** (2-1) narrow strong piece of cloth.

wed (2) marry; **a wedding** (2-1) church ceremony and feast at a marriage; *My silver wedding* = date of my wedding 25 years later; *My golden wedding* = — 50 years later.

wedge (2j) V-shaped piece of metal (or wood) driven into a piece of material so as to break it into two parts, or driven into a crack between two pieces so as to hold them firmly in place; *This is the thin end of the wedge* = this is only a beginning and more will be demanded later.

wedlock (2-5) state of being married.

wee (11) very small (Scottish).

weed (11) useless plant growing where it is not wanted; thin weak person; **to weed**, pull up weeds; *To weed out* = take out the useless things (or people) from a collection; *Widow's weeds* = black clothes worn by a woman whose husband has died.

weekday (11-21) any day except Sunday.

w'eek-'end (11 + 2) Saturday and Sunday; **weekly** (11-1) once a week, e.g. *A weekly paper*.

ween (11) think.

weep (11) let fall tears; cry.

weevil (11) small insect with a hard shell found in fruit and in grain.

weft (2) see Warp.

weigh (21) to measure the heaviness of a thing; *To weigh one's words* = speak carefully; *Weigh anchor* = pull up the *anchor* (= heavy instrument dropped to the bottom of the sea to prevent a ship from moving away); *What weighs with me most* = seems most important; n. **weight**, heaviness; importance; heavy mass, e.g. of metal used for measuring how heavy a thing is; *A weighty matter* = difficult and important matter.

weir (19) wall across a stream to make the level of the water higher.

weird (19) strange, not natural.

welcome (2-9) met or received with pleasure; *You're welcome to it* = I give it to you gladly.

weld (2) join two pieces of metal by melting the edges while pressing them together.

welfare (2-29) health; success; good condition.

welkin (2-1) sky.

well (2) deep hole made in the ground to get water or oil; spring of water; any deep hole, e.g. in the centre of a high building; **an inkwell** (1ngk-2) hole in a desk for an ink-container; the container itself; *To well up* (of liquid) = come up as from a spring.

well (2) in a good and pleasing way; cleverly; in the right way; *Well beaten* = thoroughly; *As well* = also; *You may just as well* = it would be equally good or better for you to —, I advise you to —; *Very well, then* = that is settled, I agree; *Well!* (surprise); *Well?* (= question, What next?); *Well* — (a doubt); *Well, I will tell you* — (asking the hearer to listen); adj. in good health, e.g. *I am very well*; *We are well enough where we are* = comfortable or safe; *That's all very well but* — = so you say, but I do not agree; *Well-to-do* = rich.

Welsh (2) adj. of Wales (western part of Britain); *Welsh rabbit, Welsh rarebit* = cooked cheese.

welt (2) piece of leather fixed between the upper part of a shoe and the *sole* (= flat strong leather which meets the ground); Sl. **to welt**, beat, hit.

welter (2-9) roll about in, e.g. in blood; *A welter of confusion* = great disorder; *Welterweight* = one class (by weight) in *boxing* (see Box, 3rd).

wen (2) harmless swelling below the skin.

wench (2) girl, servant girl.

wend (2) go.

went (2) p.t. of Go.

wept (2) p.t. of Weep.

wert (99) *Thou wert* = you were.

west (2) Sl. *To go west* = die; **western** (2-9) *A western* = *cinema* (= moving pictures) film about *cowboys* in U.S. in about 1880 or earlier; **westerly** (2-9-1) in or from the west.

wet (2) not dry; Am. Sl. weak, useless.

wet blanket (+ 3ngkɪ) person who spoils the happiness or hopes of others.

wether (2ŏ9) male sheep.

w'et-nurse (+ 99) woman who gives her milk to another person's child.

whack (3) sound of a blow; to hit.

WHALE

whale (21) largest sea-creature; Sl. *A whale of a* — = big thing.

wharf (55) place built on the edge of water at which ships load or unload; **wharfage** (55-1j) money paid for the use of a wharf.

whatnot (5-5) small set of shelves.

wheat (11) grain of which bread is made; plant which bears this grain.

wheedle (11) get something from a person by making oneself very pleasant to him.

wheel(s) (11-z) round things on which carriages, trains, etc., run; *To put a spoke in his wheel* = prevent him from doing what he wants to do, ruin his plans; *To put one's*

wheeze — whitlow

shoulder to the wheel = try to help on the work; *There are wheels within wheels* = there are many (secret) forces at work; *A wheel* = bicycle; *to wheel* (a cart) = push along; *Left wheel!* = order to soldiers to march round to the left; **wheel-barrow** (11-3-67) small cart with one wheel and two handles, used in a garden, etc.

wheeze (11) make a noise in breathing.

whelk (2) small shell-fish.

whelp (2) young of a lion (also of other animals); boy who behaves badly.

whence (2-s) from which place; from what place?

where- (29) **-by, -in, -of, -on, -to, -upon, -with**—in these words *where* = what or which, e.g. **whereb′y** (29-41) by which.

whereabouts (29-9-47) in what place (as nearly as you can say)?; **where′as** (29-32) since, because; **where′at** (29-3) and then (also in old books = at what, at which); **wherefore** (29-55) for what reason?, for this reason; **wherewithal** (29-1ŏ55) necessary money.

wherry (2-1) boat.

whet (2) sharpen; excite.

whether (2ŏ9) which of two; *I do not know whether —— = if ——*.

whetstone (2-67) stone used for sharpening.

whew! sound like a whistle meaning "Oh, it is hot!" or "Oh, it is unpleasant."

whey (21) clear liquid which is left after all the white solid part of milk has been taken away.

whiff (1) a slight breath of air carrying a smell, e.g. *A whiff of smoke*.

while (41) during the time that; at (during) the same time, e.g. *He got 2 while I got only 1*; n. short time; *Once in a while* = sometimes, but not often; *It is worth one's while* = it will probably pay you for the time or work given to it; *To while away time* = pass time; **whilst** (41) while.

whim (1) passing idea or wish—usually of a rather strange kind.

whimper (1-9) to cry weakly, like a small baby.

whimsy (1-z1) whim (2nd above); **whimsical**, having many strange ideas which do not last long; strange, unusual.

whine (41) cry like a dog in pain; complain like a bad child.

whinny (1-1) noise made by a horse when pleased.

whip (1) string on the end of a stick used for beating (a horse); beat with a whip; *To whip up eggs* = mix thoroughly into a light mass with air enclosed in it; *To whip out, Whip off* = pull quickly; *Whip round* = turn quickly; *To have the whip hand of* = have power over; *The Government whip* = one who arranges that members of the governing party shall be present at meetings when needed; *To whip up (persons)* = gather or collect; *A whip round* = sending round to collect money from a group of people, e.g. for the wife of a dead friend.

wh′ip ′out(+ 47) pull out quickly, e.g. a sword.

wh′ipper-snapper (1-9 + 3-9) unimportant person who thinks himself to be important.

whippet (1-1) dog used for racing.

whip-poor-will (1-79-1) American bird which flies at night and has a cry like its name.

whir(r) (99) noise made by anything passing quickly through the air.

whirl (99) turn round quickly; *My brain is in a whirl* = my thoughts are all mixed up and in disorder.

whirligig (99-1-1) thing which turns round and round quickly, e.g. child's paper fan on a stick; *The whirligig of Time*.

whirlpool (99-77) water turning round and round very quickly.

whirlwind (99-1) wind blowing in a circle.

whisk (1) brush away, e.g. *The horse whisked off the flies with its tail*; *To whisk eggs* = beat and mix; *To whisk round* = turn round quickly; a **whisk**, thing used for whisking (eggs, etc.).

whiskers (1-9z) hair growing on the sides of a man's face, or standing out from the face of an animal, e.g. a cat.

whisky (-ey) (1-1) strong drink obtained from grain.

whisper (1-9) speak with the breath only, not using the voice; speak in a low voice; any such faint sound.

whist (1) card game.

whistle (1) make a high sound by drawing the lips together and blowing through them; make such a sound by other means; instrument used for making this sound; Sl. *To wet one's whistle* = to drink.

whit (1) *I don't care a whit* = a bit, at all.

white (41) no colour, the "colour" of snow; *He is a white man* = he is good and honest; *White-collar worker* = worker in an office, not in a factory or mine; *A white night* = night without sleep.

wh′ite ′ant (+ 3) insect (not really an ant) which lives in the ground and enters houses, destroying wood, paper, etc.

whitebait (41-z1) young of certain fish, used as food; **wh′ite ′elephant** (41 + 2-1-9) useless unwanted thing.

Wh′ite H′ouse (41 + 47) home of the *President* (= head man of the government) of U.S.A. at Washington.

whitewash (41-5) mixture of water and *lime* (= form of chalk) used as a paint; *To whitewash a person* = make him seem blameless though he has perhaps done wrong.

whither (1ŏ9) in what (which) direction?

whiting (41-1) (1) small fish usually cooked with the tail bent round into the head; (2) powdered chalk for cleaning silver, or for use as a paint.

whitlow (1-67) poisoned place in the skin, usually on a finger.

Whitsun (1) Christian feast (7th Sunday after Easter = the feast of Christ's rising from the grave).

whittle (1) to cut thin pieces off a piece of wood; *To whittle down* = make less.

whiz (1) noise of something passing quickly through the air.

whoa (67) cry to a horse, meaning Stop!

whod'unit (h77-8-1) Sl. story about crime (usually murder) and finding the wrong-doer.

whole (67) (1) complete; (2) in good health; not hurt; *To go the whole hog* = hold a set of opinions completely, without disagreeing with any; act completely on an opinion without any fear or doubts.

wholesale (67-21) selling of goods in large quantities, e.g. to shops for selling again; *To do a thing wholesale* = in a large way, not bit by bit.

wholesome (67-9) good for the health; clean and nice.

wholly (67-1) whol(e)ly, completely, thoroughly.

whoop (77) loud cry; **whooping-cough** (77-1 + 5f) illness of children which causes *coughing* (= sudden pushing of air out through the throat and mouth) with a voice-sound as the breath is drawn in.

whoopee (7-11) Sl. merrymaking and noise.

whop (5) Sl. to beat; **whopper** (5-9) Sl. very large or fine; untruth; adj. Sl. **whopping**, large or fine.

whorl (99) arrangement of the *petals* (= coloured leaves) of a flower round a centre; one turn of a *spiral* (= turning round and round and up to a point, like a screw) shell.

wick (1) narrow band of cloth which draws up the oil in a lamp; string in the centre of a candle.

wicked (1-1) (act or person) bad.

wicker (1-9) basket-work, made of sticks like a basket.

wicket (1-1) small door or gate; three sticks upright in the ground used in the game of cricket.

wide (41) broad; not hitting the mark at which it is aimed; *Wide awake* = fully awake.

widgeon (1j9) sort of wild duck.

widow (1-67) woman whose husband is dead; **widower** (——9) man whose wife is dead.

width (1) wide-ness.

wield (11) have control over; use in the hand, e.g. *To wield a sword*.

wife (41) married woman.

wig (1) head-covering made of hair, used by persons who have little or no hair of their own, also by judges as a sign of office; Sl.

wigging (1-1) a scolding.

wiggle (1) move slightly.

wight (41) (in old books) person.

wigwam (1-3) hut of an American Indian.

wild (41) living in the natural state; not turned to the use of man; fierce; uncontrolled, e.g. *Wild living* = a careless and foolish way of living; *Wild with joy* = uncontrollably excited because of —; *Wild talk* = foolish uncontrolled talk; Sl. *He is wild about her* = he loves her very much.

wilderness (1-9-1) a desert.

w'ild-g'oose chase (41 + 77 + 21) a search for something which can never be found.

wile (41) a trick.

wilful (1) full of desire to see one's own wishes or plans fulfilled; *A wilful act* = done on purpose, not by accident.

will (1) (1) power of the mind to decide what to do and what not to do; (2) power of choosing one thing rather than another; (3) self-control and strength of purpose; (4) power of controlling others and making them obey; (5) wish of a person who has power expressed as an order, e.g. *It is my will that* = I order —; *To work with a will* = eagerly, keenly; *Where there's a will there's a way* = it can be done if we try hard; *Against my will* = in spite of my wish that it should not be done; *To have one's will* = get what one wants; *Take the will for the deed* = understand what he meant to do, and be grateful although he did not succeed in doing it; **a will**, paper showing to whom a man's possessions are to be given after his death; **willing** (1-1) ready and eager to act as desired.

w'ill-o'-the-wisp (1 + 9 + ðg + 1) light seen moving over wet land at night.

willow (1-67) tree which grows near water.

willowy (1-67-1) tall and graceful.

willy-nilly (1-1 + 1-1) whether (he) wants it or not.

wilt (1) *Thou wilt* = you will.

wilt (1) (of flowers) cease to be fresh; fade.

wily (41-1) full of tricks, deceiving.

wimple (1) cloth worn on the head by women in old days.

win (1) to gain; be successful; reach the place aimed at; *To win one's spurs* = do something which proves one's powers; *To win over to my side* = get a person to join my group; **winnings** (1-1-z) money won.

wince (1-s) draw back suddenly because of pain or fear.

winch (1) round, drum-like thing, to which a rope is fixed; the drum is turned by a handle and the rope is twisted on to the drum, thus lifting a heavy weight fixed to the other end of the rope.

wind (1) moving air; *To see how the wind blows* = see what will most probably happen next, discover what people are thinking; *There is something in the wind* = something being prepared secretly; Sl. *To raise the wind* = get money; *To sail close to the wind* = nearly be dishonest; *He took the wind out of my sails* = did what I was just going to do; Sl. *To get the wind up* = be afraid; *Get wind of* = hear news of; *Suffering from wind* = having wind in the

wind stomach; *His talk is all wind* = foolish, empty; **winded** (——-1) having difficulty in breathing caused by running too fast, or by being hit in the stomach; *Wind instruments (of music)* = musical instruments played by blowing.

wind (4I) move along a track which bends from side to side, e.g. *A winding road*; move upwards in circles; turn a string round and round on to (a stick); *To wind up a clock* = turn round the handle of — so as to make it go; *To wind up a speech, a business company* = bring to an end.

windbag (1-3) person who talks too much.

windfall (1-55) fruit blown down by the wind; unexpected piece of good fortune.

w'inding-sheet (4I-1 + 11) cloth bound round a dead body.

w'ind-jammer (1 + 3-9) sailing ship.

windlass (1-9) *winch* (see 7th above).

window (1-67) opening in the wall of a building to give light and air; **window-dressing** (+ 2-1) putting things in a shop window for show; making a show.

wine (4I) liquid of fruit so changed that it has an exciting effect upon the mind and the body.

wing (I) limb of a bird with which it flies; *On the wing* = flying; *To take to itself wings* = fly away; *To clip the wings of* = prevent a person from doing as much as he wants to do; *Under the wing of* — = under the protection of —; *The north wing of the house* = that part built out towards the north; *The left wing of the army* = companies of soldiers on the left; **to wing**, hurt the wing of; *To wing one's way* = go quickly, fly.

wink (Ingk) shut and open one eye quickly without moving the other; give a secret sign to a person in this way; *To wink at* = allow while pretending not to allow; *Forty winks* = short sleep.

winkle (Ingk) very small shell-fish (the meat is taken out with a pin); Sl. *To winkle him out* = get him out of a hiding-place.

winning (1-1) pleasing.

winnow (1-67) to separate off the grain from the rest of the plant by means of a stream of air; to separate what is useful from what is useless.

winsome (1-9) pleasing; charming.

winter (1-9) cold season; *To winter in France* = spend the winter in —.

wintergreen (1-9-11) plant from which a sweet-smelling oil is obtained, much used in liquids for cleaning the mouth.

wipe (4I) pass a cloth over in order to clean; Sl. *To wipe the floor with* = beat completely; *To wipe out* = destroy, cause to have no more effect.

wire (4I9) metal thread; message sent by electricity; *A wire-puller* = one who controls matters by going to great men secretly; *A live wire* = wire with electricity in it, very active person; **to wire**, put up electric wires; send a message by *telegraph* (= instrument for sending messages by electricity).

wireless (4I9-1) radio.

wiry (4I9-1) like wire, thin and having strong muscles.

wise (4Iz) having good judgment; having knowledge; n. **wisdom** (Iz-9).

wise (4Iz) *In any wise* = in any way.

-wise, e.g. **lengthwise** (2-4Iz) from end to end.

wiseacre (4Izzi-9) person who pretends to know more than he does.

wisecrack (4Iz-3) Sl. amusing play on words; clever saying.

wish (1) to want; to desire; **w'ish-bone** (1 + 67) V-shaped bone of a hen, sometimes pulled by two people while wishing for good fortune.

w'ishy-w'ashy (1-1 + 5-1) thin, tasteless, uninteresting.

wisp (1) handful of grass; a small amount of hair.

wist'aria (1-29-19) climbing plant with blue-red flowers.

wistful (1) sadly eager for; desiring what can probably not be obtained.

wit (1) power of saying clever and amusing things; **a wit**, person who says —.

witch (1) woman who does magic; **witchcraft** (1-44) magic; **w'itch-doctor** (+ 5-9) man who does magic; **witching** (1-1) charming, winning over by magic.

with (1ð) *I am with you* = I agree with you; *I am entirely with you* = I agree with you completely; *Dying with thirst* = because of —.

with'al (1ð55) also.

withdr'aw (1ð-55) pull back; go back; take away.

withe (1) see Withy.

wither (1ð9) to dry up and fade; *She withered him* = caused him to become silent and ashamed.

withers (1ðz) part of a horse's shoulder near the neck.

withh'old (1ðh67) keep back, not to give.

with'in (1ðI) in, inside.

with'out (1ð47) outside; not having; *That goes without saying* = is so clear, so well known, or well agreed, that there is no need to say it.

withst'and (1ð-3) stand against (an attack).

withy (1ðI) easily bent stick.

witness (1-I) (**1**) person who actually saw an event; (**2**) what is said by such a person about an event; **to witness**, see an event; write one's name on a paper as having actually seen another name written.

wits (1) power of mind, cleverness; *Out of one's wits* = mad; *To keep one's wits about one* = be on the watch; *At my wits' end* = very anxious and troubled; *Live by one's wits* = live by tricks and deceiving.

witticism (1-1s1z) clever and amusing saying.

wittingly (1-1-1) on purpose, knowing what one was doing.

witty (1-1) clever and amusing in speech.

wives (41-z) pl. of Wife; *An old wives' tale* = foolish and unbelievable story.

wizard (1-9) man who does magic; Sl. *A wizard (book)* = very good (book).

wizen(ed) (1) dried up, faded, wrinkled.

woad (67) blue colouring matter.

wobble (5) move unsteadily; change one's opinion often.

woe (67) grief; *Woe is me* (a cry of grief); **woebegone** (67-1-5) looking very sad.

woke (67) p.t. of Wake; **woken**, p.p. of Wake.

WOLF

wold (67) open rough grassland.

wolf (7) wild animal like a dog; *To cry wolf* = warn of danger when there is none; *A wolf in sheep's clothing* = bad man pretending to be good in outward appearance; Sl. man who goes after young women in a nasty way; *Keep the wolf from the door* = with difficulty get just enough food or money; *To wolf one's food* = eat very quickly; pl. **wolves** (7-z).

woman (7-9), pl. **women** (7-1) human female; *To play the woman* = show weakness.

wombat (5-9) Australian animal like a small bear.

won (8) p.t. and p.p. of Win.

wonder (8-9) feeling of surprise and *admiration* (n. of Admire); object which causes this feeling; *It's a wonder he's here* = it is surprising —; **to wonder**, feel surprise; to wish to know, e.g. *I wonder who he is*; **wonderful, wondrous** (8-9) causing wonder; **wonderment** (8-9-9) feeling of wonder.

won't (67) will not.

wont(-ed) (67-1) accustomed.

woo (77) try to gain the love of; try to get, e.g. *To woo sleep*.

wood (7) (1) tree-covered land; *To be out of the wood* = be out of danger or difficulty; (2) matter of which a tree is made.

woodbine (7-41) flowering bush, also called *Honeysuckle*.

woodchuck (7-8) (America) underground animal, like a very large rat; (England) bird called also green woodpecker (see 5th below).

woodcock (7-5) bird used for food.

woodcraft (7-44) art of living in the forest as a hunter.

woodcut (7-8) picture printed from a piece of cut wood.

WOODCOCK

WOODLOUSE

woodlouse (7-47) insect which lives in wood and rolls up into a ball when frightened.

woodpecker (7-2-9) bird which makes little holes in trees in eating insects from the surface.

woof (77) cross threads in cloth (see Warp).

wool (7) (1) soft hair, e.g. of sheep; Sl. *To lose one's wool* = get angry; *To pull the wool over his eyes* = deceive him; *Much cry, little wool* =

WOODPECKER

much talk but little result; (2) any material which looks like wool, e.g. *Cotton-wool* = threads of the cotton plant; *He has gone wool-gathering* = he is thinking of something else; **woolly** (——1) made of or looking like wool; not clear; **Woolsack** (7-3) bag filled with wool on which sits the *Lord Chancellor* (= chief judge of England).

word (99) sound or group of sounds, a letter or group of letters expressing an idea; *The last word in* —— = newest and best; *To have words with* —— = quarrel; *Eat one's words* = say that one is sorry for what one has said; *Receive word* = get news; *Keep one's word, Break one's word* = promise; *Word-perfect* = knowing one's words in a play; **The Word,** teaching about God; **to word,** express.

wore (55) p.t. of Wear.

work (99) act of doing things for payment; things so done, employment; *The works of Milton* = books written by ——; *Ironwork* = things made of iron; **works,** a place where things are made, e.g. *A brick works; The works of a clock* = machine inside a clock; **to work,** labour; be successful; *He has his work cut out* = he will have difficulty in doing it; *The machine is not working* = not moving, out of order; *He works one very hard* = causes one to work ——; *To work in a few words about Mr. S.* = bring into a speech; *Work up a business* = build up, make successful; *Worked up* = excited; *To work out a plan* = prepare thoroughly; **workaday** (99-9-21) such as is used every day; usual; **workhouse** (99-47) place for homeless poor people in England; **workmanlike** (99-9-41) well made; *Of good* **workmanship** (99-9-1) = well made; *Of my own workmanship* = made by me; **workshop** (99-5) building in which people make or repair things, especially machines.

world (99) the earth and sky; *Other worlds than ours* = other *planets* (Earth is one of nine planets going round the sun); the earth and its people; all people on the earth; part of life, or a group of people or things in which one is interested, e.g. *The world of school, The animal world*; *For all the world like* = exactly like; *The next world* = life after death, heaven; *A worldly* (——1) *person* = one not interested in things of the spirit.

worm (99) very common small snakelike creature which lives in the ground; other

creatures of the same form; *He's a little worm* = has no strength of character; *Worm one's way in* = enter slowly and secretly.

wormwood (99-7) plant with very bitter leaves.

worn (55) p.p. of Wear; *Worn out* = used so much as to be useless; *Looking very worn* = tired.

worry (8-1) seize and shake, e.g. *The dog worried the rat*; keep troubling a person, e.g. *He worried me by keeping on asking questions*; make anxious, e.g. *I am worried about the future*; n. feeling of being anxious; thing which makes one feel anxious.

worse (99) more bad; more badly.

worship (99-1) show great honour and respect to; to praise and pray to God; *Your Worship* = title used in speaking to a mayor and certain judges.

worst (99) most bad; in the most bad way; *If the worst comes to the worst* = if things become as bad as possible.

worsted (7-1) fine woollen thread ready for making into cloth.

worth (99) having the value of; *Worth seeing* = good enough to be seen, which should be seen; *Worth the trouble, Worth while* = worth the work or money needed; *What is he worth?* = how much money has he got?; *The game is not worth the candle* = the work costs too much and will bring in too little gain.

worthy (99ŏī) deserving of; deserving of honour; *A worthy* = well-known person of very good character.

w'ould-be (77 + 11) e.g. *A would-be poet* = person who wishes to become, wants to be thought, a poet.

wound (47) p.t. of Wind.

wound (77) cause harm to the body; harm so caused; *To wound the feelings* = cause pain in the mind, e.g. by cruel words.

wove (67) p.t. of Weave; **woven,** p.p. of Weave.

wrack (3) ruin; sea plants thrown up on the shore.

Wraf (13f) member of the Women's part of the Royal Air Force—once called Waaf.

wraith (21) spirit of a dead person (or distant living person) who visits someone to tell of death.

wrangle (3ngg) to quarrel.

wrap (3) fold cloth or paper, etc., round; *Wrapped up in his work* = interested in it and in nothing else; *a wrap*, garment to be put loosely round one to keep out the cold; a **wrapper** (3-9) a covering; light loose garment.

wrath (55) anger.

wreak (11) put into effect, e.g. *To wreak vengeance on* = do harm to a person as punishment for harm done.

wreath (11) circle of leaves and flowers; to **wreathe** (11ð) make into a circle; encircle with.

wreck (2) ship destroyed by the sea; destroy a ship; destroy anything; **wreckage** (2-1j) parts of a wreck; act of wrecking.

wren (2) small singing bird; **Wren** (2) woman serving in the British Navy (warships).

WREN

wrench (2) pull suddenly and with force; pain caused by such a pull; pain of parting from a friend; instrument for holding tight and turning things, e.g. for tightening part of a machine.

wrest (2) (1) pull away, e.g. *I wrested the sword from him*; (2) get with difficulty; *To wrest a bare living from the soil* = by hard work get just enough to live on; (3) to force words to mean what they do not naturally mean.

wrestle (2) to struggle with a person and try to throw him down; try hard.

wretch (2) sad poor person; bad person; **wretched** (2-1) deserving pity; bad.

wriggle (1) move the body about from side to side; move like a snake.

-wright, one who works at, e.g. **sh'ipwright** (1-41) ship-builder or repairer.

wring (1) to twist, e.g. *To wring clothes* = twist — so as to get the water out; *To wring one's hands* = show great sorrow; **wringer** (1-9) machine for pressing water out of clothes.

wrinkle (1ngk) small fold in the surface of material, e.g. on the face of an old man; Sl. *A wrinkle* = useful piece of advice.

wrist (1) joint between the arm and the hand.

wristlet (1-1) band worn round the *wrist* (above).

writ (1) (1) written; *Holy Writ* = the Bible; (2) written order from the king or from a lawcourt.

write (41) draw on a surface signs which make words; *Write off* = decide that a thing is of no value; *Write up* = give a full account of, to praise, e.g. in a newspaper.

writhe (41ð) turn the body from side to side as in great pain.

written (1) p.p. of Write.

wrong (5) (1) not right; not according to fact; not fitted for the purpose; *To get hold of the wrong end of the stick* = to think just the opposite of what is correct; (2) unjust; *She did him wrong* = did harm to him; *Put me in the wrong* = make it seem as if it was my fault.

wrote (67) p.t. of Write.

wroth (67) angry.

wrought (55) worked; did; done; *Wrought iron* = iron shaped and beaten when red-hot to make it strong.

wrung (8) p.t. of Wring.

wry (41) *Wry mouthed* = having the mouth pulled to one side; *To make a wry face* = show great dislike, e.g. of a very bitter drink.

X

Xmas (krɪsmǝs) Christmas (the birthday of Christ).
Xn, Xtn (krɪstɪǝn) Christian.
'X-r'ay (2ks + 2I) form of electric light able to pass through solid things.
xylo- wood, e.g. **xylophone** (z4I-9-67) musical instrument made of pieces of wood, each giving a different note when struck.
xylonite (z4I-9-4I) *celluloid* (= glass-like material which can be bent, and easily catches fire).

Y

yacht (5) ship used for pleasure; sailing ship used for racing.

yah'oo (9-77) rough and impolite person.

yak (3) animal like a cow with long hair.

yam (3) root of an African plant used for food.

yank (3ngk) pull sharply.

Yankee (3ngkI) an American (of U.S.A., especially one from the north-east).

yap (3) make a short sharp noise as does a dog when very excited.

yard (44) (1) pole to which a sail is fixed on a ship; *Yard-arm* = one end of a yard; (2) enclosed space near a house; space in which some particular business is carried on, e.g. *A builder's yard*; (3) measure of three feet.

yarn (44) (1) threads of which rope may be made; thread for use in making or repairing cloth; (2) story; *To have a yarn with* = to have a talk with.

yashmak (3sh-3) cloth worn on a Muslim's head or over the face.

yaw (55) (of a ship) move unsteadily and leave the correct course.

yawl (55) small (sailing) boat.

yawn (55) open the mouth wide as when tired or uninterested; *A yawning chasm* = wide open deep crack in the ground.

yaws (55) disease of hot countries causing hard swellings on the skin.

ye (1I) you; the, e.g. *Ye Olde Inne* = the old inn.

yea (2I) yes.

year (99) 365 or 366 days; *Reach years of discretion* = reach that age at which one ought to be wise; *Year in year out* = going on year after year; **yearling** (animal) (99-1) over one year old; less than two years; **yearly** (——1) happening each or every year.

yearn (for) (99) desire greatly.

yeast (1I) yellow material added to flour and water which, by producing gas, makes bread become light (= full of holes); yeast also makes the liquid of fruit change into wine.

yell (2) shout loudly on a high note.

yellow (2-67) colour of gold, butter, etc.; *Sl. He's yellow* = not brave; *The yellow press* = newspapers made especially exciting to work upon the lower feelings of the public.

y'ellow-hammer (+ 3-9) yellow bird.

yelp (2) sudden cry of pain of a dog; give such a cry.

yeoman (67-9) farmer; *Yeoman of the Guard* = member of the company of soldiers who live in the Tower of London; **yeomanry** (——1) farmers; certain horse-soldiers in the British Army.

yesterday (2-9-1) day before this one; *Yesteryear* = year before this one (or past times).

yet (2) (1) up to this time, up to that time; *While there is yet time* = before it is too late; *Yet more* = even more than this; (2) but.

yew (77) dark green tree often grown near churches.

Yiddish (1-1) mixed language spoken by many Jews.

yield (11) (1) to produce as the result of work; *The land yields large crops* = large crops are grown on the land; (2) give way to force, e.g. *We yielded the town to the enemy; The enemy yielded after a long battle* = ran away; *The door yielded to a strong push* = opened; *I yield to none in my love for him* = no one loves him more than I do; **the yield**, amount or gain produced; **yielding** (——1) soft, easily bent.

Y.M.C.A. (w4I + 2m + s11 + 21) Young Men's Christian Association, meeting-place for the young where they can play games and receive teaching.

yodel (67) sing, quickly changing from a high to a low note, as the Swiss do in the mountains.

yoga (67-9) certain Indian beliefs; a special way of living and form of prayer and breathing, by which a man may put his soul in unity with God; **yogi** (67-1) one who practises yoga.

yoghourt, yoghurt (67-99) sour milk used as food.

yoke (67) cross-piece put on the necks of cattle when pulling a cart; *To pass under the yoke* = be beaten in battle; *The yoke of a dress* = part which lies on the shoulders; **to yoke**, join together.

yokel (67) rough or simple man from the country.

yolk (67) yellow part of an egg.

yon (5) that (one) over there; **yonder** (5-9) over there.

yore (55) *Of yore* = in ancient times.

young (8) not old; *We need young blood* = need some younger persons in our group; *The night is young* = it is not late; **youngster** (——9) child.

youth (77) early part of life; young man; *The youth of (today)* = young men and women of —; **y'outh hostel** (77 + 5) a house where young people travelling on holiday can stay very cheaply.

yowl (47) cry aloud sadly.

Y.W.C.A. see Y.M.C.A., but this is for women.

yule (77) Christmas; **y'ule-tide** (+ 41) Christmas time.

Z

zeal (11) eagerness, keenness; **zealot** (2-9) person who is too eager and fixed in his beliefs; **zealous** (2-9) eager.

zebra (11-9) wild animal shaped like a horse with brown and white lines on the body, common in Africa; *Zebra crossing* = road marked as shown where people have the right to walk across and cars must stop to let them pass.

zen'ana (2-44-9) women's rooms in an Indian house.

Z'end-Av'esta (2 + 9-2-6) holy book of ancient Persia.

ZEBRA CROSSING

zenith (2-1) part of the sky just above you; *The zenith of fame* = highest point reached.

zephyr (2-9) **(1)** west wind; gentle wind; **(2)** fine woollen material; undergarment made of fine wool.

zeppelin (2-9-1) large *airship* (= ship filled with gas which floats in the air and is driven forward by oil-engines).

zero (19-67) 0; lowest point in measuring, e.g. the freezing-point of water is zero in the Centigrade measure of heat.

zero hour (+ 479) time from which other times (e.g. for a battle) are calculated.

zest (2) something added to give a sharp and pleasant taste; *To add zest to* = make more interesting, more pleasing and exciting: *To enter into the work with zest* = with eager enjoyment.

zigzag (1-3) shaped like a line of Zs.

zinc (ɪngk) white metal, used, e.g., to protect iron from wet.

zip (1) sound made by an object passing quickly through the air; **z'ip-fastener** (+ 44-9) **zipper** ZIGZAG

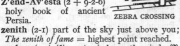

(1-9) fastener for joining two pieces of cloth or leather by fitting together two toothed metal edges by passing them through a sliding Y-shaped piece—much used for bags and clothes.

zither (1-9) musical instrument with strings which are sounded by picking them.

zodiac (67-13) plan of part of the sky divided into twelve parts showing the place of certain stars, in relation to the sun and the earth; *The signs of the Zodiac* = figures drawn on the twelve parts of this plan, from which signs each part takes its name.

ZIP-FASTENER

zone (67) band e.g. of colour; one of the five bands into which the map of the earth is divided, e.g. *The Arctic* (= very cold, northern) *zone*; any division of country in bands, e.g. for the general post, for time, etc..

zoo (77) garden in which animals of many kinds are kept for show; **zo'ologist** (77·5-9jɪ) one who studies animals, their different kinds, ways of living, etc.; **zo'ology** (77·5-9jɪ) this science; **zoo-l'ogical garden** (7-5jɪ + 44) zoo.

ZODIAC

zoom (77) deep low sound; drive an aeroplane quickly upwards.

zoophyte (679-41) plant-like sea-creature.

Zouave(s) (744-z) French soldiers who wear an *Algerian* (= of Algiers) kind of dress.

zounds (47-z) short for "God's wounds," cry of surprise or anger in past times. ZOUAVE

Zulu (77-77) member of a native race of Natal in South Africa.

PLACES AND PEOPLES

Where the name of a man who lives in the country is different from the adjective, it is added.

'Abyss'inia (3-1-1-19), -n.
Afgh'anistan (3-3-1-3), Afghan.
Africa (3-1-9), -n.
Am'erica (9-2-1-9), -n.
Ar'abia (9-21-19), -n. An Arab.
Argent'ina (44j9-11-9), -t'inian (-1-19).
Austr'alia (5-21-19), -n.
Austria (5-19), -n.
Belgium (2ljg), Belgian.
Braz'il (9-1), -ian.
Britain (1-9), British, A Briton.
Burma (99-9), Burmese, A Burman.
Canada (3-9-9), Can'adian (9-21-19).
Ceyl'on (s1-5), Sinhalese (s1nhgl11z).
China (41-9), Chinese.
Cz'echoslov'akia (ch2k6-6-3-19), Czech, Czechoslovakian, A Czech (ch2k).
Denmark (2-44), Danish (21-1), A Dane.
Egypt (11j1), Eg'yptian.
Eire (29-9) = Ireland.
'Ethi'opia (11-167-19), -n.
Europe (179-9), Europ'ean (-p119).
France (44ns), French (2).
Germany (j99-9-1), German.
Greece (11s), Greek.
Hind'u (1-77).
Holland (5-9), Dutch (8), A Dutchman.

Hungary (8ngg9-1), Hung'arian (8ngg29-19).
India (1-19), -n.
Ir'an (1-44), Iranian (1-21-19).
Ir'aq (1-44k), Ir'aqi.
Ireland (419-9), Irish (419-1), Irishman.
Israel (1z-219), Isr'aeli (1z-21-1).
Italy (1-9-1), It'alian (1-3-19).
Jap'an (9-3), J'apan'ese (3-9-11).
Jordan (55-9), Jord'anian (55-21-19).
Lebanon (2-9-9), L'eban'ese (2-9-11).
Mal'aya (9-219), Malayan.
Muslim (7z-1).
Netherlands (2ŏ9-9-z) = Holland.
Norway (55-21), Norw'egian (55-11j9).
P'akist'an (44-1-44), Pakist'ani.
Persia (99sh9), -n.
Poland (67-9), Polish (67-1), A Pole.
Portugal (55-17-9), Portuguese (-g11z).
Russia (8sh9), -n.
Sc'andin'avia (3-1-21-19), -n.
Scotland (5-9), Scottish, Scotch, A Scot, A Scotsman.
Si'am (413), S'iam'ese.
Spain (21), Spanish (3-1), A Spaniard (3-19).
Sweden (11-9), Swedish (11-1), A Swede.
Switzerland (1ts9-9), Swiss.
Syria (1-9), -n.
Thai (41) = Siam.
Turkey (99-1), Turkish, A Turk.
Wales (21-z), Welsh (2), A Welshman.
Y'ugosl'avia (177-6-44-19), -slav.

THE DEFINING VOCABULARY

THIS dictionary is written within a vocabulary of 1,490 words. This means that all the explanations of other words (over 18,000 in number, as well as 6,000 idioms) are given within these 1,490 words. A user knowing these 1,490 words will be able to understand all the explanations; they are the words most commonly introduced in the first stages of any English course.

The defining vocabulary is printed here with the exception of the following, omitted to save space:

numbers, months, days of the week, names of people, affixes, plurals and certain irregular verb forms.

THE DEFINING VOCABULARY

A

A, an
Able, Enable
About (approx., round, concerning); About to be
Above
Absent, Absence
Accept
Accident (= smash), by accident
According to, — as
Account (= narrative, and of money)
(Accustom)
Acid
(Across)
Act, — an act ; action, active
Act, Actor
Actual
Add
Address (letter); (speak to)
Adjective
Admire
Advice, Advise
Aeroplane
Afraid
After; Afterwards
Afternoon
Again
Against
Age
Ago
Agree, Agreement
Aim (= purpose), Aimlessly
Air
(Alive)
All; At all; All over; All right
Allow
Alone
Along
(Aloud)
Already
Also
(Although)
Always
Among; Amongst
Amount
Amuse, -ment
Ancient
And
Anger, Angry
Angle
Animal
(Another)
Answer
Ant
Anxious

Any; Any one; Any more
Apart
Appear; Appearance; Disappear
Apple
Appoint
Arch; Archway
(Arise)
Arm
Armour
Arms; To arm
Army
(Around)
Arrange; Arrangement (= manner in which arranged)
Arrive
Arrow
Art (= art, skill)
Article (= thing)
As (in such a way, when); As . . . as . . .; As soon as; As if; As well as
(Aside)
Ask
At; At all; At once
Attack; Attack of illness
Attempt
Attend; Attention
Autumn
(Awake)
Away
Axe

B

Baby
Back
Bad; Go bad
Bag
Bake
Ball
Band (= hoop, strip)
Bank
Bank (money)
Bar
Barrel (= tub, of gun)
Basket
Bath; Bathe
Battle
Be (all parts)
Beak (of bird)
Beam (of light, of house)
Bean
Bear, n.
Bear, — pain, child
Beard
Beat (= hit, vanquish); Beat (of heart, of music)
Beautiful; Beauty
Because

Become
Bed; (of stream)
Bee
Before (previously, in front of)
Beg
Begin
Behave; Behaviour
Behind
Believe; Belief
Bell
Belong
Below
Bend
Best
Better; Had better
Between
Beyond
Bible
Bicycle
Big
Bill (for money)
Bind
Bird
Birth
Bite; A bit of; Bit by bit
Bitter
Black
Blade (of knife, of grass)
Blame
Bless
Block of; To block (up)
Blood
Blow; To blow a horn; Blow out
Blow, A
Blue
Board
Boat
Body; Anybody, etc.; (body = mass)
Boil
Bold
Bone
Book
Boot
Border
Both
Bottle
Bottom
Bowel
Bowl
Box
Boy
Brain
Branch
Brass
Brave
Bread
Breadth

THE DEFINING VOCABULARY

Break; Break up; Break out; Break the law
Breakfast
Breast
Breath, Breathe
Brick
Bridge
Bright
Bring
Broad
Brother
Brown
Brush
Build; A building
Burn
Burst
Bush; Bushy (tail)
Business; Busy
But
Butter
Buy
By (years went by, near, agent)

C

Cage
Cake
Calculate
Call (summon, shout); Call bad names; name
Calm
Camp
Can
Candle
Cap
Captain
Car
Card, Cards (playing cards)
Care; Take care of
Carriage
Carry; Carry on work; Carry out orders
Cart
Case (receptacle)
Castle
Cat
Catch
Cattle
Cause; A good cause
Cave
Cease
Centre; Central
Ceremony, Ceremonial
Certain (= sure)
Certain, A
Chain
Chair
Chalk
Chance (= opportunity)
Change
Character; (in book or play)
Charge, In — of

Charm
Cheap
Cheer; Cheerful; Cheerless
Cheese
Chest (= part of body only)
Chief
Child
Chimney
Choice
Choose
Christmas
Church
Cigarette
Circle, Circular
City
Claim
Class
Clean
Clear
Clever
Cliff
Climb; Climbing plant
Clock; O'clock
Close to; To close; Enclose
Cloth; Clothes
Cloud
Coal
Coast
Coat
Coffee
Cold
Collect
Colour
Come
Comfort; Comfortable; Discomfort
Command (= order); In command of
Common; Common sense
Company; Business company; Companion
Compass
Complain; Complaint
Complete
Concern; Concerns; Concerning
Condition (= state)
Conquer
Consider
Contain
Content, -ed
Continue, Continuous
Control
Cook
Cool
Copper
Copy
Corn (plant)
Corner
Correct
Cost; Costly
Cotton
Could

Count; Countless
Country; Countries; The Country
Courage; Courageous
Course (of river, of work); Of course
Court (of king, of law); Court-yard
Cover
Cow
Crack (= fissure); (of gun, sound); To crack (= break)
Creature
Creep
Crop
Cross; A cross; Across
Crowd
Crown
Cruel
Cry (weep); (call)
Cup
Curl
Curse
Curtain
Curve
Custom, Accustom
Cut

D

Damage
Dance
Danger; Dangerous
Dare
Dark
Date
Daughter
Day; Daily
Dead
Deal; Deal with
Deal, A great —
Dear
Death
Debt
Decay
Deceive
Decide
Declare
Deed
Deep; Depth
Deer
Defend
Delay
Delight; Delightful
Demand
Depend
Descend; Descendants
Describe; Description
Desert, The
Desert, To
Deserve
Desire; Desirable
Destroy; Destruction

THE DEFINING VOCABULARY

Determine; Determined, adj.
Devil
Die
Difference; Different
Difficult; Difficulty
Dig; Dug
Dinner
Direct; Direction
Dirt; Dirty
(Disappear)
Discover
Disease
Dish (container; food)
Distance; Distant
Divide
Do (all parts); Do without; Have to do with; Undo
Doctor
Dog
Donkey (Ass)
Door; Door-step; Doorway; Out of doors
Doubt
Down
Draw (= pull; make picture); Draw up (army, law); Draw near
Dream
Dress
Drink; Strong drink
Drive
Drop; To drop
Drum
Dry
Duck
During
Dust
Duty

E

Each; Each other
Eager
Ear; Ear of corn
Early
Earth; (= soil)
East
Easy
Eat; Eat away
Edge
Effect
Egg
Either
Elder
Elect
Electric, Electrical, Electricity
Elephant
Else; Everyone else; Elsewhere
Empire
Employ
Empty

End
Enemy
Engine
Enjoy
Enough
Enquire; Enquiry
Enter; Entrance
Equal
Escape
(Especial)
Even, adv.
Evening
Event
Ever; -ever (whoever, etc.)
Every; Everyone, etc.; Every other one
Evil
Exact
Examine; Examination
Example; For example
Except
Excite
Exercise
Expect
Experience
Explain
Explode; Explosive
Express
Eye

F

Face; Face to face
Fact; In fact
Fade
Fail
Faint, adj.
Faint, v. (= lose consciousness)
Fair (= just)
Fairy
Faith; Faithful
Fall; Fall asleep
Fame; Famous
Family
Fancy, n.; Fancy, adj. (= not plain); Fanciful
Far; Far safer
Farm; Farmer
Fast (= strongly); Fasten
Fat
Fate
Father
Fault; Find fault with
Favour; In favour of; Favourable
Fear; Fearful
Feast
Feather
Feed
Feel; (My) feelings
Fellow; A fellow
Female
Fence

Fever
Few
Field
Fierce
Fight
Figure (= numeral)
Figure (= appearance, statue)
Fill
Find
Fine (= fine day, beautiful); (thin)
Finger
Finish
Fire; On fire; To fire (gun)
Firm
First; At first
Fish; Fisherman
Fit; Fit for; To fit
Fix
Flag
Flame
Flash
Flat
Flight
Float
Floor
Flour
Flow
Flower
Fly (insect)
Fly (in air)
Fold
Follow
Food
Fool; Foolish; Make a fool of
Foot; At the foot of; (measure); Football, Foot-step
For (for three days); (for the sake of); (in exchange for)
Forbid
Force
Foreign; Foreigner
Forest
Forget
Forgive
Form; To form
Former
Fort
Fortune; Fortunate; Misfortune
Forward
Fox
Frame
Free; Freedom
Freeze
Fresh: Freshen
Friend; Friendly; Friendship
Frighten
From
Front; In front of
Fruit
Fulfil
Full; Full of

THE DEFINING VOCABULARY

Funeral
Fur
Furniture; To furnish
Further
Future

G

Gain
Game
Garden
Garment
Gas; Gaseous
Gate
Gather
Gay
General
Generous
Gentle
Gentleman; Gentlemen
Get; Get out of; Get on with; Get wet
Gift
Girl
Give; Give way; Give up; Given to (= in habit of)
Glad; Glad to
Glass (material) (tumbler); Looking-glass
Glory
Go (all parts); Go to sleep; Go bad; Go on —ing
Goat
God
Gold; Golden
Good; Good morning
Good-bye
Goods
Govern; Government
Grace; Graceful
Grain
Grand
Grandfather; Grandmother
Grass
Grateful
Grave
Great
Green
Greet
Grey
Grief; Grieve
Ground, The —
Group
Grow; Grow up
Guard; A Guard
Guess
Guest
Guide
Gun; Gun-powder

H

Hair
Half
Hall
Hammer
Hand; Hands of clock; To hand . . . to; Handful of
Handkerchief
Handle
Hang
Happen
Happy
Harbour
Hard
Hardly
Harm
Haste; Hastily; Hasty
Hat
Hate; Hatred
Have; Have to
He
Head; adj.
Health; Healthy
Heap
Hear
Heart
Heat
Heaven
Heavy
Height
Help
Hen
Her
Here
Hide
High
Hill
Him
Hire
His
History
Hit
Hold; Take hold of; Hold (a ceremony)
Hole
Hollow
Holy
Home
Honest
Honour; Honourable
Hook
Hope
Horn (of animal, trumpet)
Horse
Hospital
Host (of guest)
Hot
Hotel
Hour
House
How?; How many?; However (much . . .)
Human
Hunger; Hungry
Hunt
Hurry
Hurt

Husband
Hut

I

I
Ice; Icy
Idea
If (condition), (whether)
Ill
Imagine; Imaginary; Imagination
Important
Impossible
Improve; Improvement
In; Inside; Into
Inch
Increase
Ink
Inn
Insect
Instead
Instrument
Intend; Intention
Interest
Invite
Iron
Island
It

J

Jelly
Jewel
Join; Joint (of limb, etc.)
Journey
Joy
Judge; Judgment
Jump
Just (= fair); Justice
Just (= exactly)

K

Keen (= sharp, eager)
Keep; Kept; Keep laws; Keep watch; Keep accounts
Key
Kick
Kill
Kind, n.
Kind, adj.
King; Kingdom
Kiss
Kitchen
Knee
Knife
Knight
Knock; Knock down
Knot
Know; Knowledge

L

Lack
Lady

THE DEFINING VOCABULARY

Lake
Lamb
Lamp
Land
Language
Large
Last; At last; To last
Late; Lately
Laugh; Laugh at; Laughable; Laughter.
Law; To keep laws; Go to law; Lawful; Lawyer
Lay (= put)
Lay (egg)
Lazy
Lead, n.
Lead, To
Leaf; (= thin piece)
Lean, v. (= incline, slope)
Learn; Learned
Least; At least
Leather
Leave; Leave out; Leave over
Left hand
Leg
Lend; Lent, v.
Length
Less; Lessen
Lesson
Let (= allow); Let us have a meal; Let go of; Let a house
Letter (note); (of aphabet)
Level
Lie (down); Prostrate, recumbent, sofa, etc.
Life
Lift
Light (not heavy)
Light, n.; adj. Light (colour)
Light, To —
Like (similar); Look like
Like (love); Dislike
Limb
Lime (powder)
Line; A line of . . .
Lion
Lip
Liquid
List
Listen
Little; A little
Live; Alive
Load; Load a gun
Loaf
Lock
Lodge; Lodger; Lodging-house
Log
Long
Look (at, in), (for); Look after
Loose; loosen
Lose; Loss

Lot; A lot of —
Loud; Aloud
Love
Low; Low (= of bad character); To lower
Loyal

M

Machine
Mad
Magic
Main
Make; (= persuade or force)
Male
Man
Manner; Manners
Many
Map
March, v.
Mark
Marriage; Marry
Mass
Master
Match, A
Material
Matter; Matter(s) (= business); To matter; The matter with
May
Meal
Mean; Mean for; Mean to do
Means; By means of
Measure
Meat
Medicine; Medicinal; Medical
Meet
Melt
Member
Memory (= power of, recollections)
Mercy
Merry; Merry-making
Message
Metal
Microscope
Middle; Mid-
Might, v.
Mile
Milk
Mill
Mind
Mine (pron.)
Minute, A
Miss (lady)
Miss (lose, not hit)
Mist
Mistake
Mix; Mixture
Moment
Money
Monkey
Month
Moon
More

Morning
Most
Mother
Motor; Motor-car
Mountain
Mouse
Mouth; Word of mouth
Move
Mr.; Mrs.
Much; Much smaller
Mud
Murder
Muscle
Music
Must
My

N

Nail (finger)
Nail (metal)
Name; Good name
Narrow
Nasty
Nation; National
Native; Native country
Nature; Natural
Near
Nearly
Neat
Necessary
Neck
Need
Needle
Neighbour; Neighbouring; Neighbourly
Neither, None, Nor, Never
Nerve
Nest
Net; Net-work
(Never)
New; News; Newspaper
Next
Nice
Night
No (negative)
Noble; Nobleman
Noise
(None)
(Nor)
North
Nose
Not
Note
Note (of music)
Notice; Take notice of
Noun
Now
Number
Nurse; A nurse; Nursery
Nut (of tree)

O

Obey
Object (= thing)

THE DEFINING VOCABULARY

Obtain
Ocean
October
Of
Off
Offer
Office; Officer
Often
Oil
Old
On
Once (one time, once upon a time); At once
One
Only
Open
Opinion
Opposite
Or (alternative; threat)
Orange
Order (command, arrangement); In order to; Disorder
Ornament; Ornamental
Other; Another; Each other
Ought
Our
Out; Outer; Outside
Over; All over . . .; Over there; Overflow
Owe
Own; To own; Ownership

P

Pack
Page (of books)
Pain; Painful
Paint
Pair
Palace
Paper
Parent
Part
Particular (= special, fussy)
Participle
Party; (social —)
Pass; (Cause to pass)
Past; The Past
Paste; Pastry
Path
Pause
Pay; My pay; Payment
Peace
Peculiar
Pen
Pencil
Penny; Pennies; Pence; A penny-half-penny
People
Perfect
Perform; Performance
Perhaps

Permit
Person
Photograph; Photography
Pick
Picture
Piece
Pig
Pillar
Pin
Pipe; Smoke a pipe
Pity
Place; In place of —
Plain (= simple, clear); A plain
Plan
Plant
Plate
Play; To play music; A play
Pleasant; Please; Please!; Pleasure
Plenty
Plural
Pocket
Poem; Poet; Poetry
Point (in reasoning; in character; in game)
Poison; Poisonous
Pole (= staff)
Police; Policeman
Polite
Poor (no money); (pitiable)
Port
Possess; Possessions
Possible
Post, The; Post-box; Postman; Postage-stamp
Post (= support)
Pot
Pound (weight); (£—)
Pour
Powder
Power; Powerful
Practise; Practice
Praise
Pray; Prayer
Precious
Prepare
Presence
Present (time); At present
Preserve
Press
Pretend
Pretty
Prevent
Price
Prick; Prickle; Prickly
Priest
Prince; Princess
Print
Prison; Prisoner
Probable
Produce; Production
Promise

Proper
Protect
Proud
Prove; Proof; (= test)
Provide
Public; In public
Pull
Punish
Pure
Purpose; On purpose
Push
Put; Put on clothes; Put off (= delay); Put out fire

Q

Quality
Quantity
Quarrel
Quarter
Queen
Question
Quick
Quiet
Quite

R

Rabbit
Race (running)
Race of
Radio
Railway
Rain
Raise
Range
Rank
Rapid
Rat
Rather (= slightly); Would rather
Reach
Read
Ready
Real, Really
Reason (= cause); To reason; Listen to reason; Reasonable
Receipt (for money)
Receive
Recognize
Red
Refuse; Refusal
Regard; In regard to
Regular
Rejoice
Relation; Related; Relative
Religion; Religious
Remain
Remember
Rent
Repair
Repeat
Report

THE DEFINING VOCABULARY

Respect; Respectful
Rest; The —
Rest (= repose)
Result
Return; In return; A return
Rich; Riches
Ride
Right (correct, you are right); Right (= quite)
Right (hand)
Ring
Ring; Ring with —
Rise; Arise
Risk; Risky
River
Road
Rock
Roll; Roller
Roof
Room; Room for — (= space for)
Root
Rope
Rose, A
Rough
Round; Around, Roundabout
Row, A row of —
Row (a boat)
Rub
Rubber
Rude
Ruin
Rule; A rule
Run; Run into; Run (= flow)
Rush

S

Sad
Safe
Sail; To sail
Salt
Same
Sand
Satisfy
Save
Say
Scatter
Scene (= part of play, stage setting; view)
School; Schoolmaster
Science; Scientist, Scientific
Scold
Screw
Sea; Seaman
Search
Season
Seat
Second
Second, A
Secret
See; See that; See about

Seed
Seem
Seize
Self; -self; Self-respect
Sell
Send; Send for
Sense (of touch); (= wisdom); Common sense; Senseless (= unconscious)
Separate; To separate
Serious
Servant; Serve; Serve food; Service
Set; Set out; Sun-set; A set of
Settle; Settle in; Settle business; Settle that
Several
Shade
Shadow
Shake
Shall
Shame; Ashamed
Shape
Share; Share in business; Shareholder
Sharp (knife, eyes)
She
Sheep
Sheet
Shelf
Shell
Shelter
Shield
Shilling
Shine
Ship
Shirt
Shock
Shoe
Shoot, A shot, Shot (= ball)
Shop
Shore
Short
Should
Shoulder
Shout
Show; A show; Showy
Shut
Sick; (= vomiting)
Side; Sideways; Aside
Sight (spectacle); Eyesight; In sight
Sign
Silence; Silent
Silk
Silly
Silver
Simple
Since (after, because)
Sing; Song
Single
Sink

Sister
Sit
Size
Skill; Skilful
Skin
Skirt
Sky
Slang
Slave
Sleep; Go to sleep; Asleep
Slide
Slight; Slightly
Slip; Slippery
Slope
Slow
Small
Smell
Smile
Smoke
Smooth
Snake
Snow
So (therefore); (so much); So ... that ...
Soap
Soft
Soil
Soldier
Solemn
Solid
Some; Some one; Somewhere; Sometimes; Somebody
Son
(Song)
Soon
Sorry; Sorrow
Sort
Soul
Sound
Sour
South
Space
Speak
Spear
Special; Especial; Especially
Speech (= speaking, oration)
Speed
Spend
Spirit (= impulse); High spirits; spirit (= ghost)
(Spite) In spite of
Splendid
Spoon
Spot
Spread
Spring (= water, time of year)
Spring, To —
Spring (metal)
Square
Stair; Stairs
Stamp (Postage)
Stand; Stand out from
Star

THE DEFINING VOCABULARY

Start
State (= condition)
Station
Stay
Steady
Steal
Steam
Steep
Stem
Step; Steps
Stick, A
Stick; Sticky; Stuck
Stiff
Still, adj.
Still, adv.
Stomach
Stone
Stop (= prevent, cease)
Store
Storm
Story
Straight
Strange; Stranger
Stream
Street
Strength
Stretch; A stretch of country
Strike
String
Stroke, A
Strong
Struggle
Study
Subject (of study)
Succeed; Success
Such
Sudden
Suffer
Sugar
Suit; Suitable
Summer
Sun
Supper
Supply
Support
Suppose
Sure
Surface
Surprise; Take by surprise
Swallow, To —.
Sweet ; Sweets
Swell; Swollen
Swift
Swim
Swing
Sword

T

Table
Tail
Take; Take off
Talk
Tall

Taste
Tea
Teach
Tear, To —
Tears
Telephone
Tell (= narrate, order)
Temper; Bad-tempered
Tender
Tense (of verb)
Tent
Terrible; Terror
Than
Thank
That; (knew that)
The
Theatre
Their
(Them)
Then
There
Therefore
These
They; Them
Thick
Thief
Thin
Thing
Think
Third
Thirst
This
Thorough
Those
Though, Although
Thought
Thread
Throat
Through
Throw; Throw away
Thumb
Thunder
Thus
Tie
Tight
Till; Until
Time (interval); Many times; Sometimes; From time to time; Time (in music).
Tin
Tire; Tired of
Title
To (direction); (want to); (went to get); (work to do)
Today; Tomorrow
Together
Tongue
Tonight
Too (excess, also)
Tooth; (= of wheel)
Top (= summit, cover)
Touch
(Towards)

Tower
Town
Track
Trade (= occupation)
Train
Train, To —
Trap
Travel
Treat
Tree
Trick
Trouble; Troublesome
Trousers
True; Truth
Trust; Trustworthy
Try; Tried; Try a prisoner; Trial
Turn; (= opportunity)
Twist

U

Ugly
Under; Underneath
Understand
Union; Unite; Unity
University
Up; Grow up; Eat up; Use up; Upon; Upper; Upright; Upside-down; Upstairs
Urge
Us
Use; Used to . . .; Used to (= accustomed to); Use; Useful; Useless
Usual; Usually

V

Valley
Value; Valuable
Various
Vegetable
Verb
Very
Vessel (= container, pipe); Blood-vessel
Victory
View (= field of vision); (= landscape)
Village
Visit
Voice

W

Waist
Wait
Wake; Waken; Awake
Walk
Wall
Wander
Want
War